Hockey Guide

Who's Who in Women's Hockey Guide 2020

hockeyMedia

JAYNA HEFFORD

Jayna Hefford won six major scoring titles during her club career, five in the National Women's Hockey League (2000-01, 2002-03, 2003-04, 2004-05, 2006-07) and one in the Canadian Women's Hockey League (the Angela James Bowl in 2008-09). Across 17 seasons in the Central Ontario Women's Hockey League, NWHL, CWHL and Women's National Championships, she scored 856 points in 444 games, more than 200 points better than the next best scorer in the *Who's Who in Women's Hockey Guide*.

Hockey Guide

EDITORIAL COMMENT

Welcome to the 2020 edition of the *Who's Who in Women's Hockey Guide*. While the women's club game continues to evolve, it was important to recognise the contributions of the now-defunct Canadian Women's Hockey League through our 2020 cover choices. As such, we have selected the league's two oldest markets for alternate covers: the Toronto Furies (Natalie Spooner cover) and Montréal Canadiennes (Hilary Knight cover).

As always, our new edition includes all the player statistics from the past season's two North American-based leagues: the 12th and final season of the Canadian Women's Hockey League and the fourth season of the American-based National Women's Hockey League.

This year, we have also gone backwards and added player statistics from the last 14 years of Hockey Canada's Women's National Championships (1995 to 2008). We hope to add the earlier years (1982 to 1994) in future editions of this guide.

Along with the CWHL, NWHL and National Championships, the 2020 guide also features the defunct Western Women's Hockey League, Central Ontario Women's Hockey League, and (Canada's old) National Women's Hockey League.

The *Who's Who in Women's Hockey Guide* is one of several publications produced by hockeyMedia over the last 15 years. Originally written in 2004, the *Who's Who in Women's Hockey Guide* has been published in book format for each of the past seven seasons. It is in fact an important legacy piece of the Angela James Bowl project.

The Angela James Bowl trophy, introduced during the CWHL's inaugural 2007-08 season, annually recognized the CWHL's top points scorer. The trophy was named in honour of Angela James, a long-time member of the North York/Beatrice Aeros and three-time scoring champion in the old Central Ontario Women's Hockey League. In 2010, she became one of the first female players inducted into the Hockey Hall of Fame.

As part of the Angela James Bowl project, hockeyMedia promised to preserve the statistical history of the CWHL and to help tell the story of women's hockey at the club level.

As members of the Professional Women's Hockey Players Association embark on their 2019-20 Dream Gap Tour, we wish all the players the best in their mission to build a better league that highlights and promotes the best of our game in North America.

hockeyMedia / Up North Productions

Who's Who in Women's Hockey

hockeyMedia / by Richard Scott
Copyright © 2004-2020 Up North Productions.
No reproduction without permission.
All rights reserved.

Published in Canada by:
Up North Productions
1995 Indian Creek Road
Limoges, ON   K0A 2M0
www.hockeyMedia.ca

An important note regarding this hockey guide: some records remain either missing or incomplete. We have done our best to gather all league statistics over the course of the past decade, including game-by-game reports in the final year of the NWHL and all years of the CWHL. Special thanks to all that have helped us gather facts and information pertaining to these leagues and players. Please send updates to books@hockeymedia.ca.

TOP SCORERS

Regular season and playoff scoring, including Women's National Championships. League scoring includes Central Ontario Women's Hockey League, (Canada's) National Women's Hockey League, Western Women's Hockey League, Canadian Women's Hockey League, and (USA's) National Women's Hockey League.

Most Points in all competitions

ALL-TIME LEADERS		GP	G	A	PTS	PPG
1.	Hefford, Jayna	444	469	387	856	1.93
2.	West, Sommer	535	297	356	653	1.22
3.	Sunohara, Vicky	392	284	328	612	1.56
4.	Ouellette, Caroline	338	254	339	593	1.75
5.	Dupuis, Lori	443	227	279	506	1.14
6.	Desrosiers, Annie	297	241	224	465	1.57
7.	Nystrom, Karen	240	201	204	405	1.69
8.	James, Angela	212	210	191	401	1.89
9.	Botterill, Jennifer	224	164	231	395	1.76
10.	Turek, Amy	272	200	189	389	1.43
11.	Heaney, Geraldine	270	116	245	361	1.34
12.	Chartrand, Cathy	435	95	264	359	.83
13.	Boyd, Stephanie	258	136	217	353	1.37
14.	Perks, Lara	313	131	213	344	1.10
15.	Breton, Lisa-Marie	438	162	176	338	.77
16.	Benoit-Wark, Amanda	242	141	187	328	1.36
17.	Pounder, Cheryl	434	62	248	310	.71
18.	Logan, Heather	300	129	169	298	.99
19.	Marin, Noémie	246	150	142	292	1.19
20.	Zamora, Kristy	429	171	116	287	.67
21.	Bettez, Ann-Sophie	195	129	156	285	1.46
22.	Wickenheiser, Hayley	140	128	152	280	2.00
23.	Kay, Stephanie	393	118	153	271	.69
24.	Piper, Cherie	210	133	137	270	1.29
25.	Apps, Gillian	217	132	113	245	1.13
26.	Goyette, Danielle	98	111	131	242	2.47
27.	Hunter, Andria	203	102	139	241	1.19
28.	Harbec, Sabrina	172	91	147	238	1.38
29.	Kingsbury, Gina	115	105	130	235	2.04
30.	Fox, Allyson	562	27	207	234	.42
31.	Hall, Kaley	168	106	121	227	1.35
32.	Vine, Lindsay	347	97	125	222	.64
33.	Campbell, Cassie	209	83	135	218	1.04
34.	Ferrari, Gillian	374	55	160	215	.57
35.	Grnak, Marianne	202	107	105	212	1.05
36.	Rourke, Erin	243	89	123	212	.87
37.	Sobek, Jeanine	169	72	135	207	1.22
38.	Poulin, Marie-Philip	107	99	107	206	1.93
39.	Dosser, Nicole	242	84	118	202	.83
40.	Russell, Rebecca	113	79	122	201	1.78
41.	Béchard, Kelly	161	85	115	200	1.24
42.	Duval, Liz	265	113	81	194	.73
43.	Cryderman, Cindy	219	90	104	194	.89
44.	Aarts, Meagan	324	98	92	190	.59
45.	Deschamps, Nancy	210	91	97	188	.90
46.	Verlaan Page, Margot	117	84	104	188	1.61
47.	Déry, Nathalie	385	46	134	180	.47
48.	Pepper, Karen	213	61	117	178	.84
49.	Drolet, Nancy	120	101	73	174	1.45
50.	Bourdeau, Nadine	260	80	89	169	.65
51.	McCormack, Kathy	218	71	98	169	.78
52.	Nadeau, Geneviève	243	91	77	168	.69

ALL-TIME LEADERS		GP	G	A	PTS	PPG
53.	Blais, Emmanuelle	233	65	103	168	.72
54.	Harrigan Head, Jana	191	86	81	167	.87
55.	Knight, Hilary	115	85	82	167	1.45
56.	Sostorics, Colleen	151	58	109	167	1.11
57.	Marchese, Teresa	153	59	107	166	1.08
58.	Haggard, Carly	149	102	62	164	1.10
59.	Stack, Kelli	115	83	77	160	1.39
60.	Spence, Karen	270	47	110	157	.58
61.	Smith, Kelly	279	32	118	150	.54
62.	Olson, Erica	156	79	67	146	.94
63.	Johnston, Rebecca	115	59	87	146	1.27
64.	Schuler, Laura	122	64	81	145	1.19
65.	Walton, Meagan	90	57	87	144	1.60
66.	Holmes-Domagala, Sam	163	72	71	143	.88
67.	Decker, Brianna	81	70	73	143	1.77
68.	Depratto, Beth	170	68	75	143	.84
69.	Campbell, Michelle	162	48	94	142	.88
70.	Rivard, Nathalie	219	51	89	140	.64
71.	Clarke, LaToya	200	54	85	139	.70
72.	Grenon, Stéphanie	178	52	87	139	.78
73.	Marvin, Gigi	123	65	73	138	1.12
74.	Jenner, Brianne	135	64	74	138	1.02
75.	Aubé, Isabelle	231	54	83	137	.59
76.	Agosta-Marciano, Meghan	59	62	73	135	2.29
77.	Rattray, Jamie-Lee	131	66	68	134	1.02
78.	Spooner, Natalie	139	76	57	133	.96
79.	Proulx, Caroline	218	61	72	133	.61
80.	Bertrand, Catherine	250	58	74	132	.53
81.	Pettersen, Jenny	238	41	91	132	.55
82.	Tabb, Jessica	135	53	78	131	.97
83.	Irwin, Haley	112	64	66	130	1.16
84.	Chu, Julie	141	28	101	129	.91
85.	Davidson, Vanessa	137	64	64	128	.93
86.	St-Louis, France	75	59	69	128	1.71
87.	Kellar Duke, Becky	257	30	98	128	.50
88.	Eustace, Joanne	242	56	71	127	.52
89.	Kauth, Kathleen	143	55	72	127	.89
90.	Williamson, Sharon	223	54	73	127	.57
91.	Collins, Delaney	151	26	101	127	.84
92.	Mikkelson-Reid, Meaghan	164	46	74	120	.73
93.	Landry, Lyne	286	31	88	119	.42
94.	Koizumi, Jessica	159	55	61	116	.73
95.	Prévost, Carolyne	183	55	61	116	.63
96.	Scanzano, Jesse	153	51	65	116	.76
97.	Ostrander, Meredith	236	42	73	115	.49
98.	Tremills, Christianne	246	38	77	115	.47
99.	Dempsey, Jillian	127	56	57	113	.89
100.	Cheverie, Kori	196	55	58	113	.58
101.	Millar, Britney	210	52	61	113	.54
102.	Knowles, Helen	188	35	78	113	.60
103.	McKay, Tara	184	46	66	112	.61
104.	Perreault, Marie-Christine	209	46	66	112	.54
105.	Schmidgall Potter, Jenny	71	40	72	112	1.58
106.	Jones, Jess	142	57	54	111	.78
107.	Bellamy, Kacey	172	22	87	109	.63
108.	Guay, Annie	99	31	76	107	1.08
109.	MacLeod, Carla	86	27	79	106	1.23
110.	Antal, Dana	72	58	47	105	1.46
111.	Powers, Christin	150	57	47	104	.69
112.	Vaillancourt, Sarah	61	43	61	104	1.70
113.	Sittler, Meaghan	101	42	62	104	1.03
114.	Lê, Mai-Lan	101	59	44	103	1.02
115.	Foley, Kate	184	43	60	103	.56
116.	Brisson, Thérèse	136	36	67	103	.76
117.	Engstrom, Molly	150	26	76	102	.68
118.	Bourgeois, A. Danielle	66	52	48	100	1.52
119.	Richardson, Heather	150	41	59	100	.67

ALL SKATERS

AARTS, MEAGAN *Forward. Shoots left. #6.*
Clarkson Cup winner with Toronto on 2014-03-22.
Born 1982-12-6, Watford, ON, CAN. 5'8". Debut at age 21 in 2004-05. Uniform #6.

Season	League	Team	GP	G	A	PTS	PM	Year	Playoffs	GP	G	A	PTS	PM
2004-05	NWHL	Durham Lightning	34	12	8	20	65							
2005-06	NWHL	Durham Lightning	35	12	12	24	32	2006	NWHL-P	2	0	0	0	0
2006-07	NWHL	Etobicoke Dolphins	28	10	14	24	28	2007	NWHL-P	3	0	1	1	0
2007	Nationals	Etobicoke Dolphins	7	0	4	4	8							
2007-08	CWHL	Vaughan Flames	24	7	7	14	26	2008	CWHL-P	2	1	0	1	0
2008-09	CWHL	Vaughan Flames	28	20	9	29	34	2009	CWHL-P	2	xx	2	2	xx
2009-10	CWHL	Vaughan Flames	24	14	10	24	24							
2010-11	CWHL	Toronto Furies	22	6	3	9	8	2011	CWHL-P	2	xx	xx	xx	xx
								2011	C-Cup	4	0	0	0	2
2011-12	CWHL	Toronto Furies	26	3	10	13	8	2012	C-Cup	3	0	1	1	0
2012-13	CWHL	Toronto Furies	24	2	2	4	12	2013	C-Cup	3	1	0	1	0
2013-14	CWHL	Toronto Furies	21	6	4	10	10	2014	C-Cup	4	1	1	2	0
2014-15	CWHL	Toronto Furies	24	3	4	7	35	2015	C-Cup	2	0	0	0	4
CWHL Regular Season			193	61	49	110	157		Clarkson Cup	16	2	2	4	6
Totals from all Competitions			**324**	**98**	**92**	**190**	**296**							

Finished 11th in the Angela James Bowl scoring race in 2008-09... scored 100th CWHL point on 2014-03-16.

ACCURSI, TAYLOR *Forward. Shoots left. #95.*
Born 1995-3-2. Grew up in Ancaster, ON, CAN. 5'8". Debut at age 22 on 2017-10-28.

Year	League	Team	GP	G	A	PTS	PM	Year	Playoffs	GP	G	A	PTS	PM
2017-18	NWHL/	Buffalo Beauts	15	6	5	11	8	2018	I-Cup	2	0	0	0	2
2018-19	NWHL/	Buffalo Beauts	13	4	2	6	2	2019	I-Cup	2	0	0	0	0

ACHERTHOLT, JENNIFER *Forward. 2004 Nationals British Columbia (5 games).*

ACHESON, SOPHIE *F. 2001-02 NWHL Wingstar de Montréal (1gp, 1pt); 2002 Nationals Québec (6 games, 3pts).*

ADAMS, CHRISTY *Forward. 2000-01 NWHL Durham Lightning (2 games).*

ADAMS, SARAH *Defence. 2007-08 CWHL Montréal #57 (1 game, 1 assist).*

ADAMS, TESS *Forward. Shoots right. #8.*
Born 1996-08-11, Calgary, AB, CAN.

Year	League	Team	GP	G	A	PTS	PM
2018-19	NWHL/	Connecticut Whale	1	0	0	0	2

ADE, RACHAEL *Defence. Shoots left. #7.*
Born 1995-2-25. Grew up in Davenport, FL, USA. 5'9". Debut at age 22 on 2017-10-28. Uniform #7.

Year	League	Team	GP	G	A	PTS	PM	Year	Playoffs	GP	G	A	PTS	PM
2017-18	NWHL/	Connecticut Whale	16	0	2	2	8	2018	I-Cup	1	0	0	0	0
2018-19	NWHL/	Connecticut Whale	15	2	2	4	12	2019	I-Cup	1	0	0	0	0

NWHL Foundation Award in 2017-18

ADOLPHE, LISA *Forward. 1995 Nationals Calgary Classics.*

AGOSTA-MARCIANO, MEGHAN *Forward. Shoots left. #87.*
Olympic champion, IIHF champion. Clarkson Cup winner with Montréal on 2012-03-25
Born 1987-2-12, Windsor, ON, CAN. Grew up in Ruthven, ON, CAN. 5'7". Debut in 2004-05 (wore #25).

Season	League	Team	GP	G	A	PTS	PM	Year	Playoffs	GP	G	A	PTS	PM
2004-05	NWHL	Toronto Aeros	1	0	0	0	0							
2011-12	CWHL	Stars de Montréal	27	41	39	80	16	2012	C-Cup	4	4	2	6	0
2012-13	CWHL	Stars de Montréal	23	16	30	46	14	2013	C-Cup	4	1	2	3	2
CWHL Regular Season			50	57	69	126	30		Clarkson Cup	8	5	4	9	2
Totals from all Competitions			**59**	**62**	**73**	**135**	**32**							

CWHL Most Valuable Player in 2011-12... Angela James Bowl in 2011-12 & 2012-13... CWHL goal-scoring leader in 2011-12... CWHL Top Forward in 2011-12... CWHL First All-Star Team in 2011-12 & 2012-13... CWHL All-Rookie Team in 2011-12... scored 100th CWHL point on 2013-01-12... selected First Decade CWHL Team in 2017.

AGOSTINELLI, SOPHIA *Forward. Shoots right. #10.*
Born 1992-10-1. Grew up in Framingham, MA, USA. 5'10". Debut at age 25 on 2018-1-20.

Year	League	Team	GP	G	A	PTS	PM
2017-18	NWHL/	Connecticut Whale	2	0	0	0	0

NWHL Fans' Three Stars Award in 2017-18

AGOZZINO, LISA *Forward. 2004 Nationals Québec (7 gp, 1 goal, 1 assist).*

AIKEN, ROBYN *Defence. Shoots left.*
Born 1975-11-13. Grew up in Kensington, PE, CAN.

Season	League	Team	GP	G	A	PTS	PM
1999	Nationals	Prince Edward Island	5	1	1	2	

Year - League - Team			GP	G	A	PTS	PM	Year - Playoff	GP	G	A	PTS	PM
2000	Nationals	Prince Edward Island											
2001	Nationals	PEI Humpty Dumpty											
2002	Nationals	PEI Humpty Dumpty	6	0	0	0	0						

AISTON, FIONA — *Ottawa, ON, CAN. Forward. 2004-05 NWHL Toronto Aeros #36 (3 gp, 1 goal, 1 assist).*

ALARY, ANNE — *D. 2002-03 NWHL Ottawa Raiders #6 (27 gp, 2 pts); 2004 Nationals Saskatchewan (6gp, 3pts).*

ALBRECHT, ASHLEY — *Defence/Forward.*

Year	League	Team	GP	G	A	PTS	PM	Year	Playoff	GP	G	A	PTS	PM
2006-07	WWHL	Minnesota Whitecaps	17	0	4	4	8	2008	WWHL-P	3	0	1	1	0

ALCORN, KRISTI — *Forward. Shoots right. #15.*

Born 1984-10-18. Grew up in Orangeville, ON, CAN. 5'7". Debut at age 24 on 2008-10-4.

Year - League - Team			GP	G	A	PTS	PM	Year - Playoff		GP	G	A	PTS	PM
2008-09	CWHL	Brampton Thunder	27	1	4	5	26	2009	CWHL-P	2	xx	2	xx	xx
								2009	C-Cup	2	0	0	0	4
2009-10	CWHL	Brampton Thunder						2010	C-Cup	1	0	0	0	0
CWHL Regular Season			27	1	4	5	26	Clarkson Cup		4	0	0	0	4
Totals from all Competitions			**33**	**1**	**4**	**5**	**32**							

Served as head coach with CWHL Brampton (see Coaches section in this guide).

ALEXANDER, KAREN — *1998 Nationals New Westminster Lightning (5gp, 1 assist).*

ALEXANDER, LAURIE — *1998 Nationals Saskatchewan (6gp, 2pts), 2003 Nationals (6gp, 10pts).*

ALFRED, BRIANNE — *Kahnawake, QC, CAN. F. 5'5". 2009-10 CWHL Montréal #77 (20 gp, 1 goal, 1 assist).*

ALIE, KARINE — *1998-99 NWHL Laval (4 games), 2000-01 NWHL Laval (2 games, 1 assist).*

ALLARD, MARIE-CLAUDE — *Forward. Shoots right.*

Born 1979-3-18. Grew up in Neufchatel, QC, CAN.

Year	League	Team	GP	G	A	PTS	PM	Year	Playoff	GP	G	A	PTS	PM
1998	Nationals	Équipe Québec	6	0	0	0	0							
1999	Nationals	Équipe Québec	5	3	5	8								
2000	Nationals	Équipe Québec	6	1	1	2								
2000-01	NWHL	Wingstar de Montréal	10	2	5	7	2							
2001	Nationals	Équipe Québec												
2001-02	NWHL	Wingstar de Montréal	4	2	5	7	0							
2002	Nationals	Équipe Québec	6	2	8	10	2							
2002-03	NWHL	Avalanche du Québec	3	0	0	0	0							
2003	Nationals	Québec	5	3	9	12	0							
2003-04	NWHL	Axion de Montréal	31	13	18	31	24							
2004	Nationals	Québec	7	3	4	7	8							
2004-05	NWHL	Axion de Montréal	17	1	2	3	8	2007	NWHL-P	x	x	x	x	x
2007-08	CWHL	Phénix du Québec	4	0	2	2	4							
2008-09	CWHL	Stars de Montréal	5	1	3	4	6							
Totals from all Competitions			**109**	**31**	**62**	**93**	**54**							

ALLARD, MARIE-JOËLLE — *Forward. Shoots left.*

Born 1992-10-02. Grew up in Victoriaville, QC, CAN. 5'7". Debut at age 26 on 2018-10-14.

Year - League - Team			GP	G	A	PTS	PM	Year - Playoff	GP	G	A	PTS	PM
2018-19	CWHL	Canadiennes de Montréal	24	0	1	1	2	2019 C-Cup	4	0	0	0	2

ALLEMOZ, MARION — *Centre. Shoots left. #39.*

Clarkson Cup winner with Montréal on 2017-03-05

Born 1989-7-4. Grew up in Chambéry, FRA. 5'5". Debut at age 27 on 2016-10-15.

Year - League - Team			GP	G	A	PTS	PM	Year - Playoff	GP	G	A	PTS	PM
2016-17	CWHL	Canadiennes de Montréal	19	1	2	3	8	2017 C-Cup	3	0	0	0	0
2017-18	CWHL	Canadiennes de Montréal	28	4	10	14	4	2018 C-Cup	2	0	1	1	0
CWHL Regular Season			47	5	12	17	12	Clarkson Cup	5	0	1	1	0
Totals from all Competitions			**52**	**5**	**13**	**18**	**12**						

ALLEN, ANSLEY — *Forward. 2010-11 WWHL Manitoba #12 (2 games).*

ALLEN, CHRISTINE — *Defence. 1996 Nationals Winnipeg Sweat Camp (6 games).*

ALLEN, JESSICA — *Defence.*

Year - League - Team			GP	G	A	PTS	PM
1995-96	COWHL	North York Aeros	1	0	0	0	0
1996-97	COWHL	North York Aeros	1	0	1	1	0
1997-98	COWHL	Scarborough Sting	19	0	2	2	23
1998-99	NWHL	Scarborough Sting	36	1	3	4	59
1999-00	NWHL	Durham Lightning	37	5	3	8	90
2000-01	NWHL	Durham Lightning	32	3	7	10	101
2001-02	NWHL	Durham Lightning	21	1	3	4	44
2002-03	NWHL	Durham Lightning					
Totals from all Competitions			**147**	**10**	**19**	**29**	**317**

ALLEN, JULIE — *Forward. Shoots right. #2.*

Clarkson Cup winner with Toronto on 2014-03-22

Born 1987-05-20 in Toronto, grew up in Brampton, ON, CAN. 5'10". Debut at age 26 on 2013-11-09.

Year - League - Team		GP	G	A	PTS	PM	Year - Playoff	GP	G	A	PTS	PM
2013-14	CWHL Toronto Furies	21	2	2	4	6	2014 C-Cup	4	0	0	0	0
2014-15	CWHL Toronto Furies	24	2	1	3	18	2015 C-Cup	2	0	0	0	0
2016-17	CWHL Toronto Furies	24	4	6	10	10	2017 C-Cup	3	0	1	1	2
2017-18	CWHL Toronto Furies	10	0	2	2	6						
2018-19	CWHL Toronto Furies	23	2	5	7	8	2019 C-Cup	3	0	0	0	0
CWHL Regular Season		102	10	16	26	48	Clarkson Cup	12	0	1	1	2
Totals from all Competitions		**114**	**10**	**17**	**27**	**50**						

ALLEN, STACY
Defence. 2003 Nationals Saskatchewan (6gp); 2009-10 WWHL Strathmore (5 gp, 1 assist).

ALLEVA, ROSE
Defence. Shoots right. #25.
Born 1992-6-16. Grew up in Red Wing, MN, USA. 5'3". Debut at age 25 on 2017-10-28.

Year - League - Team		GP	G	A	PTS	PM
2017-18	CWHL Vanke Rays	28	1	3	4	18
2018-19	CWHL KRS Vanke Rays	13	0	1	1	0

ALLGOOD, KATE
Forward. Shoots right. #16.
Born 1983-9-5. Grew up in Toronto, ON, CAN. 5'5".

Year - League - Team		GP	G	A	PTS	PM	Year - Playoff	GP	G	A	PTS	PM
2005-06	NWHL Toronto Aeros	2	2	0	2	0						
2006-07	NWHL Mississauga Aeros	16	1	2	3	2	2007 NWHL-P	3	0	0	0	0
2007	Nationals Mississauga Aeroes	6	3	7	10	4						

AMBROSE, ERIN
Defence. Shoots right. #14.
Born 1994-4-30. Grew up in Keswick, ON, CAN. 5'4". Debut at age 22 on 2016-10-15.

Year - League - Team		GP	G	A	PTS	PM	Year - Playoff	GP	G	A	PTS	PM
2016-17	CWHL Toronto Furies	17	0	8	8	8	2017 C-Cup	3	1	2	3	2
2017-18	CWHL Canadiennes de Montréal	16	2	14	16	10	2018 C-Cup	2	0	1	1	0
2018-19	CWHL Canadiennes de Montréal	26	6	18	24	20	2019 C-Cup	2	0	1	1	2
CWHL Regular Season		59	8	40	48	38	Clarkson Cup	7	1	4	5	4
Totals from all Competitions		**66**	**9**	**44**	**53**	**42**						

CWHL Defenceman of the Year in 2018-19... CWHL First All-Star Team in 2018-19... finished 15th in the Angela James Bowl scoring race in 2018-19.

AMMERMAN, BROOKE
Forward. Shoots right. #4.
Born 1990-07-13. Grew up in River Vale, NJ, USA. 5'8". Debut at age 25 on 2015-10-11.

Year - League - Team		GP	G	A	PTS	PM	Year - Playoff	GP	G	A	PTS	PM
2015-16	NWHL/ New York Riveters	15	4	10	14	26	2016 I-Cup	2	0	1	1	6

ANAKA, NICOLE
Forward. 2002 Nationals Richmond Steelers (5 gp).

ANDERSON, KAYCIE
Forward. Shoots left. #9.
Born 1991-4-29. Grew up in Maple Plain, MN, USA. 5'7". Debut at age 26 on 2017-10-28.

Year - League - Team		GP	G	A	PTS	PM	Year - Playoff	GP	G	A	PTS	PM
2017-18	NWHL/ Connecticut Whale	12	1	1	2	2	2018 I-Cup	1	0	0	0	0
2018-19	NWHL/ Connecticut Whale	6	0	0	0	0						

ANDERSON, KRISTIN
Defence. Shoots left. #7 #11.
Born 1983-10-13, Glenville, NY, USA. 5'9".

Year - League - Team		GP	G	A	PTS	PM	Year - Playoff	GP	G	A	PTS	PM
2005-06	NWHL Ottawa Raiders	26	4	4	8	20	2006 NWHL-P	1	0	0	0	0
2006-07	NWHL Oakville Ice	11	0	2	2	8						
Totals from all Competitions		**38**	**4**	**6**	**10**	**28**						

ANDERSON, LISA
Right Wing. 1995-96 with COWHL London #27 (23 gp, 2 goals, 11 assists).

ANDERSON, MELISSA
F. 2005-06 WWHL B.C. #77 (14 gp, 15 pts); 2006 Nationals BC Selects (6gp, 4 pts).

ANDERSON, NICOLE
Forward. Shoots left.
Born 1991-07-06. Grew up in Jordan, MN, USA. 6'0".

Year - League - Team		GP	G	A	PTS	PM
2018-19	CWHL Worcester Blades	24	2	2	4	4

ANDERSON, STEPHANIE
Forward. Shoots right. #12.
IIHF champion.
Born 1992-11-27. Born North St. Paul, MN, USA. 5'9". Debut at age 24 on 2017-10-21.

Year - League - Team		GP	G	A	PTS	PM	Year - Playoff	GP	G	A	PTS	PM
2017-18	CWHL Kunlun Red Star	28	8	9	17	48	2018 C-Cup	4	1	1	2	2
2018-19	CWHL KRS Vanke Rays	25	5	3	8	20						

ANDERSON, WHITNEY
Forward. 2005 Nationals Manitoba (5 games).

ANDREWS, ELLEN
Forward. 2007 Nationals Prince Edward Island (5 games, 2 pts).

ANDREWS-LARTER, KELLIE
Defence.
Born 1969-06-03.

Year - League - Team		GP	G	A	PTS	PM
1995	Nationals PEI Esso Tigers					
1996	Nationals PEI Esso Tigers	4	0	0	0	0

Year - League - Team			GP	G	A	PTS	PM	Year - Playoff	GP	G	A	PTS	PM
1999	Nationals	Prince Edward Island											
2000	Nationals	Team New Brunswick		1		1							

ANNING, LAURA

Defence. 2003 Nationals Nova Scotia Selects (6 games, 1 assist).

ANSO, HAYLEY

Defence. 2000-01 with NWHL Durham (2 games).

ANTAL, DANA

Forward. Shoots right. #14.

Olympic champion, IIHF champion. Abby Hoffman Cup winner with Calgary on 1998-03-22, 2001-03-11 and 2003-03-16. WWHL winner.
Born 1977-4-19. Grew up in Esterhazy, SK, CAN. 5'7".

Year - League - Team			GP	G	A	PTS	PM	Year - Playoff	GP	G	A	PTS	PM
1998	Nationals	Calgary Oval X-Treme	6	7	3	10	0						
1999	Nationals	Calgary Oval X-Treme	6	2	3	5							
2000	Nationals	Calgary Oval X-Treme	7	5	1	6							
2001	Nationals	Calgary Oval X-Treme											
2002-03	NWHL	Calgary Oval X-Treme	20	19	15	34	6	2003 NWHL-P	x	x	x	x	x
2003	Nationals	Calgary Oval X-Treme	5	6	7	13	2						
2003-04	NWHL	Calgary Oval X-Treme	2	1	0	1	2	2004 NWHL-P	2	0	0	0	0
2004	Nationals	Calgary Oval X-Treme	6	2	1	3	2						
2004-05	WWHL	Calgary Oval X-Treme	18	16	17	33	6	2005 WWHL-P	0	0	0	0	0
Totals from all Competitions			**72**	**58**	**47**	**105**	**18**						

ANTHONY, BELINDA

1993-94 with COWHL Hamilton #93 (2 games).

ANTHONY, KENDRA

Defence/Forward. Shoots left. #26..

Born 1981-2-16, Yorkton, SK, CAN. Grew up in Yorkton, SK, CAN. 5'3".

Year - League - Team			GP	G	A	PTS	PM	Year - Playoff	GP	G	A	PTS	PM
2004-05	NWHL	Ottawa Raiders	36	9	12	21	28						
2005-06	NWHL	Ottawa Raiders	34	6	13	19	23	2006 NWHL-P	2	2	0	2	2
2006-07	NWHL	Ottawa Raiders	35	10	11	21	51	2007 NWHL-P	2	0	2	2	6
2007-08	CWHL	Ottawa Capital Canucks	28	3	4	7	28	2008 CWHL-P	1	0	0	0	0
2008-09	CWHL	Ottawa Senators	28	1	5	6	28	2009 CWHL-P	2	1		1	2
2009-10	CWHL	Ottawa Senators	30	10	5	15	20						
CWHL Regular Season			86	14	14	28	76						
Totals from all Competitions			**198**	**42**	**52**	**94**	**188**						

AOAKI, KANAE

Defence. Shoots right.

Clarkson Cup winner with Calgary on 2016-03-14
Born 1985-2-20, Toronto, ON, CAN. Grew up in JPN. 5'5".

Year - League - Team			GP	G	A	PTS	PM	Year - Playoff	GP	G	A	PTS	PM
2015-16	CWHL	Calgary Inferno	18	1	3	4	4	2016 C-Cup	1	0	0	0	0

APPERSON, KELTY

Right wing. Shoots right. #13.

Clarkson Cup winner with Calgary on 2019-03-24.
Born 1994-9-26. Grew up in Kitchener, ON, CAN. Debut at age 23 on 2017-10-21.

Year - League - Team			GP	G	A	PTS	PM	Year - Playoff	GP	G	A	PTS	PM
2017-18	CWHL	Calgary Inferno	28	4	5	9	8	2018 C-Cup	3	0	0	0	0
2018-19	CWHL	Calgary Inferno	25	3	3	6	4	2019 C-Cup	4	0	0	0	2

APPLEGARTH, SARAH

Forward. #23.

Grew up in Burlington, ON, CAN.

Year - League - Team			GP	G	A	PTS	PM
1993-94	COWHL	Hamilton Golden Hawks	4	0	2	2	0
1995	Nationals	Mississauga Chiefs					
1995-96	COWHL	Mississauga Chiefs	22	4	4	8	26
1996-97	COWHL	Mississauga Chiefs	26	8	5	13	28
1997-98	COWHL	Mississauga Chiefs	19	4	6	10	26
1998-99	NWHL	Mississauga Chiefs	35	7	9	16	35
1999-00	NWHL	Mississauga Chiefs	6	0	2	2	4
2000-01	NWHL	Mississauga IceBears	13	1	4	5	12
Totals from all Competitions			**125**	**24**	**32**	**56**	**131**

APPS, GILLIAN

Forward. Shoots left. #10.

Olympic champion, IIHF champion, CWHL winner.
Born 1983-11-2, Toronto, ON, CAN. Grew up in Unionville, ON, CAN. 6'0".

Year - League - Team			GP	G	A	PTS	PM	Year - Playoff	GP	G	A	PTS	PM
1999-00	NWHL	Scarborough Sting	3	0	0	0	14						
2000-01	NWHL	North York Aeros	36	22	20	42	62						
2001	Nationals	North York Aeros											
2001-02	NWHL	North York Aeros	22	22	19	41	52						
2002	Nationals	North York Aeros	7	4	3	7	8						
2007-08	CWHL	Brampton Can.-Thunder	25	10	13	23	87	2008 CWHL-P	3	2	1	3	6
2008	Nationals	Brampton Can.-Thunder	3	2	1	3	6						
2008-09	CWHL	Brampton Thunder	27	15	10	25	68	2009 CWHL-P	2		1	1	2
								2009 C-Cup	2	2	0	2	4
2009-10	CWHL	Brampton Thunder	1	0	0	0	0	2010 C-Cup	2	1	1	2	8

Year - League - Team			GP	G	A	PTS	PM	Year - Playoff	GP	G	A	PTS	PM
2010-11	CWHL	Brampton Thunder	23	10	13	23	82	2011 CWHL-P	2	2	x	2	2
								2011 C-Cup	3	6	1	7	14
2011-12	CWHL	Brampton Thunder	27	19	20	39	70	2012 C-Cup	3	0	0	0	4
2012-13	CWHL	Brampton Thunder	23	14	10	24	52	2013 C-Cup	3	1	0	1	4
CWHL Regular Season			126	68	66	134	359	Clarkson Cup	13	10	2	12	34
Totals from all Competitions			**217**	**132**	**113**	**245**	**545**						

CWHL Second Team All-Star in 2011-12... Finished 5th in the Angela James Bowl scoring race in 2011-12... scored 100th CWHL point on 2012-02-25

ARAMBURU, ALEXA
Centre. Shoots right. #16.

Born 1995-3-28. Grew up in Glen Rock, NJ, USA. 5'5". Debut at age 22 on 2017-10-14.

Year - League - Team			GP	G	A	PTS	PM	Year - Playoff	GP	G	A	PTS	PM
2017-18	CWHL	Toronto Furies	28	0	0	0	0						
2018-19	NWHL/	Metropolitan Riveters	11	0	3	3	0	2019 I-Cup	1	0	0	0	0

ARBEAU, BREA
Defence. Shoots left.

Born 1984-10-04. Grew up in Lincoln, NB, CAN. 5'6".

Year - League - Team			GP	G	A	PTS	PM
2004	Nationals	Team New Brunswick	5	1	0	1	4
2005	Nationals	Team New Brunswick	6	1	1	2	8
2006	Nationals	Team New Brunswick	7	0	1	1	2
2007	Nationals	Team New Brunswick	6	0	1	1	8

ARBEAU, ELIZABETH
Defence. 2003 Nationals Team New Brunswick (4 games).

ARBEAU, LINDSAY
Forward. 1999 Nationals Team NB; 2001 Nationals 2007 Nationals (6 gp).

ARMSTRONG, AMANDA
Forward. 2008 Nationals Prince Edward Island (5 games, 3 goals, 1 assist).

ARMSTRONG, KALLEY
Forward. 2007-08 CWHL Mississauga #10 (1 game at age 17).

ARSENAULT, CHARLENE
Forward. 1995 Nationals Maritime Sports Blades.

ARSENAULT, RACHEL
Defence. 2001 Nationals PEI; 2002 Nationals (6 gp); 2005 Natoinals (4 gp).

ARSENAULT, SANDY
Defence. 1995 Nationals PEI Tigers; 1996 Nationals (4 gp, 1 a.); 1998 Nationals PEI (5 gp).

ARSENAULT, TRACY
Forward. 1996 Nationals PEI Tigers (4 gp); 1998 Nationals PEI (5 gp, 1 a.).

ARSENEAULT, EMILIE
Forward. 2008 Nationals Team New Brunswick (5 gp, 2 goals, 2 assists).

ASAY, AMANDA
Forward. 2006 Nationals BC Selects (6 games, 1 assist).

ASHLEY, DANIELLE
Defence. Shoots left. #77 #9 #97.

Abby Hoffman Cup winner with Aeros on 2005-03-13.

Born 1985-5-9. Grew up in Burlington, ON, CAN. 5'7".

Year - League - Team			GP	G	A	PTS	PM	Year - Playoff	GP	G	A	PTS	PM
2000-01	NWHL	Mississauga IceBears	38	6	5	11	84						
2001-02	NWHL	North York Aeros	18	1	13	14	34						
2001-02	NWHL	Mississauga IceBears	10	0	2	2	26						
2002	Nationals	North York Aeros	6	0	1	1	6						
2002-03	NWHL	North York Aeros						2003 NWHL-P	x	x	x	x	x
2004-05	NWHL	Toronto Aeros	35	4	11	15	104						
2005	Nationals	Toronto Aeros	7	0	6	6	16						
2005-06	NWHL	Toronto Aeros	16	1	2	3	64						
2006-07	NWHL	Brampton Thunder	31	4		4		2007 NWHL-P	0	0	0	0	0
2007-08	CWHL	Burlington Barracudas	2	0	0	0	6						
Totals from all Competitions			**163**	**16**	**40**	**56**	**340**						

ATKINSON, DEB
1995-96 COWHL Hamilton Golden Hawks #20 (2 games).

ATKINSON, CARRIE
Defence. Shoots left. #5.

Born 1994-05-06. Grew up in Fort Worth, TX, USA. 5'7". Debut at age 24 on 2018-10-20.

Year - League - Team			GP	G	A	PTS	PM
2018-19	CWHL	Worcester Blades	21	0	3	3	10

ATKINSON, OLIVIA
Forward. Shoots left. #2.

Born 1997-01-06. Grew up in Oakville, ON, CAN. 5'8". Debut at age 21 on 2018-10-13.

Year - League - Team			GP	G	A	PTS	PM	Year - Playoff	GP	G	A	PTS	PM
2018-19	CWHL	Canadiennes de Montréal	17	2	1	3	0	2019 C-Cup	4	0	0	0	0

AUBÉ, ISABELLE
Forward. Shoots left. #4.

Born 1978-5-24, Bathurst, NB, CAN. Grew up in Bathurst, NB, CAN. 5'5".

Year - League - Team			GP	G	A	PTS	PM	Year - Playoff	GP	G	A	PTS	PM
1998-99	NWHL	Ottawa Raiders	29	6	8	14	20						
1999-00	NWHL	Ottawa Raiders	31	10	6	16	24						
2000-01	NWHL	Ottawa Raiders	3	0	0	0	0						
2001-02	NWHL	Ottawa Raiders	29	9	12	21	26						
2002-03	NWHL	Ottawa Raiders	36	8	14	22	26						
2003-04	NWHL	Ottawa Raiders	20	2	8	10	23						
2004-05	NWHL	Ottawa Raiders	36	10	12	22	16						
2005	Nationals	Team New Brunswick	6	4	7	11	22						
2005-06	NWHL	Ottawa Raiders	33	4	15	19	38	2006 NWHL-P	2	0	0	0	2

Year - League - Team		GP	G	A	PTS	PM	Year - Playoff		GP	G	A	PTS	PM
2006-07	NWHL Ottawa Raiders	3	0	0	0	2	2007	NWHL-P	2	1	1	2	6
2007-08	CWHL Ottawa Capital Canucks	1	0	0	0	2							
Totals from all Competitions		**231**	**54**	**83**	**137**	**207**							

AUNGER, BOBBI
Defence. 1995 Nationals Calgary Classics.

AUSTIN, PATTY
D. 2001-02 NWHL Brampton (29 gp), 2002 Nationals (7 gp); 2002-03 NWHL Mississauga.

AUSTIN, SUSAN
Defence. #18 #21 #23.

Year - League - Team		GP	G	A	PTS	PM
1992-93	COWHL Scarborough Sting	24	8	2	10	20
1993-94	COWHL Scarborough Sting	24	3	5	8	33
1995-96	COWHL Toronto Red Wings	26	5	12	17	6
1996-97	COWHL Newtonbrook Panthers	32	13	16	29	18
Totals from all Competitions		**106**	**29**	**35**	**64**	**77**

AVERY, DANA
Defence/Forward.

Year - League - Team		GP	G	A	PTS	PM
1998-99	NWHL Ottawa Raiders	31	1	16	17	18
1999-00	NWHL Ottawa Raiders	28	5	14	19	55
2000-01	NWHL Ottawa Raiders	38	5	12	17	16
2001-02	NWHL Ottawa Raiders	24	1	5	6	12
Totals from all Competitions		**121**	**12**	**47**	**59**	**101**

AVESON, ELIZABETH
Left wing. Shoots right. #4.

Born 1995-7-18. Grew up in West Covina, CA, USA. 5'3". Debut at age 22 on 2017-10-14.

Year - League - Team		GP	G	A	PTS	PM	Year - Playoff	GP	G	A	PTS	PM
2017-18	CWHL Boston Blades	26	0	1	1	6						
2018-19	CWHL Worcester Blades	7	0	0	0	0						

AYEARST, DANIELLE
Defence. Shoots left. #2 #64.

Abby Hoffman Cup winner with Calgary on 2003-03-16.
Born 1984-11-21, Whistler, BC, CAN. Grew up in Whistler, BC, CAN.

Year - League - Team		GP	G	A	PTS	PM	Year - Playoff		GP	G	A	PTS	PM
2002-03	NWHL Calgary Oval X-Treme	14	2	1	3	6	2003	NWHL-P					
2003	Nationals Calgary Oval X-Treme	4	1	1	2	4							
2003-04	NWHL Calgary Oval X-Treme	12	2	2	4	10	2004	NWHL-P					
2004	Nationals Calgary Oval X-Treme	6	0	0	0	4							
2008-09	CWHL Vaughan Flames	29	2	11	13	22	2009	CWHL-P	2				
2009-10	CWHL Vaughan Flames	27	2	10	12	32							
CWHL Regular Season		56	4	21	25	54							
Totals from all Competitions		**94**	**9**	**25**	**34**	**78**							

AYLESWORTH, CAROLYN
Forward. #2.

Abby Hoffman Cup winner with Calgary on 1998-03-22.
Born 1976-07-28.

Year - League - Team		GP	G	A	PTS	PM
1995	Nationals Calgary Classics					
1998	Nationals Calgary Oval X-Treme	7	0	0	0	0

AZMAN, VESNA
Forward. Shoots left. #6 #26 #22.

Born 1976-07-28..

Year - League - Team		GP	G	A	PTS	PM	Year - Playoff		GP	G	A	PTS	PM
1998-99	NWHL Bonaventure	13	0	5	5	2							
2002-03	NWHL Axion de Montréal	21	2	0	2	6	2003	NWHL-P					
2003-04	NWHL Axion de Montréal	21	0	1	1	10	2004	NWHL-P	4	0	0	0	6
2004-05	NWHL Axion de Montréal	24	1	2	3	10							
2005	Nationals Axion de Montréal	6	1	1	2	0							
Totals from all Competitions		**89**	**4**	**9**	**13**	**34**							

BABCHISHIN, JANET
Sturgis, SK, CAN. Forward. 2006-07 WWHL Saskatchewan #3 (21 gp, 2 goals, 9 assists).

BABINEAU, JOSETT
Forward. 1996 Nationals Saskatchewan Selects (5 gp, 1 goal).

BABONY, ANDREA
Toronto, ON, CAN. 2001-02 NWHL Durham #24 (24 gp, 7 goals, 4 assists).

BABONY, NATALIE
Toronto, ON, CAN. 2001-02 NWHL Durham #26 (28 gp, 4 goals, 14 assists).

BABSTOCK, KELLY
Forward. Shoots right. #8.

Born 1992-8-4. Grew up in Mississauga, ON, CAN. 5'5". Debut at age 15 on 2007-11-4.

Year - League - Team		GP	G	A	PTS	PM	Year - Playoff	GP	G	A	PTS	PM
2007-08	CWHL Mississauga Chiefs	1	2	1	3	0						
2015-16	NWHL/ Connecticut Whale	18	9	13	22	24	2016 I-Cup	3	4	0	4	2
2016-17	NWHL/ Connecticut Whale	17	10	9	19	26	2017 I-Cup	1	0	0	0	2
2017-18	NWHL/ Connecticut Whale	14	4	5	9	22	2018 I-Cup	1	0	0	0	0
2018-19	NWHL/ Buffalo Beauts	16	4	6	10	22	2019 I-Cup	2	0	0	0	0
NWHL Regular Season		65	27	33	60	94	Isobel Cup	7	4	0	4	4
Totals from all Competitions		**73**	**33**	**34**	**67**	**104**						

NWHL Foundation Award in 2018-19

BACH, VICTORIA *Forward. Shoots right. #24.*

Born 1996-07-12. Grew up in Milton, ON, CAN. 5'4". Debut at age 22 on 2018-10-13.

Year - League - Team			GP	G	A	PTS	PM	Year - Playoff	GP	G	A	PTS	PM
2018-19	CWHL	Markham Thunder	26	19	13	32	6	2019 C-Cup	3	0	1	1	0

CWHL Second All-Star Team in 2018-19... CWHL Outstanding Rookie 2018-19... CWHL All-Rookie Team 2018-19... finished 4th in the Angela James Bowl scoring race in 2018-19.

BACKUS, SANDRA *1996-97 COWHL Scarborough #25 (5 games, 4 assists).*

BADGLEY, CHRISTINA *F. 2003 Nationals Host SK (5 gp, 1 goal), 2006-07 WWHL Saskatchewan (21 gp, 7 pts).*

BAECHLER, MIRJAM *Defence/Forward. #11 #4.*

Year - League - Team			GP	G	A	PTS	PM
1996-97	COWHL	Newtonbrook Panthers	33	2	20	22	8
1997-98	COWHL	Scarborough Sting	16	1	2	3	4
1998-99	NWHL	Scarborough Sting	26	0	0	0	0
1999-00	NWHL	Scarborough Sting	24	0	2	2	6
2001-02	NWHL	Durham Lightning	19	0	0	0	4
Totals from all Competitions			**118**	**3**	**24**	**27**	**22**

BAILEY, BECKIE *Left wing. Shoots left. #16.*

Born 1980-7-12, Kyle, SK, CAN. 5'8".

Year - League - Team			GP	G	A	PTS	PM	Year - Playoff	GP	G	A	PTS	PM
2003	Nationals	Saskatchewan	6	0	2	2	0						
2004	Nationals	Saskatchewan	6	3	1	4	0						
2004-05	WWHL	Saskatchewan Prairie Ice	21	1	3	4	4						
2005-06	WWHL	Saskatchewan Prairie Ice	23	6	6	12	12	2006 WWHL-P	2	0	0	0	0
2006-07	WWHL	Saskatchewan Prairie Ice	20	3	6	9	6						
Totals from all Competitions			**78**	**13**	**18**	**31**	**22**						

BAILEY, CHRISTINA *USA. Defence. 1999-00 NWHL Ottawa #93 (14 games, 2 goals, 4 assists).*

BAIN, TONI *Forward. 992-93 COWHL Scarborough #10 (22 gp, 2 goals, 10 assists).*

BALCH, SARAH *Sudbury, ON, CAN. Forward. 2007-08 CWHL Mississauga #9 (3 games, 1 assist).*

BALDIN, ALYSSA *Forward. Shoots right. #14 #57.*

Clarkson Cup winner with Toronto on 2014-03-22
Born 1991-11-19. Grew up in Waltham, MA, USA. 5'4". Debut at age 21 on 2012-12-10.

Year - League - Team			GP	G	A	PTS	PM	Year - Playoff	GP	G	A	PTS	PM
2013-14	CWHL	Toronto Furies	23	8	15	23	14	2014 C-Cup	4	0	0	0	4
2014-15	CWHL	Toronto Furies	23	3	2	5	24	2015 C-Cup	2	0	0	0	0
2015-16	CWHL	Toronto Furies	22	7	11	18	26	2016 C-Cup	2	1	1	2	4
CWHL Regular Season			**68**	**18**	**28**	**46**	**64**	**Clarkson Cup**	**8**	**1**	**1**	**2**	**8**
Totals from all Competitions			**76**	**19**	**29**	**48**	**72**						

CWHL Second All-Star Team in 2013-14... CWHL All-Rookie Team in 2013-14... finished 8th in the Angela James Bowl scoring race in 2013-14

BALFOUR, ERIN *Defence. #10.*

Born 1978-01-31.

Year - League - Team			GP	G	A	PTS	PM
1996	Nationals	Saskatchewan Selects	5	1	1	2	0
1998	Nationals	Saskatchewan Selects	6	0	1	1	4
1999	Nationals	Saskatchewan Selects	4	2	1	3	
2006-07	WWHL	Saskatchewan Prairie Ice	3	0	0	0	0
Totals from all Competitions			**18**	**3**	**3**	**6**	**4**

BALL, LINDSEY *Forward. 1998 Nationals New Westminster Lightning (5 gp, 1 assist).*

BANFIELD, ASHLEY *Defence. 1999-00 NWHL Scarborough #90 (2 gp); 2000-01 North York (5 games).*

BANNON, GENEVIÈVE *Forward. Shoots right. #18.*

Born 1995-02-03. Grew up in Candiac, QC, CAN. 5'7". Debut at age 23 on 2018-10-20.

Year - League - Team			GP	G	A	PTS	PM	Year - Playoff	GP	G	A	PTS	PM
2018-19	CWHL	Canadiennes de Montréal	26	2	5	7	4	2019 C-Cup	4	0	0	0	0

BARBARA, KRISTEN *Defence. Shoots right. #24.*

Clarkson Cup winner with Markham on 2018-03-25
Born 1992-10-30. Grew up in Mount Hope, ON, CAN. 5'8". Debut at age 23 on 2016-10-29.

Year - League - Team			GP	G	A	PTS	PM	Year - Playoff	GP	G	A	PTS	PM
2016-17	CWHL	Brampton Thunder	2	0	0	0	0						
2017-18	CWHL	Markham Thunder	28	4	8	12	28	2018 C-Cup	3	0	0	0	0
2018-19	CWHL	Markham Thunder	28	3	4	7	18	2019 C-Cup	3	0	0	0	0
CWHL Regular Season			**58**	**7**	**12**	**19**	**46**	**Clarkson Cup**	**6**	**0**	**0**	**0**	**0**
Totals from all Competitions			**64**	**7**	**12**	**19**	**46**						

BARBER, JENNA *Forward. Shoots right. #27.*

Abby Hoffman Cup winner with Calgary on 2003-03-16.
NWHL winner. Born 1982-01-20. Grew up in Saskatoon, SK, CAN.

Year - League - Team			GP	G	A	PTS	PM	Year - Playoff	GP	G	A	PTS	PM
2000	Nationals	Saskatchewan Selects											
2002	Nationals	Calgary Oval X-Treme	6	1	5	6	2						
2002-03	NWHL	Calgary Oval X-Treme	21	6	5	11	6	2003 NWHL-P					
2003	Nationals	Calgary Oval X-Treme	5	0	1	1	4						
2003-04	NWHL	Calgary Oval X-Treme	12	2	1	3	10	2004 NWHL-P					
2004	Nationals	Calgary Oval X-Treme	6	1	0	1	0						
Totals from all Competitions			**50**	**10**	**12**	**22**	**22**						

BARCELOS, MELISSA *Forward. 2008-09 WWHL Strathmore (20 gp, 4 assists, 1 playoff game).*

BARIBEAU-RONDEAU, JUANA *Forward. Shoots left. #25.*
Born 1989-4-22. Grew up in Amos, QC, CAN. 5'7". Debut at age 17 on 2006-10-7.

Year - League - Team			GP	G	A	PTS	PM	Year - Playoff	GP	G	A	PTS	PM
2006-07	NWHL	Avalanche du Québec	3	0	0	0	2						
2007-08	CWHL	Phénix du Québec	4	2	0	2	0						
2016-17	NWHL/	Connecticut Whale	8	0	0	0	4	2017 I-Cup	1	0	0	0	0
2017-18	NWHL/	Connecticut Whale	16	1	1	2	16	2018 I-Cup	1	0	0	0	0
2018-19	NWHL/	Connecticut Whale	14	1	0	1	8	2019 I-Cup	1	0	0	0	0
NWHL Regular Season			38	2	1	3	28	Isobel Cup	3	0	0	0	0
Totals from all Competitions			**48**	**4**	**1**	**5**	**30**						

BARKER, EVA *1993-94 COWHL Hamilton #10 (23 games, 3 assists).*

BARKER, STEPHANIE *Forward. 2001 Nationals Newfoundland Labrador, 2002 Nationals (5 gp).*

BARLEY-MALONEY, ERIN *Raleigh, NC, USA. Forward. 2015-16 NWHL New York (0 games).*

BARLOW, HALLEY *Forward. 2004 Nationals Saskatchewan (6 gp, 2 assists).*

BARNES, LAUREN *Forward. Shoots left. #25.*
Isobel Cup winner with Minnesota on 2019-03-17.
Born 1992-05-06. Grew up in Burnsville, MN, USA. 5'8". Debut at age 26 on 2018-10-28.

Year - League - Team			GP	G	A	PTS	PM	Year - Playoff	GP	G	A	PTS	PM
2018-19	NWHL/	Minnesota Whitecaps	8	2	1	3	2	2019 I-Cup	2	1	0	1	2

BARNES, SONYA *1996-97 COWHL Scarborough #10 (35 gp, 8 goals, 9 assists); 1997-98 (9 gp, 2 assists).*

BARNES, SUSANNE *Forward. 1995-96 COWHL London #3 (29 gp, 2 goals, 2 assists).*

BARRÉ, AMANDA *Forward. Shoots right. #3 #77 #88.*
Born 1982-4-2. Grew up in Grafton, ON, CAN. 5'6". Debut at age 23 on 2005-09-27.

Year - League - Team			GP	G	A	PTS	PM	Year - Playoff	GP	G	A	PTS	PM
2005-06	NWHL	Toronto Aeros	28	13	15	28	12						
2006-07	NWHL	Oakville Ice											
2007-08	CWHL	Burlington Barracudas	24	6	6	12	8	2008 CWHL-P	1	0	0	0	0
Totals from all Competitions			**53**	**19**	**21**	**40**	**20**						

BARRETT, KATIE *Ottawa, ON, CAN. Defence. 2002-03 NWHL Ottawa Raiders #26 (10 games).*

BARRETTE, NATALIE *Defence. Shoots right. #11.*
Born 1993-10-25. Grew up in Belle River, ON, CAN. 5'6". Debut at age 23 on 2017-10-14.

Year - League - Team			GP	G	A	PTS	PM	Year - Playoff	GP	G	A	PTS	PM
2017-18	CWHL	Canadiennes de Montréal	25	0	5	5	0	2018 C-Cup	2	0	0	0	

BARROW, MARNIE *Defence.*
Abby Hoffman Cup winner with Aeros on 1993-03-28.

Year - League - Team			GP	G	A	PTS	PM
1992-93	COWHL	Toronto Aeros	21	2	7	9	8
1993-94	COWHL	Scarborough Firefighters	8	1	2	3	2
1995	Nationals	Mississauga Chiefs	4				
1995-96	COWHL	Mississauga Chiefs	21	0	15	15	4
1996-97	COWHL	Mississauga Chiefs	28	1	10	11	0
1997-98	COWHL	Mississauga Chiefs	15	0	4	4	2
1998-99	NWHL	Mississauga Chiefs	37	1	11	12	4
1999-00	NWHL	Mississauga Chiefs	35	3	12	15	6
2000-01	NWHL	Mississauga IceBears	15	0	3	3	2
Totals from all Competitions			**184**	**8**	**64**	**72**	**28**

BARRY, CHRISTINA *Forward.*
Born 1980-12-25. Grew up in Winnipeg, MB, CAN.

Year - League - Team			GP	G	A	PTS	PM
1999	Nationals	Tazmanian Devils	4	0	0	0	
2002	Nationals	University of Manitoba	4	0	0	0	0
2003	Nationals	University of Winnipeg	4	0	1	1	0

BARRY, LEE-ANNE *Defence. 1995 Nationals Britannia Blues.*

BARTON, ABBY *Forward. 2004 Nationals Team New Brunswick (5 games).*

BATCHELOR, LISA *Forward. 2004-05 WWHL Edmonton #16 (21 gp, 1 goal, 9 assists; 3 playoff gp).*

BATES, BRIDGET *Forward. 1995-96 COWHL Mississauga #4 (7 games, 2 goals).*

BATTAGLINO, ANYA
Defence. Shoots left. #4.

Born 1991-11-19. Grew up in Waltham, MA, USA. 5'4". Debut at age 21 on 2012-12-10.

Year - League - Team			GP	G	A	PTS	PM	Year - Playoff	GP	G	A	PTS	PM
2012-13	CWHL	Boston Blades	8	0	0	0	2						
2013-14	CWHL	Boston Blades	13	0	0	0	0						
2015-16	NWHL/	Connecticut Whale	8	0	0	0	6	2016 I-Cup	1	0	0	0	2
2016-17	NWHL/	Connecticut Whale	5	0	0	0	6						
2017-18	NWHL/	Connecticut Whale	9	0	0	0	0						
NWHL Regular Season			22	0	0	0	12	Isobel Cup	1	0	0	0	2
Totals from all Competitions			**44**	**0**	**0**	**0**	**18**						

NWHL Fans' Three Stars Award in 2016-17

BAUDRIT, LORE
Centre. Shoots right. #25.

Born 1991-10-11. Grew up in Castres, FRA. 6'3". Debut at age 26 on 2017-10-14.

Year - League - Team			GP	G	A	PTS	PM	Year - Playoff	GP	G	A	PTS	PM
2017-18	CWHL	Canadiennes de Montréal	16	0	0	0	4	2018 C-Cup	1	0	0	0	0

BAUER, SARA
Forward. Shoots right. #15.

Born 1984-5-11. Grew up in St. Catharines, ON, CAN.

Year - League - Team			GP	G	A	PTS	PM
2002-03	NWHL	Mississauga IceBears	20	10	9	19	
2008-09	CWHL	Burlington Barracudas	26	4	3	7	6
Totals from all Competitions			**46**	**14**	**12**	**26**	**6**

BAUMGARDT, TARYN
Defence. Shoots left. #12.

Born 1995-1-21. Grew up in Innisfail, AB, CAN. 5'5". Debut at age 22 on 2017-10-21.

Year - League - Team			GP	G	A	PTS	PM	Year - Playoff	GP	G	A	PTS	PM
2017-18	CWHL	Calgary Inferno	28	1	4	5	4	2018 C-Cup	3	0	0	0	0

CWHL All-Rookie Team in 2017-18

BEARDSHAW, SHELLY
Forward. 1995-96 COWHL London Devilettes #21 (26 gp, 3 goals, 2 assists).

BEARE, NICOLE
Forward.

Abby Hoffman Cup winner with Calgary on 1998-03-22. Born 1979-06-22

Year - League - Team			GP	G	A	PTS	PM
1996	Nationals	Winnipeg Sweat Camp	6	3	1	4	8
1998	Nationals	Calgary Oval X-Treme	7	3	5	8	4

BEATTIE, AMBER
2009-10 CWHL Burlington Barracudas #15 (2 games).

BEATTIE, HANNA
Forward. Shoots left. #16.

Born 1995-6-1. Grew up in Whitehouse Station, NJ, USA. 5'8". Debut at age 22 on 2017-12-3.

Year - League - Team			GP	G	A	PTS	PM	Year - Playoff	GP	G	A	PTS	PM
2017-18	NWHL/	Connecticut Whale	12	0	0	0	0	2018 I-Cup	1	0	0	0	0
2018-19	NWHL/	Connecticut Whale	16	0	1	1	6	2019 I-Cup	1	0	0	0	0

BEAUBIEN, ALLISON
F. 2000 Nationals Newfoundland Labrador (5 gp), 2001 Nationals (5gp).

BEAUCHAMP, GENEVIÈVE
Forward. #17 #16 #7 #59 #98.

Born 1981-9-2, St-Jérôme, QC, CAN.

Year - League - Team			GP	G	A	PTS	PM
1999-00	NWHL	Mistral de Laval	6	0	0	0	4
2000-01	NWHL	Mistral de Laval	24	2	2	4	31
2001-02	NWHL	Wingstar de Montréal	25	1	0	1	12
2003-04	NWHL	Avalanche du Québec	34	5	10	15	24
2004-05	NWHL	Avalanche du Québec	1	0	0	0	0
Totals from all Competitions			**90**	**8**	**12**	**20**	**71**

BEAUCHEMIN, CHRISTINE
Forward. 2002-03 Wingstar de Montréal #19 (35 gp, 1 goal, 4 assists).

BEAUDOIN, DEBBIE
Centre. Shoots left. #88 #8 #6 #14.

Born 1979-3-5, White Rock, BC, CAN. Grew up in White Rock, BC, CAN. 5'5".

Year - League - Team			GP	G	A	PTS	PM	Year - Playoff	GP	G	A	PTS	PM
2004-05	NWHL	Durham Lightning	28	0	0	0	37						
2005	Nationals	British Columbia	7	0	0	0	8						
2005-06	NWHL	Avalanche du Québec	17	1	4	5	14						
2006-07	WWHL	British Columbia Breakers	12	0	5	5	16	2007 WWHL-P	2	0	0	0	6
2007-08	WWHL	British Columbia Breakers	15	0	0	0	16						
Totals from all Competitions			**81**	**1**	**9**	**10**	**97**						

BEAULIEU, LAURENCE
Defence. Shoots left. #91.

Born 1991-12-3. Grew up in Stoneham, QC, CAN. 5'6". Debut at age 25 on 2017-10-14.

Year - League - Team			GP	G	A	PTS	PM	Year - Playoff	GP	G	A	PTS	PM
2017-18	CWHL	Canadiennes de Montréal	27	1	2	3	24	2018 C-Cup	1	0	0	0	0

BEAUREGARD, BRIGITTE
Forward. 2008-09 CWHL Ottawa Senators #28 (9 gp, 1 goal, 1 assist).

BEAUREGARD, MARTINE
2000-01 NWHL Mistral de Laval #30 (5 games, 1 assist).

BEAZER, BROOKE
Forward. Shoots right. #7.

Clarkson Cup winner with Toronto on 2014-03-22
Born 1986-6-6, Kingston, ON, CAN. 5'7". Debut at age 22 on 2008-10-4.

Year - League - Team			GP	G	A	PTS	PM	Year - Playoff		GP	G	A	PTS	PM
2008-09	CWHL	Brampton Thunder	30	3	9	12	16	2009	CWHL-P	2				
								2009	C-Cup	2	0	0	0	0
2009-10	CWHL	Brampton Thunder	30	9	15	24	20	2010	C-Cup	2	0	0	0	2
2010-11	CWHL	Brampton Thunder	23	10	13	23	16	2011	CWHL-P	2		2		
								2011	C-Cup	3	1	1	2	2
2011-12	CWHL	Toronto Furies	18	5	10	15	20	2012	C-Cup	3	0	0	0	6
2012-13	CWHL	Toronto Furies	23	1	2	3	4	2013	C-Cup	3	0	0	0	0
2013-14	CWHL	Toronto Furies	9	0	1	1	0	2014	C-Cup	4	0	0	0	2
2014-15	CWHL	Toronto Furies	12	1	1	2	2	2015	C-Cup	2	0	0	0	0
2017-18	CWHL	Toronto Furies	27	1	2	3	14							
CWHL Regular Season			143	30	53	83	92	Clarkson Cup		19	1	1	2	12
Totals from all Competitions			**166**	**31**	**54**	**85**	**106**							

CWHL All-Rookie Team in 2008-09... finished 13th in the Angela James Bowl scoring race in 2010-11

BECHARD, C.
2006-07 NWHL Mississauga Aeros #15 (1 playoff game, 1 assist).

BÉCHARD, KELLY
Forward. Shoots right. #24.

Olympic champion, IIHF champion. Abby Hoffman Cup winner with Calgary on 1998-03-22, 2001-03-11 and 2003-03-16.
WWHL winner. Born 1978-1-22, Regina, SK; grew up in Sedley, SK, CAN. 5'9".

Year - League - Team			GP	G	A	PTS	PM	Year - Playoff		GP	G	A	PTS	PM
1996	Nationals	Saskatchewan Selects	5	1	2	3	2							
1998	Nationals	Calgary Oval X-Treme	7	3	4	7	8							
1999	Nationals	Calgary Oval X-Treme	6	2	4	6								
2000	Nationals	Calgary Oval X-Treme	7	1	3	4								
2001	Nationals	Calgary Oval X-Treme												
2002-03	NWHL	Calgary Oval X-Treme	20	13	26	39	26	2003	NWHL-P					
2003	Nationals	Calgary Oval X-Treme	4	4	1	5	12							
2003-04	NWHL	Calgary Oval X-Treme	8	8	3	11	14	2004	NWHL-P	4	2	5	7	0
2004	Nationals	Calgary Oval X-Treme	6	3	2	5	0							
2004-05	WWHL	Calgary Oval X-Treme	15	11	9	20	14	2005	WWHL-P	3	1	6	7	0
2005-06	NWHL	Brampton Thunder	6	2	2	4	6	2006	NWHL-P	5	0	2	2	4
2006-07	NWHL	Mississauga Aeros	30	16	12	28	56	2007	NWHL-P	3	1	0	1	4
2007	Nationals	Mississauga Aeros	8	5	3	8	4							
2007-08	WWHL	Calgary Oval X-Treme	23	12	30	42	32							
2008	Nationals	Calgary Oval X-Treme	3	0	1	1	4							
Totals from all Competitions			**161**	**85**	**115**	**200**	**186**							

Has served as an assistant coach with CWHL Calgary

BEHRENZ, VIVIAN
Defence. 1998 Nationals New Westminster Lightning (5 gp, 2 assists).

BEIKIRICH, MORGAN
Livonia, NY, USA. Forward. 2016-17 NWHL Buffalo Beauts #87 (3 games).

BELIVEAU, PENNY
Forward. 1995 Nationals Regina Sharks.

BELL (NÉE SMITH), FIONA
Defence. Shoots left. #26 #5.

IIHF champion. Abby Hoffman Cup winner with Edmonton on 1997-03-09.
Born 1973-10-31, Edam, SK, CAN. Grew up in Edmonton, AB, CAN. 5'2".

Year - League - Team			GP	G	A	PTS	PM	Year - Playoff		GP	G	A	PTS	PM
1995	Nationals	Calgary Classics												
1996	Nationals	Edmonton Chimos	7	1	2	3	0							
1997	Nationals	Edmonton Chimos												
1998	Nationals	Edmonton Chimos	7	1	0	1	4							
1999	Nationals	Calgary Oval X-Treme	6	0	1	1								
2002-03	NWHL	Ottawa Raiders	20	3	8	11	16							
2003-04	NWHL	Ottawa Raiders	1	0	0	0	0							
2005-06	WWHL	Saskatchewan Prairie Ice	10	1	1	2	8	2006	WWHL-P	2	0	2	2	2
Totals from all Competitions			**53**	**6**	**14**	**20**	**30**							

BELL, KAREN
Forward. 2000-01 NWHL Durham Lightning #68 (29 gp, 1 goal, 1 assist).

BELL, SHEILA
Forward. Shoots left.

Born 1968-04-26. Grew up in Belle River, PE, CAN.

Year - League - Team			GP	G	A	PTS	PM
1998	Nationals	Prince Edward Island	5	0	3	3	6
1999	Nationals	Prince Edward Island	5	0	0	0	
2000	Nationals	Prince Edward Island	5	0	1	1	
2001	Nationals	PEI Humpty Dumpty					
2002	Nationals	PEI Humpty Dumpty	6	2	1	3	6

BELLAMY, KACEY
Forward. Shoots left. #22.

Olympic champion, IIHF champion. Clarkson Cup winner with Boston on 2013-03-23 and 2015-03-07. Isobel Cup winner with Boston on 2016-03-12. Clarkson Cup winner with Calgary on 2019-03-24.
Born 1987-4-22. Grew up in Westfield, MA, USA. 5'8". Debut at age 24 on 2010-10-30.

Year - League - Team			GP	G	A	PTS	PM	Year - Playoff		GP	G	A	PTS	PM
2010-11	CWHL	Boston Blades	24	2	13	15	28	2011	CWHL-P	1				5
2011-12	CWHL	Boston Blades	22	5	7	12	24	2012	C-Cup	3	0	2	2	4
2012-13	CWHL	Boston Blades	24	1	8	9	22	2013	C-Cup	4	0	3	3	12
2013-14	CWHL	Boston Blades	2	0	0	0	2	2014	C-Cup	4	0	0	0	0
2014-15	CWHL	Boston Blades	18	2	9	11	16	2015	C-Cup	3	0	1	1	6
2015-16	NWHL/	Boston Pride	13	2	12	14	12	2016	I-Cup	4	0	4	4	4
2016-17	NWHL/	Boston Pride	17	3	6	9	20	2017	I-Cup	2	0	4	4	0
2018-19	CWHL	Calgary Inferno	27	6	15	21	8	2019	C-Cup	4	1	3	4	4
CWHL Regular Season			117	16	52	68	100	Clarkson Cup		18	1	9	10	26
NWHL Regular Season			30	5	18	23	32	Isobel Cup		6	0	8	8	4
Totals from all Competitions			**141**	**15**	**69**	**84**	**155**							

CWHL First All-Star Team in 2018-19 and CWHL Second All-Star Team in 2012-13... CWHL All-Rookie Team in 2010-11... finished 19th in the Angela James Bowl scoring race in 2018-19.

BELLAND, PATRICIA   *Defence. 1995 Nationals Metro Valley Selects.*

BELLEHUMEUR, KATHLEEN   *Defence. 2000-01 NWHL Durham Lightning #3 (3 games, 1 goal).*

BELYAKOVA, LYUDMILA   *Forward.*

Born 1994-08-12, Moscow, RUS. 5'7". Debut at age 21 on 2015-10-11.

Year - League - Team			GP	G	A	PTS	PM	Year - Playoff		GP	G	A	PTS	PM
2015-16	NWHL/	New York Riveters	15	5	5	10	20	2016	I-Cup	2	1	0	1	0

BENDELL, EMILEE   *Defence. 2007 Nationals Nova Scotia Selects (6 games).*

BENDER, ALEXANDRA   *Defence. Shoots right. #5.*

Born 1993-7-22. Grew up in Snohomish, WA, USA. 5'8". Debut at age 23 on 2016-10-7.

Year - League - Team			GP	G	A	PTS	PM	Year - Playoff		GP	G	A	PTS	PM
2016-17	NWHL/	Boston Pride	17	2	4	6	10	2017	I-Cup	2	1	0	1	0
2017-18	NWHL/	Boston Pride	16	0	1	1	6	2018	I-Cup	1	1	0	1	0
2018-19	NWHL/	Boston Pride	16	0	8	8	8	2019	I-Cup	1	0	0	0	0
NWHL Regular Season			49	2	13	15	24	Isobel Cup		4	2	0	2	0
Totals from all Competitions			**53**	**4**	**13**	**17**	**24**							

BENDUS, VICKI   *Forward. Shoots right. #11.*

Born 1989-4-17. Grew up in Wasaga Beach, ON, CAN. 5'2". Debut at age 23 on 2011-10-22.

Year - League - Team			GP	G	A	PTS	PM	Year - Playoff		GP	G	A	PTS	PM
2011-12	CWHL	Brampton Thunder	27	15	14	29	18	2012	C-Cup	4	1	4	5	6
2012-13	CWHL	Brampton Thunder	20	10	6	16	28	2013	C-Cup	3	0	1	1	0
2014-15	CWHL	Brampton Thunder	0	0	0	0	0							
CWHL Regular Season			47	25	20	45	46	Clarkson Cup		7	1	5	6	6
Totals from all Competitions			**54**	**26**	**25**	**51**	**52**							

Finished 12th in the Angela James Bowl scoring race in 2011-12

BENEDICT, BRITTANY   *Cornwall Island, ON, CAN. Defence. 2004-05 NWHL Ottawa Raiders #16 (9 games).*

BENNETT, KELLY   *1999-00 NWHL Durham Lightning #22 (3 games).*

BENNION, LAURA   *Forward. 1995 Nationals Britannia Blues, 1996 Brittania Blues (5 gp, 3 points).*

BENOIT-WARK, AMANDA   *Centre. Shoots left. #33.*

IIHF champion. Abby Hoffman Cup winner with Aeros on 2000-03-12 and 2004-03-14. NWHL Cup winner. Born 1976-1-22. Grew up in Welland, ON, CAN. Forward. 5'2".

Year - League - Team			GP	G	A	PTS	PM	Year - Playoff		GP	G	A	PTS	PM
1993-94	COWHL	Toronto Junior Aeros	29	15	9	24	30							
1995-96	COWHL	North York Aeros	29	16	32	48	50							
1996	Nationals	North York Aeros	5	2	3	5	8							
1996-97	COWHL	North York Aeros	24	18	34	52	28							
1997-98	COWHL	North York Aeros	20	14	11	25	28							
1998	Nationals	North York Aeros	6	9	3	12	6							
1998-99	NWHL	North York Aeros	30	16	20	36	16							
1999	Nationals	North York Aeros		3	11	14								
1999-00	NWHL	North York Aeros	32	14	25	39	39	2000	NWHL-P					
2000	Nationals	North York Aeros		6	3	9								
2000-01	NWHL	North York Aeros	26	16	24	40	16							
2001	Nationals	North York Aeros												
2001-02	NWHL	North York Aeros	7	4	2	6	8							
2002	Nationals	North York Aeros	7	4	3	7	8							
2003-04	NWHL	Toronto Aeros	6	1	1	2	2	2004	NWHL-P					
2004	Nationals	Toronto Aeros	6	1	3	4	6							
2005-06	NWHL	Toronto Aeros	4	2	3	5	6							
Totals from all Competitions			**231**	**141**	**187**	**328**	**251**							

BENSON, BRENDA   *Forward. 1996 Nationals PEI Esso Tigers (4 games, 1 goal).*

BERG, JULIA   *Forward. Shoots left.*

Born 1983-02-04. Grew up in Stavanger, NOR. 5'8".

Year - League - Team	GP	G	A	PTS	PM
2001 Nationals Vancouver Griffins					
2002-03 NWHL Vancouver Griffins	24	3	5	8	14
2003 Nationals Vancouver Griffins	7	1	4	5	4

BERGER, DESIREE *Wangen Bei Olten, SUI. D. 2008-09 CWHL Ottawa #7 (16 games; 2 playoff games, 1 assist).*

BERGERON, DEBBIE *Forward. 1995 Nationals Britannia Blues.*

BERGERON, JILLIAN *Brockville, ON, CAN. Forward. 2007-08 CWHL Ottawa Capital Canucks #7 (1 game).*

BERGIN, SHEILA *2000-01 NWHL Brampton Thunder #11 (1 game).*

BERLINGUETTE, EMILIE *Forward. #76 #9 #11.*

Born 1983-12-25, Orléans, ON, CAN. Grew up in Orléans, ON, CAN. Forward. 5'4".

Year - League - Team	GP	G	A	PTS	PM
1999-00 NWHL Ottawa Raiders	6	2	1	3	0
2000-01 NWHL Ottawa Raiders	2	2	2	4	0
2001-02 NWHL Ottawa Raiders	28	13	7	20	12
2008-09 CWHL Ottawa Senators	4	2	1	3	2
Totals from all Competitions	**40**	**19**	**11**	**30**	**14**

BERMAN, LINDSAY *Forward. Shoots right. #10 #13.*

Clarkson Cup winner with Boston on 2013-03-23
Born 1988-7-15. Grew up in Odenton, MD, USA. 5'7". Debut at age 22 on 2010-10-30.

Year - League - Team	GP	G	A	PTS	PM	Year - Playoff	GP	G	A	PTS	PM
2010-11 CWHL Boston Blades	20	2	5	7	18	2011 CWHL-P	2		1	1	
2011-12 CWHL Boston Blades	13	3	2	5	10	2012 C-Cup	3	0	0	0	0
2012-13 CWHL Boston Blades	11	1	0	1	2	2013 C-Cup	4	0	0	0	0
2013-14 CWHL Boston Blades	6	0	1	1	2	2014 C-Cup	4	0	0	0	2
2015-16 NWHL/ Connecticut Whale	3	0	1	1	0						
CWHL Regular Season	50	6	8	14	32	Clarkson Cup	11	0	0	0	2
Totals from all Competitions	**66**	**6**	**10**	**16**	**34**						

BERNARD, CARRIE *Forward. 2008 Nationals Prince Edward Island (5 games, 2 assists).*

BERRY, KIM *2003-04 NWHL Ottawa Raiders (? games).*

BERTHIAUME, MELISSA *Defence. Shoots right.*

Born 1982-09-09. Grew up in Antigonish, NS, CAN.

Year - League - Team	GP	G	A	PTS	PM
2002 Nationals Nova Scotia	5	0	0	0	0
2003 Nationals Nova Scotia Selects	6	0	0	0	0
2007 Nationals Nova Scotia Selects	7	0	0	0	6

BERTI, KATHERINE *2000-01 NWHL Brampton Thunder #11 (2 games).*

BERTRAND, CATHERINE *Forward. Shoots left. #10 #27.*

NWHL winner. Born 1976-7-15, Montréal, QC, CAN. Grew up in Sherbrooke, QC, CAN. 5'5".

Year - League - Team	GP	G	A	PTS	PM	Year - Playoff	GP	G	A	PTS	PM
1999-00 NWHL Wingstar de Montréal	33	7	8	15	16						
2000-01 NWHL Wingstar de Montréal	40	14	14	28	27						
2001 Nationals Équipe Québec											
2001-02 NWHL Wingstar de Montréal	29	9	8	17	20						
2002 Nationals Équipe Québec	6	0	1	1	2						
2002-03 NWHL Axion de Montréal	36	6	15	21	42	2003 NWHL-P					
2003-04 NWHL Axion de Montréal	35	6	10	16	24						
2004-05 NWHL Axion de Montréal	31	7	4	11	28						
2005 Nationals Axion de Montréal	6	1	2	3	17						
2005-06 NWHL Axion de Montréal	23	7	11	18	26	2006 NWHL-P	3	0	0	0	6
2006 Nationals Axion de Montréal	6	0	1	1	8						
2006-07 NWHL Axion de Montréal						2007 NWHL-P					
2007-08 CWHL Stars de Montréal	2	1	0	1	4						
Totals from all Competitions	**232**	**57**	**70**	**127**	**193**						

BÉRUBÉ, CAROLINE *Roberval, QC, CAN. F. 2006-07 NWHL Montréal (? games); 2007-08 CWHL (1 game).*

BÉRUBÉ, MARTINE *Forward. Shoots left. #17.*

Born 1971-11-02.

Year - League - Team	GP	G	A	PTS	PM
1995 Nationals Équipe Québec					
1996 Nationals Équipe Québec	6	0	2	2	0
1998 Nationals Équipe Québec	6	0	0	0	0
1999-00 NWHL Sainte-Julie Panthères	20	1	6	7	8

BERZINS, EMILY *Forward. Shoots left. #27 #17 #14.*

Born 1987-2-1, Fernie, BC, CAN. Grew up in Fort McMurray, AB, CAN. 5'5". Debut at age 23 on 2009-10-3.

Year - League - Team	GP	G	A	PTS	PM	Year - Playoff	GP	G	A	PTS	PM
2009-10 CWHL Vaughan Flames	27	8	7	15	32						
2012-13 CWHL Alberta	17	1	0	1	12						

Year - League - Team			GP	G	A	PTS	PM	Year - Playoff	GP	G	A	PTS	PM
2013-14	CWHL	Calgary Inferno	24	1	3	4	36	2014 C-Cup	3	0	0	0	6
2014-15	CWHL	Calgary Inferno	8	0	0	0	0						
CWHL Regular Season			76	10	10	20	80	Clarkson Cup	3	0	0	0	6
Totals from all Competitions			**79**	**10**	**10**	**20**	**86**						

BESNER, KARINE *Forward. 2004-05 WWHL Edmonton #11 (4 games, 1 assist; 1 playoff game).*

BESTWICK, BROOKE *Defence. #4.*
Born 1981-2-16, Nanaimo, BC, CAN. 5'3".

Year - League - Team			GP	G	A	PTS	PM	Year - Playoff	GP	G	A	PTS	PM
1999	Nationals	New Westminster Lightning	5	0	1	1							
2004-05	WWHL	British Columbia Breakers	8	1	5	6	14						
2006-07	WWHL	British Columbia Breakers	15	2	10	12	38	2007 WWHL-P	2	0	0	0	2
2007-08	WWHL	British Columbia Breakers	7	1	0	1	18						
Totals from all Competitions			**37**	**4**	**16**	**20**	**72**						

BETTEZ, ANN-SOPHIE *Forward. Shoots left. #24.*
Clarkson Cup winner with Montréal on 2017-03-05
Born 1987-10-14, Sept-Îles, QC, CAN. 5'4". Debut at age 19 on 2006-10-22.

Year - League - Team			GP	G	A	PTS	PM	Year - Playoff	GP	G	A	PTS	PM
2006-07	NWHL	Avalanche du Québec	3	0	1	1	0						
2012-13	CWHL	Stars de Montréal	23	17	16	33	2	2013 C-Cup	4	1	0	1	8
2013-14	CWHL	Stars de Montréal	23	16	24	40	12	2014 C-Cup	3	3	0	3	6
2014-15	CWHL	Stars de Montréal	22	11	12	23	4	2015 C-Cup	3	2	0	2	4
2015-16	CWHL	Canadiennes de Montréal	24	19	25	44	12	2016 C-Cup	3	1	6	7	4
2016-17	CWHL	Canadiennes de Montréal	24	18	18	36	4	2017 C-Cup	3	1	2	3	0
2017-18	CWHL	Canadiennes de Montréal	28	20	21	41	10	2018 C-Cup	2	0	0	0	0
2018-19	CWHL	Canadiennes de Montréal	26	18	30	48	16	2019 C-Cup	4	2	1	3	0
CWHL Regular Season			170	119	146	265	60	Clarkson Cup	22	10	9	19	22
Totals from all Competitions			**195**	**129**	**156**	**285**	**82**						

CWHL Most Valuable Player in 2013-14... Angela James Bowl in 2013-14... CWHL goal-scoring leader in 2012-13 (tie), 2013-14... CWHL Top Forward in 2013-14... CWHL First All-Star Team in 2013-14 and 2017-18; CWHL Second All-Star Team 2014-15, 2015-16, 2016-17, 2018-19... CWHL Rookie of the Year in 2012-13... CWHL All-Rookie Team in 2012-13... scored 100th CWHL point on 2015-10-31... scored 200th CWHL point on 2018-01-27... scored 100th CWHL goal on 2018-3-10... selected First Decade CWHL Team in 2017

BETTLES, MICHELLE *F. 2006-07 WWHL BC #7 (9 gp, 4 pts; 2 playoff games), 2007 Nationals BC (5 gp, 2pts).*

BETTS, ALICIA *Forward. 2006 Nationals Newfoundland Labrador (5 games).*

BEVAN, ANDREA *Collingwood, ON. D/F. 2005-06 NWHL Toronto (1 gp); 2010-11 CWHL Burlington (13 gp, 1 goal).*

BIANCHI, ALESSANDRA *Centre. Shoots left. #14.*
Born 1994-11-25. Grew up in Toronto, ON, CAN. 5'3". Debut at age 22 on 2017-10-15.

Year - League - Team			GP	G	A	PTS	PM
2017-18	CWHL	Toronto Furies	25	0	1	1	4

BILODEAU, DANIELLE *Defence. 2001-02 NWHL North York Aeros #15 (6 games, 2 goals, 2 assists).*

BILODEAU, VIRGINIE *Defence. Shoots left. #11.*
Born 1978-3-2, St-Etienne Lauzon, QC, CAN. 5'4".

Year - League - Team			GP	G	A	PTS	PM	Year - Playoff	GP	G	A	PTS	PM
1999	Nationals	Équipe Québec	5	0	1	1							
2000	Nationals	Équipe Québec	6	0	1	1							
2000-01	NWHL	Wingstar de Montréal	24	3	9	12	22						
2001	Nationals	Équipe Québec											
2001-02	NWHL	Wingstar de Montréal	24	7	5	12	10						
2002	Nationals	Équipe Québec	6	0	2	2	0						
2002-03	NWHL	Axion de Montréal	29	7	16	23	42	2003 NWHL-P					
2003	Nationals	Équipe Québec	5	2	2	4	2						
2003-04	NWHL	Axion de Montréal	32	4	21	25	24						
2004	Nationals	Équipe Québec	7	0	4	4	10						
Totals from all Competitions			**138**	**23**	**61**	**84**	**110**						

BINNING, MICHELLE *Oshawa, ON, CAN. Forward. 2005-06 NWHL Toronto Aeros #15 (1 game, 1 assist).*

BIRCHARD-KESSEL, COURTNEY *Defence. Shoots left. #24.*
Born 1989-7-14. Grew up in Mississauga, ON, CAN. 5'8". Debut at age 16 on 2005-10-30.

Year - League - Team			GP	G	A	PTS	PM	Year - Playoff	GP	G	A	PTS	PM
2005-06	NWHL	Toronto Aeros	2	1	0	1	0						
2011-12	CWHL	Brampton Thunder	25	3	13	16	14	2012 C-Cup	4	1	1	2	2
2012-13	CWHL	Brampton Thunder	24	0	9	9	30	2013 C-Cup	3	0	1	1	2
2014-15	CWHL	Brampton Thunder	13	0	5	5	22						
2015-16	CWHL	Brampton Thunder	24	3	17	20	10	2016 C-Cup	2	1	0	1	2
2016-17	CWHL	Brampton Thunder	20	4	11	15	12	2017 C-Cup	2	0	0	0	2
CWHL Regular Season			106	10	55	65	88	Clarkson Cup	11	2	2	4	8
Totals from all Competitions			**119**	**13**	**57**	**70**	**96**						

CWHL Second All-Star Team in 2015-16... CWHL Rookie of the Year in 2011-12... CWHL All-Rookie Team in 2011-12... finished 16th in the Angela James Bowl scoring race in 2015-16... has served as head coach with CWHL Toronto.

BIZZARI, MELISSA
Forward. Shoots right. #23.

Born 1992-3-27. Grew up in Stowe, VT, USA. 5'5". Debut at age 24 on 2016-10-15.

Year - League - Team		GP	G	A	PTS	PM
2016-17	NWHL/ Boston Pride	22	2	6	8	18
2017-18	NWHL/ Boston Pride	25	4	8	12	8
NWHL Regular Season		47	6	14	20	26

BJURMAN, NATALIE
N. Vancouver, BC. Forward. 2006-07 WWHL BC #27 (24 gp, 1 goal, 1 assist; 2 playoff gp).

BLACK, DRU
Left wing. Shoots left. #22.

Born 1980-12-8, Craven, SK, CAN. 5'5".

Year - League - Team		GP	G	A	PTS	PM	Year - Playoff		GP	G	A	PTS	PM
2004-05	WWHL Saskatchewan Prairie Ice	21	1	1	2	4							
2005-06	WWHL Saskatchewan Prairie Ice	24	3	1	4	4	2006 WWHL-P		2	0	0	0	0
2006-07	WWHL Saskatchewan Prairie Ice	21	0	3	3	2							
Totals from all Competitions		**68**	**4**	**5**	**9**	**10**							

BLACK, KRISTA
Defence. Shoots left. #15 #12.

Born 1980-6-15, Kingsclear, NB, CAN. 5'9".

Year - League - Team		GP	G	A	PTS	PM	Year - Playoff		GP	G	A	PTS	PM
1999	Nationals Team New Brunswick	6	0	0	0								
2000	Nationals Team New Brunswick	6	0	0	0								
2001	Nationals Team New Brunswick												
2003	Nationals Team New Brunswick	4	1	1	2	0							
2003-04	NWHL Ottawa Raiders	36	1	9	10	14							
2004-05	NWHL Ottawa Raiders	36	2	3	5	10							
2005	Nationals Team New Brunswick	6	2	5	7	0							
2005-06	NWHL Ottawa Raiders	36	0	11	11	8	2006 NWHL-P		0	0	0	0	0
2006-07	NWHL Ottawa Raiders	1	0	0	0	0							
Totals from all Competitions		**131**	**6**	**29**	**35**	**32**							

BLACK, TEEGON
2003-04 NWHL Ottawa Raiders #16 (14 games, 1 goal, 1 assist).

BLACKWOOD, ASHLEY
Forward. 2006 Nationals Newfoundland Labrador (5 games, 1 goal).

BLAIN, KIM
Forward. Shoots right. #22 #8.

Born 1993-09-11, Hawkesbury, ON, CAN.

Year - League - Team		GP	G	A	PTS	PM
2002	Nationals Calgary Oval X-Treme	6	1	1	2	6
2002-03	NWHL Ottawa Raiders	6	0	1	1	0
2007-08	CWHL Ottawa Capital Canucks	3	1	1	2	6

Scored first goal in CWHL history on 2007-09-15.

BLAIN, MAUDE
Magog, QC, CAN. Defence. 2007-08 CWHL Stars de Montréal #8 (2 games).

BLAINEY, JUSTINE
Defence. #9.

Year - League - Team		GP	G	A	PTS	PM
1992-93	COWHL Scarborough Sting	26	2	7	9	14
1993-94	COWHL Toronto Aeros	23	3	6	9	28
1995-96	COWHL North York Aeros	28	6	8	14	32
1996	Nationals North York Aeros	5	0	0	0	10
1996-97	COWHL Mississauga Chiefs	30	1	16	17	28
1997-98	COWHL Mississauga Chiefs	14	1	5	6	8
1998-99	NWHL Brampton Thunder	36	5	11	16	48
1999-00	NWHL Brampton Thunder	9	0	5	5	12
2001-02	NWHL Brampton Thunder	2	0	0	0	2
Totals from all Competitions		**173**	**18**	**58**	**76**	**182**

BLAIR, DESIREE
Forward. 2007 Nationals BC Outback (5 games, 1 assist).

BLAIR, LAURIE
Forward. 2005-06 WWHL Saskatchewan #25 (9 games, 1 assist, 2 playoff games).

BLAIS, EMMANUELLE
Forward. Shoots right. #47.

Clarkson Cup winner with Montréal on 2011-03-27, 2012-03-25 and 2017-03-05
Born 1987-11-7, Lasalle, QC, CAN. Grew up in Montréal, QC, CAN. 5'4".

Year - League - Team		GP	G	A	PTS	PM	Year - Playoff		GP	G	A	PTS	PM
2004-05	NWHL Axion de Montréal	15	4	5	9	10							
2005	Nationals Axion de Montréal	6	1	1	2	0							
2010-11	CWHL Stars de Montréal	26	11	21	32	30	2011 CWHL-P		2				
							2011 C-Cup		4	1	4	5	4
2011-12	CWHL Stars de Montréal	21	10	17	27	24	2012 C-Cup		4	2	3	5	4
2012-13	CWHL Stars de Montréal	23	11	14	25	18	2013 C-Cup		4	1	1	2	2
2013-14	CWHL Stars de Montréal	23	7	10	17	12	2014 C-Cup		3	1	2	3	6
2014-15	CWHL Stars de Montréal	18	5	9	14	12	2015 C-Cup		3	2	1	3	2
2015-16	CWHL Canadiennes de Montréal	23	4	4	8	12	2016 C-Cup		3	0	0	0	0

Year - League - Team			GP	G	A	PTS	PM	Year - Playoff	GP	G	A	PTS	PM
2016-17	CWHL	Canadiennes de Montréal	20	0	3	3	12	2017 C-Cup	3	0	1	1	4
2017-18	CWHL	Canadiennes de Montréal	28	4	4	8	16	2018 C-Cup	2	1	0	1	0
2018-19	CWHL	Canadiennes de Montréal	2	0	3	3	0						
CWHL Regular Season			184	52	85	137	136	Clarkson Cup	26	8	12	20	22
Totals from all Competitions			**233**	**65**	**103**	**168**	**168**						

Finished 5th in the Angela James Bowl scoring race in 2010-11... scored 100th CWHL point on 2014-03-08

BLAIS, MARIE-SOLEIL
2006-07 NWHL Axion de Montréal #74 (4 games, 1 assist).

BLAKE, ERIN
D. 2006-07 WWHL Edmonton #15 (24 gp, 1 goal, 4 assists; 2 playoff games); 2007-08 (23 games).

BLAKE, JULIE
Defence. 1998-99 NWHL Ottawa #22 (33 games, 1 goal, 4 assists).

BLANCHARD, DANIELLE
Forward. #11 #5.

Born 1985-12-3. Grew up in Newmarket, ON, CAN. Debut at age 24 on 2009-10-3.

Year - League - Team			GP	G	A	PTS	PM
2009-10	CWHL	Vaughan Flames	28	13	13	26	20
2010-11	CWHL	Burlington Barracudas	25	6	6	12	18
CWHL Regular Season			53	19	19	38	38

CWHL Rookie of the Year in 2009-10... CWHL All-Rookie Team in 2009-10... finished 13th in the Angela James Bowl scoring race in 2009-10

BLANDFORD, HEATHER
F. 1996-97 COWHL Peterborough (17 gp, 1 goal, 1 a.); 1998-99 NWHL Scarb. (7 gp).

BLANKENSHIP, KELLI
Jacksonville, FL. F. 2010-11 WWHL Minnesota #6 (7 gp, 1 goal, 4 assists; C-Cup 2 gp).

BLOW, VICKI
1998-99 NWHL Brampton (2gp); 2000-01 North York (1 gp, 1 a.); 2001-02 Mississauga (5 gp).

BLUNDY, MERRITT
2000-01 NWHL Mississauga #41 (6 games); 2001-02 NWHL #27 (6 gp, 1 assist).

BOAL, MELISSA
Forward. Shoots left. #2 #6.

Born 1986-9-6, Almonte, ON, CAN. Grew up in Pakenham, ON, CAN.

Year - League - Team			GP	G	A	PTS	PM
2004-05	NWHL	Ottawa Raiders	2	0	0	0	0
2009-10	CWHL	Ottawa Senators	24	7	9	16	14
2010-11	CWHL	Toronto Furies	11	3	0	3	4
Totals from all Competitions			**37**	**10**	**9**	**19**	**18**

BOCCHIA, EMILIE
Left wing. Shoots left. #62.

Clarkson Cup winner with Montréal on 2017-03-05
Born 1990-06-26. Grew up St-Léonard, QC, CAN. 5'3". Debut at age 23 on 2013-11-9.

Year - League - Team			GP	G	A	PTS	PM	Year - Playoff	GP	G	A	PTS	PM
2013-14	CWHL	Stars de Montréal	23	1	1	2	0	2014 C-Cup	2	0	0	0	0
2014-15	CWHL	Stars de Montréal	22	1	3	4	4	2015 C-Cup	3	0	0	0	0
2015-16	CWHL	Canadiennes de Montréal	22	3	2	5	2	2016 C-Cup	3	0	0	0	0
2016-17	CWHL	Canadiennes de Montréal	12	0	1	1	0	2017 C-Cup	2	0	0	0	0
CWHL Regular Season			79	5	7	12	6	Clarkson Cup	10	0	0	0	0
Totals from all Competitions			**89**	**5**	**7**	**12**	**6**						

BODE, JENEL
Forward. Shoots left. #18.

Abby Hoffman Cup winner with Calgary on 2003-03-16.
Born 1980-6-4. Grew up in Yorkton, SK, CAN.

Year - League - Team			GP	G	A	PTS	PM	Year - Playoff	GP	G	A	PTS	PM
1998	Nationals	Saskatchewan Selects	6	1	3	4	2						
2002-03	NWHL	Calgary Oval X-Treme	21	8	7	15	12	2003 NWHL-P					
2003	Nationals	Calgary Oval X-Treme	5	2	1	3	2						
2003-04	NWHL	Calgary Oval X-Treme	12	2	7	9	10	2004 NWHL-P					
2004	Nationals	Calgary Oval X-Treme	6	0	1	1	2						
2007-08	WWHL	Strathmore Rockies	23	5	9	14	24						
Totals from all Competitions			**73**	**18**	**28**	**46**	**52**						

BOEHM, ERIN
Forward. 2007 Nationals BC Outback (5 games, 1 assist).

BOIES, AMANDA
Defence. Shoots left..

Born 1981-12-10. Grew up in Fredericton, NB, CAN.

Year - League - Team			GP	G	A	PTS	PM	Year - Playoff	GP	G	A	PTS	PM
2004	Nationals	Team New Brunswick	5	0	0	0	4						
2005-06	NWHL	Oakville Ice	36	0	4	4	50	2006 NWHL-P	2	0	0	0	0
2007	Nationals	Team New Brunswick	6	0	1	1	20						

BOISCLAIR, VALERIE
Defence. 2005-06 NWHL Avalanche du Québec #7 (3 games, 1 goal).

BOISMENU, KIM
Forward. 2007-08 CWHL Stars de Montréal (2 games, 1 playoff game).

BOITEAU, MELANIE
Forward. 1998-99 NWHL Laval #93 (28 gp, 7 goals, 8 assists); 1999-00 #62 (2 gp, 2 a.).

BOLAND, DENISE
Defence. 2000 Nationals Newfoundland Labrador (5 games).

BOLDEN, BLAKE
Defence. Shoots right. #5 #10.

Clarkson Cup winner with Boston on 2015-03-07. Isobel Cup winner with Boston on 2016-03-12
Born 1991-03-10 in Euclid, OH, USA. Grew up in Stow, OH, USA. 5'7". Debut at age 22 on 2013-11-02.

Year - League - Team			GP	G	A	PTS	PM	Year - Playoff	GP	G	A	PTS	PM
2013-14	CWHL	Boston Blades	23	5	14	19	44	2014 C-Cup	4	0	1	1	4

Year - League - Team			GP	G	A	PTS	PM	Year - Playoff	GP	G	A	PTS	PM
2014-15	CWHL	Boston Blades	22	3	10	13	22	2015 C-Cup	3	0	1	1	4
2015-16	NWHL/	Boston Pride	18	1	8	9	10	2016 I-Cup	4	2	1	3	2
2016-17	NWHL/	Boston Pride	17	1	5	6	14	2017 I-Cup	2	0	1	1	0
2018-19	NWHL/	Buffalo Beauts	16	1	12	13	4	2019 I-Cup	2	0	2	2	0
CWHL Regular Season			45	8	24	32	66	Clarkson Cup	7	0	2	2	8
NWHL Regular Season			51	3	25	28	28	Isobel Cup	8	2	4	6	2
Totals from all Competitions			**111**	**13**	**55**	**68**	**104**						

CWHL First All-Star Team in 2013-14, 2014-15... CWHL All-Rookie Team in 2013-14... finished 11th in the Angela James Bowl scoring race in 2013-14... NWHL Defensive Player of the Year in 2018-19.

BOMBARDIER, KARRINE   *Forward. 2003-04 NWHL Québec (18 gp, 4 goals, 6 assists); 2004-05 (11 gp).*

BONANG, LISA   *Forward. 2006 Nationals British Columbia (6 gp); 2007 BC (5 gp, 1 goal).*

BOND, JESSICA   *Namur, QC. Defence. 2005-06 NWHL Québec (1 gp); 2006-07 (5 gp, 1 assist; playoffs).*

BONDY, JEANETTE   *Forward. 1996-97 COWHL Scarborough #6 (19 games, 4 goals, 5 assists).*

BONELLO, MICHELLE   *Defence. Shoots right. #4.*
Clarkson Cup winner with Toronto on 2014-03-22
Born 1985-3-10, Etobicoke, ON, CAN. Grew up in Mississauga, ON, CAN. 5'5". Debut at age 23 on 2007-11-17.

Year - League - Team			GP	G	A	PTS	PM	Year		GP	G	A	PTS	PM
2007-08	CWHL	Vaughan Flames	21	2	7	9	22	2008	CWHL-P	2	0	0	0	0
2008-09	CWHL	Vaughan Flames	27	1	7	8	32	2009	CWHL-P	2				
2009-10	CWHL	Vaughan Flames	27	10	18	28	50							
2010-11	CWHL	Toronto Furies	20	4	6	10	38	2011	CWHL-P	2		1	1	6
								2011	C-Cup	4	2	1	3	8
2011-12	CWHL	Toronto Furies	20	2	1	3	12	2012	C-Cup	1	0	0	0	0
2013-14	CWHL	Toronto Furies	22	2	10	12	39	2014	C-Cup	4	0	0	0	8
2014-15	CWHL	Toronto Furies	24	0	4	4	38	2015	C-Cup	2	0	0	0	0
2015-16	CWHL	Toronto Furies	24	0	8	8	38	2016	C-Cup	2	0	0	0	8
CWHL Regular Season			185	21	61	82	269	Clarkson Cup		13	2	1	3	24
Totals from all Competitions			**204**	**23**	**63**	**86**	**299**							

CWHL First All-Star Team in 2009-10... finished 11th in the Angela James Bowl scoring race in 2009-10

BONHOMME, TESSA   *Defence. Shoots left. #20 #25.*
Olympic champion, IIHF champion. Clarkson Cup winner with Toronto on 2014-03-22
Born 1985-7-23, Sudbury, ON, CAN. 5'7".

Year - League - Team			GP	G	A	PTS	PM	Year - Playoff		GP	G	A	PTS	PM
2008-09	WWHL	Calgary Oval X-Treme	21	12	21	33	18	2000	WWIIL-P	2	1	2	3	2
								2009	C-Cup	2	1	0	1	6
2010-11	CWHL	Toronto Furies	22	5	6	11	24	2011	CWHL-P	2	3	1	4	
								2011	C-Cup	4	2	2	4	4
2011-12	CWHL	Toronto Furies	24	4	12	16	16	2012	C-Cup	3	0	1	1	0
2012-13	CWHL	Toronto Furies	24	4	5	9	22	2013	C-Cup	3	0	3	3	4
2013-14	CWHL	Toronto Furies	11	1	3	4	10	2014	C-Cup	4	0	1	1	4
2014-15	CWHL	Toronto Furies	12	2	2	4	12	2015	C-Cup	2	1	1	2	2
CWHL Regular Season			93	16	28	44	84	Clarkson Cup		18	4	8	12	20
Totals from all Competitions			**136**	**36**	**60**	**96**	**124**							

CWHL Second All-Star Team in 2011-12 and 2012-13

BONIA, APRYL   *Defence. 2003 Nationals Nova Scotia Selects (6 games).*

BORDELEAU, MELANIE   *Forward. #11 #18 #6.*

Year - League - Team			GP	G	A	PTS	PM
1999-00	NWHL	Wingstar de Montréal	2	0	0	0	0
2000-01	NWHL	Ottawa Raiders	30	0	8	8	26
2001-02	NWHL	Ottawa Raiders	22	1	4	5	8
Totals from all Competitions			**54**	**1**	**12**	**13**	**34**

BORTON, VANESSA   *Forward. 2006 Nationals Manitoba Selects (5 games, 1 goal, 1 assist).*

BOTTERILL, JENNIFER   *Forward. Shoots left. #17.*
Olympic champion, IIHF champion. Abby Hoffman Cup winner with Calgary on 1998-03-22. Abby Hoffman Cup winner with Aeros on 2004-03-14 and 2005-03-13. Abby Hoffman Cup winner with Mississauga on 2008-03-15.
Born 1979-5-1, Ottawa, ON, CAN. Grew up in Winnipeg, MB, CAN. 5'9".

Year - League - Team			GP	G	A	PTS	PM	Year - Playoff	GP	G	A	PTS	PM
1995	Nationals	Winnipeg Sweat Camp											
1996	Nationals	Winnipeg Sweat Camp	6	1	2	3	2						
1998	Nationals	Calgary Oval X-Treme	7	6	6	12	0						
2003-04	NWHL	Toronto Aeros	36	30	31	61	16						
2004	Nationals	Toronto Aeros	6	6	5	11	0						
2004-05	NWHL	Toronto Aeros	29	22	33	55	18	2005 NWHL-P					
2005	Nationals	Toronto Aeros	7	3	10	13	2						
2005-06	NWHL	Toronto Aeros	0	0	0	0	0						
2006-07	NWHL	Mississauga Aeros	29	15	22	37	14	2007 NWHL-P	4	1	5	6	0
2007	Nationals	Mississauga Aeros	6	5	5	10	0						

Year - League - Team		GP	G	A	PTS	PM	Year - Playoff	GP	G	A	PTS	PM
2007-08	CWHL Mississauga Chiefs	26	24	37	61	22	2008 CWHL-P	5	6	1	7	2
2008	Nationals Mississauga Chiefs	3	1	3	4	0						
2008-09	CWHL Mississauga Chiefs	28	25	30	55	30	2009 CWHL-P	4	5	8	13	6
2010-11	CWHL Toronto Furies	22	13	25	38	12	2011 CWHL-P	2		5	5	
							2011 C-Cup	4	1	3	4	4
	CWHL Regular Season	76	62	92	154	64	Clarkson Cup	4	1	3	4	4
	Totals from all Competitions	**224**	**164**	**231**	**395**	**128**						

First Angela James Bowl winner in 2007-08... CWHL Top Forward in 2007-08... CWHL Central All-Star Team in 2007-08; CWHL First All-Star Team in 2008-09; CWHL Second All-Star Team in 2010-11... scored 100th CWHL point on 2009-02-07... selected First Decade CWHL Team in 2017

BOUCHARD, ANNICK
Defence. Shoots left. #14 #11 #17.

Born 1978-12-17. Grew up in St-Laurent, QC, CAN.

Year - League - Team		GP	G	A	PTS	PM
1998	Nationals Équipe Québec	6	1	1	2	6
1998-99	NWHL Mistral de Laval	34	2	17	19	51
1999	Nationals Équipe Québec	5	0	2	2	
1999-00	NWHL Mistral de Laval	32	7	8	15	91
2000-01	NWHL Mistral de Laval	36	5	13	18	110
2001	Nationals Équipe Québec					
2001-02	NWHL Cheyenne	3	0	1	1	6
2002-03	NWHL Avalanche du Québec	7	2	5	7	8
	Totals from all Competitions	**123**	**17**	**47**	**64**	**272**

BOUCHARD, K.
1999 Nationals Calgary Oval X-Treme (6 games, 1 assist)

BOUCHARD, STACY
Defence. 1995 Nationals Winnipeg Sweat Camp.

BOUCHER, ANNIE
Forward. Shoots right. #21 #4.

Born 1975-12-27. Grew up in Ste-Anne-de-Beaupré, QC, CAN.

Year - League - Team		GP	G	A	PTS	PM
1999	Nationals Équipe Québec	6	2	1	3	
2000	Nationals Équipe Québec	6	0	4	4	
2000-01	NWHL Sainte-Julie	35	13	16	29	32
2001	Nationals Équipe Québec					
2001-02	NWHL Cheyenne	7	1	0	1	0
2002-03	NWHL Avalanche du Québec	1	0	0	0	0
	Totals from all Competitions	**54**	**16**	**21**	**37**	**32**

BOUCHER, KASEY
Lewiston, ME, USA. Defence. 2012-13 CWHL Boston Blades #3 #18 (11 games, 1 goal).

BOUCHER, MARIE
Forward. 1999-00 NWHL Laval #65 (15 games, 2 goals, 2 assists).

BOUCHER, MARILYN
Defence. 1999-00 NWHL Laval #5 (24 games, 4 assists).

BOUCHER, NATHALIE

Born 1973-05-23.

Year - League - Team		GP	G	A	PTS	PM
1995	Nationals Maritime Sports Blades					
1996	Nationals Maritime Sport Blades	6	0	0	0	0
1998	Nationals Maritime Sports Blades	6	0	0	0	2

BOUDREAU, CATHERINE
Forward. 2008 Nationals Team New Brunswick (5 games, 2 points).

BOUDREAU, DANIELLE
Defence. Shoots left. #18.

Born 1990-08-29. Grew up in Whitby, ON. 5'6".

Year - League - Team		GP	G	A	PTS	PM
2013-14	CWHL Brampton Thunder	24	6	2	8	20
2014-15	CWHL Brampton Thunder	10	0	1	1	2
	CWHL Regular Season	34	6	3	9	22

BOUDREAU, MYRIAM
Defence. Shoots right. #76 #16.

Born 1980-5-4, Îles-de-la-Madeleine, QC, CAN. 5'6".

Year - League - Team		GP	G	A	PTS	PM
2003-04	NWHL Avalanche du Québec	27	1	6	7	6
2004-05	NWHL Avalanche du Québec	36	2	5	7	8
2005-06	NWHL Avalanche du Québec	35	0	2	2	2
	Totals from all Competitions	**98**	**3**	**13**	**16**	**16**

BOUDREAU, STEPHANIE
Defence. 1999 Nationals Team New Brunswick (6 games, 1 assist).

BOUETZ-ANDRIEU, VIRGINIE
Defence. Shoots right. #84.

Born 1984-3-14, FRA. Grew up in FRA. Debut at age 29 on 2012-11-24.

Year - League - Team		GP	G	A	PTS	PM	Year - Playoff	GP	G	A	PTS	PM
2012-13	CWHL Stars de Montréal	17	0	2	2	2						
2013-14	CWHL Stars de Montréal	18	1	2	3	2	2014 C-Cup	3	0	0	0	0
2014-15	CWHL Stars de Montréal	20	0	1	1	4	2015 C-Cup	0	0	0	0	0
	CWHL Regular Season	55	1	5	6	8	Clarkson Cup	3	0	0	0	0
	Totals from all Competitions	**58**	**1**	**5**	**6**	**8**						

BOULANGER, ALEXANDRA *2006-07 NWHL Montréal #17 (5 games); 2007-08 CWHL (4 games, 1 assist).*

BOULIER, AMANDA *Forward. Shoots right. #3.*
Isobel Cup winner with Minnesota on 2019-03-17.
Born 1993-3-30. Grew up in Watertown, CT, USA. 5'1". Debut at age 24 on 2017-11-4.

Year - League - Team			GP	G	A	PTS	PM	Year - Playoff	GP	G	A	PTS	PM
2017-18	NWHL/	Connecticut Whale	12	3	5	8	0	2018 I-Cup	1	0	0	0	2
2018-19	NWHL/	Minnesota Whitecaps	16	5	8	13	16	2019 I-Cup	2	1	1	2	2

NWHL Fans' Three Stars Award in 2018-19

BOURBEAU, SHARREL Defence. *2007-08 CWHL Québec #18 (27 games, 1 assist).*

BOURBEAU, STÉFANIE *Forward. #46.*
Clarkson Cup winner with Montréal on 2009-03-21
Born 1984-8-30, Charlesbourg, QC, CAN. 5'5". Debut at age 23 on 2007-9-15.

Year - League - Team			GP	G	A	PTS	PM	Year - Playoff	GP	G	A	PTS	PM
2003	Nationals	Équipe Québec	5	2	3	5	0						
2007-08	CWHL	Stars de Montréal	26	6	5	11	38	2008 CWHL-P	2	0	0	0	12
2008-09	CWHL	Stars de Montréal	30	14	15	29	42	2009 CWHL-P	2	0	0	0	0
								2009 C-Cup	3	2	2	4	4
2009-10	CWHL	Stars de Montréal	10	6	6	12	10	2010 C-Cup	1	0	0	0	0
CWHL Regular Season			66	26	26	52	90	Clarkson Cup	4	2	2	4	4
Totals from all Competitions			**79**	**30**	**31**	**61**	**106**						

Finished 12th in the Angela James Bowl scoring race in 2008-09

BOURDEAU, NADINE *Forward. Shoots left. #12 #8.*
Born 1975-4-15, Embrun, ON, CAN. 5'6".

Year - League - Team			GP	G	A	PTS	PM	Year - Playoff	GP	G	A	PTS	PM
1998-99	NWHL	Ottawa Raiders	34	11	11	22	46						
1999-00	NWHL	Ottawa Raiders	35	9	6	15	62						
2000-01	NWHL	Ottawa Raiders	38	13	20	33	72						
2001-02	NWHL	Ottawa Raiders	30	5	10	15	54	2002 NWHL-P					
2002-03	NWHL	Ottawa Raiders	33	11	16	27	36						
2003-04	NWHL	Ottawa Raiders	11	5	4	9	6						
2005-06	NWHL	Ottawa Raiders	36	9	11	20	20	2006 NWHL-P	2	0	0	0	2
2006-07	NWHL	Ottawa Raiders	35	12	8	20	44	2007 NWHL-P	2	4	0	4	4
2007-08	CWHL	Ottawa Capital Canucks	4	1	3	4	14						
Totals from all Competitions			**260**	**80**	**89**	**169**	**360**						

BOURGEOIS, ANNIK Forward. *2003 Nationals Team New Brunswick (4 games).*

BOURGEOIS, A. DANIELLE *Forward. Shoots left. #77 #88.*
Born 1981-7-15, Edmonton, AB, CAN. 5'4".

Year - League - Team			GP	G	A	PTS	PM	Year - Playoff	GP	G	A	PTS	PM
2005-06	WWHL	Edmonton Chimos	20	26	11	37	4	2006 WWHL-P	2	1	0	1	0
2006-07	WWHL	Edmonton Chimos	19	13	19	32	8	2007 WWHL-P	1	0	0	0	2
2007-08	WWHL	Edmonton Chimos	24	12	18	30	20						
Totals from all Competitions			**66**	**52**	**48**	**100**	**34**						

BOURGETTE, DANIELLE *Defence. Shoots left. #9.*
Born 1983-3-27. 5'9". Debut at age 22 on 2005-09-24.

Year - League - Team			GP	G	A	PTS	PM	Year - Playoff	GP	G	A	PTS	PM
2005-06	NWHL	Oakville Ice	36	1	14	15	28	2006 NWHL-P	2	0	0	0	0
2006-07	NWHL	Oakville Ice	35	1	7	8	62	2007 NWHL-P	3	0	0	0	4
Totals from all Competitions			**76**	**2**	**21**	**23**	**94**						

BOURS, NATHALIE Forward. *1999 Nationals Tazmanian Devils (4 games).*

BOWEN, CAROLYN Forward. *2008-09 WWHL Edmonton #81 (21 gp, 8 goals, 6 assists; 1 playoff game).*

BOWMAN, AMBER *Defence. Shoots right. #24 #15.*
Abby Hoffman Cup winner with Mississauga on 2008-03-15.
Born 1985-1-28, Barrie, ON, CAN. Grew up in Innisfil, ON, CAN. 5'8".

Year - League - Team			GP	G	A	PTS	PM	Year - Playoff	GP	G	A	PTS	PM
2001-02	NWHL	North York Aeros	2	0	0	0	0						
2007-08	CWHL	Mississauga Chiefs	29	5	13	18	20	2008 CWHL-P	5	1	1	2	10
2008	Nationals	Mississauga Chiefs	3	0	0	0	4						
2008-09	CWHL	Mississauga Chiefs	28	5	14	19	24	2009 CWHL-P	4	1		1	
2009-10	CWHL	Mississauga Chiefs	18	2	6	8	4	2010 C-Cup	1	0	0	0	0
2010-11	CWHL	Brampton Thunder	25	4	7	11	2	2011 CWHL-P	2	0	0	0	0
								2011 C-Cup	3	0	2	2	0
2011-12	CWHL	Toronto Furies	6	0	0	0	2	2012 C-Cup	3	0	0	0	0
2012-13	CWHL	Toronto Furies	13	1	0	1	6	2013 C-Cup	3	1	0	1	2
CWHL Regular Season			119	17	40	57	58	Clarkson Cup	10	1	2	3	2
Totals from all Competitions			**145**	**20**	**43**	**63**	**74**						

BOWYER, KAL Forward. *1998 Nationals New Westminster (5 gp, 2 pts), 1999 New Westminster (5 gp).*

BOYCE, DANIELLE
Forward. Shoots left. #21.

Born 1987-05-27. Grew up in Summerside, PE, CAN. 5'7".

Year	League	Team	GP	G	A	PTS	PM	Year	Playoff	GP	G	A	PTS	PM
2005	Nationals	Prince Edward Island	5	0	0	0	4							
2006	Nationals	Prince Edward Island	5	1	6	7	4							
2007	Nationals	Prince Edward Island	5	1	1	2	0							
2008	Nationals	Prince Edward Island	5	1	3	4	6							
2010-11	WWHL	Strathmore Rockies	8	0	1	1	6							

BOYD, JAMI
Forward. 2008 Nationals Manitoba (5 gp); 2009-10 CWHL Montréal #22 (9 gp, 1 assist).

BOYD, STEPHANIE
Forward. Shoots left. #22 #24.

Abby Hoffman Cup winner with Aeros on 1991-03-17, 1993-03-28 and 2004-03-14
Born 1972-12-11. Grew up in Gravenhurst, ON, CAN.

Year	League	Team	GP	G	A	PTS	PM	Year	Playoff	GP	G	A	PTS	PM
1992-93	COWHL	Toronto Aeros	24	11	13	24	23							
1993-94	COWHL	Scarborough Firefighters	29	14	26	40	20							
1995-96	COWHL	Toronto Red Wings	30	20	32	52	30							
1997-98	COWHL	Mississauga Chiefs	19	9	10	19	8							
1998-99	NWHL	Brampton Thunder	38	21	40	61	32							
1999-00	NWHL	Brampton Thunder	26	15	22	37	6							
2000-01	NWHL	Brampton Thunder	27	12	22	34	18							
2001-02	NWHL	Brampton Thunder	22	9	22	31	14	2003	NWHL-P					
2002	Nationals	Brampton Thunder	4	0	0	0	0							
2003-04	NWHL	Toronto Aeros	33	22	24	46	24	2004	NWHL-P					
2004	Nationals	Toronto Aeros	6	3	6	9	0							
Totals from all Competitions			**258**	**136**	**217**	**353**	**175**							

Served as head coach with CWHL Vaughan

BOYLE, KERRIE
Forward. Shoots right.

Born 1978-08-06. Grew up in Antigonish, NS, CAN.

Year	League	Team	GP	G	A	PTS	PM
1998	Nationals	Nova Scotia Selects	5	1	0	1	2
2000	Nationals	Nova Scotia Selects	6	1	0	1	
2002	Nationals	Nova Scotia	5	0	0	0	4
2003	Nationals	Nova Scotia Selects	6	5	0	5	14

BOZEK, MEGAN
Defence. Shoots right. #94.

IIHF champion
Clarkson Cup winner with Markham on 2018-03-25. Isobel Cup winner with Buffalo on 2017-03-19
Born 1991-03-27. Grew up in Buffalo Grove, IL, USA. 5'9". Debut at age 23 on 2014-10-18.

Year	League	Team	GP	G	A	PTS	PM	Year	Playoff	GP	G	A	PTS	PM
2014-15	CWHL	Toronto Furies	22	3	7	10	10	2015	C-Cup	2	1	0	1	2
2015-16	NWHL/	Buffalo Beauts	16	3	10	13	13	2016	I-Cup	5	3	3	6	6
2016-17	NWHL/	Buffalo Beauts	16	5	5	10	8	2017	I-Cup	2	2	2	4	0
2017-18	CWHL	Markham Thunder	10	4	5	9	10	2018	C-Cup	3	0	0	0	0
2018-19	CWHL	Markham Thunder	26	1	7	8	12	2019	C-Cup	3	0	0	0	0
CWHL Regular Season			58	8	19	27	32		Clarkson Cup	8	1	0	1	2
NWHL Regular Season			32	8	15	23	21		Isobel Cup	7	5	5	10	6
Totals from all Competitions			**105**	**22**	**39**	**61**	**61**							

NWHL Defensive Player of the Year in 2016-17... CWHL Second All-Star Team in 2017-18

BRACCO, JODIE
Bathurst, NB, CAN. Forward. 2008-09 CWHL Ottawa #5 (22 gp, 5 goals, 3 assists).

BRACKLEY, HEATHER
Defence. 1996-97 COWHL Scarborough #61 (1 game).

BRADBURN, BROOKE
Forward. Shoots right. #24 #66 #83.

Born 1980-4-17. Grew up in Brampton, ON, CAN.

Year	League	Team	GP	G	A	PTS	PM	Year	Playoff	GP	G	A	PTS	PM
2002-03	NWHL	Brampton Thunder						2003	NWHL-P					
2003	Nationals	Brampton Thunder	4	1	1	2	4							
2003-04	NWHL	Brampton Thunder												
2004-05	NWHL	Brampton Thunder	26	5	10	15	12							
2005	Nationals	Brampton Thunder	6	2	4	6	4							
2009-10	CWHL	Brampton Thunder	12	3	3	6	4							
Totals from all Competitions			**48**	**11**	**18**	**29**	**24**							

BRADFORD, AMANDA
Forward. 2004-05 NWHL Ottawa Raiders #15 (4 games).

BRADFORD, ASHLEY
Forward. 2002 Nationals Richmond Steelers (5 gp, 1 goal, 1 assist).

BRAM, BAILEY
Forward. Shoots left. #67 #27 #17.

Clarkson Cup winner with Calgary on 2016-03-14
Born 1990-9-5, Ste. Anne, MB, CAN. Grew up in Ste. Anne, MB, CAN. 5'9". Debut at age 22 on 2012-10-20.

Year	League	Team	GP	G	A	PTS	PM	Year	Playoff	GP	G	A	PTS	PM
2012-13	CWHL	Brampton Thunder	24	6	12	18	34	2013	C-Cup	3	2	0	2	2
2014-15	CWHL	Calgary Inferno	24	4	10	14	16	2015	C-Cup	2	0	0	0	2

Year - League - Team		GP	G	A	PTS	PM	Year - Playoff	GP	G	A	PTS	PM
2015-16	CWHL Calgary Inferno	16	3	11	14	18	2016 C-Cup	3	1	0	1	6
2016-17	CWHL Calgary Inferno	22	12	12	24	14	2017 C-Cup	4	0	0	0	2
CWHL Regular Season		86	25	45	70	82	Clarkson Cup	12	3	0	3	12
Totals from all Competitions		**98**	**28**	**45**	**73**	**94**						

Finished 6th in the Angela James Bowl scoring race in 2016-17

BRAM, SHELBY
Forward. Shoots left.

Born 1993-08-20. Grew up in Ste. Anne, MB, CAN. 5'1". Debut at age 22 on 2015-10-11.

Year - League - Team		GP	G	A	PTS	PM	Year - Playoff	GP	G	A	PTS	PM
2015-16	NWHL/ Buffalo Beauts	15	4	6	10	0	2016 I-Cup	5	1	1	2	2

BRAMWELL, GWEN
Forward. 1996 Nationals Saskatchewan (5 gp, 1 goal), 2003 Saskatchewan (6 gp, 1 goal).

BRAND, ERIN
Forward. Shoots right. #24.

Born 1990-12-19. Grew up in Lynbrook, NY, USA. 5'4". Debut at age 24 on 2015-10-11.

Year - League - Team		GP	G	A	PTS	PM	Year - Playoff	GP	G	A	PTS	PM
2018-19	NWHL/ Connecticut Whale	1	0	0	0	0						

BRAND, HOLLY
Forward. 1996-97 COWHL Peterborough #24 (32 games, 6 goals, 15 assists).

BRAND, MCKENNA
Forward. Shoots left. #17.

Born 1996-05-18. Grew up in Nevis, MN, USA. 5'6". Debut at age 22 on 2018-10-13.

Year - League - Team		GP	G	A	PTS	PM	Year - Playoff	GP	G	A	PTS	PM
2018-19	NWHL/ Boston Pride	16	6	11	17	6	2019 I-Cup	1	0	0	0	0

BRANDER, JOANNE
Forward. 2004 Nationals British Columbia (6 games).

BRANDT, HANNAH
Forward. Shoots right. #20.

IIHF champion. Isobel Cup winner with Minnesota on 2019-03-17.

Born 1993-11-27. Grew up in Vadnais Heights, MN, USA. 5'6". Debut at age 24 on 2018-10-06.

Year - League - Team		GP	G	A	PTS	PM	Year - Playoff	GP	G	A	PTS	PM
2018-19	NWHL/ Minnesota Whitecaps	16	5	6	11	0	2019 I-Cup	2	2	0	2	2

NWHL Foundation Award in 2018-19

BRASSARD, JANIE
Forward. 2006-07 NWHL Ottawa #44 (10 games, 1 goal).

BRAULT, SOPHIE
Defence. Shoots left. #23.

Clarkson Cup winner with Montréal on 2017-03-05.

Born 1988-11-2. Grew up in Saint-Jean-sur-Richelieu, QC, CAN. 5'5". Debut at age 19 on 2007-11-3.

Year - League - Team		GP	G	A	PTS	PM	Year - Playoff	GP	G	A	PTS	PM
2007-08	CWHL Stars de Montréal	4	0	0	0	4						
2014-15	CWHL Stars de Montréal	21	0	3	3	6	2015 C-Cup	3	0	0	0	0
2015-16	CWHL Canadiennes de Montréal	24	0	6	6	8	2016 C-Cup	3	0	0	0	0
2016-17	CWHL Canadiennes de Montréal	17	0	2	2	10	2017 C-Cup	1	0	0	0	0
2017-18	CWHL Canadiennes de Montréal	26	0	9	9	20	2018 C-Cup	2	0	0	0	0
2018-19	CWHL Canadiennes de Montréal	17	0	1	1	8	2019 C-Cup	4	0	1	1	2
CWHL Regular Season		109	0	21	21	56	Clarkson Cup	13	0	1	2	2
Totals from all Competitions		**122**	**0**	**22**	**22**	**58**						

BRAWN, JENNIFER
Forward. 2004 Nationals British Columbia (6 games).

BRAY, DEBBIE
Forward. 1996 Nationals Pictou County (4 games, 1 assist).

BREDIN, CORRENE
Defence. Shoots left. #23 #17 #2 #12 #21.

IIHF champion. WWHL winner. Abby Hoffman Cup winner with Edmonton on 1997-03-09. Abby Hoffman Cup winner with Calgary on 2007-03-10.

Born 1980-2-11, Warbury, AB, CAN. Grew up in Warburg, AB, CAN. 5'11".

Year - League - Team		GP	G	A	PTS	PM	Year - Playoff	GP	G	A	PTS	PM
1997	Nationals Edmonton Chimos											
1998	Nationals Edmonton Chimos	7	2	0	2	10						
2001-02	NWHL Mississauga IceBears	1	3	1	4	0						
2003-04	NWHL Calgary Oval X-Treme	7	3	7	10	6	2004 NWHL-P	4	1	1	2	6
2004	Nationals Calgary Oval X-Treme	6	1	3	4	6						
2004-05	WWHL Calgary Oval X-Treme	21	2	25	27	22	2005 WWHL-P	3	0	0	0	0
2006-07	WWHL Calgary Oval X-Treme	21	9	16	25	2	2007 WWHL-P	3	2	1	3	0
2007	Nationals Calgary Oval X-Treme	6	1	6	7	2						
2007-08	WWHL Strathmore Rockies	21	4	6	10	26						
Totals from all Competitions		**100**	**28**	**66**	**94**	**80**						

BREMILLER, ALANA
Forward. #18.

Born 1983-8-12. Debut at age 23 on 2006-10-27.

Year - League - Team		GP	G	A	PTS	PM	Year - Playoff	GP	G	A	PTS	PM
2006-07	WWHL British Columbia Breakers	23	7	12	19	48	2007 WWHL-P	0	0	0	0	0
2007-08	WWHL British Columbia Breakers	24	4	6	10	58						
2008-09	WWHL British Columbia Breakers	12	0	3	3	22						
Totals from all Competitions		**59**	**11**	**21**	**32**	**128**						

BRENNAN, CONNIE
Forward. 1995 Nationals PEI Esso Tigers, 1996 PEI Esso Tigers (4 games, 1 assist).

BRENNAN, MONIQUE
Defence. 2003 Nationals Saskatchewan (6 games).

BRETON-LEBREUX, LISA-MARIE
Forward/Defence. Shoots left. #26.

Clarkson Cup winner with Montréal on 2009-03-21, 2011-03-27 and 2012-03-25. NWHL winner.
Born 1977-8-3, Ste-Foy, QC, CAN. Grew up in St-Zacharie, QC, CAN. 5'3".

Year	League	Team	GP	G	A	PTS	PM	Year	Playoff	GP	G	A	PTS	PM
1998	Nationals	Équipe Québec	6	1	1	2	2							
1999	Nationals	Équipe Québec	5	1	1	2								
2000	Nationals	Équipe Québec	6	2	1	3								
2000-01	NWHL	Wingstar de Montréal	16	9	5	14	20							
2001	Nationals	Équipe Québec												
2001-02	NWHL	Wingstar de Montréal	4	1	1	2	2							
2002	Nationals	Équipe Québec	6	6	3	9	0							
2002-03	NWHL	Avalanche du Québec	36	14	10	24	44							
2003	Nationals	Équipe Québec	5	8	3	11	6							
2003-04	NWHL	Axion de Montréal	35	19	10	29	44							
2004	Nationals	Équipe Québec	7	2	3	5	16							
2004-05	NWHL	Axion de Montréal	30	14	19	33	59	2005	NWHL-P					
2005	Nationals	Axion de Montréal	6	2	7	9	0							
2005-06	NWHL	Axion de Montréal	35	16	23	39	62	2006	NWHL-P	3	2	1	3	4
2006	Nationals	Axion de Montréal	6	3	4	7	14							
2006-07	NWHL	Axion de Montréal	27	15	20	35	77	2007	NWHL-P					
2007-08	CWHL	Stars de Montréal	25	11	21	32	58	2008	CWHL-P	2	0	2	2	2
2008-09	CWHL	Stars de Montréal	26	9	11	20	50	2009	CWHL-P	2	1	0	1	6
								2009	C-Cup	3	0	1	1	0
2009-10	CWHL	Stars de Montréal	30	13	13	26	28	2010	C-Cup	1	0	0	0	2
2010-11	CWHL	Stars de Montréal	26	7	3	10	34	2011	CWHL-P	2		4		
								2011	C-Cup	4	0	0	0	2
2011-12	CWHL	Stars de Montréal	24	2	7	9	14	2012	C-Cup	4	0	2	2	2
2012-13	CWHL	Stars de Montréal	19	0	1	1	18	2013	C-Cup	4	0	1	1	2
2013-14	CWHL	Stars de Montréal	10	1	1	2	2							
2014-15	CWHL	Stars de Montréal	20	3	1	4	4	2015	C-Cup	3	0	0	0	0
CWHL Regular Season			180	46	58	104	208	Clarkson Cup		19	0	4	4	8
Totals from all Competitions			**438**	**162**	**176**	**338**	**578**							

Finished 9th in the Angela James Bowl scoring race in 2007-08... scored 100th CWHL point on 2014-01-11... has served as an assistant coach with CWHL Montréal

BRICKNER, JORDAN
Defence. Shoots left. #26.

Born 1990-10-03, Chicago, IL, USA. Grew up in Lake Forest, IL, USA. Debut at age 25 on 2015-10-11.

Year	League	Team	GP	G	A	PTS	PM	Year	Playoff	GP	G	A	PTS	PM
2015-16	NWHL/	Connecticut Whale	18	0	12	12	2	2016	I-Cup	3	0	0	0	0
2016-17	NWHL/	Connecticut Whale	14	1	3	4	2	2017	I-Cup	1	0	1	1	0
2017-18	NWHL/	Connecticut Whale	15	1	1	2	2	2018	I-Cup	1	0	0	0	0
2018-19	NWHL/	Connecticut Whale	12	0	1	1	2	2019	I-Cup	1	0	1	1	0
NWHL Regular Season			59	2	17	19	8	Isobel Cup		6	0	2	2	0
Totals from all Competitions			**65**	**2**	**19**	**21**	**8**							

BRIEN, AINSLEY
Defence. 2009-10 CWHL Burlington #77 (13 games, 1 goal, 3 assists).

BRIFFETT, KATIE
Forward. 2003 Nationals Newfoundland Labrador (5 games).

BRINE, JENNIFER
Forward. Shoots left. #11 #9.

Born 1987-4-21, Truro, NS, CAN. 5'8". Debut at age 23 on 2009-11-14.

Year	League	Team	GP	G	A	PTS	PM	Year	Playoff	GP	G	A	PTS	PM
2009-10	CWHL	Mississauga Chiefs	18	7	8	15	16	2010	C-Cup	1	0	0	0	0
2010-11	CWHL	Toronto Furies	25	8	3	11	10	2011	CWHL-P	2	1	1	2	
								2011	C-Cup	4	1	1	2	2
2011-12	CWHL	Toronto Furies	27	7	7	14	2	2012	C-Cup	3	0	0	0	4
2012-13	CWHL	Toronto Furies	23	2	3	5	6	2013	C-Cup	3	0	0	0	0
CWHL Regular Season			93	24	21	45	34	Clarkson Cup		11	1	1	2	6
Totals from all Competitions			**106**	**26**	**23**	**49**	**40**							

BRISSON, THÉRÈSE
Defence. Shoots right. #6.

Olympic champion, IIHF champion. Born 1966-10-5. Grew up in Dollard, QC, CAN. 5'7".

Year	League	Team	GP	G	A	PTS	PM	Year	Playoff	GP	G	A	PTS	PM
1995	Nationals	Équipe Québec												
1996	Nationals	Maritime Sports Blades	6	3	3	6	2							
1998	Nationals	Maritime Sports Blades	6	4	2	6	8							
1999	Nationals	Team New Brunswick	6	1	4	5								
1999-00	NWHL	Wingstar de Montréal	16	5	7	12	12							
2000	Nationals	Équipe Québec	6	2	2	4								
2001-02	NWHL	Mississauga IceBears	1	0	0	0	0							
2004-05	NWHL	Oakville Ice	27	4	15	19	26							
2005-06	NWHL	Oakville Ice	7	0	5	5	6	2006	NWHL-P	0	0	0	0	0
2000-01	NWHL	Mississauga IceBears	27	12	11	23	35							
2002-03	NWHL	Mississauga IceBears												
2003-04	NWHL	Oakville Ice	34	5	18	23	52							
Totals from all Competitions			**136**	**36**	**67**	**103**	**141**							

BRITCHARD, COURTNEY   *Forward. 2004-05 NWHL Toronto Aeros #25 (1 game).*

BROCKMAN, KRISTINE   *Defence. 1999 Nationals Saskatchewan (4 games, 1 assist).*

BRODT-ROSENTHAL, CHELSEY   *Defence. Shoots right. #3.*
Clarkson Cup winner with Minnesota on 2010-03-28. Isobel Cup winner with Minnesota on 2019-03-17.
Born 1983-12-7, Roseville, MN, USA. 5'5". Debut at age 22 on 2006-10-13.

Year	League	Team	GP	G	A	PTS	PM	Year	Playoff	GP	G	A	PTS	PM
2006-07	WWHL	Minnesota Whitecaps	22	3	1	4	20	2007	WWHL-P	3	1	1	2	4
2007-08	WWHL	Minnesota Whitecaps	13	1	4	5	24							
2008	Nationals	Minnesota Whitecaps	3	0	2	2	0							
2008-09	WWHL	Minnesota Whitecaps	8	1	2	3	16	2009	WWHL-P	2	0	1	1	2
								2009	C-Cup	3	0	1	1	4
2009-10	WWHL	Minnesota Whitecaps	11	1	7	8	16	2010	C-Cup	2	1	1	2	8
2010-11	WWHL	Minnesota Whitecaps	14	0	8	8	11	2011	C-Cup	3	0	1	1	0
2018-19	NWHL/	Minnesota Whitecaps	14	0	4	4	10	2019	I-Cup	2	0	0	0	2
Totals from all Competitions			**100**	**8**	**33**	**41**	**117**							

BRODT, WINNY   *Defence. Shoots left. #5.*
Clarkson Cup winner with Minnesota on 2010-03-28. Isobel Cup winner with Minnesota on 2019-03-17.
Born 1978-2-18, Roseville, MN, USA. 5'5".

Year	League	Team	GP	G	A	PTS	PM	Year	Playoff	GP	G	A	PTS	PM
2004-05	WWHL	Minnesota Whitecaps	12	2	8	10	16	2005	WWHL-P	2	0	1	1	0
2005-06	WWHL	Minnesota Whitecaps	8	0	3	3	16	2006	WWHL-P	3	0	2	2	2
2006-07	WWHL	Minnesota Whitecaps	24	5	11	16	22	2007	WWHL-P	3	0	1	1	0
2007-08	WWHL	Minnesota Whitecaps	19	5	5	10	14							
2008	Nationals	Minnesota Whitecaps	3	0	2	2	2							
2008-09	WWHL	Minnesota Whitecaps	14	1	8	9	16	2009	WWHL-P	0	0	0	0	0
								2009	C-Cup	3	1	1	2	2
2009-10	WWHL	Minnesota Whitecaps	12	2	8	10	4	2010	C-Cup	2	0	0	0	0
2010-11	WWHL	Minnesota Whitecaps	18	7	14	21	10	2011	C-Cup	3	0	0	0	4
2018-19	NWHL/	Minnesota Whitecaps	14	0	1	1	6	2019	I-Cup	2	0	0	0	0
Totals from all Competitions			**142**	**23**	**65**	**88**	**114**							

BROKER, AMBER   *Prince Albert, SK, CAN. Defence. 2009-10 CWHL Mississauga #16 (3 games, 1 assist).*

BROMLEY, NATALIE   *Forward. 2003 Nationals Nova Scotia Selects (5 games, 1 goal).*

BRONWEN, KELLY   *1999-00 NWHL Brampton Thunder #18 (2 games, 2 goals).*

BROOKING, CHERYL   *Defence. 2003 Nationals Newfoundland Labrador (5 games), 2006 Team NB (7 games).*

BROOKINGS, DIANE   *Forward. 1996-97 COWHL Newtonbrook Panthers #56 (1 game).*

BROWN, CELESTE   *Forward. Shoots right. #42.*
Born 1992-05-29. Grew up in Great Falls, MT, USA. 5'6". Debut at age 23 on 2015-10-11.

Year	League	Team	GP	G	A	PTS	PM	Year	Playoff	GP	G	A	PTS	PM
2015-16	NWHL/	New York Riveters	18	0	4	4	24	2016	I-Cup	2	1	0	1	4
2016-17	NWHL/	Connecticut Whale	3	0	0	0	2							

BROWN, CINDY   *Forward. 1995 Nationals Metro Valley Selects.*

BROWN, DIANA   *Defence. #2 #8.*

Year	League	Team	GP	G	A	PTS	PM
1992-93	COWHL	Scarborough Sting	23	2	2	4	12
1993-94	COWHL	Scarborough Sting	18	0	4	4	16
1996-97	COWHL	Scarborough Sting	33	6	7	13	30
1998-99	NWHL	Scarborough Sting	39	2	4	6	30
1999-00	NWHL	Scarborough Sting	36	3	3	6	44
2000-01	NWHL	Toronto Sting	38	4	5	9	52
Totals from all Competitions			**187**	**17**	**25**	**42**	**184**

BROWN, JENNIFER   *Forward. 2003 Nationals Newfoundland Labrador (5 games).*

BROWN, KENNEDY   *Left wing. Shoots left. #20.*
Born 1999-10-20. Grew up in Okotoks, AB, CAN. Debut at age 18 on 2017-10-21.

Year	League	Team	GP	G	A	PTS	PM
2017-18	CWHL	Calgary Inferno	24	2	4	6	6

BROWN, KRISTINA   *Centre. Shoots left. #24.*
Born 1991-05-01 in North Andover, MA, USA. 5'4". Debut at age 24 on 2015-10-17.

Year	League	Team	GP	G	A	PTS	PM
2015-16	CWHL	Boston Blades	22	2	2	4	8
2016-17	CWHL	Boston Blades	24	1	5	6	12
2017-18	CWHL	Boston Blades	28	1	0	1	16
2018-19	CWHL	Worcester Blades	17	0	1	1	14
CWHL Regular Season			91	4	8	12	50

BROWN, LINDSAY   *Forward. #9 #67.*
Born 1986-8-5. Grew up in Scarborough, ON, CAN. Debut at age 23 on 2009-10-3.

Year	League	Team	GP	G	A	PTS	PM	Year	Playoff	GP	G	A	PTS	PM
2009-10	CWHL	Mississauga Chiefs	23	3	6	9	26	2010	C-Cup	1	0	0	0	2

Year - League - Team		GP	G	A	PTS	PM	Year - Playoff	GP	G	A	PTS	PM
2010-11	CWHL Brampton Thunder	18	6	2	8	12	2011 CWHL-P	2	2			
							2011 C-Cup	3	0	0	0	0
CWHL Regular Season		41	9	8	17	38	Clarkson Cup	4	0	0	0	2
Totals from all Competitions		**47**	**9**	**8**	**17**	**42**						

BROWN, LISA
Forward. 1995 Nationals Calgary Classics

BROWN, NICOLE
Forward. Shoots left. #17.

Clarkson Cup winner with Markham on 2018-03-25.
Born 1994-04-19. Grew up in Oshawa, ON, CAN. 5'8". Debut at age 22 on 2016-10-08.

Year - League - Team		GP	G	A	PTS	PM	Year - Playoff	GP	G	A	PTS	PM
2016-17	CWHL Brampton Thunder	19	0	3	3	2	2017 C-Cup	2	0	0	0	4
2017-18	CWHL Markham Thunder	26	4	8	12	8	2018 C-Cup	3	1	1	2	0
2018-19	CWHL Markham Thunder	25	4	9	13	2	2019 C-Cup	3	0	0	0	2
CWHL Regular Season		70	8	20	28	12	Clarkson Cup	8	1	1	2	6
Totals from all Competitions		**78**	**9**	**21**	**30**	**18**						

BROWN, SHELLY
Forward. Shoots left.

Born 1984-08-07. Grew up in Mount Pearl, NL, CAN.

Year - League - Team		GP	G	A	PTS	PM
2002	Nationals Newfoundland Labrador	4	0	0	0	0
2003	Nationals Newfoundland Labrador	5	0	0	0	2
2006	Nationals Newfoundland Labrador	5	1	0	1	0

BROWNE, HARRISON
Forward. Shoots left. #24.

Isobel Cup winner with Buffalo on 2017-03-19 and Metropolitan on 2018-03-25.
Born 1993-05-05. Grew up in Oakville, ON, CAN. 5'4". Debut at age 22 on 2015-10-11.

Year - League - Team		GP	G	A	PTS	PM	Year - Playoff	GP	G	A	PTS	PM
2015-16	NWHL/ Buffalo Beauts	18	5	7	12	26	2016 I-Cup	5	2	2	4	10
2016-17	NWHL/ Buffalo Beauts	17	2	4	6	22	2017 I-Cup	2	0	0	0	2
2017-18	NWHL/ Metropolitan Riveters	16	3	6	9	8	2018 I-Cup	2	0	1	1	0
NWHL Regular Season		51	10	17	27	56	Isobel Cup	9	2	3	5	12
Totals from all Competitions		**60**	**12**	**20**	**32**	**68**						

NWHL Fans' Three Stars Award in 2017-18

BROWNLEE, CHRISTINE
Defence. Shoots right. #81 #24 #23.

Born 1980-12-15. Grew up in Mississauga, ON, CAN. 5'6".

Year - League - Team		GP	G	A	PTS	PM	Year - Playoff	GP	G	A	PTS	PM
1998-99	NWHL North York Aeros	2	0	0	0	0						
1999-00	NWHL Brampton Thunder	36	1	13	14	63						
2000-01	NWHL Brampton Thunder	39	6	12	18	45						
2003-04	NWHL Oakville Ice	36	2	10	12	42						
2004-05	NWHL Oakville Ice	34	2	2	4	20						
2005-06	NWHL Oakville Ice	34	2	7	9	46	2006 NWHL-P	2	0	1	1	0
2006-07	NWHL Oakville Ice	11	0	3	3	28						
Totals from all Competitions		**194**	**13**	**48**	**61**	**244**						

BROWNRIDGE, JESSICA
2000-01 NWHL Toronto Sting #55 (3 games, 2 goals).

BRUCE, CHRISTA
Forward. 1996-97 COWHL Hamilton Golden Hawks #16 (34 games, 1 assist).

BRUCE, LAURA
Forward. 1998 Nationals Tazmanian Devils (5 gp), 1999 Tazmanian Devils (4 gp).

BRULOTTE, SANDRA
Forward. 1996-97 COWHL London Devilettes #4 (1 game).

BRYKALIUK, ASHLEIGH
Defence/Forward. Shoots right. #13.

Born 1995-6-15 in Brandon, MB, CAN. 5'7". Debut at age 22 on 2017-10-28.

Year - League - Team		GP	G	A	PTS	PM
2017-18	CWHL Vanke Rays	28	8	17	25	8

CWHL All-Rookie Team in 2017-18... finished 12th in the Angela James Bowl scoring race in 2017-18

BUCHANAN, RACHEL
F. 1996-97 COWHL Hamilton #18 (36 gp, 4 g., 5 a.); 1998-99 NWHL Brampton (1 gp, 1 g.).

BUCHANAN, TARA
Defence. 2004-05 NWHL Ottawa Raiders #5 (9 games).

BUCKING, KIM
Defence. 1996-97 COWHL Peterborough Pirates #44 (25 gp, 4 goals, 4 assists).

BUDGELL, SARAH
Defence. 2005 Nationals Newfoundland Labrador (5 games, 1 goal).

BUESSER, KATE
Forward. Shoots left. #20.

Clarkson Cup winner with Boston on 2013-03-23
Born 1989-4-23. Grew up in Wolfeboro, NH, USA. 5'6". Debut at age 22 on 2011-10-22.

Year - League - Team		GP	G	A	PTS	PM	Year - Playoff	GP	G	A	PTS	PM
2011-12	CWHL Boston Blades	25	6	10	16	8	2012 C-Cup	1	0	0	0	0
2012-13	CWHL Boston Blades	23	7	11	18	16	2013 C-Cup	4	3	1	4	2
2013-14	CWHL Boston Blades	15	3	11	14	22	2014 C-Cup	4	3	4	7	4
2015-16	NWHL/ Connecticut Whale	12	3	2	5	2	2016 I-Cup	3	0	2	2	2
CWHL Regular Season		63	16	32	48	46	Clarkson Cup	9	6	5	11	6
NWHL Regular Season		12	3	2	5	2	Isobel Cup	3	0	2	2	2
Totals from all Competitions		**87**	**25**	**41**	**66**	**56**						

Finished 14th in the Angela James Bowl scoring race in 2012-13

BUIE, CORINNE   *Right wing. Shoots right. #23.*

Clarkson Cup winner on 2015-03-07. Isobel Cup winner with Boston on 2016-03-12, Buffalo on 2017-03-19
Born 1992-03-07. Grew up in Edina, MN, USA. 5'9". Debut at age 22 on 2014-11-15.

Year - League - Team		GP	G	A	PTS	PM	Year - Playoff	GP	G	A	PTS	PM
2014-15	CWHL Boston Blades	20	5	4	9	6	2015 C-Cup	3	0	2	2	0
2015-16	NWHL/ Boston Pride	18	3	4	7	12	2016 I-Cup	4	0	0	0	0
2016-17	NWHL/ Buffalo Beauts	17	9	3	12	6	2017 I-Cup	2	1	0	1	0
2017-18	NWHL/ Buffalo Beauts	15	4	6	10	8	2018 I-Cup	2	1	0	1	0
2018-19	NWHL/ Buffalo Beauts	16	3	4	7	4	2019 I-Cup	2	0	0	0	0
NWHL Regular Season		66	19	17	36	30	Isobel Cup	10	2	0	2	0
Totals from all Competitions		**99**	**26**	**23**	**49**	**36**						

BUNTON, HANNA   *Forward. Shoots right. #9.*

Born 1995-5-7. Grew up in Belleville, ON, CAN. 5'8". Debut at age 22 on 2017-10-28.

Year - League - Team		GP	G	A	PTS	PM
2017-18	CWHL Vanke Rays	28	15	11	26	18
2018-19	CWHL KRS Vanke Rays	28	10	16	26	16

CWHL All-Rookie Team in 2017-18... finished 8th in the Angela James Bowl scoring race in 2017-18

BURKE, COURTNEY   *Defence. Shoots left. #6.*

Isobel Cup winner with Metropolitan on 2018-03-25
Born 1994-9-2. Grew up in Albany, NY, USA. 5'9". Debut at age 22 on 2016-10-8.

Year - League - Team		GP	G	A	PTS	PM	Year - Playoff	GP	G	A	PTS	PM
2016-17	NWHL/ New York Riveters	13	3	8	11	2	2017 I-Cup	1	0	0	0	0
2017-18	NWHL/ Metropolitan Riveters	16	2	17	19	12	2018 I-Cup	2	0	0	0	2
2018-19	NWHL/ Metropolitan Riveters	11	0	7	7	10	2019 I-Cup	2	2	0	2	0
NWHL Regular Season		40	5	32	37	24	Isobel Cup	5	2	0	2	2
Totals from all Competitions		**45**	**7**	**32**	**39**	**26**						

NWHL Defensive Player of the Year in 2017-18

BURKE, STEPHANIE   *2003-04 NWHL Avalanche du Québec #20 (19 games).*

BURLTON, STEPHANIE   *Forward. #10 #4.*

Year - League - Team		GP	G	A	PTS	PM
2004-05	WWHL British Columbia	21	3	6	9	14
2007-08	WWHL British Columbia	11	1	1	2	2
2008-09	WWHL British Columbia	11	0	0	0	4
Totals from all Competitions		**43**	**4**	**7**	**11**	**20**

BURNS, DRU   *Defence. Shoots right. #7.*

Born 1991-02-04 in Dallas, TX, USA. 5'8". Debut at age 22 on 2013-11-02.

Year - League - Team		GP	G	A	PTS	PM	Year - Playoff	GP	G	A	PTS	PM
2013-14	CWHL Boston Blades	22	4	6	10	22	2014 C-Cup	4	0	0	0	4
2014-15	CWHL Boston Blades	1	0	0	0	0						
2015-16	CWHL Boston Blades	21	1	2	3	16						
2016-17	CWHL Boston Blades	24	0	6	6	20						
2017-18	CWHL Boston Blades	18	2	6	8	26						
CWHL Regular Season		86	7	20	27	84	Clarkson Cup	4	0	0	0	4
Totals from all Competitions		**90**	**7**	**20**	**27**	**88**						

BURNS, JORDYN   *Defence. Shoots left. #17.*

Isobel Cup winner with Buffalo on 2017-03-19
Born 1992-9-29. Grew up in Chanhassen, MN, USA. 5'7". Debut at age 24 on 2016-10-7.

Year - League - Team		GP	G	A	PTS	PM	Year - Playoff	GP	G	A	PTS	PM
2016-17	NWHL/ Buffalo Beauts	15	0	2	2	2	2017 I-Cup	2	0	0	0	0
2017-18	NWHL/ Buffalo Beauts	15	0	2	2	4	2018 I-Cup	2	0	0	0	0
2018-19	NWHL/ Buffalo Beauts	5	0	1	1	0	2019 I-Cup	2	0	0	0	0
NWHL Regular Season		35	0	5	5	6	Isobel Cup	6	0	0	0	0
Totals from all Competitions		**41**	**0**	**5**	**5**	**6**						

BURTON, BREANA   *F. 2004-05 WWHL B.C. #9 (16 gp, 1 assist), 2006 Nationals BC Selects (6 gp, 2 assists).*

BUTSCH, JENNIFER   *Centre. Shoots left. #8.*

Abby Hoffman Cup winner with Aeros on 2004-03-14 and 2005-03-13. Born 1981-09-06.

Year - League - Team		GP	G	A	PTS	PM	Year - Playoff	GP	G	A	PTS	PM
2003-04	NWHL Toronto Aeros	36	10	9	19	30	2004 NWHL-P					
2004	Nationals Toronto Aeros	6	2	4	6	14						
2004-05	NWHL Toronto Aeros	33	8	6	14	22						
2005	Nationals Toronto Aeros	7	1	3	4	8						
Totals from all Competitions		**82**	**21**	**22**	**43**	**74**						

CABANA, JEN   *Calgary, AB, CAN. Forward. 2007-08 WWHL Strathmore Rockies #71 (15 games).*

CADNEY, KAITLIN   *2007-08 CWHL Burlington #25 (1 game).*

CAHOW, CAITLIN   *Defence. Shoots left. #8.*

IIHF champion. Clarkson Cup winner with Boston on 2013-03-23.
Born 1985-5-20, Branford, CT, USA. Grew up in New Haven, CT, USA. 5'4".

Year - League - Team			GP	G	A	PTS	PM	Year - Playoff		GP	G	A	PTS	PM
2008-09	WWHL	Minnesota Whitecaps	10	3	6	9	2	2009	WWHL-P	2	0	1	1	2
								2009	C-Cup	3	2	0	2	0
2009-10	WWHL	Minnesota Whitecaps	0	0	0	0	0							
2010-11	CWHL	Boston Blades	21	2	11	13	26	2011	CWHL-P	2				
2011-12	CWHL	Boston Blades	20	4	7	11	22							
2012-13	CWHL	Boston Blades	24	2	12	14	24	2013	C-Cup	4	0	1	1	6
CWHL Regular Season			65	8	30	38	72	Clarkson Cup		7	2	1	3	6
Totals from all Competitions			**86**	**13**	**38**	**51**	**82**							

CAIAZZO, TAMMI — *1993-94 COWHL Hamilton Golden Hawks #22 (9 games, 1 goal).*

CAIRNS, COLLEN — *Forward. 2010-11 WWHL Manitoba Maple Leafs #15 (2 games, 1 goal).*

CALDWELL, AMY — *Right wing. Shoots right. #7 #21.*

Born 1980-12-23. Grew up in Cobourg, ON, CAN. 5'7".

Year - League - Team			GP	G	A	PTS	PM	Year - Playoff	GP	G	A	PTS	PM
1999-00	NWHL	Scarborough Sting	38	6	4	10	10						
2005-06	NWHL	Toronto Aeros	33	3	10	13	24						
Totals from all Competitions			**71**	**9**	**14**	**23**	**34**						

CALLAHAN, NICOLE — *Defence. 2000-01 NWHL Durham Lightning #71 (36 games, 2 assists).*

CALLEN, MICHELLE — *Defence. 2007 Nationals BC Outback (2 games).*

CALLISON, HALEIGH — *Defence. Shoots left. #16 #44 #2.*

Born 1987-5-20, Smithers, BC, CAN. Grew up in Smithers, BC, CAN. 5'6".

Year - League - Team			GP	G	A	PTS	PM	Year - Playoff		GP	G	A	PTS	PM
2005	Nationals	British Columbia	7	0	0	0	0							
2006	Nationals	British Columbia Selects	6	0	1	1	6							
2007	Nationals	British Columbia	5	0	1	1	2							
2007-08	WWHL	British Columbia Breakers	24	0	3	3	22							
2009-10	CWHL	Burlington Barracudas	25	0	7	7	28							
2010-11	CWHL	Toronto Furies	25	0	0	0	12	2011	CWHL-P	2				
								2011	C-Cup	4	0	0	0	0
2011-12	CWHL	Toronto Furies	27	0	2	2	22	2012	C-Cup	3	0	0	0	2
CWHL Regular Season			77	0	9	9	62	Clarkson Cup		7	0	0	0	2
Totals from all Competitions			**128**	**0**	**14**	**14**	**94**							

CAMERANESI, DANI — *Forward. Shoots right. #24.*

Olympic champion, IIHF champion.
Born 1995-06-30. Grew up in Plymouth, MN, USA. 5'5". Debut at age 23 on 2018-10-07.

Year - League - Team			GP	G	A	PTS	PM	Year - Playoff	GP	G	A	PTS	PM
2018-19	NWHL/	Buffalo Beauts	14	4	11	15	6	2019 I-Cup	2	1	2	3	2

CAMERON, ERIN — *Ajax, ON, CAN. Forward. 2009-10 CWHL Mississauga Chiefs #19 (1 game, 1 goal).*

CAMERON, KRISTEN — *Forward. 2006 Nationals Prince Edward Island (4 games).*

CAMERON, LISA — *Forward. Shoots left.*

Born 1981-05-17. Grew up in Kingston, PE, CAN.

Year - League - Team			GP	G	A	PTS	PM	Year - Playoff	GP	G	A	PTS	PM
2000	Nationals	Prince Edward Island	5	0	0	0							
2001	Nationals	PEI Humpty Dumpty											
2002	Nationals	PEI Humpty Dumpty	6	0	0	0	0						

CAMERON, MOIRA — *Defence. 2006 Nationals Prince Edward Island (4 games).*

CAMERON, SANDY — *2000-01 NWHL Durham Lightning #8 (27 games, 1 goal, 1 assist).*

CAMPBELL, CARLEE — *Defence. Shoots right. #15.*

Née Eusepi. Born 1988-10-23, Oakville, ON, CAN. Grew up in Sudbury, ON, CAN. 5'10".

Year - League - Team			GP	G	A	PTS	PM	Year - Playoff	GP	G	A	PTS	PM
2004-05	NWHL	Oakville Ice	2	0	0	0	0						
2005-06	NWHL	Toronto Aeros	5	1	2	3	0						
2016-17	CWHL	Toronto Furies	24	1	8	9	6	2017 C-Cup	3	0	2	2	0
2017-18	CWHL	Toronto Furies	14	0	6	6	6						
2018-19	CWHL	Toronto Furies	8	2	4	6	4	2019 C-Cup	3	0	0	0	0
Totals from all Competitions			**59**	**4**	**22**	**26**	**16**						

CAMPBELL-PASCALL, CASSIE — *Forward / Defence. Shoots left. #7 #77.*

Olympic champion, IIHF champion. Abby Hoffman Cup winner with Aeros on 2000-03-12. Abby Hoffman Cup winner with Calgary on 2001-03-11 and 2003-03-16.
NWHL Cup winner, WWHL winner.
Born 1973-11-22. Grew up in Brampton, ON, CAN. 5'6".

Year - League - Team			GP	G	A	PTS	PM	Year - Playoff	GP	G	A	PTS	PM
1993-94	COWHL	Mississauga Chiefs	22	8	6	14	10						
1995	Nationals	Mississauga Chiefs											
1995-96	COWHL	Mississauga Chiefs	19	2	7	9	12						
1996	Nationals	North York Aeros	5	0	3	3	4						

Year - League - Team			GP	G	A	PTS	PM	Year - Playoff	GP	G	A	PTS	PM
1996-97	COWHL	North York Aeros	31	9	27	36	20						
1998	Nationals	North York Aeros	6	4	6	10	4						
1998-99	NWHL	North York Aeros	29	13	15	28	20						
1999	Nationals	North York Aeros	5	1	1	2							
1999-00	NWHL	North York Aeros	34	17	18	35	18	2000 NWHL-P					
2000	Nationals	North York Aeros	6	3	6	9							
2001	Nationals	Calgary Oval X-Treme											
2002-03	NWHL	Calgary Oval X-Treme	20	4	12	16	20	2003 NWHL-P	1	3	2	5	0
2003	Nationals	Calgary Oval X-Treme	5	1	7	8	8						
2003-04	NWHL	Calgary Oval X-Treme	5	2	4	6	2	2004 NWHL-P	4	5	4	9	4
2004	Nationals	Calgary Oval X-Treme	6	3	8	11	2						
2004-05	WWHL	Calgary Oval X-Treme	8	4	7	11	6	2005 WWHL-P	3	4	2	6	0
Totals from all Competitions			**198**	**83**	**135**	**218**	**130**						

CWHL Humanitarian Award in 2013-14

CAMPBELL, DIANA *1993-94 COWHL Hamilton Golden Hawks #96 (2 games, 3 goals, 1 assist).*

CAMPBELL, GINA *2006-07 WWHL Saskatchewan Prairie Ice #21 (4 games).*

CAMPBELL, JESSICA *Forward. Shoots left. #20 #8.*

Clarkson Cup winner with Calgary on 2016-03-14
Born 1992-06-24, Moosomin, SK, CAN. Grew up in Melville, SK, CAN. 5'5". Debut at age 22 on 2014-10-18.

Year - League - Team			GP	G	A	PTS	PM	Year - Playoff	GP	G	A	PTS	PM
2014-15	CWHL	Calgary Inferno	21	12	5	17	4	2015 C-Cup	2	0	0	0	0
2015-16	CWHL	Calgary Inferno	22	10	10	20	6	2016 C-Cup	3	2	0	2	0
2016-17	CWHL	Calgary Inferno	20	7	6	13	16	2017 C-Cup	4	1	0	1	4
CWHL Regular Season			63	29	21	50	26	Clarkson Cup	9	3	0	3	4
Totals from all Competitions			**72**	**32**	**21**	**53**	**30**						

CWHL All-Rookie Team in 2014-15... finished 12th in the Angela James Bowl scoring race in 2014-15

CAMPBELL, JOCELYN *Defence. 2007 Nationals Nova Scotia Selects (7 games, 2 assists).*

CAMPBELL, LEISA *Defence.*

Year - League - Team			GP	G	A	PTS	PM
1995	Nationals	PEI Esso Tigers					
1996	Nationals	PEI Esso Tigers	4	0	0	0	2
1998	Nationals	Prince Edward Island	5	0	0	0	0
1999	Nationals	Prince Edward Island	5	0	0	0	
2000	Nationals	Prince Edward Island	5	0	0	0	

CAMPBELL, MICHELLE *Forward. #7 #24.*

Year - League - Team			GP	G	A	PTS	PM
1993-94	COWHL	Scarborough Firefighters	28	7	18	25	44
1995-96	COWHL	Toronto Red Wings	29	15	24	39	34
1996-97	COWHL	Newtonbrook Panthers	33	11	23	34	44
1997-98	COWHL	Mississauga Chiefs	19	3	7	10	18
1998-99	NWHL	Brampton Thunder	37	9	21	30	67
2000-01	NWHL	Mississauga IceBears	16	3	1	4	14
Totals from all Competitions			**162**	**48**	**94**	**142**	**221**

CAMPBELL, STEPHANIE *Defence. #16.*

Year - League - Team			GP	G	A	PTS	PM
1993-94	COWHL	Mississauga Chiefs	30	1	3	4	8
1995	Nationals	Mississauga Chiefs					
1995-96	COWHL	Mississauga Chiefs	28	2	9	11	2
1996-97	COWHL	Mississauga Chiefs	30	6	11	17	2
1998-99	NWHL	Mississauga Chiefs	38	1	7	8	12
1999-00	NWHL	Mississauga Chiefs	29	1	2	3	2
Totals from all Competitions			**155**	**11**	**32**	**43**	**26**

CAMPBELL, STÉPHANIE *2007-08 CWHL Stars de Montréal #57 (2 games).*

CAMPITELLI, JENNIFER *Scarborough, ON, CAN. Defence. 2005-06 NWHL Toronto #99 (1 game).*

CANTIN, CHLOÉ *Montréal, QC. F. 2005-06 NWHL Québec #86 (4 gp, 1 assist); 2006-07 Québec #9 (8 gp, 2 a.).*

CANTIN-DROUIN, MARIE-PIER *Defence. Shoots right.*

Born 1982-02-23. Grew up in Saint-Nicolas, QC, CAN. 5'2".

Year - League - Team			GP	G	A	PTS	PM	Year - Playoff	GP	G	A	PTS	PM
2001-02	NWHL	Wingstar de Montréal	3	0	3	3	6						
2002-03	NWHL	Wingstar de Montréal	6	0	0	0	2	2003 NWHL-P					
2003	Nationals	Équipe Québec	5	0	0	0	0						

CAPIZZANO, KRYSTIN *Forward. Shoots left. #60.*

Born 1995-01-03. Grew up in Toronto, ON, CAN. 5'2". Debut at age 24 on 2019-01-29.

Year - League - Team			GP	G	A	PTS	PM
2018-19	CWHL	Toronto Furies	3	0	0	0	0

CAPLETTE, DEENA — *Forward. Shoots left.*

Born 1984-07-25. Grew up in Winnipeg, MB, CAN. 5'2".

Year	League	Team	GP	G	A	PTS	PM
2001	Nationals	University of Manitoba					
2002	Nationals	University of Manitoba	5	1	1	2	10
2007	Nationals	Manitoba	5	4	3	7	6
2008	Nationals	Manitoba	5	1	0	1	4
2010-11	WWHL	Manitoba Maple Leafs	3	0	1	1	0

CARCARY, KIMBERLY — *Forward. Shoots left.*

Born 1985-12-27. Grew up in Newmarket, ON, CAN. 5'7".

Year	League	Team	GP	G	A	PTS	PM
2005	Nationals	Nova Scotia Selects	5	1	3	4	4
2007	Nationals	Nova Scotia Selects	7	1	2	3	14
2008	Nationals	Nova Scotia Selects	5	1	2	3	4
2010-11	CWHL	Burlington Barracudas	11	0	1	1	2

CARDELLA, JILL — *Forward. Shoots right. #4.*

Born 1991-09-24. Grew up in Rochester, NY, USA. 5'6". Debut at age 22 on 2013-11-02.

Year	League	Team	GP	G	A	PTS	PM	Year	Playoff	GP	G	A	PTS	PM
2013-14	CWHL	Boston Blades	24	4	11	15	8	2014	C-Cup	4	0	0	0	0

CWHL All-Rookie Team in 2013-14... finished 11th in the Angela James Bowl scoring race in 2013-14.

CARIERE, JACELYN — *Forward. 2002 Nationals Calgary Oval X-Treme (5 games, 1 assist).*

CARIERE, LACEY — *Defence. 2004 Nationals Nova Scotia Selects (5 games, 1 assist).*

CARIERE, TAMMY — *2000-01 NWHL Mistral de Laval #8 (1 game).*

CARLTON, JULIA — *Defence. Shoots left. #5 #12.*

Born 1981-9-24, Pointe-Claire, QC, CAN. Grew up in Pointe-Claire, QC, CAN. 5'8".

Year	League	Team	GP	G	A	PTS	PM	Year	Playoff	GP	G	A	PTS	PM
2001-02	NWHL	Wingstar de Montréal	9	0	1	1	2							
2005-06	NWHL	Avalanche du Québec	35	0	7	7	16							
2006-07	NWHL	Avalanche du Québec	31	2	6	8	42	2007	NWHL-P					
2007-08	CWHL	Phénix du Québec	2	0	0	0	0							
Totals from all Competitions			**77**	**2**	**14**	**16**	**60**							

CARNES, COURTNEY — *Winslow, ME, USA. Forward. 2015-16 NWHL Buffalo (4 games, Isobel Cup 1 game).*

CARPENTER, ALEX — *Forward. Shoots left. #9.*

IIHF champion.

Born 1994-4-13, Cambridge, MA, USA. 5'6". Debut at age 22 on 2016-10-7.

Year	League	Team	GP	G	A	PTS	PM	Year	Playoff	GP	G	A	PTS	PM
2016-17	NWHL/	Boston Pride	17	9	20	29	0	2017	I-Cup	2	3	3	6	0
2017-18	CWHL	Kunlun Red Star	13	5	7	12	0	2018	C-Cup	4	1	0	1	0
2018-19	CWHL	KRS Vanke Rays	28	17	14	31	0							
Totals from all Competitions			**64**	**35**	**44**	**79**	**0**							

Finished 6th in the Angela James Bowl scoring race in 2018-19.

CARRIE-MATTIMORE, HOLLY — *Forward. Shoots right. #77.*

Clarkson Cup winner with Toronto on 2014-03-22

Born 1991-04-30 in Stittsville, ON. Grew up in Sherwood Park, AB, CAN. 5'7". Debut at age 22 on 2013-11-09.

Year	League	Team	GP	G	A	PTS	PM	Year	Playoff	GP	G	A	PTS	PM
2013-14	CWHL	Toronto Furies	22	2	7	9	2	2014	C-Cup	4	1	0	1	0
2014-15	CWHL	Toronto Furies	15	0	1	1	4	2015	C-Cup	2	0	0	0	2
CWHL Regular Season			37	2	8	10	6	Clarkson Cup		6	1	0	1	2
Totals from all Competitions			**43**	**3**	**8**	**11**	**8**							

CARRON, COURTNEY — *2000-01 NWHL Ottawa Raiders #3 (1 game).*

CARRUTHERS, MINDY — *Defence. 1996 Nationals Pictou County (4 games).*

CARSON, JAMIE — *Defence. 2007-08 CWHL Ottawa Capital Canucks #3 (2 games).*

CARTER, CLARISSA — *2000-01 NWHL Toronto Sting (5 games, 2 assists).*

CARUFEL, CYNDY ANN — *2000-01 NWHL Mistral de Laval #18 (2 games).*

CASIAN, DESIREE — *Bow, NH, USA. Forward. 2015-16 CWHL Boston Blades #11 (20 games).*

CASORSO, SARAH — *Defence. Shoots left. #10.*

Isobel Cup winner with Buffalo on 2017-03-19

Born 1988-3-18. Grew up in Kelowna, BC, CAN. 5'7". Debut at age 27 on 2016-10-8.

Year	League	Team	GP	G	A	PTS	PM	Year	Playoff	GP	G	A	PTS	PM
2016-17	NWHL/	Buffalo Beauts	16	0	7	7	4	2017	I-Cup	2	0	0	0	4
2017-18	NWHL/	Buffalo Beauts	15	0	9	9	17	2018	I-Cup	2	1	0	1	12
2018-19	NWHL/	Buffalo Beauts	11	0	2	2	27							
NWHL Regular Season			42	0	18	18	48	Isobel Cup		4	1	0	1	16
Totals from all Competitions			**46**	**1**	**18**	**19**	**64**							

CASTONGUAY, EMILIE — *Outremont, QC. LW. 2003-04 NWHL Québec #23 (2 gp); 2004-05 (32 gp, 1 goal, 6 a.).*

CATION, TARA — *Caledon, ON, CAN. Forward. 2015-16 CWHL Brampton #44 (19 games, C-Cup 2 games).*

CAVA, MICHELA
Forward. Shoots right. #8.

Born 1994-3-26. Grew up in Thunder Bay, ON, CAN. 5'4". Debut at age 22 on 2016-10-15.

Year - League - Team			GP	G	A	PTS	PM	Year - Playoff	GP	G	A	PTS	PM
2016-17	CWHL	Toronto Furies	24	6	8	14	10	2017 C-Cup	3	0	0	0	2

CWHL All-Rookie Team in 2016-17

CAWOOD, STEPHANIE
Forward. Shoots left.

Born 1985-03-16. Grew up in Saskatoon, SK, CAN.

Year - League - Team			GP	G	A	PTS	PM
2001	Nationals	Saskatchewan Selects					
2002	Nationals	Saskatchewan	6	0	1	1	4
2003	Nationals	Saskatchewan	6	0	1	1	0
2004	Nationals	Saskatchewan	6	1	1	2	2

CECERE, ALYSSA
Forward. Shoots right. #19.

Clarkson Cup winner with Montréal on 2012-03-25

Born 1987-9-4, Brossard, QC, CAN. Grew up in Brossard, QC, CAN. 5'7". Debut at age 24 on 2011-10-22.

Year - League - Team			GP	G	A	PTS	PM	Year - Playoff	GP	G	A	PTS	PM
2011-12	CWHL	Stars de Montréal	25	2	8	10	12	2012 C-Cup	4	1	0	1	0
2012-13	CWHL	Stars de Montréal	21	0	1	1	6	2013 C-Cup	4	0	0	0	2
2013-14	CWHL	Stars de Montréal	23	3	4	7	34	2014 C-Cup	3	0	0	0	0
CWHL Regular Season			69	5	13	18	52	Clarkson Cup	11	1	0	1	2
Totals from all Competitions			**80**	**6**	**13**	**19**	**54**						

CEELAN, CANDICE
Left wing. Shoots left. #16 #27.

Born 1979-6-27. Grew up in Milton, ON, CAN. 5'5".

Year - League - Team			GP	G	A	PTS	PM
1998-99	NWHL	North York Aeros	8	1	4	5	2
2004-05	NWHL	Durham Lightning	32	5	6	11	8
2005-06	NWHL	Durham Lightning	35	0	1	1	4
2006	NWHL-P	Durham	2	0	0	0	0
Totals from all Competitions			**77**	**6**	**11**	**17**	**14**

CELIKORS, SUSAN
1996-97 COWHL Scarborough Sting #8 (9 games, 2 goals).

CELLINO, ANNMARIE
West Seneca, NY. Forward. 2015-16 NWHL Buffalo (4 games, 1 assist; I-Cup 1 game).

CHAMPOUX, CHANTAL
2000-01 NWHL Sainte-Julie (3 games).

CHANDLER, BRITNEY
Forward. 2003-04 NWHL Durham Lightning #94 (9 games, 3 assists).

CHANNELL, MELLISSA
Defence. Shoots left. #9.

Born 1994-12-16. Grew up in Oakville, ON, CAN. 5'4". Debut at age 23 on 2018-10-13.

Year - League - Team			GP	G	A	PTS	PM	Year - Playoff	GP	G	A	PTS	PM
2018-19	CWHL	Toronto Furies	28	0	12	12	16	2019 C-Cup	3	0	2	2	2

CWHL All-Rookie Team 2018-19.

CHAPDELAINE, NICOLE
Goalie.

Abby Hoffman Cup winner with Edmonton on 1997-03-09.

Born 1973-03-13.

Year - League - Team			GP	G	A	PTS	PM	Year - Playoff	GP	G	A	PTS	PM
1997	Nationals	Edmonton Chimo											

CHARBONNEAU, CINTHIA
Forward. Shoots right. #67 #25 #88 #44 71.

Born 1985-4-26, Mont-Laurier, QC, CAN. 5'8".

Year - League - Team			GP	G	A	PTS	PM	Year - Playoff	GP	G	A	PTS	PM
2003-04	NWHL	Avalanche du Québec	3	1	0	1	2						
2004	Nationals	Équipe Québec	7	1	1	2	2						
2004-05	NWHL	Avalanche du Québec	2	0	0	0	2						
2005-06	NWHL	Avalanche du Québec	6	4	5	9	10						
2006-07	NWHL	Avalanche du Québec	31	16	13	29	123	2007 NWHL-P					
2007-08	CWHL	Phénix du Québec	29	11	9	20	72						
Totals from all Competitions			**78**	**33**	**28**	**61**	**211**						

CHARBONNEAU, DOMINIQUE
1998-99 NWHL Mistral de Laval #59 (1 game).

CHARLEBOIS, BRENDA
Defence. #16 #19.

Born 1977-5-17.

Year - League - Team			GP	G	A	PTS	PM
1998-99	NWHL	Ottawa Raiders	27	2	1	3	20
1999-00	NWHL	Ottawa Raiders	35	1	3	4	46
2000-01	NWHL	Ottawa Raiders	37	4	4	8	36
2001-02	NWHL	Ottawa Raiders	27	0	3	3	12
2002-03	NWHL	Ottawa Raiders	32	0	3	3	40
2003-04	NWHL	Ottawa Raiders	19	0	2	2	12
Totals from all Competitions			**177**	**7**	**16**	**23**	**166**

CHARTIER, LISA
F. 1995-96 COWHL Hamilton (26 gp, 2 g., 10 a.); 1996-97 Scarb. (1 gp); 1998-99 NWHL (1 gp).

CHARTRAND, CATHY
Defence. Shoots left. #8.

Clarkson Cup winner with Montréal on 2017-03-05. NWHL winner
Born 1981-5-8, Verdun, QC, CAN. Grew up in Lac Nomininque, QC, CAN. 5'10". Debut at age 18 in 1999.

Year - League - Team		GP	G	A	PTS	PM	Year - Playoff		GP	G	A	PTS	PM
1999-00	NWHL	Wingstar de Montréal	34	4	11	15	22							
2000-01	NWHL	Wingstar de Montréal	38	7	24	31	56							
2001	Nationals	Équipe Québec												
2001-02	NWHL	Wingstar de Montréal	16	4	6	10	34							
2002	Nationals	Équipe Québec	6	0	0	0	4							
2002-03	NWHL	Axion de Montréal	27	11	10	21	48	2003	NWHL-P					
2003	Nationals	Équipe Québec	5	1	0	1	4							
2003-04	NWHL	Axion de Montréal	35	8	20	28	44	2004	NWHL-P	4				
2004	Nationals	Équipe Québec	7	2	4	6	2							
2004-05	NWHL	Axion de Montréal	32	8	36	44	32							
2005	Nationals	Axion de Montréal	6	3	3	6	10							
2005-06	NWHL	Axion de Montréal	34	4	26	30	60	2006	NWHL-P	3	0	0	0	2
2006-07	NWHL	Axion de Montréal	26	10	18	28	65	2007	NWHL-P					
2012-13	CWHL	Stars de Montréal	23	5	15	20	16	2013	C-Cup	4	0	2	2	4
2013-14	CWHL	Stars de Montréal	23	9	21	30	32	2014	C-Cup	3	1	1	2	4
2014-15	CWHL	Stars de Montréal	22	5	12	17	26	2015	C-Cup	3	0	0	0	0
2015-16	CWHL	Canadiennes de Montréal	24	3	12	15	14	2016	C-Cup	3	1	4	5	0
2016-17	CWHL	Canadiennes de Montréal	24	3	15	18	30	2017	C-Cup	3	1	5	6	2
2017-18	CWHL	Canadiennes de Montréal	28	5	18	23	30	2018	C-Cup	2	0	1	1	0
CWHL Regular Season			144	30	93	123	148	Clarkson Cup		18	3	13	16	10
Totals from all Competitions			**435**	**95**	**264**	**359**	**541**							

CWHL Defenceman of the Year in 2013-14 and 2017-18... CWHL First All-Star Team in 2013-14 and 2017-18; CWHL Second All-Star Team in 2016-17... NWHL Defenceman of the Year in 2004-05... scored 100th CWHL point on 2017-2-19... finished 4th in the Angela James Bowl scoring race in 2013-14... selected First Decade CWHL Team in 2017... NWHL Defenceman of the Year in 2004-05

CHARTRAND, ISABELLE
Defence. Shoots left. #73.

Olympic champion, IIHF champion. Born 1978-4-20. Grew up in Anjou, QC, CAN. 5'4".

Year - League - Team		GP	G	A	PTS	PM	Year - Playoff		GP	G	A	PTS	PM
1998-99	NWHL	Mistral de Laval	30	5	11	16	62							
1996	Nationals	Équipe Québec	6	1	2	3	2							
1998	Nationals	Équipe Québec	6	0	2	2	2							
1999	Nationals	Équipe Québec	5	0	2	2								
1999-00	NWHL	Mistral de Laval	27	10	12	22	88							
2000	Nationals	Équipe Québec	6	2	2	4								
2002	Nationals	Équipe Québec	6	0	1	1	8							
2002-03	NWHL	Axion de Montréal	3	0	0	0	17							
2003	Nationals	Équipe Québec	5	3	3	6	8							
2003-04	NWHL	Axion de Montréal	5	0	2	2	4	2004	NWHL-P	1				
2004-05	NWHL	Axion de Montréal	15	0	4	4	46							
2005	Nationals	Axion de Montréal	6	3	2	5	4							
Totals from all Competitions		**121**	**24**	**43**	**67**	**241**							

CHARTRAND, NATHALIE
Forward. 1996 Nationals Québec; 1998-99 NWHL Montréal #19 (8 games, 1 goal).

CHARTRAND, NICOLE
Defence.

Born 1984-07-15. Grew up in Winnipeg, MB, CAN. 5'8".

Year - League - Team		GP	G	A	PTS	PM
2001	Nationals	University of Manitoba					
2002	Nationals	University of Manitoba	5	0	0	0	2
2010-11	WWHL	Manitoba Maple Leafs	4	0	2	2	4

CHARTRAND, TARA
Defence.

Born 1984-11-17. Grew up in Winnipeg, MB, CAN. 5'7".

Year - League - Team		GP	G	A	PTS	PM
2001	Nationals	University of Manitoba					
2005	Nationals	Manitoba	5	0	0	0	2
2008	Nationals	Manitoba	5	0	2	2	2

CHASSIE, ERIN
Defence. Shoots left. #24 #9.

Born 1974-1-1, North Bay, ON, CAN. 5'6".

Year - League - Team		GP	G	A	PTS	PM	Year - Playoff		GP	G	A	PTS	PM
2000-01	NWHL	Ottawa Raiders	20	5	2	7	46							
2001-02	NWHL	Ottawa Raiders	29	1	1	2	77							
2002-03	NWHL	Ottawa Raiders	32	7	14	21	73							
2003-04	NWHL	Ottawa Raiders	33	11	7	18	71							
2004-05	NWHL	Ottawa Raiders	32	1	2	3	46							
2005-06	NWHL	Ottawa Raiders	32	0	1	1	12	2006	NWHL-P	0	0	0	0	0
Totals from all Competitions		**178**	**25**	**27**	**52**	**325**							

Served as interim coach with CWHL Ottawa

CHEREVATY, JACQUELINE
Mississauga. RW. 2001-02 NWHL Miss. (30 gp, 9 g., 14 a.); 2005-06 Toronto (3 gp).

CHEREWYK, LAUREN *Forward. 2006-07 WWHL Edmonton (23 gp, 6 goals, 4 assists; playoffs).*

CHESSON, LISA *Defence. Shoots left. #11.*
Isobel Cup winner with Buffalo on 2017-03-19
Born 1986-8-18. Grew up in Plainfield, IL, USA. 5'7".

Year - League - Team		GP	G	A	PTS	PM	Year - Playoff	GP	G	A	PTS	PM
2008-09	WWHL Minnesota Whitecaps	5	3	2	5	2	2009 WWHL-P	0	0	0	0	0
2016-17	NWHL/ Buffalo Beauts	7	0	3	3	0	2017 I-Cup	1	0	1	1	0
2017-18	NWHL/ Buffalo Beauts	14	1	4	5	16	2018 I-Cup	2	0	0	0	0
2018-19	NWHL/ Buffalo Beauts	16	1	8	9	6	2019 I-Cup	2	0	0	0	0
NWHL Regular Season		37	2	15	17	22	Isobel Cup	5	0	1	1	0
Totals from all Competitions		**47**	**5**	**18**	**23**	**24**						

CHEVALIER, CATHERINE *Defence. 1999-00 NWHL Mistral de Laval #59 (3 games).*

CHEVERIE, KORI *Forward. Shoots right. #44.*
Clarkson Cup winner with Toronto on 2014-03-22
Born 1987-6-18, New Glasgow, NS, CAN. 5'8". Debut at age 23 on 2010-10-23.

Year - League - Team		GP	G	A	PTS	PM	Year - Playoff	GP	G	A	PTS	PM
2003	Nationals Nova Scotia Selects	6	2	1	3	4						
2005	Nationals Nova Scotia Selects	5	6	1	7	8						
2006	Nationals Nova Scotia Selects	5	4	3	7							
2007	Nationals Nova Scotia Selects	7	3	1	4	4						
2008	Nationals Nova Scotia Selects	5	1	4	5	6						
2010-11	CWHL Toronto Furies	26	8	12	20	20	2011 CWHL-P	2	2	2	4	
							2011 C-Cup	4	0	3	3	2
2011-12	CWHL Toronto Furies	27	14	6	20	16	2012 C-Cup	3	1	0	1	0
2012-13	CWHL Toronto Furies	24	0	2	2	22	2013 C-Cup	3	0	0	0	4
2013-14	CWHL Toronto Furies	23	5	11	16	12	2014 C-Cup	4	1	0	1	0
2014-15	CWHL Toronto Furies	24	0	2	2	6	2015 C-Cup	2	0	0	0	2
2015-16	CWHL Toronto Furies	24	8	10	18	20	2016 C-Cup	2	0	0	0	0
CWHL Regular Season		148	35	43	78	96	Clarkson Cup	18	2	3	5	8
Totals from all Competitions		**196**	**55**	**58**	**113**	**128**						

CWHL All-Rookie Team in 2010-11... finished 15th in the Angela James Bowl scoring race in 2013-14

CHIASSON, ELIZABETH *Forward. Shoots left. #5.*
Born 1989-09-30.

Year - League - Team		GP	G	A	PTS	PM
1999-00	NWHL Durham Lightning	40	5	10	15	82
2000-01	NWHL Durham Lightning	38	15	21	36	51
2001-02	NWHL Durham Lightning	9	2	4	6	16
2006	Nationals Nova Scotia Selects	5	2	4	6	10
Totals from all Competitions		**87**	**22**	**35**	**57**	**149**

CHIM, LOUISE *Defence. 2004 Nationals British Columbia (6 games, 1 assist).*

CHIN, LISA *Forward. 2005 Nationals Manitoba (5 games, 1 goal).*

CHIPMAN, EMMA *Forward. 2002 Nationals Nova Scotia Selects (5 gp); 2003 Nova Scotia (6 gp, 2 pts).*

CHISWELL, LAUREN *Centre. Shoots left. #16 #9.*
Born 1987-8-11. Grew up in Edmonton, AB, CAN. 5'4. Debut at age 24 on 2011-11-19.

Year - League - Team		GP	G	A	PTS	PM
2010-11	WWHL Edmonton Chimos	17	1	0	1	4
2011-12	CWHL Alberta	12	3	0	3	2
2012-13	CWHL Alberta	23	2	1	3	8
CWHL Regular Season		35	5	1	6	10
Totals from all Competitions		**52**	**6**	**1**	**7**	**14**

CHOSE, LISA *Defence. 1998 New Westminster Lightning (5 games, 2 assists).*

CHOTOWETZ, JULIA *1998-99 NWHL Brampton Thunder #14 (1 game, 1 goal).*

CHOUINARD, VALERIE *Forward. 2004-05 NWHL Montréal (36 gp, 9 goals, 11 assists); 2005 Nationals (6 gp).*

CHOVEN, MARLIE *Forward. 2003 Nationals Saskatchewan Host (5 games, 1 goal).*

CHRISTENSEN, NAT. *Forwad. 2002-03 NWHL Vanc. (23 gp, 1 g., 1 a.); 2005-06 WWHL BC (3 gp, 1 g., 1 a.).*

CHRISTENSEN, NATALIE *Forward. Shoots left.*
Born 1971-07-23. Grew up in Abbotsford, BC, CAN. 5'3".

Year - League - Team		GP	G	A	PTS	PM
1998	Nationals New Westminster Lightning	5	0	0	0	0
2001	Nationals Vancouver Griffins					
2002-03	NWHL Vancouver Griffins	23	1	2	3	24
2003	Nationals Vancouver Griffins	7	0	0	0	4
2005-06	WWHL BC Breakers	3	1	1	2	4

CHU, JULIE *Defence/Forward. Shoots right. #17 #21.*
IIHF champion. Clarkson Cup winner with Minnesota on 2010-03-28.
Clarkson Cup winner with Montréal on 2011-03-27, 2012-03-25, and 2017-03-05.
Born 1982-3-13, New York, NY, USA. Grew up in Fairfield, CT, USA. 5'8".

Year - League - Team			GP	G	A	PTS	PM	Year - Playoff		GP	G	A	PTS	PM
2007-08	WWHL	Minnesota Whitecaps	6	3	4	7	2							
2008	Nationals	Minnesota Whitecaps	1	2	1	3	0							
2008-09	WWHL	Minnesota Whitecaps	9	2	6	8	2	2009	WWHL-P	2	0	0	0	0
								2009	C-Cup	3	0	2	2	2
2009-10	WWHL	Minnesota Whitecaps	0	0	0	0	0	2010	C-Cup	2	0	0	0	0
2010-11	CWHL	Stars de Montréal	16	5	27	32	0	2011	CWHL-P	2		3	3	4
								2011	C-Cup	4	0	4	4	0
2011-12	CWHL	Stars de Montréal	15	5	10	15	2	2012	C-Cup	4	1	3	4	4
2012-13	CWHL	Stars de Montréal	14	2	7	9	2	2013	C-Cup	4	0	1	1	0
2013-14	CWHL	Stars de Montréal	2	0	0	0	0	2014	C-Cup	3	0	1	1	2
2014-15	CWHL	Stars de Montréal	20	2	15	17	12	2015	C-Cup	3	0	0	0	0
2015-16	CWHL	Canadiennes de Montréal	15	3	9	12	4	2016	C-Cup	3	2	2	4	0
2016-17	CWHL	Canadiennes de Montréal	10	1	4	5	4	2017	C-Cup	3	0	2	2	0
CWHL Regular Season			92	18	72	90	24	Clarkson Cup		29	3	15	18	8
Totals from all Competitions			**141**	**28**	**101**	**129**	**40**							

Clarkson Cup Championship MVP in 2010... CWHL Second All-Star Team in 2015-16... finished 6th in the Angela James Bowl scoring race in 2010-11

CHURCH, AMANDA   *Durham, ON, CAN. F. 2009-10 CWHL Mississauga #6 (10 gp, 4 assists; 1 playoff gp).*

CHURCH, LAURA   *Forward. 2002-03 NWHL Durham Lightning #13 (? games).*

CHURCH, NICOLE   *Forward. 2004 Nationals Nova Scotia Selects (5 games, 1 assist).*

CHURCHMAN, SARAH   *F. 2000 Nationals Saskatchewan (7 gp, 1 assist); 2003 Saskatchewan (6 gp, 1 goal).*

CLAGGETT, BETH   *Forward. 2002-03 NWHL Mississauga #8 (? games).*

CLARK-CRUMPTON, MICHELLE   *Forward. 2001-02 NWHL Durham Lightning #4 (4 games, 1 goal, 1 assist).*

CLARK, JANE   *1995 Nationals Metro Valley Selects.*

CLARK, JAYME   *Defence. 2007 Nationals BC Outback (5 gp, 3 pts); 2011-12 CWHL Alberta #24 (7 games).*

CLARK, MARION   *Forward. Shoots left.*

Born 1973-07-03. Grew up in Morell, PE, CAN. 5'7".

Year - League - Team			GP	G	A	PTS	PM
1999	Nationals	Prince Edward Island	5	2	0	2	
2000	Nationals	Prince Edward Island	5	0	0	0	
2001	Nationals	PEI Humpty Dumpty					
2002	Nationals	PEI Humpty Dumpty	6	1	0	1	4
2005	Nationals	Prince Edward Island	5	0	0	0	2
2006	Nationals	Prince Edward Island	5	5	4	9	4
2007	Nationals	Prince Edward Island	5	0	0	0	4
2008	Nationals	Prince Edward Island	5	0	1	1	2

CLARK, MELISSA   *RW. 2004-05 NWHL Durham Lightning #19 (8 games, 1 goal, 1 assist).*

CLARK, PAM   *Forward. 1993-94 COWHL Scarborough #6 (14 gp, 2 assists); 1995-96 Peterborough (6 gp).*

CLARK, SHAWNA   *Forward. 1999 Nationals Team New Brunswick (6 games).*

CLARKE, ALYSSA   *Defence. 2006 Nationals Nova Scotia Selects (4 games).*

CLARKE, CINDY   *Defence. 1998 Nationals Nova Scotia (5 gp, 1 goal); 2000 Nationals Nova Scotia (6 games).*

CLARKE, JENN   *Forward. #20 #19.*

Born 1983-3-11. Grew up in Prescott, ON, CAN. Debut at age 27 on 2009-10-25.

Year - League - Team			GP	G	A	PTS	PM	Year - Playoff		GP	G	A	PTS	PM
2009-10	CWHL	Mississauga Chiefs	24	4	3	7	8	2010	C-Cup	1	0	0	0	2
2010-11	CWHL	Brampton Thunder	24	1	4	5	2	2011	C-Cup	3	0	0	0	0
CWHL Regular Season			48	5	7	12	10	Clarkson Cup		4	0	0	0	2
Totals from all Competitions			**52**	**5**	**7**	**12**	**12**							

CLARKE, LAYOTA   *Right wing. Shoots right. #96 #14.*

Born 1981-6-11, Pickering, ON, CAN. Grew up in Pickering, ON, CAN. 5'4".

Year - League - Team			GP	G	A	PTS	PM	Year - Playoff		GP	G	A	PTS	PM
2004-05	NWHL	Axion de Montréal	18	11	15	26	0							
2005-06	NWHL	Durham Lightning	35	12	11	23	14	2006	NWHL-P	2	0	0	0	2
2006-07	NWHL	Etobicoke Dolphins	31	7	11	18	18	2007	NWHL-P	3	1	0	1	2
2007	Nationals	Etobicoke Dolphins	7	3	0	3	2							
2007-08	CWHL	Vaughan Flames	26	4	12	16	6	2008	CWHL-P	2	0	1	1	0
2008-09	CWHL	Vaughan Flames	29	8	18	26	26	2009	CWHL-P	2		2		
2009-10	CWHL	Vaughan Flames	27	6	13	19	12							
2010-11	CWHL	Toronto Furies	18	2	4	6	6							
CWHL Regular Season			100	20	47	67	50							
Totals from all Competitions			**200**	**54**	**85**	**139**	**90**							

Finished 15th in the Angela James Bowl scoring race in 2008-09.

CLARKSON, HAILY   *F. 2008 Nationals Manitoba (5 gp, 2 goals, 4 assists) 2010-11 WWHL Manitoba #2 (2 gp).*

CLEALL, SUE   *Defence. Shoots right. #22.*

Abby Hoffman Cup winner with Brampton on 2006-03-12.
Born 1978-7-23. Grew up in Edmonton, AB, CAN. Shoots right. 5'7".

Year - League - Team			GP	G	A	PTS	PM	Year - Playoff	GP	G	A	PTS	PM
2002-03	NWHL	Edmonton Chimos	24	1	2	3	12						
2003-04	NWHL	Ottawa Raiders	14	1	1	2	8	2004 NWHL-P	3	0		0	
2004-05	NWHL	Ottawa Raiders	36	3	5	8	39						
2005-06	NWHL	Brampton Thunder	31	2	6	8	22	2006 NWHL-P	5	0	0	0	0
2006	Nationals	Brampton Thunder	3	0	0	0	0						
Totals from all Competitions			**116**	**7**	**14**	**21**	**81**						

CLEMENT-HEYDRA, KATIA　　　　　　　　　　　　　　*Forward. Shoots left. #19.*
Clarkson Cup winner with Montréal on 2017-03-05
Born 1989-11-02. Grew up in St-Bruno, QC, CAN. 5'7". Debut at age 25 on 2015-10-17.

Year - League - Team			GP	G	A	PTS	PM	Year - Playoff	GP	G	A	PTS	PM
2015-16	CWHL	Canadiennes de Montréal	24	7	13	20	2	2016 C-Cup	3	0	0	0	2
2016-17	CWHL	Canadiennes de Montréal	24	3	9	12	2	2017 C-Cup	3	2	1	3	2
2017-18	CWHL	Canadiennes de Montréal	28	12	14	26	16	2018 C-Cup	2	0	0	0	0
2018-19	CWHL	Canadiennes de Montréal	26	6	13	19	4	2019 C-Cup	4	0	0	0	0
CWHL Regular Season			102	28	49	77	24	Clarkson Cup	12	2	1	3	4
Totals from all Competitions			**114**	**30**	**50**	**80**	**28**						

CWHL All-Rookie Team in 2015-16... finished 9th in the Angela James Bowl scoring race in 2017-18

CLEMENTS, KRISTEN　　*Defence. 2005 Nationals Prince Edward Island (4 gp); 2006 Nationals PEI (5 gp, 3 assists)*

CLERMONT, JESSICA　　　　　　　　　　　　*Defence. Shoots left. #7 #2 #5.*
Born 1982-4-4, Saugeen Shores, ON, CAN. Grew up in Pickering, ON, CAN.

Year - League - Team			GP	G	A	PTS	PM	Year - Playoff	GP	G	A	PTS	PM
2000-01	NWHL	North York Aeros	8	0	3	3	4						
2001-02	NWHL	North York Aeros	28	3	4	7	8						
2002	Nationals	North York Aeros	7	0	1	1	2						
2006-07	NWHL	Etobicoke Dolphins	30	0	3	3	32	2007 NWHL-P	3	0	0	0	4
2007	Nationals	Etobicoke Dolphins	7	0	0	0							
2007-08	CWHL	Vaughan Flames	28	1	4	5	18	2008 CWHL-P	2	0	1	1	0
2008-09	CWHL	Vaughan Flames	20	0	3	3	10	2009 CWHL-P	2				
2009-10	CWHL	Vaughan Flames	23	0	5	5	34						
2010-11	CWHL	Toronto Furies	18	0	1	1	6	2011 C-Cup	3	0	0	0	2
CWHL Regular Season			89	1	13	14	68	Clarkson Cup	3	0	0	0	2
Totals from all Competitions			**179**	**4**	**25**	**29**	**120**						

CLIFF, JEN　　　　*Defence. 1995-96 COWHL Hamilton #15 (30 games, 2 assists); 1996-97 #51 (12 games).*

CLOST, CINDY　　　　*Forward. 1996-97 COWHL Newtonbrook Panthers #10 (1 game, 1 goal).*

CLOUTIER, MARIE-ÈVE　　　　　　　　　　　*Forward. Shoots left. #24 #66.*
Born 1981-6-25, St-Bruno, QC, CAN. Grew up in St-Bruno, QC, CAN. Shoots left. 5'5".

Year - League - Team			GP	G	A	PTS	PM
2000-01	NWHL	Wingstar de Montréal	9	0	1	1	2
2001-02	NWHL	Wingstar de Montréal	26	0	4	4	20
2004-05	NWHL	Avalanche du Québec	24	0	1	1	20
2005-06	NWHL	Avalanche du Québec	33	5	7	12	48
2006-07	NWHL	Avalanche du Québec	3	0	1	1	0
2007-08	CWHL	Phénix du Québec	24	1	5	6	24
Totals from all Competitions			**119**	**6**	**19**	**25**	**114**

COADY, KAYLA　　　*Defence. 2005 Nationals Prince Edward Island (5 gp, 2 pts); 2006 Nationals PEI (4gp).*

COATES, KIM　　　　　　　　　　　　　　　　　*Forward. Shoots right.*
Born 1983-10-14. Grew up in Chilliwack, BC, CAN. 5'8".

Year - League - Team			GP	G	A	PTS	PM
2002-03	NWHL	Vancouver Griffins	12	0	0	0	0
2005-06	WWHL	British Columbia Breakers	22	3	11	14	14
2006	Nationals	British Columbia	6	0	1	1	0
2007	Nationals	British Columbia	5	3	0	3	8

COATES, TARA　　　　*Forward. 2003 Nationals Newfoundland Labrador (5 games).*

COBBLEDICK, ELYSIA　　　　*Forward. 2002 Nationals Saskatchewan (6 games).*

COBURN-LANG, ASHLEY　　　*Centre. 1999-00 NWHL Ottawa (1 game); 2000-01 (14 gp, 3 goals, 1 assist).*

COCHRANE, BRADI　　　　　　　　　　　　　*Defence. Shoots right. #47 #7 #71.*
Abby Hoffman Cup winner with Aeros on 2000-03-12 and 2005-03-13. NWHL Cup winner. Born 1980-5-20. Grew up in Mississauga, ON, CAN. 5'6".

Year - League - Team			GP	G	A	PTS	PM	Year - Playoff	GP	G	A	PTS	PM
1996-97	COWHL	North York Aeros	2	0	1	1	4						
1997-98	COWHL	North York Aeros	20	0	10	10	18						
1998	Nationals	North York Aeros	6	0	4	4	4						
1998-99	NWHL	North York Aeros	37	2	21	23	12						
1999	Nationals	North York Aeros	5	0	2	2							
1999-00	NWHL	North York Aeros	32	0	7	7	34	2000 NWHL-P					
2000	Nationals	North York Aeros	6	2	0	2							
2004-05	NWHL	Toronto Aeros	34	4	9	13	52						

Year - League - Team			GP	G	A	PTS	PM	Year - Playoff		GP	G	A	PTS	PM
2005	Nationals	Toronto Aeros	7	0	3	3	0							
2005-06	NWHL	Toronto Aeros	24	4	11	15	22							
2006-07	NWHL	Mississauga Aeros	30	1	5	6	46	2007	NWHL-P	5	0	0	0	6
2007	Nationals	Mississauga Aeros	6	0	0	0	4							
Totals from all Competitions			**214**	**13**	**73**	**86**	**202**							

Served as head coach with CWHL Mississauga... served as interim coach with CWHL Burlington

COCKELL, ASHLEY
Forward. Shoots right. #21 #20.

Born 1988-10-17. Grew up in Fort Assiniboine, AB, CAN. Debut at age 18 on 2006-10-21.

Year - League - Team			GP	G	A	PTS	PM	Year - Playoff		GP	G	A	PTS	PM
2006-07	WWHL	Edmonton Chimos	22	8	10	18	48	2007	WWHL-P	2	0	1	1	0
2011-12	CWHL	Alberta	4	0	2	2	4							

COCKERILL, SHELLY
Forward. Shoots right. #2.

Born 1973-03-26. Grew up in Roblin, MB, CAN. 5'8".

Year - League - Team			GP	G	A	PTS	PM
2005	Nationals	Manitoba	5	3	4	7	2
2006	Nationals	Manitoba	5	3	5	8	2
2007	Nationals	Manitoba	5	5	2	7	12
2008	Nationals	Manitoba	5	2	2	4	10
2010-11	WWHL	Manitoba Maple Leafs	5	1	4	5	0

COENS, JACQUELINE
Forward. #6.

Year - League - Team			GP	G	A	PTS	PM
1999-00	NWHL	Durham Lightning	40	2	7	9	30
2000-01	NWHL	Durham Lightning	16	3	4	7	10
2002-03	NWHL	Durham Lightning					
Totals from all Competitions			**56**	**5**	**11**	**16**	**40**

COLE, MANDY
Forward. Shoots right. #12 #93 #14 #91.

Born 1986-8-30. Grew up in Peterborough, ON, CAN. 5'8".

Year - League - Team			GP	G	A	PTS	PM	Year - Playoff		GP	G	A	PTS	PM
2003-04	NWHL	Durham Lightning	36	5	2	7	20							
2004-05	NWHL	Durham Lightning	36	6	2	8	8							
2005-06	NWHL	Durham Lightning	2	0	0	0	2	2006	NWHL-P	0	0	0	0	0
2006-07	NWHL	Mississauga Aeros	2	0	0	0	0	2007	NWHL-P	1	0	0	0	2
2008-09	CWHL	Brampton Thunder	1					2009	CWHL-P	2				
								2009	C-Cup	2	0	0	0	4
2009-10	CWHL	Brampton Thunder	10	6	3	9	6	2010	C-Cup	1	0	0	0	0
2010-11	CWHL	Brampton Thunder	21	0	1	1	10	2011	CWHL-P	1				
								2011	C-Cup	3	0	0	0	2
2011-12	CWHL	Toronto Furies	19	0	0	0	8	2012	C-Cup	1	0	0	0	0
CWHL Regular Season			51	6	4	10	24	Clarkson Cup		7	0	0	0	6
Totals from all Competitions			**138**	**17**	**8**	**25**	**62**							

COLLINS, AIMEE
Forward. 2008 Nationals Manitoba (5 games, 4 goals, 2 assists).

COLLINS, ANGIE
Forward. #2.

Born 1978-11-3, Cobden, ON, CAN.

Year - League - Team			GP	G	A	PTS	PM
2002-03	NWHL	Ottawa Raiders	33	1	3	4	6
2003-04	NWHL	Ottawa Raiders	36	2	6	8	8
Totals from all Competitions			**69**	**3**	**9**	**12**	**14**

COLLINS, DELANEY
Defence. Shoots left. #34 #4.

IIHF champion. Abby Hoffman Cup winner with Calgary on 2001-03-11, 2003-03-16 and 2007-03-10. WWHL winner. Born 1977-5-2, Pilot Mound, MB, CAN. Grew up in Pilot Mound, MB, CAN. 5'3".

Year - League - Team			GP	G	A	PTS	PM	Year - Playoff		GP	G	A	PTS	PM
2002-03	NWHL	Calgary Oval X-Treme	24	6	20	26	12	2003	NWHL-P					
1999	Nationals	New Westminster Lightning	5	1	2	3								
2000	Nationals	Calgary Oval X-Treme	7	0	1	1								
2001	Nationals	Calgary Oval X-Treme												
2002	Nationals	Calgary Oval X-Treme	6	2	4	6	2							
2003	Nationals	Calgary Oval X-Treme	5	1	7	8	6							
2005-06	WWHL	Calgary Oval X-Treme	5	0	7	7	0	2006	WWHL-P	3	0	2	2	0
2006-07	WWHL	Calgary Oval X-Treme	16	2	14	16	4	2007	WWHL-P	3	1	2	3	0
2007	Nationals	Calgary Oval X-Treme	6	1	8	9	2							
2007-08	WWHL	Calgary Oval X-Treme	22	7	11	18	4							
2008	Nationals	Calgary Oval X-Treme	3	1	2	3	0							
2008-09	WWHL	Calgary Oval X-Treme	9	1	6	7	2							
2009-10	WWHL	Strathmore Rockies	11	3	6	9	4							
2010-11	CWHL	Brampton Thunder	21	0	8	8	8	2011	CWHL-P	2				
								2011	C-Cup	3	0	1	1	2
Totals from all Competitions			**151**	**26**	**101**	**127**	**46**							

COLLINS, JOCELYN
Forward. 2005 Nationals Manitoba (5 games, 2 goals, 1 assist).

COLLINSON, ANDREA *1992-93 Scarborough Firefighters #7 (24 games, 1 goal).*

COLOMBE, MELISSA *Defence. 2010-11 WWHL Manitoba Maple Leafs #4 (8 games, 1 goal).*

COLPITTS, KARI *Forward. Shoots right.*
Abby Hoffman Cup winner with Calgary on 2001-03-11.
Born 1976-05-30. Grew up in Calgary, AB, CAN.

Year - League - Team		GP	G	A	PTS	PM	Year - Playoff	GP	G	A	PTS	PM
1998	Nationals Équipe Québec	6	1	0	1	0						
1999	Nationals Équipe Québec	5	1	2	3							
2000	Nationals Calgary Oval X-Treme	7	3	1	4							
2001	Nationals Calgary Oval X-Treme											

COMITO, JULIE *1998-99 NWHL Scarborough Sting #98 (1 game).*

COMPTE, MELISSA *Forward. 2004 Nationals Manitoba (5 games, 3 assists).*

CONLEY, COLLEEN *Forward. 2003 Nationals Team New Brunswick (4 games).*

CONNELL, AMANDA *Forward. 2002 Nationals Nova Scotia (5 games); 2003 Nationals Nova Scotia (6 games).*

CONNERY, NICOLE *Shoots left. #27.*
Born 1994-1-27. Grew up in Scarborough, ON, CAN. 5'7". Debut at age 22 on 2016-10-9.

Year - League - Team		GP	G	A	PTS	PM	Year - Playoff	GP	G	A	PTS	PM
2016-17	NWHL/ Connecticut Whale	18	4	9	13	2	2017 I-Cup	1	0	0	0	0

CONROY, BECKY *Pembroke, ON, CAN. Forward. 2013-14 CWHL Brampton #13 (22 games, 4 assists).*

CONWAY, AUTUMN *Forward. 2007-08 WWHL Minnesota (13 gp, 2 goals, 1 a.); 2009-10 (11 gp, 5 goals, 4a.).*

COOKE, KELLY *Left wing. Shoots left. #2.*
Clarkson Cup winner with Boston on 2015-03-07 and Isobel Cup winner with Boston on 2016-03-12
Born 1990-10-29. Grew up in Andover, MA, USA. 5'1". Debut at age 23 on 2013-11-02.

Year - League - Team		GP	G	A	PTS	PM	Year - Playoff	GP	G	A	PTS	PM
2013-14	CWHL Boston Blades	23	6	8	14	8	2014 C-Cup	4	0	0	0	0
2014-15	CWHL Boston Blades	22	2	2	4	4	2015 C-Cup	3	0	0	0	0
2015-16	NWHL/ Boston Pride	18	2	2	4	2	2016 I-Cup	4	0	0	0	0
CWHL Regular Season		45	8	10	18	12	Clarkson Cup	7	0	0	0	0
NWHL Regular Season		18	2	2	4	2	Isobel Cup	4	0	0	0	0
Totals from all Competitions		**74**	**10**	**12**	**22**	**14**						

COOLIDGE, SHELLEY *Forward.*
Abby Hoffman Cup winner with Edmonton on 1997-03-09. Born 1968-02-12.

Year - League - Team		GP	G	A	PTS	PM
1996	Nationals Edmonton Chimos	7	0	1	1	0
1997	Nationals Edmonton Chimos					
1998	Nationals Edmonton Chimos	7	0	2	2	2

COOMBES, BOBBI *Forward. 1998 Nationals Tazmanian Devils (5 games).*

COOMBES, CHERYL *1995-96 COWHL Peterborough Skyway #25 (2 games).*

COOPER, CAROL *Defence. #8.*

Year - League - Team		GP	G	A	PTS	PM
1992-93	COWHL Guelph Eagles	28	3	13	16	6
1993-94	COWHL Mississauga Chiefs	27	2	4	6	7
1995	Nationals Mississauga Chiefs					
1995-96	COWHL Mississauga Chiefs	28	4	12	16	12
1996-97	COWHL Mississauga Chiefs	35	3	17	20	10
1997-98	COWHL Mississauga Chiefs	19	2	3	5	6
1998-99	NWHL Mississauga Chiefs	36	2	9	11	12
1999-00	NWHL Mississauga Chiefs	18	0	2	2	8
2000-01	NWHL Mississauga IceBears	35	2	5	7	10
2001-02	NWHL Mississauga IceBears	22	0	3	3	12
Totals from all Competitions		**248**	**18**	**68**	**86**	**83**

Served as interim coach with CWHL Brampton

COOPER, KATHY *Defence. 2000 Nationals Britannia Blues (5 gp, 4 pts); 2003 Nationals Vancouver Griffins (7 gp).*

CORBEIL, MELANIE *LW. 2000-01 NWHL Laval #96 (10 gp, 3 goals); 2004-05 Québec #20 (26 games, 3 assists).*

CORBETT, MEGHAN *Forward. Shoots right. #20.*
Abby Hoffman Cup winner with Calgary on 2007-03-10. WWHL winner. Born 1988-6-19, Winnipeg, MB, CAN. 5'4".
Debut at age 18 on 2006-10-21.

Year - League - Team		GP	G	A	PTS	PM	Year - Playoff	GP	G	A	PTS	PM
2006-07	WWHL Calgary Oval X-Treme	15	6	4	10	8	2007 WWHL-P	1	0	0	0	2
2007	Nationals Calgary Oval X-Treme	5	1	3	4	4						
2007-08	WWHL Calgary Oval X-Treme	13	4	8	12	8						
2008	Nationals Calgary Oval X-Treme	3	0	0	0	2						

CORMIER, LOUISE *Forward. 1995 Nationals Maritime Sports Blades; 1996 Maritime Sport Blades (6 gp, 1 assist).*

CORMIER, NADINE *1998-99 NWHL Bonaventure Wingstar #31 (5 gp, 2 goals, 1 assist).*

CORMIER, PAULETTE *D. 1996 Nationals Maritime Sport Blades (6 gp, 8 pts); 2000 Nationals Team NB (6 gp).*

CORMIER, TINA   *Forward. 2000 Nationals Team New Brunswick (6 gp, 3 pts); 2001 Nationals Team NB.*

CORNELSSEN, TARYN   *Forward. 2005-06 WWHL Calgary #33 (6 games); 2006 Nationals (1 game).*

CORRIERO, NICOLE   *Forward. Shoots right. #34 #77.*
NWHL Cup winner.
Born 1983-10-27. Grew up in Thornhill, ON, CAN.

Year - League - Team		GP	G	A	PTS	PM	Year - Playoff	GP	G	A	PTS	PM
1999-00	NWHL Beatrice Aeros	1	0	1	1	0	2000 NWHL-P					
2000-01	NWHL Beatrice Aeros	8	4	15	19	0						
2001	Nationals North York Aeros											

CORRIVEAU, SONIA   *Forward. 2003 Nationals Équipe Québec (5 games, 2 goals, 1 assist)*

COSSAR, JANICE   *1995 Nationals Metro Valley Selects.*

COSTAGLIOLA, NATHALIE   *Defence. #27.*

Year - League - Team		GP	G	A	PTS	PM
1998-99	NWHL Mistral de Laval	23	0	1	1	32
1999-00	NWHL Mistral de Laval	27	0	3	3	18
Totals from all Competitions		**50**	**0**	**4**	**4**	**50**

COSTIE, MIRANDA   *Cambridge, ON, CAN. F. 2009-10 CWHL Vaughan Flames #72 (7 games, 1 goal, 1 assist).*

CÔTÉ-RIOUX, GENEVIÈVE   *Forward. 2009-10 CWHL Montréal #12 (7 games).*

CÔTÉ, MARIE-JOSÉE   *Forward. 2001 Nationals Équipe Québec.*

CÔTÉ, TARA   *Forward. 2002 Nationals Saskatchewan (6 games).*

COTTINGHAM, MARIANNE   *Forward. 2004 Nationals British Columbia (6 games, 1 goal).*

COTTRELL, ASHLEY   *Forward. Shoots right. #16 #20.*
Clarkson Cup winner with Boston on 2015-03-07.
Born 1990-04-04. Grew up in Sterling Heights, MI, USA. 5'6". Debut at age 23 on 2013-11-02.

Year - League - Team		GP	G	A	PTS	PM	Year - Playoff	GP	G	A	PTS	PM
2013-14	CWHL Boston Blades	24	5	2	7	6	2014 C-Cup	4	0	0	0	0
2014-15	CWHL Boston Blades	12	1	2	3	0	2015 C-Cup	0	0	0	0	0
2015-16	CWHL Boston Blades	2	0	0	0	2						
CWHL Regular Season		38	6	4	10	8	Clarkson Cup	4	0	0	0	0
Totals from all Competitions		**42**	**6**	**4**	**10**	**8**						

COUGHLAN, JODY   *Forward. 2005 Nationals Alberta (6 games, 1 assist)*

COULOMBE, JULIE   *Defence. #19 #99 #4.*

Year - League - Team		GP	G	A	PTS	PM
2001-02	NWHL Wingstar de Montréal	26	1	2	3	18
2002-03	NWHL Avalanche du Québec	28	1	4	5	16
2003-04	NWHL Avalanche du Québec	28	1	2	3	20
2004-05	NWHL Avalanche du Québec	27	0	3	3	18
Totals from all Competitions		**109**	**3**	**11**	**14**	**72**

COULOMBE, MELISSA   *Defence. 2007 Nationals Manitoba (5 games, 2 goals, 4 assists).*

COULTER, LINDA   *Left wing. #12.*

Year - League - Team		GP	G	A	PTS	PM
1995-96	COWHL London Devilettes	30	23	12	35	34
1996-97	COWHL London Devilettes	25	18	17	35	28
1998	Nationals Edmonton Chimos	7	3	2	5	0
Totals from all Competitions		**62**	**44**	**31**	**75**	**62**

COURNOYER, AUDREY   *Forward. Shoots left. #10 #77.*
Born 1990-9-10, Montréal, QC, CAN. Debut at age 16 on 2006-9-23.

Year - League - Team		GP	G	A	PTS	PM
2006-07	NWHL Avalanche du Québec	26	17	11	28	10
2007-08	CWHL Phénix du Québec	3	1	1	2	0

COURNOYER, JOSÉE   *Forward #7 #20.*

Year - League - Team		GP	G	A	PTS	PM
1998-99	NWHL Mistral de Laval	20	4	7	11	2
1999-00	NWHL Mistral de Laval	26	0	4	4	0
2000-01	NWHL Mistral de Laval	7	2	0	2	2
2001-02	NWHL Cheyenne	6	0	0	0	0
Totals from all Competitions		**59**	**6**	**11**	**17**	**4**

COUSINEAU, NANCY   *Forward. 2007-08 CWHL Québec #19 (29 gp, 3 goals, 4 assists).*

COUTURIER, MARIE-EVE   *2003-04 NWHL Québec #90 (3 games).*

COVENY, MARION   *1995-96 COWHL Hamilton Golden Hawks #16 (3 games).*

COWLING, SHARLA   *D. 2005 Nationals Manitoba (5 gp, 2 assists); 2006 Nationals Manitoba (5 gp, 1 goal).*

COYNE SCHOFIELD, KENDALL   *Forward. Shoots left. #26.*
IIHF champion. Isobel Cup winner with Minnesota on 2019-03-17.
Born 1992-05-25. Grew up in Palos Heights, IL, USA. 5'2". Debut at age 26 on 2018-10-06.

Year - League - Team		GP	G	A	PTS	PM	Year - Playoff	GP	G	A	PTS	PM
2018-19	NWHL/ Minnesota Whitecaps	13	7	8	15	4	2019 I-Cup	2	0	2	2	2

CRAMM, JANET *Defence. 1995 Nationals Calgary Classics.*

CRANE, JULIE *1993-94 COWHL Hamilton Golden Hawks #19 (1 game).*

CREARY, JENI *Forward. #6.*
WWHL winner. Born 1983-9-28. Grew up in Shell Lake, SK, CAN. 5'5". Debut at age 23 on 2006-10-13.

Year - League - Team		GP	G	A	PTS	PM	Year - Playoff	GP	G	A	PTS	PM
2000	Nationals Saskatchewan Selects	7	3	4	7							
2006-07	WWHL Calgary Oval X-Treme	14	16	13	29	10	2007 WWHL-P	1	0	0	0	0

CREED, SANDRA *Forward.*
Born 1979-11-14. Grew up in Gaspereaux, PE, CAN.

Year - League - Team		GP	G	A	PTS	PM
1999	Nationals Prince Edward Island	5	0	0	0	
2000	Nationals Prince Edward Island	5	0	0	0	
2001	Nationals PEI Humpty Dumpty					

CROSSMAN, DEMI *Forward. Shoots left. #9.*
Born 1994-12-14. Grew up in Livonia, MI, USA. 5'7". Debut at age 23 on 2018-10-20.

Year - League - Team		GP	G	A	PTS	PM	Year - Playoff	GP	G	A	PTS	PM
2018-19	CWHL Worcester Blades	22	2	3	5	30						

CROWE, HILLARY *Forward. Shoots right. #12.*
Born 1992-9-18. Grew up in Eden Prairie, MN, USA. 5'11". Debut at age 25 on 2018-2-25.

Year - League - Team		GP	G	A	PTS	PM
2017-18	NWHL/ Metropolitan Riveters	3	0	0	0	0

CROWE, LISA *Forward. 2003 Nationals Host Saskatchewan (5 games).*

CROWE, TRACY *Forward. 1995 Nationals Britannia Blues.*

CROZIER-ROUX, VALERIANNE *2000-01 NWHL Laval (1 game).*

CRUICKSHANK, RAYNA *Defence. 2008-09 WWHL British Columbia (1 game).*

CRYDERMAN, CINDY *Defence/Forward. Shoots left. #2 #4.*
Born 1974-05-28. Grew up in Grimsby, ON, CAN.

Year - League - Team		GP	G	A	PTS	PM
1992-93	COWHL Guelph Eagles	21	5	7	12	36
1993-94	COWHL Toronto Junior Aeros	28	13	13	26	44
1995-96	COWHL North York Aeros	25	6	16	22	30
1996	Nationals North York Aeros	5	0	1	1	15
1996-97	COWHL North York Aeros	33	22	18	40	32
1997-98	COWHL North York Aeros	18	8	6	14	20
1998	Nationals North York Aeros	6	3	2	5	0
1998-99	NWHL North York Aeros	39	18	17	35	50
1999	Nationals North York Aeros	5	1	3	4	
2000-01	NWHL North York Aeros	39	14	21	35	42
2001	Nationals North York Aeros					
Totals from all Competitions		**219**	**90**	**104**	**194**	**269**

CUDMORE, HAYLEIGH *Defence. Shoots right. #24.*
Clarkson Cup winner with Calgary on 2016-03-14
Born 1992-05-25. Grew up in Oakville, ON, CAN. 5'4". Debut at age 22 on 2014-10-18.

Year - League - Team		GP	G	A	PTS	PM	Year - Playoff	GP	G	A	PTS	PM
2014-15	CWHL Calgary Inferno	24	2	5	7	20	2015 C-Cup	2	0	0	0	0
2015-16	CWHL Calgary Inferno	24	2	13	15	8	2016 C-Cup	3	0	1	1	0
2016-17	CWHL Calgary Inferno	24	2	3	5	32	2017 C-Cup	4	0	0	0	2
2017-18	CWHL Calgary Inferno	19	2	5	7	2	2018 C-Cup	3	0	0	0	4
CWHL Regular Season		91	8	26	34	62	Clarkson Cup	12	0	1	1	6
Totals from all Competitions		**103**	**8**	**27**	**35**	**68**						

CUDMORE, KIM *Forward. 1996 Nationals Saskatchewan (5 games).*

CULLIGAN, JAMIE *Forward. 1999 Nationals Team New Brunswick (6 games).*

CUMMING, KOBI *Defence. 2000 Nationals Team New Brunswick (5 games).*

CUNNINGHAM, JENNA *Forward. Shoots right. #22 #14.*
Clarkson Cup winner with Calgary on 2016-03-14
Born 1988-8-19. Grew up in Medicine Hat, AB, CAN. 5'5". Debut at age 23 on 2011-10-28.

Year - League - Team		GP	G	A	PTS	PM	Year - Playoff	GP	G	A	PTS	PM
2011-12	CWHL Alberta	15	9	3	12	30						
2012-13	CWHL Alberta	23	4	4	8	18						
2013-14	CWHL Calgary Inferno	18	10	7	17	10	2014 C-Cup	3	0	3	3	4
2014-15	CWHL Calgary Inferno	24	6	8	14	8	2015 C-Cup	2	0	0	0	2
2015-16	CWHL Calgary Inferno	24	7	4	11	20	2016 C-Cup	3	0	0	0	2
2016-17	CWHL Calgary Inferno	4	2	2	4	2						
CWHL Regular Season		108	38	28	66	88	Clarkson Cup	8	0	3	3	8

Totals from all Competitions	116	38	31	69	96

CWHL Second All-Star Team in 2013-14... finished 12th in the Angela James Bowl scoring race in 2013-14

CURRIE, CHARLA
Forward. Shoots right.

Born 1974-06-18. Grew up in Summerside, PE, CAN.

Year - League - Team		GP	G	A	PTS	PM
1995	Nationals PEI Esso Tigers					
1996	Nationals PEI Esso Tigers	4	0	0	0	0
1998	Nationals Prince Edward Island	5	1	2	3	4
1999	Nationals Prince Edward Island	5	1	3	4	
2000	Nationals Prince Edward Island	5	1		1	
2001	Nationals PEI Humpty Dumpty					
2002	Nationals PEI Humpty Dumpty	6	0	1	1	4

CURRIE, JENNY
Left wing. Shoots left. #20.

Born 1994-1-18. Grew up in Chelmsford, MA, USA. F5'4". Debut at age 22 on 2016-10-29.

Year - League - Team		GP	G	A	PTS	PM
2016-17	CWHL Boston Blades	4	0	0	0	0

CURTIN, RENÉE
Forward. 2004-05 WWHL Minnesota #11 (1 game); 2007-08 (0 games).

CURTIN, RONDA
Defence. #9 #19.

Born 1980-11-2, Roseville, MN, USA.

Year - League - Team		GP	G	A	PTS	PM	Year - Playoff	GP	G	A	PTS	PM
2004-05	WWHL Minnesota Whitecaps	10	6	5	11	0	2005 WWHL-P	2	0	1	1	0
2006-07	NWHL Etobicoke Dolphins	26	7	6	13	14	2007 NWHL-P	3	0	0	0	4
2007	Nationals Etobicoke Dolphins	7	0	0	0							
Totals from all Competitions		**48**	**13**	**12**	**25**	**18**						

CURTIS, JONNA
Forward. Shoots right. #24.

Isobel Cup winner with Minnesota on 2019-03-17.

Born 1994-02-28. Grew up in Elk River, MN, USA. 5'4". Debut at age 24 on 2018-10-06.

Year - League - Team		GP	G	A	PTS	PM	Year - Playoff	GP	G	A	PTS	PM
2018-19	NWHL/ Minnesota Whitecaps	16	8	11	19	12	2019 I-Cup	2	0	1	1	0

NWHL Rookie of the Year in 2018-19

CURTIS, LINDSEY
Forward. 2006 Nationals British Columbia (6 games, 1 assist).

CUTHBERT, BOBBIE
Defence. 2003 Nationals Host Saskatchewan (5 games, 1 assist).

CUTKNIFE, RAYLENE
Forward. 2010-11 WWHL Strathmore Rockies #18 (8 games, 3 goals, 2 assists).

CUVELÉ, NATHALIE
2003-04 NWHL Québec #12 (20 games, 1 goal).

CZEREWATY, AMIE
1996-97 COWHL Hamilton Golden Hawks #14 (1 game).

D'ANGELO, CARLA
Hamilton, ON, CAN. D. 2007-08 CWHL Burlington #88 (2 games; 2 playoff games, 1 goal).

DAGENAIS, SARA
Forward. Shoots left. #22 #4.

Born 1987-12-1, Montréal, QC, CAN. Grew up in Montréal, QC, CAN. 5'6". Debut at age 20 on 2007-12-8.

Year - League - Team		GP	G	A	PTS	PM	Year - Playoff	GP	G	A	PTS	PM
2007-08	CWHL Stars de Montréal	5	2	2	4	2						
2012-13	CWHL Stars de Montréal	21	1	4	5	10	2013 C-Cup	4	0	0	0	0
2013-14	CWHL Stars de Montréal	23	0	4	4	12	2014 C-Cup	3	0	0	0	0
2014-15	CWHL Stars de Montréal	22	1	2	3	10						
CWHL Regular Season		71	4	12	16	34	Clarkson Cup	7	0	0	0	0
Totals from all Competitions		**78**	**4**	**12**	**16**	**34**						

DAGG, KIM
Forward. #9 #21

Year - League - Team		GP	G	A	PTS	PM
1993-94	COWHL Hamilton Golden Hawks	22	1	4	5	16
1995-96	COWHL Hamilton Golden Hawks	26	2	11	13	26
Totals from all Competitions		**48**	**3**	**15**	**18**	**42**

DAGG, SARAH
Forward. Shoots right. #21.

Born 1989-7-23, Hamilton, ON, CAN. Grew up in Paris, ON, CAN. 5'2". Debut at age 22 on 2011-10-28.

Year - League - Team		GP	G	A	PTS	PM
2011-12	CWHL Burlington Barracudas	25	3	4	7	6
2012-13	CWHL Brampton Thunder	12	0	0	0	6
CWHL Regular Season		37	3	4	7	12

DAL COLLE, DANIELA
Woodbridge, ON, CAN. Forward. 2007-08 CWHL Mississauga #16 (1 game, 1 assist).

DANDURAND, CASSANDRE
2002-03 NWHL Québec (21 gp, 1 goal, 1 assist); 2003-04 (24 gp, 1 assist).

DANEAU, JESSICA
1998-99 NWHL Montréal Jofa-Titan #4 (8 games, 2 goals, 1 assist).

DANEAU, MYLENE
Defence/Forward. #24 #25.

Year - League - Team		GP	G	A	PTS	PM
1998-99	NWHL Montréal Jofa-Titan	31	2	5	7	14
2000-01	NWHL Mistral de Laval	27	3	3	6	42
Totals from all Competitions		**58**	**5**	**8**	**13**	**56**

DANEAU, STÉPHANIE
Defence. 2003-04 NWHL Québec (5 gp); 2004-05 (2 gp, 1 assist); 2005-06 (1 game).

DANIEL, SARAH *Forward. #3.*
Born 1985-11-20. Grew up in Calgary, AB, CAN.

Year - League - Team		GP	G	A	PTS	PM	Year - Playoff	GP	G	A	PTS	PM
2007-08	WWHL Strathmore Rockies	20	1	3	4	2						
2008-09	WWHL Strathmore Rockies	20	3	3	6	4	2009 WWHL-P	1	0	0	0	0
2009-10	WWHL Strathmore Rockies	18	4	0	4	8						
Totals from all Competitions		**59**	**8**	**6**	**14**	**14**						

DANIELS, MICHELLE *Scarb., ON. 2005-06 NWHL Toronto (3 gp, 4 a.); 2009-10 CWHL Vaughan (12 gp, 1 g., 1 a.).*

DANIELS, SYDNEY *Forward. Shoots left. #19.*
Born 1995-4-19. Grew up in Southwick, MA,USA. 5'8". Debut at age 22 on 2017-10-28.

Year - League - Team		GP	G	A	PTS	PM	Year - Playoff	GP	G	A	PTS	PM
2017-18	NWHL/ Boston Pride	7	4	2	6	2	2018 I-Cup	1	0	0	0	0

DANIS, TAWNYA *Defence. #8.*
Clarkson Cup winner with Montréal on 2009-03-21 and 2011-03-27.
Born 1983-9-13, Newmarket, ON, CAN. Grew up in Pointe-Claire, QC, CAN. 5'6". Debut at age 25 on 2008-10-18.

Year - League - Team		GP	G	A	PTS	PM	Year - Playoff	GP	G	A	PTS	PM
2008-09	CWHL Stars de Montréal	26	3	7	10	8	2009 CWHL-P	2	0	0	0	0
							2009 C-Cup	3	0	0	0	2
2009-10	CWHL Stars de Montréal	13	0	2	2	4						
2010-11	CWHL Stars de Montréal	17	1	0	1	0	2011 C-Cup	1	0	0	0	0
CWHL Regular Season		56	4	9	13	12						
Clarkson Cup 4 0		0	0	2								
Totals from all Competitions		**62**	**4**	**9**	**13**	**14**						

DANN, DAYNA *Right wing. #9.*

Year - League - Team		GP	G	A	PTS	PM
1995-96	COWHL London Devilettes	29	5	8	13	16
1996-97	COWHL London Devilettes	30	3	6	9	32
Totals from all Competitions		**59**	**8**	**14**	**22**	**48**

DANYLYK, INGRID *Defence. #8 #88.*

Year - League - Team		GP	G	A	PTS	PM
1993-94	COWHL Hamilton Golden Hawks	27	4	4	8	38
1995-96	COWHL London Devilettes	26	1	5	6	38
1996-97	COWHL London Devilettes	27	4	5	9	16
1999-00	NWHL Scarborough Sting	33	2	9	11	51
Totals from all Competitions		**113**	**11**	**23**	**34**	**143**

DANZIG, JENA *D. 2002-03 NWHL Vancouver Griffins (22 gp, 3 pts); 2003 Nationals Vanc. Griffins (7 gp, 1 goal).*

DAOUST, CATHERINE *Defence. Shoots right.*
Born 1995-06-18. Grew up in Île-Bizard, QC, CAN. 5'5". Debut at age 23 on 2018-10-13.

Year - League - Team		GP	G	A	PTS	PM	Year - Playoff	GP	G	A	PTS	PM
2018-19	CWHL Canadiennes de Montréal	27	2	3	5	2	2019 C-Cup	4	1	1	2	2

DAOUST, MÉLODIE *Forward. Shoots left.*
Olympic champion.
Born 1992-1-7. Grew up in Valleyfield, QC, CAN. 5'6". Debut at age 19 on 2011-1-8.

Year - League - Team		GP	G	A	PTS	PM	Year - Playoff	GP	G	A	PTS	PM
2010-11	CWHL Stars de Montréal	2	0	3	3	0						
2018-19	CWHL Canadiennes de Montréal	14	11	9	20	24	2019 C-Cup	4	2	3	5	2
Totals from all Competitions		**20**	**13**	**15**	**28**	**26**						

Finished 20th in the Angela James Bowl scoring race in 2018-19

DARKANGELO, SHIANN *Forward. Shoots left. #27.*
Isobel Cup winner with Buffalo on 2017-03-19
Born 1993-11-28. Grew up in Brighton, MI, USA. 5'9". Debut at age 21 on 2015-10-11.

Year - League - Team		GP	G	A	PTS	PM	Year - Playoff	GP	G	A	PTS	PM
2015-16	NWHL/ Connecticut Whale	13	10	3	13	0	2016 I-Cup	3	0	2	2	0
2016-17	NWHL/ Buffalo Beauts	16	7	5	12	6	2017 I-Cup	2	0	1	1	0
2017-18	CWHL Kunlun Red Star	27	10	8	18	32	2018 C-Cup	4	1	0	1	6
2018-19	CWHL Toronto Furies	27	6	4	10	22	2019 C-Cup	3	0	1	1	0
Totals from all Competitions		**95**	**34**	**24**	**58**	**66**						

DARVILL, MARY *Forward. 2006-07 WWHL B.C. #16 (16 games; 2 playoff games); 2008-09 (1 game).*

DARWITZ, NATALIE *Forward. Shoots right. #22.*
IIHF champion. Born 1983-10-13, Eagan, MN, USA. 5'3". Debut at age 23 on 2006-10-13.

Year - League - Team		GP	G	A	PTS	PM	Year - Playoff	GP	G	A	PTS	PM
2006-07	WWHL Minnesota Whitecaps	10	11	10	21	10	2007 WWHL-P	3	2	3	5	2
2007-08	WWHL Minnesota Whitecaps	7	4	7	11	2						
2008	Nationals Minnesota Whitecaps											

DAVID, GENEVIÈVE *Defence. Shoots left. #71 #59 #12.*
Born 1988-3-16. Grew up in Acton Vale, QC, CAN. Debut at age 19 on 2006-11-11.

Year - League - Team	GP	G	A	PTS	PM	Year - Playoff	GP	G	A	PTS	PM
2006-07 NWHL Avalanche du Québec	10	0	2	2	10	2007 NWHL-P					
2007-08 CWHL Phénix du Québec	27	2	4	6	44						
Totals from all Competitions	**37**	**2**	**6**	**8**	**54**						

DAVID, MELISSA
2000-01 NWHL Laval #16 (4 games).

DAVIDSON, GABRIELLE
Pointe-Claire, QC. Forward. 2011-12 CWHL Montréal #4 (2 gp, 1 goal, 2 assists).

DAVIDSON, VANESSA
Forward. Shoots left. #61 #25.

Clarkson Cup winner with Montréal on 2011-03-27 and 2012-03-25.
Born 1984-8-15, Pointe-Claire, QC, CAN. Grew up in Kirkland, QC, CAN. 5'8".

Year - League - Team	GP	G	A	PTS	PM	Year - Playoff	GP	G	A	PTS	PM
2004-05 NWHL Avalanche du Québec	32	8	3	11	44						
2010-11 CWHL Stars de Montréal	24	12	7	19	22	2011 CWHL-P	2		1	1	2
						2011 C-Cup	4	2	0	2	2
2011-12 CWHL Stars de Montréal	27	24	25	49	26	2012 C-Cup	4	1	2	3	6
2012-13 CWHL Stars de Montréal	14	5	6	11	6	2013 C-Cup	4	1	0	1	10
2013-14 CWHL Stars de Montréal	23	11	20	31	20	2014 C-Cup	3	0	0	0	6
CWHL Regular Season	88	52	58	110	74	Clarkson Cup	15	4	2	6	24
Totals from all Competitions	**137**	**64**	**64**	**128**	**144**						

CWHL Second All-Star Team in 2011-12... finished 3rd in the Angela James Bowl scoring race in 2011-12... scored 100th CWHL point on 2014-02-08

DAVIES MICHAEL, REBECCA
Forward. Shoots left. #67.

Abby Hoffman Cup winner with Mississauga on 2008-03-15.
Born 1985-11-8, Toronto, ON, CAN. Grew up in Toronto, ON, CAN. 5'4". Debut at age 22 on 2007-9-22.

Year - League - Team	GP	G	A	PTS	PM	Year - Playoff	GP	G	A	PTS	PM
2007-08 CWHL Mississauga Chiefs	29	4	14	18	34	2008 CWHL-P	5	0	0	0	8
2008 Nationals Mississauga Chiefs	3	1	1	2	4						
2008-09 CWHL Mississauga Chiefs	28	6	10	16	24	2009 CWHL-P	4	2	4	6	2
2009-10 CWHL Mississauga Chiefs	30	17	14	31	56	2010 C-Cup	1	0	0	0	0
2010-11 CWHL Toronto Furies	18	4	2	6	29	2011 CWHL-P	2	1		1	2
						2011 C-Cup	4	0	3	3	0
2011-12 CWHL Toronto Furies	21	1	3	4	22	2012 C-Cup	3	0	0	0	6
CWHL Regular Season	126	32	43	75	165	Clarkson Cup	8	0	3	3	6
Totals from all Competitions	**148**	**36**	**51**	**87**	**187**						

Finished 10th in the Angela James Bowl scoring race in 2009-10... served as a general manager with CWHL Toronto... has served as Director of Hockey Operations with the Canadian Women`s Hockey League.

DAVIS, COURTNEY
Forward. 1998-99 NWHL Ottawa Raiders #9 (30 games, 1 goal); 1999-00 #56 (1 game).

DAVIS, JESSI
Defence. 2000 Nationals University of Manitoba (5 games).

DAVIS, PATTY
Forward. 1999-00 NWHL Durham #7 (36 games, 5 assists); 2000-01 #77 (31 games, 4 assists).

DAVIS, ROBYN
Defence. #6.

Year - League - Team	GP	G	A	PTS	PM
1993-94 COWHL Mississauga Chiefs	29	5	7	12	4
1995 Nationals Mississauga Chiefs					
1995-96 COWHL Mississauga Chiefs	27	4	5	9	6
Totals from all Competitions	**56**	**9**	**12**	**21**	**10**

DAVIS, SARAH
Forward. Shoots left. #9.

Clarkson Cup winner with Calgary on 2016-03-14
Born 1992-06-23. Grew up in Paradise, NL, CAN. 5'4". Debut at age 22 on 2014-10-18.

Year - League - Team	GP	G	A	PTS	PM	Year - Playoff	GP	G	A	PTS	PM
2014-15 CWHL Calgary Inferno	24	7	6	13	16	2015 C-Cup	2	0	0	0	2
2015-16 CWHL Calgary Inferno	21	4	9	13	8	2016 C-Cup	3	0	1	1	4
2016-17 CWHL Calgary Inferno	20	3	12	15	6	2017 C-Cup	4	0	2	2	2
CWHL Regular Season	65	14	27	41	30	Clarkson Cup	9	0	3	3	8
Totals from all Competitions	**74**	**14**	**30**	**44**	**38**						

DAVIS, VICKI
F. 2008-09 WWHL Edmonton #25 (21 gp, 6 goals, 4 a.; 1 playoff gp); 2009-10 (6 gp, 3 g., 5 a.).

DAVISON, KATHRYN
Forward. Shoots left. #28.

Abby Hoffman Cup winner with Calgary on 2007-03-10. WWHL winner. Born 1982-8-8. Canmore, AB, CAN. 5'9".

Year - League - Team	GP	G	A	PTS	PM	Year - Playoff	GP	G	A	PTS	PM
2005-06 WWHL Calgary Oval X-Treme	17	1	4	5	4	2006 WWHL-P	1	0	0	0	0
2006 Nationals Calgary Oval X-Treme	5	0	0	0	0						
2006-07 WWHL Calgary Oval X-Treme	13	4	6	10	4	2007 WWHL-P	0	0	0	0	0
2007 Nationals Calgary Oval X-Treme	3	1	2	3	2						
Totals from all Competitions	**39**	**6**	**12**	**18**	**10**						

DAWSON, AMY
Defence. Shoots right.

Born 1987-04-29. Grew up in Fall River, NS, CAN. 5'5".

Year - League - Team	GP	G	A	PTS	PM	Year - Playoff	GP	G	A	PTS	PM
2005 Nationals Nova Scotia Selects	5	0	1	1	4						
2006 Nationals Nova Scotia Selects	5	1	2	3	2						
2008 Nationals Nova Scotia Selects	5	0	1	1	0						

DAWSON, CINDY *1995-96 COWHL Mississauga Chiefs #3 (1 game).*

DAY, ROZ *2000 Nationals Nova Scotia Selects (6 games, 1 goal).*

DE ABREU, CATHERINE *Defence. Shoots right. #24.*

NWHL winner. Born 1978-12-24. Grew up in Roxboro, QC, CAN. 5'6".

Year - League - Team		GP	G	A	PTS	PM	Year - Playoff	GP	G	A	PTS	PM
2004-05	NWHL Axion de Montréal	34	0	12	12	12						
2005	Nationals Axion de Montréal	6	0	0	0	0						
2005-06	NWHL Axion de Montréal	36	0	4	4	12	2006 NWHL-P	3	0	1	1	0
2006	Nationals Axion de Montréal	6	3	1	4	6						
2006-07	NWHL Axion de Montréal	26	2	2	4	12	2007 NWHL-P					
2007-08	CWHL Stars de Montréal	15	1	4	5	4						
Totals from all Competitions		**126**	**6**	**24**	**30**	**46**						

DE BREE, AMY *Defence. 2008-09 WWHL British Columbia #19 (14 games, 1 goal).*

DEBLOIS, MARIE-HÉLÈNE *Forward. #19.*

Year - League - Team		GP	G	A	PTS	PM
1999-00	NWHL Wingstar de Montréal	30	4	9	13	16
2000-01	NWHL Wingstar de Montréal	24	3	5	8	6
2003-04	NWHL Avalanche du Québec	0	0	0	0	0
Totals from all Competitions		**54**	**7**	**14**	**21**	**22**

DEBRUYNE, MELISSA *1995-96 COWHL London Devilettes #11 (26 games, 6 goals, 9 assists).*

DECKER, BRIANNA *Forward. Shoots right. #13 #14.*

Olympic champion, IIHF champion. Clarkson Cup winner with Boston on 2015-03-07 and Isobel Cup winner with Boston on 2016-03-12. Clarkson Cup winner with Calgary on 2019-03-24.
Born 1991-05-13. Grew up in Dousman, WI, USA. 5'4". Debut at age 23 on 2015-01-17.

Year - League - Team		GP	G	A	PTS	PM	Year - Playoff	GP	G	A	PTS	PM
2014-15	CWHL Boston Blades	12	16	16	32	10	2015 C-Cup	3	5	3	8	10
2015-16	NWHL/ Boston Pride	16	14	15	29	20	2016 I-Cup	4	5	4	9	6
2016-17	NWHL/ Boston Pride	17	14	17	31	14	2017 I-Cup	2	1	4	5	2
2018-19	CWHL Calgary Inferno	23	12	14	26	18	2019 C-Cup	4	3	0	3	4
CWHL Regular Season		35	28	30	58	28	Clarkson Cup	7	8	3	11	14
NWHL Regular Season		33	6	8	14	8	Isobel Cup	6	6	8	14	8
Totals from all Competitions		**81**	**70**	**73**	**143**	**84**						

CWHL First All-Star Team in 2014-15 and 2018-19... CWHL Outstanding Rookie in 2014-15... CWHL All-Rookie Team in 2014-15... finished 2nd in the Angela James Bowl scoring race in 2014-15... NWHL Most Valuable Player in 2015-16 and 2018-19... NWHL Scoring Champion in 2016-17

DEER, JOELLENE *1999-00 NWHL Sainte-Julie #19 (6 games, 1 assist).*

DEERING, MARCIE *Forward. #7 #21 #9.*

Year - League - Team		GP	G	A	PTS	PM
1993-94	COWHL Toronto Junior Aeros	30	5	9	14	10
1999-00	NWHL North York Aeros	38	7	12	19	8
2000-01	NWHL Durham Lightning	3	0	0	0	4
Totals from all Competitions		**71**	**12**	**21**	**33**	**22**

DE GRAZIA, JENNA *Forward. 2004-05 NWHL Ottawa Raiders #2 (1 game).*

DE HOEY, COURTNEY *Forward. Shoots right. #3.*

Born 1986-1-2, Chatham, ON, CAN. 5'3". Debut at age 23 on 2008-10-11.

Year - League - Team		GP	G	A	PTS	PM	Year - Playoff	GP	G	A	PTS	PM
2008-09	CWHL Ottawa Senators	26	3	4	7	12	2009 CWHL-P	2	1		1	
2009-10	CWHL Ottawa Senators	26	5	3	8	22						
Totals from all Competitions		**54**	**9**	**7**	**16**	**34**						

DELAINEY, CASSIDY *Left wing. Shoots left. #93.*

Born 1993-9-4. Grew up in Edmonton, AB, CAN. 5'7". Debut at age 24 on 2017-10-14.

Year - League - Team		GP	G	A	PTS	PM
2017-18	CWHL Toronto Furies	27	2	2	4	2

DELANEY, BRIANNA *Sittsville, ON, CAN. Forward. 2007-08 CWHL Ottawa Capital Canucks #9 (2 games).*

DELAY, MEGAN *Defence. Shoots right. #11.*

Born 1997-4-8. Grew up in Fort Erie, ON, CAN. Debut at age 20 on 2017-10-14.

Year - League - Team		GP	G	A	PTS	PM
2017-18	CWHL Markham Thunder	21	0	1	1	4

DELLA PORTA, BIANCA *Defence. Shoots left. #8.*

Clarkson Cup winner with Montréal on 2012-03-25
Born 1991-3-23, Montréal, QC, CAN. Grew up in Dorval, QC, CAN. 5'7". Debut at age 21 on 2011-10-22.

Year - League - Team		GP	G	A	PTS	PM	Year - Playoff	GP	G	A	PTS	PM
2011-12	CWHL Stars de Montréal	27	2	7	9	20	2012 C-Cup	3	0	0	0	5

DELONG, HANNAH *Forward. 1999 Nationals Team New Brunswick (6 games, 3 goals, 2 assists).*

DELUCE, MALLORY
Forward. Shoots left. #97 #7.

Born 1989-4-13, London, ON, CAN. Grew up in London, ON, CAN. 5'7". Debut at age 17 on 2006-9-16.

Year - League - Team			GP	G	A	PTS	PM	Year - Playoff	GP	G	A	PTS	PM
2006-07	NWHL	Mississauga Aeros	33	18	9	27	16	2007 NWHL-P	4	2	1	3	4
2007	Nationals	Mississauga Aeros	1	0	0	0	0						
2011-12	CWHL	Toronto Furies	20	12	9	21	12	2012 C-Cup	3	0	2	2	2
2012-13	CWHL	Toronto Furies	23	6	14	20	10	2013 C-Cup	3	0	1	1	6
2014-15	CWHL	Toronto Furies	6	2	0	2	0	2015 C-Cup	0	0	0	0	0
CWHL Regular Season			49	20	23	43	22	Clarkson Cup	6	0	3	3	8
Totals from all Competitions			**93**	**40**	**36**	**76**	**50**						

Finished 12th in the Angela James Bowl scoring race in 2012-13

DEMETRICK, EMBER
Defence. 2001 Nationals Saskatchewan.

DEMEULE, KARINE
Forward. #48 #42 #22.

Born 1984-8-30, Montréal, QC, CAN.

Year - League - Team			GP	G	A	PTS	PM	Year - Playoff	GP	G	A	PTS	PM
2003-04	NWHL	Axion de Montréal	36	13	13	26	40	2004 NWHL-P	4	4	1	5	1
2004-05	NWHL	Axion de Montréal	7	1	1	2	10						
2009-10	CWHL	Stars de Montréal	8	2	1	3	14						
Totals from all Competitions			**55**	**20**	**16**	**36**	**65**						

DEMPSEY, JILLIAN
Centre. Shoots right. #14.

Clarkson Cup winner with Boston on 2015-03-07 and Isobel Cup winner with Boston on 2016-03-12.
Born 1991-01-19. Grew up in Winthrop, MA, USA. 5'4". Debut at age 22 on 2013-11-02.

Year - League - Team			GP	G	A	PTS	PM	Year - Playoff	GP	G	A	PTS	PM
2013-14	CWHL	Boston Blades	24	14	14	28	8	2014 C-Cup	4	0	1	1	0
2014-15	CWHL	Boston Blades	22	9	10	19	2	2015 C-Cup	2	0	0	0	0
2015-16	NWHL/	Boston Pride	18	7	7	14	10	2016 I-Cup	4	2	3	5	4
2016-17	NWHL/	Boston Pride	17	5	10	15	0	2017 I-Cup	2	1	0	1	0
2017-18	NWHL/	Boston Pride	16	7	8	15	2	2018 I-Cup	1	1	0	1	0
2018-19	NWHL/	Boston Pride	16	10	4	14	0	2019 I-Cup	1	0	0	0	2
CWHL Regular Season			46	23	24	47	10	Clarkson Cup	6	0	1	1	0
NWHL Regular Season			67	29	29	58	12	Isobel Cup	8	4	3	7	6
Totals from all Competitions			**127**	**56**	**57**	**113**	**28**						

CWHL First All-Star Team in 2013-14... CWHL Rookie of the Year in 2013-14... CWHL All-Rookie Team in 2013-14... finished 5th in the Angela James Bowl scoring in 2013-14... NWHL Denna Laing Perseverance Award in 2017-18 and 2018-19.

DEMPSEY, STEPHANIE
Defence. 1998-99 NWHL Scarborough #88 (20 games).

DENBY, JOANNE
Defence. Shoots left. #77 #21.

Born 1982-10-2. Grew up in Sterling Heights, MI, USA. 5'10".

Year - League - Team			GP	G	A	PTS	PM	Year - Playoff	GP	G	A	PTS	PM
2004-05	NWHL	Durham Lightning	7	0	2	2	4						
2005-06	NWHL	Durham Lightning	34	1	6	7	28	2006 NWHL-P	2	1	0	1	0
Totals from all Competitions			**43**	**2**	**8**	**10**	**32**						

DENINO, STEPHANIE
Defence. Shoots left. #24.

Clarkson Cup winner with Montréal on 2011-03-27 and 2012-03-25.
Born 1987-7-6, Montréal, QC, CAN. Grew up in St-Laurent, QC, CAN. 5'5". Debut at age 23 on 2010-10-23.

Year - League - Team			GP	G	A	PTS	PM	Year - Playoff	GP	G	A	PTS	PM
2010-11	CWHL	Stars de Montréal	24	1	3	4	16	2011 CWHL-P	2				
								2011 C-Cup	3	0	2	2	2
2011-12	CWHL	Stars de Montréal	25	3	11	14	16	2012 C-Cup	4	0	3	3	0
CWHL Regular Season			49	4	14	18	32	Clarkson Cup	7	0	5	5	2
Totals from all Competitions			**58**	**4**	**19**	**23**	**34**						

DENIS, SHAUNA
Forward. Shoots left. #77 #22.

Clarkson Cup winner with Montréal on 2009-03-21
Born 1984-9-17, Stittsville, ON, CAN. Debut at age 24 on 2008-10-11.

Year - League - Team			GP	G	A	PTS	PM	Year - Playoff	GP	G	A	PTS	PM
2008-09	CWHL	Stars de Montréal	7	4	3	7		2009 CWHL-P	1	0	0	0	0
								2009 C-Cup	2	1	0	1	0

DENNER, RACHEL
Forward. Shoots right.

Born 1978-02-28. Grew up in Kelowna, BC, CAN. 5'6".

Year - League - Team			GP	G	A	PTS	PM
1996-97	COWHL	Hamilton Golden Hawks	29	11	10	21	16
2007	Nationals	BC Outback	5	2	0	2	2

DEPRATTO, BETH
Centre. Shoots left. #55 #3 #5.

Born 1982-8-31, Alexandria, ON, CAN. Grew up in Alexandria, ON, CAN. 5'5".

Year - League - Team			GP	G	A	PTS	PM	Year - Playoff	GP	G	A	PTS	PM
2002-03	NWHL	Ottawa Raiders	34	11	11	22	18						
2003-04	NWHL	Axion de Montréal	32	15	10	25	16	2004 NWHL-P	4				
2004-05	NWHL	Ottawa Raiders	31	12	4	16	10						

Year - League - Team			GP	G	A	PTS	PM	Year - Playoff	GP	G	A	PTS	PM
2005-06	NWHL	Ottawa Raiders	35	22	31	53	16	2006 NWHL-P	2	0	2	2	0
2006-07	NWHL	Ottawa Raiders	31	8	17	25	84	2007 NWHL-P	1	0	0	0	0
Totals from all Competitions			**170**	**68**	**75**	**143**	**144**						

DERMOTT, KRISTA *Milton, ON, CAN. Forward. 2006-07 NWHL Brampton #55 (2 games).*

DEROUIN, VALERIE *1998-99 NWHL Laval #69 (1 game).*

DÉRY, NATHALIE *Defence. Shoots left. #25 #44.*

Clarkson Cup winner with Montréal on 2009-03-21, 2011-03-27 and 2012-03-25.
Born 1976-6-8, Cap-Santé, QC, CAN. 5'6". Debut at age 24 in 2000-01.

Year - League - Team			GP	G	A	PTS	PM	Year - Playoff	GP	G	A	PTS	PM
1999	Nationals	Équipe Québec	5		3	3							
2000	Nationals	Équipe Québec	6	1	2	3							
2000-01	NWHL	Sainte-Julie	31	5	11	16	36						
2001	Nationals	Équipe Québec											
2001-02	NWHL	Cheyenne	11	1	2	3	12						
2002	Nationals	Équipe Québec	6	0	2	2	4						
2002-03	NWHL	Avalanche du Québec	36	5	11	16	42						
2003	Nationals	Équipe Québec	5	1	2	3	4						
2003-04	NWHL	Avalanche du Québec	35	6	9	15	80						
2004	Nationals	Équipe Québec	5	0	1	1	6						
2004-05	NWHL	Avalanche du Québec	36	1	5	6	48						
2005-06	NWHL	Avalanche du Québec	35	5	9	14	82						
2006-07	NWHL	Axion de Montréal	22	4	12	16	38	2007 NWHL-P					
2007-08	CWHL	Stars de Montréal	27	7	20	27	72	2008 CWHL-P	2	0	1	1	6
2008-09	CWHL	Stars de Montréal	26	4	14	18	40	2009 CWHL-P	2	0	1	1	0
								2009 C-Cup	3	0	0	0	2
2009-10	CWHL	Stars de Montréal	29	4	21	25	36	2010 C-Cup	1	0	0	0	0
2010-11	CWHL	Stars de Montréal	26	1	2	3	28	2011 CWHL-P	2		2		
								2011 C-Cup	4	0	0	0	2
2011-12	CWHL	Stars de Montréal	26	1	5	6	36	2012 C-Cup	4	0	1	1	6
CWHL Regular Season			134	17	62	79	212	Clarkson Cup	12	0	1	1	10
Totals from all Competitions			**385**	**46**	**134**	**180**	**582**						

CWHL Eastern All-Star Team in 2007-08... finished 12th in the Angela James Bowl scoring race in 2007-08... served as interim coach with CWHL Montréal...

DESCHAMPS, LEE-ANN *Defence. 2002 Nationals PEI Humpty Dumpty (6 games).*

DESCHAMPS, NANCY *Forward. Shoots right. #19 #13.*

Born 1972-11-06. Grew up in Montreal, QC, CAN.

Year - League - Team			GP	G	A	PTS	PM						
1992-93	COWHL	Guelph Eagles	27	7	7	14	16						
1995	Nationals	Équipe Québec											
1996	Nationals	Équipe Québec	6	5	2	7	0						
1998	Nationals	Équipe Québec	6	4	3	7	2						
1998-99	NWHL	Montréal Jofa-Titan	30	13	15	28	33						
1999	Nationals	Équipe Québec	5	1	3	4							
1999-00	NWHL	Sainte-Julie	34	14	15	29	22	2000 NWHL-P					
2000-01	NWHL	Sainte-Julie	37	23	27	50	20						
2001-02	NWHL	Cheyenne	29	13	9	22	20						
2002	Nationals	Équipe Québec	6	1	1	2	0						
2002-03	NWHL	Avalanche du Québec	30	10	15	25	11						
Totals from all Competitions			**210**	**91**	**97**	**188**	**124**						

DESCHÊNES, JOSÉE-ANN *Defence. #20.*

Clarkson Cup winner with Montréal on 2009-03-21
Born 1988-8-20, Rouyn-Noranda, QC, CAN. 5'8". Debut at age 20 on 2008-10-11.

Year - League - Team			GP	G	A	PTS	PM	Year - Playoff	GP	G	A	PTS	PM
2008-09	CWHL	Stars de Montréal	26	1	7	8	8	2009 CWHL-P	2	0	0	0	2
								2009 C-Cup	3	0	0	0	0

DESCHÊNES, KIM *Right wing. Shoots left. #9.*

Clarkson Cup winner with Montréal on 2017-03-05
Born 1991-08-17. Grew up in Saint-Quentin, NB, CAN. 5'10". Debut at age 23 on 2014-10-18.

Year - League - Team			GP	G	A	PTS	PM	Year - Playoff	GP	G	A	PTS	PM
2008	Nationals	Team New Brunswick	5	3	1	4	0						
2014-15	CWHL	Stars de Montréal	22	8	6	14	12	2015 C-Cup	3	1	1	2	2
2015-16	CWHL	Canadiennes de Montréal	24	13	20	33	6	2016 C-Cup	3	1	1	2	2
2016-17	CWHL	Canadiennes de Montréal	20	4	6	10	14	2017 C-Cup	3	3	0	3	4
2017-18	CWHL	Canadiennes de Montréal	22	5	5	10	14	2018 C-Cup	2	0	0	0	4
2018-19	CWHL	Canadiennes de Montréal	28	4	7	11	12	2019 C-Cup	4	0	0	0	2
CWHL Regular Season			116	34	44	78	58	Clarkson Cup	15	5	2	7	14
Totals from all Competitions			**136**	**42**	**47**	**89**	**72**						

Finished 3rd in the Angela James Bowl scoring race in 2015-16

DESFORGES, FANNIE
Left wing. Shoots left. #23 #28.

Born 1990-02-27. Grew up in Fournier, ON, CAN. 5'6". Debut at age 23 on 2013-11-09.

Year - League - Team			GP	G	A	PTS	PM	Year - Playoff	GP	G	A	PTS	PM
2013-14	CWHL	Stars de Montréal	19	6	1	7	12	2014 C-Cup	3	0	0	0	0
2014-15	CWHL	Stars de Montréal	20	0	1	1	12	2015 C-Cup	3	0	0	0	4
CWHL Regular Season			39	6	2	8	24	Clarkson Cup	6	0	0	0	4
Totals from all Competitions			**45**	**6**	**2**	**8**	**28**						

DÉSILETS, LYSANNE
Defence/Forward. Shoots left. #7 #4.

Born 1984-9-14, Trois-Rivières, QC, CAN. 5'5". Debut at age 21 on 2006-01-29.

Year - League - Team			GP	G	A	PTS	PM
2005-06	NWHL	Avalanche du Québec	1	1	0	1	0
2006-07	NWHL	Avalanche du Québec	32	9	7	16	10
2007-08	CWHL	Phénix du Québec	28	4	6	10	8
Totals from all Competitions			**61**	**14**	**13**	**27**	**18**

DESMET, TRISTAN
Forward. Shoots right. #27 #91.

Abby Hoffman Cup winner with Calgary on 2001-03-11.
WWHL winner. Born 1983-11-16. Grew up in Strathmore, AB, CAN.

Year - League - Team			GP	G	A	PTS	PM	Year - Playoff	GP	G	A	PTS	PM
2001	Nationals	Calgary Oval X-Treme											
2005-06	WWHL	Calgary Oval X-Treme	24	12	15	27	24	2006 WWHL-P	3	3	3	6	0
2006	Nationals	Calgary Oval X-Treme	7	2	2	4	0						
2007-08	WWHL	Strathmore Rockies	5	1	2	3	10						
Totals from all Competitions			**39**	**18**	**22**	**40**	**34**						

DESMIER, ELYSIA
Right wing. Shoots left. #4.

CWHL winner. Born 1986-4-23, Halifax, NS; grew up in Orléans, ON, CAN. 5'9". Debut at age 19 on 2005-12-10.

Year - League - Team			GP	G	A	PTS	PM	Year - Playoff	GP	G	A	PTS	PM
2005-06	NWHL	Brampton Thunder	3	2	2	4	0						
2007-08	CWHL	Burlington Barracudas	1	0	0	0	0						
2007-08	CWHL	Brampton Can.-Thunder	4	0	1	1	0	2008 CWHL-P	2	0	1	1	0
2008	Nationals	Brampton Can.-Thunder	3	0	0	0	0						
2008-09	CWHL	Brampton Thunder	29	10	9	19	18	2009 CWHL-P	2	0	1	1	
								2009 C-Cup	2	0	0	0	0
2009-10	CWHL	Brampton Thunder	30	10	17	27	16	2010 C-Cup	2	0		0	
2010-11	CWHL	Brampton Thunder	22	4	4	8	14	2011 CWHL-P	2				
								2011 C-Cup	3	0	0	0	0
CWHL Regular Season			86	24	31	55	48	Clarkson Cup	7	0	0	0	0
Totals from all Competitions			**105**	**26**	**35**	**61**	**48**						

Finished 12th in the Angela James Bowl scoring race in 2009-10

DESPIEGELAERE, CHANTAL
Defence. Shoots left.

Born 1986-05-27. Grew up in Winnipeg, MB, CAN. 5'7".

Year - League - Team			GP	G	A	PTS	PM
2005	Nationals	Manitoba	5	0	0	0	2
2006	Nationals	Manitoba	5	0	1	1	2
2007	Nationals	Manitoba	5	0	1	1	2

DESROCHERS, MELANIE
Defence. Shoots left. #11.

Born 1992-4-15. Grew up in Welland, ON, CAN. 5'4". Debut at age 24 on 2016-10-15.

Year - League - Team			GP	G	A	PTS	PM	Year - Playoff	GP	G	A	PTS	PM
2016-17	CWHL	Canadiennes de Montréal	10	0	1	1	4						
2017-18	CWHL	Canadiennes de Montréal	28	3	6	9	16	2018 C-Cup	2	0	0	0	0
2018-19	CWHL	Canadiennes de Montréal	28	1	6	7	18	2019 C-Cup	3	0	1	1	4
Totals from all Competitions			**71**	**4**	**14**	**18**	**44**						

DESROSIERS, ANNIE
Forward. Shoots left. #96 #27 #48 #57.

Abby Hoffman Cup winner with Aeros on 2004-03-14. NWHL winner. Born 1980-7-29. Grew up in Saint-Antoine-sur-Richelieu, QC, CAN. 5'8".

Year - League - Team			GP	G	A	PTS	PM	Year - Playoff	GP	G	A	PTS	PM
1998-99	NWHL	Mistral de Laval	32	28	12	40	40						
1999	Nationals	Équipe Québec	5	3	7	10							
1999-00	NWHL	Mistral de Laval	33	29	16	45	30						
2000	Nationals	Équipe Québec	6	1	2	3							
2000-01	NWHL	Mistral de Laval	2	2	0	2	0						
2000-01	NWHL	Wingstar de Montréal	24	18	13	31	6						
2001	Nationals	Équipe Québec											
2001-02	NWHL	North York Aeros	27	20	16	36	31						
2002	Nationals	North York Aeros	7	1	6	7	0						
2002-03	NWHL	North York Aeros		24	15	39	16	2003 NWHL-P	5	1	2	3	4
2003-04	NWHL	Toronto Aeros	34	26	34	60	57						
2004	Nationals	Toronto Aeros	6	5	7	12	18						
2004-05	NWHL	Axion de Montréal	35	30	28	58	40						
2005	Nationals	Axion de Montréal	6	3	7	10	4						
2005-06	NWHL	Axion de Montréal	33	25	20	45	60	2006 NWHL-P	3	2	2	4	2

Year - League - Team	GP	G	A	PTS	PM	Year - Playoff	GP	G	A	PTS	PM
2006 Nationals Axion de Montréal	6	6	8	14	0						
2006-07 NWHL Axion de Montréal	29	15	26	41	32	2007 NWHL-P					
2007-08 CWHL Stars de Montréal	4	2	3	5	0						
Totals from all Competitions	**297**	**241**	**224**	**465**	**340**						

Women's National Championships Most Valuable Player in 2006.

DESROSIERS, MARIE-HÉLÈNE *F. 2003 Nationals Équipe Québec (5 gp, 6 pts); 2007-08 CWHL Québec (6 gp).*

DEVEREAUX, KATHY *Centre. Shoots left. #44 #26.*

Abby Hoffman Cup winner with Calgary on 1998-03-22 and 2001-03-11. Abby Hoffman Cup winner with Brampton on 2006-03-12.
Born 1979-8-3. Grew up in Seaforth, ON, CAN. 5'6".

Year - League - Team	GP	G	A	PTS	PM	Year - Playoff	GP	G	A	PTS	PM
1996-97 COWHL London Devilettes	2	1	0	1	0						
1998 Nationals Calgary Oval X-Treme	7	0	2	2	0						
1999 Nationals Calgary Oval X-Treme	6	0	3	3							
2000 Nationals Calgary Oval X-Treme	7	4	1	5							
2001 Nationals Calgary Oval X-Treme											
2004-05 NWHL Brampton Thunder	22	4	8	12	2						
2005 Nationals Brampton Thunder	6	1	0	1	0						
2005-06 NWHL Brampton Thunder	28	4	8	12	4	2006 NWHL-P	5	0	0	0	0
2006 Nationals Brampton Thunder	6	0	1	1	2						
2006-07 NWHL Brampton Thunder		2		2		2007 NWHL-P	6	1	1	2	4
Totals from all Competitions	**95**	**17**	**24**	**41**	**12**						

DEVEREAUX, KIM *Defence. #24.*

Seaforth, ON, CAN. Debut on 2006-09-19.

Year - League - Team	GP	G	A	PTS	PM	Year - Playoff	GP	G	A	PTS	PM
2006-07 NWHL Brampton Thunder	31	0	4	4	51	2007 NWHL-P	6	0	0	0	2

DEVRIES, RACHEL *Defence. 2002 Nationals Nova Scotia.*

DI STASI, ANGELA *Forward. Shoots left. #15.*

Born 1985-5-7, Toronto, ON, CAN. Grew up in Toronto, ON, CAN. 5'3". Debut at age 23 on 2008-10-4.

Year - League - Team	GP	G	A	PTS	PM	Year - Playoff	GP	G	A	PTS	PM
2008-09 CWHL Mississauga Chiefs	27	4	7	11	8	2009 CWHL-P	4	1	2	3	
2009-10 CWHL Mississauga Chiefs	27	13	10	23	8						
2010 C-Cup Mississauga	1	0	0	0	0						
2010-11 CWHL Toronto Furies	26	3	6	9	8	2011 CWHL-P	2	0	1	1	
						2011 C-Cup	4	1	2	3	2
CWHL Regular Season	80	20	23	43	24	Clarkson Cup	5	1	2	3	2
Totals from all Competitions	**91**	**22**	**28**	**50**	**26**						

Finished 20th in the Angela James Bowl scoring race in 2009-10

DIAMOND, SARA *Defence. 2006 Nationals Newfoundland Labrador (5 games).*

DIAZ, DANIELA *Forward. Shoots right. #4*

Born 1982-06-16, Zug, SUI. 5'7".

Year - League - Team	GP	G	A	PTS	PM	Year - Playoff	GP	G	A	PTS	PM
2006-07 NWHL Etobicoke Dolphins	29	10	11	21	26	2007 NWHL-P	3	0	0	0	4
2007 Nationals Etobicoke Dolphins	7	3	1	4	4						

DICKINSON, LAURA *Forward. 2002-03 NWHL Vancouver Griffins #5 (1 game).*

DICKSON, HEATHER *Defence. 2004 Nationals Nova Scotia (5 games).*

DIDUCK, JUDY *Defence. Shoots left.*

Abby Hoffman Cup winner with Edmonton on 1997-03-09. Abby Hoffman Cup winner with Calgary on 2001-03-11.
Born 1966-04-21. Grew up in Sherwood Park, AB, CAN.

Year - League - Team	GP	G	A	PTS	PM
1995 Nationals Calgary Classics					
1996 Nationals Edmonton Chimos	7	0	3	3	6
1997 Nationals Edmonton Chimos					
1998 Nationals Edmonton Chimos	6	2	3	5	2
1999 Nationals Calgary Oval X-Treme	6	3	4	7	
2000 Nationals Calgary Oval X-Treme	7	1	2	3	
2001 Nationals Calgary Oval X-Treme					

DILLABOUGH, JESSICA *1999-00 NWHL Ottawa Raiders #9 (35 games, 3 goals, 11 assists).*

DIMASI, MAGGIE *Defence. Shoots left. #18.*

Born 1991-05-06. Grew up in Burlington, ON, CAN. Debut at age 24 on 2015-10-17.

Year - League - Team	GP	G	A	PTS	PM
2015-16 CWHL Boston Blades	22	1	1	2	8
2016-17 CWHL Boston Blades	11	0	1	1	6

DINGELDEIN, JENNA *Forward. Shoots left. #44.*

Born 1992-10-8. Grew up in Toronto, ON, CAN. 5'10". Debut at age 24 on 2016-10-15.

Year - League - Team	GP	G	A	PTS	PM	Year - Playoff	GP	G	A	PTS	PM
2016-17 CWHL Toronto Furies	21	4	0	4	8	2017 C-Cup	3	0	0	0	0
2017-18 CWHL Toronto Furies	28	9	6	15	34						
2018-19 CWHL Toronto Furies	8	0	0	0	0						
Totals from all Competitions	**60**	**13**	**6**	**19**	**50**						

DIONNE, ANDRÉ-ANNE *2003-04 NWHL Ottawa Raiders #11 (16 games, 3 goals; ? playoff games, 1 goal).*

DIONNE, KRISTY *Forward. 2000 Nationals Newfoundland Labrador (5 games, 1 goal).*

DIX-COOPER, LINDA *Defence. 2002 Nationals Richmond Steelers (5 games).*

DIXON, LAURA *Forward. 2001 Nationals Saskatchewan.*

D'OENCH, MIYE *Forward. Shoots right. #19.*
Isobel Cup winner with Metropolitan on 2018-03-25
Born 1994-1-26. Grew up in New York, NY, USA. 5'4". Debut at age 22 on 2016-10-8.

Year - League - Team	GP	G	A	PTS	PM	Year - Playoff	GP	G	A	PTS	PM
2016-17 NWHL/ New York Riveters	18	5	9	14	10	2017 I-Cup	1	0	1	1	2
2017-18 NWHL/ Metropolitan Riveters	9	7	6	13	0	2018 I-Cup	2	0	2	2	0
2018-19 NWHL/ Metropolitan Riveters	9	1	6	7	4	2019 I-Cup	2	0	2	2	4
NWHL Regular Season	36	13	21	34	14	Isobel Cup	5	0	5	5	6
Totals from all Competitions	**41**	**13**	**26**	**39**	**20**						

DOBBIE, KRISTIE *Defence. Shoots left. #20 #24.*
Born 1982-2-13. Grew up in Brampton, ON, CAN. 5'5".

Year - League - Team	GP	G	A	PTS	PM	Year - Playoff	GP	G	A	PTS	PM
2000-01 NWHL North York Aeros	16	1	2	3	10						
2001 Nationals North York Aeros											
2001-02 NWHL North York Aeros	29	0	11	11	32	2003 NWHL-P					
2002 Nationals North York Aeros	7	0	1	1	2						
2004-05 NWHL Brampton Thunder	22	0	2	2	26						
2005 Nationals Brampton Thunder	6	0	1	1	6						
2005-06 NWHL Brampton Thunder	21	0	0	0	34						
Totals from all Competitions	**101**	**1**	**17**	**18**	**110**						

DOHM, LISA *Forward. #4*
Born 1982-11-21. Grew up in Saskatoon, SK, CAN.

Year - League - Team	GP	G	A	PTS	PM	Year - Playoff	GP	G	A	PTS	PM
2003 Nationals Saskatchewan	6	1	4	5	2						
2004-05 WWHL Saskatchewan Prairie Ice	11	0	0	0	2						
2005-06 WWHL Saskatchewan Prairie Ice	19	5	7	12	8	2006 WWHL-P	2	0	0	0	0
Totals from all Competitions	**38**	**6**	**11**	**17**	**12**						

DOIRON, MICHELLE *Forward. 2001 Nationals Team New Brunswick.*

DOLAN, ANDREA *Centre. #96 #14.*

Year - League - Team	GP	G	A	PTS	PM	Year - Playoff	GP	G	A	PTS	PM
2001-02 NWHL Wingstar de Montréal	28	1	2	3	4						
2002-03 NWHL Axion de Montréal	31	3	10	13	16	2003 NWHL-P					
Totals from all Competitions	**59**	**4**	**12**	**16**	**20**						

DOMARCHUK, KATE *D. 2007 Nationals Prince Edward Island (5 gp, 1 assist); 2008 Nationals PEI (5 gp, 2 assists).*

DOMENICO, ALISON *Forward. #6 #8.*
Born 1987-3-22, Ottawa, ON, CAN. Grew up in Nepean, ON, CAN.

Year - League - Team	GP	G	A	PTS	PM	Year - Playoff	GP	G	A	PTS	PM
2003-04 NWHL Ottawa Raiders	36	11	17	28	48	2004 NWHL-P	3	0	2	2	4
2004-05 NWHL Ottawa Raiders	31	11	26	37	58						
Totals from all Competitions	**70**	**22**	**45**	**67**	**110**						

DONALDSON, DAWNA *Forward. Shoots left.*
Born 1967-04-22

Year - League - Team	GP	G	A	PTS	PM	Year - Playoff	GP	G	A	PTS	PM
1998 Nationals Prince Edward Island	5	1	2	3	0						
2000 Nationals Prince Edward Island	5	1	0	1							
2001 Nationals PEI Humpty Dumpty											
2002 Nationals PEI Humpty Dumpty	6	1	0	1	4						

DONALDSON, JAIME *D. 2006 Nationals Prince Edward Island (5 gp, 1 assist); 2008 Nationals PEI (5 gp, 1 assist).*

DONALDSON, KARLEY *Forward. 2008-09 CWHL Ottawa Senators #14 (2 games, 1 goal).*

DONINCX, KRISTY *Forward. 2000 Nationals Saskatchewan (7 gp, 4 goals, 3 assists).*

DONNELLY, JENNIFER *Defence. 1995 Nationals Britannia Blues.*

DONOHUE, KATHERINE *Forward. Shoots right. #20.*
Born 1994-1-27. Grew up in Rochester, NY, USA. 5'5". Debut at age 23 on 2017-11-4.

Year - League - Team	GP	G	A	PTS	PM
2017-18 NWHL/ Buffalo Beauts	6	1	0	1	0

DONOVAN, SAM   *Forward. Shoots right. #32.*

Born 1996-1-3. Grew up in New Brighton, MN, USA. 5'2". Debut at age 22 on 2018-3-3.

Year - League - Team		GP	G	A	PTS	PM	Year - Playoff	GP	G	A	PTS	PM
2017-18	NWHL/ Connecticut Whale	2	0	1	1	0	2018 I-Cup	1	0	0	0	0
2018-19	NWHL/ Connecticut Whale	4	0	0	0	0						

DORRION, ALYNN   *Defence. 2006 Nationals Nova Scotia Selects (5 games, 1 assist); 2008 Nationals (5 gp).*

DOSDALL, KIIRA   *Defence/Forward. Shoots right. #26.*

Isobel Cup winner with Metropolitan on 2018-03-25
Born 1987-07-31. Grew up in Fairfield, CT, USA. 5'8". Debut at age 26 on 2013-11-02.

Year - League - Team		GP	G	A	PTS	PM	Year - Playoff	GP	G	A	PTS	PM
2013-14	CWHL Boston Blades	11	0	0	0	8	2014 C-Cup	4	0	1	1	6
2015-16	NWHL/ New York Riveters	18	1	6	7	20	2016 I-Cup	2	1	0	1	2
2016-17	NWHL/ New York Riveters	17	2	3	5	16	2017 I-Cup	1	0	0	0	0
2017-18	NWHL/ Metropolitan Riveters	16	0	10	10	8	2018 I-Cup	2	0	0	0	4
2018-19	NWHL/ Metropolitan Riveters	16	0	1	1	6	2019 I-Cup	2	0	0	0	0
NWHL Regular Season		67	3	20	23	50	Isobel Cup	7	1	0	1	6
Totals from all Competitions		**89**	**4**	**21**	**25**	**70**						

DOSSER, NICOLE   *Forward. Shoots right. #19.*

Born 1978-7-12, Hamilton, ON, CAN. Grew up in Jarvis, ON, CAN. 5'4". Debut at age 17 in 1995-96.

Year - League - Team		GP	G	A	PTS	PM	Year - Playoff	GP	G	A	PTS	PM
1995-96	COWHL Mississauga Chiefs	2	4	1	5	0						
1996-97	COWHL Mississauga Chiefs	33	11	16	27	8						
2000-01	NWHL Toronto Sting	29	11	12	23	18						
2001-02	NWHL Brampton Thunder	28	11	4	15	10						
2002	Nationals Brampton Thunder	7	0	1	1	2						
2002-03	NWHL Brampton Thunder						2003 NWHL-P					
2003	Nationals Brampton Thunder	5	3	2	5	0						
2003-04	NWHL Brampton Thunder	36	17	19	36	14						
2004-05	NWHL Brampton Thunder	34	10	25	35	12						
2005-06	NWHL Brampton Thunder	33	5	19	24	20	2006 NWHL-P	5	1	7	8	2
2006-07	NWHL Brampton Thunder	24	9	10	19	12	2007 NWHL-P	6	2	2	4	6
Totals from all Competitions		**242**	**84**	**118**	**202**	**104**						

DOSTALER, LAURA   *Forward/Defence. Shoots right. #2.*

Born 1991-9-17. Grew up in Beaumont, AB, CAN. 5'7". Debut at age 20 on 2011-10-28.

Year - League - Team		GP	G	A	PTS	PM	Year - Playoff	GP	G	A	PTS	PM
2009-10	WWHL Edmonton Chimos	13	3	3	6	8						
2010-11	WWHL Edmonton Chimos	17	4	4	8	0						
2011-12	CWHL Alberta	15	2	1	3	2						
2012-13	CWHL Alberta	23	2	0	2	4						
2013-14	CWHL Calgary Inferno	24	1	3	4	14	2014 C-Cup	3	0	0	0	0
2014-15	CWHL Calgary Inferno	6	0	0	0	0						
2015-16	CWHL Calgary Inferno	2	1	0	1	0						
2016-17	CWHL Calgary Inferno	16	0	0	0	2	2017 C-Cup	4	0	0	0	0
2017-18	CWHL Calgary Inferno	23	4	3	7	8						
2018-19	CWHL Calgary Inferno	16	0	1	1	2						
CWHL Regular Season		125	10	8	18	32	Clarkson Cup	7	0	0	0	0
Totals from all Competitions		**162**	**17**	**15**	**32**	**40**						

DOUCET, CELESTE *F. 2005 Nationals Team New Brunswick (6 gp, 1 goal); 2006 Team NB (7 gp, 1 goal, 2 assists).*
DOUCET, MARGOT *Forward. 2004 Nationals Newfoundland (5 gp, 1 assist); 2005 Newfoundland (5 gp, 1 assist).*
DOUCET, NOLA   *1996-97 COWHL Newtonbrook Panthers (2 games)..*
DOUGHERTY, BRITTANY *Chesterfield, MI, USA. 2015-16 NWHL Connecticut (17 gp, 1 goal, 4 assists; I-Cup 3 gp).*
DOUGLAS, COURTNEY   *Defence. 1999 Nationals Team New Brunswick (6 games).*
DOULL, TANIA   *1993-94 COWHL Hamilton Golden Hawks #32 (4 games, 1 goal).*
DOVASTON, STEPHANIE   *Forward. 2009-10 CWHL Mississauga Chiefts #9 (1 game, 1 goal).*
DOW, REBECCA   *Ottawa, ON, CAN. Defence. 2008-09 CWHL Ottawa Senators #24 (4 games, 1 goal, 1 assist).*

DOWDALL, KATIE   *Forward. Shoots left. #21.*

Born 1985-7-9. Debut at age 23 on 2008-10-4.

Year - League - Team		GP	G	A	PTS	PM	Year - Playoff	GP	G	A	PTS	PM
2008-09	CWHL Brampton Thunder	25	2	8	10	2	2009 CWHL-P	2				
							2009 C-Cup	2	0	0	0	0
2009-10	CWHL Brampton Thunder						2010 C-Cup	1	0		0	
CWHL Regular Season		25	2	8	10	2	Clarkson Cup	4	0	0	0	0
Totals from all Competitions		**31**	**2**	**8**	**10**	**2**						

DOYLE, JENNIFER   *1998-99 NWHL Mistral de Laval #81 (1 game).*
DOYLE, JULIE   *Defence. 2001 Nationals Team New Brunswick.*
DOYLE, KATHLEEN   *Defence. 1996 Nationals PEI Esso Tigers (4 games).*
DOYLE, LISA   *Forward. 1995 Nationals PEI Esso Tigers.*

DOYLE, RICKIE-LEE
Forward. Shoots right. #7 #22.

Born 1981-2-5, Calgary, AB, CAN. 5'4".

Year - League - Team			GP	G	A	PTS	PM	Year - Playoff		GP	G	A	PTS	PM
2004-05	NWHL	Ottawa Raiders	36	11	14	25	78							
2005-06	NWHL	Ottawa Raiders	33	12	11	23	34	2006	NWHL-P	2	0	0	0	0
2006-07	NWHL	Ottawa Raiders	34	6	12	18	82	2007	NWHL-P	2	0	1	1	4
Totals from all Competitions			**107**	**29**	**38**	**67**	**198**							

DOYLE, SHANNON
Defence. Shoots right. #6.

Born 1993-03-14. Grew up in Peterborough, NH, USA. 5'6". Debut at age 22 on 2015-10-11.

Year - League - Team			GP	G	A	PTS	PM	Year - Playoff		GP	G	A	PTS	PM
2015-16	NWHL/	Connecticut Whale	18	2	3	5	12	2016 I-Cup		3	0	1	1	2
2016-17	NWHL/	Connecticut Whale	15	0	7	7	22							
2017-18	NWHL/	Connecticut Whale	15	0	5	5	20	2018 I-Cup		1	0	0	0	4
2018-19	NWHL/	Connecticut Whale	13	3	5	8	10	2019 I-Cup		1	0	1	1	2
NWHL Regular Season			61	5	20	25	64	Isobel Cup		5	0	2	2	8
Totals from all Competitions			**66**	**5**	**22**	**27**	**72**							

DOYON, SOPHIE
Defence. 2003-04 NWHL Québec #89 (1 game); 2004 Nationals 2004-05 #25 (1 game).

DOYON, SOPHIE
Defence / Forward.

Year - League - Team			GP	G	A	PTS	PM	Year - Playoff	GP	G	A	PTS	PM
2003-04	NWHL	Avalanche du Québec	1	0	0	0	0						
2004	Nationals	Équipe Québec	5	0	0	0	2						
2004-05	NWHL	Avalanche du Québec	1	0	0	0	0						

DRAZAN, RACHAEL
Orono, MN. D. 2009-10 WWHL Minnesota (6 gp, 3 goals, 5 a.); 2010-11 (2 gp; C-Cup 2 gp).

DREWS, KAITLIN
Forward. 2010-11 WWHL Manitoba Maple Leafs (2 games).

DROLET, NANCY
Forward. Shoots left. #18.

IIHF champion. Born 1973-8-2, Drummondville, QC, CAN. 5'6".

Year - League - Team			GP	G	A	PTS	PM	Year - Playoff		
1995	Nationals	Équipe Québec								
1996	Nationals	Équipe Québec	6	10	7	17	2			
1997	Nationals	Équipe Québec								
1998	Nationals	Équipe Québec	6	6	6	12	2			
1998-99	NWHL	Montréal Jofa-Titan	19	15	6	21	29			
1999	Nationals	Équipe Québec	5	5	5	10				
1999-00	NWHL	Sainte-Julie	29	26	17	43	16	2000 NWHL-P		
2000	Nationals	Équipe Québec	6	5	8	13				
2000-01	NWHL	Sainte-Julie	2	0	4	4	0			
2001	Nationals	Vancouver Griffins								
2002-03	NWHL	Vancouver Griffins	23	19	10	29	14			
2003	Nationals	Vancouver Griffins	7	8	3	11	8			
2003-04	NWHL	Avalanche du Québec	17	7	7	14	12			
Totals from all Competitions			**120**	**101**	**73**	**174**	**83**			

DROOG, KAREN
Right wing. Shoots right. #26 #14 #15.

Abby Hoffman Cup winner with Brampton on 2006-03-12.

Born 1982-3-25, Listowel, ON, CAN. Grew up in Listowel, ON, CAN. 5'11".

Year - League - Team			GP	G	A	PTS	PM	Year - Playoff		GP	G	A	PTS	PM
1998-99	NWHL	Brampton Thunder	8	2	0	2	0							
2004-05	NWHL	Brampton Thunder	34	8	12	20	33							
2005	Nationals	Brampton Thunder	6	1	4	5	0							
2005-06	NWHL	Brampton Thunder	34	22	16	38	40	2006	NWHL-P	5	1	0	1	4
2006	Nationals	Brampton Thunder	6	2	2	4	4							
2006-07	NWHL	Brampton Thunder	25	7	12	19	54							
Totals from all Competitions			**118**	**43**	**46**	**89**	**135**							

DROVER, ASHLEE
Defence. Shoots left. #11.

Born 1984-09-17, Bay Roberts, NL, CAN. Grew up in Harbour Grace, NL, CAN. 5'8".

Year - League - Team			GP	G	A	PTS	PM	Year - Playoff		GP	G	A	PTS	PM
2000	Nationals	Newfoundland Labrador	5	0	0	0								
2001	Nationals	Newfoundland Labrador												
2002	Nationals	Newfoundland Labrador	5	0	0	0	6							
2006-07	NWHL	Avalanche du Québec	31	2	15	17	53	2007	NWHL-P					

DRUMMOND, KATHY
Defence. 1995 Nationals PEI Esso Tigers; 1996 Nationals PEI Esso Tigers (4 games).

DUBORD, ISABELLE
Sainte-Julie, QC, CAN. Forward. 2005-06 NWHL Québec #2 (17 games, 2 goals).

DUFOUR, SANDRA
Forward. 1998-99 NWHL Montréal (31 gp, 7 goals, 7 a.); 1999-00 Sainte-Julie (16 gp, 2 a.).

DUFRESNE, KARINE
1999-00 NWHL Laval #71 (4 games); 2000-01 #11 (29 gp, 1 goal, 1 assist).

DUGGAN, CARSON
Forward. #26.

Born 1986-12-26, Ma-Me-O Beach, AB, CAN.

Year - League - Team			GP	G	A	PTS	PM	Year - Playoff		GP	G	A	PTS	PM
2003-04	NWHL	Edmonton Chimos	9	1	1	2	0	2004	NWHL-P	2	0	0	0	0

Year - League - Team		GP	G	A	PTS	PM	Year - Playoff	GP	G	A	PTS	PM
2004	Nationals Edmonton Chimos	7	3	1	4	0						
2004-05	WWHL Edmonton Chimos	20	9	9	18	4	2005 WWHL-P	3	0	1	1	0
Totals from all Competitions		**41**	**13**	**12**	**25**	**4**						

DUGGAN, ERIN
Defence. Shoots right. #26 #9 #21.

Born 1983-2-21, Beaumont, AB, CAN. 5'6".

Year - League - Team		GP	G	A	PTS	PM	Year - Playoff	GP	G	A	PTS	PM
2005-06	WWHL Edmonton Chimos	24	2	9	11	16	2006 WWHL-P	2	0	0	0	0
2007-08	WWHL Edmonton Chimos	24	8	14	22	20						
2008-09	WWHL Edmonton Chimos	23	5	6	11	14	2009 WWHL-P	1	0	0	0	0
2009-10	WWHL Edmonton Chimos	17	1	6	7	20						
2010-11	WWHL Edmonton Chimos	15	6	6	12	6						
2012-13	CWHL Alberta	22	1	2	3	2						
2013-14	CWHL Calgary Inferno	23	1	4	5	12	2014 C-Cup	3	0	1	1	0
CWHL Regular Season		45	2	6	8	14	Clarkson Cup	3	0	1	1	0
Totals from all Competitions		**154**	**24**	**48**	**72**	**90**						

DUGGAN, MEGHAN
Forward. Shoots right. #17.

Olympic champion, IIHF champion. Clarkson Cup winner with Boston on 2013-03-23 and 2015-03-07.
Born 1987-9-3. Grew up in Danvers, MA, USA. 5'9". Debut at age 24 on 2012-1-7.

Year - League - Team		GP	G	A	PTS	PM	Year - Playoff	GP	G	A	PTS	PM
2011-12	CWHL Boston Blades	4	0	0	0	0						
2012-13	CWHL Boston Blades	14	5	8	13	24	2013 C-Cup	4	0	2	2	4
2013-14	CWHL Boston Blades	1	0	0	0	0						
2014-15	CWHL Boston Blades	7	1	5	6	12						
2015-16	NWHL/ Buffalo Beauts	13	6	10	16	14	2016 I-Cup	2	0	1	1	4
2016-17	NWHL/ Boston Pride	17	13	7	20	24	2017 I-Cup	2	0	1	1	0
CWHL Regular Season		26	6	13	19	36	Clarkson Cup	4	0	2	2	4
NWHL Regular Season		30	19	17	36	38	Isobel Cup	4	0	2	2	4
Totals from all Competitions		**64**	**25**	**34**	**59**	**82**						

CWHL Second All-Star Team in 2012-13

DUGUAY, ASHLEY
Forward. Shoots left.

Born 1986-08-19. Grew up in Quispamsis, NB, CAN. 5'3".

Year - League - Team		GP	G	A	PTS	PM
2004	Nationals Team New Brunswick	5	1	0	1	0
2005	Nationals Team New Brunswick	6	2	2	4	6
2006	Nationals Team New Brunswick	7	0	0	0	2
2007	Nationals Team New Brunswick	6	0	1	1	10
2008	Nationals Team New Brunswick	5	0	0	0	2

DUGUAY, LOUIS
1998-99 NWHL Mistral de Laval #80 (1 game).

DUHAMEL, MANDI
Forward. Shoots left. #4 #41.

Born 1984-5-15, Lively, ON, CAN. 5'7". Debut at age 28 on 2012-1-7.

Year - League - Team		GP	G	A	PTS	PM	Year - Playoff	GP	G	A	PTS	PM
2008-09	CWHL Ottawa Senators	25	2	5	7	8	2009 CWHL-P	2				
2009-10	CWHL Ottawa Senators	17	3	10	13	12						
CWHL Regular Season		42	5	15	20	20						

Has served as an assistant coach with CWHL Calgary.

DUMAIS, CAMILLE
Forward. Shoots left. #96 #7.

Born 1990-8-15. Grew up in Beaconsfield, QC, CAN. Debut at age 17 on 2007-10-27.

Year - League - Team		GP	G	A	PTS	PM	Year - Playoff	GP	G	A	PTS	PM
2007-08	CWHL Stars de Montréal	2	0	1	1	0						
2013-14	CWHL Stars de Montréal	19	0	1	1	10	2014 C-Cup	3	0	0	0	0
CWHL Regular Season		21	0	2	2	10	Clarkson Cup	3	0	0	0	0
Totals from all Competitions		**24**	**0**	**2**	**2**	**10**						

DUMAIS, GENEVIÈVE
Defence. #2.

Year - League - Team		GP	G	A	PTS	PM
1998-99	NWHL Bonaventure	31	1	5	6	20
1999-00	NWHL Wingstar de Montréal	22	1	4	5	14
Totals from all Competitions		**53**	**2**	**9**	**11**	**34**

DUNA, KAYLA
Forward. 2008 Nationals Manitoba (5 games, 1 assist).

DUNCAN, SARAH
Dedham. Defence. 2015-16 CWHL Boston Blades #16 (24 games).

DUNLAP, MEGHAN
2001-02 NWHL Ottawa Raiders #5 (3 games, 1 assist).

DUNN, ASHLEY
F. 2004 Nationals Nova Scotia (5 gp, 1 assist); 2004-05 NWHL Durham Lightning #19 (1 gp).

DUNN, CUMLEY
Defence.

Abby Hoffman Cup winner with Calgary on 1998-03-22. Born 1972-11-23.

Year - League - Team		GP	G	A	PTS	PM
1996	Nationals Edmonton Chimos	7	1	0	1	0
1998	Nationals Calgary Oval X-Treme	7	0	2	2	8
1999	Nationals Calgary Oval X-Treme	6	0	3	3	

DUNN, MICHELLE
1995-96 COWHL Mississauga Chiefs #73 (1 game).

DUNN, TARA
Right wing. Shoots right. #11 #55.

Born 1979-5-7. Grew up in New Glasgow, NS, CAN. 5'5".

Year - League - Team			GP	G	A	PTS	PM
1996	Nationals	Pictou County Sobey's	4	1	0	1	0
2004	Nationals	Nova Scotia	5	4	4	8	0
2004-05	NWHL	Durham Lightning	36	10	17	27	2
2005	Nationals	Nova Scotia Selects	5	5	4	9	2
2005-06	NWHL	Toronto Aeros	11	2	3	5	0
2006	Nationals	Nova Scotia Selects	5	1	2	3	0
2007	Nationals	Nova Scotia Selects	7	1	3	4	0
2008	Nationals	Nova Scotia Selects	5	1	1	2	0
Totals from all Competitions			**78**	**25**	**34**	**59**	**4**

DUNN-LUOMA, TRICIA
Forward. Shoots left. #25 #21 #22.

Olympic champion. Born 1974-4-25, Derry, NH, USA. 5'8".

Year - League - Team			GP	G	A	PTS	PM	Year - Playoff		GP	G	A	PTS	PM
2004-05	WWHL	Minnesota Whitecaps						2005	WWHL-P	0	0	0	0	0
2005-06	WWHL	Minnesota Whitecaps	24	22	13	35	28	2006	WWHL-P	3	1	5	6	6
2006-07	WWHL	Minnesota Whitecaps	12	3	13	16	2	2007	WWHL-P	0	0	0	0	0
2008-09	WWHL	Minnesota Whitecaps	1	0	0	0	0							
2009-10	WWHL	Minnesota Whitecaps	3	0	2	2	4							
Totals from all Competitions			**43**	**26**	**33**	**59**	**40**							

DUNNE, CASSIE
Defence. Shoots right. #13.

Born 1994-10-12. Grew up in Philadelphia, PA, USA. 5'3". Debut at age 23 on 2017-10-28.

Year - League - Team			GP	G	A	PTS	PM
2017-18	NWHL/	Connecticut Whale	5	0	0	0	0

DUNPHY, ASHLEY
Forward. 2005 Nationals Newfoundland (5 games), 2006 Nationals Newfoundland (5 games).

DUPUIS, CASSANDRA
Forward. Shoots right. #17 #42.

Born 1990-1-5. Debut at age 18 on 2007-12-30.

Year - League - Team			GP	G	A	PTS	PM	Year - Playoff		GP	G	A	PTS	PM
2007-08	CWHL	Phénix du Québec	7	1	2	3	8							
2013-14	CWHL	Stars de Montréal	23	5	10	15	8	2014	C-Cup	3	0	0	0	0
2014-15	CWHL	Stars de Montréal	22	1	4	5	16	2015	C-Cup	3	0	0	0	6
CWHL Regular Season			52	7	16	23	32	Clarkson Cup		6	0	0	0	6
Totals from all Competitions			**58**	**7**	**16**	**23**	**38**							

Finished 18th in the Angela James Bowl scoring race in 2013-14

DUPUIS, CHRISTINE
Defence. #2.

Year - League - Team			GP	G	A	PTS	PM	Year - Playoff	
1998-99	NWHL	Montréal Jofa-Titan	29	0	5	5	20		
1999-00	NWHL	Sainte-Julie	34	2	7	9	16	2000	NWHL-P
2000-01	NWHL	Sainte-Julie	37	3	9	12	22		
2001-02	NWHL	Cheyenne	27	2	3	5	12		
Totals from all Competitions			**127**	**7**	**24**	**31**	**70**		

DUPUIS, GENEVIÈVE
Forward. Shoots left. #11.

Born 1981-12-23. Grew up in St-Laurent, QC, CAN. 5'4".

Year - League - Team			GP	G	A	PTS	PM	Year - Playoff		GP	G	A	PTS	PM
2000-01	NWHL	Wingstar de Montréal	1	0	0	0	0							
2006-07	NWHL	Axion de Montréal	18	2	5	7	38	2007	NWHL-P					
2007-08	CWHL	Phénix du Québec	21	2	6	8	36							
Totals from all Competitions			**40**	**4**	**11**	**15**	**74**							

DUPUIS, KRISTA
Defence. 2000 Nationals Team New Brunswick (6 games).

DUPUIS, LORI
Forward. Shoots left. #12.

Olympic champion, IIHF champion. Abby Hoffman Cup winner with Brampton on 2006-03-12. CWHL winner, WWHL winner. Born 1972-11-14, Cornwall, ON, CAN. Grew up in Cornwall, ON, CAN. 5'7".

Year - League - Team			GP	G	A	PTS	PM	Year - Playoff		GP	G	A	PTS	PM
1995-96	COWHL	Toronto Red Wings	14	5	3	8	15							
1996-97	COWHL	Newtonbrook Panthers	18	13	12	25	18							
1998-99	NWHL	Brampton Thunder	22	15	20	35	18							
1999-00	NWHL	Brampton Thunder	31	25	15	40	28							
2000-01	NWHL	Brampton Thunder	28	23	17	40	50							
2002	Nationals	Brampton Thunder	7	7	3	10	10							
2002-03	NWHL	Brampton Thunder						2003	NWHL-P					
2003	Nationals	Brampton Thunder	5	5	8	13	2							
2003-04	NWHL	Brampton Thunder	35	20	24	44	52	2004	NWHL-P	5	2	6	8	2
2004-05	NWHL	Brampton Thunder	9	6	9	15	14							
2004-05	WWHL	Calgary Oval X-Treme	8	8	5	13	12	2005	WWHL-P	3	1	3	4	0
2005-06	NWHL	Brampton Thunder	34	17	24	41	56	2006	NWHL-P	3	0	0	0	2
2006	Nationals	Brampton Thunder	6	1	5	6	10							

Year	League	Team	GP	G	A	PTS	PM
2006-07	NWHL	Brampton Thunder	33	12	24	36	70
2007-08	CWHL	Brampton Can.-Thunder	25	17	12	29	18
2008	Nationals	Brampton Can.-Thunder	3	1	1	2	6
2008-09	CWHL	Brampton Thunder	28	13	24	37	44
2009-10	CWHL	Brampton Thunder	27	14	24	38	44
2010-11	CWHL	Brampton Thunder	23	9	13	22	22
2011-12	CWHL	Brampton Thunder	26	7	6	13	36
2012-13	CWHL	Brampton Thunder	24	3	7	10	32
CWHL Regular Season			153	63	86	149	196
Totals from all Competitions			**443**	**227**	**279**	**506**	**611**

Year - Playoff	GP	G	A	PTS	PM
2007 NWHL-P	5	0	5	5	6
2008 CWHL-P	3	2	4	6	6
2009 CWHL-P	2				
2009 C-Cup	2	0	0	0	4
2010 C-Cup	2	0	0	0	2
2011 CWHL-P	2				
2011			4		
2011	3	0	3	3	16
2012 C-Cup	4	1	2	3	8
2013 C-Cup	3	0	0	0	4
Clarkson Cup	14	1	5	6	34

CWHL Second All-Star Team in 2009-10... CWHL Championship Game MVP in 2008... finished 4th in the Angela James Bowl scoring race in 2009-10... scored 100th CWHL point on 2010-03-10... has served as general manager with CWHL Brampton

DUPUIS, MONICA
Defence. Shoots left. #19.

Abby Hoffman Cup winner with Calgary on 2007-03-10. WWHL winner. Born 1981-5-2, Memramcook, NB, CAN. 5'10".

Year	League	Team	GP	G	A	PTS	PM
2003-04	NWHL	Calgary Oval X-Treme	12	0	2	2	6
2004-05	WWHL	Calgary Oval X-Treme	21	6	7	13	4
2005-06	WWHL	Calgary Oval X-Treme	21	5	4	9	6
2006-07	WWHL	Calgary Oval X-Treme	14	5	4	9	16
2007	Nationals	Calgary Oval X-Treme	3	1	0	1	2
2007-08	CWHL	Ottawa Capital Canucks	21	9	8	17	18
2008-09	CWHL	Ottawa Senators	25	9	7	16	40
2009-10	CWHL	Ottawa Senators	3	0	1	1	4
CWHL Regular Season			49	18	16	34	62
Totals from all Competitions			**132**	**38**	**37**	**75**	**108**

Year - Playoff	GP	G	A	PTS	PM
2004 NWHL-P	2	0	1	1	2
2005 WWHL-P	3	0	1	1	2
2006 WWHL-P	2	0	2	2	4
2007 WWHL-P	2	2	0	2	4
2008 CWHL-P	1	1	0	1	0
2009 CWHL-P	2				

DUPUIS, ROXANNE
Defence. Shoots left. #73 #21 #5.

NWHL winner. Born 1980-1-11. Grew up in Montréal, QC, CAN. 5'4". Debut at age 25 on 2005-09-17.

Year	League	Team	GP	G	A	PTS	PM
2005-06	NWHL	Axion de Montréal	34	0	3	3	26
2006	Nationals	Axion de Montréal	6	0	0	0	16
2006-07	NWHL	Axion de Montréal	18	2	5	7	20
2008-09	CWHL	Stars de Montréal	4	0	0	0	0
Totals from all Competitions			**65**	**2**	**8**	**10**	**66**

Year - Playoff	GP	G	A	PTS	PM
2006 NWHL-P	3	0	0	0	4
2007 NWHL-P					

DURHAM, CHRISTINE
Defence. 2005 Nationals Manitoba (5 games, 1 assist).

DURUPT, LISA
Forward. 2000 Nationals U. Manitoba (5 games); 2001 Nationals U. Manitoba.

DUVAL, JANIQUE
Val d'Or, QC, CAN. Defence. 2007-08 CWHL Montréal #8 (1 game).

DUVAL, LIZ
Defence. #21 #23 #25 #27 #32.

Year	League	Team	GP	G	A	PTS	PM
1992-93	COWHL	Guelph Eagles	27	18	4	22	18
1993-94	COWHL	Mississauga Chiefs	28	11	7	18	16
1995	Nationals	Mississauga Chiefs					
1995-96	COWHL	Mississauga Chiefs	30	20	11	31	26
1996-97	COWHL	Mississauga Chiefs	36	29	25	54	44
1998-99	NWHL	Mississauga Chiefs	39	12	8	20	46
1999-00	NWHL	Mississauga Chiefs	39	4	13	17	60
2000-01	NWHL	Mississauga IceBears	37	12	7	19	66
2001-02	NWHL	Mississauga IceBears	29	7	6	13	18
Totals from all Competitions			**265**	**113**	**81**	**194**	**294**

DZIENGELEWSKI, RAYLEN
Southwick, MA. D. 2011-12 CWHL Boston (23 games, 3 assists; C-Cup 3 games).

ECKEBRECHT, NIKKI
Forward. #21.

Born 1983-3-27. Grew up in Hamilton, ON, CAN. 5'6".

Year	League	Team	GP	G	A	PTS	PM
2000-01	NWHL	North York Aeros	7	1	2	3	2
2007-08	CWHL	Burlington Barracudas	10	0	0	0	20
2008-09	CWHL	Burlington Barracudas	2				
2009-10	CWHL	Burlington Barracudas	6	0	2	2	0

ECKMEIER, MONICA
Forward. 2000 Nationals Britannia Blues (5 games, 1 goal).

EDGAR, ALISON
Defence. Shoots left. #10.

Abby Hoffman Cup winner with Aeros on 2005-03-13. Born 1981-5-28. Grew up in Brigden, ON, CAN. 5'6".

Year	League	Team	GP	G	A	PTS	PM
2004-05	NWHL	Toronto Aeros	26	1	6	7	10
2005	Nationals	Toronto Aeros	7	0	3	3	0
2005-06	NWHL	Toronto Aeros	31	6	13	19	53

Year - League - Team	GP	G	A	PTS	PM	Year - Playoff	GP	G	A	PTS	PM
2006-07 NWHL Mississauga Aeros	25	1	4	5	12	2007 NWHL-P	4	1	1	2	0
2007 Nationals Mississauga Aeros	4	0	2	2	0						
2007-08 CWHL Mississauga Chiefs	2	0	0	0	0						
Totals from all Competitions	**88**	**9**	**24**	**33**	**75**						

EDGAR, MICHELLE *Niagara Falls, ON. 2007-08 CWHL Burlington #88 (1 game).*

EDINGTON-HRYB, MERRYL *Forward. 2006-07 WWHL British Columbia #93 (24 gp, 6 goals, 7 assists).*

EDISON, RENEE *Forward. 2006 Nationals Newfoundland (5 gp); 2008 Nationals Team NB (5 gp, 2 goals).*

EDMONDSON, KATIE *Defence. 2005-06 WWHL British Columbia #7 (11 games).*

EDNEY, SARAH *Defence. Shoots left. #3.*
Born 1993-09-02, Mississauga, ON, CAN. 5'6". Debut at age 22 on 2015-10-17.

Year - League - Team	GP	G	A	PTS	PM	Year - Playoff	GP	G	A	PTS	PM
2015-16 CWHL Brampton Thunder	24	5	5	10	8	2016 C-Cup	2	1	1	2	0
2016-17 CWHL Brampton Thunder	14	4	6	10	6						
2017-18 NWHL/ Buffalo Beauts	14	3	3	6	6	2018 I-Cup	2	1	1	2	0
2018-19 NWHL/ Buffalo Beauts	10	0	1	1	2						
Totals from all Competitions	**66**	**14**	**17**	**31**	**22**						

CWHL All-Rookie Team in 2015-16

EGLI, AMY *Forward. 2003-04 NWHL Durham Lightning #88 (5 games).*

EINARSON, BROOKE *Forward. 2003 Nationals University of Winnipeg (4 games, 1 assist).*

EISENSCHMID, TANJA *Defence. Shoots right. #23.*
Born 1993-04-20. Grew up in Marktoberdorf, GER. 5'7". Debut at age 25 on 2018-10-20.

Year - League - Team	GP	G	A	PTS	PM
2018-19 NWHL/ Minnesota Whitecaps	5	0	0	0	0

ELIA, MADDIE *Forward. Shoots right. #16.*
Born 1995-5-31. Grew up in Lewiston, NY, USA. 5'10". Debut at age 22 on 2017-10-28.

Year - League - Team	GP	G	A	PTS	PM	Year - Playoff	GP	G	A	PTS	PM
2017-18 NWHL/ Buffalo Beauts	14	5	9	14	18	2018 I-Cup	2	0	1	1	0
2018-19 NWHL/ Buffalo Beauts	16	12	7	19	32	2019 I-Cup	2	1	0	1	0

NWHL Most Valuable Player in 2018-19.

ELLA, THERESA *Defence. Shoots left. #13 #7.*
Born 1983-01-15. Grew up in Schomberg, ON, CAN.

Year - League - Team	GP	G	A	PTS	PM
2000-01 NWHL Durham Lightning	35	2	9	11	32
2001-02 NWHL Brampton Thunder	21	2	4	6	22
2002 Nationals Brampton Thunder	7	0	0	0	6

ELLIOTT, NICOLE *2000-01 NWHL Toronto Sting (5 games).*

ELLIS, MIKAELA *Forward. 2007 Nationals Prince Edward Island (5 gp, 4 pts); 2008 Nationals PEI (5 gp, 1 assist).*

ELLIS, MISSY *1995-96 COWHL Peterborough Skyway #21 (25 games, 3 goals, 6 assists).*

ELLIS, SANDRA *Forward. 1995 Nationals PEI Esso Tigers.*

ÉMARD, KARELL *Forward. Shoots left. #76.*
Clarkson Cup winner with Montréal on 2017-03-05
Born 1988-4-18, Richelieu, QC, CAN. 5'6". Debut at age 17 on 2005-11-26.

Year - League - Team	GP	G	A	PTS	PM	Year - Playoff	GP	G	A	PTS	PM
2005-06 NWHL Axion de Montréal	3	0	0	0	2						
2006-07 NWHL Avalanche du Québec	4	3	1	4	10	2007 NWHL-P					
2015-16 CWHL Canadiennes de Montréal	24	7	6	13	42	2016 C-Cup	3	0	1	1	2
2016-17 CWHL Canadiennes de Montréal	24	7	10	17	22	2017 C-Cup	3	2	1	3	2
2017-18 CWHL Canadiennes de Montréal	27	7	14	21	48	2018 C-Cup	1	0	0	0	2
2018-19 CWHL Canadiennes de Montréal	28	6	8	14	28	2019 C-Cup	3	1	0	1	4
CWHL Regular Season	103	27	38	65	140	Clarkson Cup	10	3	2	5	10
Totals from all Competitions	**120**	**33**	**41**	**74**	**162**						

Finished 16th in the Angela James Bowl scoring race in 2016-17

EMSLIE, TERYN *Forward. 2002 Nationals Richmond Steelers (5 games, 1 assist).*

ENDICOTT, MADDIE *Defence. 2005-06 NWHL Toronto Aeros #15 (6 games, 1 assist).*

ENDRIZZI, JAMIE *2007-08 CWHL Vaugham #25 (18 games; 2 playoff games).*

ENGSTROM, MOLLY *Defence. Shoots right. #9.*
IIHF champion, CWHL winner.
Born 1983-3-1, Siren, WI, USA. Grew up in Grantsburg, WI, USA. 5'9". Debut at age 25 on 2007-9-16.

Year - League - Team	GP	G	A	PTS	PM	Year - Playoff	GP	G	A	PTS	PM
2007-08 CWHL Brampton Can.-Thunder	28	9	11	20	32	2008 CWHL-P	3	1	1	2	2
2008 Nationals Brampton Can.-Thunder	3	1	2	3	2						
2008-09 WWHL Minnesota Whitecaps	13	3	9	12	8	2009 WWHL-P	2	0	1	1	0
						2009 C-Cup	3	0	2	2	0
2009-10 WWHL Brampton Thunder	0	0	0	0	0	2010 C-Cup	2	0		0	2

Year - League - Team			GP	G	A	PTS	PM	Year - Playoff	GP	G	A	PTS	PM
2010-11	CWHL	Brampton Thunder	24	2	18	20	14	2011 CWHL-P	2		1	1	2
								2011 C-Cup	3	0	1	1	6
2011-12	CWHL	Brampton Thunder	27	4	23	27	22	2012 C-Cup	4	1	1	2	4
2012-13	CWHL	Boston Blades	8	1	2	3	6						
2015-16	NWHL/	Connecticut Whale	15	3	2	5	21	2016 I-Cup	3	0	0	0	2
2016-17	NWHL/	Connecticut Whale	10	1	2	3	4						
CWHL Regular Season			87	16	54	70	74	Clarkson Cup	12	1	4	5	12
NWHL Regular Season			25	4	4	8	25	Isobel Cup	3	0	0	0	2
Totals from all Competitions			150	26	76	102	129						

CWHL Central All-Star Team in 2007-08; CWHL First All-Star Team in 2011-12; CWHL Second All-Star Team in 2010-11... CWHL All-Rookie Team in 2007-08... finished 15th in the Angela James Bowl scoring race in 2011-12... selected First Decade CWHL Team in 2017

ESPOSITO, BRITTANY
Forward. Shoots right. #7.

Born 1991-04-15. Grew up in Edmonton, AB, CAN. Debut at age 23 on 2014-10-18.

Year - League - Team			GP	G	A	PTS	PM	Year - Playoff	GP	G	A	PTS	PM
2014-15	CWHL	Calgary Inferno	24	10	15	25	8	2015 C-Cup	2	0	0	0	0
2015-16	CWHL	Calgary Inferno	24	6	14	20	4	2016 C-Cup	3	0	0	0	2
2016-17	CWHL	Calgary Inferno	20	4	9	13	6	2017 C-Cup	4	0	0	0	2
2017-18	CWHL	Calgary Inferno	25	16	9	25	6						
CWHL Regular Season			93	36	47	83	24	Clarkson Cup	9	0	0	0	4
Totals from all Competitions			102	36	47	83	28						

Finished 4th in the Angela James Bowl scoring race in 2014-15

ETELE, CHRISTINE
Centre. 1992-93 COWHL Scarborough (26 gp, 5 goals, 4 a.); 1993-94 (25 gp, 3 goals, 11 a.).

ÉTHIER, MARIE-FRANCE
Forward. #6 #26.

Year - League - Team			GP	G	A	PTS	PM
1998-99	NWHL	Ottawa Raiders	34	5	9	14	2
1999-00	NWHL	Ottawa Raiders	29	4	7	11	2
2000-01	NWHL	Ottawa Raiders	37	4	2	6	6
2001-02	NWHL	Ottawa Raiders	30	1	0	1	8
Totals from all Competitions			130	14	18	32	18

ÉTHIER, ROXANNE
Forward. #77 #11.

Year - League - Team			GP	G	A	PTS	PM
1995	Nationals	Équipe Québec					
1996	Nationals	Équipe Québec	6	1	5	6	0
1998	Nationals	Équipe Québec	6	1	0	1	0
1998-99	NWHL	Bonaventure	13	2	9	11	14
1999-00	NWHL	Wingstar de Montréal	29	8	15	23	18
2000-01	NWHL	Mistral de Laval	8	0	2	2	8
Totals from all Competitions			62	12	31	43	40

ÉTHIER, SANDRA
2002-03 NWHL Québec #59 (12 games).

EUSTACE, JOANNE
Forward. Shoots right. #9.

Born 1981-1-20, St. John's, NL, CAN. Grew up in Torbay, NL, CAN. 5'6".

Year - League - Team			GP	G	A	PTS	PM	Year - Playoff	GP	G	A	PTS	PM
2003-04	NWHL	Durham Lightning	34	7	7	14	26						
2004	Nationals	Newfoundland Labrador	4	3	6	9	8						
2004-05	NWHL	Durham Lightning	34	9	13	22	32						
2005	Nationals	Newfoundland Labrador	5	2	4	6	6						
2005-06	NWHL	Durham Lightning	35	16	18	34	46	2006 NWHL-P	2	0	0	0	6
2006-07	NWHL	Etobicoke Dolphins	25	5	8	13	40	2007 NWHL-P	3	0	0	0	6
2007	Nationals	Etobicoke Dolphins	7	3	2	5	4						
2007-08	CWHL	Vaughan Flames	24	2	4	6	32	2008 CWHL-P	2	0	0	0	2
2008-09	CWHL	Vaughan Flames	29	4	5	9	40	2009 CWHL-P	2	0	0	0	6
2009-10	CWHL	Vaughan Flames	14	3	0	3	12						
2011-12	CWHL	Burlington Barracudas	22	2	4	6	14						
CWHL Regular Season			89	11	13	24	98						
Totals from all Competitions			242	56	71	127	280						

Served as interim coach with CWHL Vaughan

EVANS, HEATHER
Forward. #11.

Year - League - Team			GP	G	A	PTS	PM
1995-96	COWHL	Peterborough Skyway	30	7	8	15	14
1996-97	COWHL	Peterborough Pirates	31	7	21	28	82
Totals from all Competitions			61	14	29	43	96

EVELYN, SAMANTHA
Defence. 2004-05 NWHL Ottawa Raiders #95 (2 games).

EVERS, TINA
2001-02 NWHL Durham Lightning #6 (17 games, 7 goals, 6 assists).

FAASSE, TONYA
2010-11 WWHL Strathmore Rockies #14 (11 games, 4 goals, 2 assists).

FABER, SAM
Forward. Shoots right. #28.

IIHF champion. Born 1987-5-8. Grew up in Chestwood, NY, USA. 5'4". Debut at age 23 on 2010-10-30.

Year	League	Team	GP	G	A	PTS	PM	Year	Playoff	GP	G	A	PTS	PM
2010-11	CWHL	Boston Blades	21	14	14	28	28	2011	CWHL-P	2	0	1	1	0
2015-16	NWHL/	Connecticut Whale	13	3	3	6	14	2016	I-Cup	3	1	1	2	2
2016-17	NWHL/	Connecticut Whale	18	3	5	8	10	2017	I-Cup	1	0	0	0	0
2017-18	NWHL/	Connecticut Whale	13	3	2	5	14	2018	I-Cup	1	0	0	0	2
	NWHL Regular Season		44	9	10	19	38		Isobel Cup	5	1	1	2	4
	Totals from all Competitions		**72**	**24**	**26**	**50**	**70**							

CWHL Second All-Star Team in 2010-11... CWHL All-Rookie Team in 2010-11... finished 8th in the Angela James Bowl scoring race in 2010-11

FABBRI, ROBERTA
Defence. 1998 Nationals Tazmanian Devils (5 games).

FAGNAN, GENEVIÈVE
Defence.

Year	League	Team	GP	G	A	PTS	PM
1999	Nationals	Équipe Québec	5	0	2	2	
2000	Nationals	Équipe Québec	6	0	1	1	
2000-01	NWHL	Wingstar de Montréal	37	2	16	18	4

FAHEY, REBECCA
Defence.

Born 1975-01-31. Grew up in Sackville, NB, CAN.

Year	League	Team	GP	G	A	PTS	PM
1995	Nationals	Maritime Sports Blades					
1996	Nationals	Maritime Sports Blades	6	1	0	1	0
1998	Nationals	Maritime Sports Blades	6	1	1	2	8
1999	Nationals	Calgary Oval X-Treme	6	3	1	4	

FAHLENBOCK, ANNIE
Forward. #14 #57 #22.

Year	League	Team	GP	G	A	PTS	PM
1995-96	COWHL	North York Aeros	1	1	0	1	0
1996-97	COWHL	North York Aeros	2	1	1	2	0
1997-98	COWHL	North York Aeros	1	0	0	0	0
1998-99	NWHL	Mississauga Chiefs	37	10	22	32	8
	Totals from all Competitions		**41**	**12**	**23**	**35**	**8**

FAIRFIELD, KATELYN
Rexdale, ON, CAN. RW. 2005-06 NWHL Oakville Ice #22 (1 game, 1 assist).

FALCONER, CHRIS
Left wing.

Year	League	Team	GP	G	A	PTS	PM
1992-93	COWHL	Scarborough Firefighters	20	4	4	8	6
1993-94	COWHL	Scarborough Firefighters	26	12	8	20	13
2000-01	NWHL	Toronto Sting	1	0	0	0	0
	Totals from all Competitions		**47**	**16**	**12**	**28**	**19**

FANG XIN
Centre. Shoots right. #23.

Born 1994-5-10. Grew up in Harbin, CHN. 5'5". Debut at age 23 on 2017-10-28.

Year	League	Team	GP	G	A	PTS	PM
2017-18	CWHL	Vanke Rays	28	5	3	8	16
2018-19	CWHL	KRS Vanke Rays	28	0	2	2	0

FARDELMANN, MEGHAN
Forward. 2015-16 NWHL New York (18 gp, 6 goals, 1 a.; Isobel Cup 2 gp).

FARREL, RACHEL
Forward. 2015-16 CWHL Boston #8 (19 games, 1 assist).

FASENKO, KATHY
Forward. 1995 Nationals Briannia Blues; 1996 Nationals Britannia (5 gp, 2 goals, 1 assist).

FAST, JILL
Forward. 2005 Nationals Manitoba (5 games); 2006 Nationals Manitoba (5 games, 1 goal).

FAST, RENATA
Defence. Shoots right. #21.

Born 1994-10-6. Grew up in Burlington, ON, CAN. 5'7". Debut at age 22 on 2016-10-15.

Year	League	Team	GP	G	A	PTS	PM	Year	Playoff	GP	G	A	PTS	PM
2016-17	CWHL	Toronto Furies	22	4	5	9	38	2017	C-Cup	3	0	1	1	4
2018-19	CWHL	Toronto Furies	26	2	6	8	48	2019	C-Cup	3	0	1	1	6

CWHL Second All-Star Team in 2016-17 and 2018-19... CWHL All-Rookie Team in 2016-17

FAULK, CHRIS
2004-05 NWHL Durham Lightning #17 (1 game).

FAURSCHOU, TRISH
Forward. 2005 Nationals Manitoba (5 games, 1 goal, 4 assists).

FAUTEUX, MICHELLE
Forward. #10 #18.

Year	League	Team	GP	G	A	PTS	PM
1998-99	NWHL	Bonaventure	30	6	6	12	12
1999-00	NWHL	Mistral de Laval	30	1	5	6	26
2000-01	NWHL	Mistral de Laval	14	2	1	3	24
	Totals from all Competitions		**74**	**9**	**12**	**21**	**62**

FAVORETTO, MIA
Oakville, ON, CAN. Defence. 2009-10 CWHL Mississauga #20 (2 games).

FAWCETT, DIANE
Forward.

Abby Hoffman Cup winner with Calgary on 1998-03-22.

Year - League - Team			GP	G	A	PTS	PM
1995	Nationals	Calgary Classics					
1998	Nationals	Calgary Oval X-Treme	4	0	1	1	0

FAYE, JODI — *Defence. 2004-05 WWHL British Columbia #18 (21 gp, 9 goals, 5 assists).*

FEDESKI, JULIA — *Defence. Shoots left. #4.*
Born 1996-11-08. Grew up in Haliburton, ON, CAN. 5'11". Debut at age 21 on 2018-10-14.

Year - League - Team			GP	G	A	PTS	PM	Year - Playoff	GP	G	A	PTS	PM
2018-19	CWHL	Toronto Furies	24	0	2	2	24	2019 C-Cup	3	0	0	0	2

FEDIUK, LISA — *Forward. 1996 Nationals Edmonton Chimos (7 games).*

FEDORUK, STEPH — *Forward. 2007-08 WWHL Edmonton Chimos #77 (21 games, 3 goals).*

FELDMAN, SARAH — *Forward. 2008-09 CWHL Burlington #12 (19 gp, 6 goals, 4 assists).*

FENERTY, SUZANNE — *Defence. 2004 Nationals Nova Scotia (5 games, 1 assist).*

FENTON, KATRINA — *Forward. 2004-05 NWHL Ottawa #94 (3 games, 2 assists).*

FERGUSON, BRAYDEN — *Forward. Shoots left. #24.*
Grew up in Toronto, ON, CAN. 5'7". Debut on 2010-10-23.

Year - League - Team			GP	G	A	PTS	PM
2010-11	CWHL	Burlington Barracudas	22	5	10	15	10
2011-12	CWHL	Burlington Barracudas	23	5	3	8	30
CWHL Regular Season			45	10	13	23	40

FERGUSON, LINDSAY — *Defence. 2004 Nationals Saskatchewan (6 games).*

FERGUSON, TARA — *Forward. 1998-99 NWHL Ottawa #11 (26 gp, 6 goals, 3 assists); 1999-00 #71 (2 gp, 1 assist).*

FERGUSON, TERRI — *Forward. 1996 Nationals Pictou County (4 games).*

FERRARI, GILLIAN — *Defence. Shoots right. #9 #18 #79.*
Olympic champion, IIHF champion. Abby Hoffman Cup winner with Aeros on 2000-03-12 and 2004-03-14. Abby Hoffman Cup winner with Calgary on 2007-03-10. NWHL Cup winner, WWHL winner. Born 1980-6-23, Thornhill, ON, CAN. 5'8".

Year - League - Team			GP	G	A	PTS	PM	Year - Playoff	GP	G	A	PTS	PM
1996-97	COWHL	North York Aeros	20	2	5	7	30						
1997-98	COWHL	North York Aeros	20	3	5	8	30						
1998	Nationals	North York Aeros	6	1	3	4	0						
1998-99	NWHL	North York Aeros	38	2	13	15	51						
1999	Nationals	North York Aeros	5		1	1							
1999-00	NWHL	North York Aeros	36	2	14	16	50	2000 NWIIL-P					
2000	Nationals	North York Aeros	6	1	2	3							
2000-01	NWHL	North York Aeros	28	5	14	19	46						
2001	Nationals	North York Aeros											
2001-02	NWHL	North York Aeros	23	7	10	17	25						
2002	Nationals	North York Aeros	7	0	3	3	4						
2002-03	NWHL	North York Aeros	22	2	12	14	62	2003 NWHL-P	1	0	0	0	2
2003-04	NWHL	Toronto Aeros	33	7	9	16	18	2004 NWHL-P	2	0	0	0	0
2004	Nationals	Toronto Aeros	6	0	5	5	2						
2004-05	NWHL	Brampton Thunder	34	3	22	25	28						
2005	Nationals	Brampton Thunder	6	0	1	1	6						
2005-06	NWHL	Brampton Thunder	1	0	0	0	0	2006 NWHL-P	5	0	1	1	0
2006-07	WWHL	Calgary Oval X-Treme	14	2	10	12	12	2007 WWHL-P	3	0	3	3	0
2007	Nationals	Calgary Oval X-Treme	6	1	1	2	6						
2007-08	WWHL	Calgary Oval X-Treme	22	9	15	24	12						
2008	Nationals	Calgary Oval X-Treme	3	0	1	1	4						
2008-09	WWHL	Calgary Oval X-Treme	20	7	9	16	10	2009 WWHL-P	2	1	1	2	0
								2009 C-Cup	2	0	0	0	4
2012-13	CWHL	Stars de Montréal	3	0	0	0	2						
Totals from all Competitions			**374**	**55**	**160**	**215**	**404**						

FERRER, ERICA — *Forward. 2008-09 WWHL Calgary Oval X-Treme #41 (3 games, 2 goals).*

FICKEL, JESSICA — *Fort Erie, ON, CAN. Forwad. 2015-16 NWHL Buffalo (14 games, 2 assists; I-Cup 5 games).*

FIDDLER, JOELL — *Defence. Shoots left. #19.*
Born 1971-8-14, Regina, SK, CAN. 5'5".

Year - League - Team			GP	G	A	PTS	PM	Year - Playoff	GP	G	A	PTS	PM
1996	Nationals	Saskatchewan Selects	5	0	1	1	10						
1998	Nationals	Saskatchewan Selects	6	0	2	2	6						
1999	Nationals	Saskatchewan Selects	4	0	0	0							
2001	Nationals	Saskatchewan Selects											
2004-05	WWHL	Saskatchewan Prairie Ice	18	0	1	1	26						
2005-06	WWHL	Saskatchewan Prairie Ice	21	1	5	6	30	2006 WWHL-P	2	0	0	0	2
Totals from all Competitions			**56**	**1**	**9**	**10**	**74**						

FIELD, EMILY — *Forward. Shoots left. #15.*
Isobel Cup winner with Boston on 2016-03-12.
Born 1993-04-06, Littleton, MA, USA. 5'6". Debut at age 22 on 2015-10-11.

Year - League - Team		GP	G	A	PTS	PM	Year - Playoff	GP	G	A	PTS	PM
2015-16	NWHL/ Boston Pride	18	4	3	7	10	2016 I-Cup	4	0	0	0	2
2016-17	NWHL/ Boston Pride	15	3	3	6	8	2017 I-Cup	2	0	0	0	0
2017-18	NWHL/ Boston Pride	16	5	7	12	10	2018 I-Cup	1	0	0	0	4
2018-19	NWHL/ Boston Pride	15	2	3	5	4	2019 I-Cup	1	0	0	0	0
NWHL Regular Season		64	14	16	30	32	Isobel Cup	8	0	0	0	6
Totals from all Competitions		**72**	**14**	**16**	**30**	**38**						

FIFIELD, CATHERINE   *Defence. 2002 Nationals Newfoundland Labrador (4 games).*

FIGUERIA, LIZ   *Forward. 2002-03 NWHL Durham Lightning #19 (? games).*

FIGUEROA, GABIE   *Defence. Shoots right. #21.*
Born 1992-02-21. Grew up in Branchburg, NJ, USA. 5'5". Debut at age 23 on 2015-10-11.

Year - League - Team		GP	G	A	PTS	PM	Year - Playoff	GP	G	A	PTS	PM
2015-16	NWHL/ New York Riveters	18	1	0	1	18	2016 I-Cup	2	0	0	0	4
2016-17	NWHL/ New York Riveters	3	0	0	0	2						

FILEY, LAURA-LEA   *1993-94 COWHL Hamilton #20 (5 gp); 1995-96 COWHL London #16 (28 gp, 1 goal, 2 a.).*

FINDLAY, AMY   *Toronto, ON, CAN. Defence. 2009-10 CWHL Ottawa Senators #8 (27 games, 1 assist).*

FINGLAND, DEVON   *Defence. 2002 Nationals U. Manitoba (5 gp, 2 pts); 2008 Nationals Manitoba (5 gp, 3 pts).*

FINLAYSON, JESSICA   *Defence. Shoots right. #13.*
NWHL winner. Born 1982-12-7. Grew up in Seaforth, ON, CAN. 5'8". Debut at age 22 on 2005-10-2.

Year - League - Team		GP	G	A	PTS	PM	Year - Playoff	GP	G	A	PTS	PM
2005-06	NWHL Axion de Montréal	27	0	1	1	14	2006 NWHL-P	3	0	0	0	0
2006	Nationals Axion de Montréal	6	0	1	1	2						

FINNIE, ANGIE   *Edmonton, AB, CAN. Forward. 2002-03 NWHL Edmonton #11 (21 games).*

FISCHER, COURTNEY   *Defence. 2009-10 WWHL Strathmore Rockies (3 games).*

FISCHER, REAGAN   *Forward. 2009-10 WWHL Strathmore Rockies #19 (18 gp, 7 goals, 7 assists).*

FISHER, BRANDY   *Forward. 1999-00 NWHL Ottawa Raiders #66 (13 gp, 5 goals, 3 assists).*

FISHER, MAGGIE   *Forward. #27.*
Clarkson Cup winner with Minnesota on 2010-03-28
Born 1986-12-26.

Year - League - Team		GP	G	A	PTS	PM	Year - Playoff	GP	G	A	PTS	PM
2009-10	WWHL Minnesota Whitecaps	12	6	1	7	6	2010 C-Cup	2	2	1	3	0
2010-11	WWHL Minnesota Whitecaps	0	0	0	0	0	2011 C-Cup	2	0	0	0	0

FJELD, TARYN   *Forward. Shoots left. #12 #25.*
Born 1979-4-1, Grimshaw, AB, CAN. 5'7".

Year - League - Team		GP	G	A	PTS	PM	Year - Playoff	GP	G	A	PTS	PM
2005-06	WWHL Edmonton Chimos	23	5	8	13	37	2006 WWHL-P	2	0	0	0	0
2006-07	WWHL Edmonton Chimos	24	3	12	15	26	2007 WWHL-P	2	0	0	0	2
2007-08	WWHL Calgary Oval X-Treme	6	2	0	2	0						
2008	Nationals Calgary Oval X-Treme	3	0	0	0	0						
2008-09	WWHL Strathmore Rockies	11	1	1	2	10	2009 WWHL-P	1	0	0	0	2
2009-10	WWHL Strathmore Rockies	7	4	2	6	10						
2010-11	WWHL Strathmore Rockies	5	0	1	1	0						
Totals from all Competitions		**84**	**15**	**24**	**39**	**87**						

FLEMING, REBECCA   *Forward. Shoots right. #24.*
Born 1992-07-20. Grew up in Boston, MA, USA. 5'4". Debut at age 26 on 2018-10-13.

Year - League - Team		GP	G	A	PTS	PM
2018-19	CWHL Worcester Blades	26	0	0	0	2

FLOER, MEGHAN   *Forward. 2004 Nationals British Columbia (6 games).*

FLOOD, STACEY   *Forward. 2006 Nationals Prince Edward Island (5 games).*

FLORES, NICOLE   *Forward. 2015-16 CWHL Boston Blades #10 (14 games).*

FLUKE, EMILY   *Forward. Shoots right. #11.*
Born 1992-9-3. Grew up in Bourne, MA, USA. 5'5". Debut at age 25 on 2017-10-28.

Year - League - Team		GP	G	A	PTS	PM	Year - Playoff	GP	G	A	PTS	PM
2017-18	NWHL/ Connecticut Whale	16	4	7	11	20	2018 I-Cup	1	0	0	0	0
2018-19	NWHL/ Connecticut Whale	16	3	8	11	4	2019 I-Cup	1	1	0	1	0

FLYNN, LYNDSEY   *Forward. 2007 Nationals Prince Edward Island (5 gp, 4 pts); 2008 Nationals PEI (5 gp, 2 pts).*

FOISY, JANINE   *Forward. 2000 Nationals Britannia Blues (5 games, 1 assist).*

FOLEY, KATE   *Forward. #11 #22 #26.*

Year - League - Team		GP	G	A	PTS	PM
1995-96	COWHL Toronto Red Wings	23	7	10	17	16
1996-97	COWHL Mississauga Chiefs	36	14	19	33	42
1998-99	NWHL Scarborough Sting	34	5	6	11	60
1999-00	NWHL Scarborough Sting	26	1	6	7	36
2000-01	NWHL Toronto Sting	39	7	11	18	70

Year - League - Team			GP	G	A	PTS	PM	Year - Playoff	GP	G	A	PTS	PM
2001-02	NWHL	Mississauga IceBears	26	9	8	17	55						
2002-03	NWHL	Mississauga IceBears											
Totals from all Competitions			**184**	**43**	**60**	**103**	**279**						

FOLEY, SARA   *Defence. 2002 Nationals Nova Scotia (5 gp); 2003 Nationals (6 gp); 2008 Nationals (5 gp).*

FOLLETT, SARA JANE   *Forward. 2001 Nationals Newfoundland; 2002 Nationals Newfoundland (5 gp, 1 assist).*

FONG, JENNIFER   *Defence. 2002 Nationals Richmond Steelers (5 gp, 1 assist); 2004 Natoinals B.C. (6 gp).*

FORBES, DONNA   *Defence. #91 #11.*

Year - League - Team			GP	G	A	PTS	PM
1993-94	COWHL	Hamilton Golden Hawks	4	0	1	1	0
1995-96	COWHL	Hamilton Golden Hawks	26	0	3	3	2
1996-97	COWHL	Hamilton	8	0	2	2	0
Totals from all Competitions			**38**	**0**	**6**	**6**	**2**

FORD, FIONA   *Defence. Shoots right. #8.*

Born 1984-5-9. Grew up in Lions Bay, BC, CAN. 5'9".

Year - League - Team			GP	G	A	PTS	PM	Year - Playoff	GP	G	A	PTS	PM
2003-04	NWHL	Calgary Oval X-Treme	3	0	1	1	2						
2004-05	WWHL	British Columbia Breakers	18	0	0	0	20						
2005	Nationals	British Columbia	7	0	1	1	8						
2005-06	WWHL	British Columbia Breakers	16	2	1	3	22						
2006-07	WWHL	British Columbia Breakers	23	2	12	14	32	2007 WWHL-P	0	0	0	0	0
2007	Nationals	British Columbia	5	0	2	2	0						
2007-08	WWHL	British Columbia Breakers	24	0	0	0	24						
Totals from all Competitions			**84**	**4**	**14**	**18**	**100**						

FORFAR, AILISH   *Forward. Shoots left. #11.*

Born 1994-07-11. Grew up in East Gwillimbury, ON, CAN . 5'6". Debut at age 24 on 2018-10-13.

Year - League - Team			GP	G	A	PTS	PM
2018-19	CWHL	Markham Thunder	25	1	3	4	10

FORSYTH, KAILEY   *Forward. 2006 Nationals Manitoba (3 games).*

FORTIER, JOSÉE   *Forward. #55.*

Year - League - Team			GP	G	A	PTS	PM
1998-99	NWHL	Bonaventure	32	5	8	13	10
1999-00	NWHL	Wingstar de Montréal	30	14	14	28	6
2000-01	NWHL	Wingstar de Montréal	37	13	15	28	12
2001-02	NWHL	Wingstar de Montréal	28	5	8	13	4
Totals from all Competitions			**127**	**37**	**45**	**82**	**32**

FORTIER, MICHELLE   *Forward. 2000 Nationals Nova Scotia (6 gp, 4 assists); 2001 Nationals Nova Scotia.*

FORTIN, ALEXANDRA   *2000-01 NWHL Mistral de Laval #26 (2 games).*

FORTINO, LAURA   *Defence. Shoots left. #8.*

Olympic champion. Clarkson Cup winner with Markham on 2018-03-25
Born 1991-1-30, Hamilton, ON, CAN. 5'6". Debut at age 18 on 2008-11-29.

Year - League - Team			GP	G	A	PTS	PM	Year - Playoff	GP	G	A	PTS	PM
2008-09	CWHL	Burlington Barracudas	3	0	1	1	2						
2014-15	CWHL	Brampton Thunder	24	5	10	15	8						
2015-16	CWHL	Brampton Thunder	24	8	20	28	10	2016 C-Cup	2	0	0	0	0
2016-17	CWHL	Brampton Thunder	20	6	13	19	34	2017 C-Cup	2	0	0	0	0
2017-18	CWHL	Markham Thunder	2	0	1	1	0	2018 C-Cup	3	0	1	1	0
2018-19	CWHL	Markham Thunder	26	5	13	18	4	2019 C-Cup	1	0	0	0	0
CWHL Regular Season			99	24	58	82	58	Clarkson Cup	8	0	1	1	0
Totals from all Competitions			**107**	**24**	**59**	**83**	**58**						

CWHL Top Defender in 2015-16... CWHL First All-Star Team in 2015-16 and 2016-17; CWHL Second All-Star Team in 2014-15... CWHL All-Rookie Team in 2014-15... finished 8th in the Angela James Bowl scoring race in 2015-16... selected First Decade CWHL Team in 2017

FOSTER, JULIE   *Centre. Shoots right. #17.*

Born 1969-1-12, Regina, SK, CAN. 5'5".

Year - League - Team			GP	G	A	PTS	PM	Year - Playoff	GP	G	A	PTS	PM
1995	Nationals	Regina Sharks											
1996	Nationals	Saskatchewan Selects	5	0	1	1	4						
1998	Nationals	Saskatchewan Selects	6	0	2	2	4						
1999	Nationals	Saskatchewan Selects	4	0	2	2							
2000	Nationals	Saskatchewan Selects	7	0	2	2							
2001	Nationals	Saskatchewan Selects											
2003	Nationals	Saskatchewan	6	6	6	12	0						
2004	Nationals	Saskatchewan	6	2	3	5	10						
2004-05	WWHL	Saskatchewan Prairie Ice	21	4	10	14	10						
2005-06	WWHL	Saskatchewan Prairie Ice	19	3	8	11	6	2006 WWHL-P	2	1	1	2	0
2006-07	WWHL	Saskatchewan Prairie Ice	24	2	6	8	26						
Totals from all Competitions			**100**	**18**	**41**	**59**	**60**						

FOURACRES, BRITTNEY
Defence. Shoots right. #14.

Clarkson Cup winner with Montréal on 2017-03-05
Born 1993-3-22. Grew up in Calgary, AB, CAN. 5'2". Debut at age 2016-10-15.

Year - League - Team		GP	G	A	PTS	PM	Year - Playoff	GP	G	A	PTS	PM
2016-17	CWHL Canadiennes de Montréal	21	0	1	1	12	2017 C-Cup	3	0	0	0	2
2017-18	CWHL Calgary Inferno	25	2	5	7	4	2018 C-Cup	3	1	0	1	2
CWHL Regular Season		46	2	6	8	16	Clarkson Cup	6	1	0	1	4
Totals from all Competitions		**52**	**3**	**6**	**9**	**20**						

FOURNIER, NATHALIE
Forward. #4.

Year - League - Team		GP	G	A	PTS	PM
1998-99	NWHL Bonaventure	33	14	21	35	25
1999-00	NWHL Wingstar de Montréal	30	5	17	22	20
2000-01	NWHL Wingstar de Montréal	38	11	10	21	28
2001-02	NWHL Wingstar de Montréal	28	3	6	9	26
Totals from all Competitions		**129**	**33**	**54**	**87**	**99**

FOWLER, KORRIN
Forward. 2006 Nationals Newfoundland Labrador (5 games).

FOWLIE, DIANA
Forward. #88 #18.

Year - League - Team		GP	G	A	PTS	PM
1993-94	COWHL Hamilton Golden Hawks	19	4	1	5	10
1995-96	COWHL Hamilton Golden Hawks	28	3	11	14	24
Totals from all Competitions		**47**	**7**	**12**	**19**	**34**

FOX, ALLYSON
Defence. Shoots left. #20.

Abby Hoffman Cup winner with Brampton on 2006-03-12.
NWHL winner, CWHL winner.
Born 1975-3-30. Grew up in Toronto, ON, CAN. 5'5".

Year - League - Team		GP	G	A	PTS	PM	Year - Playoff	GP	G	A	PTS	PM
1993-94	COWHL Toronto Junior Aeros	29	0	11	11	24						
1996-97	COWHL North York Aeros	33	5	6	11	26						
1997-98	COWHL North York Aeros	20	0	8	8	10						
1998	Nationals North York Aeros	6	0	1	1	0						
1998-99	NWHL Brampton Thunder	39	2	16	18	48						
1999-00	NWHL Brampton Thunder	38	4	18	22	58						
2000-01	NWHL Brampton Thunder	35	2	14	16	36						
2001-02	NWHL Brampton Thunder	28	0	14	14	28						
2002	Nationals Brampton Thunder	7	0	2	2	2						
2002-03	NWHL Brampton Thunder						2003 NWHL-P					
2003	Nationals Brampton Thunder	5	3	1	4	2						
2003-04	NWHL Brampton Thunder	36	3	29	32	58						
2004-05	NWHL Brampton Thunder	36	0	15	15	38						
2005	Nationals Brampton Thunder	6	0	1	1	4						
2005-06	NWHL Brampton Thunder	34	0	9	9	70	2006 NWHL-P	5	0	3	3	2
2006	Nationals Brampton Thunder	6	0	1	1	2						
2006-07	NWHL Brampton Thunder	33	0	7	7	58	2007 NWHL-P	6	0	1	1	8
2007-08	CWHL Brampton Can.-Thunder	30	2	9	11	18	2008 CWHL-P	3	0	4	4	2
2008	Nationals Brampton Can.-Thunder	3	0	0	0	0						
2008-09	CWHL Brampton Thunder	29	1	6	7	20	2009 CWHL-P	2		1	1	
							2009 C-Cup	2	0	0	0	0
2009-10	CWHL Brampton Thunder	29	2	19	21	40	2010 C-Cup	1	0	0	0	0
2010-11	CWHL Brampton Thunder	25	1	7	8	18	2011 CWHL-P	2	1		1	2
							2011 C-Cup	3	0	0	0	0
2011-12	CWHL Brampton Thunder	27	0	3	3	10	2012 C-Cup	4	1	1	2	0
CWHL Regular Season		140	6	44	50	106	Clarkson Cup	10	1	1	2	0
Totals from all Competitions		**562**	**27**	**207**	**234**	**584**						

Helped establish Canadian Women's Hockey League

FRANCIS, BRITTANY
Etobicoke, ON, CAN. RW. 2005-06 NWHL Toronto Aeros #6 (6 games, 1 assist).

FRANCOEUR, CINDY
Defence. 1995 Nationals Québec; 1996 Nationals (6 gp); 1998 Nationals (6 gp, 2 pts).

FRASER, SHERILYN
Forward. 2002 Nationals PEI Humpty Dumpty (6 games, 1 assist).

FRATKIN, KALEIGH
Defence. Shoots right. #13.

Clarkson Cup winner with Boston on 2015-03-07
Born 1992-03-24. Grew up in Burnaby, BC, CAN. Debut at age 22 on 2014-10-18.

Year - League - Team		GP	G	A	PTS	PM	Year - Playoff	GP	G	A	PTS	PM
2014-15	CWHL Boston Blades	22	1	7	8	10	2015 C-Cup	3	0	1	1	4
2015-16	NWHL/ Connecticut Whale	18	5	12	17	40	2016 I-Cup	3	0	1	1	6
2016-17	NWHL/ New York Riveters	18	1	5	6	20	2017 I-Cup	1	0	0	0	0
2017-18	NWHL/ Boston Pride	11	0	5	5	20	2018 I-Cup	1	0	0	0	2
2018-19	NWHL/ Boston Pride	16	2	7	9	26	2019 I-Cup	1	0	0	0	2
NWHL Regular Season		63	8	29	37	106	Isobel Cup	6	0	1	1	10
Totals from all Competitions		**94**	**9**	**38**	**47**	**130**						

FRAUTSCHI, ANGELA
D. 2008-09 WWHL Calgary (21 gp, 4 goals, 5 a.; 2 playoff gp; C-Cup 2 gp, 1 goal, 2 a.).

FRECHETTE, ANNIE   *LW. 2003-04 NWHL Québec (2 games); 2004-05 (31 games, 1 goal, 2 assists).*

FREDERICK, ABBY   *Ottawa, ON, CAN. Forward. 2008-09 CWHL Ottawa (21 games, 1 goal, 3 assists).*

FRENCH, TARA   *Defence. Shoots right. #4 #34 #11 #22.*
Abby Hoffman Cup winner with Mississauga on 2008-03-15.
Born 1985-9-12, Halifax, NS, CAN. Grew up in Truro, NS, CAN. 5'8". Debut at age 22 on 2007-9-22.

Year - League - Team		GP	G	A	PTS	PM	Year - Playoff	GP	G	A	PTS	PM
2001	Nationals Nova Scotia Selects											
2007-08	CWHL Mississauga Chiefs	28	2	8	10	44	2008 CWHL-P	2	0	0	0	0
2008	Nationals Mississauga Chiefs	3	0	1	1	2						
2008-09	CWHL Mississauga Chiefs	5	0	1	1	6						
2012-13	CWHL Brampton Thunder	23	1	6	7	18	2013 C-Cup	3	0	0	0	2
2013-14	CWHL Brampton Thunder	22	1	0	1	36						
2014-15	CWHL Toronto Furies	20	0	3	3	16	2015 C-Cup	2	0	0	0	2
2015-16	CWHL Toronto Furies	22	0	3	3	22	2016 C-Cup	2	0	0	0	0
CWHL Regular Season		120	4	21	25	142	Clarkson Cup	7	0	0	0	4
Totals from all Competitions		**132**	**4**	**22**	**26**	**148**						

FRIDFINNSON, LAURA   *Forward. Shoots left. #4.*
Abby Hoffman Cup winner with Calgary on 2007-03-10. WWHL winner. Born 1988-2-2, Arborg, MB, CAN. 5'8".

Year - League - Team		GP	G	A	PTS	PM	Year - Playoff	GP	G	A	PTS	PM
2004	Nationals Manitoba	5	3	2	5	0						
2005-06	WWHL Calgary Oval X-Treme	23	11	10	21	20	2006 WWHL-P	3	1	1	2	2
2006	Nationals Calgary Oval X-Treme	7	3	3	6	2						
2006-07	WWHL Calgary Oval X-Treme	22	7	3	10	28	2007 WWHL-P	2	1	1	2	0
2007	Nationals Calgary Oval X-Treme	5	1	2	3	2						
Totals from all Competitions		**67**	**27**	**22**	**49**	**54**						

FRIER, MEGAN   *Forward. 2004-05 NWHL Durham Lightning #91 (3 games, 1 goal).*

FRIESEN, BONNIE   *Forward. 2002 Nationals Manitoba (5 gp); 2003 Nationals (4 gp, 1 g); 2004 Nationals (5 gp).*

FRIESEN, JACKIE   *F. 2000 Nationals Saskatchewan (7 gp, 5 pts); 2004-05 WWHL Sask. (21gp); 2005-06 (3 gp).*

FRIESEN, MARGARET   *Forward. 2003 Nationals University Winnipeg (4 gp); 2004 Nationals Manitoba (5 gp).*

FRIGON, CAROLINE   *1998-99 NWHL Mistral de Laval #37 (12 games, 3 assists).*

FRITZ-WARD, MORGAN   *Forward. Shoots right. #11.*
Born 1993-09-14. Mason City, IA, USA. 5'7". Debut at age 22 on 2015-10-11.

Year - League - Team		GP	G	A	PTS	PM
2015-16	NWHL/ New York Riveters	17	4	2	6	8
2016-17	NWHL/ New York Riveters	8	0	0	0	0

FRIZZELL, MEGHAN   *Forward. 2005 Nationals Newfoundland Labrador (5 gp, 1 goal, 1 assist).*

FROST, SHANA   *Forward. 1998-99 NWHL North York #82 (1 game); 2003-04 Durham #11 (11 gp, 2 goals).*

FRYER, NATASHA   *Forward. #9.*
Born 1991-05-02 in Rugby, ENG. Grew up in Oakville, ON, CAN. 5'7". Debut at age 22 on 2013-11-02.

Year - League - Team		GP	G	A	PTS	PM
2013-14	CWHL Brampton Thunder	21	4	3	7	2
2014-15	CWHL Brampton Thunder	19	1	3	4	12
CWHL Regular Season		40	5	6	11	14

FRYKLUND, AMBER   *Forward. #15.*
Born 1980-5-31. 5'4".

Year - League - Team		GP	G	A	PTS	PM	Year - Playoff	GP	G	A	PTS	PM
2004-05	WWHL Minnesota Whitecaps	3	0	1	1	0	2005 WWHL-P	2	0	0	0	2
2005-06	WWHL Minnesota Whitecaps	6	0	1	1	2	2006 WWHL-P	3	0	0	0	2
2006-07	WWHL Minnesota Whitecaps	6	1	1	2	0	2007 WWHL-P	0	0	0	0	0

FUJIMOTO, NACHI   *Defence. Shoots right. #7.*
Boston 1991-5-7, JPN. 5'2". Debut at age 25 on 2016-10-29.

Year - League - Team		GP	G	A	PTS	PM
2016-17	CWHL Boston Blades	22	1	0	1	8
2017-18	CWHL Canadiennes de Montréal	17	0	1	1	0

FULTON, EMILY   *Forward. Shoots left. #17.*
Born 1993-02-11. Grew up in Stratford, ON, CAN. 5'5". Debut at age 22 on 2015-10-17.

Year - League - Team		GP	G	A	PTS	PM	Year - Playoff	GP	G	A	PTS	PM
2015-16	CWHL Toronto Furies	22	5	10	15	10	2016 C-Cup	2	0	0	0	0
2016-17	CWHL Toronto Furies	24	4	3	7	8	2017 C-Cup	3	0	0	0	2
2017-18	CWHL Toronto Furies	25	12	5	17	20						
2018-19	CWHL Toronto Furies	15	2	2	4	22	2019 C-Cup	3	0	0	0	2
CWHL Regular Season		86	23	20	43	60	Clarkson Cup	8	0	0	0	4
Totals from all Competitions		**94**	**23**	**20**	**43**							

FULTON, MELISSA   *Forward. 1995 Nationals Winnipeg Sweat Camp.*

FUNK, CHELSEY   *Forward. 2001 Nationals Saskatchewan; 2002 Nationals Saskatchewan (6 gp, 1 goal).*

FUNK, KALLI — Forward. Shoots left. #22.

Isobel Cup winner with Minnesota on 2019-03-17.
Born 1993-03-06. Grew up in Roseville, MN, USA. 5'5". Debut at age 25 on 2018-10-06.

Year - League - Team	GP	G	A	PTS	PM	Year - Playoff	GP	G	A	PTS	PM
2018-19 NWHL/ Minnesota Whitecaps	6	1	1	2	0	2019 I-Cup	2	0	0	0	0

GABLE, JENNIFER — Forward. 1995 Nationals Britannia Blues.

GAGLIARDI, ALYSSA — Defence. Shoots left. #2.

Clarkson Cup winner with Boston on 2015-03-07 and Isobel Cup winner with Boston on 2016-03-12.
Born 1992-04-02. Grew up in Raleigh, NC, USA. 5'5". Debut at age 22 on 2014-10-18.

Year - League - Team	GP	G	A	PTS	PM	Year - Playoff	GP	G	A	PTS	PM
2014-15 CWHL Boston Blades	21	2	2	4	14	2015 C-Cup	3	0	0	0	0
2015-16 NWHL/ Boston Pride	17	0	6	6	10	2016 I-Cup	4	0	0	0	0
2016-17 NWHL/ Boston Pride	17	0	5	5	8	2017 I-Cup	2	0	0	0	0
2017-18 NWHL/ Boston Pride	16	2	6	8	12	2018 I-Cup	1	0	0	0	2
2018-19 NWHL/ Boston Pride	15	1	5	6	6	2019 I-Cup	1	0	0	0	0
NWHL Regular Season	65	3	22	25	36	Isobel Cup	8	0	0	0	2
Totals from all Competitions	**97**	**5**	**24**	**29**	**52**						

NWHL Foundation Award in 2016-17

GAGNÉ, DANIELLE — Forward. Shoots right. #18.

Born 1993-8-31. Grew up in Brampton, ON, CAN. 5'5". Debut at age 23 on 2016-11-19.

Year - League - Team	GP	G	A	PTS	PM	Year - Playoff	GP	G	A	PTS	PM
2016-17 CWHL Toronto Furies	14	0	1	1	6	2017 C-Cup	3	0	0	0	0
2017-18 CWHL Toronto Furies	22	1	1	2	12						
CWHL Regular Season	36	1	2	3	18	Clarkson Cup	3	0	0	0	0
Totals from all Competitions	**39**	**1**	**2**	**3**	**18**						

GAGNÉ, JESSICA — Rock Forest, QC, CAN. Forward. 2007-08 CWHL Québec #15 (5 games, 3 goals).

GAGNÉ, MANON — 1999-00 NWHL Laval (24 gp, 1 assist); 2000-01 (5 gp); 2000-01 Sainte-Julie (1 game).

GAGNON, MELANIE — Defence. Shoots right. #34.

WWHL winner. Born 1986-6-11, St. Adolphe, MB, CAN. 5'5".

Year - League - Team	GP	G	A	PTS	PM	Year - Playoff	GP	G	A	PTS	PM
2001 Nationals University of Manitoba											
2002 Nationals University of Manitoba	5	0	1	1	4						
2003 Nationals University of Winnipeg	4	0	2	2	4						
2003-04 NWHL Calgary Oval X-Treme	10	1	3	4	4	2004 NWHL-P					
2004 Nationals Calgary Oval X-Treme	6	0	1	1	2						
2004-05 WWHL Calgary Oval X-Treme	16	0	9	9	6	2005 WWHL-P	3	1	0	1	0

GAGNON, PATRICIA — Forward. 2004 Nationals Équipe Québec (7 gp, 3 goals, 2 assists).

GAGNON, VANESSA — Forward. Shoots left. #21 #2.

Born 1990-10-28. Grew u pin St-Constant, QC, CAN. 5'2". Debut at age 17 on 2008-10-25.

Year - League - Team	GP	G	A	PTS	PM
2008-09 CWHL Stars de Montréal	4	0	2	2	4
2018-19 NWHL/ Connecticut Whale	3	0	0	0	0

GALARNEAU, MARILENE — Defence. 1999-00 NWHL Laval #16 (3 games); 2000-01 #27 (38 games, 1 assist).

GALBRAITH, HEATHER — 1996-97 COWHL Scarborough (9 gp, 1 assist); 1999-00 NWHL Durham (37 gp, 1 assist).

GALLANT, AMBYR — Forward. Shoots right.

Born 1981-10-01. Grew up in Elmwood, PE, CAN.

Year - League - Team	GP	G	A	PTS	PM
1998 Nationals Prince Edward Island	5	0	0	0	4
1999 Nationals Prince Edward Island	5	0	1	1	
2000 Nationals Prince Edward Island	5	0	0	0	
2001 Nationals PEI Humpty Dumpty					
2002 Nationals PEI Humpty Dumpty	6	0	0	0	2
2005 Nationals Prince Edward Island	5	0	1	1	2
2006 Nationals Prince Edward Island	5	0	0	0	6

GAMBLE, ANISSA — Forward. Shoots right.

Born 1993-5-21. Grew up in Fredericton, NB, CAN. 5'5". Debut at age 16 on 2009-11-14.

Year - League - Team	GP	G	A	PTS	PM	Year - Playoff	GP	G	A	PTS	PM
2009-10 CWHL Mississauga Chiefs	2	0	0	0	0						
2018-19 CWHL Toronto Furies	19	0	2	2	2	2019 C-Cup	2	0	0	0	0

GAMBLE, WENDY — Defence. 1996-97 Newtonbrook Panthers #18 (1 game).

GAMMIE, SHANTEL — Forward. 1995-96 COWHL Mississauga #23 (26 gp, 1 goal, 2 assists).

GAO HAN — Left wing. Shoots right. #89.

Born 1998-6-23. Grew up in Harbin, CHN. 5'2". Debut at age 19 on 2017-10-28.

Year - League - Team	GP	G	A	PTS	PM
2017-18 CWHL Vanke Rays	28	0	0	0	0

GARDNER, CARA *Defence. #21 #77 #22.*
Born 1978-7-31. 5'5".

Year - League - Team			GP	G	A	PTS	PM	Year - Playoff		GP	G	A	PTS	PM
1996-97	COWHL	London Devilettes	30	7	10	17	26							
2002-03	NWHL	Axion de Montréal	32	4	11	15	22	2003	NWHL-PMontréal					
2003-04	NWHL	Axion de Montréal	8	0	5	5	2							
2003-04	NWHL	Brampton Thunder												
Totals from all Competitions			**70**	**11**	**26**	**37**	**50**							

GARDNER, KAYLA *Centre. Shoots left. #18.*
Born 1994-11-16. Grew up in Eagle Lake, ON, CAN. Debut at age 22 on 2017-10-21.

Year - League - Team			GP	G	A	PTS	PM	Year - Playoff		GP	G	A	PTS	PM
2017-18	CWHL	Calgary Inferno	25	6	5	11	10	2018	C-Cup	3	0	0	0	0

GARLAND, MARTINE *Defence. Shoots right. #12.*
Clarkson Cup winner with Toronto on 2014-03-22
Born 1984-9-25, Toronto, ON, CAN. 5'10".

Year - League - Team			GP	G	A	PTS	PM	Year - Playoff		GP	G	A	PTS	PM
2001-02	NWHL	Mississauga IceBears	5	0	1	1	2							
2002-03	NWHL	Brampton Thunder	34	5	12	17	4	2003	NWHL-P					
2003	Nationals	Brampton Thunder	5	1	3	4	2							
2008-09	CWHL	Vaughan Flames	17	9	7	16	8							
2010-11	CWHL	Toronto Furies	22	4	8	12	4	2011	CWHL-P	2				
								2011	C-Cup	4	0	0	0	2
2011-12	CWHL	Toronto Furies	26	2	11	13	8	2012	C-Cup	3	0	0	0	0
2012-13	CWHL	Toronto Furies	19	0	2	2	10	2013	C-Cup	3	0	0	0	2
2013-14	CWHL	Toronto Furies	12	0	4	4	2	2014	C-Cup	4	0	0	0	2
CWHL Regular Season			96	15	32	47	32	Clarkson Cup		14	0	0	0	6
Totals from all Competitions			**156**	**21**	**48**	**69**	**46**							

GARNEAU, JOSIANNE *Aylmer, QC, CAN. Forward. 2002-03 NWHL Ottawa #11 (35 games, 2 assists).*

GARTNER, TAMARA *2003-04 NWHL Edmonton #6 (10 games, ? playoffs).*

GARTNER, TAMARA *Forward. Shoots right. #6.*
Born 1972-12-19.

Year - League - Team			GP	G	A	PTS	PM	Year - Playoff		GP	G	A	PTS	PM
2003-04	NWHL	Edmonton Chimos	10	0	0	0	8	2004	NWHL-P					
2004	Nationals	Edmonton Chimos	7	3	1	4	6							
2005	Nationals	Alberta	6	0	0	0	10							

GASKA, HEATHER *2009-10 WWHL Strathmore Rockies #98 (17 games, 1 goal).*

GASKIN, KATIE *Defence. Shoots right. #20.*
Born 1992-04-06. Grew up in Pickering, ON, CAN. 5'6". Debut at age 23 on 2015-10-17.

Year - League - Team			GP	G	A	PTS	PM	Year - Playoff		GP	G	A	PTS	PM
2015-16	CWHL	Toronto Furies	18	0	4	4	4	2016	C-Cup	2	0	0	0	0
2016-17	CWHL	Toronto Furies	14	0	0	0	0	2017	C-Cup	3	0	0	0	0
2017-18	CWHL	Toronto Furies	21	0	8	8	8							
CWHL Regular Season			53	0	12	12	12	Clarkson Cup		5	0	0	0	0
Totals from all Competitions			**58**	**0**	**12**	**12**	**12**							

GASTMAN, STEPHANIE *Richmond Hill, ON, CAN. Forward. 2007-08 CWHL Burlington #77 (4 games).*

GATTO, RHEA *Slave Lake, AB, CAN. F. 2004-05 NWHL Ottawa #44 (31 gp, 3 goals, 6 a.); 2005-06 (9 gp, 1 goal).*

GAUDET, CLARA *Forward. 2006 Nationals Nova Scotia Selects (5 gp, 2 goals, 2 assists).*

GAUDET, KATRINA *Forward. Shoots right.*
Born 1984-11-18. Grew up in Summerside, PE, CAN.

Year - League - Team			GP	G	A	PTS	PM
2005	Nationals	Prince Edward Island	5	2	1	3	10
2006	Nationals	Prince Edward Island	5	0	2	2	2
2007	Nationals	Prince Edward Island	5	0	1	1	4
2008	Nationals	Prince Edward Island	5	0	2	2	4

GAUDETTE, AMBER *Forward. 2008 Nationals Prince Edward Island (5 games, 1 assist).*

GAUTHIER, NATALIE *Forward. 2003 Nationals Team New Brunswick (4 gp, 1 goal); 2003 Nationals (5 games).*

GAUTREAU, TINA *Forward. 2001 Nationals Team New Brunswick.*

GAUVIN, CHANTAL *2003-04 NWHL Avalanche du Québec (4 gp); 2004 Nationals Équipe Québec (6 gp).*

GAVIN, CATHERINE *2006 Nationals Nova Scotia Selects (5 gp, 1 goal).*

GAVRILOVA, IYA *Forward. Shoots left. #25.*
Born 1987-9-3. Grew up in Krasnoyarsk, RUS. 5'8".

Year - League - Team			GP	G	A	PTS	PM	Year - Playoff		GP	G	A	PTS	PM
2010-11	WWHL	Minnesota Whitecaps	3	1	4	5	0	2011	C-Cup	3	0	1	1	6
2016-17	CWHL	Calgary Inferno	20	11	10	21	8	2017	C-Cup	4	3	0	3	2
2017-18	CWHL	Calgary Inferno	28	6	18	24	10	2018	C-Cup	3	1	0	1	4

CWHL Regular Season	48	17	28	45	18	Clarkson Cup	10	4	1	5	12
Totals from North America	61	22	33	55	30					

Finished 9th in the Angela James Bowl scoring race in 2016-17

GAWLEY, BRITTANY *Pakenham, ON, CAN. RW. 2007-08 CWHL Ottawa #22 #37 (15 gp, 1 goal, 1 playoff gp).*

GEDMAN, MARISSA *Defence. Shoots left. #12.*

Isobel Cup winner with Boston on 2016-03-12
Born 1992-03-12, Framingham, MA, USA. Debut at age 23 on 2015-10-11.

Year - League - Team	GP	G	A	PTS	PM	Year - Playoff	GP	G	A	PTS	PM
2015-16 NWHL/ Boston Pride	18	0	6	6	16	2016 I-Cup	4	0	2	2	12
2016-17 NWHL/ Boston Pride	3	0	0	0	2						
2017-18 NWHL/ Boston Pride	12	0	0	0	4						
Totals from all Competitions	**37**	**0**	**8**	**8**	**34**						

GEE, LAUREN *Defence. 2002 Nationals Richmond Steelers (5 gp); 2004 Nationals B.C. (6 gp, 2 goals).*

GEIGER, KRISTA *1993-94 COWHL Hamilton Golden Hawks #3 (28 games, 2 goals, 4 assists).*

GELDNER, RYANN *Forward. Shoots right. #8 #39 #4.*

Born 1978-10-4. Grew up in Mankato, MN, USA. 5'1".

Year - League - Team	GP	G	A	PTS	PM	Year - Playoff	GP	G	A	PTS	PM
2002-03 NWHL Vancouver Griffins	12	0	0	0	6						
2003 Nationals Vancouver Griffins	7	0	2	2	2						
2003-04 NWHL Durham Lightning	31	2	7	9	47						
2004-05 WWHL Minnesota Whitecaps	1	0	1	1	0	2005 WWHL-P	2	0	0	0	0
2005-06 WWHL Minnesota Whitecaps	12	8	8	16	6	2006 WWHL-P	3	1	0	1	2
2006-07 WWHL Minnesota Whitecaps	18	5	4	9	14	2007 WWHL-P	3	0	2	2	4
Totals from all Competitions	**89**	**16**	**24**	**40**	**81**						

GÉLINAS, MAUDE *Forward. Shoots left. #22.*

Born 1992-02-27. Grew up in St-Bruno-de-Montarville, QC, CAN. 5'7". Debut at age 26 on 2018-10-13.

Year - League - Team	GP	G	A	PTS	PM	Year - Playoff	GP	G	A	PTS	PM
2018-19 CWHL Canadiennes de Montréal	25	3	1	4	2	2019 C-Cup	4	0	0	0	0

GEMMITI, ELIZABETH *Etobicoke, ON, CAN. Defence. 2009-10 CWHL Brampton #15 (1 game).*

GENDRON, JACINTHE *Forward. #9.*

Year - League - Team	GP	G	A	PTS	PM	
1998-99 NWHL Montréal Jofa-Titan	34	10	9	19	46	
1999-00 NWHL Sainte-Julie	35	8	13	21	14	2000 NWHL-P
2000-01 NWHL Sainte-Julie	30	3	11	14	30	
2002-03 NWHL Avalanche du Québec	11	0	0	0	4	
Totals from all Competitions	**110**	**21**	**33**	**54**	**94**	

GIAMO, MAGGIE *Orchard Park, NY, USA. Forward. 2015-16 NWHL Buffalo (5 games).*

GIANNINO, NICOLE *Forward. Shoots right. #27.*

Born 1993-09-19. Grew up in Bay Shore, NY, USA. 5'2". Debut at age 22 on 2015-10-17.

Year - League - Team	GP	G	A	PTS	PM
2015-16 CWHL Boston Blades	22	0	1	1	8
2016-17 CWHL Boston Blades	24	2	1	3	2
2017-18 CWHL Boston Blades	24	0	0	0	0
2018-19 CWHL Worcester Blades	10	0	0	0	0
CWHL Regular Season	80	2	2	4	10

GIBSON, HALEY *Richmond Hill, ON, CAN. Defence. 2008-09 CWHL Ottawa Senators #28 (2 games).*

GIBSON, S. *1999-00 NWHL Scarborough Sting #92 (1 game).*

GIGUÈRE, ISABELLE *Forward. 1999-00 Laval #93 (14 gp, 2 goals, 4 assists); 2000-01 (2 games, 1 goal).*

GILBERT, BRIANNE *Forward. 2004-05 NWHL Toronto Aeros #25 (3 games).*

GILBERT, CHELSEA *Forward. Shoots left.*

Born 1985-09-02. Grew up in Fredericton, NB, CAN.

Year - League - Team	GP	G	A	PTS	PM	Year - Playoff	GP	G	A	PTS	PM
2001 Nationals Team New Brunswick											
2003 Nationals Team New Brunswick	4	3	2	5	0						
2005 Nationals Team New Brunswick	6	5	7	12	6						
2006 Nationals Team New Brunswick	7	1	4	5	2						
2007 Nationals Team New Brunswick	6	1	1	2	4						

GILDERDALE, PAM *Defence. 2007 Nationals BC Outback (5 games, 1 assist).*

GILLESPIE, DANA *Forward. 1995 Nationals Winnipeg Sweat Camp.*

GILLESPIE, KYLA *Right wing. Shoots right. #14 #10.*

Born 1980-11-25. Grew up in Nanaimo, BC, CAN. 5'4".

Year - League - Team	GP	G	A	PTS	PM	Year - Playoff	GP	G	A	PTS	PM
1999 Nationals New Westminster Lightning		1	1	2							
2002-03 NWHL Vancouver Griffins	15	3	4	7	6						
2003 Nationals Vancouver Griffins	7	1	0	1	4						

Year - League - Team			GP	G	A	PTS	PM	Year - Playoff		GP	G	A	PTS	PM
2004-05	WWHL	British Columbia Breakers	14	9	9	18	6							
2005	Nationals	British Columbia	7	1	0	1	2							
2005-06	NWHL	Durham Lightning	34	9	2	11	1	2006	NWHL-P	0	0	0	0	0
2008-09	WWHL	British Columbia Breakers	14	2	1	3	8							
Totals from all Competitions			**96**	**26**	**17**	**43**	**44**							

GILLESPIE, SHAWNA *Forward. 1998 Nationals Tazmanian Devils (5 games); 1999 Nationals (4 games).*

GILLETTE, GINELLE *Defence. 1999 Nationals Saskatchewan (4 games, 1 goal, 1 assist).*

GILLINGHAM, SUZETTE *Forward. #27.*
Born 1973-7-11, Fort McMurray, AB, CAN.

Year - League - Team			GP	G	A	PTS	PM	Year - Playoff		GP	G	A	PTS	PM
2002-03	NWHL	Edmonton Chimos	24	2	4	6	12							
2003-04	NWHL	Edmonton Chimos	11	1	2	3	4	2004	NWHL-P	2	0	0	0	0
2004-05	WWHL	Edmonton Chimos	21	8	7	15	10	2005	WWHL-P	3	0	0	0	0
2005-06	WWHL	Edmonton Chimos	21	7	6	13	10	2006	WWHL-P	2	0	0	0	2
2006-07	WWHL	Edmonton Chimos	0	0	0	0	0	2007	WWHL-P	0	0	0	0	0
2008-09	WWHL	Edmonton Chimos	24	4	6	10	24	2009	WWHL-P	1	0	0	0	0
Totals from all Competitions			**109**	**22**	**25**	**47**	**62**							

GILLIS, JANNA *D. 1998 Nationals Prince Edward Island (5 gp); 2001 Nationals; 2002 Nationals (6 gp, 1 assist).*

GINZEL, HEATHER *Forward. #93.*
IIHF champion. Abby Hoffman Cup winner with Aeros on 1991-03-17 and 1993-03-28. Born 1962-08-14.

Year - League - Team			GP	G	A	PTS	PM
1992-93	COWHL	Toronto Aeros	26	12	10	22	2
1992-93	COWHL	Toronto Aeros	7	1	3	4	2
1995	Nationals	Mississauga Chiefs					
1997-98	COWHL	North York Aeros	1	0	0	0	0
Totals from all Competitions			**34**	**13**	**13**	**26**	**4**

GIRARD, CAROLINE *Forward. #5 #21.*

Year - League - Team			GP	G	A	PTS	PM	Year - Playoff		GP	G	A	PTS	PM
1999-00	NWHL	Sainte-Julie	33	5	9	14	12	2000	NWHL-P					
2000-01	NWHL	Wingstar de Montréal	38	14	12	26	20							
2001-02	NWHL	Wingstar de Montréal	30	14	9	23	4							
2002-03	NWHL	Axion de Montréal	25	6	6	12	4	2003	NWHL-P					
Totals from all Competitions			**126**	**39**	**36**	**75**	**40**							

GIRTZ, ANNE *2008-09 WWHL British Columbia #6 (14 games, 6 goals, 2 assists).*

GLAZER, JODI *Defence. #12.*
Abby Hoffman Cup winner with Aeros on 1991-03-17, 1993-03-28.

Year - League - Team			GP	G	A	PTS	PM
1992-93	COWHL	Toronto Aeros	25	2	2	4	10
1992-93	COWHL	Toronto Aeros	23	6	10	16	2
Totals from all Competitions			**48**	**8**	**12**	**20**	**12**

GLENDINING, MICHELLE *F. 2009-10 WWHL Strathmore (1 gp, 1 goal, 1 a.); 2010-11 (10 gp, 1 goal, 2 assists).*

GODBOUT, MARIE-EVE *2000-01 NWHL Laval (1 game); 2001-02 Montréal (9 games).*

GODEL, KELLY *Forward. 2010-11 WWHL Edmonton #5 (16 gp, 2 goals, 3 assists).*

GOEMANS, HEATHER *Forwad. 2000-01 NWHL Brampton (2 gp); 2001-02 (1 gp); 2005-06 (4 gp, 2 assists).*

GOGUEN, NICOLE *Defence. 2001 Nationals Nova Scotia; 2002 Nationals (5 games).*

GOIN, MICHELLE *Defence. 2005 Nationals Alberta (6 games).*

GOLDBERG, CHELSEY *Centre. Shoots right. #22.*
Born 1993-1-30. Grew up in Agoura Hills, CA, USA. 5'5". Debut at age 23 on 2016-10-15.

Year - League - Team			GP	G	A	PTS	PM
2016-17	CWHL	Boston Blades	20	0	2	2	0
2017-18	CWHL	Boston Blades	26	3	2	5	2
2018-19	CWHL	Worcester Blades	27	2	1	3	2
CWHL Regular Season			73	5	5	10	4

GOLDSMITH, JAMIE *Forward. Shoots left. #12.*
Born 1990-12-11. Grew up in Media, PA, USA. 5'5". Debut at age 26 on 2017-10-28.

Year - League - Team			GP	G	A	PTS	PM	Year - Playoff		GP	G	A	PTS	PM
2017-18	NWHL/	Connecticut Whale	14	3	1	4	8	2018	I-Cup	1	0	0	0	0
2018-19	NWHL/	Connecticut Whale	12	1	0	1	6	2019	I-Cup	1	0	0	0	4

GOODING, NICOLE *Milton, ON, CAN. F. 2011-12 CWHL Burlington Barracudas #20 (8 games, 1 goal, 1 assist).*

GOODMAN, ALLY *Defence. Shoots right. #11 #7 #15 #8.*
Born 1981-4-22.

Year - League - Team			GP	G	A	PTS	PM	Year - Playoff		GP	G	A	PTS	PM
1999-00	NWHL	Brampton Thunder	15	0	3	3	6							
2001-02	NWHL	Mississauga IceBears	2	0	0	0	2							

Year - League - Team			GP	G	A	PTS	PM	Year - Playoff		GP	G	A	PTS	PM
2004-05	NWHL	Brampton Thunder	35	0	12	12	24							
2005	Nationals	Brampton Thunder	6	0	1	1	2							
2007-08	WWHL	Strathmore Rockies	23	1	6	7	32							
2008-09	WWHL	Strathmore Rockies	17	1	3	4	26	2009	WWHL-P	1	0	0	0	2
2010-11	WWHL	Strathmore Rockies	0	0	0	0	0							
Totals from all Competitions			**99**	**2**	**25**	**27**	**94**							

GORE, MADDIE — *Forward. 2015-16 CWHL Boston Blades #26 (16 games).*

GORRILL, RANDI — *Forward. 1998 Nationals Saskatchewan (6 games, 1 assist).*

GOSLING, KAITLYN — *Defence. Shoots left. #51.*

Clarkson Cup winner with Calgary on 2019-03-24.
Born 1993-10-5. Grew up in London, ON, CAN. 5'5". Debut at age 23 on 2016-10-9.

Year - League - Team			GP	G	A	PTS	PM	Year - Playoff		GP	G	A	PTS	PM
2016-17	CWHL	Calgary Inferno	19	6	5	11	4	2017	C-Cup	4	0	2	2	0
2017-18	CWHL	Calgary Inferno	28	7	11	18	18	2018	C-Cup	3	0	0	0	0
2018-19	CWHL	Calgary Inferno	25	9	7	16	12	2019	C-Cup	4	0	2	2	0
CWHL Regular Season			72	22	27	49	34	Clarkson Cup		11	0	4	4	0
Totals from all Competitions			**83**	**22**	**27**	**49**	**34**							

CWHL Second All-Star Team in 2017-18... CWHL All-Rookie Team in 2016-17

GOSSE, JODI — *New Glasgow, NS, CAN. F. 2006-07 NWHL Montréal #10 (13 gp, 2 goals, 2 assists).*

GOULD, MELANIE — *Forward. 2002 Nationals Newfoundland (5 games); 2004 Nationals (5 games, 1 goal).*

GOULDEN, ALANA — *Newmarket, ON, CAN. F. 2007-08 CWHL Mississauga #9 (1 game).*

GOULET, JANINE — *Left wing. Shoots left. #18.*

Born 1981-12-2. Grew up in Ottawa, ON, CAN. 5'7".

Year - League - Team			GP	G	A	PTS	PM	Year - Playoff		GP	G	A	PTS	PM
1999-00	NWHL	Ottawa Raiders	35	3	7	10	22							
2004-05	NWHL	Ottawa Raiders	16	3	6	9	2							
2005-06	NWHL	Ottawa Raiders	9	0	1	1	0	2006	NWHL-P	0	0	0	0	0
Totals from all Competitions			**60**	**6**	**14**	**20**	**24**							

GOULET, JENNIFER — *Forward. #5 #16 #11 #18 #9.*

Year - League - Team			GP	G	A	PTS	PM
1996-97	COWHL	Peterborough Pirates	1	0	0	0	0
1997-98	COWHL	Mississauga Chiefs	17	3	7	10	26
1998-99	NWHL	Mississauga Chiefs	21	2	5	7	16
1999-00	NWHL	Durham Lightning	38	9	6	15	46
2004-05	NWHL	Oakville Ice	30	3	3	6	12
Totals from all Competitions			**107**	**17**	**21**	**38**	**100**

GOW, MARY-ANN — *F. 1995 Nationals Manitoba; 1996 Nationals (6 gp, 2 pts); 2000 Nationals (5 gp, 1 assist).*

GOYETTE, DANIELLE — *Forward. Shoots left. #15.*

Hockey Hall of Fame honoured member, Class of 2017
Olympic champion, IIHF champion. Abby Hoffman Cup winner with Calgary on 2001-03-11, 2003-03-16 and 2007-03-10. WWHL winner.
Born 1966-1-30, St-Nazaire, QC, CAN. 5'6".

Year - League - Team			GP	G	A	PTS	PM	Year - Playoff		GP	G	A	PTS	PM
1995	Nationals	Équipe Québec												
1996	Nationals	Équipe Québec	6	11	8	19	2							
1998	Nationals	Équipe Québec	6	5	6	11	0							
1999	Nationals	Calgary Oval X-Treme	6	4	2	6								
2000	Nationals	Calgary Oval X-Treme	7	3	11	14								
2001	Nationals	Calgary Oval X-Treme												
2002-03	NWHL	Calgary Oval X-Treme	17	23	20	43	21	2003	NWHL-P					
2003	Nationals	Calgary Oval X-Treme	5	5	10	15	0							
2003-04	NWHL	Calgary Oval X-Treme	6	7	4	11	6	2004	NWHL-P	0	0	0	0	0
2004	Nationals	Calgary Oval X-Treme	6	6	8	14	2							
2004-05	WWHL	Calgary Oval X-Treme	18	22	33	55	12	2005	WWHL-P	3	1	3	4	2
2006-07	WWHL	Calgary Oval X-Treme	10	9	17	26	18	2007	WWHL-P	3	8	4	12	2
2007	Nationals	Calgary Oval X-Treme	5	7	5	12	0							
2008	Nationals	Calgary Oval X-Treme												
Totals from all Competitions			**98**	**111**	**131**	**242**	**65**							

Women's National Championships Most Valuable Player in 2003.

GRAAT, JILL — *LW. 1995-96 COWHL London Devliettes #5 (28 games, 8 goals, 8 assists).*

GRABAS, JODY — *Forward.*

Born 1975-12-01.

Year - League - Team			GP	G	A	PTS	PM
1996	Nationals	Edmonton Chimos	7	0	0	0	0
1998	Nationals	Edmonton Chimos	7	2	1	3	2
2000	Nationals	Calgary Oval X-Treme	7	3	3	6	

GRAHAM-MACKAY, AMY   *Defence. 2005 Nationals Nova Scotia (5 games, 1 assist).*

GRANATO, CAMMI   *Forward. Shoots right. #21.*
Hockey Hall of Fame honoured member, Class of 2010
Olympic champion, IIHF champion.
Born 1971-3-25, Downers Grove, IL, USA. 5'7".

Year - League - Team			GP	G	A	PTS	PM
2002-03	NWHL	Vancouver Griffins	24	23	23	46	12
2003	Nationals	Vancouver Griffins	7	3	7	10	2
2004-05	WWHL	British Columbia Breakers	21	8	11	19	30
Totals from all Competitions			**52**	**34**	**41**	**75**	**44**

GRANT, CHRISTINE   *Forward. 2009-10 CWHL Mississauga #16 (2 games).*

GRANT, HEATHER   *Defence. 2007-08 CWHL Burlington #88 (2 games).*

GRANT, LAURA   *Defence. 2011-12 CWHL Burlington #5 (17 games, 1 assist).*

GRATTON, DANIELLE   *Defence. 1998 Nationals Manitoba (5 gp); 1999 Nationals (4 gp); 2000 Nationals (5 gp).*

GRAVEL, NATHALIE   *Forward. 2003-04 NWHL Québec (4 games, 2 assists); 2004-05 (1 game).*

GRAY, ALANA   *Forward. Shoots right. #12.*
Born 1974-12-14. 5'5".

Year - League - Team			GP	G	A	PTS	PM
2000	Nationals	Britannia Blues	5	0	1	1	
2001	Nationals	Vancouver Griffins					
2002-03	NWHL	Vancouver Griffins	19	1	0	1	2

GRAY, ANDREA   *Forward. 2004-05 WWHL British Columbia #17 (21 games, 2 goals, 2 assists).*

GRAY, ERIN   *Defence. 2005 Nationals Alberta (6 games, 1 goal).*

GRAY, KATE   *Forward. 2015-16 CWHL Boston Blades #17 (23 games).*

GRAY, KATIE   *Forward. #7 #18 #6.*
Born 1984-8-18. Grew up in Cambridge, ON, CAN. 5'7".

Year - League - Team			GP	G	A	PTS	PM
2001-02	NWHL	Mississauga IceBears	2	0	1	1	0
2007-08	CWHL	Vaughan Flames	2	0	1	1	2
2009-10	WWHL	Strathmore Rockies	16	0	5	5	8
2009-10	CWHL	Vaughan Flames	2	0	0	0	0

GRAY, TARA   *Defence. Shoots right. #16 #2 #43.*
Born 1988-7-6, Toronto, ON, CAN. 5'10". Debut at age 17 on 2005 10 01.

Year - League - Team			GP	G	A	PTS	PM	Year - Playoff	GP	G	A	PTS	PM
2005-06	NWHL	Toronto Aeros	10	1	1	2	8						
2006-07	NWHL	Mississauga Aeros	32	2	8	10	22	2007 NWHL-P	4	0	0	0	0
2007	Nationals	Mississauga Aeros	6	0	1	1	6						
2011-12	CWHL	Brampton Thunder	27	1	6	7	20	2012 C-Cup	4	0	0	0	0
2012-13	CWHL	Brampton Thunder	21	1	4	5	10	2013 C-Cup	3	0	0	0	4
2013-14	CWHL	Brampton Thunder	18	0	0	0	4						
2014-15	CWHL	Brampton Thunder	0	0	0	0	0						
CWHL Regular Season			66	2	10	12	34	Clarkson Cup	7	0	0	0	4
Totals from all Competitions			**125**	**5**	**20**	**25**	**74**						

GRECO, EMMA   *Defence. Shoots left. #17.*
Born 1995-3-6. Grew up in Burlington, ON, CAN. 5'9". Debut at age 22 on 2018-1-27.

Year - League - Team			GP	G	A	PTS	PM	Year - Playoff	GP	G	A	PTS	PM
2017-18	NWHL/	Connecticut Whale	6	0	2	2	4	2018 I-Cup	1	0	0	0	0
2018-19	CWHL	Toronto Furies	23	0	3	3	12						

GRECO, JACQUIE   *Defence. Shoots right. #25.*
Isobel Cup winner with Buffalo on 2017-03-19
Born 1991-5-30. Grew up in Buffalo, NY, USA. 5'7". Debut at age 25 on 2016-10-7.

Year - League - Team			GP	G	A	PTS	PM	Year - Playoff	GP	G	A	PTS	PM
2016-17	NWHL/	Buffalo Beauts	15	1	0	1	2	2017 I-Cup	2	0	0	0	0
2017-18	NWHL/	Buffalo Beauts	14	0	2	2	2	2018 I-Cup	2	0	0	0	2
2018-19	NWHL/	Buffalo Beauts	9	0	0	0	0	2019 I-Cup	2	0	0	0	0
NWHL Regular Season			38	1	2	3	4	Isobel Cup	6	0	0	0	2
Totals from all Competitions			**44**	**1**	**2**	**3**	**6**						
NWHL Foundation Award in 2017-18													

GREEN, LEE   *Defence. 2001 Nationals University of Manitoba.*

GREENE, ALISON   *Defence. 2006 Nationals Newfoundland Labrador (5 games, 1 assist).*

GREENE, JILLIAN   *Forward. 2006 Nationals Newfoundland Labrador (5 games, 1 assist).*

GREENHAM, SHELLEY   *Forward. 2001 Nationals Manitoba; 2002 Nationals University of Manitoba (5 games).*

GRENON, MEGAN   *Defence. Shoots left. #6.*
Born 1994-8-16. Grew up in Calgary, AB, CAN. Debut at age 23 on 2017-10-21.

Year - League - Team			GP	G	A	PTS	PM	Year - Playoff	GP	G	A	PTS	PM
2017-18	CWHL	Calgary Inferno	25	1	1	2	8	2018 C-Cup	3	0	0	0	0

GRENON, STÉPHANIE
Forward. Shoots left. #16.

Born 1974-10-30. Grew up in Terrebonne, QC, CAN.

Year - League - Team			GP	G	A	PTS	PM		
1998-99	NWHL	Montréal Jofa-Titan	34	8	6	14	16		
1999-00	NWHL	Sainte-Julie	34	3	19	22	35	2000	NWHL-P
2000-01	NWHL	Sainte-Julie	38	21	30	51	32		
2001-02	NWHL	Cheyenne	29	8	14	22	10		
2002	Nationals	Équipe Québec	6	1	0	1	2		
2002-03	NWHL	Avalanche du Québec	32	10	17	27	20		
2003-04	NWHL	Avalanche du Québec	5	1	1	2	2		
Totals from all Competitions			**178**	**52**	**87**	**139**	**117**		

GRIBBONS, KELLY
Forward. Shoots left. #18.

Born 1995-09-07. Grew up in Port Elgin, ON, CAN. 5'10". Debut at age 23 on 2018-10-20.

Year - League - Team			GP	G	A	PTS	PM	Year - Playoff		GP	G	A	PTS	PM
2018-19	CWHL	Markham Thunder	25	1	3	4	0	2019	C-Cup	3	0	0	0	2

GRIEVES, MEGHAN
Right wing. Shoots right. #17.

Born 1994-5-3. Grew up in Cary, NC, USA. 5'8". Debut at age 22 on 2016-10-15.

Year - League - Team			GP	G	A	PTS	PM
2016-17	CWHL	Boston Blades	22	5	8	13	16
2017-18	CWHL	Boston Blades	28	6	8	14	12
2018-19	CWHL	Worcester Blades	27	3	5	8	2
CWHL Regular Season			**77**	**14**	**21**	**35**	**30**

GRIGG, LINDSAY
Forward. Shoots right. #23.

Clarkson Cup winner with Markham on 2018-03-25

Born 1993-5-26. Grew up in Oakville, ON, CAN. 5'6". Debut at age 16 on 2009-10-18.

Year - League - Team			GP	G	A	PTS	PM	Year - Playoff		GP	G	A	PTS	PM
2009-10	CWHL	Mississauga Chiefs	1	0	0	0	0							
2015-16	NWHL/	Buffalo Beauts	15	0	2	2	6	2016	I-Cup	5	0	1	1	6
2017-18	CWHL	Markham Thunder	28	0	5	5	6	2018	C-Cup	3	0	0	0	0
Totals from all Competitions			**21**	**0**	**3**	**3**	**12**							

GRIGNON L'ANGLAIS, ANOUK
Forward. Shoots left. #11 #12 #19.

NWHL winner. Born 1980-6-2. Grew up in Outremont, QC, CAN. 5'7". Debut at age 24 in 2004-05.

Year - League - Team			GP	G	A	PTS	PM	Year - Playoff		GP	G	A	PTS	PM
2004-05	NWHL	Axion de Montréal	21	1	7	8	4							
2005	Nationals	Axion de Montréal	6	0	1	1	0							
2005-06	NWHL	Axion de Montréal	22	3	1	4	8	2006	NWHL-P	3	0	0	0	0
2006	Nationals	Axion de Montréal	6	0	0	0	0							
2006-07	NWHL	Axion de Montréal	7	1	0	1	2	2007	NWHL-P					
2007-08	CWHL	Stars de Montréal	16	1	1	2	12							
2008-09	CWHL	Stars de Montréal	4	0	0	0	6							

GRILLS, CHELSEA
Forward. #14.

Born 1985-3-21.

Year - League - Team			GP	G	A	PTS	PM
2001-02	NWHL	Ottawa Raiders	30	7	13	20	18
2002-03	NWHL	Ottawa Raiders	27	11	18	29	28
Totals from all Competitions			**57**	**18**	**31**	**49**	**46**

GRIMBLY, SHANNON
Forward. #21 #9.

Year - League - Team			GP	G	A	PTS	PM
1997-98	COWHL	North York Aeros	1	2	0	2	0
1998-99	NWHL	Mississauga Chiefs	38	5	7	12	32
1999-00	NWHL	Mississauga Chiefs	40	7	13	20	48
2000-01	NWHL	Mississauga IceBears	39	3	8	11	47
2001-02	NWHL	Mississauga IceBears	29	12	12	24	28
2002-03	NWHL	Mississauga IceBears					
Totals from all Competitions			**147**	**29**	**40**	**69**	**155**

GRNAK (O'MARA), MARIANNE
Forward. #16 #67.

IIHF champion. Abby Hoffman Cup winner with Aeros on 1991-03-17, 1993-03-28.

Born 1967-9-1. Grew up in North York, ON, CAN.

Year - League - Team			GP	G	A	PTS	PM
1992-93	COWHL	Toronto Aeros	24	10	5	15	22
1992-93	COWHL	Toronto Aeros	25	20	24	44	10
1995-96	COWHL	North York Aeros	26	19	7	26	8
1996	Nationals	North York Aeros	5	2	2	4	0
1996-97	COWHL	North York Aeros	32	20	18	38	29
1997-98	COWHL	North York Aeros	16	7	7	14	10
1998	Nationals	North York Aeros	4	0	1	1	0
1998-99	NWHL	Brampton Thunder	36	19	18	37	40
1999-00	NWHL	Brampton Thunder	34	10	23	33	32
Totals from all Competitions			**202**	**107**	**105**	**212**	**151**

GROULX, KARINE *Forward. Shoots right. #6.*
Born 1984-4-28.

Year - League - Team		GP	G	A	PTS	PM	Year - Playoff		GP	G	A	PTS	PM
2002-03	NWHL Axion de Montréal	27	3	3	6	8	2003	NWHL-P					
2003-04	NWHL Axion de Montréal	35	6	3	9	20							
2004-05	NWHL Axion de Montréal	31	4	5	9	41							
2005	Nationals Axion de Montréal	6	0	1	1	2							
Totals from all Competitions		**99**	**13**	**12**	**25**	**71**							

GROULX, VALERIANN *2000-01 NWHL Mistral de Laval (3 games).*

GRUHN, LORI *Forward. 1999 Nationals Tazmanian Devils (4 games, 1 goal).*

GRUNDY, DANIELLE *Forward. Shoots right. #3 #26 #16.*
Born 1993-09-06. Grew up in Kelowna, BC, CAN.

Year - League - Team		GP	G	A	PTS	PM
2001	Nationals Vancouver Griffins					
2004-05	WWHL British Columbia Breakers	21	4	2	6	8
2007-08	WWHL British Columbia Breakers	6	1	3	4	14
2008-09	WWHL British Columbia Breakers	12	2	5	7	16
Totals from all Competitions		**39**	**7**	**10**	**17**	**38**

GRUSCHOW, ALEXA *Forward. Shoots right. #11.*
Isobel Cup winner with Metropolitan on 2018-03-25
Born 1994-4-16. Grew up in Mechanicburgh, PA, USA. 5'7". Debut at age 22 on 2016-10-8.

Year - League - Team		GP	G	A	PTS	PM	Year - Playoff		GP	G	A	PTS	PM
2016-17	NWHL/ New York Riveters	18	2	8	10	12	2017	I-Cup	1	0	1	1	0
2017-18	NWHL/ Metropolitan Riveters	16	9	13	22	26	2018	I-Cup	2	1	0	1	0
2018-19	NWHL/ Metropolitan Riveters	16	2	2	4	12	2019	I-Cup	2	2	0	2	2
NWHL Regular Season		50	13	23	36	50	Isobel Cup		5	3	1	4	2
Totals from all Competitions		**55**	**16**	**24**	**40**	**52**							

NWHL Most Valuable Player in 2017-18... NWHL Scoring Champion in 2017-18

GUAY, ANNIE *Defence. Shoots left. #73 #4.*
Clarkson Cup winner with Montréal on 2009-03-21 and 2011-03-27.
Born 1985-6-29, Rouyn-Noranda, QC, CAN. 5'8". Debut at age 23 on 2008-10-18.

Year - League - Team		GP	G	A	PTS	PM	Year - Playoff		GP	G	A	PTS	PM
2004	Nationals Équipe Québec	7	0	4	4	6							
2008-09	CWHL Stars de Montréal	28	10	16	26	20	2009	CWHL-P	2	0	2	2	0
							2009	C-Cup	3	0	1	1	2
2009-10	CWHL Stars de Montréal	26	8	30	38	26	2010	C-Cup	1	0	1	1	0
2010-11	CWHL Stars de Montréal	26	13	18	31	14	2011	CWHL-P	2		1	1	
							2011	C-Cup	4	0	3	3	8
2011-12	CWHL Stars de Montréal	0	0	0	0	0							
CWHL Regular Season		80	31	64	95	60	Clarkson Cup		8	0	5	5	10
Totals from all Competitions		**99**	**31**	**76**	**107**	**76**							

CWHL Top Defender in 2009-10... CWHL First All-Star Team in 2009-10 and 2010-11... CWHL All-Rookie Team in 2008-09... finished 5th in the Angela James Bowl scoring race in 2009-10... selected First Decade CWHL Team in 2017

GUENETTE, ANNICK *Forward. #7 #12 #22.*

Year - League - Team		GP	G	A	PTS	PM	Year - Playoff	
1998-99	NWHL Bonaventure	11	1	3	4	12		
1999-00	NWHL Sainte-Julie	21	0	1	1	22	2000	NWHL-P
2004-05	NWHL Avalanche du Québec	21	0	1	1	22		
Totals from all Competitions		**53**	**1**	**5**	**6**	**56**		

GUEST, TRICIA *Forward. Shoots left. #14.*
Born 1982-4-23, Estevan, SK, CAN. 5'7".

Year - League - Team		GP	G	A	PTS	PM	Year - Playoff		GP	G	A	PTS	PM
1998	Nationals Saskatchewan Selects	6	0	2	2	10							
2004-05	WWHL Edmonton Chimos						2005	WWHL-P	3	1	0	1	2
2005-06	WWHL Edmonton Chimos	19	10	9	19	28	2006	WWHL-P	2	1	0	1	4

GUÊVREMONT, CHANTAL *Defence. Shoots left. #9*
NWHL winner. Born 1977-2-18. Grew up in St-Laurent, QC, CAN. 5'1".

Year - League - Team		GP	G	A	PTS	PM	Year - Playoff		GP	G	A	PTS	PM
1998	Nationals Équipe Québec	6	0	2	2	4							
1998-99	NWHL Bonaventure	33	1	6	7	38							
1999	Nationals Équipe Québec	5	1	2	3								
1999-00	NWHL Wingstar de Montréal	33	2	5	7	56							
2000	Nationals Équipe Québec	6	0	1	1								
2000-01	NWHL Wingstar de Montréal	35	3	11	14	46							
2001	Nationals Équipe Québec												
2001-02	NWHL Wingstar de Montréal	27	0	8	8	40							
2002	Nationals Équipe Québec	6	0	0	0	2							

Year - League - Team		GP	G	A	PTS	PM	Year - Playoff		GP	G	A	PTS	PM
2002-03	NWHL Axion de Montréal	34	1	4	5	73	2003	NWHL-P					
2003	Nationals Équipe Québec	5	1	2	3	4							
2003-04	NWHL Axion de Montréal	35	3	2	5	72							
2004-05	NWHL Axion de Montréal	20	1	4	5	26							
2005	Nationals Axion de Montréal	6	0	0	0	10							
2005-06	NWHL Axion de Montréal	14	1	5	6	22	2006	NWHL-P	3	0	0	0	2
2006-07	NWHL Axion de Montréal	1	0	0	0	2							
Totals from all Competitions		**269**	**14**	**52**	**66**	**397**							

GUILLEMETTE, MELANIE   *Forward. 2009-10 CWHL Mississauga #7 (15 games, 5 goals, 3 assists).*

GUNSOLUS, MELISSA   *Peterborough, ON. D. 2007-08 CWHL Ottawa (23 games, 1 goal, 6 a.); 2009-10 (6 gp).*

GYSEL, NICOLE   *Defence. 2002 Nationals Manitoba (5 gp); 2003 Nationals (4 gp); 2004 Nationals (5 gp, 1 goal).*

HACHÉ, GUYLAINE   *Forward. 2000 Nationals Team New Brunswick (6 gp, 2 goals, 1 assist).*

HAGERMAN, JAMIE   *Defence. Shoots right. #8.*

IIHF champion. Born 1981-5-7, North Andover, MA, USA. 5'9".

Year - League - Team		GP	G	A	PTS	PM
2003-04	NWHL Brampton Thunder	31	8	22	30	34
Totals from all Competitions		**31**	**8**	**22**	**30**	**34**

HAGG, KRISTEN   *Forward. Shoots right. #16.*

Clarkson Cup winner with Calgary on 2016-03-14
Born 1983-8-23. Grew up in Edmonton, AB, CAN. 5'4". Debut at age 23 on 2006-10-21.

Year - League - Team		GP	G	A	PTS	PM	Year - Playoff		GP	G	A	PTS	PM
2006-07	WWHL Edmonton Chimos	24	10	20	30	15	2007	WWHL-P	2	1	0	1	2
2008-09	WWHL Edmonton Chimos	24	14	18	32	14	2009	WWHL-P	1	0	0	0	2
2009-10	WWHL Edmonton Chimos	4	2	1	3	2							
2010-11	WWHL Edmonton Chimos	3	0	0	0	0							
2014-15	CWHL Calgary Inferno	18	0	2	2	4	2015	C-Cup	2	0	0	0	2
2015-16	CWHL Calgary Inferno	21	2	3	5	4	2016	C-Cup	3	0	0	0	0
CWHL Regular Season		39	2	5	7	8	Clarkson Cup		5	0	0	0	2
Totals from all Competitions		**102**	**29**	**44**	**73**	**45**							

Has served as a general manager with CWHL Calgary

HAGGARD, CARLY   *Forward. Shoots right. #7.*

Born 1981-4-12. Grew up in Port Alberni, BC, CAN. 5'6".

Year - League - Team		GP	G	A	PTS	PM	Year - Playoff		GP	G	A	PTS	PM
1998	Nationals New Westminster Lightning	5	4	3	7	2							
1999	Nationals New Westminster Lightning	5	3	1	4								
2003-04	NWHL Oakville Ice	31	26	13	39	32							
2004-05	NWHL Oakville Ice	35	21	14	35	68							
2005-06	NWHL Oakville Ice	36	26	13	39	52	2006	NWHL-P	2	1	1	2	4
2006-07	NWHL Oakville Ice	25	16	10	26	42	2007	NWHL-P	3	0	2	2	8
2007	Nationals Etobicoke Dolphins	7	5	5	10	4							
Totals from all Competitions		**132**	**90**	**53**	**143**	**206**							

HAGGE, TIFFANY   *Forward. Shoots right. #20.*

CWHL winner.
Born 1984-5-3, Minneapolis, MN, USA. Grew up in Coon Rapids, MN, USA. 5'9". Debut at age 22 on 2006-9-16.

Year - League - Team		GP	G	A	PTS	PM	Year - Playoff		GP	G	A	PTS	PM
2006-07	NWHL Mississauga Aeros	27	9	8	17	34	2007	NWHL-P	2	1	1	2	0
2007	Nationals Mississauga Aeros	6	3	6	9	8							
2007-08	CWHL Brampton Can.-Thunder	30	12	15	27	36	2008	CWHL-P	3	1	1	2	0
2008	Nationals Brampton Can.-Thunder	3	1	1	2	4							
2008-09	CWHL Brampton Thunder	30	5	16	21	42	2009	CWHL-P	2		2		
							2009	C-Cup	2	0	2	2	4
CWHL Regular Season		60	17	31	48	78	Clarkson Cup		2	0	2	2	4
Totals from all Competitions		**105**	**32**	**50**	**82**	**130**							

Finished 11th in the Angela James Bowl scoring race in 2007-08

HAHN, MARIE   *Defence. 2000-01 NWHL Durham Lightning #2 (32 games, 1 goal, 2 assists).*

HAIGHT, RACHELLE   *Forward. 2000 Nationals Saskatchewan (7 games); 2001 Nationals Saskatchewan.*

HAIN, LANDA   *Defence. 2006-07 WWHL Saskatchewan Prairie Ice #18 (4 games).*

HAINS, JESSICA   *Forward. 2007-08 CWHL Montréal #96 (1 game).*

HALL, CAROLINE   *Forward. 2001 Nationals Vancouver Griffins.*

HALL, CAROLYN   *Forward. 1996 Nationals Saskatchewan (6 games, 2 assists).*

HALL, ERIN   *Defence. Shoots right. #10.*

Born 1994-11-18. Grew up in Pembroke, MA, USA. 5'3". Debut at age 22 on 2017-10-14.

Year - League - Team		GP	G	A	PTS	PM
2017-18	CWHL Boston Blades	15	0	0	0	2
2018-19	CWHL Worcester Blades	2	0	0	0	0

HALL, KALEY Forward. Shoots left. #7.
Abby Hoffman Cup winner with Calgary on 2003-03-16 and 2007-03-10. NWHL winner, WWHL winner. Born 1984-5-14, Calgary, AB, CAN. 5'7".

Year - League - Team			GP	G	A	PTS	PM	Year - Playoff		GP	G	A	PTS	PM
2002-03	NWHL	Calgary Oval X-Treme	22	13	17	30	18	2003	NWHL-P					
2003	Nationals	Calgary Oval X-Treme	5	6	2	8	2							
2003-04	NWHL	Calgary Oval X-Treme	9	6	4	10	6	2004	NWHL-P	4	2	1	3	6
2004	Nationals	Calgary Oval X-Treme	6	0	2	2	2							
2004-05	WWHL	Calgary Oval X-Treme	19	15	15	30	40	2005	WWHL-P	3	1	1	2	10
2005-06	WWHL	Calgary Oval X-Treme	21	12	17	29	42	2006	WWHL-P	3	3	1	4	0
2006-07	WWHL	Calgary Oval X-Treme	22	15	24	39	54	2007	WWHL-P	3	1	1	2	2
2007	Nationals	Calgary Oval X-Treme	6	6	5	11	6							
2007-08	WWHL	Calgary Oval X-Treme	18	11	12	23	26							
2008	Nationals	Calgary Oval X-Treme	3	2	0	2	0							
2008-09	WWHL	Calgary Oval X-Treme	21	13	18	31	65	2009	WWHL-P	1	0	0	0	0
								2009	C-Cup	2	0	1	1	4
Totals from all Competitions			**168**	**106**	**121**	**227**	**283**							

HALL, VAL Centre. Shoots right. #88 #91 #93.
Born 1981-7-14. Grew up in Niagara Falls, ON, CAN. 5'6".

Year - League - Team			GP	G	A	PTS	PM	Year - Playoff		GP	G	A	PTS	PM
2004-05	NWHL	Oakville Ice	30	9	9	18	24							
2005-06	NWHL	Oakville Ice	29	11	10	21	28	2006	NWHL-P	2	1	0	1	4
2006-07	NWHL	Oakville Ice	27	6	8	14	59	2007	NWHL-P	3	0	1	1	10
2007-08	CWHL	Burlington Barracudas	23	4	9	13	46	2008	CWHL-P	3	2	0	2	2
2008-09	CWHL	Burlington Barracudas	6	2	0	2	2							
2009-10	CWHL	Burlington Barracudas	6	5	0	5	2							
CWHL Regular Season			35	11	9	20	50							
Totals from all Competitions			**129**	**40**	**37**	**77**	**177**							

HALLER, MADISON Defence. Shoots left. #6 #5.
Born 1996-5-21. Grew up in Calgary, AB, CAN. Debut at age 16 on 2012-10-29.

Year - League - Team			GP	G	A	PTS	PM	Year - Playoff		GP	G	A	PTS	PM
2012-13	CWHL	Alberta	13	0	1	1	2							
2013-14	CWHL	Calgary Inferno	24	0	6	6	10	2014	C-Cup	3	0	0	0	0
2014-15	CWHL	Calgary Inferno	17	1	4	5	4	2015	C-Cup	0	0	0	0	0
CWHL Regular Season			54	1	11	12	16	Clarkson Cup		3	0	0	0	0
Totals from all Competitions			**57**	**1**	**11**	**12**	**16**							

HALLIDAY, KAREN 2001-02 NWHL Mississauga Ice Bears #14 (3 games).

HALVORSON, KELSEY Defence. 2007 Nationals BC Outback (5 games, 2 assists).

HAMBLY, CATHY Forward. Shoots left. #27.
CWHL winner. Born 1978-2-10. Grew up in Alliston, ON, CAN. 5'7". Debut at age 30 on 2007-10-6.

Year - League - Team			GP	G	A	PTS	PM			GP	G	A	PTS	PM
2007-08	CWHL	Brampton Can.-Thunder	26	3	2	5	6	2008	CWHL-P	3	0	0	0	2
2008	Nationals	Brampton Can.-Thunder	3	0	0	0	0							

HAMEL, VALERIE Left wing. Shoots left. #16 #20.
NWHL winner. Born 1978-9-28, Danville, QC; grew up in Montréal, QC, CAN. 5'5". Debut at age 26 on 2005-09-17.

Year - League - Team			GP	G	A	PTS	PM			GP	G	A	PTS	PM
2005-06	NWHL	Axion de Montréal	28	3	2	5	8	2006	NWHL-P	3	0	0	0	0
2006	Nationals	Axion de Montréal	6	0	0	0	2							
2006-07	NWHL	Axion de Montréal	24	3	5	8	32	2007	NWHL-P					

HAMILTON, CHERYL Forward. 2007 Nationals Nova Scotia (7 gp); 2008 Nationals Nova Scotia (1 game).

HAMILTON, LINDSAY Defence. 2000 Nationals Saskatchewan (7 games).

HAMILTON, MELISSA 1998-99 NWHL Mississauga Chiefs #87 (1 game).

HAMMER, TARA Forward. #14 #11.
Born 1979-5-25. Grew up in Crowsnest Pass, BC, CAN.

Year - League - Team			GP	G	A	PTS	PM	Year - Playoff		GP	G	A	PTS	PM
2002-03	NWHL	Edmonton Chimos	24	8	3	11	10							
2007-08	WWHL	Strathmore Rockies	23	8	7	15	14							
2008-09	WWHL	Strathmore Rockies	20	5	3	8	22	2009	WWHL-P	1	0	0	0	0
2009-10	WWHL	Strathmore Rockies	16	5	6	11	18							
Totals from all Competitions			**84**	**26**	**19**	**45**	**64**							

HAMPTON, JORDAN Defence. Shoots right. #91.
Born 1994-2-17. Grew up in Foxborough, MA, USA. 5'6". Debut at age 23 on 2017-10-14.

Year - League - Team			GP	G	A	PTS	PM
2017-18	CWHL	Boston Blades	20	1	1	2	4
2018-19	CWHL	Toronto Furies	6	0	1	1	6

HANDLEY, CARRIE 2001-02 NWHL Durham Lightning #17 (23 games, 3 assists).

HANLON, LISA
Forward. #6 #17 #67.

Abby Hoffman Cup winner with Aeros on 1993-03-28.

Year - League - Team		GP	G	A	PTS	PM
1992-93	COWHL Toronto Aeros	23	2	11	13	28
1993-94	COWHL Toronto Junior Aeros	29	7	15	22	20
1995-96	COWHL North York Aeros	30	12	18	30	42
1996	Nationals North York Aeros	5	0	3	3	2
1996-97	COWHL North York Aeros	4	3	4	7	6
1997-98	COWHL Scarborough Sting	1	0	0	0	0
Totals from all Competitions		**92**	**24**	**51**	**75**	**98**

HANN, CHRISTINE
Forward. 2000 Nationals Newfoundland Labrador (5 games).

HANNAH-HORNE, WHITNEY
Forward. 2015-16 CWHL Brampton #37 (24 gp; C-Cup 2 gp).

HANNAH, KATHERINE
Forward. 2000-01 NWHL Ottawa Raiders (2 gp, 1 goal, 1 assist).

HANNAH, RAE
Forward. 2003 Nationals Saskatchewan (5 games, 2 goals).

HANNAM, MARYELLE
Forward. 2005 Nationals Nova Scotia Selects (5 games).

HANRAHAN, BETH
Forward. 2015-16 NWHL New York (18 gp, 2 g., 1 a., I-Cup 2 gp, 1 a.).

HANRAHAN, MORGAN
Defence. 2004 Nationals Newfoundland Labrador (5 gmes, 1 assist).

HANSON, TIA
Forward. Shoots left. #23 #24.

NWHL winner, WWHL winner. Born 1986-11-29. Grew up in Calgary, AB, CAN. 5'4".

Year - League - Team		GP	G	A	PTS	PM	Year - Playoff	GP	G	A	PTS	PM
2003-04	NWHL Calgary Oval X-Treme	7	1	2	3	8	2004 NWHL-P					
2004	Nationals Calgary Oval X-Treme	2	0	2	2	0						
2004-05	WWHL Calgary Oval X-Treme	10	4	2	6	4	2005 WWHL-P	2	0	0	0	0
2012-13	CWHL Alberta	14	1	2	3	4						
Totals from all Competitions		**35**	**6**	**8**	**14**	**16**						

HARBEC, SABRINA
Forward. Shoots right. #96.

Clarkson Cup winner with Montréal on 2009-03-21, 2011-03-27 and 2012-03-25.
Born 1985-3-20, Greenfield Park, QC, CAN. Grew up in Montréal, QC, CAN. 5'8".

Year - League - Team		GP	G	A	PTS	PM	Year - Playoff	GP	G	A	PTS	PM
2002-03	NWHL Axion de Montréal	24	16	11	27	2	2003 NWHL-P					
2003-04	NWHL Axion de Montréal	36	14	23	37	22	2004 NWHL-P	4	2	5	7	2
2004	Nationals Équipe Québec	7	3	4	7	8						
2008-09	CWHL Stars de Montréal	27	20	26	46	20	2009 CWHL-P	2	1	2	3	0
							2009 C-Cup	3	2	2	4	2
2009-10	CWHL Stars de Montréal	29	15	40	55	34	2010 C-Cup	1	0	2	2	2
2010-11	CWHL Stars de Montréal	12	6	8	14	6	2011 CWHL-P	2	1	1	2	2
							2011 C-Cup	4	1	5	6	0
2011-12	CWHL Stars de Montréal	17	8	16	24	2	2012 C-Cup	4	2	2	4	4
CWHL Regular Season		85	49	90	139	62	Clarkson Cup	12	5	11	16	8
Totals from all Competitions		**172**	**91**	**147**	**238**	**130**						

CWHL Most Valuable Player in 2009-10... Angela James Bowl in 2009-10... CWHL Top Forward in 2009-10... CWHL First All-Star Team in 2009-10; CWHL Second All-Star Team in 2008-09... scored 100th CWHL point on 2010-02-06

HARDILL, KERRI
LW. 1995-96 COWHL Peterborough #4 (22 games, 3 assists).

HARDING, LESLIE
Forward. 2000 Nationals Team New Brunswick (6 games, 1 assist).

HARDY, GENEVIÈVE
Defence.

Year - League - Team		GP	G	A	PTS	PM
2000-01	NWHL Wingstar de Montréal	13	3	3	6	2
2001-02	NWHL Wingstar de Montréal	26	0	1	1	10
2002-03	NWHL Axion de Montréal	4	1	0	1	0
Totals from all Competitions		**43**	**4**	**4**	**8**	**12**

HARKENSON, NICOLE
Defence. 1999 Nationals Saskatchewan (4 games).

HARMENS, MARTE
Defence. 2005-06 WWHL B.C. #93 (19 gp); 2007-08 CWHL Vaughan #42 (6 gp).

HARMON, SAVANNAH
Forward. Shoots right. #24.

Born 1995-10-27. Grew up in Downers Grove, IL, USA. 5'5". Debut at age 22 on 2018-10-07..

Year - League - Team		GP	G	A	PTS	PM	Year - Playoff	GP	G	A	PTS	PM
2018-19	NWHL/ Buffalo Beauts	16	3	4	7	6	2019 I-Cup	2	0	0	0	2

HARRIGAN (HEAD), JANA
Forward. Shoots right. #19 #11 #27 #32.

Born 1983-7-20, Edmonton, AB, CAN. Grew up in Burlington, ON, CAN. 5'9".

Year - League - Team		GP	G	A	PTS	PM	Year - Playoff	GP	G	A	PTS	PM
2000-01	NWHL Mississauga IceBears	6	1	0	1	2						
2001-02	NWHL Mississauga IceBears	3	0	1	1	2						
2006-07	NWHL Oakville Ice	25	13	3	16	36	2007 NWHL-P	3	3	0	3	4
2007	Nationals Etobicoke Dolphins	7	1	4	5	10						
2007-08	CWHL Burlington Barracudas	27	18	17	35	32	2008 CWHL-P	3	2	1	3	2
2008-09	CWHL Burlington Barracudas	28	19	19	38	26	2009 CWHL-P	4	3	2	5	6
2009-10	CWHL Burlington Barracudas	22	16	21	37	26						
2010-11	CWHL Burlington Barracudas	23	4	4	8	18						

Year - League - Team	GP	G	A	PTS	PM
2011-12 CWHL Burlington Barracudas	23	5	5	10	18
2013-14 CWHL Brampton Thunder	17	1	4	5	10
CWHL Regular Season	140	63	70	133	130
Totals from all Competitions	**191**	**86**	**81**	**167**	**192**

CWHL Central All-Star Team in 2007-08; CWHL Second All-Star Team in 2008-09 and 2009-10... finished 6th in the Angela James Bowl scoring race in 2007-08... scored 100th CWHL point on 2010-01-02

HARRINGTON, PAIGE

Defence. Shoots left. #44.

Isobel Cup winner with Buffalo on 2017-03-19
Born 1993-05-28. Grew up in Mansfield, MA, USA. 5'11". Debut on 2015-10-11.

Year - League - Team	GP	G	A	PTS	PM	Year - Playoff	GP	G	A	PTS	PM
2015-16 NWHL/ Buffalo Beauts	18	0	3	3	12	2016 I-Cup	5	0	0	0	2
2016-17 NWHL/ Buffalo Beauts	17	0	0	0	14	2017 I-Cup	2	0	0	0	0
2017-18 NWHL/ Buffalo Beauts	14	0	3	3	15	2018 I-Cup	1	0	0	0	0
NWHL Regular Season	49	0	6	6	41	Isobel Cup	8	0	0	0	2
Totals from all Competitions	**57**	**0**	**6**	**6**	**43**						

HARRIS, BRIANNE

Defence. #5.

Born 1987-5-4, North Vancouver, BC, CAN.

Year - League - Team	GP	G	A	PTS	PM	Year - Playoff	GP	G	A	PTS	PM
2005-06 WWHL British Columbia Breakers	23	1	1	2	12						
2006-07 WWHL British Columbia Breakers	20	0	2	2	10	2007 WWHL-P	2	0	0	0	2
2007-08 WWHL British Columbia Breakers	24	0	1	1	16						
Totals from all Competitions	**69**	**1**	**4**	**5**	**40**						

HARRIS, DAWN

Forward. #4 #5.

Year - League - Team	GP	G	A	PTS	PM
1995-96 COWHL Peterborough Skyway	27	2	5	7	28
1996-97 COWHL Peterborough Pirates	22	6	5	11	14
Totals from all Competitions	**49**	**8**	**10**	**18**	**42**

HARRIS, FRAN

Defence. 1999 Nationals Saskatchewan (6 games).

HARRIS, MELISSA

Forward. #19.

Year - League - Team	GP	G	A	PTS	PM
2000-01 NWHL Durham Lightning	38	4	8	12	24
2001-02 NWHL Durham Lightning	28	1	2	3	10
Totals from all Competitions	**66**	**5**	**10**	**15**	**34**

HARRIS, SHANNON

Defence. 1995 Nationals Metro Valley Selects.

HARRIS, TARYN

Defence. Shoots right. #18.

Born 1994-11-1. Grew up in Morrison, CO, USA. 5'9". Debut at age 22 on 2017-10-14.

Year - League - Team	GP	G	A	PTS	PM
2017-18 CWHL Boston Blades	24	0	0	0	4
2018-19 CWHL Worcester Blades	26	0	2	2	24

HARRIS, WENDY

Forward. 1995 Nationals PEI Esso Tigers.

HARRIS-MURRAY, SHERRY

Defence.

Year - League - Team	GP	G	A	PTS	PM
1995 Nationals Maritime Sports Blades					
1996 Nationals Maritime Sports Blades	6	0	3	3	2
1998 Nationals Maritime Sports Blades	6	1	1	2	2

HARRISON, RACHEL

Forward. #4 #5.

Year - League - Team	GP	G	A	PTS	PM
1995-96 COWHL Peterborough Skyway	29	2	16	18	6
1996-97 COWHL Peterborough Pirates	34	3	16	19	10
Totals from all Competitions	**63**	**5**	**32**	**37**	**16**

HARRON, LYNN

Defence. #2.

Year - League - Team	GP	G	A	PTS	PM	Year - Playoff	GP	G	A	PTS	PM
2003 Nationals Host Saskatchewan	5	0	0	0	8						
2004-05 WWHL Saskatchewan Prairie Ice	21	0	0	0	8						
2005-06 WWHL Saskatchewan Prairie Ice	22	1	0	1	34	2006 WWHL-P	2	0	0	0	0

HART, KELLY

Forward. Shoots right. #44 #7.

Born 1985-2-15. Grew up in Oakville, ON, CAN. 5'7".

Year - League - Team	GP	G	A	PTS	PM	Year - Playoff	GP	G	A	PTS	PM
2000-01 NWHL Durham Lightning	1	0	0	0	0						
2001-02 NWHL Durham Lightning	3	0	0	0	0						
2007-08 CWHL Burlington Barracudas	30	8	13	21	24	2008 CWHL-P	3	0	1	1	2
2008-09 CWHL Burlington Barracudas	30	11	11	22	18	2009 CWHL-P	4	1	3	4	2
2009-10 CWHL Burlington Barracudas	30	10	24	34	20						
2010-11 CWHL Burlington Barracudas	25	0	7	7	12						
2011-12 CWHL Burlington Barracudas	21	0	4	4	6						
2013-14 CWHL Brampton Thunder	8	1	2	3	2						

CWHL Regular Season	144	30	61	91	82
Totals from all Competitions	**155**	**31**	**65**	**96**	**86**

Finished 8th in the Angela James Bowl scoring race in 2009-10

HART, MARTHA   *Forward. 1995-96 COWHL London Devilettes #2 (21 games, 3 goals, 8 assists).*

HARTE, PATRICIA   *Forward. 1993-94 COWHL Mississauga Chiefs #10 (27 gp, 4 goals, 1 assist).*

HARTNOLL, CHRISTINE   *Markham. F. 2001-02 NWHL Durham (1 gp); 2010-11 CWHL Burlington (3 gp, 1 goal).*

HARTWICK, JESSICA   *Forward/Defence. Shoots right. #18.*

Born 1993-8-3. Grew up in Brampton, ON, CAN. 5'3". Debut at age 23 on 2016-10-8.

Year - League - Team	GP	G	A	PTS	PM	Year - Playoff	GP	G	A	PTS	PM
2016-17 CWHL Brampton Thunder	24	0	1	1	10	2017 C-Cup	2	0	0	0	2
2017-18 CWHL Markham Thunder	25	0	1	1	37						
CWHL Regular Season	49	0	2	2	47	Clarkson Cup	2	0	0	0	2
Totals from all Competitions	**51**	**0**	**2**	**2**	**49**						

HARVEY, NATALIE   *Forward. 2004 Nationals Team New Brunswick (5 gp, 1 goal, 3 assists).*

HATANAKA, AKIKO   *Defence. 2000-01 NWHL Mississauga Ice Bears (32 games, 4 goals, 6 assists).*

HAUCK, CORA-LEE   *Defence. 2002 Nationals Richmond (5 gp); 2002-03 NWHL Vancouver Griffins #5 (3 gp).*

HAWKINS, JACLYN   *Forward. Shoots left. #19 #21.*

Born 1985-2-28, Manotick, ON, CAN. Grew up in Manotick, ON, CAN. 5'8". Debut at age 26 on 2011-1-8.

Year - League - Team	GP	G	A	PTS	PM	Year - Playoff	GP	G	A	PTS	PM
2010-11 CWHL Boston Blades	6	0	0	0	0	2011 CWHL-P	1				
2011-12 CWHL Boston Blades	18	5	6	11	4	2012 C-Cup	3	1	1	2	0
2012-13 CWHL Boston Blades	1	0	0	0	0						
CWHL Regular Season	25	5	6	11	4	Clarkson Cup	3	1	1	2	0

HAWKINS, LYDIA   *Defence. 2000 Nationals Team New Brunswick (6 games).*

HAWRISH, TANYA   *D/F. 1995 Nationals Britannia; 1996 Nationals (5 gp, 5 pts); 2001 Nationals Vancouver Griffins.*

HAYES, JAYNE   *Forward. 2004 Nationals Saskatchewan (6 games, 1 goal).*

HAYNES, ASPEN   *Defence. Shoots left.*

Born 1982-10-07.

Year - League - Team	GP	G	A	PTS	PM	Year - Playoff	GP	G	A	PTS	PM
2003-04 NWHL Calgary Oval X-Treme											
2005-06 WWHL Calgary Oval X-treme	17	0	3	3	2	2007 WWHL-P	0	0	0	0	0
2006 Nationals Calgary Oval X-Treme	2	0	1	1	0						

HAZ, MELANIE

Abby Hoffman Cup winner with Edmonton on 1997-03-09.
Born 1975-11-26, Edmonton, AB, CAN. 5'8".

Year - League - Team	GP	G	A	PTS	PM
1995 Nationals Calgary Classics					
1996 Nationals Edmonton Chimos	7	0	3	3	0
1997 Nationals Edmonton Chimos					
1998 Nationals Edmonton Chimos	7	1	2	3	2

As a soccer goalkeeper, represented Canada at the FIFA Women's World Cup USA 1999.

HE XIN   *Left wing. Shoots right. #10.*

Born 1996-7-24. Grew up in Harbin, CHN. 5'5". Debut at age 21 on 2017-10-28.

Year - League - Team	GP	G	A	PTS	PM
2017-18 CWHL Vanke	28	1	0	1	6

HEAD, FALLON   *Forward. 2002 Nationals Saskatchewan (6 games, 1 assist).*

HEANEY, ANN   *Defence. 1996-97 COWHL London Devilettes #3 (31 games, 1 goal, 1 assist).*

HEANEY, GERALDINE   *Defence. #91.*

Hockey Hall of Fame honoured member, Class of 2013
Olympic champion, IIHF champion. Abby Hoffman Cup winner with Aeros on 1991-03-17, 1993-03-28, 2000-03-12 and 2004-03-14. NWHL Cup winner. Born 1967-10-1. Grew up in Weston, ON, CAN.

Year - League - Team	GP	G	A	PTS	PM	Year - Playoff	GP	G	A	PTS	PM
1992-93 COWHL Toronto Aeros	21	8	12	20	14						
1992-93 COWHL Toronto Aeros	28	13	28	41	27						
1995 Nationals Mississauga Chiefs											
1995-96 COWHL North York Aeros	29	21	28	49	20						
1996 Nationals North York Aeros	5	1	4	5	4						
1996-97 COWHL North York Aeros	32	21	45	66	18						
1997 Nationals Ontario											
1998 Nationals North York Aeros	6	3	3	6	4						
1998-99 NWHL North York Aeros	29	8	25	33	22						
1999 Nationals North York Aeros	5	4	4	8							
1999-00 NWHL North York Aeros	37	13	38	51	18	2000 NWHL-P					
2000 Nationals North York Aeros	6	1	7	8							
2000-01 NWHL North York Aeros	27	8	27	35	25						
2001 Nationals North York Aeros											

Year - League - Team			GP	G	A	PTS	PM	Year - Playoff		GP	G	A	PTS	PM
2002	Nationals	North York Aeros	7	3	2	5	4							
2002-03	NWHL	North York Aeros						2003	NWHL-P					
2003-04	NWHL	Toronto Aeros	32	8	19	27	30	2004	NWHL-P					
2004	Nationals	Toronto Aeros	6	4	3	7	0							
Totals from all Competitions			**270**	**116**	**245**	**361**	**186**							

HEATON, SHEENA   *D. 2006 Nationals British Columbia (6 gp, 1 goal); 2007 Nationals BC Outback (5 gp, 4 assists).*

HEBEL, MANUELA   *Forward. 2010-11 WWHL Edmonton Chimos #77 (16 gp, 2 goals, 1 assist).*

HEBERT, JENNIFER   *Forward. 1998-99 NWHL Laval (33 gp, 1 goal, 4 a.); 1999-00 Sainte-Julie (19 games).*

HEBERT, JULIE   *Forward. 2007-08 CWHL Mississauga #9 (1 game).*

HÉBERT, MONELLE   *Forward. Shoots left.*
Born 1975-12-27. Grew up in Montréal, QC, CAN.

Year - League - Team			GP	G	A	PTS	PM
2000-01	NWHL	Sainte-Julie Panthères	33	13	15	28	44
1995	Nationals	Winnipeg Sweat Camp					
2001	Nationals	Équipe Québec					

HEDLEY, ANN   *Forward. 2001 Nationals Manitoba; 2007 Nationals Manitoba (5 gp).*

HEFFORD, JAYNA   *Forward. Shoots left. #16.*
Hockey Hall of Fame honoured member, Class of 2018
Olympic champion, IIHF champion, CWHL winner.
Born 1977-5-14, Trenton, ON, CAN. Grew up in Kingston, ON, CAN. 5'5".

Year - League - Team			GP	G	A	PTS	PM	Year - Playoff		GP	G	A	PTS	PM
1996-97	COWHL	Mississauga Chiefs	30	32	34	66	20							
1998-99	NWHL	Brampton Thunder	27	34	19	53	30							
1999	Nationals	North York Aeros	5	7	5	12								
1999-00	NWHL	Brampton Thunder	31	25	31	56	53							
2000-01	NWHL	Brampton Thunder	31	36	33	69	36							
2002	Nationals	Brampton Thunder	7	4	6	10	12							
2002-03	NWHL	Brampton Thunder	30	37	25	62	32	2003	NWHL-P	1	0	0	0	6
2003	Nationals	Brampton Thunder	5	7	8	15	2							
2003-04	NWHL	Brampton Thunder	35	41	23	64	42	2004	NWHL-P	5	7	4	11	8
2004-05	NWHL	Brampton Thunder	33	39	34	73	26	2005	NWHL-P	2	2	1	3	0
2005	Nationals	Brampton Thunder	6	10	10	20	6							
2005-06	NWHL	Brampton Thunder	1	0	2	2	0	2006	NWHL-P	5	5	2	7	10
2006-07	NWHL	Brampton Thunder	33	40	30	70	46	2007	NWHL-P	5	2	2	4	12
2007-08	CWHL	Brampton Can.-Thunder	27	26	32	58	56	2008	CWHL-P	3	3	2	5	2
2008	Nationals	Brampton Can.-Thunder	3	2	2	4	6							
2008-09	CWHL	Brampton Thunder	28	44	25	69	36	2009	CWHL-P	2	2		2	2
								2009	C-Cup	2	1	2	3	0
2009-10	CWHL	Brampton Thunder	1	0	0	0	2	2010	C-Cup	2	1	2	3	2
2010-11	CWHL	Brampton Thunder	24	24	22	46	26	2011	CWHL-P	2	1		1	4
								2011	C-Cup	3	0	5	5	4
2011-12	CWHL	Brampton Thunder	27	21	13	34	28	2012	C-Cup	4	1	0	1	6
2012-13	CWHL	Brampton Thunder	21	15	12	27	18	2013	C-Cup	3	0	1	1	4
CWHL Regular Season			**128**	**130**	**104**	**234**	**166**		Clarkson Cup	15	3	10	13	16
Totals from all Competitions			**444**	**469**	**387**	**856**	**537**							

CWHL Most Valuable Player in 2007-08... Angela James Bowl in 2008-09... CWHL goal-scoring leader in 2007-08, 2008-09, 2010-11... CWHL Top Forward in 2008-09... CWHL Central All-Star Team in 2007-08; CWHL First All-Star Team in 2008-09 and 2010-11; CWHL Second All-Star Team in 2011-12 and 2012-13... NWHL Player of the Year in 2004-05... COWHL Rookie of the Year in 1996-97.. Scored 100th CWHL point on 2009-01-17... scored 100th CWHL goal on 2011-12-18... scored 200th CWHL point on 2012-03-03... selected First Decade CWHL Team in 2017

HEGGESTAD, CAILEE   *Forward. 1998 Nationals Saskatchewan (6 gp, 1 goal); 2004 Nationals (6 gp, 1 goal)*

HEGLAND, AMBER   *Forward. 2004-05 WWHL Minnesota (6 gp, 1 goal, 5 a.; 1 playoff gp); 2006-07 (13 gp, 3 a.)*

HEIGHTON, BECKY   *Forward. 1996 Nationals Pictou County (4 games).*

HEINHUIS, MYRIA   *Defence. Shoots right. #27.*
Abby Hoffman Cup winner with Mississauga on 2008-03-15.
Born 1984-8-24. Grew up in Chatham, ON, CAN. 5'10". Debut at age 22 on 2006-9-16.

Year - League - Team			GP	G	A	PTS	PM	Year - Playoff		GP	G	A	PTS	PM
2006-07	NWHL	Mississauga Aeros	33	3	11	14	68	2007	NWHL-P	5	0	1	1	10
2007	Nationals	Mississauga Aeros	6	1	2	3	4							
2007-08	CWHL	Mississauga Chiefs	29	4	12	16	68	2008	CWHL-P	5	0	3	3	36
2008	Nationals	Mississauga Chiefs	3	0	1	1	8							
Totals from all Competitions			**81**	**8**	**30**	**38**	**194**							

HEINRICHS, KENDRA   *Forward. 2006 Nationals Manitoba (5 gp, 2 goals); 2007 Nationals (4 gp, 1 assist).*

HEINTZ, KYLE   *Forward. 2004-05 WWHL Saskatchewan Prairie Ice #11 (18 games, 2 goals, 3 assists).*

HEITT, CANDACE   *Forward. 2004-05 WWHL Saskatchewan Prairie Ice #21 (21 games, 1 assist).*

HEITZMAN, MELISSA *Defence. 2000-01 NWHL Brampton Thunder #21 (13 gp, 6 goals, 3 assists).*

HEMPEL, JENNIFER *2004-05 WWHL Minnesota Whitecaps #3 (7 games).*

HEMPHILL, BRENDA *Forward. Shoots left.*
Born 1971-02-25. Grew up in Montréal, QC, CAN.

Year - League - Team			GP	G	A	PTS	PM
1998	Nationals	Prince Edward Island	5	2	1	3	2
1999	Nationals	Prince Edward Island	5	3	0	3	
2000	Nationals	Prince Edward Island	5	0	2	2	
2001	Nationals	PEI Humpty Dumpty					
2002	Nationals	PEI Humpty Dumpty	6	0	1	1	0
2005	Nationals	Prince Edward Island	5	1	1	2	0

HENDRICKSON, CHERIE *Defence/Forward. Shoots right. #25 #24.*
Clarkson Cup winner with Boston on 2013-03-23
Born 1986-1-23. Grew up in Boxford, MA, USA. 5'7". Debut at age 23 on 2008-10-5.

Year - League - Team			GP	G	A	PTS	PM	Year - Playoff		GP	G	A	PTS	PM
2008-09	CWHL	Burlington Barracudas	27	2	9	11	6	2009	CWHL-P	4	1		1	
2009-10	CWHL	Burlington Barracudas	16	1	3	4	16							
2010-11	CWHL	Boston Blades	21	0	0	0	14	2011	CWHL-P	2		2		
2011-12	CWHL	Boston Blades	21	0	1	1	8	2012	C-Cup	3	0	0	0	0
2012-13	CWHL	Boston Blades	20	2	5	7	10	2013	C-Cup	4	0	0	0	0
2015-16	NWHL/	Boston Pride	3	0	0	0	0							
CWHL Regular Season			105	5	18	23	54	Clarkson Cup		7	0	0	0	0
Totals from all Competitions			**121**	**6**	**18**	**24**	**56**							

HENNIGAR, ALYSSA *Defence. 2008 Nationals Nova Scotia Selects (5 games).*

HENRY, ASHLEY *Defence. 2007 Nationals British Columbia (5 games, 1 assist).*

HENRY, EMILY *Defence. 2006-07 WWHL Saskatchewan Prairie Ice #4 (21 games, 3 assists).*

HERMAN, KALEY *Forward. 2009-10 WWHL Strathmore #7 (16 gp, 5 goals, 9 a.); 2010-11 (11 gp, 1 goal, 3 a.).*

HERN, JACLYN *Defence. 2004-05 WWHL Saskatchewan #15 (19 gp); 2005-06 (17 gp, 1 assist; 1 playoff gp).*

HERON, COURTNEY *Forward. 2009-10 WWHL Edmonton Chimos #17 (12 games, 1 assist).*

HERR, JULIA CHEEKY *Forward. Shoots left. #20.*
Born 1993-11-27. Grew up in Princeton, NJ, USA. 5'3". Debut at age 22 on 2016-11-20.

Year - League - Team			GP	G	A	PTS	PM
2016-17	NWHL/	New York Riveters	2	0	0	0	0
2017-18	NWHL/	Metropolitan Riveters	3	0	0	0	0

HERRINGTON, TIFFANY *Defence. 1996-97 COWHL Peterborough #10 (36 games, 13 goals, 16 assists).*

HERSIKOM, DENISE *Defence. 1996 Nationals Saskatchewan (5 games).*

HEUCHERT, LEANNE *Forward. Shoots left.*
Born 1982-04-22. Grew up in Winnipeg, MB, CAN.

Year - League - Team			GP	G	A	PTS	PM
2001	Nationals	University of Manitoba					
2002	Nationals	University of Manitoba	5	0	0	0	6
2003	Nationals	University of Winnipeg	4	1	0	1	4
2004	Nationals	Manitoba	5	2	0	2	4

HEUKSHORST, ELISA *F. 1996 Nationals Pictou County (4 gp, 1 goal); 2000 Nationals Nova Scotia (6 gp, 3 goals).*

HEWINGS, MEG *Right wing. #6 #19.*

Year - League - Team			GP	G	A	PTS	PM
2000-01	NWHL	Wingstar de Montréal	37	4	5	9	2
2006-07	NWHL	Avalanche du Québec	3	0	0	0	2
Totals from all Competitions			**40**	**4**	**5**	**9**	**4**

Has served as general manager with CWHL Montréal

HEWITT, AMY *Defence. #93 #12.*

Year - League - Team			GP	G	A	PTS	PM
1998-99	NWHL	Ottawa Raiders	34	3	6	9	26
1999-00	NWHL	Ottawa Raiders	29	0	4	4	24
Totals from all Competitions			**63**	**3**	**10**	**13**	**50**

HEWITT, NICOLE *Forward. 1998 Nationals Tazmanian Devils (5 games).*

HEYES, KRISTINA *Defence. 2000-01 NWHL Ottawa Raiders #3 (6 games).*

HEYWOOD, CHELSEA *Forward. 2003 Nationals Saskatchewan (6 games, 1 goal, 2 assists).*

HEYS, JACQUIE *Defence. 1993-94 COWHL Toronto Jr. Aeros #15 (26 games, 4 assists).*

HICKEL, TORI *Defence. Shoots right. #3.*
Clarkson Cup winner with Calgary on 2019-03-24.
Born 1994-03-04. Grew up in Anchorage, AK, USA. 5'4'. Debut at age 24 on 2018-10-13.

Year - League - Team			GP	G	A	PTS	PM	Year - Playoff		GP	G	A	PTS	PM
2018-19	CWHL	Calgary Inferno	27	1	4	5	6	2019	C-Cup	4	0	0	0	0

HICKEL, ZOE
Forward. Shoots right. #44.

Isobel Cup winner with Boston on 2016-03-12. Clarkson Cup winner with Calgary on 2019-03-24.
Born 1992-07-10, Anchorage, AK, USA. 5'6". Debut at age 23 on 2015-10-11.

Year - League - Team			GP	G	A	PTS	PM	Year - Playoff	GP	G	A	PTS	PM
2015-16	NWHL/	Boston Pride	15	3	4	7	14	2016 I-Cup	4	1	3	4	4
2016-17	NWHL/	Boston Pride	12	1	5	6	8						
2016-17	NWHL/	Connecticut Whale	4	3	0	3	6	2017 I-Cup	1	0	0	0	0
2017-18	CWHL	Kunlun Red Star	28	12	26	38	16	2018 C-Cup	4	0	1	1	6
2018-19	CWHL	Calgary Inferno	24	7	16	23	10	2019 C-Cup	4	2	2	4	4
CWHL Regular Season			52	19	42	61	26	Clarkson Cup	8	2	3	5	10
NWHL Regular Season			31	7	9	16	28	Isobel Cup	5	1	3	4	4
Totals from all Competitions			**96**	**29**	**57**	**86**	**68**						

CWHL Second All-Star Team in 2017-18... finished 5th in the Angela James Bowl scoring race in 2017-18

HICKEY, SHANNON
Forward. Shoots right. #71.

Born 1995-08-24. Grew up in Arlington, MA, USA. 5'11". Debut at age 23 on 2018-10-13.

Year - League - Team		GP	G	A	PTS	PM
2018-19	CWHL Worcester Blades	24	0	0	0	4

HICKOX, RANDI *Defence. 1996-97 COWHL North York #92 (1 gp); 1998-99 NWHL Brampton (39 gp, 16 assists).*

HIGGINS, STEPHANIE *Cornwall, ON, CAN. Forward. 2008-09 CWHL Ottawa #25 (3 games, 1 goal).*

HILDERMAN, TANIELLE *Forward. 2003 Nationals Saskatchewan (6 games, 1 assist).*

HILL, CARLY
Defence. Shoots right. #7 #16 #6.

Clarkson Cup winner with Montréal on 2012-03-25 and 2017-03-05.
Born 1986-3-6, Beaconsfield, QC, CAN. Grew up in Pointe-Claire, QC, CAN. 5'6". Debut at age 20 on 2005-12-17.

Year - League - Team			GP	G	A	PTS	PM	Year - Playoff	GP	G	A	PTS	PM
2005-06	NWHL	Avalanche du Québec	2	0	1	1	0						
2011-12	CWHL	Stars de Montréal	22	1	6	7	22	2012 C-Cup	4	0	4	4	2
2012-13	CWHL	Stars de Montréal	23	0	12	12	18	2013 C-Cup	4	0	0	0	0
2013-14	CWHL	Montréal	20	1	8	9	6	2014 C-Cup	3	0	0	0	0
2014-15	CWHL	Stars de Montréal	14	0	1	1	2	2015 C-Cup	3	0	3	3	2
2015-16	CWHL	Canadiennes de Montréal	22	0	6	6	8	2016 C-Cup	3	0	0	0	0
2016-17	CWHL	Canadiennes de Montréal	18	0	10	10	16	2017 C-Cup	3	0	0	0	0
CWHL Regular Season			119	2	43	45	72	Clarkson Cup	20	0	7	7	4
Totals from all Competitions			**141**	**2**	**51**	**53**	**76**						

HILL, JAMIE *2002-03 NWHL Durham Lightning #17 (? games).*

HILL, LAUREL *Huntsville, ON. Defence. 2014-15 CWHL Toronto (14 gp, 1 assist; C-Cup 2 gp); 2015-16 (9 gp).*

HINKS, WENDY *1992-93 COWHL Guelph #17 (14 gp, 1 goal, 2 a.); 1993-94 COWHL Miss. (27 gp, 7 goals, 2 a.).*

HOBSON, SUSAN
Centre. Shoots right. #24.

Abby Hoffman Cup winner with Aeros on 2005-03-13.
Born 1982-2-12. Grew up in Mississauga, ON, CAN. 5'9".

Year - League - Team			GP	G	A	PTS	PM
2004-05	NWHL	Toronto Aeros	36	14	14	28	38
2005	Nationals	Toronto Aeros	7	5	5	10	2
2005-06	NWHL	Toronto Aeros	31	7	17	24	40
Totals from all Competitions			**74**	**26**	**36**	**62**	**80**

HODGKINSON, VICKI *Forward. 2001-02 NWHL Ottawa Raiders #11 (27 games, 1 goal, 6 assists).*

HOFFMEYER, LEXIE
Defence. Shoots right. #18.

Clarkson Cup winner with Toronto on 2014-03-22
Born 1988-8-23, Grand Blanc, MI, USA. Grew up in Dettroit, MI, USA. 5'4". Debut at age 22 on 2010-10-23.

Year - League - Team			GP	G	A	PTS	PM	Year - Playoff	GP	G	A	PTS	PM
2010-11	CWHL	Toronto Furies	25	1	5	6	22	2011 CWHL-P	2				
								2011 C-Cup	4	0	0	0	0
2011-12	CWHL	Toronto Furies	27	4	3	7	32	2012 C-Cup	3	0	0	0	4
2012-13	CWHL	Toronto Furies	22	1	2	3	38	2013 C-Cup	3	0	0	0	2
2013-14	CWHL	Toronto Furies	23	1	3	4	33	2014 C-Cup	4	0	0	0	12
2014-15	CWHL	Toronto Furies	23	0	1	1	16	2015 C-Cup	2	0	0	0	0
CWHL Regular Season			120	7	14	21	141	Clarkson Cup	16	0	0	0	18
Totals from all Competitions			**138**	**7**	**14**	**21**	**159**						

Has served as assistant coach with CWHL Toronto

HOFFMAN, PAM
Forward. #7 #26.

Year - League - Team			GP	G	A	PTS	PM	Year - Playoff	GP	G	A	PTS	PM
2001-02	NWHL	Mississauga IceBears	2	0	0	0	0						
2002-03	NWHL	Durham Lightning											
2003-04	NWHL	Durham Lightning	18	1	0	1	4						

HOGAN, ANNIE *Medford, MA, USA. F. 2010-11 CWHL Boston #91 (22 gp, 3 goals, 3 assists; playoffs 2gp).*

HOGAN, ASHTON *Elmira, ON, CAN. Forward. 2015-16 CWHL Toronto Furies #16 (22 gp, 2 goals, 3 assists).*

HOGG, KELLY *Forward. 2003 Nationals Team New Brunswick (4 games).*

HOLDER, MELISSA *Forward. #77. #6. #51.*

Year - League - Team		GP	G	A	PTS	PM
1996-97	COWHL Newtonbrook Panthers	8	2	5	7	10
1999	Nationals Calgary Oval X-Treme	6	0	1	1	
1999-00	NWHL Brampton Thunder	2	2	0	2	0

HOLLAND, JODI *Forward. 2010-11 Manitoba Maple Leafs #17 (9 games, 4 goals, 3 assists).*

HOLLDORF, CARRIE *Forward. Shoots left. #33.*
Born 1982-11-6, New Richmond, WI, USA. Grew up in Glenwood City, WI, USA. 5'7".

Year - League - Team		GP	G	A	PTS	PM	Year - Playoff	GP	G	A	PTS	PM
2005-06	WWHL Minnesota Whitecaps	23	5	14	19	10	2006 WWHL-P	3	4	3	7	0
2006-07	WWHL Minnesota Whitecaps	22	2	3	5	10	2007 WWHL-P	3	0	1	1	0
2007-08	WWHL Minnesota Whitecaps	10	1	2	3	4						
2008	Nationals Minnesota Whitecaps	3	0	0	0	2						
Totals from all Competitions		**64**	**12**	**23**	**35**	**26**						

HOLLIDAY, LEAH *Defence. 1995 Nationals Regina Sharks.*

HOLMES, MICHELLE *D. 1992-93 COWHL Guelph (14 gp, 3 assists); 1993-94 Mississauga (26 gp, 2 assists).*

HOLMES, MICHELLE *Defence.*

Year - League - Team		GP	G	A	PTS	PM	Year - Playoff	GP	G	A	PTS	PM
1992-93	COWHL Guelph Eagles	14	0	3	3	4						
1993-94	COWHL Mississauga Chiefs	26	0	2	2	16						
1995	Nationals Mississauga Chiefs											
1995-96	COWHL Mississauga Chiefs	0	0	0	0	0						

HOLMES-DOMAGALA, SAMANTHA *Forward. Shoots right. #8 #20.*
Abby Hoffman Cup winner with Calgary on 2003-03-16.
WWHL winner. Born 1977-6-23. Grew up in Mississauga, ON, CAN.

Year - League - Team		GP	G	A	PTS	PM	Year - Playoff	GP	G	A	PTS	PM
2000-01	NWHL Brampton Thunder	33	18	15	33	34						
2002-03	NWHL Calgary Oval X-Treme	24	13	11	24	20	2003 NWHL-P					
2003	Nationals Calgary Oval X-Treme	5	4	3	7	2						
2003-04	NWHL Calgary Oval X-Treme	12	4	11	15	16	2004 NWHL-P	4	3	3	6	0
2004	Nationals Calgary Oval X-Treme	6	2	1	3	0						
2004-05	WWHL Calgary Oval X-Treme	21	15	16	31	18	2005 WWHL-P	3	0	1	1	0
2007-08	WWHL Strathmore Rockies	22	5	4	9	16						
2008-09	WWHL Strathmore Rockies	19	3	3	6	30	2009 WWHL-P	1	0	0	0	2
2009-10	WWHL Strathmore Rockies	13	5	3	8	16						
Totals from all Competitions		**163**	**72**	**71**	**143**	**154**						

CWHL Humanitarian Award in 2012-13

HOLT, JESSICA *Defence. 2006 Nationals Team New Brunswick (7 games).*

HOLUBOWICH, SHARON *Defence. 1996 Nationals Britannia Blues (5 games, 2 goals, 2 assists).*

HOLZE, TAYLOR *Forward. Shoots right. #24.*
Born 1990-12-19. Grew up in Lynbrook, NY, USA. 5'4". Debut at age 24 on 2015-10-11.

Year - League - Team		GP	G	A	PTS	PM	Year - Playoff	GP	G	A	PTS	PM
2015-16	NWHL/ New York Riveters	7	0	1	1	2	2016 I-Cup	2	0	0	0	0
2016-17	NWHL/ New York Riveters	9	1	0	1	4						

HOMANS, ROBYN *2000 Nationals Nova Scotia Selects (? games).*

HOOGSTRATEN, LINDSAY *2008-09 CWHL Burlington (2 games, 1 assist; 3 playoff games).*

HOOVER, ANGIE *LW. 1995-96 COWHL Peterborough Skyway #42 (2 games).*

HOOVER, JAN *Centre. 1992-93 COWHL Scarborough (10 gp, 2 goals, 2 assists); 1996-97 Newtonbrook (1 gp).*

HOPKINS, NADINE *Forward. 1998 Nationals Nova Scotia (5 games, 1 goal); 2000 Nationals (6 games).*

HORNSBY, JULIE *Forward. 2000-01 NWHL Montréal #5 (10 games, 3 goals, 5 assists).*

HORROCKS, KIM *Forward. 2000 Nationals U. Manitoba (5 games, 1 assist).*

HORWOOD, KRISTEN *Forward. 1995 Nationals Britannia Blues; 1996 Nationals Britannia (5 games).*

HOSOYAMADA, AKANE *Defence. Shoots right. #14.*
Born 1992-9-3. Grew up in Banff, AB, CAN. 5'4". Debut at age 24 on 2016-11-26.

Year - League - Team		GP	G	A	PTS	PM
2016-17	CWHL Calgary Inferno	5	0	2	2	4

HOSSIE, HEATHER *2001-02 NWHL Ottawa Raiders #9 (2 games).*

HOU YUE *Defence. Shoots right. #19.*
Born 1998-2-9. Grew up in Harbin, CHN. 5'4". Debut at age 19 on 2017-10-28.

Year - League - Team		GP	G	A	PTS	PM
2017-18	CWHL Kunlun Red Star	2	0	0	0	0
2017-18	CWHL Vanke	28	0	0	0	22

HOUDE, KIM *Forward. Shoots left. #18.*
Born 1979-01-29. Grew up in Winnipeg, MB, CAN. 5'8".

Year - League - Team		GP	G	A	PTS	PM
2006	Nationals Manitoba	5	5	6	11	6
2007	Nationals Manitoba	5	2	8	10	6
2009-10	CWHL Mississauga Chiefs	1	0	0	0	0

HOULDEN, JEN *2000-01 NWHL Toronto Sting #20 (10 games, 1 assist).*

HOVI, VENLA *Forward. Shoots left. #7.*
Clarkson Cup winner with Calgary on 2019-03-24.
Born 1987-10-28, Tampere, FIN. 5'7". North American debut at age 30 on 2018-10-13.

Year - League - Team		GP	G	A	PTS	PM	Year - Playoff	GP	G	A	PTS	PM
2018-19	CWHL Calgary Inferno	25	4	10	14	4	2019 C-Cup	4	0	0	0	2

HOWALD, SARAH *Defence. Shoots right.*
Born 1974-10-31. Grew up in Regina, SK, CAN.

Year - League - Team		GP	G	A	PTS	PM
1998	Nationals Saskatchewan Selects	6	3	0	3	8
1999	Nationals Saskatchewan Selects	4	0	3	3	
2001	Nationals Saskatchewan Selects					
2003	Nationals Saskatchewan	6	1	3	4	0

HOWARD, BRITTANY *Forward. Shoots right. #3.*
Born 1995-11-20. Grew up in St. Thomas, ON, CAN. 5'4". Debut at age 22 on 2018-10-13.

Year - League - Team		GP	G	A	PTS	PM	Year - Playoff	GP	G	A	PTS	PM
2018-19	CWHL Toronto Furies	25	5	8	13	20	2019 C-Cup	3	0	0	0	4

HOWARD, LINDSEY *RW. 1995-96 COWHL London (29 games, 1 assisst); 1996-97 (3 games).*

HOYLE-LEVY, CHARDE *Forward. 2009-10 CWHL Vaughan Flames #18 (2 games).*

HRADSKY, AMELIA *Calgary, AB. Forward. 2007-08 WWHL Strathmore #98 (21 gp, 6 goals, 2 assists).*

HUBBARD, JENNIFER *Forward. 2007 Nationals Manitoba (5 games).*

HUDSON, JANET *Defence. 1992-93 COWHL Scarborough (18 gp, 1 assist); 1993-94 (27 gp, 3 goals, 13 assists).*

HUERTAS, MEGHAN *Forward. Shoots left. #43.*
Born 1992-7-30. Grew up in Boynton Beach, FL, USA. 5'6". Debut at age 24 on 2017-1-7.

Year - League - Team		GP	G	A	PTS	PM	Year - Playoff	GP	G	A	PTS	PM
2016-17	NWHL/ Connecticut Whale	9	1	3	4	14	2017 I-Cup	1	0	0	0	0
2017-18	NWHL/ Connecticut Whale	7	2	2	4	6						

HUGHES, ASHLEY *Forward. 2000-01 NWHL Brampton #18 (1 game); 2004-05 #34 (1 game).*

HUGHES, KAREN *1992-93 Scarborough Sting #11 (4 games, 1 assist).*

HUGHSON, SARAH *Forward. Shoots left. #24.*
Born 1995-01-02. Grew up in East Haddam, CT, USA. 5'4". Debut at age 23 on 2018-10-07.

Year - League - Team		GP	G	A	PTS	PM	Year - Playoff	GP	G	A	PTS	PM
2018-19	NWHL/ Connecticut Whale	12	0	0	0	4	2019 I-Cup	1	0	0	0	0

NWHL Foundation Award in 2018-19

HUIZINGH, RANDALL *Defence. 2001-02 NWHL Mississauga #28 (27 games, 3 assists).*

HULSHOF, TRINA *Right wins. Shoots right. #14 #12 #18.*
Born 1983-5-4. Grew up in Cedar Valley, ON, CAN. 5'4".

Year - League - Team		GP	G	A	PTS	PM
2001-02	NWHL Durham Lightning	13	0	1	1	2
2002-03	NWHL Durham Lightning					
2005-06	NWHL Toronto Aeros	35	5	8	13	28

HUNT, SAMANTHA *Calgary, AB. Forward. 2011-12 CWHL Alberta #71 (15 games, 5 goals, 9 assists).*

HUNTER, ANDRIA *Forward. #11 #12 #55 #25.*
IIHF champion. Born 1967-12-22, Peterborough, ON, CAN. 5'6".

Year - League - Team		GP	G	A	PTS	PM
1993-94	COWHL Scarborough Firefighters	24	13	19	32	4
1995-96	COWHL Toronto Red Wings	10	1	6	7	2
1996-97	COWHL Newtonbrook Panthers	6	6	9	15	0
1997-98	COWHL Mississauga Chiefs	17	7	7	14	0
1998-99	NWHL Mississauga Chiefs	40	20	21	41	2
1999-00	NWHL Mississauga Chiefs	37	20	29	49	0
2000-01	NWHL Mississauga IceBears	39	18	27	45	0
2001-02	NWHL Mississauga IceBears	30	17	21	38	8
Totals from all Competitions		**203**	**102**	**139**	**241**	**16**

HUNTER, MEGHAN *Forward. Shoots left. #89 #8.*
Born 1981-4-20. Grew up in Oil Springs, ON, CAN. 5'9". Debut at age 26 on 2007-10-6.

Year - League - Team		GP	G	A	PTS	PM
2007-08	CWHL Vaughan Flames	3	2	0	2	4
2011-12	CWHL Alberta	4	1	0	1	2
2012-13	CWHL Alberta	2	0	0	0	4

HURLBURT, LESLIE — *2001-02 NWHL Durham Lightning #58 (1 game).*

HURREN, BETH — *Defence. 2002-03 NWHL Durham Lightning #4 (? games).*

HUSSEY, MELISSA — *1996-97 COWHL Scarborough #88 (3 games, 1 goal).*

HUSTLER, CORINNE — *Defence. 1993-94 COWHL Scarb. (30 gp, 3 assists); 1995-96 Toronto (23 gp, 8 assists).*

HUSTLER, SANDY *Defence. #55 #5.*

Year - League - Team		GP	G	A	PTS	PM
1992-93	COWHL Guelph Eagles	5	0	0	0	0
1993-94	COWHL Scarborough Sting	28	6	1	7	18
1995-96	COWHL Toronto Red Wings	27	5	6	11	16
1996-97	COWHL Scarborough Sting	6	0	0	0	2
Totals from all Competitions		**66**	**11**	**7**	**18**	**36**

HUTCHINSON, TERESA *F. 1996-97 COWHL Newtonbrook (2 gp, 1 goal, 1 assist); 1997-98 Scarb. (15 gp, 2 goals).*

HUYGHEBAERT, DEANA *Defence. 1996 Nationals Saskatchewan (5 gp); 2001 Nationals Saskatchewan.*

HYLWA, LINDSEY *Forward. Shoots right. #45.*
Born 1994-6-14. Grew up in Cary, NC, USA. 5'9". Debut at age 2017-10-28.

Year - League - Team		GP	G	A	PTS	PM
2017-18	NWHL/ Metropolitan Riveters	5	0	0	0	0

IAFALLO, JULIANNA *Forward. Shoots left. #18.*
Born 1996-03-30. Grew up in Eden, NY, USA. 5'8". Debut at age 22 on 2018-10-07.

Year - League - Team		GP	G	A	PTS	PM	Year - Playoff		GP	G	A	PTS	PM
2018-19	NWHL/ Buffalo Beauts	16	6	7	13	4	2019	I-Cup	2	0	0	0	2

INSALACO, KIM *Defence. Shoots left. #10.*
IIHF champion. Born 1980-11-4, Rochester, NY, USA. 5'6".

Year - League - Team		GP	G	A	PTS	PM	Year - Playoff		GP	G	A	PTS	PM
2003-04	NWHL Oakville Ice	25	10	9	19	40							
2004-05	NWHL Oakville Ice	30	6	7	13	34							
2005-06	NWHL Oakville Ice	1	0	0	0	0	2006	NWHL-P	0	0	0	0	0
Totals from all Competitions		**56**	**16**	**16**	**32**	**74**							

IRELAND, C.J. *Forward. Shoots left. #17.*
Born 1980-6-23, Capreol, ON, CAN. 5'6". Debut at age 26 on 2006-11-4.

Year - League - Team		GP	G	A	PTS	PM	Year - Playoff		GP	G	A	PTS	PM
2006-07	NWHL Ottawa Raiders	22	3	7	10	12	2007	NWHL-P	2	0	2	2	0
2007-08	CWHL Ottawa Capital Canucks	25	3	8	11	34							
2008-09	CWHL Ottawa Senators	27	1	8	9	24	2009	CWHL-P	2		2		
2009-10	CWHL Ottawa Senators	28	3	10	13	28							
CWHL Regular Season		80	7	26	33	86							
Totals from all Competitions		**106**	**10**	**35**	**45**	**100**							

IRONSIDE, ANDREA *Forward. Shoots right. #66.*
Born 1987-8-27. Grew up in Collingwood, ON, CAN. 5'4". Debut at age 23 on 2010-10-23.

Year - League - Team		GP	G	A	PTS	PM	Year - Playoff		GP	G	A	PTS	PM
2010-11	CWHL Brampton Thunder	21	5	7	12	8	2011	CWHL-P	2		2		
							2011	C-Cup	3	0	0	0	0
2011-12	CWHL Brampton Thunder	25	3	3	6	16	2012	C-Cup	4	1	1	2	0
CWHL Regular Season		46	8	10	18	24	Clarkson Cup		7	1	1	2	0
Totals from all Competitions		**55**	**9**	**11**	**20**	**26**							

IRVEN, KAYLA *Winchester, ON, CAN. Forward. 2006-07 NWHL Ottawa Raiders #24 (2 games, 1 goal).*

IRVINE, BECKY *Forward.*
Born 1984-05-09.

Year - League - Team		GP	G	A	PTS	PM	Year - Playoff		GP	G	A	PTS	PM
2000	Nationals Nova Scotia Selects			2	2								
2001	Nationals Nova Scotia Selects												
2002	Nationals Nova Scotia	5	1	1	2	4							
2008-09	WWHL Strathmore Rockies	13	1	3	4	9	2009	WWHL-P	1	0	0	0	2

IRVINE, LINDA *Defence. Shoots left.*
Born 1963-07-09. Grew up in Summerside, PE, CAN.

Year - League - Team		GP	G	A	PTS	PM	Year - Playoff		GP	G	A	PTS	PM
1995	Nationals PEI Esso Tigers												
1996	Nationals PEI Esso Tigers	4	0	0	0	4							
1998	Nationals Prince Edward Island	5	0	0	0	2							
1999	Nationals Prince Edward Island	5	0	2	2								
2000	Nationals Prince Edward Island	5	1	1	2								
2001	Nationals PEI Humpty Dumpty												
2002	Nationals PEI Humpty Dumpty	6	0	0	0	2							

IRWIN, HALEY *Forward. Shoots left. #98 #16 #21 #12.*
Olympic champion. Abby Hoffman Cup winner with Aeros on 2005-03-13.
Born 1988-6-6, Thunder Bay, ON, CAN. 5'7".

Year - League - Team		GP	G	A	PTS	PM	Year - Playoff	GP	G	A	PTS	PM
2004-05	NWHL Toronto Aeros	0	0	0	0	0	2005 NWHL-P					
2005	Nationals Toronto Aeros	7	4	3	7	12						
2005-06	NWHL Toronto Aeros	7	9	6	15	6						
2006-07	NWHL Mississauga Aeros	27	20	21	41	36	2007 NWHL-P	5	0	1	1	2
2007	Nationals Mississauga Aeros	6	7	4	11	6						
2012-13	CWHL Stars de Montréal	20	10	11	21	16	2013 C-Cup	4	1	1	2	10
2014-15	CWHL Calgary Inferno	13	8	12	20	2	2015 C-Cup	0	0	0	0	0
2016-17	CWHL Calgary Inferno	19	3	7	10	14	2017 C-Cup	4	2	0	2	2
CWHL Regular Season		52	21	30	51	32	Clarkson Cup	8	3	1	4	12
Totals from all Competitions		**112**	**64**	**66**	**130**	**106**						

Finished 11th in the Angela James Bowl scoring race in 2012-13

ISEN, CELINA
1996-97 COWHL London Devilettes #41 (4 games, 1 goal, 2 assists).

IV YUE
Right wing. Shoots right. #17.

Born 1995-5-30. Grew up in Harbin, CHN. 5'5". Debut at age 22 on 2017-10-28.

Year - League - Team		GP	G	A	PTS	PM
2017-18	CWHL Vanke Rays	28	0	0	0	4

JACK, AMY
Forward. #26 #16 #11.

Born 1984-3-30, Cheltenham, ON, CAN. 5'8".

Year - League - Team		GP	G	A	PTS	PM	Year - Playoff	GP	G	A	PTS	PM
2000-01	NWHL Brampton Thunder	2	0	1	1	0						
2007-08	CWHL Vaughan Flames	26	3	5	8	22	2008 CWHL-P	2	0	0	0	5
2008-09	CWHL Vaughan Flames	13	3	2	5							

Year - League - Team		GP	G	A	PTS	PM	Year - Playoff	GP	G	A	PTS	PM
2009-10	CWHL Vaughan Flames	10	1	4	5	8						
2011-12	CWHL Toronto Furies	4	0	0	0	0						
CWHL Regular Season		53	7	11	18	30						
Totals from all Competitions		**57**	**7**	**12**	**19**	**35**						

JACQUARD-SOWA, JAIMI
Forward. 2004-05 WWHL British Columbia #5 (21 games, 2 goals, 5 assists).

JACQUES, MELISSA
Forward. 2010-11 WWHL Manitoba Maple Leafs #13 (6 games, 4 goals, 4 assists).

JAFFRAY, ASHLEY
Forward. 2008 Nationals Manitoba (5 games, 3 goals, 2 assists).

JAFKA, KATHERINE
Forward. 1998-99 NWHL Brampton Thunder #66 (2 games).

JAILLET, CHANTAL
Defence. Shoots right.

Born 1987-03-15. Grew up in St-Edouard-de-Kent, NB, CAN.

Year - League - Team		GP	G	A	PTS	PM	Year - Playoff	GP	G	A	PTS	PM
2003	Nationals Team New Brunswick	4	0	0	0	0						
2004	Nationals Team New Brunswick	5	0	2	2	0						
2005	Nationals Team New Brunswick	6	0	6	6	0						

JAILLETT, NADINE
Forward. Shoots right.

Born 1975-05-30. Grew up in Bouctouche, NB, CAN.

Year - League - Team		GP	G	A	PTS	PM	Year - Playoff	GP	G	A	PTS	PM
1995	Nationals Maritime Sports Blades											
1996	Nationals Maritime Sports Blades	6	0	0	0	4						
1998	Nationals Maritime Sports Blades	6	3	3	6	2						
1999	Nationals Team New Brunswick	6	1	2	3							
2000	Nationals Team New Brunswick	6		3	3							
2001	Nationals Team New Brunswick											

JAMES, ANGELA
Forward. #8.

Hockey Hall of Fame honoured member, Class of 2010
IIHF champion. Abby Hoffman Cup winner with Aeros on 1991-03-17, 1993-03-28 and 2000-03-12. NWHL Cup winner. Born 1964-12-22. Grew up in Thornhill, ON, CAN. 5'6".

Year - League - Team		GP	G	A	PTS	PM	Year - Playoff	GP	G	A	PTS	PM
1992-93	COWHL Toronto Aeros	23	16	18	34	67						
1993-94	COWHL Toronto Aeros	28	40	30	70	41						
1995-96	COWHL Toronto Red Wings	29	35	35	70	37						
1996-97	COWHL Newtonbrook Panthers	28	29	29	58	57						
1997-98	COWHL North York Aeros	9	6	3	9	19						
1998	Nationals North York Aeros	6	2	2	4	8						
1998-99	NWHL North York Aeros	31	36	19	55	47						
1999	Nationals North York Aeros	5	3	5	8							
1999-00	NWHL North York Aeros	27	22	22	44	10	2000 NWHL-P					
2000	Nationals North York Aeros	6	5	6	11							
2000-01	NWHL North York Aeros	18	7	17	24	22						
2004-05	NWHL Toronto Aeros	2	0	0	0	4						
Totals from all Competitions		**212**	**201**	**186**	**387**	**312**						

COWHL scoring champion in 1992-93, 1993-94, 1995-96... NWHL goal-scoring champion in 1998-99

JANIGA, EMILY   *Forward. Shoots right. #4.*

Isobel Cup winner with Buffalo on 2017-03-19
Born 1994-3-4. Grew up in East Aurora, NY, USA. 5'8". Debut at age 22 on 2016-10-7.

Year - League - Team		GP	G	A	PTS	PM	Year - Playoff	GP	G	A	PTS	PM
2016-17	NWHL/ Buffalo Beauts	17	6	5	11	8	2017 I-Cup	2	3	1	4	2
2017-18	CWHL Vanke Rays	28	8	6	14	26						
2018-19	NWHL/ Buffalo Beauts	16	4	2	6	14	2019 I-Cup	2	1	0	1	0
Totals from all Competitions		**65**	**22**	**14**	**36**	**50**						

JANUS, MICHELLE   *Forward. 2009-10 CWHL Burlington #88 (28 games, 3 goals, 5 assists).*

JANUSC, MORGAN   *D. 1999-00 NWHL Mississauga (2 gp, 1 goal, 2 a.); 2000-01 (3 gp); 2001-02 North York (1 gp).*

JACQUES, MELISSA   *Forward. 2004 Nationals Manitoba (5 games, 6 goals, 2 assists).*

JARDINE, KELLY   *Forward. 2003 Nationals Host Saskatchewan (5 games, 1 goal, 1 assist).*

JARRELL, JACKIE   *Belleville, ON. Forward. 2002-03 NWHL Durham Lightning #9 (? games).*

JARVIS, DARCIE   *2001-02 NWHL Durham Lightning #58 (1 game).*

JAWORSKI, ALEX   *Cambridge, ON, CAN. Forward. 2009-10 CWHL Burlington #15 (2 games).*

JEDDRY, DANIELLE   *Defence. 1995 Nationals Metro Valley Selects.*

JEFFERIES, ROBYN   *1993-94 COWHL Hamilton Golden Hawks #29 (2 games, 1 assist).*

JEFFREY, JENNIFER   *Defence. Shoots left. #21 #27.*

Born 1980-9-14. 5'7".

Year - League - Team		GP	G	A	PTS	PM	Year - Playoff	GP	G	A	PTS	PM
2003-04	NWHL Edmonton Chimos	6	0	1	1	20	2004 NWHL-P	2	0	0	0	2
2004	Nationals Edmonton Chimos	7	1	3	4	6						
2004-05	WWHL Edmonton Chimos	20	1	5	6	22	2005 WWHL-P	3	0	2	2	0
2005-06	WWHL Edmonton Chimos	24	3	9	12	20	2006 WWHL-P	2	0	0	0	4
2006-07	WWHL Edmonton Chimos	21	1	9	10	22	2007 WWHL-P	2	0	0	0	2
2007-08	WWHL Edmonton Chimos	23	2	11	13	33						
2009-10	WWHL Edmonton Chimos	3	0	1	1	2						
Totals from all Competitions		**113**	**8**	**41**	**49**	**133**						

JELINSKI, RANDIE   *Defence. 2001 Nationals Saskatchewan; 2002 Nationals Saskatchewan (6 games).*

JENKINS, CAITLIN   *Forward. 2007-08 WWHL Edmonton Chimos #81 (24 gp, 3 goals, 3 assists).*

JENNER, BRIANNE   *Defence. Shoots left. #11.*

Olympic champion. Abby Hoffman Cup winner with Mississauga on 2008-03-15. Clarkson Cup winner with Calgary on 2016-03-14 and 2019-03-24.
Born 1991-5-4, Oakville, ON, CAN. Grew up in St. Catharines, ON, CAN. 5'9". Debut at age 17 on 2008-10-4.

Year - League - Team		GP	G	A	PTS	PM	Year - Playoff	GP	G	A	PTS	PM
2008	Nationals Mississauga Chiefs	3	0	0	0	0						
2008-09	CWHL Mississauga Chiefs	26	6	4	10	10	2009 CWHL-P	4	3	0	3	4
2009-10	CWHL Burlington Barracudas	13	11	11	22	0						
2015-16	CWHL Calgary Inferno	24	10	18	28	6	2016 C-Cup	3	2	4	6	2
2016-17	CWHL Calgary Inferno	20	9	18	27	6	2017 C-Cup	4	1	3	4	0
2017-18	CWHL Calgary Inferno	4	1	1	2	4	2018 C-Cup	3	0	2	2	0
2018-19	CWHL Calgary Inferno	27	19	13	32	8	2019 C-Cup	4	2	0	2	2
CWHL Regular Season		114	56	65	121	34	Clarkson Cup	14	5	9	14	4
Totals from all Competitions		**135**	**64**	**74**	**138**	**42**						

CWHL Second All-Star Team in 2015-16 and 2016-17... finished 4th in the Angela James Bowl scoring in 2018-19.

JENNISON, BECKY   *Left wing. Shoots left. #77 #67.*

Born 1982-11-28, Grand Bend, ON, CAN. Grew up in Hamilton, ON, CAN. 5'8". Debut at age 22 on 2005-09-17.

Year - League - Team		GP	G	A	PTS	PM	Year - Playoff	GP	G	A	PTS	PM
2005-06	NWHL Ottawa Raiders	34	5	7	12	12	2006 NWHL-P	2	0	0	0	0
2007-08	CWHL Burlington Barracudas	26	3	5	8	32	2008 CWHL-P	3	0	1	1	2
2008-09	CWHL Burlington Barracudas	27	1	3	4	34	2009 CWHL-P	4	0	0	0	8
CWHL Regular Season		53	4	8	12	66						
Totals from all Competitions		**96**	**9**	**16**	**25**	**88**						

JENSEN, CHRISTIE   *Delta, BC, CAN. Defence. 2013-14 CWHL Boston Blades #9 (23 games, 7 assists).*

JENSEN, RENEE   *2010-11 WWHL Manitoba Maple Leafs #11 (3 games).*

JENTNER, BRIANA   *Defence. Shoots left. #7.*

Born 1982-3-14, Akron, OH, USA. 5'6".

Year - League - Team		GP	G	A	PTS	PM	Year - Playoff	GP	G	A	PTS	PM
2004-05	WWHL Minnesota Whitecaps	12	1	4	5	4	2005 WWHL-P	2	0	0	0	0
2005-06	WWHL Minnesota Whitecaps	22	0	16	16	6	2006 WWHL-P	3	0	2	2	0
2006-07	WWHL Minnesota Whitecaps	23	2	6	8	14	2007 WWHL-P	3	0	4	4	2
2007-08	WWHL Minnesota Whitecaps	16	2	3	5	6						
2008	Nationals Minnesota Whitecaps	3	0	0	0	0						

Year - League - Team			GP	G	A	PTS	PM	Year - Playoff	GP	G	A	PTS	PM
2008-09	WWHL	Minnesota Whitecaps	14	1	5	6	2	2009 WWHL-P	0	0	0	0	0
								2009 C-Cup	3	0	0	0	0
2009-10	WWHL	Minnesota Whitecaps	11	0	4	4	0						
2010-11	WWHL	Minnesota Whitecaps	16	1	9	10	10	2011 C-Cup	3	0	0	0	0
Totals from all Competitions			**131**	**7**	**53**	**60**	**44**						

JEREBIC, SHANNON *Bon Accord, AB, CAN. Defence. 2002-03 NWHL Edmonton #6 (24 games, 1 goal).*

JESSOP, JENN *2000-01 NWHL Toronto Sting #9 (5 games, 3 goals).*

JEWERS, JAMIE *Forward. 2000 Nationals Newfoundland Labrador (5 games, 1 goal).*

JIANG BOWEN *Left wing. Shoots right. #7.*
Born 1997-2-19. Grew up in Harbin, CHN. 5'4". Debut at age 20 in 2017-10-28.

Year - League - Team			GP	G	A	PTS	PM
2017-18	CWHL	Vanke Rays	27	0	0	0	2

JIN FENGLING *Harbin, CHN. Forward. 2007-08 WWHL Strathmore #6 (20 games, 8 goals, 3 assists).*

JOHANSSON, MICH. *D. 1996 Nationals Équipe Québec (6 gp, 2 a.); 1998 Nationals New Westminster (5 gp, 1 a.).*

JOHNSON, AMANDA *Defence. 2007 Nationals Manitoba (5 games).*

JOHNSON, KALIYA *Defence. Shoots right. #10.*
Born 1994-12-2. Grew up in Chandler, AZ, USA. 5'7". Debut at age 21 on 2016-10-9.

Year - League - Team			GP	G	A	PTS	PM	Year - Playoff	GP	G	A	PTS	PM
2016-17	NWHL/	Connecticut Whale	14	0	3	3	2	2017 I-Cup	1	0	0	0	0
2017-18	NWHL/	Boston Pride	16	0	2	2	4	2018 I-Cup	1	0	0	0	0
2018-19	NWHL/	Boston Pride	2	0	0	0	0						
Totals from all Competitions			**34**	**0**	**5**	**5**	**6**						

JOHNSTON, ASHLEY *Defence. Shoots left. #10.*
Isobel Cup winner with Metropolitan on 2018-03-25
Born 1992-7-17. Grew up in Burlington, ON, CAN. 6'0". Debut at age 16 on 2009-3-8.

Year - League - Team			GP	G	A	PTS	PM	Year - Playoff	GP	G	A	PTS	PM
2008-09	CWHL	Burlington Barracudas						2009 CWHL-P	3	0	1	1	2
2009-10	CWHL	Burlington Barracudas	17	1	7	8	8						
2015-16	NWHL/	New York Riveters	16	1	6	7	8	2016 I-Cup	2	0	0	0	0
2016-17	NWHL/	New York Riveters	17	2	1	3	6	2017 I-Cup	1	0	0	0	0
2017-18	NWHL/	Metropolitan Riveters	14	1	1	2	10	2018 I-Cup	2	0	1	1	0
NWHL Regular Season			47	4	8	12	24	Isobel Cup	5	0	1	1	0
Totals from all Competitions			**72**	**5**	**17**	**22**	**34**						

CWHL All-Rookie Team in 2009-10... NWHL Denna Laing Perseverance Award in 2016-17... NWHL Fans' Three Stars Award in 2018-19

JOHNSTON, KAREN *Forward. 1995 Nationals Prince Edward Island; 1996 Nationals (4 gp); 1998 Nationals (5 gp).*

JOHNSTON, MALLORY *Defence. Shoots right. #51 #15.*
Born 1986-7-18. Grew up in Chatham, ON, CAN. 5'7". Debut at age 22 on 2008-10-5.

Year - League - Team			GP	G	A	PTS	PM	Year - Playoff	GP	G	A	PTS	PM
2008-09	CWHL	Burlington Barracudas	28	1	6	7	14	2009 CWHL-P	4	1	1	2	4
2009-10	CWHL	Burlington Barracudas	30	4	14	18	18						
2010-11	CWHL	Burlington Barracudas	23	0	1	1	14						
2011-12	CWHL	Burlington Barracudas	27	1	1	2	28						
2012-13	CWHL	Brampton Thunder	24	1	7	8	12	2013 C-Cup	3	0	0	0	2
2013-14	CWHL	Brampton Thunder	22	0	4	4	16						
2014-15	CWHL	Brampton Thunder	14	0	0	0	8						
CWHL Regular Season			168	7	33	40	110	Clarkson Cup	3	0	0	0	2
Totals from all Competitions			**175**	**8**	**34**	**42**	**116**						

JOHNSTON, REBECCA *Forward. Shoots left. #6.*
Olympic champion. Clarkson Cup winner with Calgary on 2016-03-14 and 2019-03-24.
Born 1989-9-24, Sudbury, ON, CAN. 5'9". Debut at age 23 on 2012-10-20.

Year - League - Team			GP	G	A	PTS	PM	Year - Playoff	GP	G	A	PTS	PM
2012-13	CWHL	Toronto Furies	24	8	17	25	4	2013 C-Cup	3	2	0	2	2
2014-15	CWHL	Calgary Inferno	24	17	20	37	10	2015 C-Cup	2	0	0	0	0
2015-16	CWHL	Calgary Inferno	4	4	2	6	2	2016 C-Cup	3	4	5	9	2
2016-17	CWHL	Calgary Inferno	20	7	15	22	2	2017 C-Cup	4	0	2	2	0
2018-19	CWHL	Calgary Inferno	27	15	24	39	8	2019 C-Cup	4	2	2	4	0
CWHL Regular Season			99	51	78	129	26	Clarkson Cup	16	8	9	17	4
Totals from all Competitions			**115**	**59**	**87**	**146**	**30**						

CWHL Most Valuable Player in 2014-15... Angela James Bowl in 2014-15... CWHL goal-scoring leader in 2014-15... CWHL Top Forward in 2014-15... CWHL First All-Star Team in 2014-15 and 2018-19; CWHL Second All-Star Team in 2012-13... CWHL All-Rookie Team in 2012-13... selected First Decade CWHL Team in 2017

JOLLIMORE, SANDRA *Forward. 1995 Nationals PEI Esso Tigers.*

JONES, DANIKA *2010-11 WWHL Manitoba Maple Leafs #12 (3 games).*

JONES, JESS
Forward. Shoots left. #22.

Born 1990-08-30 in Demorestville ,ON, CAN. Grew up in Picton, ON, CAN. 5'4". Debut at age 23 on 2013-11-02.

Year - League - Team			GP	G	A	PTS	PM	Year - Playoff		GP	G	A	PTS	PM
2013-14	CWHL	Brampton Thunder	23	5	4	9	26							
2014-15	CWHL	Brampton Thunder	24	7	9	16	12							
2015-16	CWHL	Brampton Thunder	24	14	10	24	36	2016	C-Cup	2	0	0	0	0
2016-17	CWHL	Brampton Thunder	24	17	20	37	28	2017	C-Cup	2	1	0	1	0
2017-18	NWHL/	Buffalo Beauts	14	4	5	9	11	2018	I-Cup	2	0	0	0	0
2018-19	CWHL	Markham Thunder	25	9	6	15	20	2019	C-Cup	2	0	0	0	0
CWHL Regular Season			120	52	49	101	122	Clarkson Cup		6	1	0	1	0
Totals in North America			**142**	**57**	**54**	**111**	**133**							

Angela James Bowl in 2016-17... CWHL First All-Star Team in 2016-17

JONES, KATIE
Centre. 2004-05 NWHL Durham Lightning #7 (36 games, 2 goals, 4 assists).

JONES, LORI
Forward. 2003 Nationals Newfoundland Labrador (5 games).

JONES, STEPHANIE
Born 1983. Forward. 2004 Nationals Manitoba (2 games).

JONES, STEPHANIE
Forward. Shoots right. #25 #27.

Born 1986-6-20. Grew up in Grand Prairie, AB, CAN. 5'4".

Year - League - Team			GP	G	A	PTS	PM	Year - Playoff		GP	G	A	PTS	PM
2003-04	NWHL	Edmonton Chimos	9	0	2	2	2	2004	NWHL-P					
2004	Nationals	Edmonton Chimos	6	4	3	7	2							
2008-09	CWHL	Vaughan Flames	25	8	7	15	29	2009	CWHL-P	2		2	2	2

JONES, SUZIE
Forward. 2005 Nationals Alberta (6 games).

JONES, TAMRA
1993-94 COWHL Toronto Jr. Aeros (19 gp, 4 goals, 3 a.); 1995-96 Miss. (2 gp, 1 g., 3 a.).

JONSSON, JENNIFER
Forward. 2008-09 WWHL Calgary #4 (13 games, 5 assists; 2 playoff gp; C-Cup 2 gp).

JORDAN, LISA
Forward. 1996 Nationals Pictou County (4 games, 1 goal).

JOSEPH, MANDY
2000-01 NWHL North York Aeros #15 (9 games, 1 assist).

JOSEPHS, KATY
Forward. 2008-09 WWHL Calgary Oval X-Treme #6 (3 games, 1 goal, 1 assist).

JOSLIN, JAMIE
Richmond Hill, ON, CAN. Defence. 2007-08 CWHL Burlington #25 (1 game).

JUBINVILLE, CHANTEL
Forward. 2010-11 WWHL Manitoba Maple Leafs #17 (3 games).

JUBINVILLE, JULIANNE
Defence/Forward. #12 #17.

Born 1985-8-7. Grew up in Edmonton, AB, CAN.

Year - League - Team			GP	G	A	PTS	PM	Year - Playoff		GP	G	A	PTS	PM
2002-03	NWHL	Edmonton Chimos	23	6	5	11	28							
2008-09	WWHL	Edmonton Chimos	23	8	9	17	54	2009	WWHL-P	1	0	0	0	2

Has served as an assistant coach with CWHL Calgary

JUE, MELANIE
Forward. Shoots left. #6.

Born 1988-3-30. Grew up in Richmond, BC, CAN. Debut at age 29 on 2017-10-21.

Year - League - Team			GP	G	A	PTS	PM	Year - Playoff		GP	G	A	PTS	PM
2002	Nationals	Richmond Steelers	5	0	1	1	4							
2004	Nationals	British Columbia	5	1	1	2	8							
2006	Nationals	British Columbia	6	2	1	3	6							
2017-18	CWHL	Kunlun Red Star	28	6	4	10	24	2018	C-Cup	4	0	0	0	6
2018-19	CWHL	KRS Vanke Rays	28	1	10	11	16							
Totals from all Competitions			**76**	**10**	**17**	**27**	**64**							

JULIEN, NATHALIE
Forward. 1998-99 NWHL Laval #26 (4 gp, 2 goals); 1999-00 #8 (30 gp, 1 assist).

JURON, JORDAN
Forward. Shoots right. #7.

Born 1995-6-10. Grew up in Latham, NY, USA. 5'8". Debut at age 22 on 2018-3-10.

Year - League - Team			GP	G	A	PTS	PM	Year - Playoff		GP	G	A	PTS	PM
2017-18	NWHL/	Buffalo Beauts	2	1	1	2	0	2018	I-Cup	1	0	0	0	0
2018-19	NWHL/	Buffalo Beauts	2	0	0	0	0							

JUSZKIEWICZ, WHITNEY
Defence. 2005 Nationals Alberta (6 games).

KACHUR, MICHELLE
Forward. 2003 Nationals Saskatchewan (5 games, 1 assist).

KAIP, CHANDY
Defence. 1998 Nationals Saskatchewan (6 games, 1 goal).

KALDMA, TIINA
Forward. 1996-97 COWHL Hamilton Golden Hawks #10 (34 games, 3 assists).

KAMO, KIM
1999-00 NWHL Ottawa Raiders #11 (19 games, 2 goals).

KANNIS, DAYNA
Georgetown, ON. F. 2006-07 NWHL Oakville (2 gp, 1 assists); 2011-12 CWHL Burlington (3 gp).

KANTOR, ESTHER
Vienna, AUT. LW. 2005-06 NWHL Québec #23 (32 games, 3 goals, 4 assists).

KAUTH, KATHLEEN
Forward. Shoots left. #18.

IIHF champion, Abby Hoffman Cup winner with Brampton on 2006-03-12. CWHL winner.

Born 1979-3-28, Saratoga Springs, NY, USA. 5'8".

Year - League - Team			GP	G	A	PTS	PM	Year - Playoff		GP	G	A	PTS	PM
2003-04	NWHL	Brampton Thunder	19	10	9	19	10	2004	NWHL-P	5	5	3	8	6
2004-05	NWHL	Brampton Thunder	0	0	0	0	0	2005	NWHL-P	2	0	1	1	
2005	Nationals	Brampton Thunder	6	1	2	3	2							

Year - League - Team			GP	G	A	PTS	PM	Year - Playoff	GP	G	A	PTS	PM
2005-06	NWHL	Brampton Thunder	1	0	2	2	0	2006 NWHL-P	5	2	2	4	4
2006	Nationals	Brampton Thunder	6	2	2	4	2						
2006-07	NWHL	Brampton Thunder	29	14	15	29	36	2007 NWHL-P	6	3	1	4	4
2007-08	CWHL	Brampton Can.-Thunder	26	9	8	17	10	2008 CWHL-P	3	0	2	2	0
2008	Nationals	Brampton Can.-Thunder	3	0	1	1	2						
2008-09	CWHL	Brampton Thunder	28	9	22	31	20	2009 CWHL-P	2				
								2009 C-Cup	2	0	2	2	0
CWHL Regular Season			54	18	30	48	30	Clarkson Cup	2	0	2	2	0
Totals from all Competitions			**143**	**55**	**72**	**127**	**96**						

Finished 10th in the Angela James Bowl scoring race in 2008-09

KAWAMOTO, KOBI

Defence. Shoots left. #77.

Born 1980-9-7, Surrey, BC, CAN. 5'7".

Year - League - Team			GP	G	A	PTS	PM	Year - Playoff	GP	G	A	PTS	PM
1996	Nationals	Britannia Blues	5	2	1	3	2						
1997	Nationals	British Columbia											
2000	Nationals	Britannia Blues	5	4	0	4							
2004-05	WWHL	Minnesota Whitecaps	12	4	6	10	14	2005 WWHL-P	2	0	1	1	0
2005-06	WWHL	Minnesota Whitecaps	23	8	10	18	28	2006 WWHL-P	3	2	1	3	2
2006-07	WWHL	Minnesota Whitecaps	20	0	3	3	18	2007 WWHL-P	3	0	1	1	4
2007-08	WWHL	Minnesota Whitecaps	11	0	2	2	4						
Totals from all Competitions			**84**	**20**	**25**	**45**	**72**						

KAY, KRISTEN

1993-94 COWHL Hamilton Golden Hawks #14 (25 games, 3 goals, 4 assists).

KAY, STEPHANIE

Forward. Shoots right. #5 #55 #14 #17.

Abby Hoffman Cup winner with Aeros on 2000-03-12. Abby Hoffman Cup winner with Brampton on 2006-03-12. NWHL Cup winner. Born 1975-9-16. Grew up in Toronto, ON, CAN. 5'6".

Year - League - Team			GP	G	A	PTS	PM	Year - Playoff	GP	G	A	PTS	PM
1993-94	COWHL	Toronto Junior Aeros	30	2	6	8	46						
1995-96	COWHL	North York Aeros	24	3	4	7	52						
1996	Nationals	North York Aeros	5	0	2	2	4						
1996-97	COWHL	North York Aeros	32	15	18	33	68						
1997-98	COWHL	North York Aeros	19	6	12	18	30						
1998	Nationals	North York Aeros	6	2	3	5	4						
1998-99	NWHL	North York Aeros	34	12	12	24	52						
1999	Nationals	North York Aeros	5	2	1	3							
1999-00	NWHL	North York Aeros	39	22	26	48	64	2000 NWHL-P					
2000	Nationals	North York Aeros	6	3	8	11							
2000-01	NWHL	Brampton Thunder	31	11	15	26	79						
2001-02	NWHL	Brampton Thunder	27	6	9	15	102						
2002	Nationals	Brampton Thunder	6	3	0	3	6						
2002-03	NWHL	Brampton Thunder						2003 NWHL-P					
2003	Nationals	Brampton Thunder	5	1	4	5	8						
2003-04	NWHL	Brampton Thunder	34	8	13	21	62						
2004-05	NWHL	Brampton Thunder	28	9	3	12	73						
2005	Nationals	Brampton Thunder	6	0	1	1	8						
2005-06	NWHL	Brampton Thunder	34	12	10	22	74	2006 NWHL-P	5	0	1	1	4
2006	Nationals	Brampton Thunder	6	1	3	4	4						
2006-07	NWHL	Brampton Thunder	11	0	2	2	4						
Totals from all Competitions			**393**	**118**	**153**	**271**	**744**						

KAYE, MELINDA

Defence. Shoots left.

Born 1984-02-29. Grew up in Colpitts Settlement, NB, CAN. 5'10".

Year - League - Team			GP	G	A	PTS	PM	Year - Playoff	GP	G	A	PTS	PM
2003	Nationals	Team New Brunswick	4	0	0	0	2						
2005	Nationals	Team New Brunswick	6	1	0	1	0						
2006	Nationals	Team New Brunswick	7	2	0	2	8						
2007	Nationals	Team New Brunswick	6	0	1	1	6						
2008	Nationals	Team New Brunswick	5	2	3	5	12						

KAYE, SUZANNE

Defence. Shoots left. #14 #10.

Born 1980-2-8. Grew up in Truro, NS, CAN. 5'7".

Year - League - Team			GP	G	A	PTS	PM
1996	Nationals	Pictou County Sobey's	4	0	0	0	0
1998	Nationals	Nova Scotia Selects	5	0	3	3	2
1999	Nationals	Prince Edward Island	5	0	0	0	
2000	Nationals	Nova Scotia Selects	6	0	0	0	
2001	Nationals	Nova Scotia Selects					
2002	Nationals	Nova Scotia Selects	5	0	2	2	2
2003	Nationals	Nova Scotia Selects	6	1	3	4	6
2003-04	NWHL	Avalanche du Québec	15	1	1	2	6
2004-05	NWHL	Avalanche du Québec	18	1	1	2	8

Year - League - Team		GP	G	A	PTS	PM	Year - Playoff	GP	G	A	PTS	PM
2006	Nationals Nova Scotia Selects	5	2	3	5	4						
2007-08	CWHL Phénix du Québec	3	0	0	0	14						
Totals from all Competitions		**72**	**5**	**13**	**18**	**42**						

KEADY, LIZ   *Boston, MA, USA. F. 2010-11 CWHL Boston Blades #3 (22 gp, 4 goals, 11 a.; 2 playoff gp, 1 goal).*

KEARNEY, JENNIFER   *Defence. #8.*

Year - League - Team		GP	G	A	PTS	PM
2002-03	NWHL Durham Lightning					
2003-04	NWHL Durham Lightning	30	3	2	5	18
2004-05	NWHL Durham Lightning	29	0	2	2	26
Totals from all Competitions		**59**	**3**	**4**	**7**	**44**

KEARNS, EMILY   *2004-05 WWHL Minnesota #29 (2 games; 2 playoff games).*

KEATING, ANDREA   *Forward. 2007 Nationals Manitoba (5 games); 2008 Nationals (4 games).*

KEAY, BRIDEN   *Defence. 1996 Nationals Pictou County (4 gp); 2000 Nationals N.S. (6 gp, 2 pts); 2001 Nationals.*

KEEFE, OLIVIA   *Ottawa, ON, CAN. Forward. 2015-16 CWHL Boston Blades #21 (18 games).*

KEEN, KATHLEEN   *Defence. 2003 Nationals Host Saskatchewan (5 games).*

KEERS, ALORA   *Forward. #5.*

Born 1991-4-26. Grew up in Everett. 5'4". Debut at age 18 on 2009-10-24.

Year - League - Team		GP	G	A	PTS	PM
2009-10	CWHL Brampton Thunder	2	0	0	0	0
2013-14	CWHL Toronto Furies	4	0	0	0	2
2014-15	CWHL Toronto Furies	7	0	0	0	0
CWHL Regular Season		13	0	0	0	2

KEHOE, MAEVE   *Ottawa, ON, CAN. Defence. 2009-10 CWHL Ottawa Senators #25 (20 games, 2 assists).*

KELL, MELANIE   *Edmonton. F. 2002-03 NWHL Edmonton (18 gp, 2 a.); 2006-07 WWHL Sask. (20 gp, 4 g., 3 a.).*

KELLAR DUKE, BECKY   *Defence. Shoots left. #71 #44 #4.*

Olympic champion, IIHF champion. Abby Hoffman Cup winner with Aeros on 2000-03-12 and 2004-03-14. NWHL Cup winner. Born 1975-1-1. Grew up in Burlington, ON, CAN. 5'7".

Year - League - Team		GP	G	A	PTS	PM	Year - Playoff	GP	G	A	PTS	PM
1998	Nationals North York Aeros	6	0	3	3	0						
1998-99	NWHL North York Aeros	32	7	9	16	2						
1999	Nationals North York Aeros	6	0	0	0							
1999-00	NWHL North York Aeros	30	4	14	18	33	2000 NWHL-P					
2000	Nationals North York Aeros	5	1	4	5							
2000-01	NWHL North York Aeros	34	4	18	22	14	2003 NWHL-P					
2001	Nationals North York Aeros											
2002	Nationals North York Aeros	7	2	2	4	2						
2003-04	NWHL Toronto Aeros	26	1	14	15	24	2004 NWHL-P					
2004	Nationals Toronto Aeros	6	0	3	3	2						
2004-05	NWHL Oakville Ice	17	2	5	7	4	2005 NWHL-P					
2005-06	NWHL Oakville Ice	1	0	0	0	2	2006 NWHL-P	2	1	0	1	0
2006-07	NWHL Oakville Ice						2007 NWHL-P	1	0	0	0	0
2007-08	CWHL Burlington Barracudas	28	2	10	12	42	2008 CWHL-P	3	0	2	2	2
2008-09	CWHL Burlington Barracudas	27	4	10	14	26	2009 CWHL-P	4	1	2	3	4
2009-10	CWHL Burlington Barracudas	1	0	0	0	0						
2010-11	CWHL Burlington Barracudas	21	1	2	3	16						
CWHL Regular Season		77	7	22	29	84						
Totals from all Competitions		**257**	**30**	**98**	**128**	**173**						

CWHL Top Defender in 2007-08 and 2008-09... CWHL Central All-Star Team in 2007-08; CWHL First All-Star Team in 2008-09... selected First Decade CWHL Team in 2017

KELLER, KRISTIE   *Forward. 2006 Nationals British Columbia (6 games, 2 assists).*

KELLY, LAURA   *2000-01 NWHL Ottawa Raiders (1 game).*

KELLY, LAUREN   *Defence. Shoots right. #6.*

Born 1992-1-31. Grew up in Milton, ON, CAN. 5'8". Debut at age 25 on 2017-11-4.

Year - League - Team		GP	G	A	PTS	PM
2017-18	CWHL Vanke Rays	23	1	1	2	6
2018-19	NWHL/ Boston Pride	15	1	2	3	6

KELLY, SARAH   *Forward. 1998 Nationals Nova Scotia (5 games, 1 goal).*

KELLY, SHARON   *Defence. Shoots right. #19.*

Clarkson Cup winner with Montréal on 2011-03-27
Born 1985-3-20. Grew up in Riverview, NB, CAN. Debut at age 25 on 2009-10-3.

Year - League - Team		GP	G	A	PTS	PM	Year - Playoff	GP	G	A	PTS	PM
2003	Nationals Team New Brunswick	4	0	0	0	4						
2009-10	CWHL Ottawa Senators	30	1	7	8	58						
2010-11	CWHL Stars de Montréal	24	1	3	4	24	2011 CWHL-P	2		2		
							2011 C-Cup	4	0	0	0	0

						Clarkson Cup	4	0	0	0	0
CWHL Regular Season	54	2	10	12	82						
Totals from all Competitions	**64**	**2**	**10**	**12**	**88**						

CWHL All-Rookie Team in 2009-10

KELLY, SHEILA   *D. 2001 Nationals Newfoundland; 2002 Nationals (5 gp); 2009-10 WWHL Strathmore #21 (1 gp).*

KELLY-MURPHY, JACQUELINE   *Forward.*
Born 1969-08-14.

Year - League - Team		GP	G	A	PTS	PM
1996	Nationals PEI Esso Tigers	4	0	0	0	0
1998	Nationals Prince Edward Island	5	1	0	1	6
1999	Nationals Prince Edward Island	5	0	0	0	
2000	Nationals Prince Edward Island	5	0	0	0	

KENNEDY, COURTNEY   *Defence. Shoots left. #77.*
IIHF champion. Born 1979-3-29, Woburn, MA, USA. 5'9".

Year - League - Team		GP	G	A	PTS	PM
2002-03	NWHL Vancouver Griffins	8	4	4	8	8
2003	Nationals Vancouver Griffins	5	0	0	0	8

KENNEDY, WHITNEY   *Mississauga, ON. Forward. 2007-08 CWHL Mississauga #20 (1 game, 2 goals, 1 assist).*

KENNEY, ALISON   *Forward. #7.*
Born 1978-06-08.

Year - League - Team		GP	G	A	PTS	PM
2001-02	NWHL North York Aeros	28	14	23	37	18
2002	Nationals North York Aeros	7	3	2	5	2

KENWORTHY, LAURISSA   *Forward. 2004-05 NWHL Toronto Aeros #89 (3 games, 1 goal).*

KERNALEGUEN, GUEN   *Defence. 2000 Nationals Saskatchewan (7 gp, 1 assist); 2001 Nationals Saskatchewan.*

KERR, KIM   *2002-03 NWHL Ottawa (33 gp, 3 goals, 5 a.); 2009-10 CWHL (9 gp, 2 goals, 3 a.).*

KERR, TAMMY   *Forward. 1996-97 COWHL Newtonbrook #42 (1 game, 1 assist).*

KESSEL, AMANDA   *Forward. Shoots right. #28.*
IIHF champion
Born 1991-8-28, Madison, WI, USA. 5'5". Debut at age 25 on 2016-10-8.

Year - League - Team		GP	G	A	PTS	PM	Year - Playoff	GP	G	A	PTS	PM
2016-17	NWHL/ New York Riveters	8	4	14	18	4	2017 I-Cup	1	0	1	1	0
2018-19	NWHL/ Metropolitan Riveters	13	2	15	17	6	2019 I-Cup	1	0	0	0	0

KETCHUM, BRAY   *Right wing. Shoots left. #17.*
Clarkson Cup winner with Boston on 2015-03-07 and Isobel Cup winner with Metropolitan on 2018-03-25.
Born 1989-3-18. Grew up in Greenwich, CT, USA. 5'8". Debut at age 23 on 2011-10-22.

Year - League - Team		GP	G	A	PTS	PM	Year - Playoff	GP	G	A	PTS	PM
2011-12	CWHL Boston Blades	20	0	6	6	2	2012 C-Cup	3	0	0	0	0
2012-13	CWHL Boston Blades	1	0	0	0	0						
2014-15	CWHL Boston Blades	20	3	1	4	0	2015 C-Cup	3	0	0	0	0
2015-16	NWHL New York Riveters	18	10	4	14	18	2016 I-Cup	2	0	0	0	0
2016-17	NWHL/ New York Riveters	17	2	5	7	2	2017 I-Cup	1	0	0	0	0
2017-18	NWHL/ Metropolitan Riveters	16	5	6	11	4	2018 I-Cup	2	1	0	1	0
CWHL Regular Season		41	3	7	10	2	Clarkson Cup	6	0	0	0	0
NWHL Regular Season		51	17	15	32	24	Isobel Cup	5	1	0	1	0
Totals from all Competitions		**103**	**21**	**22**	**43**	**26**						

KETT, KAREN   *Forward. 2001-02 NWHL Durham Lightning #13 (29 games, 2 goals, 7 assists).*

KEYOWSKI, STACEY   *Forward. 1995 Nationals Regina Sharks; 2001 Nationals Saskatchewan.*

KEYS, ERIN   *Forward. #19.*
Clarkson Cup winner with Minnesota on 2010-03-28

Year - League - Team		GP	G	A	PTS	PM	Year - Playoff	GP	G	A	PTS	PM
2008-09	WWHL Minnesota Whitecaps	4	3	4	7	2	2009 WWHL-P	2	2	0	2	0
2009-10	WWHL Minnesota Whitecaps	11	8	5	13	18	2010 C-Cup	2	1	1	2	0
2010-11	WWHL Minnesota Whitecaps	5	5	4	9	0	2011 C-Cup	2	0	0	0	0

KHAN, TARA   *Forward. 2004 Nationals British Columbia (6 games).*

KICKHAM, ERIN   *Forward. Shoots right. #6.*
Born 1992-09-16. Grew up in Needham, MA, USA. 5'5". Debut at age 23 on 2015-10-17.

Year - League - Team		GP	G	A	PTS	PM
2015-16	CWHL Boston Blades	22	1	6	7	12
2016-17	CWHL Boston Blades	22	3	1	4	16
2017-18	CWHL Boston Blades	27	1	3	4	6
2018-19	CWHL Worcester Blades	27	1	0	1	10
CWHL Regular Season		98	6	10	16	44

KIDD, SYDNEY   *Defence. Shoots left. #8.*
Born 1992-10-30. Grew up in Sundridge, ON, CAN. 5'8". Debut at age 22 on 2015-10-11.

Year - League - Team			GP	G	A	PTS	PM	Year - Playoff	GP	G	A	PTS	PM
2015-16	NWHL/	Boston Pride	15	0	4	4	4	2016 I-Cup	2	0	0	0	2
2017-18	CWHL	Toronto Furies	26	3	3	6	18						
2018-19	CWHL	Toronto Furies	12	0	0	0	4	2019 C-Cup	3	0	0	0	0

KIIPELI, SATU *2004-05 WWHL Minnesota Whitecaps #33 (12 games, 3 assists; 1 playoff game).*

KIKUCHI, SATO *Defence. Shoots left. #8.*
Born 1989-5-18. Grew up in Tokyo, JPN. 5'3". Debut at age 27 on 2016-10-29.

Year - League - Team			GP	G	A	PTS	PM
2016-17	CWHL	Boston Blades	22	0	0	0	12
2017-18	CWHL	Boston Blades	28	1	1	2	22

KILFOY, GWEN *Forward. 2002-03 NWHL Durham Lightning #12 (? games).*

KINDRET, JENNIFER *Winnipeg, MB. F. 2007-08 WWHL B.C. #93 (24 gp, 1 g., 3a.); 2008-09 (14 gp, 1 g., 4 a.).*

KING, ASHLEY *Winnipeg, MB. Forward. 2010-11 WWHL Manitoba Maple Leafs #11 (3 games).*

KING, BECCA *Forward. Shoots right. #2.*
Clarkson Cup winner with Markham on 2018-03-25
Born 1986-09-21. Grew up in Thunder Bay, ON, CAN. 5'5". Debut at age 29 on 2015-10-17.

Year - League - Team			GP	G	A	PTS	PM	Year - Playoff	GP	G	A	PTS	PM
2015-16	CWHL	Brampton Thunder	24	2	4	6	4	2016 C-Cup	2	0	2	2	0
2016-17	CWHL	Brampton Thunder	20	3	0	3	0	2017 C-Cup	2	0	0	0	2
2017-18	CWHL	Markham Thunder	28	0	3	3	10	2018 C-Cup	3	0	0	0	0
2018-19	CWHL	Markham Thunder	27	1	4	5	10	2019 C-Cup	3	0	0	0	0
CWHL Regular Season			99	6	11	17	24	Clarkson Cup	10	0	2	2	2
Totals from all Competitions			**109**	**6**	**13**	**19**	**26**						

KING, DANENE *Forward. 2003 Nationals Host Saskatchewan (5 games, 1 assist).*

KING, DAYNA *Defence. 2005-06 WWHL Saskatchewan (24 gp, 2 goals, 5 assists; 1 playoff gp).*

KING, KRISTIN *Forward. Shoots right. #14 #2.*
IIHF champion. Born 1979-7-21, Piqua, OH, USA. 5'4".

Year - League - Team			GP	G	A	PTS	PM	Year - Playoff	GP	G	A	PTS	PM
2002-03	NWHL	Mississauga IceBears											
2003-04	NWHL	Oakville Ice	28	12	9	21							
2004-05	NWHL	Oakville Ice	30	9	6	15	35						
2005-06	NWHL	Oakville Ice	0	0	0	0	0	2006 NWHL-P	2	0	0	0	0
2006-07	WWHL	Minnesota Whitecaps	12	6	3	9	12	2007 WWHL-P	3	3	2	5	4
2007-08	WWHL	Minnesota Whitecaps	14	4	1	5	8						
2008	Nationals	Minnesota Whitecaps	3	2	2	4	4						
Totals from all Competitions			**92**	**36**	**23**	**59**	**63**						

KINGSBURY, GINA *Forward.*
Olympic champion, IIHF champion. Abby Hoffman Cup winner with Calgary on 2007-03-10. NWHL winner, WWHL winner.
Born 1981-11-26, Uranium City, SK, CAN. Grew up in Rouyn-Noranda, QC, CAN. 5'7".

Year - League - Team			GP	G	A	PTS	PM	Year - Playoff	GP	G	A	PTS	PM
2004-05	NWHL	Axion de Montréal	30	31	29	60	16	2006 NWHL-P	0	0	0	0	0
2005	Nationals	Axion de Montréal	6	4	4	8	0						
2006-07	WWHL	Calgary Oval X-Treme	19	11	20	31	8	2007 WWHL-P	3	4	7	11	4
2007	Nationals	Calgary Oval X-Treme	6	7	12	19	2						
2007-08	WWHL	Calgary Oval X-Treme	23	20	25	45	8						
2008	Nationals	Calgary Oval X-Treme	3	1	2	3	4						
2008-09	WWHL	Calgary Oval X-Treme	21	24	30	54	10	2009 WWHL-P	2	1	1	2	0
								2009 C-Cup	2	2	0	2	4
Totals from all Competitions			**115**	**105**	**130**	**235**	**56**						

KINNEAR, KATIE *Forward. 1995-96 COWHL Hamilton #6 (18 games, 1 goal); 1996-97 #99 (3 games, 1 assist).*

KINSMAN, ALICIA *Forward. 1998-99 NWHL Brampton Thunder #8 (8 games, 1 goal).*

KIRBY, BRITTANY *Forward. 2004 Nationals British Columbia (6 games).*

KIRCHNER, JILL *Frankfort, IL, USA. Forward. 2011-12 CWHL Boston #18 (20 gp, 2 goals, 7 a.; C-Cup 3 games).*

KIRK, JENNIFER *Forward. Shoots left. #21 #6 #9 #71.*
Born 1983-6-14. Grew up in Brampton, ON, CAN. Debut at age 16 in 1999-00.

Year - League - Team			GP	G	A	PTS	PM	Year - Playoff	GP	G	A	PTS	PM
1999-00	NWHL	Brampton Thunder	3	0	1	1	0						
2009-10	CWHL	Brampton Thunder	30	4	7	11	67	2010 C-Cup	2	0		0	
2010-11	CWHL	Brampton Thunder	25	11	5	16	32	2011 CWHL-P	2		1	1	2
								2011 C-Cup	2	3	1	4	8
2011-12	CWHL	Brampton Thunder	9	1	0	1	6						
2012-13	CWHL	Brampton Thunder	12	0	1	1	16						
2013-14	CWHL	Brampton Thunder	20	2	6	8	32						
2014-15	CWHL	Brampton Thunder	20	1	3	4	18						
CWHL Regular Season			116	19	22	41	171	Clarkson Cup	4	3	1	4	8
Totals from all Competitions			**125**	**22**	**25**	**47**	**181**						

KIRKORIAN, MARG   RW. 1993-94 COWHL Hamilton (17 gp, 1 assist); 1996-97 London (29 gp, 9 goals, 3 assists).

KIRWAN, AMANDA   Mississauga, ON, CAN. Defence. 2005-06 NWHL Oakville Ice #18 (1 game).

KISIL, LEANNE   Winnipeg, MB, CAN. Forward. 201-12 CWHL Alberta #25 (2 games).

KISSICK, LISA   F. 2004 Nationals Manitoba (5 gp, 1 goal); 2010-11 WWHL Manitoba Maple Leafs #18 (6 gp, 2 g.).

KITLAR, BLAIR   Defence. Shoots left.
Born 1988-01-10. Grew up in North Bay, ON, CAN. 5'7".

Year - League - Team		GP	G	A	PTS	PM	Year - Playoff
2008-09	CWHL Ottawa Senators	30	2	6	8	40	2009 CWHL-P
2008	Nationals Nova Scotia Selects	5	0	1	1	4	

KITTREDGE, KELLY   Defence. Shoots right. #71.
Born 1992-1-23. Grew up in Mahwah, NJ, USA. 5'7". Debut at age 25 on 2017-10-22.

Year - League - Team		GP	G	A	PTS	PM
2017-18	CWHL Boston Blades	24	0	3	3	6

KITTS, BIANCA   Defence. 2002-03 NWHL Ottawa (7 gp); 2005-06 Brampton (5 gp); 2006-07 Oakville (1 gp).

KLASSEN, AMANDA   Winnipeg, MB. Forward. 2011-12 CWHL Toronto #5 (26 games, 1 goal; C-Cup 2 games).

KLASSEN, CINDY   Defence.
Born 1979-08-12, Winnipeg, MB, CAN.

Year - League - Team		GP	G	A PTS	PM	Year - Playoff	GP	G	A PTS PM
1995	Nationals Winnipeg Sweat Camp								
1996	Nationals Winnipeg Sweat Camp								
1998	Nationals Manitoba Tazmanian Devils	5	1	3	4	10			

As a speed skater, won an Olympic gold medals at Salt Lake City 2002 and Rio 2006.

KLEIN-SWORMINK, BECKY   Forward. Shoots left. #11.
Abby Hoffman Cup winner with Calgary on 2001-03-11 and 2003-03-16.
WWHL winner. Born 1981-9-10, Winchester, ON, CAN.

Year - League - Team		GP	G	A PTS	PM	Year - Playoff	GP	G	A PTS PM
2000	Nationals Calgary Oval X-Treme	7	1	0	1				
2001	Nationals Calgary Oval X-Treme								
2002	Nationals Calgary Oval X-Treme	6	4	0	4	0			
2002-03	NWHL Calgary Oval X-Treme	22	4	18	22	8	2003 NWHL-P		
2003	Nationals Calgary Oval X-Treme	5	0	1	1	0			
2003-04	NWHL Calgary Oval X-Treme	12	8	4	12	4	2004 NWHL-P	4	1	1 2 2
2004	Nationals Calgary Oval X-Treme	6	2	1	3	0			
Totals from all Competitions		**62**	**20**	**25**	**45**	**14**			

KLEIN-SWORMINK, CHELSEA   Defence. 2004-05 Calgary Oval X-Treme (? games).

KLEINSASSER, HEIDI   LW. 2007-08 WWHL Strathmore Rockies #7 (5 games).

KLIENBACH, GRACE   Left wing. Shoots right. #94.
Born 1996-4-1. Grew up in Acton, MA, USA. Debut at age 21 on 2017-10-28.

Year - League - Team		GP	G	A	PTS	PM
2017-18	NWHL/ Connecticut Whale	13	1	1	2	4

KLINKOSZ, CORA   Forward. 2002 Nationals Richmond Steelers (5 games, 1 assist).

KNIGHT, HILARY   Right wing. Shoots right. #21.
Olympic champion, IIHF champion.
Clarkson Cup winner with Boston on 2013-03-23 and 2015-03-07. Isobel Cup winner with Boston on 2016-03-12.
Born 1989-7-21, Palo Alto, CA, USA. 5'11". Debut at age 23 on 2012-10-20.

Year - League - Team		GP	G	A	PTS	PM	Year - Playoff	GP	G	A	PTS	PM
2012-13	CWHL Boston Blades	24	17	15	32	10	2013 C-Cup	4	1	4	5	0
2013-14	CWHL Boston Blades	4	4	4	8	0	2014 C-Cup	4	5	1	6	0
2014-15	CWHL Boston Blades	13	8	14	22	4	2015 C-Cup	3	4	3	7	6
2015-16	NWHL/ Boston Pride	17	15	18	33	8	2016 I-Cup	4	7	2	9	0
2016-17	NWHL/ Boston Pride	10	8	7	15	4	2017 I-Cup	2	3	2	5	2
2017-18	CWHL Canadiennes de Montréal	1	0	0	0	2	2018 C-Cup	2	0	0	0	0
2018-19	CWHL Canadiennes de Montréal	23	9	8	17	4	2019 C-Cup	4	4	4	8	0
CWHL Regular Season		65	38	41	79	20	Clarkson Cup	17	14	12	26	6
NWHL Regular Season		27	23	25	48	12	Isobel Cup	6	10	4	14	2
Totals from all Competitions		**115**	**85**	**82**	**167**	**40**						

CWHL Most Valuable Player in 2012-13... CWHL goals leader in 2012-13 (tie)... CWHL Top Forward in 2012-13...
CWHL First All-Star Team in 2012-13, 2014-15... CWHL All-Rookie Team in 2012-13... finished 3rd in the Angela
James Bowl scoring in 2012-13... NWHL Leading Scorer in 2015-16... selected First Decade CWHL Team in 2017

KNIGHT, KERI   Defence. 1995 Nationals Winnipeg; 1996 Nationals (6 gp, 1 assist); 2000 Nationals (5 gp).

KNIGHT, SHANNON   Forward. 2007 Nationals BC Outback (5 games, 3 goals, 1 assist).

KNITTIG, NICOLE   Forward.
Born 1980-03-08.

Year - League - Team		GP	G	A	PTS	PM
1996	Nationals Saskatchewan Selects	5	0	0	0	0
1998	Nationals Saskatchewan Selects	6	1	3	4	2
2000	Nationals Calgary Oval X-Treme	7	3	4	7	

KNOWLES, HELEN
Defence. #5.

Year - League - Team		GP	G	A	PTS	PM
1995	Nationals Mississauga Chiefs					
1995-96	COWHL Mississauga Chiefs	25	2	18	20	26
1996-97	COWHL Mississauga Chiefs	35	12	19	31	50
1997-98	COWHL Mississauga Chiefs	17	4	7	11	18
1998-99	NWHL Mississauga Chiefs	36	4	15	19	62
1999-00	NWHL Mississauga Chiefs	38	11	14	25	89
2000-01	NWHL Mississauga IceBears	37	2	5	7	61
Totals from all Competitions		**188**	**35**	**78**	**113**	**306**

KNOWLES, JAYNE
Forward. Shoots left.

Born 1986-03-21. Grew up in Newport, NS, CAN. 5'3".

Year - League - Team		GP	G	A	PTS	PM
2003	Nationals Nova Scotia Selects	6	0	0	0	2
2004	Nationals Nova Scotia Selects	5	1	0	1	0
2005	Nationals Nova Scotia Selects	5	1	1	2	4
2008	Nationals Nova Scotia Selects	5	3	1	4	0

KNOWLES, TRACY
Forward. Shoots right.

Born 1973-09-26. Grew up in Bathurst, NB, CAN. 5'4".

Year - League - Team		GP	G	A	PTS	PM
1995	Nationals PEI Esso Tigers					
1996	Nationals PEI Esso Tigers	4	0	0	0	2
2002	Nationals PEI Humpty Dumpty	6	1	0	1	6
2005	Nationals Prince Edward Island	5	0	0	0	0
2007	Nationals Prince Edward Island	1	0	0	0	0
2008	Nationals Prince Edward Island	5	2	0	2	12

KOCAY, SHEILA
Forward. 2006 Nationals Manitoba (5 gp, 2 goals, 3 assists); 2006 Nationals (5 gp)

KODATSKY, KIM
Left wing. #16 #29.

Born 1984-1-30.

Year - League - Team		GP	G	A	PTS	PM	Year		GP	G	A	PTS	PM
2000-01	NWHL Brampton Thunder	1	0	0	0	0							
2001-02	NWHL Mississauga IceBears	30	6	10	16	40							
2002-03	NWHL Mississauga IceBears												
2005-06	NWHL Oakville Ice	0	0	0	0	0	2006	NWHL-P	0	0	0	0	0
2006-07	NWHL Oakville Ice	32	1	1	2	24	2007	NWHL-P	3	0	0	0	0
Totals from all Competitions		**66**	**7**	**11**	**18**	**64**							

KOELZER, KELSEY
Defence. Shoots right. #55.

Isobel Cup winner with Metropolitan on 2018-03-25
Born 1995-06-16. Grew up in Horsham, PA, USA. 5'9". Debut at age 21 on 2017-3-17.

Year - League - Team		GP	G	A	PTS	PM	Year - Playoff		GP	G	A	PTS	PM
2016-17	NWHL New York Riveters	0	0	0	0	0	2017	I-Cup	1	0	0	0	0
2017-18	NWHL Metropolitan Riveters	15	5	9	14	10	2018	I-Cup	2	0	1	1	2
2018-19	NWHL/ Metropolitan Riveters	13	0	0	0	12	2019	I-Cup	1	0	0	0	0

KOHANCHUK, JENELLE
Forward. Shoots left. #25 #91.

Clarkson Cup winner with Toronto on 2014-03-22
Born 1990-10-03 in Winnipeg, MB, CAN. Debut at age 23 on 2014-01-05.

Year - League - Team		GP	G	A	PTS	PM	Year - Playoff		GP	G	A	PTS	PM
2013-14	CWHL Toronto Furies	14	7	3	10	10	2014	C-Cup	4	1	0	1	2
2014-15	CWHL Toronto Furies	21	7	10	17	8	2015	C-Cup	0	0	0	0	0
2016-17	CWHL Toronto Furies	22	3	7	10	8	2017	C-Cup	3	4	0	4	0
CWHL Regular Season		57	17	20	37	26	Clarkson Cup		7	5	0	5	2
Totals from all Competitions		**64**	**22**	**20**	**42**	**28**							

CWHL Second All-Star Team in 2014-15... finished 13th in the Angela James Bowl scoring race in 2014-15

KOIZUMI, JESSICA
Forward. Shoots left. #27 #14 #56.

Year - League - Team		GP	G	A	PTS	PM	Year - Playoff		GP	G	A	PTS	PM

IIHF champion. Clarkson Cup winner with Boston on 2013-03-23 and 2015-03-07.
Born 1985-4-15, Honolulu, HI, USA. Grew up in Simi Valley, CA, USA. 5'5". Debut at age 22 in 2007-08.

Year - League - Team		GP	G	A	PTS	PM	Year - Playoff		GP	G	A	PTS	PM
2007-08	WWHL Minnesota Whitecaps	14	2	8	10	16							
2008	Nationals Minnesota Whitecaps	3	0	0	0	4							
2008-09	WWHL Minnesota Whitecaps	13	11	5	16	14	2009	WWHL-P	2	0	1	1	8
							2009	C-Cup	3	1	0	1	2
2009-10	CWHL Stars de Montréal	16	11	11	22	4	2010	C-Cup	1	0	0	0	2
2010-11	CWHL Boston Blades	17	9	10	19	4	2011	CWHL-P	2				
2011-12	CWHL Boston Blades	18	7	5	12	10	2012	C-Cup	3	1	2	3	4
2012-13	CWHL Boston Blades	15	2	3	5	4	2013	C-Cup	4	0	0	0	4
2013-14	CWHL Boston Blades	12	7	8	15	10	2014	C-Cup	4	0	0	0	2
2014-15	CWHL Boston Blades	9	2	1	3	2	2015	C-Cup	3	0	1	1	0

Year - League - Team	GP	G	A	PTS	PM	Year - Playoff	GP	G	A	PTS	PM
2015-16 NWHL/ Connecticut Whale	15	2	5	7	8	2016 I-Cup	3	0	1	1	0
2018-19 NWHL/ Connecticut Whale	1	0	0	0	0	2019 I-Cup	1	0	0	0	2
CWHL Regular Season	87	38	38	76	34	Clarkson Cup	18	2	3	5	14
NWHL Regular Season	16	2	5	7	8	Isobel Cup	4	0	1	1	2
Totals from all Competitions	**159**	**55**	**61**	**116**	**100**						

Finished 17th in the Angela James Bowl scoring race in 2013-14

KOMENDA, BRIAR *LW. 2005-06 NWHL Brampton Thunder #17 (2 games, 2 assists).*

KONDO, YOKO *Aomori, JPN. Defence. 2005-06 NWHL Ottawa #3 (36 gp, 3 goals, 11 assists; 2 playoff gp).*

KONG MINGHUI *Right Wing. Shoots right. #15*

Born 1992-04-21. Grew up in Harbin, CHN. 5'4". Debut at age 25 on 2017-10-28.

Year - League - Team	GP	G	A	PTS	PM
2017-18 CWHL Vanke Rays	28	1	1	2	10
2018-19 CWHL KRS Vanke Rays	28	1	1	2	0

KORDLOFF, KRISTINA *1999-00 NWHL Durham Lightning #28 (1 game).*

KORN, HILARY *Defence. 1999-00 NWHL Ottawa Raiders #5 (35 games, 2 goals, 7 assists).*

KOSHER, MICHELLE *Forward. 1997-98 COWHL Scarborough Sting #9 (18 games, 1 assist).*

KOSTA, NICOLE *Forward. Shoots right. #22.*

Clarkson Cup winner with Markham on 2018-03-25
Born 1993-2-27. Grew up in Mississauga, ON, CAN. 5'5". Debut at age 17 on 2009-10-11.

Year - League - Team	GP	G	A	PTS	PM	Year - Playoff	GP	G	A	PTS	PM
2009-10 CWHL Mississauga Chiefs	1	1	0	1	2						
2016-17 NWHL/ Connecticut Whale	18	6	11	17	6	2017 I-Cup	1	0	0	0	0
2017-18 CWHL Markham Thunder	12	2	6	8	2	2018 C-Cup	3	1	3	4	2
2018-19 CWHL Markham Thunder	13	1	5	6	2						
Totals from all Competitions	**48**	**11**	**25**	**36**	**14**						

KOYANAGI, ALISON *Forward. 2004-05 WWHL B.C. #4 (20 gp); 2005-06 (24 gp, 4 goals, 6 assists).*

KOZAK, STACY *Forward.*

Abby Hoffman Cup winner with Calgary on 1998-03-22.

Year - League - Team	GP	G	A	PTS	PM	Year - Playoff	GP	G	A	PTS	PM
1998 Nationals Calgary Oval X-Treme	7	2	1	3	0						
1999 Nationals Calgary Oval X-Treme	6	1	0	1							

KRATCHMER, JOCELYN *Watrous, SK, CAN. F. 2006-07 WWHL Saskatchewan #19 (24 gp, 3 goals, 1 assist).*

KRAUSE, LORI *Forward. 2005 Nationals Alberta (6 games, 1 goal).*

KRETZ, ANDREA *2001-02 NWHL Durham #7 (28 gp, 3 goals, 1 a.); 2007-08 CWHL Burlington (3 gp; playoff 3gp).*

KRISTENSEN, TINA *Forward. 1996 Nationals Edmonton Chimos (7 gp, 6 goals, 5 assists).*

KRIZOVA, DENISA *Forward. Shoots left. #41.*

Born 1994-11-03. Grew up in Horní Cerekev, CZE. 5'6". Debut at age 23 on 2018-10-13.

Year - League - Team	GP	G	A	PTS	PM	Year - Playoff	GP	G	A	PTS	PM
2018-19 NWHL/ Boston Pride	16	6	8	14	4	2019 I-Cup	1	0	0	0	0

KROEKER, BONNIE *Defence. 2008 Nationals Manitoba (5 games, 1 goal).*

KROG, JEN *Forward. Shoots right. #17 #11 #10.*

Born 1977-6-13. Grew up in Fernie, BC, CAN.

Year - League - Team	GP	G	A	PTS	PM
1996-97 COWHL North York Aeros	2	5	3	8	0
2000-01 NWHL Mississauga IceBears	7	0	0	0	0
2001-02 NWHL Brampton Thunder	29	0	4	4	10
2002 Nationals Brampton Thunder	7	1	2	3	2
Totals from all Competitions	**45**	**6**	**9**	**15**	**12**

KROMM, ERICA *Defence. Shoots left. #8*

Clarkson Cup winner with Calgary on 2016-03-14 and 2019-03-24.
Born 1989-3-25. Grew up in Penticton, BC, CAN. 5'9". Debut at age 24 on 2012-10-27.

Year - League - Team	GP	G	A	PTS	PM	Year - Playoff	GP	G	A	PTS	PM
2012-13 CWHL Alberta	23	2	2	4	8						
2013-14 CWHL Calgary Inferno	24	1	2	3	16	2014 C-Cup	3	0	0	0	0
2014-15 CWHL Calgary Inferno	23	3	2	5	6	2015 C-Cup	2	0	0	0	0
2015-16 CWHL Calgary Inferno	23	1	5	6	16	2016 C-Cup	3	0	0	0	4
2018-19 CWHL Calgary Inferno	22	0	1	1	6	2019 C-Cup	4	0	0	0	0
CWHL Regular Season	165	12	24	36	70	Clarkson Cup	19	0	0	0	10
Totals from all Competitions	**184**	**12**	**24**	**36**	**80**						

KROOKS, SARI *Forward. Shoots left. #71 #17.*

Abby Hoffman Cup winner with Aeros on 1991-03-17. Born 1968-02-02, Vaasa, FIN. 5'3".

Year - League - Team	GP	G	A	PTS	PM
1995-96 COWHL North York Aeros	14	15	7	22	16
1996 Nationals North York Aeros	5	3	4	7	4

Year - League - Team			GP	G	A	PTS	PM
1996-97	COWHL	North York Aeros	25	24	21	45	16
1998-99	NWHL	North York Aeros	22	10	11	21	18
1999	Nationals	North York Aeros	5	1	1	2	
1999-00	NWHL	North York Aeros	2	2	0	2	0
Totals from all Competitions			**63**	**51**	**39**	**90**	**50**

KRZYZANIAK, HALLI *Defence. Shoots right. #21.*

Clarkson Cup winner with Calgary on 2019-03-24.
Born 1995-02-05. Grew up in Neepawa, MB, CAN. 5'7". Debut at age 23 on 2018-10-13.

Year - League - Team			GP	G	A	PTS	PM	Year - Playoff	GP	G	A	PTS	PM
2018-19	CWHL	Calgary Inferno	27	4	9	13	26	2019 C-Cup	4	1	1	2	2

CWHL All-Rookie Team 2018-19.

KUBER, MELISSA *Forward. 2008-09 WWHL Edmonton Chimos #71 (0 games).*

KUBO, HANAE *Forward. 2005-06 NWHL Oakville Ice #49 (36 gp, 15 goals, 19 assists; 2 playoff gp).*

KULAK, MARLOW *D. 2002-03 NWHL Edmonton (24 gp, 2 a.); 2003-04 (8 gp, 1 goal); 2004 Nationals (6 gp, 2 a.).*

KUNICHIKA, KOURTNEY *Forward. Shoots right. #36.*

Isobel Cup winner with Buffalo on 2017-03-19
Born 1991-11-07. Grew up in Fullerton, CA, USA. 5'5". Debut at age 23 on 2015-10-11.

Year - League - Team			GP	G	A	PTS	PM	Year - Playoff	GP	G	A	PTS	PM
2015-16	**NWHL/**	**Buffalo Beauts**	**18**	**9**	**8**	**17**	**4**	**2016 I-Cup**	**5**	**0**	**1**	**1**	**2**
2016-17	NWHL/	Buffalo Beauts	17	2	9	11	6	2017 I-Cup	2	0	0	0	0
2017-18	NWHL/	Buffalo Beauts	15	4	10	14	8	2018 I-Cup	2	0	1	1	2
NWHL Regular Season			50	15	27	42	18	Isobel Cup	9	0	2	2	4
Totals from all Competitions			**59**	**15**	**29**	**44**	**22**						

KURATA, TOMOMI *Osaka, JPN. Forward. 2015-16 CWHL Toronto Furies #18 (24 games; C-Cup 2 games).*

KURIO, RHIANNA *Forward. Shoots right. #10.*

Clarkson Cup winner with Calgary on 2019-03-24.
Born 1991-10-18. Grew up in Calgary, AB, CAN. 5'4". Debut at age 22 on 2013-11-09.

Year - League - Team			GP	G	A	PTS	PM	Year - Playoff	GP	G	A	PTS	PM
2013-14	CWHL	Calgary Inferno	24	3	3	6	8	2014 C-Cup	3	0	0	0	0
2014-15	CWHL	Calgary Inferno	20	5	8	13	2	2015 C-Cup	2	0	0	0	0
2015-16	CWHL	Calgary Inferno	12	1	0	1	0						
2016-17	CWHL	Calgary Inferno	5	0	2	2	0						
2017-18	CWHL	Calgary Inferno	24	9	5	14	4	2018 C-Cup	3	0	0	0	0
2018-19	CWHL	Calgary Inferno	14	0	1	1	0	2019 C-Cup	4	0	0	0	0
CWHL Regular Season			99	18	19	37	14	Clarkson Cup	12	0	0	0	0
Totals from all Competitions			**111**	**18**	**19**	**37**	**14**						

KURTH, KATELYN *High Bridge, NJ. D. 2011-12 CWHL Boston Blades #9 (26 gp, 1 goal, 3 a.; C-Cup 3 gp, 2 a.).*

KURYK, JACKIE *Defence. Shoots left.*

Born 1973-11-09. Grew up in Winnipeg, MB, CAN.

Year - League - Team			GP	G	A	PTS	PM	Year - Playoff	GP	G	A	PTS	PM
1995	Nationals	Winnipeg Sweat Camp											
1996	Nationals	Winnipeg Sweat Camp	6	3	1	4	4						
2000	Nationals	University of Manitoba	5										
2001	Nationals	University of Manitoba											

KWASNICKI, KAREENA *Forward. 1995 Nationals Regina Sharks.*

LABONNE, MÉLANIE *Forward. 2000-01 NWHL Mistral de Laval (1 game); 2001 Nationals Équipe Québec.*

LABRIE, KRISTINA *Forward. Shoots right. #71*

Born 1988-11-23. Grew up in St. Quentin, NB, CAN.

Year - League - Team			GP	G	A	PTS	PM
2006	Nationals	Team New Brunswick	7	3	1	4	4
2007	Nationals	Team New Brunswick		0	0	0	
2012-13	CWHL	Alberta	11	1	2	3	4

LACASSE, KATY *Forward. #19 #9.*

Born 1987-9-9. Forward.

Year - League - Team			GP	G	A	PTS	PM	Year - Playoff	GP	G	A	PTS	PM
2005-06	WWHL	British Columbia Breakers	24	0	1	1	12						
2006-07	WWHL	British Columbia Breakers	24	3	3	6	16	2007 WWHL-P	2	0	0	0	0
2007-08	WWHL	British Columbia Breakers	24	5	4	9	14						
2008-09	WWHL	British Columbia Breakers	14	1	4	5	2						
Totals from all Competitions			**88**	**9**	**12**	**21**	**44**						

LACELLE, KRISTINE *Forward. 2002 Nationals Saskatchewan (6 games, 2 assists).*

LACEY, TRICIA *RW. 1995-96 COWHL Peterborough #18 (28 games, 2 goals, 4 assists).*

LACHANCE, SARA *Forward. 2015-16 CWHL Montréal (18 games, 1 assist).*

LACHAPELLE, SOPHIE *Forward. Shoots right. #89.*
Born 1984-8-28, Laval, QC, CAN. Grew up in Laval, QC, CAN. 5'11".

Year - League - Team			GP	G	A	PTS	PM
2003-04	NWHL	Avalanche du Québec	1	0	0	0	
2005-06	NWHL	Avalanche du Québec	8	3	2	5	4
2006-07	NWHL	Avalanche du Québec	13	1	3	4	6

LACQUETTE, BRIGETTE *Defence. Shoots right. #4.*
Clarkson Cup winner with Calgary on 2016-03-14 and 2019-03-24.
Born 1992-10-11. Grew up in Waterhen, MB, CAN. 5'7". Debut at age 18 on 2010-11.

Year - League - Team			GP	G	A	PTS	PM	Year - Playoff		GP	G	A	PTS	PM
2010-11	WWHL	Manitoba Maple Leafs	6	2	2	4	8							
2015-16	CWHL	Calgary Inferno	10	2	8	10	12	2016	C-Cup	3	1	3	4	4
2016-17	CWHL	Calgary Inferno	19	4	10	14	30	2017	C-Cup	4	0	1	1	2
2018-19	CWHL	Calgary Inferno	24	2	16	18	34	2019	C-Cup	4	1	2	3	18
CWHL Regular Season			53	8	34	42	76	Clarkson Cup		11	2	6	8	24
Totals from all Competitions			**70**	**12**	**42**	**54**	**108**							

CWHL Second All-Star Team in 2018-19... CWHL All-Rookie Team in 2015-16

LACROIX, DANIELLE *Forward. 2002 Nationals Richmond Steelers (5 games).*
LACROIX, MELLISSA *RW. 2005-06 NWHL Toronto Aeros #15 (2 games, 1 assist).*

LAFLAMME, BRIGITTE *Forward. Shoots left.*
Born 1982-11-04. Grew up in St-Augustin, QC, CAN.

Year - League - Team			GP	G	A	PTS	PM	Year - Playoff		GP	G	A	PTS	PM
2003	Nationals	Équipe Québec	5	0	5	5	0							
2007-08	CWHL	Stars de Montréal	14	3	3	6	12	2008	CWHL-P	2	0	0	0	4

LAFLEUR, KATIE *Defence. Shoots left. #77 #66 #27.*
Born 1981-8-21. Grew up in Gatineau, QC, CAN. 5'9".

Year - League - Team			GP	G	A	PTS	PM	Year - Playoff		GP	G	A	PTS	PM
2004-05	NWHL	Ottawa Raiders	26	1	4	5	6							
2005-06	NWHL	Ottawa Raiders	4	0	1	1	0	2006	NWHL-P	2	0	0	0	0
2006-07	NWHL	Ottawa Raiders	14	0	3	3	28							
Totals from all Competitions			**46**	**1**	**8**	**9**	**34**							

LAFORGE, CAROLINE *Forward.*
Born 1987-11-16, Brossard, QC, CAN. 5'5". Debut at age 17 on 2005-09-17.

Year - League - Team			GP	G	A	PTS	PM	Year - Playoff		GP	G	A	PTS	PM
2005-06	NWHL	Axion de Montréal	8	2	4	6	2							
2006-07	NWHL	Avalanche du Québec	31	9	26	35	50	2007	NWHL-P					
2007-08	CWHL	Stars de Montréal	23	12	20	32	34							
2008	CWHL-P	Montréal	2	0	1	1	4							
Totals from all Competitions			**64**	**23**	**51**	**74**	**90**							

Finished 8th in the Angela James Bowl scoring race in 2007-08

LAGACÉ, JANE *Forward. #16.*
IIHF champion. Abby Hoffman Cup winner with Edmonton on 1997-03-09.
Also played Jane Robinson. Born 1963-07-29, St-Jérôme, QC, CAN.

Year - League - Team			GP	G	A	PTS	PM	Year - Playoff		GP	G	A	PTS	PM
1996	Nationals	Edmonton Chimos	7	8	3	11	2							
1997	Nationals	Edmonton Chimos												
1998	Nationals	Edmonton Chimos	7	2	4	6	2							
2002-03	NWHL	Edmonton Chimos	23	2	7	9	18							
2003-04	NWHL	Edmonton Chimos	2	1	0	1	0	2004	NWHL-P	1	1	0	1	0
2004	Nationals	Edmonton Chimos	7	0	0	0	0							

LAGUEUX, CLAUDIE *Forward. #61 #20 #8.*

Year - League - Team			GP	G	A	PTS	PM
1999-00	NWHL	Mistral de Laval	2	0	0	0	0
2000-01	NWHL	Mistral de Laval	5	1	0	1	2
2001-02	NWHL	Cheyenne	19	0	0	0	6

LAING, AMANDA *Defence. 2006 Nationals Manitoba (5 games, 2 assists).*
LAING, DENNA *Forward. Shoots right. #24.*
Clarkson Cup winner with Boston on 2015-03-07.
Born 1991-05-12. Grew up in Marblehead, MA, USA. 5'9". Debut at age 23 on 2014-10-18.

Year - League - Team			GP	G	A	PTS	PM	Year - Playoff		GP	G	A	PTS	PM
2014-15	CWHL	Boston Blades	18	1	1	2	0	2015	C-Cup	3	0	0	0	0
2015-16	NWHL/	Boston Pride	2	0	0	0	0							

NWHL Foundation Award in 2015-16... NWHL Perseverance Award in 2015-16

LAIRD, ERIKA *Defence. 2004 Nationals Saskatchewan (6 games).*
LAKING, ABYGAIL *Forward. 2013-14 CWHL Calgary #15 (22 gp, 4 goals, 2 a.; C-Cup 3 gp, 1 g., 1 a.).*
LALLY, ERIN *Calgary, AB, CAN. Forward. 2014-15 CWHL Montréal #19 (6 games).*
LALOI, JENNIFER *FRA. Defence. 2013-14 CWHL Montréal #9 (13 games).*

LAMBERT, JULIE

Forward. #19 #29 #20.

Year - League - Team			GP	G	A	PTS	PM			
1998-99	NWHL	Bonaventure	3	1	0	1	2			
1999-00	NWHL	Sainte-Julie	31	9	6	15	30	2000	NWHL-P	
2000-01	NWHL	Sainte-Julie	10	3	0	3	12			
2001-02	NWHL	Cheyenne	24	3	13	16	30			
2002-03	NWHL	Avalanche du Québec	17	3	3	6	10			
2003-04	NWHL	Avalanche du Québec	2	0	0	0	2			
Totals from all Competitions			**87**	**19**	**22**	**41**	**86**			

LAMBERT, MADELAINE

Forward. 1998 Nationals Tazmanian Devils (5 gp, 1 assist); 1999 Nationals (4 gp).

LAMBERT, NATHALIE

Defence. 2002-03 NWHL Vancouver Griffins #44 (24 gp); 2003 Nationals Vancouver (7 gp).

LAMBERT, STÉPHANIE

Forward. Shoots left. #9.

Born 1981-8-6, Grande-Rivière, QC, CAN. Grew up in Montréal, QC, CAN. 5'3".

Year - League - Team			GP	G	A	PTS	PM
2002-03	NWHL	Avalanche du Québec	3	0	0	0	4
2003	Nationals	Équipe Québec	5	1	1	2	0
2003-04	NWHL	Avalanche du Québec	9	3	1	4	8
2004-05	NWHL	Avalanche du Québec	36	6	14	20	32
2005-06	NWHL	Avalanche du Québec	20	2	5	7	32
Totals from all Competitions			**73**	**12**	**21**	**33**	**76**

LAMER, MARTINE

Forward. #22.

Year - League - Team			GP	G	A	PTS	PM
1998-99	NWHL	Mistral de Laval	34	3	7	10	26
1999-00	NWHL	Mistral de Laval	33	3	5	8	28
2000-01	NWHL	Sainte-Julie	1	0	0	0	0
Totals from all Competitions			**68**	**6**	**12**	**18**	**54**

LAMOUREUX, MONIQUE

Defence. Shoots right. #15.

Olympic champion, IIHF champion. Clarkson Cup winner with Boston on 2015-03-07
Born 1989-07-03, Grand Forks, ND, USA. 5'7". Debut at age 25 on 2014-11-15.

Year - League - Team			GP	G	A	PTS	PM	Year - Playoff		GP	G	A	PTS	PM
2014-15	CWHL	Boston Blades	17	6	12	18	23	2015	C-Cup	3	0	5	5	0

CWHL Second All-Star Team in 2014-15... CWHL All-Rookie Team in 2014-15... finished 11th in the Angela James Bowl scoring race in 2014-15

LAMOUREUX, TANIS

Forward. Shoots left. #20.

Born 1992-11-18, Stuttgart, GER. 5'4". Debut at age 22 on 2014-11-30.

Year - League - Team			GP	G	A	PTS	PM	Year - Playoff		GP	G	A	PTS	PM
2014-15	CWHL	Toronto Furies	7	1	2	3	2	2015	C-Cup	2	1	0	1	0
2015-16	CWHL	Toronto Furies	13	1	2	3	6							
2016-17	CWHL	Toronto Furies	19	2	3	5	2	2017	C-Cup	3	0	0	0	0
CWHL Regular Season			39	4	7	11	10	Clarkson Cup		5	1	0	1	0
Totals from all Competitions			**44**	**5**	**7**	**12**	**10**							

LAMPRON, CHANTAL

Forward. Shoots left.

Born 1984-01-30. Grew up in St-Boniface, QC, CAN.

Year - League - Team			GP	G	A	PTS	PM
2002-03	NWHL	Avalanche du Québec	4	1	2	3	0
2003	Nationals	Équipe Québec	5	2	5	7	4
2003-04	NWHL	Avalanche du Québec	3	0	1	1	6
2004	Nationals	Équipe Québec	7	3	4	7	12

LANDRY, KAYLA

Defence. 2008 Nationals Team New Brunswick (5 games).

LANDRY, LYNE

Defence. Shoots left. #16.

Born 1978-10-5, Memramcook, NB, CAN. Grew up in Memramcook, NB, CAN. 5'7".

Year - League - Team			GP	G	A	PTS	PM	Year - Playoff		GP	G	A	PTS	PM
1996	Nationals	Maritime Sports Blades	6	1	2	3	4							
1998	Nationals	Maritime Sports Blades	6	0	2	2	4							
1999	Nationals	Team New Brunswick	6	1	2	3								
1999-00	NWHL	Ottawa Raiders	31	3	5	8	30							
2000-01	NWHL	Ottawa Raiders	38	1	13	14	44							
2001-02	NWHL	Ottawa Raiders	29	2	10	12	14							
2002-03	NWHL	Ottawa Raiders	35	10	12	22	16							
2003-04	NWHL	Ottawa Raiders	21	2	4	6	6							
2005-06	NWHL	Ottawa Raiders	36	4	13	17	22	2006	NWHL-P	2	0	0	0	2
2006-07	NWHL	Ottawa Raiders	33	5	12	17	46	2007	NWHL-P	2	1	1	2	2
2007-08	CWHL	Ottawa Capital Canucks	25	1	9	10	20	2008	CWHL-P	1	0	0	0	0
2008-09	CWHL	Ottawa Senators	15	0	3	3	6							
CWHL Regular Season			40	1	12	13	26							
Totals from all Competitions			**286**	**31**	**88**	**119**	**216**							

CWHL Eastern All-Star Team in 2007-08... NWHL Defenceman of the Year in 2005-06... served as interim coach with CWHL Ottawa... served as general manager with CWHL Ottawa

LANE, CHRISTINE *Forward. 1998-99 NWHL Ottawa Raiders #19 (30 games, 6 goals, 10 assists).*

LANG, DEANNE *Forward.*
Abby Hoffman Cup winner with Edmonton on 1997-03-09.

Year - League - Team		GP	G	A	PTS	PM
1997	Nationals Edmonton Chimos					
1998	Nationals Edmonton Chimos	7	5	2	7	4

LANG, VERONICA *Defence. 2008-09 WWHL British Columbia #77 (14 games, 1 assist).*

LANGLOIS, JACINTHE *2006-07 NWHL Québec #5 (7 games).*

LANKTON, LAURA *Houghton, MI. F. 2008-09 CWHL Ottawa #21 (19 games, 2 assists; 2 playoff gp, 1 assist).*

LANNING, CARRIE *Forward. #14 #99 #41.*

Year - League - Team		GP	G	A	PTS	PM
1992-93	COWHL Scarborough Firefighters	26	3	5	8	2
1993-94	COWHL Scarborough Firefighters	8	0	0	0	0
1996-97	COWHL Newtonbrook Panthers	1	0	1	1	0
1998-99	NWHL Mississauga Chiefs	1	1	0	1	0
Totals from all Competitions		**36**	**4**	**6**	**10**	**2**

LANSING, DANI JO *Defence. Shoots left. #8 #11.*
Born 1984-2-6, Red Deer, AB, CAN. Grew up in Coronation, AB, CAN. 5'5". Debut at age 23 on 2006-9-30.

Year - League - Team		GP	G	A	PTS	PM	Year		GP	G	A	PTS	PM
2002	Nationals Calgary Oval X-Treme	4	0	0	0	2							
2006-07	NWHL Etobicoke Dolphins	30	3	7	10	32	2007	NWHL-P	3	0	0	0	2
2007	Nationals Etobicoke Dolphins	7	1	3	4	4							
2007-08	CWHL Vaughan Flames	17	1	2	3	28	2008	CWHL-P	2	0	0	0	0
2008-09	CWHL Vaughan Flames	24	2	7	9	20	2009	CWHL-P	2		4		
CWHL Regular Season		41	3	9	12	48							
Totals from all Competitions		**89**	**7**	**19**	**26**	**92**							

LANZL, MICHAELA *F. 2008-09 WWHL Minnesota #77 (11 gp, 3 goals, 1 assist; 2 playoff gp, 1 a.; C-Cup 2 gp).*

LAPAGE-BARRETTE, VALERIE *Forward. 2004-05 NWHL Québec #45 (3 games, 1 goal).*

LAPIERRE, VÉRONIQUE *Centre. Shoots left. #21.*
Born 1981-6-8, Lac Mégantic, QC, CAN. Grew up in Lac Mégantic, QC, CAN. 5'4". Debut at age 24 on 2005-09-25.

Year - League - Team		GP	G	A	PTS	PM	Year - Playoff		GP	G	A	PTS	PM
2005-06	NWHL Avalanche du Québec	35	10	5	15	36							
2006-07	NWHL Avalanche du Québec	30	7	10	17	37	2007	NWHL-P					
2007-08	CWHL Phénix du Québec	29	5	8	13	46							
CWHL Regular Season		29	5	8	13	46							
Totals from all Competitions		**94**	**22**	**23**	**45**	**119**							

LAPLANTE, ALEXIA *Ste-Thérèse, QC, CAN. Forward. 2007-08 Québec #15 (2 games, 1 goal, 1 assist).*

LARADE, SHELLEY *Forward. 1995 Nationals Metro Valley Selects.*

LARAMÉE-PAQUETTE, VERNONIQUE *Forward. Shoots left. #91 #96.*
Born 1988-11-10, St-Jovite, QC, CAN. Grew up in Mont Tremblay, QC, CAN. 5'8". Debut at age 16 on 2005-09-25.

Year - League - Team		GP	G	A	PTS	PM
2005-06	NWHL Avalanche du Québec	35	9	6	15	10
2007-08	CWHL Stars de Montréal	4	2	1	3	2
Totals from all Competitions		**39**	**11**	**7**	**18**	**12**

LAROCHE, DOMINIQUE *Forward. #22.*
Born 1979-5-12.

Year - League - Team		GP	G	A	PTS	PM	Year - Playoff		GP	G	A	PTS	PM
1999-00	NWHL Ottawa Raiders	34	7	2	9	18							
2000-01	NWHL Ottawa Raiders	35	16	12	28	10							
2001-02	NWHL Ottawa Raiders	30	14	8	22	8							
2002-03	NWHL Ottawa Raiders	6	1	0	1	0							
2003-04	NWHL Ottawa Raiders	16	3	3	6	4							
2003-04	NWHL Avalanche du Québec	16	3	3	6	4	2004	NWHL-P	0	0	0	0	0
Totals from all Competitions		**137**	**44**	**28**	**72**	**44**							

LAROCQUE, CHANTAL *Forward. Shoots left. #10.*
Abby Hoffman Cup winner with Calgary on 2007-03-10. WWHL winner. Born 1986-12-22. Grew up in Ste. Anne, MB, CAN. 5'2".

Year - League - Team		GP	G	A	PTS	PM	Year - Playoff		GP	G	A	PTS	PM
2004	Nationals Manitoba	5	3	4	7	2							
2005-06	WWHL Calgary Oval X-Treme	23	10	19	29	20	2006	WWHL-P	3	2	2	4	4
2006	Nationals Calgary Oval X-Treme	7	5	7	12	8							
2006-07	WWHL Calgary Oval X-Treme	18	8	9	17	26	2007	WWHL-P	3	0	2	2	6
2007	Nationals Calgary Oval X-Treme	6	2	1	3	0							
2010-11	WWHL Manitoba	12	6	8	14	2							
Totals from all Competitions		**77**	**36**	**52**	**88**	**68**							

LAROCQUE, JOCELYNE

Defence. Shoots left. #3.

Olympic champion. Abby Hoffman Cup winner with Calgary on 2007-03-10. Clarkson Cup winner with Markham on 2018-03-25. WWHL winner.

Born 1988-5-19. Grew up in Ste. Anne, MB, CAN. 5'7". Debut at age 26 in 2004-05.

Year	League	Team	GP	G	A	PTS	PM	Year	Playoff	GP	G	A	PTS	PM
2004	Nationals	Manitoba	5	0	2	2	16							
2004-05	WWHL	Calgary Oval X-Treme	17	2	6	8	18	2005	WWHL-P	3	0	0	0	2
2005-06	WWHL	Calgary Oval X-Treme	21	2	8	10	66	2006	WWHL-P	3	0	4	4	8
2006	Nationals	Calgary Oval X-Treme	7	0	3	3	12							
2006-07	WWHL	Calgary Oval X-Treme	21	3	15	18	43	2007	WWHL-P	3	0	0	0	6
2007	Nationals	Calgary Oval X-Treme	6	0	1	1	4							
2012-13	CWHL	Alberta	23	1	2	3	44							
2014-15	CWHL	Brampton Thunder	24	3	2	5	38							
2015-16	CWHL	Brampton Thunder	24	2	5	7	32	2016	C-Cup	2	0	1	1	4
2016-17	CWHL	Brampton Thunder	20	0	4	4	38	2017	C-Cup	2	0	0	0	12
2017-18	CWHL	Markham Thunder	4	1	1	2	2	2018	C-Cup	3	0	0	0	2
2018-19	CWHL	Markham Thunder	23	2	8	10	28	2019	C-Cup	3	0	2	2	4
CWHL Regular Season			118	9	22	31	182	Clarkson Cup		10	0	3	3	22
Totals from all Competitions			**214**	**16**	**64**	**80**	**379**							

LAROCQUE, RAELYN

Forward. Shoots left. #44 #28.

Born 1986-12-28, The Pas, MB, CAN. Grew up in The Pas, MB, CAN. 5'6".

Year	League	Team	GP	G	A	PTS	PM	Year	Playoff	GP	G	A	PTS	PM
2004-05	WWHL	Edmonton Chimos	21	2	1	3	12	2005	WWHL-P	3	1	0	1	0
2005-06	WWHL	Edmonton Chimos	21	5	2	7	14	2006	WWHL-P	2	0	0	0	0
2010-11	CWHL	Brampton Thunder	25	2	4	6	8	2011	CWHL-P	2				
								2011	C-Cup	3	0	0	0	2
CWHL Regular Season			25	2	4	6	8	Clarkson Cup		3	0	0	0	2
Totals from all Competitions			**77**	**10**	**7**	**17**	**36**							

LARSEN, KRISTA

Forward. #19.

Born 1985-5-7. Grew up in Winnipeg, MB, CAN.

Year	League	Team	GP	G	A	PTS	PM	Year	Playoff	GP	G	A	PTS	PM
2007-08	WWHL	Strathmore Rockies	20	1	2	3	0							
2008-09	WWHL	Strathmore Rockies	20	1	1	2	4	2009	WWHL-P	1	0	0	0	0
2009-10	WWHL	Strathmore Rockies	1	0	0	0	0							
Totals from all Competitions			**42**	**2**	**3**	**5**	**4**							

LASCELLE, JENNA

Cornwall, ON, CAN. Forward. 2008-09 CWHL Ottawa #14 (3 games, 2 assists).

LASH, SARAH

Defence. Shoots left.

Born 1974-06-25. Grew up in Vancouver, BC, CAN.

Year	League	Team	GP	G	A	PTS	PM
1996	Nationals	Britannia Blues	5	1	0	1	4
1998	Nationals	New Westminster Lightning	5	0	0	0	2
1999	Nationals	New Westminster Lightning	5	1	2	3	
2000	Nationals	Britannia Blues	5	0	1	1	
2002	Nationals	Richmond Steelers	5	0	0	0	4
2004	Nationals	British Columbia	6	0	0	0	2

LASKA, SUSIE

Defence. Shoots left. #14.

Born 1979-11-1, Cobden, ON, CAN. 5'8".

Year	League	Team	GP	G	A	PTS	PM	Year	Playoff	GP	G	A	PTS	PM
2003-04	NWHL	Ottawa Raiders	33	4	8	12	18	2004	NWHL-P		1		1	
2004-05	NWHL	Ottawa Raiders	35	6	9	15	36							
2005-06	NWHL	Ottawa Raiders	36	3	10	13	38	2006	NWHL-P	2	0	0	0	4
2006-07	NWHL	Ottawa Raiders	35	4	6	10	64	2007	NWHL-P	2	0	0	0	0
2008-09	CWHL	Ottawa Senators	2	0	0	0	2							
Totals from all Competitions			**145**	**18**	**33**	**51**	**162**							

LATOURES, ESTHER

Forward. #26 #16.

Year	League	Team	GP	G	A	PTS	PM	Year	Playoff
2001-02	NWHL	Wingstar de Montréal	30	2	1	3	10		
2002-03	NWHL	Axion de Montréal	35	1	0	1	8	2003	NWHL-PMontréal
2003-04	NWHL	Axion de Montréal	36	4	3	7	24		
Totals from all Competitions			**101**	**7**	**4**	**11**	**42**		

LATREILLE, NICOLE

Left wing. #3 #5 #17.

Born 1986-8-19.

Year	League	Team	GP	G	A	PTS	PM
2001-02	NWHL	Ottawa Raiders	3	0	0	0	0
2003-04	NWHL	Ottawa Raiders	35	3	6	9	80
2005-06	NWHL	Brampton Thunder	3	1	0	1	4
Totals from all Competitions			**41**	**4**	**6**	**10**	**84**

LAUER, MEGAN

Forward. 2009-10 WWHL Edmonton Chimos #18 (12 games, 1 assist).

LAURINAITIS, JESSICA   *Defence. 2008-09 WWHL Minnesota #33 (5 games, 1 goal).*

LAUNCELOTTE, ZOË   *Forward. 2006 Nationals Nova Scotia (5 gp, 3 assists); 2008 Nationals (5 gp, 2 g., 1 a.).*

LAUZON, LIZ   *Forward. 1999-00 NWHL Ottawa Raiders #7 (29 games, 2 goals, 5 assists).*

LAVALLEE, ANN   *Burlington, ON, CAN. D. 2009-10 CWHL Burlington #6 (2 games).*

LAVALLEE, ANDREA   *1996-97 COWHL London #15 (2 games, 1 assist); 2002-03 NWHL North York (playoffs).*

LAVERS, DANA   *Defence. 2007 Nationals Prince Edward Island (5 games).*

LAVERS, SALLY *Defence. 2003 Nationals Newfoundland (5 gp); 2005 Nationals (5 gp, 1 a.); 2006 Nationals (5 gp).*

LAVIGNE, TRACY ANN   *Centre. Shoots left. #78.*

Born 1992-03-07. Grew up in Montréal, QC, CAN. 5'3". Debut at age 25 on 2017-10-14.

Year - League - Team	GP	G	A	PTS	PM	Year - Playoff	GP	G	A	PTS	PM
2017-18 CWHL Canadiennes de Montréal	27	2	3	5	14	2018 C-Cup	2	0	0	0	0
2018-19 CWHL Canadiennes de Montréal	28	1	1	2	4	2019 C-Cup	3	1	0	1	0

LAVIOLETTE, MELISSA   *Forward. #22.*

Year - League - Team	GP	G	A	PTS	PM
1995-96 COWHL London Devilettes	30	22	24	46	62
1996-97 COWHL London Devilettes	23	11	21	32	28
1998 Nationals Edmonton Chimos	7	1	3	4	0
Totals from all Competitions	**60**	**34**	**48**	**82**	**90**

LAVIOLETTE, MISSY
Abby Hoffman Cup winner with Aeros on 1991-03-17.

LAVOIE, GENEVIÈVE   *LW. 2004-05 NWHL Québec #25 (4 goals, 1 goal); 2005-06 #59 (1 goal).*

LAVOIE, KRISTINA   *Defence. Shoots left. #8.*

Born 1990-12-27. Grew up in Foothill, ON, CAN. 5'9". Debut at age 25 on 2016-10-7.

Year - League - Team	GP	G	A	PTS	PM
2016-17 NWHL/ Buffalo Beauts	10	0	0	0	4

LAVOIE, STEPHANIE   *1998-99 NWHL Mistral de Laval #30 (5 games).*

LAW, KELLY   *Defence. 2001-02 NWHL North York Aeros #23 (5 games, 1 assist).*

LAWLER, ERIKA   *Forward. Shoots right. #2.*

IIHF champion. Isobel Cup winner with Metropolitan on 2018-03-25
Born 1987-2-5, Fitchburg, MA, USA. 5'0". Debut at age 24 on 2010-10-31.

Year - League - Team	GP	G	A	PTS	PM	Year - Playoff	GP	G	A	PTS	PM
2010-11 CWHL Boston Blades	4	2	3	5	4						
2011-12 CWHL Boston Blades	26	11	22	33	10	2012 C-Cup	3	2	2	4	0
2012-13 CWHL Boston Blades	1	0	0	0	0						
2017-18 NWHL/ Metropolitan Riveters	14	1	7	8	10	2018 I-Cup	2	1	2	3	0
2018-19 NWHL/ Metropolitan Riveters	15	0	1	1	4	2019 I-Cup	2	0	0	0	0
Totals from all Competitions	**67**	**17**	**37**	**54**	**28**						

CWHL All-Rookie Team in 2011-12... finished 9th in the Angela James Bowl scoring race in 2011-12

LAYDEN, MANDY   *Forward. Shoots right. #24.*

Born 1976-12-1, Drayton Valley, AB, CAN. 5'6".

Year - League - Team	GP	G	A	PTS	PM	Year - Playoff	GP	G	A	PTS	PM
2003-04 NWHL Edmonton Chimos	11	0	1	1	0	2004 NWHL-P					
2004 Nationals Edmonton Chimos	7	1	0	1	4						
2004-05 WWHL Edmonton Chimos	20	4	2	6	4	2005 WWHL-P	3	0	0	0	0
2005-06 WWHL Edmonton Chimos	24	2	3	5	12	2006 WWHL-P	2	0	0	0	0
2006-07 WWHL Edmonton Chimos	24	1	0	1	2	2007 WWHL-P	2	0	0	0	2
Totals from all Competitions	**93**	**8**	**6**	**14**	**24**						

LÊ, MAI-LAN   *Forward. #23 #22.*

IIHF champion. Born 1971-07-31.

Year - League - Team	GP	G	A	PTS	PM	Year - Playoff
1998 Nationals Équipe Québec	6	0	1	1	4	
1998-99 NWHL Montréal Jofa-Titan	21	12	10	22	28	
1999 Nationals Équipe Québec	5	3	4	7		
1999-00 NWHL Sainte-Julie	31	16	15	31	97	2000 NWHL-P
2000 Nationals Équipe Québec	6	5	3	8		
2000-01 NWHL Sainte-Julie	28	22	10	32	46	
2001-02 NWHL Cheyenne	4	1	1	2	14	
Totals from all Competitions	**101**	**59**	**44**	**103**	**189**	

LEAHY, SHELLEY   *Forward. Shoots left.*

Born 1967-07-19. Grew up in Fredericton, NB, CAN.

Year - League - Team	GP	G	A	PTS	PM
1995 Nationals Maritime Sports Blades					
1996 Nationals Maritime Sports Blades	6	0	4	4	8
1998 Nationals Maritime Sports Blades	6	0	0	0	2
2000 Nationals Team New Brunswick	6	0	0	0	
2001 Nationals Team New Brunswick					

LEARY, BRENNA — *Defence. 2004 Nationals Manitoba (5 games).*
LEARY, JAYMIE — *Defence. 1996 Nationals Winnipeg (6 gp); 2000 Nationals U. Manitoba (5 games).*

LEARY, KATE — Forward. Shoots right. #28.
Born 1993-8-10. Grew up in Seabrook, NH, USA. 5'2". Debut at age 23 on 2016-10-15.

Year - League - Team			GP	G	A	PTS	PM
2016-17	CWHL	Boston Blades	24	10	6	16	6
2017-18	CWHL	Boston Blades	28	7	9	16	18
CWHL Regular Season			52	17	15	32	24

CWHL All-Rookie Team in 2016-17... finished 17th in the Angela James Bowl scoring race in 2016-17

LEBEAU, JESSICA — Forward. #3.
Born 1987-10-8, Gatineau, QC, CAN. 5'7".

Year - League - Team			GP	G	A	PTS	PM	Year - Playoff		GP	G	A	PTS	PM
2003-04	NWHL	Ottawa Raiders	16	2	2	4	14	2004 NWHL-P		1			1	
2004-05	NWHL	Ottawa Raiders	27	1	0	1	12							
Totals from all Competitions			**43**	**4**	**2**	**6**	**26**							

LEBLANC, CAROLE — *Forward. 2006 Nationals Team New Brunswick (7 gp, 1 goal, 2 assists).*
LEBLANC, CAROLINE — *Defence. 1999-00 NWHL Laval #37 (7 games); 2000-01 (6 games).*
LEBLANC, GUYLAINE — *F. 1999 Nationals Team N.B. (6 gp, 1 goal); 2000 Nationals (6 gp, 5 pts); 2001 Nationals.*
LEBLANC, JOCELYN — *Forward. 2008 Nationals Nova Scotia Selects (5 games, 3 goals, 2 assists).*
LEBLANC, JULIE — *Forward. 2001 Nationals Team New Brunswick.*
LEBLOND, NATHALIE — *Defence. 1995 Nationals Équipe Québec; 1996 Nationals (6 gp, 4 goals, 2 assists).*
LEBRUN, LAURA — *Forward. 2005 Nationals British Columbia (7 games, 2 assists).*
LECLAIR, PAM — *Forward. 2005 Nationals Prince Edward Island (4 games, 1 goal, 1 assist).*
LECLAIRE, CHANTAL — *Defence. 1995 Nationals Équipe Québec.*
LECLERC-AUGER, MARIE-ANDRÉE — *2005-06 NWHL Québec #7 (1 game); 2006-07 #94 (1 game, 1 goal).*
LE DONNE, ANDIE — *Defence. 2013-14 CWHL Brampton #21 (22 games, 1 goal, 1 assist).*
LEDUC, MARTINE — *Centre. 2005-06 NWHL Québec #88 (1 game); 2007-08 CWHL #11 (1 game).*

LEE, CHERYL — Forward. Shoots right. #18.
Born 1978-07-14. Grew up in New Westminster, BC, CAN.

Year - League - Team			GP	G	A	PTS	PM
2002	Nationals	Richmond Steelers	5	2	1	3	8
2004	Nationals	British Columbia	6	0	0	0	2
2005-06	WWHL	British Columbia Breakers	13	0	0	0	6

LEE, CHRISTINA — *Forward. 2010-11 WWHL Minnesota #29 (11 gp, 6 goals, 5 assists; C-Cup 2 games).*
LEFEBVRE, VÉRONIQUE — *F. 2002-03 NWHL Québec (1 gp); 2003-04 (4 gp); 2005-06 (7 gp, 4 goals, 1 assist).*

LEFORT, SARAH — Left wing. Shoots left. #16.
Clarkson Cup winner with Montréal on 2017-03-05
Born 1994-02-09. Grew up in Ormstown, QC,CAN. 5'8". Debut at age 22 on 2016-10-15.

Year - League - Team			GP	G	A	PTS	PM			GP	G	A	PTS	PM
2016-17	CWHL	Canadiennes de Montréal	22	9	6	15	28	2017 C-Cup		3	1	2	3	4
2017-18	CWHL	Canadiennes de Montréal	28	18	12	30	24	2018 C-Cup		2	1	0	1	0
2018-19	CWHL	Canadiennes de Montréal	26	7	9	16	16	2019 C-Cup		4	0	2	2	4
CWHL Regular Season			76	34	27	61	68	Clarkson Cup		9	2	4	6	8
Totals from all Competitions			**85**	**36**	**31**	**67**	**76**							

Finished 7th in the Angela James Bowl scoring race in 2017-18

LEGAULT, GENEVIÈVE — *Sainte-Julie, QC. D. 2009-10 CWHL Montréal (26 gp, 2 goals, 2 a.); 2011-12 (2 games).*
LEGERE, CHANTAL — *Forward. 2001 Nationals Team N.B.; 2005 Nationals (6 gp, 2 a.); 2007 Nationals.*

LEGRESLEY, CAROLINE — Defence. Shoots right.
Born 1977-06-19. Grew up in Grande Digille, NB, CAN.

Year - League - Team			GP	G	A	PTS	PM
1996	Nationals	Maritime Sports Blades	6	0	0	0	2
1998	Nationals	Maritime Sports Blades	6	0	1	1	4
2000	Nationals	Team New Brunswick			1	1	
2001	Nationals	Team New Brunswick					

LEHRKE, ALI — Forward. Shoots right.
Born 1983-11-29. Grew up in Bloomington, MN, USA. 5'8".

Year - League - Team			GP	G	A	PTS	PM		
2006-07	WWHL	Minnesota Whitecaps	24	3	12	15	42	2007	WWHL-P
2007-08	WWHL	Minnesota Whitecaps	14	0	1	1	6		
2008	Nationals	Minnesota Whitecaps							

LEITOLD, JILL — *Forward. 1995 Nationals Winnipeg; 1996 Nationals Winnipeg (6 gp, 2 assists).*
LEMAIRE, KEIRSTEN — *Defence. 2002-03 NWHL Durham Lightning #3 (? games).*

LEMAIRE, SHEREE
Forward.

Year - League - Team			GP	G	A	PTS	PM
1996-97	COWHL	Peterborough Pirates	36	5	14	19	22
2000-01	NWHL	Durham Lightning	1	0	1	1	0

LEMIEUX, GWEN
Forward. 1998 Nationals New Westminster Lightning (5 games, 1 goal).

LEMIEUX, MARIE-MICHEL
2008-09 CWHL Montréal (2 games).

LEN, KELLEY
Defence. 2002 Nationals Saskatchewan (6 gp); 2003 Nationals Saskatchewan (6 gp, 1 goal).

LEONE, NIKKI
Defence. #2 #17.

Year - League - Team			GP	G	A	PTS	PM
2002-03	NWHL	Durham Lightning					
2003-04	NWHL	Durham Lightning	35	3	10	13	60
2004-05	NWHL	Durham Lightning	28	5	3	8	69
Totals from all Competitions			**63**	**8**	**13**	**21**	**129**

LEONE, TANYA
Forward/Defence. Shoots left. #16.

Born 1972-7-28. Grew up in Vancouver, BC, CAN. 5'6".

Year - League - Team			GP	G	A	PTS	PM
1998	Nationals	New Westminster Lightning	5	1	2	3	6
1999	Nationals	New Westminster Lightning	5	0	0	0	
2000	Nationals	Britannia Blues	5	2	3	5	
2002	Nationals	Richmond Steelers	5	4	1	5	6
2002-03	NWHL	Vancouver Griffins	24	6	11	17	12
2003	Nationals	Vancouver Griffins	7	2	2	4	12
2004-05	WWHL	British Columbia Breakers	21	0	0	0	0
2005	Nationals	British Columbia	7	1	0	1	0
2007	Nationals	British Columbia	5	4	2	6	12
Totals from all Competitions			**84**	**20**	**21**	**41**	**48**

LEROY, EVE
Forward. 1998 Nationals New Westminster (5 gp, 5 pts); 1999 Nationals (5 games).

LESLIE, ERIN
Defence. Shoots left.

Born 1975-04-04. Grew up in Calgary, AB, CAN. 5'8".

Year - League - Team			GP	G	A	PTS	PM
2000	Nationals	Britannia Blues	5	0	2	2	
2002-03	NWHL	Vancouver Griffins	21	0	2	2	10
2003	Nationals	Vancouver Griffins	7	0	0	0	2

LESLIE, LAURA
Forward. #91 #19.

IIHF champion. Born 1960-05-17.

Year - League - Team			GP	G	A	PTS	PM
1995	Nationals	Équipe Québec					
1996	Nationals	Équipe Québec	6	1	5	6	0
1998-99	NWHL	Bonaventure	0	0	0	0	0
2000-01	NWHL	Mistral de Laval	31	8	10	18	50
Totals from all Competitions			**31**	**8**	**10**	**18**	**50**

LESLIE, REBECCA
Forward. Shoots right. #16.

Clarkson Cup winner with Calgary on 2019-03-24.
Born 1996-05-08. Grew up in Ottawa, ON, CAN. 5'6". Debut at age 22 on 2018-10-13.

Year - League - Team			GP	G	A	PTS	PM	Year - Playoff		GP	G	A	PTS	PM
2018-19	CWHL	Calgary Inferno	27	11	15	26	16	2019	C-Cup	4	0	2	2	4

CWHL All-Rookie Team 2018-19... finished 11th in the Angela James Bowl scoring race in 2018-19.

LETENDRE, LUCE
Forward. Shoots left. #8 #7

IIHF champion. Born 1971-04-19. Grew up in Brossard, QC, CAN. 5'5"

Year - League - Team			GP	G	A	PTS	PM
1995	Nationals	Équipe Québec					
1996	Nationals	Équipe Québec	6	1	1	2	0
1998	Nationals	Équipe Québec	6	0	0	0	4
1998-99	NWHL	Bonaventure	9	0	3	3	18
1999-00	NWHL	Wingstar de Montréal	1	0	0	0	0
2003-04	NWHL	Avalanche du Québec	6	0	0	0	8

LEUNG, JUSTINE
Forward. 2005-06 WWHL British Columbia #3 (21 games, 1 goal).

LEUSZLER, KRISTIN
Forward. 2006-07 WWHL British Columbia #87 (24 gp, 12 goals, 9 assists; 2 playoff games).

LEUSZLER, KRISTIN
Forward. Shoots right. #87

Born 1982-07-12. Grew up in Surrey, BC, CAN. 6'0".

Year - League - Team			GP	G	A	PTS	PM	Year - Playoff		GP	G	A	PTS	PM
2006-07	WWHL	British Columbia Breakers	24	12	9	21	18	2007	WWHL-P	2	0	0	0	2
2007	Nationals	British Columbia	5	0	2	2	2							

LÉVESQUE, CAROLINE
Forward. Shoots left. #55.

Born 1982-4-14, St-Georges-de-Champlain, QC, CAN. Grew up in Rosemont, QC, CAN. 5'5".

Year - League - Team			GP	G	A	PTS	PM	Year - Playoff		GP	G	A	PTS	PM
2004-05	NWHL	Avalanche du Québec	31	4	3	7	83							
2005-06	NWHL	Avalanche du Québec	33	1	1	2	70							
2006-07	NWHL	Avalanche du Québec	28	7	6	13	86	2007	NWHL-P					
2007-08	CWHL	Phénix du Québec	27	8	3	11	79							
Totals from all Competitions			**119**	**20**	**13**	**33**	**318**							

LEVESQUE, KRISTEN
Forward. Shoots right. #25.
Born 1994-03-31. Grew up in Sandwich, MA, USA. 5'2". Debut at age 22 on 2016-11-26.

Year - League - Team			GP	G	A	PTS	PM
2016-17	CWHL	Boston Blades	2	0	0	0	0

LEVESQUE, VALÉRIE
Defence/Forward. #7.

Year - League - Team			GP	G	A	PTS	PM
1998-99	NWHL	Mistral de Laval	34	0	6	6	36
1999-00	NWHL	Mistral de Laval	34	4	9	13	60
Totals from all Competitions			**68**	**4**	**15**	**19**	**96**

LEVINE, MICHAELA
Forward. Shoots right. #18.
Born 1994-05-04. Grew up in Lititz, PA, USA. 5'7". Debut at age 22 on 2016-11-20.

Year - League - Team			GP	G	A	PTS	PM	Year - Playoff		GP	G	A	PTS	PM
2016-17	NWHL/	Boston Pride	6	0	0	0	0	2017	I-Cup	1	0	0	0	0
2017-18	NWHL/	Boston Pride	6	0	0	0	2							

LEWICKI, KRISTIN
Forward. Shoots right. #27.
Born 1995-06-10. Grew up in Moundsville, WV, USA. 5'2". Debut at age 22 on 2017-10-28.

Year - League - Team			GP	G	A	PTS	PM	Year - Playoff		GP	G	A	PTS	PM
2017-18	NWHL/	Buffalo Beauts	14	5	2	7	2	2018	I-Cup	2	0	1	1	0
2018-19	NWHL/	Metropolitan Riveters	16	1	0	1	2	2019	I-Cup	2	0	0	0	0

LIEN, IDA
NOR. Defence. 2007-08 WWHL British Columbia #7 (24 games, 1 assist)

LIMACHER, JENNIFER
Forward. 1999 Nationals Saskatchewan (4 games, 1 goal, 1 assist).

LIPPITT, SUE
Forward. 2002 Nationals Calgary Oval X-Treme (6 games, 2 goals).

LITTLE, SARA
Defence. 2000 Nationals Newfoundland (5 gp); 2002 Nationals Newfoundland (5 gp).

LIU ZHIXIN
Defence. Shoots right. #93.
Born 1993-04-25, Qiqihar, Heilongjiang, CHN. 5'8". Debut at age 24 on 2017-10-21.

Year - League - Team			GP	G	A	PTS	PM	Year - Playoff		GP	G	A	PTS	PM
2017-18	CWHL	Kunlun Red Star	28	3	3	6	12	2018	C-Cup	4	0	0	0	4
2018-19	CWHL	KRS Vanke Rays	28	0	2	2	16							

LLANES, RACHEL
Right Wing. Shoots right. #91.
Clarkson Cup winner with Boston on 2015-03-07. Isobel Cup winner with Boston on 2016-03-12
Born 1991-04-29. Grew up in San Jose, CA, USA. 5'5". Debut at age 22 on 2013-11-02.

Year - League - Team			GP	G	A	PTS	PM	Year - Playoff		GP	G	A	PTS	PM
2013-14	CWHL	Boston Blades	23	6	6	12	10	2014	C-Cup	3	0	0	0	2
2014-15	CWHL	Boston Blades	22	6	5	11	6	2015	C-Cup	3	0	0	0	2
2015-16	NWHL/	Boston Pride	17	3	4	7	20	2016	I-Cup	4	0	0	0	0
2016-17	NWHL/	Boston Pride	16	3	1	4	6	2017	I-Cup	2	0	0	0	2
2017-18	CWHL	Kunlun Red Star	28	5	5	10	24	2018	C-Cup	4	0	0	0	2
2018-19	CWHL	KRS Vanke Rays	19	6	9	15	16							
CWHL Regular Season			92	23	25	48	56	Clarkson Cup		10	0	0	0	6
NWHL Regular Season			33	6	5	11	26	Isobel Cup		6	0	0	0	2
Totals from all Competitions			**141**	**29**	**30**	**59**	**90**							

LLOYD, LAURA
Defence. #3.

Year - League - Team			GP	G	A	PTS	PM
1992-93	COWHL	Scarborough Sting	25	0	0	0	22
1993-94	COWHL	Scarborough Sting	29	0	3	3	34

LOCICERO, DEANDRA
Forward. Shoots left. #3 #63 #94 #71.
Born 1979-6-16, Mississauga, ON, CAN. Grew up in Mississauga, ON, CAN. 5'7".

Year - League - Team			GP	G	A	PTS	PM	Year - Playoff		GP	G	A	PTS	PM
1996-97	COWHL	Scarborough Sting	35	5	7	12	16							
1997-98	COWHL	Scarborough Sting	16	1	0	1	6							
1998-99	NWHL	Scarborough Sting	27	2	1	3	42							
1999-00	NWHL	Scarborough Sting	35	4	10	14	50							
2000-01	NWHL	Toronto Sting	29	6	9	15	47							
2004-05	NWHL	Durham Lightning	32	4	7	11	16							
2005-06	NWHL	Durham Lightning	33	4	6	10	4	2006	NWHL-P	2	0	0	0	0
2006-07	NWHL	Etobicoke Dolphins	20	2	4	6	30	2007	NWHL-P	3	0	0	0	2
2007	Nationals	Etobicoke Dolphins	7	0	0	0								
2007-08	CWHL	Vaughan Flames	2	1	0	1	4							
2008-09	CWHL	Vaughan Flames	3	1	1	2	4	2009	CWHL-P	2	1		1	
2009-10	CWHL	Vaughan Flames	5	0	3	3	0							
Totals from all Competitions			**251**	**31**	**48**	**79**	**221**							

LOCK, JEN — *Forward. 1996-97 COWHL London Devilettes #18 (10 games).*

LODER, KELLIE — *Forward. 2006 Nationals Newfoundland Labrador (5 games).*

LOFTUS, LORI — *Left wing. Shoots left. #22 #8.*

Abby Hoffman Cup winner with Brampton on 2006-03-12. CWHL winner.
Born 1977-12-15, Mississauga, ON, CAN. 5'8".

Year - League - Team		GP	G	A	PTS	PM	Year - Playoff		GP	G	A	PTS	PM
1995-96	COWHL	Mississauga Chiefs	1	0	0	0	0							
2000-01	NWHL	Mississauga IceBears	24	5	5	10	47							
2001-02	NWHL	Brampton Thunder	27	10	1	11	10							
2002	Nationals	Brampton Thunder	7	2	0	2	2							
2005-06	NWHL	Brampton Thunder	32	5	8	13	26	2006	NWHL-P	5	0	0	0	2
2006	Nationals	Brampton Thunder	6	0	1	1	2							
2006-07	NWHL	Brampton Thunder	33	0	4	4	28	2007	NWHL-P	6	0	0	0	14
2007-08	CWHL	Brampton Can.-Thunder	28	0	10	10	38	2008	CWHL-P	3	0	0	0	4
2008	Nationals	Brampton Can.-Thunder	3	0	1	1	2							
Totals from all Competitions		**175**	**22**	**30**	**52**	**175**							

Served as head coach with CWHL Brampton

LOGAN, HEATHER — *Forward. Shoots left. #22 #20.*

Abby Hoffman Cup winner with Aeros on 2000-03-12 and 2004-03-14. Abby Hoffman Cup winner with Mississauga on 2008-03-15. CWHL winner, NWHL Cup winner, WWHL winner.
Born 1982-5-14, Smooth Rock Falls, ON; grew up in Thessalon, ON, CAN. 5'10".

Year - League - Team		GP	G	A	PTS	PM	Year - Playoff		GP	G	A	PTS	PM
1998-99	NWHL	North York Aeros	1	0	1	1	0							
1999-00	NWHL	North York Aeros	4	3	2	5	2	2000	NWHL-P					
2000	Nationals	North York Aeros	6	3	4	7								
2000-01	NWHL	North York Aeros	38	12	21	33	10							
2001	Nationals	North York Aeros												
2001-02	NWHL	North York Aeros	28	16	14	30	12	2002	NWHL-P					
2002	Nationals	North York Aeros	7	2	3	5	2							
2002-03	NWHL	North York Aeros						2003	NWHL-P					
2003-04	NWHL	Toronto Aeros	31	17	22	39	12	2004	NWHL-P					
2004	Nationals	Toronto Aeros	6	4	6	10	0							
2004-05	NWHL	Toronto Aeros	36	15	29	44	20	2005	NWHL-P					
2005-06	WWHL	Calgary Oval X-Treme	22	21	15	36	14	2006	WWHL-P	3	1	2	3	2
2006-07	NWHL	Mississauga Aeros	34	8	19	27	24	2007	NWHL-P	5	0	1	1	0
2007	Nationals	Mississauga Aeros	6	5	8	13	2							
2007-08	CWHL	Mississauga Chiefs	24	13	4	17	28	2008	CWHL-P	5	2	2	4	6
2008	Nationals	Mississauga Chiefs	3	1	0	1	0							
2008-09	CWHL	Mississauga Chiefs	22	2	8	10	10	2009	CWHL-P	2	2	1	3	
2009-10	CWHL	Mississauga Chiefs	14	2	7	9	22							
2010-11	CWHL	Brampton Thunder	1	0	0	0	0	2011	C-Cup	2	0	0	0	0
CWHL Regular Season		61	17	19	36	60	Clarkson Cup		2	0	0	0	0
Totals from all Competitions		**300**	**129**	**169**	**298**	**166**							

LOIGNON, LINDA — *Forward. 1998-99 NWHL Montréal (30 gp, 4 goals, 9 a.); 1999-00 Sainte-Julie (4 gp, 2 a.).*

LONDON, KAYE — *Forward. #21 #12.*

Born 1984-6-2.

Year - League - Team		GP	G	A	PTS	PM	Year - Playoff		GP	G	A	PTS	PM
2007-08	WWHL	Edmonton Chimos	24	0	4	4	20							
2008-09	WWHL	Edmonton Chimos	24	7	12	19	10	2009	WWHL-P	1	0	0	0	0
2009-10	WWHL	Edmonton Chimos	3	1	1	2	0							
Totals from all Competitions		**52**	**8**	**17**	**25**	**30**							

LONG, MICAELA — *Forward. Shoots left. #16.*

Born 1987-11-16, Boston, MA, USA. Grew up in South Boston, MA, USA. 5'4". Debut at age 23 on 2010-10-30.

Year - League - Team		GP	G	A	PTS	PM	Year - Playoff		GP	G	A	PTS	PM
2010-11	CWHL	Boston Blades	23	8	9	17	2	2011	CWHL-P	2	1	0	1	2
2011-12	CWHL	Boston Blades	13	3	4	7	2							
2015-16	NWHL/	Connecticut Whale	17	3	7	10	27	2016	I-Cup	3	0	2	2	2
2016-17	NWHL/	Connecticut Whale	17	3	7	10	6	2017	I-Cup	1	0	0	0	0
CWHL Regular Season		36	11	13	24	4							
NWHL Regular Season		34	6	14	20	33	Isobel Cup		4	0	2	2	2
Totals from all Competitions		**76**	**18**	**29**	**47**	**41**							

Finished 20th in the Angela James Bowl scoring race in 2010-11

LONG, MICHELLE — *Forward. 2008 Nationals Nova Scotia Selects (5 games).*

LONG, PATRICIA — *Forward. #2 #12 #21.*

Year - League - Team		GP	G	A	PTS	PM
1995-96	COWHL	Mississauga Chiefs	1	0	0	0	0
1996-97	COWHL	Scarborough Sting	33	6	8	14	8
2001-02	NWHL	Mississauga IceBears	18	0	5	5	2
Totals from all Competitions		**52**	**6**	**13**	**19**	**10**

LONGLOIS, DEANNE
Abby Hoffman Cup winner with Edmonton on 1997-03-09.

Year - League - Team			GP	G	A	PTS	PM
1997	Nationals	Edmonton Chimos					

LOONEY, SHELLEY
Forward. Shoots right. #15.

Olympic champion, IIHF champion. Born 1972-1-21, Brownstown Township, MI, USA. 5'5".

Year - League - Team			GP	G	A	PTS	PM
2002-03	NWHL	Vancouver Griffins	24	10	25	35	12
2003	Nationals	Vancouver Griffins	7	2	7	9	2

Has served as head coach with NWHL Buffalo

LORENZ, KRYSTY
Forward. #18.

Born 1978-9-23. Grew up in Sherwood Park, AB, CAN.

Year - League - Team			GP	G	A	PTS	PM	Year - Playoff		GP	G	A	PTS	PM
2002-03	NWHL	Edmonton Chimos	24	3	5	8	10							
2003-04	NWHL	Edmonton Chimos	8	1	0	1	4	2004	NWHL-P					
2005	WWHL-P	3	0	0	0									
Totals from all Competitions			**35**	**4**	**5**	**9**	**14**							

LORION, MICHELLE
Forward. Shoots left.

Born 1981-3-16, Etobicoke, ON, CAN. Grew up in Mississauga, ON, CAN. 5'6".

Year - League - Team			GP	G	A	PTS	PM	Year - Playoff		GP	G	A	PTS	PM
2003-04	NWHL	Oakville Ice	35	10	6	16	48							
2004-05	NWHL	Oakville Ice	35	3	4	7	18							
2005-06	NWHL	Oakville Ice	35	8	10	18	48	2006	NWHL-P	2	0	0	0	2
2006-07	NWHL	Oakville Ice	34	6	4	10	36	2007	NWHL-P	3	0	0	0	2
2007-08	CWHL	Burlington Barracudas	28	4	8	12	42							
CWHL Regular Season			28	4	8	12	42							
Totals from all Competitions			**172**	**31**	**32**	**63**	**196**							

LORMS, HOLLY
Forward. Shoots right. #29.

Born 1988-10-6. Grew up in Wauwatosa, WS, USA. 5'7". Debut at age 23 on 2011-10-22.

Year - League - Team			GP	G	A	PTS	PM	Year - Playoff		GP	G	A	PTS	PM
2011-12	CWHL	Boston Blades	24	2	3	5	14	2012	C-Cup	3	0	0	0	2
2012-13	CWHL	Boston Blades	8	0	0	0	0							
CWHL Regular Season			32	2	3	5	14	Clarkson Cup		3	0	0	0	2
Totals from all Competitions			**35**	**2**	**3**	**5**	**16**							

LOVE, MANDY
2007-08 CWHL Brampton Thunder #14 (1 game).

LOVELL, ELANA
Forward. Shoots left. #15.

Clarkson Cup winner with Calgary on 2016-03-14
Born 1990-02-17. Grew up in Kamloops, BC, CAN. Debut at age 25 on 2015-10-24.

Year - League - Team			GP	G	A	PTS	PM	Year - Playoff		GP	G	A	PTS	PM
2015-16	CWHL	Calgary Inferno	24	14	12	26	8	2016	C-Cup	3	0	0	0	0
2016-17	CWHL	Calgary Inferno	10	1	2	3	29							
2017-18	CWHL	Calgary Inferno	19	3	4	7	4	2018	C-Cup	3	0	1	1	2
CWHL Regular Season			53	18	18	36	41	Clarkson Cup		6	0	1	1	2
Totals from all Competitions			**59**	**18**	**19**	**37**	**43**							

CWHL Outstanding Rookie in 2015-16... CWHL All-Rookie Team in 2015-16... finished 10th in the Angela James Bowl scoring race in 2015-16

LOWE, JAIME
Defence. 1998 Nationals Tazmanian Devils (5 gp); 1999 Nationals (4 gp).

LÖWENHIELM, MICHELLE
Forward. Shoots left. #67.

Born 1995-03-22. Grew up in Sollentuna, SWE. 5'8". Debut at age 23 on 2018-10-07.

Year - League - Team			GP	G	A	PTS	PM	Year - Playoff		GP	G	A	PTS	PM
2018-19	NWHL/	Connecticut Whale	16	3	3	6	8	2019	I-Cup	1	0	0	0	0

LUCK, EMILIE
Forward. Shoots left. #12.

Clarkson Cup winner with Montréal on 2011-03-27
Born 1990-2-12. Grew up in Pointe Claire, QC, CAN. 5'9". Debut at age 21 on 2010-10-23.

Year - League - Team			GP	G	A	PTS	PM	Year - Playoff		GP	G	A	PTS	PM
2010-11	CWHL	Stars de Montréal	22	0	0	0	6	2011	CWHL-P	2				
								2011	C-Cup	4	1	0	1	2

LUCKY, BRITTANY
Kanata, ON, CAN. Defence. 2008-09 CWHL Ottawa (4 games).

LUDWIG, MIRJAM
GER. Forward. 2007-08 CWHL Québec #17 (8 games).

LUHOWY, TRACY
Forward. Shoots left.

Abby Hoffman Cup winner with Calgary on 2001-03-11.
Born 1971-06-17. Grew up in Thompson, MB, CAN.

Year - League - Team			GP	G	A	PTS	PM
1995	Nationals	Winnipeg Sweat Camp					
1999	Nationals	Calgary Oval X-Treme	6	2		2	
2000	Nationals	Calgary Oval X-Treme	7	3		3	
2001	Nationals	Calgary Oval X-Treme					

LUM, LEAH   Forward. Shoots left. #7.
Born 1996-05-12. Grew up in Richmond, BC, CAN. 5'5". Debut at age 22 on 2018-10-13.

Year - League - Team		GP	G	A	PTS	PM
2018-19	CWHL KRS Vanke Rays	28	4	6	10	14

LUND, MARGO   Forward. Shoots right. #16.
Born 1993-05-23. Grew up in White Bear Lake, MN, USA. 5'9'. Debut at age 25 on 2018-10-07.

Year - League - Team		GP	G	A	PTS	PM
2018-19	NWHL/ Minnesota Whitecaps	2	0	0	0	0

LUNDQUIST, SADIE   Forward. Shoots right. #17.
Born 1991-06-18. Grew up in Cloquet, MN, USA. 5'9". Debut at age 27 on 2018-10-27.

Year - League - Team		GP	G	A	PTS	PM
2018-19	NWHL/ Minnesota Whitecaps	3	0	0	0	0

LUNN, JENN   Forward. 2005 Nationals Alberta (6 games).

LYNCH, SARA   Forward. 2011-12 CWHL Burlington #16 (21 games, 1 goal, 6 assist).

LYONS, BRITTANY   Shoots left.
Born 1990-10-11. Grew up in Canton, MA, USA. Debut at age 25 on 2015-11-01.

Year - League - Team		GP	G	A	PTS	PM
2015-16	CWHL Boston Blades	1	0	0	0	0

LYONS, SHELBY   2008 Nationals Team New Brunswick (5 games, 1 goal, 4 assists).

MACASKILL, JENNIFER   Forward. Shoots right. #11.
Born 1996-02-09. Grew up in Valley, NS, CAN. 5'5". Debut at age 22 on 2018-10-13.

Year - League - Team		GP	G	A	PTS	PM
2018-19	CWHL Worcester Blades	7	0	0	0	2

MACAULAY, SHANNON   Forward. Shoots left. #21.
Born 1994-06-22. Grew up in Mount Herbert, PE, CAN. 5'11". Debut at age 22 on 2016-10-08.

Year - League - Team		GP	G	A	PTS	PM	Year - Playoff		GP	G	A	PTS	PM
2016-17	CWHL Brampton Thunder	23	4	7	11	16	2017 C-Cup		2	0	0	0	4

MACAULEY, DAWN   Defence. Shoots right. #24 #18 #81.
Born 1982-10-11, Comox, BC, CAN. Grew up in Courtenay, BC, CAN. 5'7".

Year - League - Team		GP	G	A	PTS	PM	Year - Playoff		GP	G	A	PTS	PM
1999	Nationals Tazmanian Devils												
2004-05	NWHL Oakville Ice	36	2	6	8	50							
2005-06	NWHL Durham Lightning	35	2	11	13	42	2006 NWHL-P		?	0	0	0	8
2006-07	NWHL Avalanche du Québec	7	0	2	2	8							
	Totals from all Competitions	80	4	19	23	108							

MACAULEY, SARAH   Defence. Shoots right.
Born 1987-06-06. Grew up in Charlottetown, PE, CAN

Year - League - Team		GP	G	A	PTS	PM
2006	Nationals Prince Edward Island	3	0	0	0	0
2007	Nationals Prince Edward Island	5	1	2	3	4
2008	Nationals Prince Edward Island	5	0	1	1	6

MACDONALD, GAYLE   Defence. 2000 Nationals Nova Scotia Selects (6 games); 2001 Nationals Nova Scotia.

MACDONALD, HEATHER   Forward. 2001 Nationals Nova Scotia Selects; 2003 Nationals Nova Scotia.

MACDONALD, JANELLE   Forward.
Born 1966-08-22.

Year - League - Team		GP	G	A	PTS	PM
1996	Nationals PEI Esso Tigers	4	0	0	0	4
1998	Nationals Prince Edward Island	5	2	0	2	6
1999	Nationals Prince Edward Island	5	0	0	0	

MACDONALD, KENDRA   Forward.
Born 1981-12-29. Grew up in Peakes, PE, CAN.

Year - League - Team		GP	G	A	PTS	PM
1998	Nationals Prince Edward Island	5	2	2	4	0
1999	Nationals Prince Edward Island	5	0	0	0	
2000	Nationals Prince Edward Island	5	1	1	2	
2001	Nationals PEI Humpty Dumpty					

MACDONALD, LEANNE   Defence. Shoots right.
Born 1978-02-11. Grew up in Mabou, NS, CAN.

Year - League - Team		GP	G	A	PTS	PM
1996	Nationals Pictou County Sobey's	4	0	0	0	0
2000	Nationals Nova Scotia Selects	6	0	0	0	
2001	Nationals Nova Scotia Selects					

MACDONALD, NANCY   Centre. 2006-07 WWHL British Columbia #14 (18 games, 4 assists; 2 playoff games).

MACDONALD, ROBYN   Defence. 2005 Nationals Prince Edward Island (5 gp, 3 pts); 2006 Nationals (5 pts).

MACDONALD, SHELLEY   Forward. 1996 Nationals Pictou County (4 games).

MACDONALD, TAMMY   *D. 1992-93 COWHL Scarborough #4 (20 gp, 1 assist); 1993-94 (13 games, 2 assists).*

MACDONNELL, SARAH   *2008 Nationals Team New Brunswick (5 games, 1 goal, 1 assist).*

MACDOUGALL, COURTNEY   *Forward. 2006-07 WWHL Saskatchewan #15 (21 games, 2 goals, 2 assists).*

MACDOUGALL, MARIANNE   *Defence/Forward. Shoots left.*

Abby Hoffman Cup winner with Calgary on 2001-03-11.
Born 1979-09-01. Grew up in Lumsden, SK, CAN.

Year - League - Team			GP	G	A	PTS	PM
2000	Nationals	Calgary Oval X-Treme		1	2	3	
2001	Nationals	Calgary Oval X-Treme					

MACFARLANE, LESLIE   *Forward. Shoots right.*

Born 1964-03-20. Grew up in Montréal, QC, CAN

Year - League - Team			GP	G	A	PTS	PM
1995	Nationals	Winnipeg Sweat Camp					
1996	Nationals	Winnipeg Sweat Camp	6	0	1	1	4
2000	Nationals	University of Manitoba	5	0	0	0	
2001	Nationals	University of Manitoba					
2002	Nationals	University of Manitoba	5	0	1	1	0

MACHT, GRETCHEN   *Forward. 1995 Nationals Britannia Blues.*

MACINNIS, JEN   *Forward. 2000 Nationals Nova Scotia Selects (6 games).*

MACINTOSH, LEISA   *F. 1999 Nationals P.E.I. (5 gp, 4 pts); 2000 Nationals (5 gp, 1 a.); 2001 Nationals.*

MACKAY, NICOLE   *Defence. 2007 Nationals Prince Edward Island (5 gp); 2008 Nationals (2 gp).*

MACKENZIE, JESSICA   *Forward. 2008 Nationals Nova Scotia Selects (5 games, 1 goal).*

MACKENZIE, KAREN   *Forward. 1995 Nationals Metro Valley Selects.*

MACKENZIE, LAURA   *F. 1995-96 COWHL Mississauga (2 gp); 2000-01 NWHL Mississauga #17 (38 gp, 11 pts).*

MACKENZIE, VICTORIA   *Forward. Shoots right. #55*

Born 1994-04-20. Grew up in Toronto, ON, CAN. 5'8". Debut at age 22 on 2016-10-29.

Year - League - Team			GP	G	A	PTS	PM
2016-17	CWHL	Toronto Furies	2	0	0	0	0

MACKINNON, KARI   *Forward. 1995 Nationals Metro Valley Selects.*

MACLEAN, JANE   *Forward. 1995 Nationals PEI Esso Tigers.*

MACLEAN, LAURA   *1993-94 COWHL Hamilton Golden Hawks #95 (5 goals).*

MACLEAN, SAMANTHA   *Defence. Shoots left. #12.*

Born 1988-5-19, Montréal, QC, CAN. 5'6".

Year - League - Team			GP	G	A	PTS	PM	Year - Playoff		GP	G	A	PTS	PM
2004-05	NWHL	Oakville Ice	1	0	0	0	0							
2005-06	NWHL	Oakville Ice	1	0	0	0	0	2006	NWHL-P	0	0	0	0	0
2006-07	NWHL	Oakville Ice	33	0	1	1	20	2007	NWHL-P	3	0	0	0	4
Totals from all Competitions			**38**	**0**	**1**	**1**	**24**							

MACLEAN, SANDRA   *D. 1995 Nationals Maritime Sport Blades; 1996 Nationals (6 gp, 1 a.); 2001 Nationals.*

MACLELLAN, MONICA   *Forward. 2009-10 CWHL Ottawa Senators #14 (25 gp, 3 goals, 4 assists).*

MACLEOD, CARLA   *Defence. Shoots right. #8.*

Olympic champion, IIHF champion. Abby Hoffman Cup winner with Calgary on 1998-03-22, 2001-03-11 and 2007-03-10. WWHL winner.
Born 1982-6-16, Spruce Grove, AB, CAN. 5'4". Debut at age 24 on 2006-10-14.

Year - League - Team			GP	G	A	PTS	PM	Year - Playoff		GP	G	A	PTS	PM
1998	Nationals	Calgary Oval X-Treme	7	0	4	4	2							
1999	Nationals	Calgary Oval X-Treme	6	0	0	0								
2000	Nationals	Calgary Oval X-Treme	7	0	6	6								
2001	Nationals	Calgary Oval X-Treme												
2006-07	WWHL	Calgary Oval X-Treme	7	4	10	14	2	2007	WWHL-P	3	1	2	3	0
2007	Nationals	Calgary Oval X-Treme	6	3	5	8	2							
2007-08	WWHL	Calgary Oval X-Treme	23	4	22	26	16							
2008	Nationals	Calgary Oval X-Treme	3	1	3	4	2							
2008-09	WWHL	Calgary Oval X-Treme	21	12	23	35	16	2009	WWHL-P	2	1	4	5	4
								2009	C-Cup	1	1	0	1	2
Totals from all Competitions			**86**	**27**	**79**	**106**	**46**							

MACLEOD, KATIE   *F. 2004 Nationals Nova Scotia (5 gp, 1 goal); 2005 Nationals (5 gp); 2006 Nationals (4 gp).*

MACLEOD, RENA   *Forward. 1995 Nationals PEI Esso Tigers.*

MACMILLAN, CARLA   *Forward. Shoots right.*

Born 1974-10-22. Grew up in Thompson, MB, CAN.

Year - League - Team			GP	G	A	PTS	PM
1998	Nationals	Tazmanian Devils	5	0	0	0	4
1999	Nationals	Tazmanian Devils	4				
2000	Nationals	University of Manitoba	5	1		1	
2001	Nationals	University of Manitoba					

Year - League - Team			GP	G	A	PTS	PM	Year - Playoff	GP	G	A	PTS	PM
2002	Nationals	University of Manitoba	5	1	2	3	0						
2003	Nationals	University of Winnipeg	4	1	0	1	4						
2004	Nationals	Manitoba	5	2	3	5	4						

MACMILLAN, JODY   *Forward. 1999-00 NWHL Ottawa #53 (3 games); 2000-01 #11 (35 gp, 2 goals, 5 assists).*

MACMILLAN, LAUREN   *Forward. Shoots left.*
Born 1980-08-21. Grew up in Winnipeg, MB, CAN. 5'4".

Year - League - Team			GP	G	A	PTS	PM
2003	Nationals	University of Winnipeg	4	0	1	1	0
2005	Nationals	Manitoba	5	2	3	5	6
2007	Nationals	Manitoba	5	4	1	5	2
2008	Nationals	Manitoba	5	1	2	3	4

MACNAMARA, KATE   *Forward. 1999-00 NWHL Brampton (7 gp, 3 goals); 2001-02 Mississauga (6 gp, 1 assist).*

MACNAULL, MARLA   *1992-93 COWHL Scarborough Sting #88 (1 game).*

MACNEIL, MACKENZIE   *Forward. Shoots right. #28.*
Born 1996-11-01. Grew up in Richmond Hill, ON, CAN. 5'8". Debut at age 21 on 2018-10-13.

Year - League - Team			GP	G	A	PTS	PM	Year - Playoff	GP	G	A	PTS	PM
2018-19	CWHL	Toronto Furies	25	2	2	4	0	2019 C-Cup	3	0	0	0	0

MACPHEE, SHANA   *Forward. 2004 Nationals Team New Brunswick (5 games, 2 assists).*

MACRI, LIZ   *Defence. Shoots left. #4.*
Abby Hoffman Cup winner with Brampton on 2006-03-12.
Born 1979-3-11, Oyster Bay, NY, USA. 6'0".

Year - League - Team			GP	G	A	PTS	PM	Year - Playoff	GP	G	A	PTS	PM
2001-02	NWHL	Mississauga IceBears	27	1	4	5	14						
2002-03	NWHL	Mississauga IceBears											
2003-04	NWHL	Oakville Ice	29	1	5	6	34						
2004-05	NWHL	Brampton Thunder	31	4	9	13	32						
2005	Nationals	Brampton Thunder	6	1	1	2	0						
2005-06	NWHL	Brampton Thunder	33	6	12	18	30	2006 NWHL-P	5	0	0	0	6
2006	Nationals	Brampton Thunder	6	0	1	1	2						
2006-07	NWHL	Brampton Thunder	28	7	13	20	36	2007 NWHL-P	6	1	2	3	8
Totals from all Competitions			**171**	**21**	**47**	**68**	**162**						

MACY, LINDSAY   *Forward. 2008-09 WWHL Minnesota (15 gp, 8 goals, 6 a.; playoffs 2 gp, 1 g.; C-Cup 3 gp).*

MADIGAN, EMMA   *Forward. 2010-11 CWHL Brampton (6 gp, C-Cup 1 gp); 2011-12 Burlington (10 gp, 2 a.).*

MADOWER, WANDA   *Defence. 2004 Nationals Nova Scotia Selects (5 games).*

MAGNUSSON, JAMIE LEE   *Defence. 2006-07 WWHL Saskatchewan #12. (11 games).*

MAGUIRE, MEGHAN   *Defence. Shoots left.*
Born 1979-08-27. Grew up in Amherst, NH, USA. 5'6".

Year - League - Team			GP	G	A	PTS	PM	Year - Playoff	GP	G	A	PTS	PM
2004-05	NWHL	Axion de Montréal	36	3	7	10	22						
2005	Nationals	Axion de Montréal	6	0	1	1	6						
2005-06	NWHL	Axion de Montréal	8	0	3	3	4	2006 NWHL-P					

MAH, KAREN   *Forward. 1999 Nationals New Westminster Lightning (5 games).*

MAHONEY, SHANNON   *Forward. 2013-14 CWHL Boston Blades #13 (18 gp, 1 goal; C-Cup 1 game).*

MAHOVLICH, JENNIFER   *Forward. Shoots right.*
Born 1987-01-27. Grew up in Vancouver, BC, CAN.

Year - League - Team			GP	G	A	PTS	PM
2004-05	WWHL	British Columbia Breakers	11	1	3	4	4
2006	Nationals	British Columbia	6	0	0	0	0
2007	Nationals	British Columbia	5	1	1	2	0

MAIK, LISA   *Defence/Forward. #99 #7 #27 #14.*

Year - League - Team			GP	G	A	PTS	PM
1992-93	COWHL	Guelph Eagles	16	2	1	3	12
1996-97	COWHL	Scarborough Sting	29	6	9	15	22
1997-98	COWHL	Scarborough Sting	19	1	2	3	10
1998-99	NWHL	Scarborough Sting	35	1	1	2	74
1999-00	NWHL	Durham Lightning	37	0	3	3	78
2000-01	NWHL	Durham Lightning	33	3	5	8	73
Totals from all Competitions			**169**	**13**	**21**	**34**	**269**

MAILLOUX, GUYLAINE   *Forward. 1999-00 NWHL Mistral de Laval #36 (9 games).*

MAILLOUX, PAULA   *Forward. 2002 Nationals Équipe Québec (6 gp); 2004-05 NWHL Ottawa Raiders (27 gp, 4 a.).*

MAISONNEUVE, SHERI   *Forward. #87 #71 #18.*
NWHL Cup winner. Born 1981-12-7.

Year - League - Team			GP	G	A	PTS	PM	Year - Playoff	GP	G	A	PTS	PM
1999-00	NWHL	Beatrice Aeros	2	0	1	1	0	2000 NWHL-P					

MALCHER, KIM
Defence. Shoots left. #5 #71 #18.

Abby Hoffman Cup winner with Aeros on 2004-03-14 and 2005-03-13.
Born 1980-1-28. Grew up in Bolton, ON, CAN. 5'8".

Year - League - Team			GP	G	A	PTS	PM	Year - Playoff	GP	G	A	PTS	PM
2003-04	NWHL	Toronto Aeros	36	3	17	20	26	2004 NWHL-P					
2004	Nationals	Toronto Aeros	6	2	3	5	12						
2004-05	NWHL	Toronto Aeros	36	7	15	22	52						
2005	Nationals	Toronto Aeros	7	0	1	1	2						
2005-06	NWHL	Toronto Aeros	24	3	12	15	50						
2006-07	NWHL	Mississauga Aeros	20	1	5	6	44						
2007	Nationals	Mississauga Aeros	2	0	0	0	0						
2009-10	CWHL	Mississauga Chiefs	7	1	2	3	18	2010 C-Cup	1	0	0	0	0
Totals from all Competitions			**139**	**17**	**55**	**72**	**204**						

MALCOLM, JANELLE
Forward. 2007-08 WWHL Edmonton Chimos #24 (24 games, 2 goals, 2 assists).

MALENFANT, SYLVIE
Defence.

Born 1965-02-02.

Year - League - Team			GP	G	A	PTS	PM	Year - Playoff	GP	G	A	PTS	PM
1995	Nationals	Équipe Québec											
1996	Nationals	Équipe Québec	6	0	2	2	2						
1998-99	NWHL	Montréal Jofa-Titan	8	2	2	4	0						
1999-00	NWHL	Sainte-Julie	26	0	6	6	2	2000 NWHL-P					
2000-01	NWHL	Sainte-Julie	1	0	0	0	0						

MAMCHUK, KAREN
Forward. 2003 Nationals U. Winnipeg (4 gp, 1 goal, 1 assist).

MANGENE, MEAGAN
Defence. Shoots right. #57.

Born 1992-08-21, Manorville, NY, USA. Grew up in Miller Place, NY, USA. 5'6". Debut at age 23 on 2015-10-18.

Year - League - Team			GP	G	A	PTS	PM	Year - Playoff	GP	G	A	PTS	PM
2015-16	NWHL/	Boston Pride	7	0	1	1	0						
2016-17	NWHL/	Connecticut Whale	16	1	3	4	10	2017 I-Cup	1	0	0	0	0
2017-18	NWHL/	Boston Pride	15	2	1	3	2	2018 I-Cup	1	0	0	0	0
NWHL Regular Season			38	3	5	8	12	Isobel Cup	2	0	0	0	0
Totals from all Competitions			**40**	**3**	**5**	**8**	**12**						

MANNING, LINDSAY
Defence. 2008 Nationals Prince Edward Island (5 games, 1 goal).

MANSEAU, JULIE
1998-99 NWHL Laval (11 gp, 1 goal, 1 a.); 1999-00 Sainte-Julie (2 gp); 2000-01 (4 gp, 4 a.).

MANSHOLT, TERRY
Centre. #17.

Year - League - Team			GP	G	A	PTS	PM
1992-93	COWHL	Scarborough Sting	28	8	11	19	16
1993-94	COWHL	Scarborough Sting	28	7	8	15	60
Totals from all Competitions			**56**	**15**	**19**	**34**	**76**

MANTHA, ÉLIZABETH
Defence. #22.

Born 1990-8-3. Debut at age 17 on 2007-10-27.

Year - League - Team			GP	G	A	PTS	PM
2007-08	CWHL	Stars de Montréal	6	0	2	2	4
2009-10	CWHL	Stars de Montréal	2	0	0	0	6

MANTHA, MELANIE
Forward. 2005-06 Montréal (33 gp, 6 assists, 2 playoff games); 2006 Nationals (6 gp).

MANUEL, KELLY
Forward. 2003 Nationals Team New Brunswick (4 games).

MANUEL, PENNY
Forward. 1996 Nationals Pictou County (4 games).

MARCHESE, TERESA
Forward. Shoots right. #11 #41.

Born 1982-1-11, Toronto, ON, CAN. Grew up in Brampton, ON, CAN. 5'7".

Year - League - Team			GP	G	A	PTS	PM	Year - Playoff	GP	G	A	PTS	PM
1998-99	NWHL	Brampton Thunder	15	2	7	9	14						
1999-00	NWHL	Brampton Thunder	38	14	31	45	28						
2000-01	NWHL	Brampton Thunder	40	17	27	44	55						
2005-06	NWHL	Durham Lightning	35	17	22	39	78	2006 NWHL-P	2	0	1	1	0
2006-07	NWHL	Etobicoke Dolphins	23	9	19	28	52						
Totals from all Competitions			**153**	**59**	**107**	**166**	**227**						

MARCHIN, TAYLOR
Defence. Shoots right. #11.

Born 1994-01-26. Grew up in Algonac, MI, USA. 5'7". Debut at age 23 on 2017-11-14.

Year - League - Team			GP	G	A	PTS	PM	Year - Playoff	GP	G	A	PTS	PM
2017-18	CWHL	Kunlun Red Star	22	0	9	9	6	2018 C-Cup	4	1	0	1	2
2018-19	NWHL/	Connecticut Whale	13	0	0	0	6	2019 I-Cup	1	0	0	0	0

MARCOTTE, KELLY
Forward.

Year - League - Team			GP	G	A	PTS	PM	Year - Playoff	GP	G	A	PTS	PM
2003-04	NWHL	Calgary Oval X-Treme	9	0	7	7	12	2004 NWHL-P	4	0	0	0	0
2004	Nationals	Calgary Oval X-Treme	5	0	0	0	0						
2004-05	WWHL	Calgary Oval X-Treme	4	3	0	3	8	2005 NWHL-P					

MARIN, NOÉMIE

Forward/Defence. Shoots left. #10.

Clarkson Cup winner with Montréal on 2009-03-21, 2011-03-27, 2012-03-25 and 2017-03-05
Born 1984-4-5, Acton Vale, QC, CAN. Grew up in Acton Vale, QC, CAN. 5'6". Debut at age 18 in 2002-03.

Year - League - Team		GP	G	A	PTS	PM
2002-03	NWHL Axion de Montréal	7	4	2	6	2
2003	Nationals Équipe Québec	5	2	4	6	4
2008-09	CWHL Stars de Montréal	26	23	26	49	12
2009-10	CWHL Stars de Montréal	28	25	18	43	16
2010-11	CWHL Stars de Montréal	17	21	14	35	10
2011-12	CWHL Stars de Montréal	24	12	22	34	16
2012-13	CWHL Stars de Montréal	14	7	7	14	6
2013-14	CWHL Stars de Montréal	7	1	3	4	2
2014-15	CWHL Stars de Montréal	18	13	5	18	2
2015-16	CWHL Canadiennes de Montréal	22	7	8	15	6
2016-17	CWHL Canadiennes de Montréal	19	6	6	12	8
2017-18	CWHL Canadiennes de Montréal	26	17	14	31	12
CWHL Regular Season		201	132	123	255	90
Totals from all Competitions		**246**	**150**	**142**	**292**	**108**

Year - Playoff	GP	G	A	PTS	PM
2003 NWHL-P					
2009 CWHL-P	2	4	2	6	0
2009 C-Cup	3	0	2	2	4
2010 C-Cup	1	1	0	1	0
2011 CWHL-P	2	1	1	2	
2011 C-Cup	4	3	3	6	0
2012 C-Cup	4	0	0	0	0
2013 C-Cup	4	0	1	1	0
2014 C-Cup	3	0	0	0	0
2015 C-Cup	3	1	0	1	4
2016 C-Cup	3	1	1	2	2
2017 C-Cup	3	1	3	4	0
2018 C-Cup	1	0	0	0	2
Clarkson Cup	29	7	10	17	12

CWHL goal-scoring leader in 2009-10... CWHL Second All-Star Team in 2009-10 and 2010-11... CWHL All-Rookie Team in 2008-09... finished 3rd in the Angela James Bowl scoring race in 2009-10... scored CWHL record 10 points (5g-5a) on 2009-03-09... scored 100th CWHL point on 2010-10-31... scored 100th CWHL goal on 2015-02-21... scored 200th CWHL point on 2015-12-13... scored CWHL record 132nd goal on 2018-03-11... selected First Decade CWHL Team in 2017

MAKRIS, MELISSA

2000-01 NWHL Durham Lightning (1 game).

MARLING, SUNNY

Defence.

Abby Hoffman Cup winner with Aeros on 2000-03-12.

Year - League - Team		GP	G	A	PTS	PM
1998-99	NWHL North York Aeros	8	1	2	3	4
1999-00	NWHL North York Aeros	38	1	11	12	24
2000	Nationals North York Aeros					

MARLYK, TANYA

Forward. Shoots left.

Year - League - Team		GP	G	A	PTS	PM
1998-99	NWHL North York Aeros	8	1	2	3	4
2000	Nationals Britannia Blues	5	0	0	0	
2001	Nationals Saskatchewan					
2003	Nationals Saskatchewan	6	3	2	5	2
2004	Nationals Saskatchewan	6	1	0	1	2
2004-05	WWHL Saskatchewan Prairie Ice	20	0	1	1	22
2005-06	WWHL Saskatchewan Prairie Ice	24	3	2	5	32

Year - Playoff	GP	G	A	PTS	PM
2006 WWHL-P	2	0	0	0	0

MARNOCH, STACY

Defence. 1992-93 COWHL Scarborough #20 (27 gp, 1 goal, 6 a.); 1993-94 (20 gp, 4 a.).

MARRINER, HEATHER

Defence. 2001-02 NWHL Ottawa Raiders #12 (27 games, 2 goals, 1 assist).

MARSHALL, CHERA

Forward. 1998-99 NWHL Ottawa Raiders #8 (28 games, 11 goals, 7 assists).

MARSOLAIS, SYLVIA

2007-08 CWHL Québec #34 (1 game).

MARSON, KRISTEN

Defence. Shoots right. #78 #3 #11.

Born 1987-7-4, Toronto, ON, CAN. Grew up in Ajax, ON, CAN. 5'9".

Year - League - Team		GP	G	A	PTS	PM
2004-05	NWHL Durham Lightning	1	1	0	1	0
2011-12	CWHL Burlington Barracudas	14	0	2	2	18
2012-13	CWHL Toronto Furies	7	0	0	0	0
2013-14	CWHL Toronto Furies	15	0	3	3	4
CWHL Regular Season		36	0	5	5	22

MARTELL, LEANNE

Defence. Shoots right. #19.

NWHL winner. Born 1978-4-5. Grew up in Trenton, NS, CAN. 5'8".

Year - League - Team		GP	G	A	PTS	PM	Year - Playoff	GP	G	A	PTS	PM
1996	Nationals Pictou County Sobey's	4	1	1	2	4						
1998	Nationals Nova Scotia Selects	5	0	1	1	2						
2000	Nationals Nova Scotia Selects	6	1	3	4							
2000-01	NWHL Wingstar de Montréal	1	0	1	1	0						
2001	Nationals Nova Scotia Selects											
2002	Nationals Nova Scotia Selects	5	1	2	3	0						
2003	Nationals Nova Scotia Selects	6	0	4	4	0						
2003-04	NWHL Axion de Montréal	23	3	4	7	8						
2004-05	NWHL Axion de Montréal	36	2	7	9	6						
2005	Nationals Axion de Montréal	6	2	1	3	2						
2005-06	NWHL Axion de Montréal	27	1	2	3	2	2006 NWHL-P	3	0	0	0	0
Totals from all Competitions		**122**	**11**	**26**	**37**	**24**						

MARTIN, EMMA — *Defence. Shoots left. #72.*
Born 1996-01-12. grew up in Winsloe, PE, CAN. 5'9". Debut at age 22 on 2018-11-17.

Year - League - Team			GP	G	A	PTS	PM	Year - Playoff	GP	G	A	PTS	PM
2018-19	CWHL	Canadiennes de Montréal	12	1	2	3	4	2019 C-Cup	3	0	0	0	0

MARTIN, JENNIFER — *Forward. 2003 Nationals Newfoundland Labrador (5 games).*

MARTINDALE, REBECCA — *Forward. Shoots left. #12.*
Clarkson Cup winner with Montréal on 2012-03-25
Born 1987-8-31, Kingston, ON, CAN. 5'5". Debut at age 24 on 2011-10-22.

Year - League - Team			GP	G	A	PTS	PM	Year - Playoff	GP	G	A	PTS	PM
2011-12	CWHL	Stars de Montréal	12	1	1	2	0	2012 C-Cup	4	0	0	0	2

MARTINSON, LISA — *Forward. Shoots right. #11.*
Isobel Cup winner with Minnesota on 2019-03-17.
Born 1991-05-29. Grew up in St. Louis Park, MN, USA. 5'5". Debut at age 27 on 2018-10-20.

Year - League - Team			GP	G	A	PTS	PM	Year - Playoff	GP	G	A	PTS	PM
2018-19	NWHL/	Minnesota Whitecaps	4	0	1	1	0	2019 I-Cup	1	0	0	0	0

MARVIN, GIGI — *Defence. Shoots right. #19.*
Olympic champion, IIHF champion. Clarkson Cup winner on 2013-03-23. Isobel Cup winner on 2016-03-12.
Born 1987-3-7, Warroad, MN, USA. 5'8". Debut at age 23 in 2010-11.

Year - League - Team			GP	G	A	PTS	PM	Year - Playoff	GP	G	A	PTS	PM
2010-11	WWHL	Minnesota Whitecaps	17	27	14	41	8	2011 C-Cup	3	1	0	1	2
2011-12	CWHL	Boston Blades	27	10	21	31	24	2012 C-Cup	3	2	3	5	0
2012-13	CWHL	Boston Blades	15	2	3	5	6	2013 C-Cup	4	1	1	2	8
2014-15	CWHL	Boston Blades	0	0	0	0	0						
2015-16	NWHL/	Boston Pride	16	5	9	14	12	2016 I-Cup	4	2	5	7	2
2016-17	NWHL/	Boston Pride	16	4	10	14	8	2017 I-Cup	2	1	1	2	0
2018-19	NWHL/	Boston Pride	15	10	6	16	8	2019 I-Cup	1	0	0	0	0
CWHL Regular Season			42	12	24	36	30	Clarkson Cup	10	4	4	8	10
NWHL Regular Season			47	19	25	44	28	Isobel Cup	7	3	6	9	2
Totals from all Competitions			**123**	**65**	**73**	**138**	**78**						

CWHL First All-Star Team in 2012-13; CWHL Second All-Star Team in 2011-12... finished 10th in the Angela James Bowl scoring race in 2011-12... NWHL Defender of the Year in 2015-16

MARYNICK, ALYSE — *Forward. 2006-07 WWHL British Columbia #26 (22 gp, 1 goal, 1 a.; 2 playoff gp).*

MARZIALI, MORGAN — *St. Mary's, ON. Centre. 2004-05 NWHL Oakville Ice #91.*

MASCHMEYER, BRITTANEY — *Defence. Shoots right. #8 #14 #19.*
Born 1989-1-20, Bruderheim, AB, CAN. Grew up in Bruderheim, AB, CAN. 5'7".

Year - League - Team			GP	G	A	PTS	PM	Year - Playoff	GP	G	A	PTS	PM
2004-05	WWHL	Edmonton Chimos	21	1	7	8	22	2005 WWHL-P	3	0	1	1	0
2005-06	WWHL	Edmonton Chimos	23	2	10	12	10	2006 WWHL-P	2	0	1	1	0
2010-11	WWHL	Edmonton Chimos	14	0	3	3	4						
2011-12	CWHL	Alberta	15	0	1	1	6						
Totals from all Competitions			**78**	**3**	**23**	**26**	**42**						

MASHIFTER, SHANNON — *2000-01 NWHL North York Aeros (1 game, 1 goal, 1 assist).*

MASHINTER, AMANDA — *Bradford, ON. LW. 2005-06 NWHL Toronto Aeros #27 (20 gp, 5 goals, 2 assists).*

MASKALL, PATTI — *Defence. 2001 Nationals Vancouver Griffins.*

MASON, MARIESA — *Forward. Shoots left.*
Born 1985-03-04. Grew up in Saskatoon, SK, CAN

Year - League - Team			GP	G	A	PTS	PM	Year - Playoff	GP	G	A	PTS	PM
2002	Nationals	Saskatchewan	6	0	0	0	0						
2003	Nationals	Host Saskatchewan	5	0	2	2	0						
2004	Nationals	British Columbia	6	0	0	0	12						

MASON, PATRICE — *Calgary, AB, CAN. Defence. 2007-08 WWHL Strathmore (18 games, 1 goal, 5 assists).*

MATCHERN, ASHLEY — *F. 2000 Nationals Newfoundland (5 gp); 2001 Nationals; 2002 Nationals (5 gp, 1 goal).*

MATHESON, MALLORY — *Forward. #8.*

Year - League - Team			GP	G	A	PTS	PM	Year - Playoff	GP	G	A	PTS	PM
2008-09	WWHL	Edmonton Chimos	24	3	2	5	14	2009 WWHL-P	1	0	0	0	0
2009-10	WWHL	Edmonton Chimos	15	1	5	6	12						
2010-11	WWHL	Edmonton Chimos	13	0	4	4	6						
Totals from all Competitions			**53**	**4**	**11**	**15**	**32**						

MATHESON, SARA — *Forward. Shoots right.*
Born 1978-03-03.

Year - League - Team			GP	G	A	PTS	PM	Year - Playoff	GP	G	A	PTS	PM
2000	Nationals	Nova Scotia Selects											
2001	Nationals	Nova Scotia Selects											
2004	Nationals	Nova Scotia Selects	5	1	3	4	4						
2005	Nationals	Team New Brunswick	6	4	2	6	4						
2006	Nationals	Team New Brunswick	7	0	1	1	0						

MATTEUCCI, ELLA *Defence. Shoots right. #71.*
Born 1993-08-02, Kelowna, BC, CAN. Grew up in Fruitvale, BC, CAN. 5'7". Debut at age 25 on 2018-10-13.

Year - League - Team		GP	G	A	PTS	PM	Year - Playoff	GP	G	A	PTS	PM
2018-19	CWHL Markham Thunder	28	1	4	5	8	2019 C-Cup	3	1	0	1	0

MATTHEWS, ALYCIA *Defence. 2004 Nationals British Columbia (6 gp, 1 g., 1 a.); 2005 Nationals (7 gp, 1 a.).*

MATTHEWS, KELLY *Forward. 2003 Nationals Newfoundland (5 gp); 2004 Nationals (5 gp, 1 goal).*

MATHISON, AMANDA *Newport, MN. 2004-05 WWHL Minnesota (11 gp, 2 goals, 1 assist; 2 playoff games).*

MATT, KIM *Sutton, ON. Defence. 2005-06 NWHL Toronto Aeros #12 (34 games, 6 goals, 8 assists).*

MAXWELL, DANIELLE *Defence. 2010-11 WWHL Manitoba Maple Leafs #33 (1 game).*

MAY, URSZALA *Forward. 1995-96 COWHL North York (1 game); 1996-97 COWHL (1 game, 1 assist).*

MCALLISTER, RENEE *1992-93 COWHL Guelph #12 (26 gp, 1 goal, 3 a.); 1996-97 London #14 (1 game).*

MCALPINE, LINDSAY *Forward. #16.*
Born 1983-11-9.

Year - League - Team		GP	G	A	PTS	PM
2007-08	WWHL Edmonton Chimos	9	6	6	12	4
2009-10	WWHL Edmonton Chimos	17	7	5	12	18
2010-11	WWHL Edmonton Chimos	3	0	0	0	0

MCANDREW, *2002-03 NWHL Ottawa Raiders (1 game, 1 assist).*

MCARTHUR, KRISTA *Defence. Shoots left. #6 #42.*
CWHL winner. Born 1983-2-14, Collingwood, ON, CAN. Grew up in Aliston, ON, CAN. 5'10".

Year - League - Team		GP	G	A	PTS	PM	Year - Playoff	GP	G	A	PTS	PM
1998-99	NWHL Brampton Thunder	8	1	1	2	19						
1999-00	NWHL Brampton Thunder	39	2	13	15	54						
2000-01	NWHL Brampton Thunder	38	7	13	20	72						
2001-02	NWHL Brampton Thunder	24	2	3	5	38						
2002	Nationals Brampton Thunder	7	1	1	2	10						
2006-07	NWHL Brampton Thunder	34	3	16	19	42	2007 NWHL-P	6	0	3	3	10
2007-08	CWHL Brampton Can.-Thunder	28	2	13	15	36	2008 CWHL-P	2	1	0	1	2
2008-09	CWHL Vaughan Flames	28	5	7	12	40	2009 CWHL-P	2		4		
2009-10	CWHL Vaughan Flames	2	0	0	0	4						
CWHL Regular Season		58	7	20	27	80						
Totals from all Competitions		**218**	**24**	**70**	**94**	**331**						

MCARTHUR, LESLEY *Forward. Shoots right. #15.*
Born 1985-2-1, Mississauga, ON, CAN. Grew up in Kanata, ON, CAN. 5'7". Debut at age 23 on 2007-9-1.

Year - League - Team		GP	G	A	PTS	PM	Year - Playoff	GP	G	A	PTS	PM
2007-08	CWHL Ottawa Capital Canucks	24	4	5	9	24	2008 CWHL-P	1	0	0	0	0
2008-09	CWHL Ottawa Senators	23	5	6	11	8	2009 CWHL-P	2		1	1	
2009-10	CWHL Ottawa Senators	26	3	7	10	20						
CWHL Regular Season		73	12	18	30	52						
Totals from all Competitions		**76**	**12**	**19**	**31**	**52**						

MCAULIFFE, JESSA *Defence. Shoots left. #20.*
Abby Hoffman Cup winner with Aeros on 2005-03-13.
Born 1993-11-29, Odessa, ON, CAN. 5'8". Debut at age 22 on 2016-10-15.

Year - League - Team		GP	G	A	PTS	PM
2016-17	CWHL Brampton Thunder	4	0	0	0	0

MCAULIFFE, LAUREN *Right wing. Shoots right. #33.*
Born 1981-12-06.

Year - League - Team		GP	G	A	PTS	PM	Year - Playoff	GP	G	A	PTS	PM
2004-05	NWHL Toronto Aeros	36	15	9	24	12	2005 NWHL-P					
2005	Nationals Toronto Aeros	7	5	3	8	0						

Served as head coach with CWHL Boston... CWHL Coach of the Year in 2011-12

MCCABE, KATIE *1993-94 COWHL Hamilton #11 (30 games, 1 goal, 1 assist).*

MCCABE, SARAH *Forward. 1996 Nationals Pictou County (4 gp, 2 goals, 1 assist); 1998 Nationals (5 gp).*

MCCARTHY, MEGAN *Forward. #22.*
Clarkson Cup winner with Minnesota on 2010-03-28. Born 1987-6-28. Forward.

Year - League - Team		GP	G	A	PTS	PM	Year - Playoff	GP	G	A	PTS	PM
2009-10	WWHL Minnesota Whitecaps	10	2	1	3	2	2010 C-Cup	2	0	1	1	0
2010-11	WWHL Minnesota Whitecaps	13	4	5	9	12	2011 C-Cup	3	0	0	0	0

MCCARVILLE, PATSY *1995 Nationals PEI Esso Tigers.*

MCCLINTOCK, JAIMIE *Forward. 2004 Nationals Manitoba (5 games).*

MCCONNELL, GRETCHEN *Forward. 1996 Britannia Blues (5 games).*

MCCONNELL, STACEY *Defence. 007-08 CWHL Burlington Barracudas #25 (2 games, 1 playoff game).*

MCCORMACK, KATHY *Forward. Shoots left. #20.*
Born 1974-2-16. Grew up in Blackville, NB, CAN. 5'9".

Year - League - Team			GP	G	A	PTS	PM	Year - Playoff		GP	G	A	PTS	PM
1995	Nationals	Maritime Sports Blades												
1996	Nationals	Maritime Sports Blades												
1998	Nationals	Maritime Sports Blades	6	1	2	3	4							
1999	Nationals	Team New Brunswick	6	3	0	3								
1999-00	NWHL	Mississauga Chiefs	33	19	16	35	43							
2000-01	NWHL	Mississauga IceBears	35	14	20	34	40							
2001-02	NWHL	Mississauga IceBears	28	6	14	20	27							
2002-03	NWHL	Mississauga IceBears												
2003-04	NWHL	Oakville Ice	23	6	12	18	18	2004	NWHL-P	2				
2004-05	NWHL	Oakville Ice	35	7	11	18	20							
2005-06	NWHL	Oakville Ice	35	11	15	26	36	2006	NWHL-P	2	0	1	1	0
2006-07	NWHL	Oakville Ice	10	4	6	10	14	2007	NWHL-P	3	0	1	1	2
Totals from all Competitions			**218**	**71**	**98**	**169**	**204**							

MCCORMICK, E.   *1999-00 NWHL Scarborough Sting #55 (1 game).*

MCCREA, KOLBEE   *Forward. 2009-10 CWHL Burlington #6 (1 game).*

MCCULLOUCH, LINDSAY   *Forward. 1999-00 NWHL Scarborough (1 game); 2000-01 Toronto (11 gp, 1 assist).*

MCCULLOUGH, KIM   *Defence/Forward. Shoots right. #8 #11.*
Born 1979-10-9, Toronto, ON, CAN. Grew up in Toronto, ON, CAN. 5'9".

Year - League - Team			GP	G	A	PTS	PM	Year - Playoff		GP	G	A	PTS	PM
2002-03	NWHL	Brampton Thunder						2003	NWHL-P					
2003	Nationals	Brampton Thunder	5	1	7	8	2							
2003-04	NWHL	Calgary Oval X-Treme	11	1	2	3	18	2004	NWHL-P					
2004	Nationals	Calgary Oval X-Treme	6	0	0	0	0							
2004-05	NWHL	Oakville Ice	36	3	12	15	20							
2005-06	NWHL	Oakville Ice	36	1	12	13	38	2006	NWHL-P	2	0	0	0	2
2006-07	NWHL	Oakville Ice	34	0	7	7	62	2007	NWHL-P	3	0	0	0	6
2007-08	CWHL	Burlington Barracudas	29	4	5	9	34	2008	CWHL-P	3	0	0	0	2
Totals from all Competitions			**165**	**10**	**45**	**55**	**184**							

MCCULLOUGH, SARAH   *F. 2003 Nationals Newfoundland Labrador (5 games).*

MCCUMBER, DINA   *Defence/Forward. Shoots left.*
Born 1984-12-12. Grew up in North Tonawanda, NY, USA.

Year - League - Team			GP	G	A	PTS	PM
2001-02	NWHL	Brampton Thunder	28	1	9	10	34
2002	Nationals	Brampton Thunder	7	0	2	2	0
2002-03	NWHL	Brampton Thunder					
2002-03	NWHL	Mississauga Ice Bears					

MCCURDY, MANDY   *Defence. 1998-99 Ottawa Raiders #66 (34 games, 2 goals, 3 assists).*

MCCUSKY, LINDSAY   *Kirkland Lake, QC. Defence. 2007-08 CWHL Montréal #86 (6 games).*

MCCUTCHEON, SUE   *Forward. Shoots right. #7.*
CWHL winner. Born 1982-9-10. Grew up in Ottawa, ON, CAN. 5'7". Debut at age 24 on 2006-11-15.

Year - League - Team			GP	G	A	PTS	PM	Year - Playoff		GP	G	A	PTS	PM
2006-07	NWHL	Brampton Thunder	14	1	0	1	10	2007	NWHL-P	5	2	0	2	2
2007-08	CWHL	Brampton Can.-Thunder	26	1	2	3	22	2008	CWHL-P	3	0	0	0	2
2008	Nationals	Brampton Can.-Thunder	3	0	0	0	0							

MCDONALD, FAITH   *Forward. Shoots right.*
Born 1979-09-22. Grew up in Nelson House, MB, CAN.

Year - League - Team			GP	G	A	PTS	PM
2002	Nationals	Calgary Oval X-Treme	6	0	2	2	0
2005	Nationals	Manitoba	5	3	2	5	0
2006	Nationals	Manitoba	0	0	0	0	

MCDONALD, JODIE   *2007-08 CWHL Ottawa Capital Canucks #18 (5 games, 1 goal).*

MCDONALD, KATHLEEN   *Forward. 2008-09 WWHL British Columbia (1 game).*

MCDONALD, KELLY   *Defence. 2015-16 NWHL Buffalo (17 gp, 9 assists; I-Cup 5 gp, 2 assists).*

MCDONALD, NICOLE   *Forward. 2004-05 NWHL Ottawa Raiders #11 (26 gp, 3 goals, 3 assists).*

MCDONALD, SARA   *Forward. 2006-07 NWHL Oakville Ice #15 (34 gp, 8 goals, 7 a.; 3 playoff gp).*

MCDONALD, TANYA   *F. 1996 Nationals Pictou County (4 gp, 1 goal); 1998 Nationals Nova Scotia (5 gp, 2pts).*

MCELREA, ANDRIANE   *Forward. 2002 Nationals Manitoba (4 games).*

MCFARLANE, TARA   *2007-08 CWHL Burlington Barracudas #82 (1 game).*

MCGEE, BECKY   *Defence. 2004-05 WWHL Calgary #11 (5 games, 2 goals, 2 assists).*

MCGEE, TAYLOR   *Defence. Shoots right. #14.*
Born 1994-02-08. Grew up in Pearl River, NY, USA. 5'5". Debut at age 22 on 2016-10-15.

Year - League - Team			GP	G	A	PTS	PM
2016-17	CWHL	Boston Blades	6	0	0	0	2

MCGEOUGH, KARA *Forward. 2003 Nationals Host Saskatchewan (5 games).*

MCGOVERN, KATIE *Forward. Shoots left. #13.*
Isobel Cup winner with Minnesota on 2019-03-17.
Born 1994-11-29. Grew up in Scottsdale, AZ, USA. 5'4". Debut at age 23 on 2018-10-06.

Year - League - Team		GP	G	A	PTS	PM	Year - Playoff	GP	G	A	PTS	PM
2018-19	NWHL/ Minnesota Whitecaps	16	6	5	11	2	2019 I-Cup	2	1	1	2	0

MCGOWAN, HANNAH *Forward. 2015-16 NWHL Buffalo (18 gp, 1 goal, 2 a.; I-Cup 5 gp, 1 a.).*

MCGRATH-AGG, EMILY *Forward. Shoots left.*
Born 1984-01-27. Grew up in New Westminster, BC, CAN.

Year - League - Team		GP	G	A	PTS	PM
2005-06	WWHL B	22	6	4	10	
2006	Nationals British Columbia	6	0	2	2	4
2007	Nationals British Columbia	5	1	3	4	2
2008-09	WWHL B	14	1	2	3	

MCGRORY, PAIGE *RW. 1993-94 COWHL Mississauga #14 (5 gp, 2 a.) & Hamilton (8 gp, 1 goal, 1 a.).*

MCGUIRE, DAWN *Defence.*
IIHF champion. Abby Hoffman Cup winner with Aeros on 1991-03-17. Abby Hoffman Cup winner with Edmonton on 1997-03-09.
Born 1960, 03-26, Edmonton, AB, CAN. 5'4".

Year - League - Team		GP	G	A	PTS	PM
1996	Nationals Edmonton Chimos	7	0	2	2	4
1997	Nationals Edmonton Chimos					

MCGURK, STACEY *1993-94 Hamilton Golden Hawks #92 (3 games).*

MCHATTIE, BETH *1999-00 NWHL Ottawa Raiders #86 (2 games).*

MCINTOSH, LAURA *Forward. Shoots left. #15.*
Clarkson Cup winner with Markham on 2018-03-25
Born 1990-1-21. Grew up in Waterloo, ON, CAN. 5'5". Debut at age 18 on 2008-2-7.

Year - League - Team		GP	G	A	PTS	PM	Year - Playoff	GP	G	A	PTS	PM
2007-08	CWHL Mississauga Chiefs	1	1	0	1	0						
2012-13	CWHL Brampton Thunder	24	6	18	24	22	2013 C-Cup	3	0	2	2	6
2013-14	CWHL Brampton Thunder	9	4	1	5	2						
2015-16	CWHL Brampton Thunder	15	1	7	8	6						
2017-18	CWHL Markham Thunder	17	5	13	18	8	2018 C-Cup	3	0	1	1	2
2018-19	CWHL Markham Thunder	3	0	1	1	2						
CWHL Regular Season		69	17	40	57	40	Clarkson Cup	6	0	3	3	8
Totals from all Competitions		**75**	**17**	**43**	**60**	**48**						

Finished 9th in the Angela James Bowl scoring race in 2012-13

MCINTYRE, ANNIE *Forward. 2008 Nationals Team New Brunswick (5 games).*

MCKAY, AMANDA *Defence. 2005-06 NWHL Québec #89 (7 games); 2006-07 #7 (16 games, 1 assist).*

MCKAY, TARA *Forward. Shoots right. #10 #17 #71 #27.*
Born 1972-3-21, Toronto, ON, CAN. Grew up in Pickering, ON, CAN. 5'4".

Year - League - Team		GP	G	A	PTS	PM	Year - Playoff	GP	G	A	PTS	PM
1993-94	COWHL Scarborough Sting	13	5	2	7	4						
1995-96	COWHL Mississauga Chiefs	27	14	5	19	29						
1996-97	COWHL Mississauga Chiefs	29	6	15	21	12						
1997-98	COWHL Mississauga Chiefs	18	1	7	8	8						
1998-99	NWHL Brampton Thunder	38	10	21	31	20						
2000-01	NWHL Brampton Thunder	7	1	2	3	8						
2001-02	NWHL Brampton Thunder	29	4	10	14	10						
2002	Nationals Brampton Thunder	7	1	1	2	4						
2002-03	NWHL Brampton Thunder						2003 NWHL-P					
2003	Nationals Brampton Thunder	5	1	3	4	4						
2003-04	NWHL Brampton Thunder											
2009-10	CWHL Brampton Thunder	11	3	0	3	4						
Totals from all Competitions		**184**	**46**	**66**	**112**	**103**						

MCKENNA, FIONA *Forward. Shoots right. #24.*
Born 1995-06-01. Grew up in Burr Ridge, IL, USA. 5'8". Debut at age 23 on 2018-10-06.

Year - League - Team		GP	G	A	PTS	PM
2018-19	NWHL/ Metropolitan Riveters	6	0	0	0	2

MCKERNAN, TAMARA *Defence. 1996 Nationals Edmonton Chimos (7 games).*

MCKIMM, CLAIRE *Defence. 2009-10 CWHL Vaughan Flames #39 (13 games, 1 goal, 1 assist).*

MCKINNON, MARY *Forward. 2005 Nationals Prince Edward island (5 gp, 4 pts); 2006 Nationals (5 gp, 8 pts).*

MCLAUGHLIN, KAREN *Forward. #12 #28 #14.*
Born 1982-3-25.

Year - League - Team		GP	G	A	PTS	PM	Year - Playoff	GP	G	A	PTS	PM
2007-08	CWHL Burlington Barracudas	13	5	2	7	20						

Year - League - Team		GP	G	A	PTS	PM	Year - Playoff		GP	G	A	PTS	PM
2007-08	WWHL Calgary Oval X-Treme	9	5	3	8	6							
2008	Nationals Calgary Oval X-Treme	3	0	0	0	0							
2008-09	WWHL Calgary Oval X-Treme	21	21	11	32	20	2009	WWHL-P	2	1	0	1	2
							2009	C-Cup	2	0	0	0	0
2009-10	WWHL Strathmore Rockies	1	0	0	0	0							
2010-11	WWHL Strathmore Rockies	1	0	1	1	0							
Totals from all Competitions		**52**	**32**	**17**	**49**	**48**							

MCLEAN, BRENNA *Forward. 2008-09 WWHL Strathmore Rockies (20 games, 2 assists; playoff 1 game).*

MCLEAN, NANCY *Forward. 1996-97 COWHL Newtonbrook #13 (4 games, 1 goal, 4 assists).*

MCLEAN, STEFANIE *Defence. #3 #5 #11.*
Born 1983-5-24, Edmonton, AB, CAN.

Year - League - Team		GP	G	A	PTS	PM	Year - Playoff		GP	G	A	PTS	PM
2001-02	NWHL Ottawa Raiders	29	3	2	5	28	2002	NWHL-P					
2002-03	NWHL Ottawa Raiders	29	5	3	8	30							
2007-08	CWHL Ottawa Capital Canucks	21	4	3	7	24	2008	CWHL-P	1	0	0	0	0
Totals from all Competitions		**80**	**12**	**8**	**20**	**82**							

MCLEARY, MICHELLE *Forward. 2001 Nationals Vancouver Griffins.*

MCLEOD, FIONA *Defence. #17 #27.*
Born 1979-5-7.

Year - League - Team		GP	G	A	PTS	PM	Year - Playoff		GP	G	A	PTS	PM
1995-96	COWHL North York Aeros	1	0	0	0	0							
1996-97	COWHL Scarborough Sting	33	3	10	13	24							
1997-98	COWHL Scarborough Sting	19	0	2	2	6							
2004-05	WWHL Minnesota Whitecaps	11	2	0	2	16	2005	WWHL-P	1	0	0	0	0
Totals from all Competitions		**65**	**5**	**12**	**17**	**46**							

MCLEOD, L. *Defence. 1996-97 COWHL Scarborough #81 (1 game).*

MCLEOD, TAYLOR *Forward. 2007 Nationals BC Outback (5 games, 1 assist).*

MCMEEKIN, HAYLEY *Forward. Shoots left. #36 #89.*
Abby Hoffman Cup winner with Aeros on 2005-03-13.
Born 1986-06-18, Waterloo, ON, CAN. 5'5".

Year - League - Team		GP	G	A	PTS	PM
2004-05	NWHL Toronto Aeros	5	1	0	1	2
2005	Nationals Toronto Aeros	7	4	4	8	2

MCMILLAN, KELSIE *Defence. 2009-10 WWHL Edmonton #81 (16 gp, 1 g., 3 a.); 2010-11 (17 gp, 2 g., 1 a.).*

MCMILLAN, MARLEY *Forward. 2009-10 WWHL Minnesota #24 (1 game, 1 assist).*

MCMILLEN, MILICA *Defence. Shoots left. #73.*
Born 1993-07-13. Grew up in St. Paul, MN, USA. 5'10". Debut at age 23 on 2016-10-08.

Year - League - Team		GP	G	A	PTS	PM	Year - Playoff		GP	G	A	PTS	PM
2016-17	NWHL/ New York Riveters	18	3	6	9	21	2017	I-Cup	1	0	0	0	0

MCMURRAY, REBECCA *Forward. 2010-11 WWHL Manitoba Maple Leafs #33 (3 games).*

MCNAMARA, CARMEN *Forward. 1996-97 COWHL Peterborough #88. (33 games, 1 goal, 7 assists).*

MCNUTT, KAITLYN *Defence. 2007 Nationals Nova Scotia Selects (7 games).*

MCPARLAND, JENNA *Forward. Shoots right. #91.*
Clarkson Cup winner with Markham on 2018-03-25
Born 1992-05-12. Grew up in Schreiber, ON, CAN. 5'9". Debut at age 23 on 2015-10-17.

Year - League - Team		GP	G	A	PTS	PM	Year - Playoff		GP	G	A	PTS	PM
2015-16	CWHL Brampton Thunder	24	8	11	19	8	2016	C-Cup	2	1	0	1	0
2016-17	CWHL Brampton Thunder	24	4	6	10	28	2017	C-Cup	2	0	0	0	4
2017-18	CWHL Markham Thunder	21	8	10	18	6	2018	C-Cup	3	3	0	3	0
2018-19	CWHL Markham Thunder	24	10	6	16	6	2019	C-Cup	3	3	0	3	12
CWHL Regular Season		**93**	**30**	**33**	**63**	**48**	Clarkson Cup		10	7	0	7	16
Totals from all Competitions		**103**	**37**	**33**	**70**	**64**							

Finished 17th in the Angela James Bowl scoring race in 2015-16

MCPHAIL, FRANCES *Forward. Shoots right. #15 #16.*
Born 1989-4-13, Richmond, BC, CAN. Grew up in Oakville, ON, CAN. 5'7". Debut at age 16 on 2005-10-19.

Year - League - Team		GP	G	A	PTS	PM	Year - Playoff		GP	G	A	PTS	PM
2005-06	NWHL Toronto Aeros	3	0	0	0	0							
2010-11	CWHL Toronto Furies	23	2	4	6	20	2011	CWHL-P	2		4		
							2011	C-Cup	4	2	0	2	6
2011-12	CWHL Toronto Furies	25	6	3	9	12	2012	C-Cup	3	1	0	1	2
CWHL Regular Season		**48**	**8**	**7**	**15**	**32**	Clarkson Cup		7	3	0	3	8
Totals from all Competitions		**60**	**11**	**7**	**18**	**44**							

MCPHERSON, MORAG *Forward. #21.*
Born 1977-12-10. 5'5".

Year - League - Team		GP	G	A	PTS	PM
2000-01	NWHL Ottawa Raiders	36	13	10	23	24
2001-02	NWHL Ottawa Raiders	27	2	8	10	19
2002-03	NWHL Ottawa Raiders	31	7	10	17	18
2003-04	NWHL Ottawa Raiders	9	3	2	5	8
Totals from all Competitions		**103**	**25**	**30**	**55**	**69**

MCPHEE, LEANNE   *F. 2001 Nationals Nova Scotia; 2002 Nationals (5 gp, 1 goal); 2003 Nationals (6 gp, 1 g.).*

MCQUAID, KATE   *Forward. 1998 Nationals Prince Edward Island (5 games).*

MCRAE, JENNIFER   *RW. 2004-05 NWHL Oakville Ice #44 (32 games, 1 goal, 4 assists).*

MCRENNEY   *2002-03 NWHL Ottawa Raiders (1 game).*

MEDHURST, KAREN   *Forward. Shoots left.*
Abby Hoffman Cup winner with Calgary on 2003-03-16.
Born 1978-11-29. Grew up in Calgary, AB, CAN.

Year - League - Team		GP	G	A	PTS	PM	Year - Playoff	GP	G	A	PTS	PM
2002	Nationals Calgary Oval X-Treme	6	1	2	3	0						
2002-03	NWHL Calgary Oval X-Treme	21	2	9	11	12	2003 NWHL-P					
2003	Nationals Calgary Oval X-Treme	5	1	2	3	0						

MEEHAN, PATTI   *Forward. 1995 Nationals Metro Valley Selects.*

MENARD, HÉLÈNE   *Forward. 1998 Nationals Nova Scotia Selects (5 games, 2 assists).*

MÉNARD, LAURIE-ANNE   *Defence. #24 #12.*
Clarkson Cup winner with Montréal on 2009-03-21
Born 1992-3-21, Chicoutimi, QC, CAN. Debut at age 17 on 2008-10-11.

Year - League - Team		GP	G	A	PTS	PM	Year - Playoff	GP	G	A	PTS	PM
2008-09	CWHL Stars de Montréal	22	1	6	7	16	2009 CWHL-P	2	0	0	0	0
							2009 C-Cup	3	0	0	0	4
2009-10	CWHL Stars de Montréal	2	0	0	0	2						
2010-11	CWHL Stars de Montréal	9	0	0	0	2						
CWHL Regular Season		33	1	6	7	20	Clarkson Cup	3	0	0	0	4
Totals from all Competitions		**38**	**1**	**6**	**7**	**24**						

MENEGHIN, KAYLA   *Forward. Shoots right. #3.*
Born 1994-12-22. Grew up in Clifton, NJ, USA. 5'4". Debut at age 23 on 2018-10-13.

Year - League - Team		GP	G	A	PTS	PM
2018-19	NWHL/ Connecticut Whale	10	1	1	2	6

MENKE, AMY   *Forward. Shoots right. #21.*
Isobel Cup winner with Minnesota on 2019-03-17.
Born 1995-04-09. Grew up in Shakopee, MN, USA. 5'6". Debut at age 23 on 2018-10-07.

Year - League - Team		GP	G	A	PTS	PM	Year - Playoff	GP	G	A	PTS	PM
2018-19	NWHL/ Minnesota Whitecaps	15	4	6	10	10	2019 I-Cup	2	1	1	2	0

MERCER, CARLY   *Exeter, ON. Forward. 2014-15 CWHL Brampton #21 (24 games, 6 goals, 2 assists).*

MERCER, CAYLEY   *Left wing. Shoots right. #18.*
Born 1994-01-18. Grew up in Exeter, ON, CAN. 5'8". Debut at age 23 on 2017-10-28.

Year - League - Team		GP	G	A	PTS	PM
2017-18	CWHL Vanke Rays	28	15	26	41	20
2018-19	CWHL KRS Vanke Rays	28	7	14	21	12

CWHL Second Team All-Star in 2017-18... CWHL All-Rookie Team in 2017-18... finished 3rd in the Angela James Bowl scoring race in 2017-18.

MERKLEY, LEAH   *Forward. 2007 Nationals Nova Scotia (7 gp, 2 pts); 2008 Nationals (1 gp).*

MERRIFIELD, GILLIAN   *Defence. Shoots left. #14 #21 #16.*
Clarkson Cup winner with Montréal on 2009-03-21 and 2011-03-27.
Born 1985-2-22, London, ON, CAN. Grew up in London, ON, CAN. 5'6". Debut at age 24 on 2008-10-18.

Year - League - Team		GP	G	A	PTS	PM	Year - Playoff	GP	G	A	PTS	PM
2008-09	CWHL Stars de Montréal	26	1	6	7	4	2009 CWHL-P	2	0	0	0	0
							2009 C-Cup	3	0	0	0	0
2009-10	CWHL Stars de Montréal	22	2	6	8	2	2010 C-Cup	1	0	0	0	0
2010-11	CWHL Stars de Montréal	24	1	4	5	4	2011 CWHL-P	1				
							2011 C-Cup	4	0	0	0	0
CWHL Regular Season		72	4	16	20	10	Clarkson Cup	8	0	0	0	0
Totals from all Competitions		**83**	**4**	**16**	**20**	**10**						

MERZ, SUE   *Defence. #7.*

Year - League - Team		GP	G	A	PTS	PM	Year - Playoff	GP	G	A	PTS	PM

Olympic champion. Born 1972-4-10, USA.

Year - League - Team		GP	G	A	PTS	PM
1996-97	COWHL Newtonbrook Panthers	19	11	16	27	18
1998-99	NWHL Brampton Thunder	27	6	22	28	61
1999-00	NWHL Brampton Thunder	10	2	10	12	9
Totals from all Competitions		**56**	**19**	**48**	**67**	**88**

MESCHINO, LAUREN   *Defence. #17 #77 #89.*
Born 1984-2-1, Toronto, ON, CAN. Debut at age 21 on 2005-09-27.

Year - League - Team		GP	G	A	PTS	PM
2005-06	NWHL Toronto Aeros	1	0	0	0	0
2008-09	CWHL Stars de Montréal	6	2			
2009-10	CWHL Vaughan Flames	18	2	7	9	8

MESSNER, STEPHANIE   *Forward. Shoots left.*
Born 1985-11-08, Winnipeg, MB, CAN. 5'5".

Year - League - Team		GP	G	A	PTS	PM	Year - Playoff	GP	G	A	PTS	PM
2003	Nationals University of Winnipeg	4	2	2	4	2						
2010-11	WWHL Manitoba Maple leafs	5	1	1	2	0						

METCALF, VERONICA   *Forward. 2002 Nationals Richmond Steelers (5 games).*

METCALFE, HEIDI   *Defence. 1998 Nationals Nova Scotia Selects (5 games).*

METZGER, SANDY   *1999-00 NWHL Scarborough (5 games, 1 goal); 2000-01 Toronto (40 games, 2 assists).*

MEUNIER-PELLETIER, KARINE   *Defence. 2008 Natioals Team New Brunswick (5 gp, 1 assist).*

MEZZERA, ANNABELLE   *RW. 1993-94 COWHL Mississauga #21 (25 games, 2 goals, 8 assists).*

MIANO, TONI ANN   *Defence. Shoots right. #18.*
Born 1996-05-17. Grew up in Bronx, NY, USA. 5'4". Debut at age 22 on 2018-10-13.

Year - League - Team		GP	G	A	PTS	PM	Year - Playoff	GP	G	A	PTS	PM
2018-19	NWHL/ Boston Pride	15	3	2	5	10	2019 I-Cup	1	0	0	0	0

MICHALEK, ANNIE   *2007-08 CWHL Ottawa Capital Canucks (1 game).*

MICHAUD, TINA   *Forward. 1998 Nationals Maritime Sport Blades (6 games).*

MIHALCHEON, KIRSTEN   *Defence. 2006 Nationals B.C. (6 gp, 2 pts); 2007 Nationals B.C. (5 gp, 2 pts).*

MIKKELSON-REID, MEAGHAN   *Defence. Shoots right. #12.*
Olympic champion. Abby Hoffman Cup winner with Calgary on 2003-03-16. Clarkson Cup champion with Calgary.
Born 1985-1-4. Grew up in St. Albert, AB, CAN. 5'9.

Year - League - Team		GP	G	A	PTS	PM	Year - Playoff	GP	G	A	PTS	PM
2002-03	NWHL Calgary Oval X-Treme	22	7	10	17	14	2003 NWHL-P					
2003	Nationals Calgary Oval X-Treme	3	2	0	2	0						
2007-08	WWHL Edmonton Chimos	24	10	9	19	44						
2008-09	WWHL Edmonton Chimos	22	9	20	29	32	2009 WWHL-P	1	0	0	0	0
2010-11	WWHL Edmonton Chimos	14	7	8	15	12						
2011-12	CWHL Alberta	15	2	9	11	20						
2012-13	CWHL Alberta	23	2	4	6	40						
2015-16	CWHL Calgary Inferno	11	1	0	1	2	2016 C-Cup	3	1	2	3	0
2016-17	CWHL Calgary Inferno	22	5	10	15	6	2017 C-Cup	4	0	2	2	8
	CWHL Regular Season	71	10	23	33	68	Clarkson Cup	7	1	4	5	8
	Totals from all Competitions	164	46	74	120	178						

CWHL First All-Star Team in 2016-17... finished 16th in the Angela James Bowl scoring race in 2016-17.

MIKULA, SANDY   *Forward. 1995 Nationals Calgary Classics.*

MILANO, CHLOE   *2006-07 NWHL Etobicoke (1 gp); 2007-08 CWHL Vaughan (1 gp); 2009-10 (1 gp).*

MILLAR, BRITNEY   *Forward. Shoots left. #4 #33.*
Born 1981-7-21, Kingston, ON, CAN. 5'9".

Year - League - Team		GP	G	A	PTS	PM	Year - Playoff	GP	G	A	PTS	PM
1998-99	NWHL Mississauga Chiefs	31	9	11	20	30						
1999-00	NWHL Mississauga Chiefs	35	9	7	16	18						
2004-05	WWHL Edmonton Chimos	21	2	8	10	24	2005 WWHL-P	3	0	0	0	2
2005-06	WWHL Edmonton Chimos	22	8	8	16	36	2006 WWHL-P	2	0	0	0	6
2006-07	WWHL Edmonton Chimos	24	11	5	16	56	2007 WWHL-P	2	0	1	1	2
2007-08	WWHL Edmonton Chimos	24	5	6	11	36						
2008-09	WWHL Edmonton Chimos	24	7	7	14	34	2009 WWHL-P	1	0	0	0	0
2009-10	WWHL Edmonton Chimos	13	1	5	6	30						
2010-11	WWHL Edmonton Chimos	8	0	3	3	4						
	Totals from all Competitions	210	52	61	113	278						

MILLARD, ANDREA   *LW. 1995-96 COWHL Peterborough #44. (27 games, 7 goals, 4 assists).*

MILLARD, HEATHER   *1995-96 COWHL Peterborough #5. (11 games, 3 goals, 3 assists).*

MILLER, ALEXIS   *Forward. Shoots left. #25.*
Born 1994-04-07. Grew up in Cole Harbour, NS, CAN. 5'8". Debut at age 24 on 2018-10-20.

Year - League - Team		GP	G	A	PTS	PM
2018-19	CWHL Worcester Blades	22	0	2	2	8

MILLER, ASHLEY   *2003-04 NWHL Durham Lightning #7 (34 games, 1 goal, 1 assist).*

MILLER, HANNAH   *Forward. Shoots left. #34.*
Born 1996-02-16. Grew up in North Vancouver, BC, CAN. 5'8". Debut at age 22 on 2018-10-13.

Year - League - Team		GP	G	A	PTS	PM
2018-19	CWHL KRS Vanke Rays	21	10	5	15	16

MILLER, MEGAN   *Defence. 2005-06 WWHL Calgary #14 (21 gp, 1 goal, 3 a.; 3 playoff gp); 2006 Nationals (7 gp).*

MILLER, SARA   *Defence. 2006 Nationals Newfoundland Labrador (5 gp).*

MILLER, STEPHANIE   *Defence. 2010-11 WWHL Manitoba Maple Leafs #22 (6 games, 1 assist).*

MILLER, TARRA   *Forward. 2005 Nationals Nova Scotia Selects (5 games, 1 goal).*

MILLIUS, CARLA   *2000-01 NWHL Toronto Sting (1 game, 1 assist).*

MILLS, BRITTANY   *Forward. 2009-10 WWHL Strathmore Rockies #8 (18 gp, 3 goals, 1 assist).*

MILLS, MELANIE   Forward. #11.
Born 1984-7-24, Hamilton, ON, CAN.

Year - League - Team			GP	G	A	PTS	PM
2004-05	NWHL	Toronto Aeros	4	0	0	0	6
2009-10	CWHL	Vaughan Flames	19	8	3	11	38
2010-11	CWHL	Toronto Furies	18	2	0	2	14
Totals from all Competitions			**41**	**10**	**3**	**13**	**58**

MIKIOWETZ, KIRA   Forward. #25 #4 #88 #27.

Year - League - Team			GP	G	A	PTS	PM
1995-96	COWHL	Hamilton Golden Hawks	28	10	5	15	10
1996-97	COWHL	Scarborough Sting	31	10	10	20	12
1997-98	COWHL	Scarborough Sting	15	1	3	4	4
2002-03	NWHL	Mississauga IceBears					
2003-04	NWHL	Oakville Ice	31	14	21	35	64
Totals from all Competitions			**105**	**35**	**39**	**74**	**90**

MINTZLER, TANIS   *Defence. 1999 Nationals Saskatchewan (4 gp, 1 a.); 2003 Nationals (6 gp, 1 a.).*

MITCHELL, ANN   *Forward. 2004 Nationals Newfoundland Labrador (5 gp); 2005 Nationals (5 gp, 2 assists).*

MITCHELL, RHONDA   *2000-01 NWHL Wingstar de Montréal #7 (33 games, 7 assists).*

MIYAUCHI, KRISTIN   *2009-10 WWHL Strathmore (1 game); 2010-11 (11 games, 1 goal, 2 assists).*

MIZUKAMI (NÉE TAKEUCHI), AINA   Defence. Shoots left. #18.
Clarkson Cup winner with Calgary on 2016-03-14 and 2019-03-24.
Born 1991-08-16. Grew up in Kushiro, JPN. 5'5". Debut at age 23 on 2014-10-25.

Year - League - Team			GP	G	A	PTS	PM	Year - Playoff	GP	G	A	PTS	PM
2014-15	CWHL	Calgary Inferno	8	0	4	4	8	2015 C-Cup	2	0	0	0	2
2015-16	CWHL	Calgary Inferno	20	1	3	4	14	2016 C-Cup	3	0	2	2	4
2016-17	CWHL	Calgary Inferno	10	1	0	1	6	2017 C-Cup	1	0	0	0	0
2018-19	CWHL	Calgary Inferno	18	1	1	2	4	2019 C-Cup	4	0	0	0	2
CWHL Regular Season			56	3	8	11	32	Clarkson Cup	10	0	2	2	8
Totals from all Competitions			**66**	**3**	**10**	**13**	**40**						

MOCK, STEPHANIE   Forward. Shoots right. #5.
Born 1992-02-10. Grew up in Cape Coral, FL, USA. 5'4. Debut at age 25 on 2017-10-28.

Year - League - Team			GP	G	A	PTS	PM
2017-18	NWHL/	Connecticut Whale	11	0	0	0	4

MODESTE, MARY   Defence. Shoots left. #14.
Abby Hoffman Cup winner with Mississauga on 2008-03-15.
Born 1986-3-2, Toronto, ON, CAN. Grew up in Oshawa, ON, CAN. 5'6". Debut at age 22 on 2007-9-22.

Year - League - Team			GP	G	A	PTS	PM	Year - Playoff	GP	G	A	PTS	PM
2007-08	CWHL	Mississauga Chiefs	20	0	2	2	14	2008 CWHL-P	4	0	1	1	2
2008	Nationals	Mississauga Chiefs	3	0	0	0	2						
2008-09	CWHL	Mississauga Chiefs	26	1	2	3	24	2009 CWHL-P	4	1		1	
2009-10	CWHL	Mississauga Chiefs	26	0	10	10	26	2010 C-Cup	1	0	0	0	2
CWHL Regular Season			72	1	14	15	64	Clarkson Cup	1	0	0	0	2
Totals from all Competitions			**84**	**2**	**15**	**17**	**70**						

MOE, JENNIFER   *F. 2010-11 WWHL Edmonton #11 (16 gp, 1 goal, 1 assist); 2015-16 CWHL Calgary (2 games).*

MOE, SARAH   Forward. Shoots right. #27.
Born 1980-6-10. Grew up in West Des Moines, IA, USA. Debut at age 32 on 2012-10-20.

Year - League - Team			GP	G	A	PTS	PM	Year - Playoff	GP	G	A	PTS	PM
2012-13	CWHL	Brampton Thunder	23	4	2	6	18	2013 C-Cup	3	0	0	0	0
2013-14	CWHL	Brampton Thunder	19	3	1	4	2						
CWHL Regular Season			42	7	3	10	20	Clarkson Cup	3	0	0	0	0
Totals from all Competitions			**45**	**7**	**3**	**10**	**20**						

MOFFAT, TARYN   Forward. #23.
Born 1988-9-15, Maple Ridge, BC, CAN. Debut at age 18 on 2006-10-27.

Year - League - Team			GP	G	A	PTS	PM	Year - Playoff	GP	G	A	PTS	PM
2006-07	WWHL	British Columbia Breakers	24	2	1	3	10	2007 WWHL-P	2	0	0	0	0
2007-08	WWHL	British Columbia Breakers	24	2	1	3	29						
Totals from all Competitions			**50**	**4**	**2**	**6**	**39**						

MOIR, ALANA   *Forward. 2008-09 WWHL Edmonton Chimos #7.*

MOLITOR, INES   *Defence. 1993-94 COWHL Toronto Jr Aeros #8 (27 games, 4 assists).*

MOLOUGHNEY, ASHLEY
Forward. Shoots left. #21 #9.

Born 1984-3-6, Ottawa, ON, CAN. Grew up in Winchester, ON, CAN. 5'6". Debut at age 23 on 2006-9-16.

Year - League - Team			GP	G	A	PTS	PM	Year - Playoff	GP	G	A	PTS	PM
2006-07	NWHL	Ottawa Raiders	35	3	0	3	28	2007 NWHL-P	2	0	0	0	0
2007-08	CWHL	Ottawa Capital Canucks	2	0	0	0	2						
2008-09	CWHL	Ottawa Senators	2	0	0	0	0						

MONNEY, SANDRA
Forward. 1998 Nationals Tazmanian Devils (5 games).

MONTEITH, LIZ
Forward. 1996-97 COWHL North York #66 (1 game, two goals, 4 assists).

MONTGOMERY, FIELDING
Forward. Shoots left. #16.

Born 1991-02-21, Toronto, ON, CAN. 5'5". Debut at age 23 on 2014-10-19.

Year - League - Team			GP	G	A	PTS	PM	Year - Playoff	GP	G	A	PTS	PM
2014-15	CWHL	Brampton Thunder	17	3	0	3	4						
2015-16	CWHL	Brampton Thunder	23	3	3	6	8	2016 C-Cup	2	0	0	0	2
2016-17	CWHL	Brampton Thunder	24	0	1	1	2	2017 C-Cup	2	0	0	0	0
2017-18	CWHL	Markham Thunder	24	0	1	1	0						
CWHL Regular Season			88	6	5	11	14	Clarkson Cup	4	0	0	0	2
Totals from all Competitions			**92**	**6**	**5**	**11**	**16**						

MOORE, AMBER
Sunnyvale, CA. Defence. 2015-16 NWHL New York (13 game, 2 assists, I-Cup 1 game).

MOORE, GEORGIA
Forward. #12.

Year - League - Team			GP	G	A	PTS	PM	Year - Playoff	GP	G	A	PTS	PM
2008-09	WWHL	Strathmore Rockies	20	0	0	0	12	2009 WWHL-P	1	0	0	0	2
2009-10	WWHL	Strathmore Rockies	17	0	0	0	14						
2010-11	WWHL	Strathmore Rockies	3	0	0	0	0						

MOORE, HAYLEY
Forward. Shoots right. #9.

Grew up in Chelmsford, MA, USA. Debut on 2010-10-30.

Year - League - Team			GP	G	A	PTS	PM	Year - Playoff	GP	G	A	PTS	PM
2010-11	CWHL	Boston Blades	24	8	5	13	4	2011 CWHL-P	2	0	0	0	2
2015-16	NWHL/	Boston Pride	1	0	0	0	0						
Totals from all Competitions			**27**	**8**	**5**	**13**	**6**						

MORAND, AUDREY
Montréal, QC. F. 2015-16 CWHL Montréal #17 (4 games, 1 assist).

MORDEN, HEATHER
1999-00 NWHL Durham #4 (32 gp, 1 assist); 2000-01 Toronto #6 (8 gp, 1 g., 2 a.).

MORGAN, ANNETTE
Defence. 1995-96 COWHL Hamilton #7 (19 games); 1996-97 (33 games, 1 assist).

MORISSON, KATHY
Forward. 1995 Nationals Équipe Québec.

MORK, LISA
Forward. 1998 Nationals Tazmanian Devils (5 gp, 3 goals); 1999 Nationals (4 games).

MORRISETTE, AUDREY
2005-06 NWHL Québec #88 (2 games).

MORRISON, JODY
Defence. 1996 Nationals Pictou County (4 games).

MORSE, REBECCA
Defence. Shoots left. #9.

Born 1992-03-04, Westfield, NJ, USA. 5'8". Debut at age 24 on 2016-11-12.

Year - League - Team			GP	G	A	PTS	PM	Year - Playoff	GP	G	A	PTS	PM
2016-17	NWHL/	New York Riveters	7	0	1	1	2						
2017-18	NWHL/	Metropolitan Riveters	13	2	0	2	2						
2018-19	NWHL/	Minnesota Whitecaps	15	4	6	10	10	2019 I-Cup	2	0	0	0	0
NWHL Regular Season			31	3	1	4	12	Isobel Cup	2	0	0	0	0

MORTAN, NIKKI
Defence. 1998 Nationals Tazmanian Devils (5 games, 1 assist).

MORTON, KATELYN
Forward. 2005 Nationals Nova Scotia (5 gp, 1 goal, 1 assist); 2006 Nationals (4 gp)

MOSHER, TRACY
Forward. 2001 Nationals PEI Humpty Dumpty; 2002 Nationals (6 games).

MOSS, LYNSEY
2003-04 NWHL Brampton Thunder #24 (? games).

MOSS, SHERI
Defence. 1998 Nationals Tazmanian Devils (5 games).

MOSSOP, NICOLE
Forward. Shoots right.

Born 1979-05-28. Grew up in Saskatoon, SK, CAN. 5'0".

Year - League - Team			GP	G	A	PTS	PM
2001	Nationals	Saskatchewa					
2002	Nationals	Saskatchewan	6	0	0	0	4
2003	Nationals	Saskatchewan	3	0	0	0	0
2004	Nationals	Saskatchewan	6	2	1	3	2
2004-05	WWHL	Saskatchewan Prairie Ice	21	2	2	4	2

MOULD, JOANNA
Forward. 1998 Nationals Saskatchewan (6 gp, 2 pts); 1999 Nationals (4 gp, 3 pts).

MOULSON, SHANNON
Defence. Shoots left. #23.

Clarkson Cup winner with Toronto on 2014-03-22
Born 1986-4-15, Mississauga, ON, CAN. 5'9". Debut at age 22 on 2008-10-4.

Year - League - Team			GP	G	A	PTS	PM	Year - Playoff	GP	G	A	PTS	PM
2008-09	CWHL	Mississauga Chiefs	30		5	5	24	2009 CWHL-P	4	1		1	2
2009-10	CWHL	Mississauga Chiefs	30	6	15	21	36	2010 C-Cup	1	0	0	0	0
2010-11	CWHL	Burlington Barracudas	13	2	0	2	6						

Year - League - Team			GP	G	A	PTS	PM	Year - Playoff	GP	G	A	PTS	PM
2011-12	CWHL	Burlington Barracudas	27	3	6	9	42						
2012-13	CWHL	Toronto Furies	24	1	1	2	24	2013 C-Cup	3	0	1	1	8
2013-14	CWHL	Toronto Furies	23	2	5	7	22	2014 C-Cup	3	0	0	0	0
2014-15	CWHL	Toronto Furies	24	1	3	4	24	2015 C-Cup	2	0	0	0	0
2015-16	CWHL	Toronto Furies	24	0	7	7	28	2016 C-Cup	2	0	2	2	6
2016-17	CWHL	Toronto Furies	23	0	2	2	34	2017 C-Cup	3	0	0	0	0
2017-18	CWHL	Toronto Furies	28	2	5	7	24	2019 C-Cup	3	0	0	0	0
2018-19	CWHL	Toronto Furies	16	0	0	0	2						
CWHL Regular Season			262	17	49	66	266	Clarkson Cup	17	0	3	3	14
Totals from all Competitions			**283**	**18**	**52**	**70**	**282**						

CWHL Second All-Star Team in 2009-10... CWHL All-Rookie Team in 2008-09

MOWAT, KATHERINE   *Forward. 1996-97 COWHL Hamilton Golden Hawks #9 (33 gp, 6 goals, 7 assists).*

MOXLEY, CANDICE   *Forward. Shoots right. #15.*

Born 1982-10-4, Markham, ON, CAN. 5'7".

Year - League - Team			GP	G	A	PTS	PM	Year - Playoff	GP	G	A	PTS	PM
2000-01	NWHL	Toronto Sting	10	2	2	4	12						
2005-06	NWHL	Durham Lightning	35	8	15	23	38	2006 NWHL-P	2	0	0	0	2
2006-07	NWHL	Etobicoke Dolphins	30	14	15	29	38	2007 NWHL-P	3	0	1	1	8
2007	Nationals	Etobicoke Dolphins	7	1	0	1	4						
2007-08	CWHL	Vaughan Flames	27	12	9	21	50	2008 CWHL-P	2	0	1	1	4
Totals from all Competitions			**116**	**37**	**43**	**80**	**156**						

Finished 17th in Angela James Bowl scoring in 2007-08... has served as an assistant coach with CWHL Markham

---

MOYLAN, SARAH   *Ottawa, ON. Forward. 2006-07 NWHL Ottawa Raiders #7. (9 games, 1 goal, 3 assists).*

MRÁZOVÁ, KATEŘINA   *Forward. Shoots left. #16.*

Clarkson Cup winner with Boston on 2013-03-23
Born 1992-10-19, Prague, CZE. Debut at age 20 on 2012-10-21.

Year - League - Team			GP	G	A	PTS	PM	Year - Playoff	GP	G	A	PTS	PM
2012-13	CWHL	Boston Blades	21	1	1	2	4	2013 C-Cup	4	0	0	0	2
2018-19	NWHL/	Connecticut Whale	15	6	6	12	4	2019 C-Cup	1	1	1	2	0

NWHL Fans' Three Stars Award in 2018-19

MUCCI, MIA   *Forward. 2009-10 WWHL Edmonton #6 (16 games, 6 goals, 6 assists); 2010-11 (3 games).*

MUHARUMA, SAFIYA   *Toronto. D. 1996-97 COWHL Scarborough (1 gp); 2004-05 NWHL Oakville (34 gp, 2 a.).*

MUIR, EMILY   *1999-00 NWHL Durham Lightning #12 (1 game).*

MUIR, HANNAH   *Forward. 2006 Nationals Team New Brunswick (7 games).*

MULICK, JENNIFER   *Forward. Shoots right. #67.*

Born 1982-11-18, Aurora, ON, CAN. Grew up in Aurora, ON, CAN. 5'8".

Year - League - Team			GP	G	A	PTS	PM	Year - Playoff	GP	G	A	PTS	PM
1999-00	NWHL	Scarborough Sting	1	0	0	0	0						
2000-01	NWHL	Toronto Sting	9	3	2	5	2						
2005-06	NWHL	Durham Lightning	35	0	6	6	10	2006 NWHL-P	2	0	0	0	0
2006-07	NWHL	Etobicoke Dolphins	21	1	2	3	16	2007 NWHL-P	1	0	0	0	0
2007	Nationals	Etobicoke Dolphins	7	0	1	1	0						
2007-08	CWHL	Vaughan Flames	19	1	1	2	12	2008 CWHL-P	1	0	0	0	0
Totals from all Competitions			**96**	**5**	**12**	**17**	**40**						

MULLAN, LISA   *Forward. Shoots left. #20.*

Clarkson Cup winner with Toronto on 2014-03-22
Born 1989-07-14 in Brentwood Bay, BC, CAN. Grew up in Victoria, BC, CAN. 5'9". Debut at age 24 on 2013-11-16.

Year - League - Team			GP	G	A	PTS	PM	Year - Playoff	GP	G	A	PTS	PM
2013-14	CWHL	Toronto Furies	13	1	0	1	6	2014 C-Cup	1	0	0	0	0

MULVIHILL, LEAH   *Defence. 2000 Nationals Manitoba (5 gp); 2005 Nationals (5 gp); 2006 Nationals (5 gp; 1 a.).*

MUNHOFEN, JEN   *2006-07 NWHL Québec #16 (15 games, 1 goal, 6 assists).*

MUNNINGS, SANDY   *2008-09 WWHL Strathmore Rockies (4 games).*

MURANKO, CHERYL   *Forward. Shoots right. #8 #27 #16 #16.*

Abby Hoffman Cup winner with Aeros on 2000-03-12. Abby Hoffman Cup winner with Mississauga on 2008-03-15. NWHL Cup winner.
Born 1982-4-24. Grew up in Cambridge, ON, CAN.

Year - League - Team			GP	G	A	PTS	PM	Year - Playoff	GP	G	A	PTS	PM
1996-97	COWHL	North York Aeros	1	0	0	0	0						
1998-99	NWHL	North York Aeros	8	2	0	2	2						
1999-00	NWHL	North York Aeros	38	16	10	26	26	2000 NWHL-P					
2000	Nationals	North York Aeros			2	2							
2000-01	NWHL	North York Aeros	33	18	18	36	28						
2001	Nationals	North York Aeros											
2007-08	CWHL	Mississauga Chiefs	6	1	5	6	8	2008 CWHL-P	4	2	0	2	2
2008	Nationals	Mississauga Chiefs	3	0	0	0	4						
Totals from all Competitions			**99**	**39**	**35**	**74**	**70**						

MURAO, LINDSAY   Forward. 1999 Nationals New Westminster Lightning (5 games).

NAME   Forward. Shoots right. #37.

Grew up in Roseau, MN, USA. 5'5". Debut on 2019-02-08.

Year - League - Team	GP	G	A	PTS	PM
2018-19 NWHL/ Boston Pride	2	0	0	0	0

MURPHY, COLLEEN   Defence. Shoots right. #4.

Born 1993-10-08. Grew up in Cary, NC, USA. 5'4". Debut at age 24 on 2017-11-04.

Year - League - Team	GP	G	A	PTS	PM	Year - Playoff	GP	G	A	PTS	PM
2017-18 NWHL/ Buffalo Beauts	14	0	2	2	10	2018 I-Cup	2	0	1	1	2
2018-19 NWHL/ Connecticut Whale	9	0	1	1	12	2019 I-Cup	1	0	0	0	0

MURPHY, GRACE   Montclair, VA. Forward. 2015-16 CWHL Boston Blades (22 games, 1 assist).

MURPHY, SHANNON   2012-13 CWHL Alberta #16 (11 games).

MURRAY, EDEN   Forward. Shoots left. #11.

Born 1995-11-30. Grew up in Medicine Hat, AB, CAN. 5'3". Debut at age 22 on 2018-10-13.

Year - League - Team	GP	G	A	PTS	PM
2018-19 CWHL Calgary Inferno	17	1	3	4	6

MURRAY, KAREN   1992-93 COWHL Scarborough Sting #5 (2 games, 1 goal).

MURRAY, KELLY   Defence. Shoots left. #5.

Clarkson Cup winner with Calgary on 2019-03-24.
Born 1994-04-26. Grew up in Medicine Hat, AB, CAN. Debut at age 23 on 2017-10-21.

Year - League - Team	GP	G	A	PTS	PM	Year - Playoff	GP	G	A	PTS	PM
2017-18 CWHL Calgary Inferno	25	2	6	8	26	2018 C-Cup	3	0	0	0	0
2018-19 CWHL Calgary Inferno	27	0	2	2	12	2019 C-Cup	4	0	0	0	2

MUZERALL, TRACY   Defence. 1999-00 NWHL Mississauga (1 gp); 2000-01 (1 gp); 2001-02 #38 (30 gp, 4 assists).

MYERS, LISA   Forward. 2000 Nationals Prince Edward Island (5 games).

MYERS, MEGAN   Forward. Shoots right. #15.

Clarkson Cup winner with Boston on 2015-03-07
Born 1992-06-24. Grew up in Las Vegas, NV, USA. 5'6". Debut at age 22 on 2014-10-18.

Year - League - Team	GP	G	A	PTS	PM	Year - Playoff	GP	G	A	PTS	PM
2014-15 CWHL Boston Blades	12	0	2	2	0	2015 C-Cup	3	0	0	0	0
2015-16 CWHL Boston Blades	17	4	3	7	12						
2016-17 CWHL Boston Blades	14	0	2	2	10						
2017-18 CWHL Boston Blades	20	3	6	9	10						
2018-19 CWHL Worcester Blades	21	2	1	3	10						
CWHL Regular Season	84	9	14	23	42	Clarkson Cup	3	0	0	0	0

MYERS, SHANNON   1992-93 COWHL Guelph #40 (10 games); 1993-94 Toronto Jr. ssist).

NADEAU, GENEVIÈVE   Forward. Shoots right. #10 #22.

Born 1975-7-29, Plessisville, QC, CAN. Grew up in Plessisville, QC, CAN. 5'5".

Year - League - Team	GP	G	A	PTS	PM	Year - Playoff	GP	G	A	PTS	PM
1996 Nationals Équipe Québec	6	2	2	4	0						
1999-00 NWHL Sainte-Julie	32	12	6	18	38	2000 NWHL-P					
2000-01 NWHL Sainte-Julie	36	14	21	35	53						
2001-02 NWHL Cheyenne	28	15	8	23	26						
2002-03 NWHL Avalanche du Québec	36	17	12	29	46						
2003-04 NWHL Avalanche du Québec	33	15	9	24	46						
2004 Nationals Équipe Québec	7	3	4	7	6						
2004-05 NWHL Avalanche du Québec	35	10	9	19	52						
2005-06 NWHL Avalanche du Québec	22	1	2	3	28						
2007-08 CWHL Stars de Montréal	7	2	4	6	10	2008 CWHL-P	1	0	0	0	2
Totals from all Competitions	**243**	**91**	**77**	**168**	**307**						

NAGYMAROSI, DEE   Uxbridge, ON. Forward. 2008-09 CWHL Brampton #8 (12 gp, 1 goal, 2 assists).

NAKONECHNY, STACEY   F. 1995 Nationals Regina; 1996 Saskatchewan (5 games, 2 g.); 1999 Nationals (4 gp, 1 a.).

NANJI, SASHA   Defence. Shoots right. #25 #77 #24 #11.

Born 1992-1-8. Grew up in Markham, ON, CAN. 5'5". Debut at age 15 on 2007-10-7.

Year - League - Team	GP	G	A	PTS	PM
2007-08 CWHL Burlington Barracudas	2	0	0	0	0
2008-09 CWHL Burlington Barracudas	5	1	3	4	4
2013-14 CWHL Toronto Furies	3	0	0	0	6
2013-14 CWHL Brampton Thunder	11	4	4	8	2
CWHL Regular Season	21	5	7	12	12

NANTAIS, JENNIFER   Defence/Forward. #17.

Year - League - Team	GP	G	A	PTS	PM
1998-99 NWHL Scarborough Sting	38	5	3	8	22
1999-00 NWHL Scarborough Sting	39	2	2	4	4
Totals from all Competitions	**77**	**7**	**5**	**12**	**26**

NASH, KELLY Forward. Shoots right. #22.

Isobel Cup winner with Metropolitan on 2018-03-25
Born 1989-01-09. Grew up in Bonita, CA, USA. 5'6". Debut at age 28 on 2017-12-03.

Year - League - Team			GP	G	A	PTS	PM	Year - Playoff	GP	G	A	PTS	PM
2017-18	NWHL/	Metropolitan Riveters	8	2	3	5	2	2018 I-Cup	2	1	0	1	0
2018-19	NWHL/	Metropolitan Riveters	4	0	0	0	2						

NASLUND, WHITNEY Forward. Shoots right. #11.

Clarkson Cup winner with Boston on 2013-03-23
Born 1988-6-8. Grew up in Bloomington, MN, USA. 5'4". Debut at age 23 on 2011-10-22.

Year - League - Team			GP	G	A	PTS	PM						
2011-12	CWHL	Boston Blades	26	9	8	17	8	2012 C-Cup	3	1	1	2	2
2012-13	CWHL	Boston Blades	24	5	3	8	12	2013 C-Cup	4	0	1	1	0
2013-14	CWHL	Boston Blades	23	1	5	6	6	2014 C-Cup	4	0	0	0	2
	CWHL Regular Season		73	15	16	31	26	Clarkson Cup	11	1	2	3	4
	Totals from all Competitions		**84**	**16**	**18**	**34**	**30**						

Finished 20th in the Angela James Bowl scoring race in 2011-12

NEAL, ANDREA 2000-01 NWHL Toronto Sting (3 games, 1 goal).

NEAL, DANIELLE 1993-94 COWHL Hamilton #2 (17 games, 2 assists).

NEAL, DAPHNE Forward. 2007 Nationals BC Outback (5 games, 1 goal, 1 assist).

NEAL, JEN D. 1996-97 COWHL North York #87 (2 games, 2 assists); 1998-99 NWHL (7 games, 2 assists).

NELSON, DANIELLE Defence. 2008 Nationals Manitoba (5 games).

NELSON, NIKKI Forward. 2001-02 NWHL Durham #9 (1 game); 2007-08 CWHL Burlington #25 (1 game).

NERENBERG, PEARLE Forward. 2005-06 NWHL Québec #8 (3 games, 1 goal).

NEUWALD, BRYANNA Defence. 2009-10 CWHL Brampton Thunder #11 (1 game).

NEWHOOK, VICTORIA Forward. 2004 Nationals Newfoundland (5 gp, 1 assist); 2005 Nationals (5 gp).

NEWMAN, ANNE 2000-01 NWHL Toronto Sting (4 games); 2001-02 Mississauga (5 games, 1 goal).

NEWMAN, JESSICA Forward. #8 #17.

Born 1988-04-09.

Year - League - Team			GP	G	A	PTS	PM
2017-18	CWHL	Boston Blades	20	4	5	9	12
2002-03	NWHL	Vancouver Griffins	1	0	0	0	0
2004	Nationals	British Columbia	6	0	1	1	4
2005-06	WWHL	British Columbia Breakers	24	0	5	5	73

NEWTON, JEN Forward. 2009-10 Edmonton #11 (8 gp, 2 goals, 2 assists); 2010-11 (3 gp, 1 assist).

NEWTON, LYNN Defence. #19.

Abby Hoffman Cup winner with Aeros on 1991-03-17 and 1993-03-28.

Year - League - Team			GP	G	A	PTS	PM
1992-93	COWHL	Toronto Aeros	26	2	12	14	12
1992-93	COWHL	Toronto Aeros	28	4	13	17	6
2000-01	NWHL	Brampton Thunder	36	1	7	8	26
	Totals from all Competitions		**90**	**7**	**32**	**39**	**44**

NG, MICHELLE Centre. Shoots right. #5.

Born 1991-04-21. Grew up in Milton, MA, USA. 5'2". Debut at age 26 on 2017-10-14.

Year - League - Team			GP	G	A	PTS	PM
2017-18	CWHL	Boston Blades	20	4	5	9	12
2018-19	CWHL	KRS Vanke Rays	28	1	2	3	10

NICHOLS, ANDREA Forward. Shoots left. #15.

Clarkson Cup winner with Minnesota on 2010-03-28
Born 1984-9-28. Grew up in Monut Iron, MN, USA.

Year - League - Team			GP	G	A	PTS	PM	Year - Playoff	GP	G	A	PTS	PM
2007-08	WWHL	Minnesota Whitecaps	13	1	2	3	10						
2008	Nationals	Minnesota Whitecaps											
2008-09	WWHL	Minnesota Whitecaps	5	1	1	2	2	2009 WWHL-P	0	0	0	0	0
2009-10	WWHL	Minnesota Whitecaps	7	0	2	2	2	2010 C-Cup	2	0	0	0	0

NICHOLSON, CHERYL 1995-96 COWHL London #10 (26 gp, 2 goals); 1996-97 (29 gp, 3 goals, 8 assists).

NICHOLSON, ROBYN 2008 Nationals Nova Scotia Selects (5 games, 2 assists).

NICKEL, KRISTIN Left wing. Shoots left. #45.

Born 1982-9-11. Grew up in Solsgirth, MB, CAN. 5'7". Debut at age 23 on 2005-09-24.

Year - League - Team			GP	G	A	PTS	PM	Year - Playoff	GP	G	A	PTS	PM
2005-06	NWHL	Oakville Ice	36	9	19	28	10	2006 NWHL-P	2	0	0	0	0
2006-07	NWHL	Oakville Ice	30	3	5	8	10	2007 NWHL-P	3	0	0	0	0
	Totals from all Competitions		**71**	**12**	**24**	**36**	**20**						

NIXON, SAM Forward. #2.

Clarkson Cup winner with Minnesota on 2010-03-28

Year - League - Team			GP	G	A	PTS	PM	Year - Playoff	GP	G	A	PTS	PM
2009-10	WWHL	Minnesota Whitecaps	11	9	7	16	14	2010 C-Cup	2	0	0	0	0
2010-11	WWHL	Minnesota Whitecaps	12	8	12	20	8	2011 C-Cup	3	0	0	0	2

NOBLE, TASHA — *Forward. Shoots left. #7 #77.*

Born 1977-10-28, Lahr, GER. Grew up in Lower Sackville, NS, CAN. 5'7".

Year - League - Team			GP	G	A	PTS	PM	Year - Playoff	GP	G	A	PTS	PM
1998	Nationals	Nova Scotia Selects	5	1	2	3	0						
2000	Nationals	Nova Scotia Selects	6	2	1	3							
2001	Nationals	Nova Scotia Selects											
2002-03	NWHL	Axion de Montréal	32	8	7	15	20	2003 NWHL-PMontréal					
2003-04	NWHL	Oakville Ice	36	12	5	17	12						
2004-05	NWHL	Oakville Ice	36	4	6	10	4						
2005-06	NWHL	Oakville Ice	35	15	13	28	16	2006 NWHL-P	2	0	0	0	0
2006-07	NWHL	Oakville Ice	21	0	5	5	12						
Totals from all Competitions			**173**	**42**	**39**	**81**	**64**						

NOËL, MARIE — *2000-01 NWHL Mistral de Laval (1 game).*

NOELMANS, MERCEDES — *1998-99 NWHL Mistral de Laval #19 (6 games, 1 assist).*

NONIS, AMANDA — *Forward. Shoots right. #14 #55 #13.*

Born 1984-1-6. Grew up in Brampton, ON, CAN. 5'3". Debut at age 26 on 2009-10-4.

Year - League - Team			GP	G	A	PTS	PM	Year - Playoff	GP	G	A	PTS	PM
2009-10	CWHL	Brampton Thunder	29	5	6	11	30	2010 C-Cup	2	0		0	
2010-11	WWHL	Strathmore Rockies	10	0	2	2	8						
2011-12	CWHL	Burlington Barracudas	7	0	0	0	8						
2011-12	CWHL	Toronto Furies	3	0	0	0	0						
CWHL Regular Season			39	5	6	11	38	Clarkson Cup	2	0	0	0	0
Totals from all Competitions			**51**	**5**	**8**	**13**	**46**						

NORMORE, ALEX — *Forward. 2007 Nationals Nova Scotia Selects (7 games).*

NORMORE, ERIN — *Defence. 2010-11 CWHL Boston Blades #6 (9 gp, 1 a.; C-Cup 2 gp, 1 a.).*

NOSEWORTHY, ERINN — *Left wing. Shoots left. #22.*

Born 1993-03-30. Grew up in Appin, ON, USA. 5'5". Debut at age 24 on 2017-10-15.

Year - League - Team			GP	G	A	PTS	PM	Year - Playoff	GP	G	A	PTS	PM
2017-18	CWHL	Canadiennes de Montréal	17	2	2	4	0	2018 C-Cup	1	0	0	0	0

NOSKEY, ALANA — *Defence. 2009-10 WWHL Edmonton Chimos #5 (13 games, 3 goals, 5 assists).*

NOVELLI, KAYLA — *Defence. 2006 Nationals British Columbia (6 games, 1 goal).*

NOYES, MONTANNA — *F. 2006-07 WWHL Edmonton #17 (19 gp, 1 a.; 2 playoff gp); 2007-08 (24 gp, 3 goals, 2 a.).*

NUGENT, JILLIAN — *Defence. 2002 Nationals Nova Scotia Selects (5 games).*

NURSE, SARAH — *Forward. Shoots left. #16.*

Born 1995-01-04. Grew up in Hamilton, ON, CAN. 5'8". Debut at age 23 on 2018-10-13.

Year - League - Team			GP	G	A	PTS	PM	Year - Playoff	GP	G	A	PTS	PM
2018-19	CWHL	Toronto Furies	26	14	12	26	16	2019 C-Cup	3	1	0	1	0

CWHL All-Rookie Team 2018-19... finished 9th in the Angela James Bowl scoring race in 2018-19.

NYSTROM, KAREN — *Forward. Shoots right. #15 #89.*

IIHF champion. Abby Hoffman Cup winner with Aeros on 1991-03-17.

Born 1969-6-17. Grew up in Scarborough, ON, CAN. Forward. Shoots right.

Year - League - Team			GP	G	A	PTS	PM	Year - Playoff	GP	G	A	PTS	PM
1992-93	COWHL	Scarborough Firefighters	27	21	11	32	28						
1993-94	COWHL	Scarborough Firefighters	28	22	24	46	38						
1995	Nationals	Mississauga Chiefs											
1995-96	COWHL	Toronto Red Wings	29	23	20	43	42						
1996-97	COWHL	Newtonbrook Panthers	31	36	48	84	54						
1998-99	NWHL	Brampton Thunder	25	23	14	37	38						
1999-00	NWHL	Brampton Thunder	36	34	30	64	30						
2000-01	NWHL	Brampton Thunder	34	21	34	55	46						
2001-02	NWHL	Brampton Thunder	23	18	17	35	31						
2002	Nationals	Brampton Thunder	7	3	6	9	2						
2002-03	NWHL	Brampton Thunder						2003 NWHL-P					
2003-04	NWHL	Brampton Thunder											
Totals from all Competitions			**240**	**201**	**204**	**405**	**309**						

OATWAY, BOBBI JO — *Forward. 1996 Nationals PEI Esso Tigers (4 games).*

O'DOHERTY, COLLEEN — *2000-01 NWHL Toronto Sting (1 game).*

O'DOHERTY, SHARYN — *Forward. #13.*

Year - League - Team			GP	G	A	PTS	PM
1992-93	COWHL	Scarborough Firefighters	29	5	9	14	22
1999-00	NWHL	Mississauga Chiefs	1	1	1	2	0
2000-01	NWHL	Brampton Thunder	2	1	0	1	2
Totals from all Competitions			**32**	**7**	**10**	**17**	**24**

O'DONNELL, KELSEY — *Forward. 2008 Nationals Prince Edward Island (5 gp, 8 goals, 2 assists).*

ODELL, BELINDA — *Defence. Shoots left. #24 #2.*
Born 1985-10-11. Grew up in Priceville, ON, CAN. 5'7". Debut at age 22 on 2007-11-10.

Year - League - Team			GP	G	A	PTS	PM	Year - Playoff	GP	G	A	PTS	PM
2007-08	CWHL	Brampton Can.-Thunder	1	0	1	1	0						
2008-09	CWHL	Brampton Thunder	14	1	1	2	6	2009 C-Cup	2	0	0	0	0
2009-10	CWHL	Brampton Thunder	30	0	6	6	18	2010 C-Cup	2	0		0	
CWHL Regular Season			45	1	8	9	24	Clarkson Cup	4	0	0	0	0

O'GRADY, ERIN — *2006-07 WWHL Minnesota Whitecaps.*

O'GRADY, JESSICA — *Forward. Shoots left. #29.*
Born 1987-11-12. Grew up in Ottawa, ON, CAN. 5'6". Debut at age 20 on 2007-10-20.

Year - League - Team			GP	G	A	PTS	PM	Year - Playoff	GP	G	A	PTS	PM
2007-08	CWHL	Ottawa Capital Canucks	17	3	2	5	4	2008 CWHL-P	1	0	0	0	0
2013-14	CWHL	Calgary Inferno	16	0	1	1	2						
2017-18	CWHL	Toronto Furies	9	0	0	0	0						

O'HANLON, KELLY — *Forward. 2014-15 CWHL Brampton #27 (20 games, 1 assist).*

O'HARA, CAITLIN — *Defence. 2005-06 WWHL Calgary #8 (9 games, 1 assist); 2006 Nationals (1 game).*

O'HARA, KERRI LYNN — *Defence. 2002-03 NWHL Brampton #5 (? games); 2003 Nationals (5 games).*

O'KEEFE, CRYSTAL — *Defence. 2000 Nationals Newfoundland (5 gp); 2001 Nationals; 2005 Nationals (5 gp).*

O'KEEFE, PAIGE — *Defence. Shoots right. #24.*
Born 1983-06-08. Grew up in Souris, PE, CAN.

Year - League - Team			GP	G	A	PTS	PM	Year - Playoff	GP	G	A	PTS	PM
2000	Nationals	Prince Edward Island	5	0	0	0							
2001	Nationals	PEI Humpty Dumpty											
2002	Nationals	PEI Humpty Dumpty	6	0	0	0	4						
2003-04	NWHL	Axion de Montréal											

OLES, LESLIE — *Forward. Shoots left. #71.*
Born 1990-11-18, Beaconsfield, QC, CAN. 5'3". Debut at age 17 on 2007-9-15.

Year - League - Team			GP	G	A	PTS	PM	Year - Playoff	GP	G	A	PTS	PM
2007-08	CWHL	Stars de Montréal	20	16	16	32	28	2008 CWHL-P	2	1	3	4	4
2008-09	CWHL	Stars de Montréal	2	1	1	2							
2009-10	CWHL	Stars de Montréal	28	14	17	31	50	2010 C-Cup	1	0	0	0	0
2015-16	CWHL	Canadiennes de Montréal	22	3	4	7	22	2016 C-Cup	2	0	0	0	0
2016-17	CWHL	Canadiennes de Montréal	15	1	2	3	10						
CWHL Regular Season			87	35	40	75	110	Clarkson Cup	3	0	0	0	0
Totals from all Competitions			**92**	**36**	**43**	**79**	**114**						

CWHL Eastern All-Star Team in 2007-08... CWHL All-Rookie Team in 2007-08... finished 7th in the Angela James Bowl scoring race in 2007-08

OLIVIER, ERIKA — *2003-04 NWHL Québec (22 games, 2 goals, 3 assists).*

OLIVER, SARAH — *Defence. #28.*

Year - League - Team			GP	G	A	PTS	PM
2002-03	NWHL	Ottawa Raiders	31	1	9	10	64
2003-04	NWHL	Ottawa Raiders	21	4	8	12	4
Totals from all Competitions			**52**	**5**	**17**	**22**	**68**

OLSEN, CARRIE — *Defence. #10 #71.*

Year - League - Team			GP	G	A	PTS	PM	Year - Playoff	GP	G	A	PTS	PM
2008-09	WWHL	Calgary Oval X-Treme	22	5	12	17	32	2009 C-Cup	2	0	0	0	0
2009-10	WWHL	Strathmore Rockies	13	0	2	2	14						
2010-11	WWHL	Strathmore Rockies	11	0	4	4	28						
Totals from all Competitions			**50**	**5**	**18**	**23**	**74**						

OLSON, COLLEEN — *Forward. Shoots right. #24 #27.*
Born 1988-8-21. Grew up in Sherwood Park, AB, CAN. 5'10". Debut at age 23 on 2011-10-28.

Year - League - Team			GP	G	A	PTS	PM	Year - Playoff	GP	G	A	PTS	PM
2008-09	WWHL	Edmonton Chimos	11	0	2	2	18	2009 WWHL-P	1	0	0	0	0
2009-10	WWHL	Edmonton Chimos	1	0	0	0	0						
2010-11	WWHL	Edmonton Chimos	17	9	8	17	18						
2011-12	CWHL	Alberta	15	0	2	2	8						
Totals from all Competitions			**45**	**9**	**12**	**21**	**44**						

OLSON, ERICA — *Forward. Shoots left. #24.*
Born 1979-8-13, Minneapolis, MN, USA. 5'4".

Year - League - Team			GP	G	A	PTS	PM	Year - Playoff	GP	G	A	PTS	PM
2002-03	NWHL	Ottawa Raiders	34	16	8	24	24						
2003-04	NWHL	Ottawa Raiders	35	20	15	35	26	2004 NWHL-P	3	3	2	5	
2004-05	NWHL	Ottawa Raiders	35	20	19	39	36	2005 NWHL-P	2	1	0	1	
2005-06	NWHL	Ottawa Raiders	36	18	21	39	50	2006 NWHL-P	2	0	0	0	4
2006-07	WWHL	Minnesota Whitecaps	9	1	2	3	4	2007 WWHL-P	0	0	0	0	0
Totals from all Competitions			**156**	**79**	**67**	**146**	**144**						

OLSON, GLENDA *D/F. 1998-99 NWHL Mistral de Laval #49 (25 gp, 2 g., 2 a.); 2001 Nationals Vancouver.*

O'NEIL, JACKIE *2000-01 NWHL North York (1 gp); 2001-02 (1 gp); 2007-08 CWHL Vaughan (3 gp, 1 goal).*

O'NEIL, SHAUN *Forward. 1995 Nationals Metro Valley Selects.*

OPELA, CASSANDRA *Defence. Shoots right. #12.*
Born 1994-01-02. Grew up in Penfield, NY, USA. 5'8". Debut at age 22 on 2016-10-15.

Year - League - Team		GP	G	A	PTS	PM
2016-17	CWHL Boston Blades	10	0	0	0	0

ORCHARD, KATE *Defence. 2000 Nationals Britannia Blues (5 goals).*

ORLANDO, ELENA *Forward. Shoots left. #14.*
Born 1992-06-15. San Jose, CA, USA. 5'7". Debut at age 23 on 2015-10-11.

Year - League - Team		GP	G	A	PTS	PM	Year - Playoff		GP	G	A	PTS	PM
2015-16	NWHL/ New York Riveters	17	0	1	1	12	2016	I-Cup	2	0	0	0	4
2016-17	NWHL/ Connecticut Whale	12	0	0	0	4							
2017-18	NWHL/ Connecticut Whale	16	0	1	1	2	2018	I-Cup	1	0	0	0	0
2018-19	NWHL/ Connecticut Whale	16	0	1	1	4	2019	I-Cup	1	0	0	0	2
	NWHL Regular Season	61	0	3	3	22		Isobel Cup	4	0	0	0	6

NWHL Foundation Award in 2016-17

ORR, TRACEY *Defence. 2010-11 WWLH Manitoba Maple Leafs #15 (4 games).*

OSTERMANN, LISA *Defence. 1995 Nationals Winnipeg; 1996 Nationals (6 gp, 1 a.); 2001 Nationals.*

OSTRANDER, MEREDITH *Defence. Shoots left. #23.*
Abby Hoffman Cup winner with Brampton on 2006-03-12. CWHL winner. Born 1979-5-14, Prescott, ON, CAN. 6'0".

Year - League - Team		GP	G	A	PTS	PM	Year - Playoff		GP	G	A	PTS	PM
2002-03	NWHL Brampton Thunder						2003	NWHL-P					
2003	Nationals Brampton Thunder	5	2	3	5	4							
2003-04	NWHL Brampton Thunder	36	3	14	17	46							
2004-05	NWHL Brampton Thunder	34	11	8	19	56							
2005	Nationals Brampton Thunder	6	3	0	3	4							
2005-06	NWHL Brampton Thunder	32	6	15	21	54	2006	NWHL-P	5	0	1	1	4
2006	Nationals Brampton Thunder	6	0	1	1	8							
2006-07	NWHL Brampton Thunder	32	2	8	10	58	2007	NWHL-P	6	0	2	2	4
2007-08	CWHL Brampton Can.-Thunder	28	4	10	14	54	2008	CWHL-P	3	1	0	1	2
2008	Nationals Brampton Can.-Thunder	3	0	0	0	8							
2008-09	CWHL Brampton Thunder	27	8	10	18	56	2009	CWHL-P	2	1	0	1	6
							2009	C-Cup	2	0	0	0	4
2009-10	CWHL Brampton Thunder	8	1	1	2	8	2010	C-Cup	1	0		0	
	CWHL Regular Season	63	13	21	34	118		Clarkson Cup	4	0	0	0	4
	Totals from all Competitions	**236**	**42**	**73**	**115**	**376**							

O'TOOLE, ERIN *Defence. 2008-09 WWHL Strathmore Rockies (1 game).*

O'TOOLE, SARA *Forward. Shoots left.*
Born 1987-05-01. Grew up in Burton, MB, CAN.

Year - League - Team		GP	G	A	PTS	PM
2003	Nationals Team New Brunswick	4	1	4	5	0
2004	Nationals Team New Brunswick	5	1	0	1	0
2005	Nationals Team New Brunswick	6	3	6	9	0

OTT, JORDAN *Forward. Shoots left. #2.*
Born 1995-09-23. Grew up in Hilton, NY, USA. 5'9". Debut at age 22 on 2017-11-04.

Year - League - Team		GP	G	A	PTS	PM
2017-18	NWHL/ Buffalo Beauts	7	0	2	2	2

OUELLETTE, CAROLINE *Forward. Shoots left. #13.*
Olympic champion, IIHF champion.
Clarkson Cup winner with Montréal on 2009-03-21, 2011-03-27, 2012-03-25, 2017-03-05. NWHL winner.
Born 1979-5-25, Montréal, QC, CAN. 5'11". Debut at age 19 in 1998-99

Year - League - Team		GP	G	A	PTS	PM	Year - Playoff		GP	G	A	PTS	PM
1998	Nationals Équipe Québec	6	2	3	5	2							
1998-99	NWHL Bonaventure	27	32	28	60	6							
1999	Nationals Équipe Québec	6	8	4	12								
1999-00	NWHL Wingstar de Montréal	25	26	27	53	6							
2000	Nationals Équipe Québec	5	4	4	8								
2000-01	NWHL Wingstar de Montréal	31	22	37	59	28							
2001	Nationals Équipe Québec												
2001-02	NWHL Wingstar de Montréal	1	0	0	0	0							
2002	Nationals Équipe Québec	6	2	2	4	0							
2005-06	NWHL Axion de Montréal						2006	NWHL-P	2	0	3	3	0
2006-07	WWHL Minnesota Whitecaps	8	0	2	2	4	2007	WWHL-P	1	0	0	0	0
2007-08	WWHL Minnesota Whitecaps	9	7	9	16	0							
2008	Nationals Minnesota Whitecaps	1	1	3	4	0							

Year - League - Team			GP	G	A	PTS	PM	Year - Playoff	GP	G	A	PTS	PM
2008-09	CWHL	Stars de Montréal	24	26	33	59	6	2009 CWHL-P	2	2	4	6	0
								2009 C-Cup	3	3	4	7	4
2009-10	CWHL	Stars de Montréal	0	0	0	0	0	2010 C-Cup	1	1	0	1	0
2010-11	CWHL	Stars de Montréal	26	22	46	68	14	2011 CWHL-P	2	1	1	2	2
								2011 C-Cup	4	1	5	6	4
2011-12	CWHL	Stars de Montréal	27	30	36	66	12	2012 C-Cup	4	5	3	8	0
2012-13	CWHL	Stars de Montréal	23	12	13	25	14	2013 C-Cup	4	1	1	2	6
2013-14	CWHL	Stars de Montréal	2	2	0	2	4	2014 C-Cup	3	0	3	3	2
2014-15	CWHL	Stars de Montréal	22	8	18	26	18	2015 C-Cup	3	1	2	3	0
2015-16	CWHL	Canadiennes de Montréal	24	15	17	32	18	2016 C-Cup	3	4	6	10	0
2016-17	CWHL	Canadiennes de Montréal	22	15	16	31	21	2017 C-Cup	3	0	4	4	0
2017-18	CWHL	Canadiennes de Montréal	6	1	5	6	2	2018 C-Cup	2	0	0	0	0
CWHL Regular Season			**176**	**131**	**184**	**315**	**109**	Clarkson Cup	30	16	28	44	16
Totals from all Competitions			**338**	**254**	**339**	**593**	**173**						

CWHL Most Valuable Player in 2008-09 and 2010-11... Angela James Bowl in 2010-11... CWHL Top Forward in 2010-11... CWHL First All-Star Team in 2008-09, 2010-11, 2011-12, 2012-13, 2016-17 and CWHL Second All-Star Team in 2014-15... Clarkson Cup Championship MVP in 2012... scored 100th CWHL point on 2011-01-16... scored 200th CWHL point on 2013-01-05... Became CWHL's all-time leading scorer on 2015-02-07... scored 100th CWHL goal on 2015-02-22... selected First Decade CWHL Team in 2017... Women's National Championships Most Valuable Player in 2001... has served as head coach with CWHL Montréal.

OUELLETTE, STÉPHANIE
Forward. #22.

Year - League - Team			GP	G	A	PTS	PM
1995	Nationals	Équipe Québec					
1996	Nationals	Équipe Québec	6	1	2	3	0
1998	Nationals	Équipe Québec	6	1	4	5	0
1998-99	NWHL	Bonaventure	26	6	5	11	26
1999-00	NWHL	Wingstar de Montréal	33	6	7	13	66
2000	Nationals	Équipe Québec	6	3	0	3	
2000-01	NWHL	Wingstar de Montréal	39	4	12	16	48
2001-02	NWHL	Wingstar de Montréal	29	6	8	14	26
2002-03	NWHL	Axion de Montréal	4	0	1	1	4
Totals from all Competitions			**149**	**27**	**39**	**66**	**170**

OUIMET, VÉRONIQUE
Laval, QC. Defence. 2013-14 CWHL Montréal #4 (6 games).

OVERGUARD, KARLEE
Sundre, AB. Forward. 2011-12 CWHL Alberta #10 (8 gp, 4 goals, 3 a.); 2012-13 (1 gp).

PACHAL, PAMELA
Defence. Shoots right. #81.

Born 1981-6-1, Yorkton, SK, CAN. Grew up in Saltcoats, SK, CAN. 5'6".

Year - League - Team			GP	G	A	PTS	PM	Year - Playoff	GP	G	A	PTS	PM
1998	Nationals	Saskatchewan Selects	6	1	1	2	4						
1999	Nationals	Saskatchewan Selects	4	0	1	1							
2004-05	NWHL	Durham Lightning	10	2	3	5	4						
2005-06	NWHL	Durham Lightning	35	3	15	18	14	2006 NWHL-P	2	0	0	0	2
2006-07	NWHL	Oakville Ice	35	5	13	18	34	2007 NWHL-P	3	0	1	1	2
2007	Nationals	Etobicoke Dolphins	7	0	3	3	10						
Totals from all Competitions			**102**	**11**	**37**	**48**	**70**						

PACHOLOK, SAIGE
Defence. #6.

Born 1991-4-5. Debut at age 15 on 2006-10-21.

Year - League - Team			GP	G	A	PTS	PM	Year - Playoff	GP	G	A	PTS	PM
2006-07	WWHL	Edmonton Chimos	24	2	10	12	26	2007 WWHL-P	0	0	0	0	0
2007-08	WWHL	Edmonton Chimos	24	1	5	6	29						
2008-09	WWHL	Edmonton Chimos	21	4	6	10	48	2009 WWHL-P	1	0	0	0	0
Totals from all Competitions			**70**	**7**	**21**	**28**	**103**						

PACKER, MADISON
Forward. Shoots right. #14.

Isobel Cup winner with Metropolitan on 2018-03-25
Born 1991-06-25. Grew up in Detroit, MI, USA. 5'9". Debut at age 24 on 2015-10-11.

Year - League - Team			GP	G	A	PTS	PM	Year - Playoff	GP	G	A	PTS	PM
2015-16	NWHL/	New York Riveters	16	3	4	7	22	2016 I-Cup	2	1	0	1	4
2016-17	NWHL/	New York Riveters	17	8	5	13	22	2017 I-Cup	1	0	1	1	2
2017-18	NWHL/	Metropolitan Riveters	12	10	8	18	12	2018 I-Cup	2	1	2	3	4
2018-19	NWHL/	Metropolitan Riveters	15	8	5	13	35	2019 I-Cup	2	0	0	0	2
NWHL Regular Season			**60**	**29**	**22**	**51**	**91**	Isobel Cup	7	2	3	5	12

NWHL Fans' Three Stars Award in 2018-19

PADMORE, CLARE
Toronto, ON. Forward. 2008-09 CWHL Mississauga Chiefs #9 (1 game).

PAETSCH, JULIE
Forward. Shoots right. #10 #16.

Born 1984-02-22. Grew up in Lanigan, SK, CAN. 5'3".

Year - League - Team			GP	G	A	PTS	PM	Year - Playoff	GP	G	A	PTS	PM
2004-05	WWHL	Saskatchewan Prairie Ice	21	6	8	14	6						
2005-06	WWHL	Saskatchewan Prairie Ice	22	1	10	11	10	2006 WWHL-P	2	1	1	2	0

Year - League - Team	GP	G	A	PTS	PM	Year - Playoff	GP	G	A	PTS	PM
2013-14 CWHL Calgary Inferno	24	13	9	22	10	2014 C-Cup	3	2	2	4	2
Totals from all Competitions	**72**	**23**	**30**	**53**	**28**						

Finished 9th in the Angela James Bowl scoring race in 2013-14

PAGE, SIMONE
Defence. 1998 Nationals Nova Scotia Selects (5 games).

PAGNIELLO, CARLA
Forward. 1999-00 NWHL Brampton Thunder #88 (2 games, 1 assist).

PAIANO, ALLISON
Forward. Shoots left. #44 #24 #5 #2.

Born 1983-6-20, Montréal, QC, CAN. Grew up in Orléans, ON, CAN. 5'5".

Year - League - Team	GP	G	A	PTS	PM
1999-00 NWHL Ottawa Raiders	5	0	1	1	4
2000-01 NWHL Ottawa Raiders	1	0	0	0	2
2001-02 NWHL Ottawa Raiders	24	5	6	11	18
2008-09 CWHL Ottawa Senators	13	1	4	5	16
Totals from all Competitions	**43**	**6**	**11**	**17**	**40**

PALAZETI, TAYLOR
Forward. #4.

Born 1986-5-23. Grew up in Calgary, AB, CAN.

Year - League - Team	GP	G	A	PTS	PM	Year - Playoff	GP	G	A	PTS	PM
2007-08 WWHL Strathmore Rockies	23	4	5	9	6						
2008-09 WWHL Strathmore Rockies	20	6	5	11	10	2009 WWHL-P	1	0	0	0	0
Totals from all Competitions	**44**	**10**	**10**	**20**	**16**						

PALINSKI, TRACY
Forward. #15 #11.

Year - League - Team	GP	G	A	PTS	PM
1999-00 NWHL Mississauga Chiefs	38	9	14	23	8
2001-02 NWHL Mississauga IceBears	10	0	1	1	0
Totals from all Competitions	**48**	**9**	**15**	**24**	**8**

PALMA, MELISSA
Winnipeg, MB. Defence. 2010-11 WWHL Manitoba Maple Leafs #9 (7 games, 2 goals).

PALMER, KERRI
Defence. Shoots right. #8 #16 #27.

Born 1988-7-14. Grew up in Holland Landing, ON, CAN. 5'6". Debut at age 17 on 2005-10-04.

Year - League - Team	GP	G	A	PTS	PM	Year - Playoff	GP	G	A	PTS	PM
2005-06 NWHL Toronto Aeros	4	0	1	1	0						
2008-09 CWHL Mississauga Chiefs	17	3	2	5	16	2009 CWHL-P	4				
2009-10 CWHL Mississauga Chiefs	2	0	1	1	4						
2010-11 CWHL Brampton Thunder	25	1	2	3	14	2011 CWHL-P	2		2		
						2011 C-Cup	3	0	1	1	2
2011-12 CWHL Brampton Thunder	27	2	3	5	24	2012 C-Cup	4	0	0	0	6
2012-13 CWHL Brampton Thunder	1	0	0	0	0						
CWHL Regular Season	72	6	8	14	58	Clarkson Cup	7	0	1	1	8
Totals from all Competitions	**89**	**6**	**10**	**16**	**68**						

PANCHUCK, BRYANNE
Forward. 2008-09 WWHL Calgary Oval X-Treme #29 (4 games, 2 assists).

PAQUETTE, NICKI
Forward. 1996 Nationals Pictou County (4 games, 1 goal).

PAQUETTE, VALÉRIE
Forward. #27.

Born 1983-9-24. 5'3". Debut at age 24 on 2007-9-15.

Year - League - Team	GP	G	A	PTS	PM	Year - Playoff	GP	G	A	PTS	PM
2007-08 CWHL Stars de Montréal	10	4	3	7	12						
2008-09 CWHL Stars de Montréal	20	6	9	15	18	2009 CWHL-P	1	0	0	0	0

PARADIS, STÉPHANIE
Forward. #77 #9.

Born 1985-5-2. Debut at age 21 on 2006-10-7.

Year - League - Team	GP	G	A	PTS	PM	Year - Playoff	GP	G	A	PTS	PM
2006-07 NWHL Axion de Montréal	25	0	0	0	18	2007 NWHL-P Montréal					
2007-08 CWHL Stars de Montréal	14	1	1	2	4						

PARENT, STÉPHANIE
Forward. #17 #67.

Born 1974-01-07.

Year - League - Team	GP	G	A	PTS	PM
1995 Nationals Maritime Sports Blades					
1996 Nationals Maritime Sports Blades	6	0	1	1	0
1998 Nationals Maritime Sports Blades	6	1	3	4	0
1998-99 NWHL Montréal Jofa-Titan	3	0	2	2	2

PARENT, VANESSA
Forward.

Year - League - Team	GP	G	A	PTS	PM
2000-01 NWHL Mistral de Laval	37	6	17	23	22
2001-02 NWHL Cheyenne	25	0	4	4	12
2002-03 NWHL Avalanche du Québec	10	0	1	1	12
Totals from all Competitions	**72**	**6**	**22**	**28**	**46**

PARKER, ELIZABETH
Defence. Shoots left. #6.

Born 1991-07-29. Grew up in Milton, MA, USA. 5'9". Debut at age 26 on 2017-12-02.

Year - League - Team	GP	G	A	PTS	PM
2017-18 NWHL/ Boston Pride	4	0	0	0	0

PARKER, LORI   D. 1995 Nationals Britannia; 1996 Nationals (5 gp, 1 g.); 2002-03 NWHL Vancouver (2 gp).

PARKER, MARY   Forward. Shoots left. #7.
Born 1993-09-02. Grew up in Milton, MA, USA. 5'9". Debut at age 23 on 2017-03-12.

Year - League - Team	GP	G	A	PTS	PM	Year - Playoff	GP	G	A	PTS	PM
2016-17 NWHL/ Boston Pride	1	0	0	0	0	2017 I-Cup	2	0	0	0	0
2017-18 NWHL/ Boston Pride	15	1	2	3	6	2018 I-Cup	1	0	2	2	0
2018-19 NWHL/ Boston Pride	9	3	0	3	0	2019 I-Cup	1	0	0	0	0
NWHL Regular Season	25	4	2	6	6	Isobel Cup	4	0	2	2	0

PARKINS, AMANDA   Forward. #72 #24 #91.
Born 1986-2-20. Grew up in Cambridge, ON, CAN.

Year - League - Team	GP	G	A	PTS	PM	Year - Playoff	GP	G	A	PTS	PM
2004-05 NWHL Brampton Thunder	1	0	1	1	0						
2007-08 CWHL Burlington Barracudas	5	2	4	6	8						
2008-09 CWHL Burlington Barracudas	29	7	7	14	14	2009 CWHL-P	4				
2009-10 CWHL Burlington Barracudas	5	3	0	3	0						
2010-11 CWHL Burlington Barracudas	24	4	9	13	18						
2011-12 CWHL Burlington Barracudas	14	5	2	7	10						
CWHL Regular Season	77	21	22	43	50						
Totals from all Competitions	**82**	**21**	**23**	**44**	**50**						

CWHL All-Rookie Team in 2008-09

PARKMAN, STACY   Defence. 2007 Nationals Manitoba (5 games).
PARROTT, JANEIL   Forward. 2006 Nationals Newfoundland Labrador (5 games).

PARSONS, KAYLA   Defence. Shoots left. #22.
Born 1992-03-31. Grew up in Anchorage, AK, USA. 5'8". Debut at age 24 on 2016-11-13.

Year - League - Team	GP	G	A	PTS	PM
2016-17 NWHL/ Buffalo Beauts	10	0	0	0	0
2017-18 NWHL/ Buffalo Beauts	3	0	0	0	0

PARSONS, SHELLEY   Forward. 1995 Nationals Metro Valley Selects.

PARTINGTON, VICTORIA   F. 1995-96 COWHL Hamilton Golden Hawks #10 (15 games, 3 goals, 3 assists).
PASQUARIELLO, TORI   Forward. 2009-10 CWHL Brampton Thunder #13 (1 game).
PATENAUDE, AMANDA   Forward. 1995 Nationals Winnipeg; 1996 Nationals Winnipeg (6 games).
PATER, LISA   Forward. 1996-97 COWHL Scarborough #15 (32 gp, 17 goals, 11 a.); 1997-98 (4 games).
PATERSON, DINEEN   Defence. 1995 Nationals Regina Sharks; 1996 Nationals Saskatchewan (5 gp, 1 a.).
PATRY, EMILY   Forward. 2008-09 CWHL Vaughan #89 (28 games, 3 goals, 4 a.; 2 playoff gp, 1 goal).

PATTERSON, PAM   Forward. Shoots right. #28.
Born 1986-08-10. Grew up in Miramichi, NB, CAN.

Year - League - Team	GP	G	A	PTS	PM	Year - Playoff	GP	G	A	PTS	PM
2003 Nationals Team New Brunswick	4	1	0	1	2						
2004 Nationals Team New Brunswick	5	3	4	7	0						
2009-10 WWHL Strathmore Rockies	10	1	2	3	2						

PATTERSON, TRACY   Forward. 1996 Nationals Winnipeg Sweat Camp (6 games)).
PATTON, LEAH   1995-96 COWHL Hamilton #3 (29 gp, 1 goal, 3 a.); 1996-97 (34 gp, 3 goals, 2 a.).
PAUL, DONNA   Forward. 1998-99 NWHL Ottawa Raiders #18 (33 games, 1 goal, 4 a.).
PAUL, GILLIAN   Forward. 2004 Nationals Team New Brunswick (5 gp, 7 goals, 1 a.); 2007 Nationals (6 gp, 4 g.).
PAYNE, NATALIE   Defence. 2010-11 CWHL Burlington #28 (10 games, 1 goal).
PAYTON, ASHLEY   F. 2006-07 WWHL British Columbia #9 (20 gp, 15 goals, 9 assists; 2 playoff gp, 1 assist).
PEACOCK, JILL   Centre. 1992-93 COWHL Toronto Aeros #4 (2 games, 1 assist).

PEACOCK, TARYN   Forward. Shoots left. #15 #21.
Born 1988-3-13. Grew up in Calgary, AB, CAN. 5'4. Debut at age 24 on 2011-10-28.

Year - League - Team	GP	G	A	PTS	PM	Year - Playoff	GP	G	A	PTS	PM
2010-11 WWHL Strathmore Rockies	4	2	1	3	2						
2011-12 CWHL Alberta	15	2	6	8	22						
2013-14 CWHL Calgary Inferno	23	3	9	12	16	2014 C-Cup	3	1	4	5	2
2014-15 CWHL Calgary Inferno	21	0	4	4	12	2015 C-Cup	2	0	0	0	2
CWHL Regular Season	59	5	19	24	50	Clarkson Cup	5	1	4	5	4
Totals from all Competitions	**68**	**8**	**24**	**32**	**56**						

PEARSON, EMMA   Forward. Shoots left. #97.
Born 1994-03-06. Grew up in Richmond Hill, ON, CAN. 5'5". Debut at age 24 on 2019-02-09.

Year - League - Team	GP	G	A	PTS	PM	Year - Playoff	GP	G	A	PTS	PM
2018-19 CWHL Toronto Furies	3	0	0	0	0						

PEAVOY, BEVERLY   Forward. 2004-05 WWHL British Columbia (6 games, 1 goal); 2005 Nationals B.C. (7 games).

PELKEY, AMANDA   Forward. Shoots right. #16.
Olympic champion. Isobel Cup winner with Boston on 2016-03-12.
Born 1993-05-29. Grew up in Montpellier, VT, USA. 5'3". Debut at age 22 on 2015-10-11.

Year - League - Team	GP	G	A	PTS	PM	Year - Playoff	GP	G	A	PTS	PM
2015-16 NWHL/ Boston Pride	16	7	3	10	12	2016 I-Cup	4	1	3	4	2
2016-17 NWHL/ Boston Pride	17	2	5	7	10	2017 I-Cup	2	0	0	0	2
2018-19 NWHL/ Boston Pride	16	5	7	12	4	2019 I-Cup	1	0	0	0	4
NWHL Regular Season	49	14	15	29	26	Isobel Cup	7	1	3	4	8

PELLAND, GABRIELLE *Forward. 2005 Nationals Alberta (6 games).*

PELLATT, NATASHIA *Forward. Shoots left. #22 #20.*
Born 1985-8-4. Grew up in Burnaby, BC, CAN. Forward. Shoots left. 5'5".

Year - League - Team	GP	G	A	PTS	PM
2002-03 NWHL Vancouver Griffins	24	2	4	6	15
2003 Nationals Vancouver Griffins	7	0	0	0	4
2008-09 WWHL British Columbia Breakers	14	1	1	2	16
Totals from all Competitions	**45**	**3**	**5**	**8**	**35**

PELLERIN, NATHALIE *Forward. Shoots left.*
Born 1980-05-23. Grew up in Haute-Aboujagane, NB, CAN.

Year - League - Team	GP	G	A	PTS	PM
1996 Nationals Maritime Sports Blades	6	0	0	0	0
1998 Nationals Maritime Sports Blades	6	0	1	1	6
1999 Nationals Team New Brunswick	6	1	6	7	
2000 Nationals Team New Brunswick	6	0	3	3	
2001 Nationals Team New Brunswick					
2002 Nationals PEI Humpty Dumpty	6	1	2	3	2
2004 Nationals Team New Brunswick	5	2	7	9	2
2005 Nationals Team New Brunswick	6	4	3	7	24

PELLETIER, JULIE *Forward. #28.*

Year - League - Team	GP	G	A	PTS	PM		
1998-99 NWHL Mistral de Laval	33	15	15	30	26		
2000-01 NWHL Mistral de Laval	33	12	6	18	54	2000 NWHL-P
Totals from all Competitions	**66**	**27**	**21**	**48**	**80**		

PELLETIER, MARIE-CLAUDE *Defence. #41 #4.*

Year - League - Team	GP	G	A	PTS	PM
1998 Nationals Équipe Québec	6	0	2	2	4
1998-99 NWHL Montréal Jofa-Titan	5	0	0	0	0
1999-00 NWHL Sainte-Julie	34	2	7	9	20
2000-01 NWHL Sainte-Julie	37	0	10	10	42
Totals from all Competitions	**82**	**2**	**19**	**21**	**66**

PELLETIER, NICOLE *Forward. 1995 Nationals Équipe Québec.*

PENDLETON, ASHLEY *Defence. Shoots left. #18 #34 #43.*
Born 1984-6-1, Orton, ON, CAN. Grew up in Orton, ON, CAN. 5'9".

Year - League - Team	GP	G	A	PTS	PM	Year - Playoff	GP	G	A	PTS	PM
2000-01 NWHL Brampton Thunder	2	0	1	1	2						
2001-02 NWHL Brampton Thunder	29	1	5	6	44						
2002 Nationals Brampton Thunder	7	2	1	3	10						
2002-03 NWHL Brampton Thunder						2003 NWHL-P					
2003 Nationals Brampton Thunder	5	1	1	2	8						
2007-08 CWHL Vaughan Flames	30	7	9	16	74	2008 CWHL-P	2	0	0	0	2
2008-09 CWHL Brampton Thunder	30	5	14	19	58	2009 CWHL-P	2				
						2009 C-Cup	1	0	0	0	2
2009-10 CWHL Brampton Thunder	25	2	3	5	30	2010 C-Cup	2	0		0	
2010-11 CWHL Brampton Thunder	16	3	5	8	24	2011 CWHL-P	2		6		
						2011 C-Cup	3	0	2	2	2
2011-12 CWHL Brampton Thunder	8	0	0	0	4						
2013-14 CWHL Brampton Thunder	22	1	9	10	32						
CWHL Regular Season	131	18	40	58	222	Clarkson Cup	6	0	2	2	4
Totals from all Competitions	**186**	**22**	**50**	**72**	**298**						

CWHL Second All-Star Team in 2008-09

PENNEL, JESSICA *Defence. 2006-07 WWHL Saskatchewan #23 (4 games).*

PEPELS, MARION *Forward. 1996-97 COWHL London Devilettes #17 (31 games, 3 goals, 11 assists).*

PEPPER, KAREN *Forward. #14.*
Abby Hoffman Cup winner with Aeros on 1993-03-28.

Year - League - Team	GP	G	A	PTS	PM
1992-93 COWHL Toronto Aeros	27	3	15	18	12
1992-93 COWHL Toronto Aeros	26	7	21	28	22
1995 Nationals Mississauga Chiefs					
1995-96 COWHL Mississauga Chiefs	30	9	15	24	36
1996-97 COWHL Mississauga Chiefs	33	16	25	41	50
1997-98 COWHL Mississauga Chiefs	19	6	5	11	18
1998-99 NWHL Mississauga Chiefs	32	8	14	22	71

Year - League - Team			GP	G	A	PTS	PM	Year - Playoff		GP	G	A	PTS	PM
1999-00	NWHL	Mississauga Chiefs	39	12	21	33	48							
2000-01	NWHL	Mississauga IceBears	7	0	1	1	6							
Totals from all Competitions			**213**	**61**	**117**	**178**	**263**							

PERKINS, SUE
1993-94 COWHL Hamilton Golden Hawks #90 (6 games, 4 goals, 2 assists).

PERKS, LARA
Forward. Shoots right. #19 #13.

Abby Hoffman Cup winner with Aeros on 2000-03-12 and 2004-03-14. Abby Hoffman Cup winner with Mississauga on 2008-03-15. NWHL Cup winner. Born 1981-9-8, Trenton, ON, CAN. 5'8".

Year - League - Team			GP	G	A	PTS	PM	Year - Playoff		GP	G	A	PTS	PM
1995-96	COWHL	North York Aeros	1	0	0	0	0							
1996-97	COWHL	North York Aeros	2	2	1	3	0							
1997-98	COWHL	North York Aeros	20	5	15	20	18							
1998	Nationals	North York Aeros	6	2	3	5	2							
1998-99	NWHL	North York Aeros	35	16	19	35	16	1999	NWHL-P					
1999	Nationals	North York Aeros	5	1	3	4								
1999-00	NWHL	North York Aeros	37	13	27	40	4	2000	NWHL-P					
2000	Nationals	North York Aeros	6	1	7	8								
2000-01	NWHL	North York Aeros	27	18	16	34	20							
2001	Nationals	North York Aeros												
2001-02	NWHL	North York Aeros	24	6	21	27	12	2003	NWHL-P					
2002	Nationals	North York Aeros	7	3	5	8	6							
2003-04	NWHL	Toronto Aeros	33	18	29	47	8	2004	NWHL-P					
2004	Nationals	Toronto Aeros	6	2	3	5	6							
2004-05	NWHL	Toronto Aeros	13	3	10	13	4	2005	NWHL-P					
2005-06	NWHL	Toronto Aeros	0	0	0	0	0							
2006-07	NWHL	Mississauga Aeros	33	8	19	27	44	2007	NWHL-P	5	3	0	3	2
2007	Nationals	Mississauga Aeros	6	3	7	10	10							
2007-08	CWHL	Mississauga Chiefs	10	5	3	8	6	2008	CWHL-P	1	0	0	0	0
2008	Nationals	Mississauga Chiefs	1	0	0	0	0							
2008-09	CWHL	Mississauga Chiefs	27	20	23	43	30	2009	CWHL-P	4	2	2	4	2
2010-11	CWHL	Burlington Barracudas	4	0	0	0	0							
CWHL Regular Season			41	25	26	51	36							
Totals from all Competitions			**313**	**131**	**213**	**344**	**190**							

CWHL Second All-Star Team in 2008-09... finished 6th in the Angela James Bowl scoring race in 2008-09

PEROFF, JORDANNA
Forward. Shoots left. #20.

Clarkson Cup winner with Toronto on 2014-03-22 and Montréal on 2017-03-05
Born 1989-7-4. Grew up in Keswick, ON, CAN. 5'6". Debut at age 23 on 2012-10-20.

Year - League - Team			GP	G	A	PTS	PM	Year - Playoff		GP	G	A	PTS	PM
2012-13	CWHL	Toronto Furies	20	0	0	0	2	2013	C-Cup	3	0	0	0	2
2013-14	CWHL	Toronto Furies	22	1	2	3	4	2014	C-Cup	4	0	0	0	0
2015-16	CWHL	Canadiennes de Montréal	22	3	6	9	4	2016	C-Cup	3	0	0	0	0
2016-17	CWHL	Canadiennes de Montréal	24	2	0	2	2	2017	C-Cup	3	0	0	0	2
2017-18	CWHL	Canadiennes de Montréal	22	2	2	4	10							
CWHL Regular Season			110	8	10	18	22	**Clarkson Cup**		13	0	0	0	4
Totals from all Competitions			**123**	**8**	**10**	**18**	**26**							

PERREAULT, MARIE-CHRISTINE
Centre. Shoots left. #13.

Born 1979-09-29. Grew up in Montréal, QC, CAN. 5'5".

Year - League - Team			GP	G	A	PTS	PM	Year - Playoff		GP	G	A	PTS	PM
1998-99	NWHL	Bonaventure	33	9	12	21	2							
1999	Nationals	Équipe Québec	5	0	2	2								
1999-00	NWHL	Wingstar de Montréal	32	10	10	20	35							
2000	Nationals	Équipe Québec	6	0	1	1								
2000-01	NWHL	Wingstar de Montréal	25	10	8	18	6							
2001	Nationals	Équipe Québec												
2001-02	NWHL	Wingstar de Montréal	23	4	3	7	12							
2002-03	NWHL	Axion de Montréal	27	6	5	11	14	2003	NWHL-P					
2003-04	NWHL	Axion de Montréal	30	4	19	23	12							
2004-05	NWHL	Axion de Montréal	22	3	6	9	6							
2005	Nationals	Axion de Montréal	6	0	0	0	0							
Totals from all Competitions			**209**	**46**	**66**	**112**	**87**							

PERRON, MELISSA
1998-99 NWHL Mistral de Laval #9 (27 games, 2 goals, 3 assists).

PETERSON, DANETTE
1996-97 COWHL Newtonbrook Panthers #21 (1 game, 1 assist).

PETRI, SHERRI
Forward. 1995 Nationals Britannia Blues.

PETTERSEN, JENNY
Forward.

Year - League - Team			GP	G	A	PTS	PM
1992-93	COWHL	Guelph Eagles	29	2	14	16	22
1993-94	COWHL	Mississauga Chiefs	29	5	13	18	31
1995	Nationals	Mississauga Chiefs					
1995-96	COWHL	Mississauga Chiefs	30	11	14	25	28

			GP	G	A	PTS	PM
1996-97	COWHL	Mississauga Chiefs	33	9	20	29	24
1997-98	COWHL	Mississauga Chiefs	18	2	5	7	25
1998-99	NWHL	Mississauga Chiefs	32	5	11	16	33
1999-00	NWHL	Mississauga Chiefs	32	6	10	16	20
2000-01	NWHL	Mississauga IceBears	35	1	4	5	34
Totals from all Competitions			**238**	**41**	**91**	**132**	**217**

PEZON, MEAGHAN
Forward/Defence. Shoots right. #8 #15.

Isobel Cup winner with Minnesota on 2019-03-17. Born 1988-02-07. Grew up in Eden Prairie, MN, USA. 5'6".

Year - League - Team			GP	G	A	PTS	PM	Year - Playoff	GP	G	A	PTS	PM
2010-11	WWHL	Minnesota Whitecaps	18	10	14	24	6	2011 I-Cup	3	0	0	0	0
2018-19	NWHL/	Minnesota Whitecaps	9	1	1	2	4	2019 I-Cup	1	0	0	0	0

PEW, KELSEY
Forward. 2007 Nationals BC Outback (4 games, 1 assist).

PHELAN, GENNA
Forward. 2005 Nationals Prince Edward Island (5 gp, 5 pts); 2006 (5 gp, 3 pts); 2007 (5 gp, 1 a.).

PFALZER, EMILY
Defence. Shoots right. #7.

Olympic champion, IIHF champion. Isobel Cup winner with Buffalo on 2017-03-19

Born 1993-06-14, Getville, NY, USA. 5'2". Debut at age 22 on 2015-10-11.

Year - League - Team			GP	G	A	PTS	PM	Year - Playoff	GP	G	A	PTS	PM
2015-16	NWHL/	Buffalo Beauts	17	2	10	12	6	2016 I-Cup	5	1	4	5	2
2016-17	NWHL/	Buffalo Beauts	15	1	6	7	6	2017 I-Cup	2	0	0	0	6
2018-19	NWHL/	Buffalo Beauts	16	2	4	6	19	2019 I-Cup	2	2	1	3	0
NWHL Regular Season			48	5	20	25	31	Isobel Cup	9	3	5	8	8

PHARAND, MARIE-ÈVE
Forward. #27 #59 #16.

Born 1986-4-6.

Year - League - Team			GP	G	A	PTS	PM
2004-05	NWHL	Avalanche du Québec	3	0	0	0	0
2005-06	NWHL	Avalanche du Québec	2	0	0	0	0
2007-08	CWHL	Phénix du Québec	28	7	14	21	18
Totals from all Competitions			**33**	**7**	**14**	**21**	**18**

Finished 20th in the Angela James Bowl scoring race in 2007-08

PHILLION, MARLIES
Defence. 2007-08 CWHL Ottawa Capital Canucks #20 (1 game).

PICARD, MICHELLE
Defence. Shoots left. #27.

Isobel Cup winner with Metropolitan on 2018-03-25

Born 1993-05-27. Grew up in Fall River, MA, USA. 5'4". Debut at age 23 on 2016-10-08.

Year - League - Team			GP	G	A	PTS	PM	Year - Playoff	GP	G	A	PTS	PM
2016-17	NWHL/	New York Riveters	18	2	6	8	4	2017 I-Cup	1	0	0	0	0
2017-18	NWHL/	Metropolitan Riveters	16	0	4	4	12	2018 I-Cup	2	0	0	0	2
2018-19	NWHL/	Metropolitan Riveters	16	0	2	2	8	2019 I-Cup	2	0	0	0	0
NWHL Regular Season			50	2	12	14	24	Isobel Cup	5	0	0	0	2

NWHL Foundation Award in 2016-17 and 2017-18

PICKETT, CASEY
Left wing. Shoots left. #16.

Clarkson Cup winner with Boston on 2015-03-07

Born 1986-12-13. Grew up Wilmington, MA, USA. Forward. Shoots left. 5'4". Debut at age 26 on 2013-11-02.

Year - League - Team			GP	G	A	PTS	PM	Year - Playoff	GP	G	A	PTS	PM
2013-14	CWHL	Boston Blades	22	9	6	15	10	2014 C-Cup	4	0	0	0	0
2014-15	CWHL	Boston Blades	21	6	2	8	6	2015 C-Cup	3	1	1	2	0
2015-16	NWHL/	Boston Pride	7	0	0	0	2						
2016-17	CWHL	Boston Blades	3	1	1	2	2						
CWHL Regular Season			46	16	9	25	18	Clarkson Cup	7	1	1	2	0
Totals from all Competitions			**60**	**17**	**10**	**27**	**20**						

Finished 16th in the Angela James Bowl scoring race in 2013-14

PICKFORD, TAMARA
Forward. Shoots left. #27.

Abby Hoffman Cup winner with Edmonton on 1997-03-09.

Born 1975-1-31, Moose Jaw, SK, CAN. Grew up in Chilliwack, BC, CAN. 5'7".

Year - League - Team			GP	G	A	PTS	PM
1995	Nationals	Calgary Classics					
1996	Nationals	Edmonton Chimos	7	4	2	6	2
1997	Nationals	Edmonton Chimos					
1998	Nationals	Edmonton Chimos	7	1	3	4	0
1999	Nationals	New Westminster Lightning	5	0	1	1	
2001	Nationals	Vancouver Griffins					
2002-03	NWHL	Vancouver Griffins	24	2	12	14	26
2003	Nationals	Vancouver Griffins	7	1	4	5	4
2003-04	NWHL	Ottawa Raiders	34	0	4	4	32
2004-05	WWHL	British Columbia Breakers	20	1	6	7	16
2005	Nationals	British Columbia	7	0	1	1	12
2005-06	WWHL	British Columbia Breakers	23	4	6	10	34
2007	Nationals	British Columbia	5	2	5	7	10
Totals from all Competitions			**139**	**15**	**44**	**59**	**136**

PIEPER, ERIN   Forward. Shoots left. #27.
Abby Hoffman Cup winner with Edmonton on 1997-03-09.   Born 1976-03-23.

Year - League - Team		GP	G	A	PTS	PM
1996	Nationals Edmonton Chimos	7	0	2	2	0
1997	Nationals Edmonton Chimos					
1998	Nationals Edmonton Chimos	7	0	0	0	2

PIERRI, JACQUIE   Defence. Shoots right. #11.
Clarkson Cup winner with Calgary on 2016-03-14
Born 1994-06-10. Grew up in Montclair, NJ, USA. 5'4". Debut at age 19 on 2013-11-09.

Year - League - Team		GP	G	A	PTS	PM	Year - Playoff		GP	G	A	PTS	PM
2013-14	CWHL Calgary Inferno	24	0	2	2	44	2014	C-Cup	3	0	1	1	4
2014-15	CWHL Calgary Inferno	24	0	5	5	22	2015	C-Cup	2	0	0	0	2
2015-16	CWHL Calgary Inferno	24	0	0	0	18	2016	C-Cup	3	0	2	2	4
2016-17	CWHL Calgary Inferno	23	0	3	3	48	2017	C-Cup	3	0	0	0	0
2017-18	CWHL Calgary Inferno	28	4	7	11	26	2018	C-Cup	3	0	0	0	12
	CWHL Regular Season	123	4	17	21	158		Clarkson Cup	14	0	3	3	22
	Totals from all Competitions	**137**	**4**	**20**	**24**	**180**							

PIETRANGELO, LOUISE   Defence. 1999-00 NWHL Mississauga #17 (31 games, 2 goals, 5 assists).

PIPER, CHERIE   Forward. Shoots right. #18 #97 #14 #9 #7.
*Olympic champion, IIHF champion. Abby Hoffman Cup winner with Aeros on 2000-03-12. Abby Hoffman Cup win-
ner with Mississauga on 2008-03-15. NWHL Cup winner.*
Born 1981-6-29, East York (Toronto). Grew up in Scarborough, ON, CAN. 5'6". Debut at age 16 in 1997-98.

Year - League - Team		GP	G	A	PTS	PM	Year - Playoff		GP	G	A	PTS	PM
1997-98	COWHL North York Aeros	2	0	0	0	2							
1998-99	NWHL North York Aeros	9	4	3	7	13							
1999-00	NWHL North York Aeros	35	26	19	45	49	2000	NWHL-P					
2000	Nationals North York Aeros	6	6	2	8								
2000-01	NWHL North York Aeros	29	22	22	44	40							
2001	Nationals North York Aeros												
2002	Nationals North York Aeros	7	3	4	7	8							
2007-08	CWHL Mississauga Chiefs	17	9	14	23	10	2008	CWHL-P	5	4	4	8	6
2008	Nationals Mississauga Chiefs	3	5	0	5	8							
2008-09	WWHL Calgary Oval X-Treme	21	15	22	37	18	2009	WWHL-P	2	1	2	3	2
							2009	C-Cup	2	0	2	2	2
2010-11	CWHL Brampton Thunder	13	13	12	25	6	2011	CWHL-P	2		2	2	
							2011	C-Cup	3	3	3	6	6
2011-12	CWHL Brampton Thunder	25	12	21	33	10	2012	C-Cup	4	1	1	2	4
2012-13	CWHL Brampton Thunder	22	9	4	13	14	2013	C-Cup	3	0	0	0	6
	CWHL Regular Season	77	43	51	94	40		Clarkson Cup	12	4	6	10	18
	Totals from all Competitions	**210**	**133**	**137**	**270**	**204**							

Finished 8th in the Angela James Bowl scoring race in 2011-12

PIPER, HEATHER   Defence. 1996 Nationals Saskatchewan (5 games).

PIRIE, MELISSA   Forward. 1997-98 COWHL North York #17 (1 game); 1998-99 #88 (6 gp, 3 goals, 2 assists).

PITRE, KAREN   RW. 1992-93 COWHL Scarborough #15 (7 games, 1 goal, 1 assist); 1993-94 (2 games).

PITRE, SHERRI   Forward. Shoots right. #10.
Born 1973-11-23. Grew up in North Vancouver, BC, CAN.

Year - League - Team		GP	G	A	PTS	PM
1996	Nationals Edmonton Chimos	7	0	2	2	0
1996	Nationals Britannia Blues	5	2	2	4	0
1998	Nationals New Westminster Lightning	5	2	1	3	2
2001	Nationals Vancouver Griffins					
2005-06	WWHL British Columbia	17	4	1	5	10

PITUSHKA, JACLYN   2000-01 NWHL Toronto Sting #7 (3 games).

PLATT, JESSICA   Forward. Shoots left. #11.
Born 1989-05-08. Grew up in Sarnia, ON, USA. 5'9". Debut at age 27 on 2016-10-29.

Year - League - Team		GP	G	A	PTS	PM
2016-17	CWHL Toronto Furies	4	0	0	0	0
2017-18	CWHL Toronto Furies	27	2	0	2	14
2018-19	CWHL Toronto Furies	18	0	1	1	0

PLOURDE, MARIE-HÉLÈNE   Forward. 2006 Nationals Team New Brunswick (7 gp, 5 pts); 2007 Nationals.

PODLOSKI, TARIN   Forward. Shoots right. #21 #11 #71.
Born 1986-8-28. Grew up in Wetaskiwin, AB, CAN. 5'5".

Year - League - Team		GP	G	A	PTS	PM	Year - Playoff		GP	G	A	PTS	PM
2002-03	NWHL Edmonton Chimos	24	1	4	5	14							
2003-04	NWHL Edmonton Chimos	11	2	1	3	20	2004	NWHL-P					
2004	Nationals Edmonton Chimos	7	1	1	2	2							
2007-08	CWHL Mississauga Chiefs	7	7	1	8	0							
	Totals from all Competitions	**49**	**11**	**7**	**18**	**36**							

PODOLSKY, AMY — *Forward. 1996 Nationals Winnipeg (6 gp, 1 goal); 2000 Nationals (5 gp, 1 assist).*

PODOVINNKOFF, SHEENA — *Forward. 2000 Nationals Saskatchewan (7 gp, 3 goals, 9 assists).*

POIRIER, KAREN — *Defence. 1999-00 NWHL Durham #2 (4 games), 2000-01 (29 games, 1 goal, 4 assists).*

POIRIER, MARIE-MICHÈLE — *Forward. #41 #5 #8.*
Born 1987-4-6, Gaspé, QC, CAN. Debut at age 18 on 2005-11-05.

Year - League - Team		GP	G	A	PTS	PM	Year - Playoff	GP	G	A	PTS	PM
2005-06	NWHL Avalanche du Québec	2	0	0	0	4						
2006-07	NWHL Avalanche du Québec	7	4	1	5	2	2007 NWHL-P					
2007-08	CWHL Phénix du Québec	5	2	3	5	6						

POIRIER, SARAH — *Pickering. D. 2001-02 NWHL Durham #58 (2 gp); 2008-09 CWHL Vaughan #3 (14 gp, 1 goal).*

POLCI, BREE — *London, ON. Forward. 2010-11 CWHL Brampton #2 (19 games, 4 goals, 3 assists).*

POLLETT, JENNIFER — *Forward. Shoots right. #86.*
Born 1986-3-7, St. John's, NL, CAN. Grew up in New Harbour, NL, CAN. 5'4". Debut at age 19 on 2005-09-24.

Year - League - Team		GP	G	A	PTS	PM	Year - Playoff	GP	G	A	PTS	PM
2002	Nationals Newfoundland Labrador	5	0	0	0	0						
2004	Nationals Newfoundland Labrador	5	7	5	12	0						
2005	Nationals Newfoundland Labrador	5	3	3	6	2						
2005-06	NWHL Durham Lightning	35	7	9	16	6	2006 NWHL-P	2	0	0	0	2
2006-07	NWHL Etobicoke Dolphins	31	10	11	21	40	2007 NWHL-P	3	1	0	1	4
2007	Nationals Etobicoke Dolphins	7	3	1	4	4						
Totals from all Competitions		**93**	**31**	**29**	**60**	**58**						

POORT, LINDA — *LW. 1995-96 COWHL London Devilettes #17 (14 games, 3 assists).*

POROCHNAVY, GALE — *Forward. 1995 Nationals Calgary Classics.*

POSCENTE, MIA — *Forward. #26 #11 #24.*

Year - League - Team		GP	G	A	PTS	PM
1996-97	COWHL Newtonbrook Panthers	2	0	2	2	4
1999-00	NWHL Mississauga Chiefs	1	0	1	1	0
2000-01	NWHL Brampton Thunder	2	0	1	1	0
2001-02	NWHL Brampton Thunder	4	2	2	4	0

POTTER (NÉE SCHMIDGALL), JENNY — *Forward. Shoots left. #16 #20.*
Olympic champion, IIHF champion. Clarkson Cup winner with Minnesota on 2010-03-28
Born 1979-1-12, Edina, MN, USA. 5'4". Debut at age 27 on 2006-11-17.

Year - League - Team		GP	G	A	PTS	PM	Year - Playoff	GP	G	A	PTS	PM
2006-07	WWHL Minnesota Whitecaps	1	0	0	0	0	2007 WWHL-P	3	1	1	2	4
2007-08	WWHL Minnesota Whitecaps	20	8	26	34	14						
2008	Nationals Minnesota Whitecaps	3	3	5	8	2						
2008-09	WWHL Minnesota Whitecaps	16	16	19	35	16	2009 WWHL-P	2	0	2	2	0
							2009 C-Cup	3	0	2	2	0
2009-10	WWHL Minnesota Whitecaps	0	0	0	0	0	2010 C-Cup	2	2	0	2	6
2010-11	WWHL Minnesota Whitecaps	12	8	13	21	6	2011 C-Cup	3	1	1	2	0
2014-15	CWHL Boston Blades	6	1	3	4	4						
Totals from all Competitions		**71**	**40**	**72**	**112**	**52**						

Clarkson Cup Championship MVP in 2009

POTVIN, MELANIE — *Forward. 1999-00 NWHL Mistral de Laval #49 (3 games).*

POUDRIER, CASSANDRA — *Defence. Shoots left. #51.*
Clarkson Cup winner with Montréal on 2017-03-05
Born 1992-12-05. Grew up in Mont-Laurier, QC, CAN. 5'5". Debut at age 23 on 2016-10-15.

Year - League - Team		GP	G	A	PTS	PM	Year - Playoff	GP	G	A	PTS	PM
2007-08	CWHL Phénix du Québec											
2016-17	CWHL Canadiennes de Montréal	24	3	8	11	10	2017 C-Cup	3	0	1	1	0
2017-18	CWHL Canadiennes de Montréal	18	1	11	12	12						

POULIN, ANNE — *Forward. #8 #6 #9.*

Year - League - Team		GP	G	A	PTS	PM
2000-01	NWHL Mistral de Laval	7	1	1	2	6
2001-02	NWHL Wingstar de Montréal	27	4	9	13	28
2002-03	NWHL Avalanche du Québec	33	8	3	11	16
2003-04	NWHL Avalanche du Québec	1	0	0	0	0
Totals from all Competitions		**68**	**13**	**13**	**26**	**50**

POULIN, JULIE — *Defence. 2003 Nationals Équipe Québec (5 games, 1 goal, 2 assists).*

POULIN, MARIE-PHILIP — *Forward. Shoots left. #29.*
Olympic champion. Clarkson Cup winner with Montréal on 2009-03-21 and 2017-03-05
Born 1991-3-28, Beauceville, QC, CAN. 5'6". Debut at age 16 on 2007-9-23.

Year - League - Team		GP	G	A	PTS	PM	Year - Playoff	GP	G	A	PTS	PM
2007-08	CWHL Stars de Montréal	16	22	21	43	16	2008 CWHL-P	2	2	1	3	4
2008-09	CWHL Stars de Montréal	6	4	4	8	8	2009 C-Cup	3	2	3	5	2
2009-10	CWHL Stars de Montréal	0	0	0	0	0	2010 C-Cup	1	0	0	0	0

Year - League - Team			GP	G	A	PTS	PM	Year - Playoff	GP	G	A	PTS	PM
2015-16	CWHL	Canadiennes de Montréal	22	23	23	46	10	2016 C-Cup	3	4	4	8	2
2016-17	CWHL	Canadiennes de Montréal	23	15	22	37	6	2017 C-Cup	3	4	2	6	0
2018-19	CWHL	Canadiennes de Montréal	26	23	27	50	12	2019 C-Cup	1	0	0	0	0
CWHL Regular Season			93	87	97	184	52	Clarkson Cup	11	10	9	19	4
Totals from all Competitions			**107**	**99**	**107**	**206**	**60**						

CWHL Most Valuable Player in 2015-16, 2016-17 and 2018-19... CWHLPA Jayna Hefford Trophy in 2015-16, 2016-17, 2018-19... Angela James Bowl winner in 2015-16, 2016-17, 2018-19... CWHL Top Forward in 2015-16 and 2016-17... CWHL First All-Star Team in 2015-16, 2016-17, 2018-19; CWHL Eastern All-Star Team in 2007-08... CWHL Outstanding Rookie in 2007-08... CWHL All-Rookie Team in 2007-08... scored 100th CWHL point on 2016-10-16... selected First Decade CWHL Team in 2017.

POULIOT, ERIKA
Left wing. Shoots left. #22.

NWHL winner. Born 1985-7-3. Grew up in Montréal, QC, CAN. 5'8". Debut at age 20 on 2005-09-17.

Year - League - Team			GP	G	A	PTS	PM	Year - Playoff	GP	G	A	PTS	PM
2005-06	NWHL	Axion de Montréal	36	4	8	12	42	2006 NWHL-P	3	1	0	1	6
2006	Nationals	Axion de Montréal	6	1	1	2	6						
2006-07	NWHL	Axion de Montréal	20	3	3	6	28	2007 NWHL-P					
Totals from all Competitions			**65**	**9**	**12**	**21**	**82**						

POUNDER, CHERYL
Defence. Shoots right. #11.

Olympic champion, IIHF champion. Abby Hoffman Cup winner with Aeros on 1993-03-28, 2000-03-12, 2004-03-14 and 2005-03-13. Abby Hoffman Cup winner with Mississauga on 2008-03-15. NWHL Cup winner. Born 1976-6-21, Montréal, QC, CAN. Grew up in Mississauga, ON, CAN. 5'6".

Year - League - Team			GP	G	A	PTS	PM	Year - Playoff	GP	G	A	PTS	PM
1992-93	COWHL	Toronto Aeros	24	4	8	12	6						
1993-94	COWHL	Toronto Junior Aeros	29	9	12	21	20						
1995-96	COWHL	North York Aeros	26	1	20	21	4						
1996	Nationals	North York Aeros	5	2	2	4	6						
1996-97	COWHL	North York Aeros	32	8	24	32	16						
1997-98	COWHL	North York Aeros	16	1	17	18	8						
1998	Nationals	North York Aeros	6	1	3	4	2						
1998-99	NWHL	North York Aeros	25	0	15	15	4						
1999	Nationals	North York Aeros	5	2		2							
1999-00	NWHL	North York Aeros	31	1	15	16	32	2000 NWHL-P					
2000	Nationals	North York Aeros	6	1	4	5							
2000-01	NWHL	North York Aeros	30	6	21	27	14						
2001	Nationals	North York Aeros											
2002	Nationals	North York Aeros	7	3	3	6	2						
2002-03	NWHL	North York Aeros	34	3	17	20	40	2003 NWHL-P	1	0	0	0	0
2003-04	NWHL	Toronto Aeros	36	4	33	37	30	2004 NWHL-P	2	0	1	1	0
2004	Nationals	Toronto Aeros	6	0	2	2	4						
2004-05	NWHL	Toronto Aeros	33	8	8	16	14	2005 NWHL-P					
2005	Nationals	Toronto Aeros	7	1	7	8	2						
2005-06	NWHL	Toronto Aeros	0	0	0	0	0						
2006-07	NWHL	Mississauga Aeros	29	2	7	9	18	2007 NWHL-P	4	0	0	0	0
2007	Nationals	Mississauga Aeros	6	1	8	9	4						
2007-08	CWHL	Mississauga Chiefs	0	0	0	0	0	2008 CWHL-P	2	0	0	0	0
2008	Nationals	Mississauga Chiefs	3	0	1	1	4						
2008-09	CWHL	Mississauga Chiefs	25	3	15	18	16	2009 CWHL-P	4	1	5	6	0
CWHL Regular Season			25	3	15	18	16						
Totals from all Competitions			**434**	**62**	**248**	**310**	**246**						

CWHL First All-Star Team in 2008-09... Women's National Championships Most Valuable Player in 2005.

POW, BOBBI
Forward. 1995 Nationals Regina Sharks.

POWELL, LYNNCY
Forward.

Born 1958-01-05.

Year - League - Team			GP	G	A	PTS	PM
1995	Nationals	Britannia Blues					
1996	Nationals	Britannia Blues	5	0	1	1	6
2000	Nationals	Britannia Blues	5	1	1	2	

POWERS, ASHLEY
Ottawa, ON. D. 2009-10 CWHL Ottawa Senators #9 (24 games, 1 goal, 2 assists).

POWERS, CHRISTIN
Forward. Shoots right. #11 #10.

Born 1983-2-24, Potsdam, NY, United States. Grew up in Canton, NY, USA. 5'2". Debut at age 22 on 2005-09-17.

Year - League - Team			GP	G	A	PTS	PM	Year - Playoff	GP	G	A	PTS	PM
2005-06	NWHL	Ottawa Raiders	36	17	6	23	56	2006 NWHL-P	2	0	0	0	0
2006-07	NWHL	Ottawa Raiders	36	12	14	26	84	2007 NWHL-P	2	0	2	2	8
2007-08	CWHL	Ottawa Capital Canucks	24	5	5	10	26	2008 CWHL-P	1	0	0	0	0
2008-09	CWHL	Ottawa Senators	21	11	6	17	32	2009 CWHL-P	2		2		
2009-10	CWHL	Ottawa Senators	26	12	14	26	46						
CWHL Regular Season			71	28	25	53	104						
Totals from all Competitions			**150**	**57**	**47**	**104**	**254**						

Finished 15th in the Angela James Bowl scoring race in 2009-10

POWER, HEATHER — *1999 Nationals Prince Edward Island (5 games).*

POWER, JENNIFER — *Forward. Shoots left.*
Born 1979-02-13. Grew up in Montague, PE, CAN. 5'9".

Year - League - Team			GP	G	A	PTS	PM
1999	Nationals	Prince Edward Island	5				
2000	Nationals	Prince Edward Island	5				
2001	Nationals	PEI Humpty Dumpty					
2008	Nationals	Prince Edward Island	5	1	3	4	2

POWERS, ROSEMARY — *LW. 1993-94 COWHL Scarborough Sting #11 (18 games, 5 goals, 5 assists).*

POYTON, SAMANTHA — *Hamilton, ON. Forward. 2010-11 CWHL Toronto Furies #3 (9 games).*

PRALL, BARB — *Defence. 2002-03 NWHL Mississauga Ice Bears #9 (? games).*

PRATT, DIANE — *Forward. Shoots left.*

Year - League - Team			GP	G	A	PTS	PM			GP	G	A	PTS	PM
2003-04	WWHL	Edmonton Chimos	10	0	0	0	24	2004	WWHL-P					
2004	Nationals	Edmonton Chimos	7	1	2	3	2							
2004-05	WWHL	Edmonton Chimos	21	0	1	1	54	2005	WWHL-P	3	0	0	0	2

PREFONTAINE, MARIE — *1998-99 NWHL Mistral de Laval #67 (1 game).*

PRESLEY, ROBYN — *Defence. 2006-07 WWHL Saskatchewan Prairie Ice #5 (22 games).*

PRETTY, DANA — *Defence. Shoots left.*
Abby Hoffman Cup winner with Calgary on 2001-03-11.
Born 1982-01-15. 5'6".

Year - League - Team			GP	G	A	PTS	PM
1998	Nationals	New Westminster Lightning	5	0	1	1	0
1999	Nationals	New Westminster Lightning	5	0	5	5	
2000	Nationals	Calgary Oval X-Treme	7	0	3	3	
2001	Nationals	Calgary Oval X-Treme					
2002	Nationals	Calgary Oval X-Treme	6	1	0	1	4

PRÉVOST, CAROLYNE — *Forward. Shoots left. #27.*
Clarkson Cup winner with Toronto on 2014-03-22
Born 1990-1-6, Sarnia, ON, CAN. 5'4". Debut at age 23 on 2012-10-20.

Year - League - Team			GP	G	A	PTS	PM	Year - Playoff	GP	G	A	PTS	PM
2012-13	CWHL	Stars de Montréal	21	5	10	15	4	2013 C-Cup	4	1	0	1	0
2013-14	CWHL	Toronto Furies	23	11	12	23	6	2014 C-Cup	4	0	2	2	12
2014-15	CWHL	Toronto Furies	24	9	7	16	0	2015 C-Cup	2	0	1	1	0
2015-16	CWHL	Toronto Furies	24	7	7	14	4	2016 C-Cup	2	0	0	0	0
2016-17	CWHL	Toronto Furies	24	5	2	7	4	2017 C-Cup	3	0	0	0	4
2017-18	CWHL	Toronto Furies	28	10	12	22	10						
2018-19	CWHL	Toronto Furies	21	6	6	12	2	2019 C-Cup	3	1	2	3	0
CWHL Regular Season			165	53	56	109	30	Clarkson Cup	18	2	5	7	16
Totals from all Competitions			**183**	**55**	**61**	**116**	**46**						

CWHL Second All-Star Team in 2013-14... finished 7th in the Angela James Bowl scoring race in 2013-14

PRÉVOST, MELINDA — *Montréal, QC. F. 2015-16 CWHL Montréal (2 games).*

PRICE, LAURA — *Defence. 2007 Nationals Nova Scotia Selects (7 games).*

PRIVÉE, BRITTANY — *Forward. #7.*
Clarkson Cup winner with Montréal on 2009-03-21
Born 1982-3-8. 5'9". Debut at age 26 on 2007-9-15.

Year - League - Team			GP	G	A	PTS	PM	Year - Playoff	GP	G	A	PTS	PM
2007-08	CWHL	Stars de Montréal	25	3	6	9	28	2008 CWHL-P	2	0	0	0	0
2008-09	CWHL	Stars de Montréal	19	3	4	7	16	2009 CWHL-P	2	0	0	0	0
								2009 C-Cup	3	0	0	0	2
2009-10	CWHL	Stars de Montréal	3	0	0	0	6						
CWHL Regular Season			47	6	10	16	50	Clarkson Cup	3	0	0	0	2
Totals from all Competitions			**54**	**6**	**10**	**16**	**52**						

PROCYSHYN, CARLY — *Defence. Shoots left. #19.*
Abby Hoffman Cup winner with Calgary on 1998-03-22.
Born 1979-03-31. Grew up in Aberdeen, SK, CAN.

Year - League - Team			GP	G	A	PTS	PM
1996	Nationals	Saskatchewan Selects	5	0	1	1	2
1998	Nationals	Calgary Oval X-Treme	7	0	4	4	2
1999	Nationals	Calgary Oval X-Treme ·	6	0	0	0	0
2002	Nationals	Calgary Oval X-Treme	6	1	2	3	2
2002-03	NWHL	Calgary Oval X-Treme	2	0	0	0	0

PROSDOCIMO, ATHENA — *2000-01 NWHL Brampton Thunder #26 (3 games, 1 assist).*

PROULX, CAROLINE — *Forward. Shoots right. #5.*
Born 1976-8-8, Boisbriand, QC, CAN. Grew up in Montréal, QC, CAN. 5'4".

Year - League - Team			GP	G	A	PTS	PM	Year - Playoff	GP	G	A	PTS	PM
1999	Nationals	Équipe Québec	5	3	0	3							
2000-01	NWHL	Sainte-Julie	35	15	21	36	22						
2001	Nationals	Équipe Québec											
2001-02	NWHL	Cheyenne	27	8	8	16	14						
2002	Nationals	Équipe Québec	6	0	0	0	0						
2002-03	NWHL	Avalanche du Québec	34	12	16	28	30						
2003	Nationals	Équipe Québec	5	0	2	2	0						
2003-04	NWHL	Avalanche du Québec	35	6	9	15	36						
2004	Nationals	Équipe Québec	7	0	1	1	6						
2004-05	NWHL	Avalanche du Québec	36	14	8	22	14						
2005-06	NWHL	Avalanche du Québec	22	2	5	7	16						
2007-08	CWHL	Stars de Montréal	5	1	2	3	8	2008 CWHL-P	1	0	0	0	0
Totals from all Competitions			**218**	**61**	**72**	**133**	**146**						

PROULX-DUPERRÉ, LAURIE   *Lévis, QC. D. 2013-14 CWHL Montréal #28 (23 games, 1 assist, C-Cup 3 games).*

PROVOST, MARIÈVE   *Forward. Shoots left. #77 #97 #88 #44 #55.*
Born 1985-4-15, Laval, QC, CAN. Grew up in Laval, QC, CAN. 5'5".

Year - League - Team			GP	G	A	PTS	PM	Year - Playoff	GP	G	A	PTS	PM
2003-04	NWHL	Axion de Montréal	1	0	0	0	0						
2004	Nationals	Équipe Québec	5	0	0	0	6						
2004-05	NWHL	Axion de Montréal	0	0	0	0	0						
2005-06	NWHL	Avalanche du Québec	2	0	0	0	4						
2007	Nationals	Team New Brunswick											
2012-13	CWHL	Stars de Montréal	20	4	0	4	4	2013 C-Cup	4	0	1	1	2
2013-14	CWHL	Stars de Montréal	22	8	11	19	12	2014 C-Cup	3	0	0	0	2
2014-15	CWHL	Stars de Montréal	17	2	3	5	12	2015 C-Cup	3	1	2	3	0
CWHL Regular Season			59	14	14	28	28	Clarkson Cup	10	1	3	4	4
Totals from all Competitions			**77**	**15**	**17**	**32**	**42**						
Finished 10th in the Angela James Bowl scoring race in 2013-14

PRUDEN, BARBIE   *Defence. Shoots left.*
Born 1981-01-27. Grew up in Winnipeg, MB, CAN.

Year - League - Team			GP	G	A	PTS	PM
2000	Nationals	University of Manitoba	5	0	1	1	
2002	Nationals	University of Manitoba	5	0	0	0	0
2003	Nationals	University of Winnipeg	4	0	0	0	0
2004	Nationals	Manitoba	5	1	0	1	4

PRUD'HOMME, MARYLENE   *RW. 2003-04 NWHL Québec (13 gp, 5 goals, 2 a.); 2004-05 (36 gp, 3 goals, 3 a.).*

PUCHNIAK, CAITLIN   *Defence. 2006 Nationals Manitoba (5 games, 1 goal, 1 assist).*

PUDSEY, MELANIE   *Forward. Shoots left. #89 #16 #22.*
Born 1982-7-6. Grew up in Erin, ON, CAN. 5'8".

Year - League - Team			GP	G	A	PTS	PM
1999-00	NWHL	Scarborough Sting	7	3	1	4	2
2000-01	NWHL	North York Aeros	6	0	1	1	2
2005-06	NWHL	Toronto Aeros	35	6	15	21	20
Totals from all Competitions			**48**	**9**	**17**	**26**	**24**

PURCELL, CHELSEA   *Forward. Shoots right. #18.*
Born 1987-5-24. Grew up in Hudson Bay, SK, CAN. 5'6". Debut at age 24 on 2011-10-28.

Year - League - Team			GP	G	A	PTS	PM	Year - Playoff	GP	G	A	PTS	PM
2010-11	WWHL	Edmonton Chimos	17	9	11	20	6						
2011-12	CWHL	Alberta	15	6	2	8	16						
2012-13	CWHL	Alberta	23	0	5	5	22						
2013-14	CWHL	Calgary Inferno	24	4	6	10	12	2014 C-Cup	3	0	0	0	2
CWHL Regular Season			62	10	13	23	50	Clarkson Cup	3	0	0	0	2
Totals from all Competitions			**82**	**19**	**24**	**43**	**58**						
Has served as a general manager with CWHL Markham

PURYEAR, SARA   *Sugarland, TX, USA. LW. 2004-05 NWHL Durham #26 (35 games); 2005-06 #24 (23 games).*

PYKE, ERIKA   *Halifax, NS. Forward. 2009-10 CWHL Mississauga Chiefs #11 (1 game).*

QI XUETING   *Harbin, CHN. Defence. 2007-08 WWHL Strathmore Rockies #55 (20 games, 1 goal, 3 assists).*

QUENNEVILLE, LIANE   *Montréal, QC. 2007-08 CWHL Ottawa #4 (24 gp, 6 a.; 1 playoff gp); 2009-10 (22 gp, 3 a.).*

QUINLAN, CATHIE   *Defence. 2000 Nationals Newfoundland Labrador (5 games).*

QUINN, ERIN   *Defence. 2005-06 NWHL Brampton Thunder #5 (3 games, 2 assists).*

QUINN, KATIE   *Defence/Forward. #88 #7 #16.*

Year - League - Team			GP	G	A	PTS	PM
1995-96	COWHL	Peterborough Skyway	6	2	3	5	6
1997-98	COWHL	Scarborough Sting	12	0	0	0	2
1999-00	NWHL	Durham Lightning	33	8	3	11	50

Year - League - Team		GP	G	A	PTS	PM	Year - Playoff	GP	G	A	PTS	PM
2000-01	NWHL Durham Lightning	19	2	8	10	46						
2001-02	NWHL Durham Lightning	29	2	3	5	34						
2002-03	NWHL Durham Lightning											
Totals from all Competitions		**99**	**14**	**17**	**31**	**138**						

QUINN, MEGAN
Forward. Shoots right. #21.

Born 1994-09-11. Grew up in Belleville, ON, CAN. 5'9". Debut at age 24 on 2018-10-13.

Year - League - Team		GP	G	A	PTS	PM	Year - Playoff	GP	G	A	PTS	PM
2018-19	CWHL Toronto Furies	28	1	3	4	8	2019 C-Cup	3	0	0	0	4

RAFTER, TATIANA
Forward. Shoots right. #7.

Isobel Cup winner with Metropolitan on 2018-03-25

Born 1992-02-27. Grew up in Winnipeg, MB, CAN. 5'10". Debut at age 23 on 2015-10-11.

Year - League - Team		GP	G	A	PTS	PM	Year - Playoff	GP	G	A	PTS	PM
2015-16	NWHL/ Buffalo Beauts	17	2	1	3	12	2016 I-Cup	4	0	0	0	0
2016-17	NWHL/ New York Riveters	18	6	1	7	0	2017 I-Cup	1	1	0	1	0
2017-18	NWHL/ Metropolitan Riveters	16	4	2	6	6	2018 I-Cup	2	0	0	0	0
NWHL Regular Season		51	12	4	16	18	Isobel Cup	7	1	0	1	0

RAIMONDI MOAD, JENNIFER
Forward. Shoots right. #12.

Abby Hoffman Cup winner with Mississauga on 2008-03-15.

Born 1985-4-12. Grew up in Langley, BC, CAN. 5'9". Debut at age 21 on 2006-9-16.

Year - League - Team		GP	G	A	PTS	PM	Year - Playoff	GP	G	A	PTS	PM
2006-07	NWHL Mississauga Aeros	35	18	11	29	16	2007 NWHL-P	4	1	0	1	2
2007	Nationals Mississauga Aeros	6	2	8	10	0						
2007-08	CWHL Mississauga Chiefs	28	4	18	22	20	2008 CWHL-P	5	0	4	4	2
2008	Nationals Mississauga Chiefs	3	1	0	1	0						
CWHL Regular Season		28	4	18	22	20						
Totals from all Competitions		**81**	**26**	**41**	**67**	**40**						

Finished 16th in the Angela James Bowl scoring race in 2007-08

RAJAHUHTA, ANNINA
Forward. Shoots left. #9.

Born 1989-3-8, Helsinki, FIN. 5'5". Debut at age 23 on 2011-10-28.

Year - League - Team		GP	G	A	PTS	PM	Year - Playoff	GP	G	A	PTS	PM
2011-12	CWHL Burlington Barracudas	8	3	1	4	2						
2017-18	CWHL Kunlun Red Star	10	3	6	9	10						

RALPH, BRITTNY
Defence. Shoots left. #14.

Born 1978-3-14. Grew up in Brooklyn Center, MN, USA.

Year - League - Team		GP	G	A	PTS	PM	Year - Playoff	GP	G	A	PTS	PM
2004-05	WWHL Minnesota Whitecaps	12	2	2	4	10	2005 WWHL-P	2	0	0	0	0
2007-08	WWHL Minnesota Whitecaps	17	1	3	4	6						
2008	Nationals Minnesota Whitecaps	3	0	0	0	0						
Totals from all Competitions		**34**	**3**	**5**	**8**	**16**						

RAMBO, EMMA
Joliet, IL, USA. Defence. 2013-14 CWHL Boston Blades #17 (22 games, 2 goals, 1 assist).

RAMOLLA, ALICIA
2001-02 NWHL Durham Lightning #3 (3 games).

RAMSAY, MARGARET
Forwad. Shoots left.

Born 1983-01-22. Grew up in Scarborough, ON, CAN.

Year - League - Team		GP	G	A	PTS	PM
2000-01	NWHL North York Aeros	7	0	0	0	6
2001-02	NWHL North York Aeros	25	7	13	20	20
2002	Nationals North York Aeros	5	1	0	1	2

RAMSAY, STEPHANIE
Defence. Shoots right. #23.

WWHL winner. Born 1990-4-19, Charlottetown, PE, CAN.

Year - League - Team		GP	G	A	PTS	PM	Year - Playoff	GP	G	A	PTS	PM
2005-06	WWHL Calgary Oval X-Treme	24	5	14	19	48	2006 WWHL-P	3	1	1	2	2
2006	Nationals Calgary Oval X-Treme	7	0	1	1	6						
2006-07	WWHL Calgary Oval X-Treme	16	1	7	8	32	2007 WWHL-P	0	0	0	0	0
2007-08	WWHL Calgary Oval X-Treme	22	3	13	16	44						
2008	Nationals Calgary Oval X-Treme	3	0	1	1	4						
2010-11	WWHL Strathmore Rockies	2	0	0	0	2						
Totals from all Competitions		**77**	**10**	**37**	**47**	**138**						

RAMSLEY, ALISON
Forward.

Abby Hoffman Cup winner with Edmonton on 1997-03-09. Abby Hoffman Cup winner with Calgary on 1998-03-22.

Born 1963-01-04.

Year - League - Team		GP	G	A	PTS	PM
1995	Nationals Calgary Classics					
1996	Nationals Edmonton Chimos	7	0	6	6	0
1997	Nationals Edmonton Chimos					
1998	Nationals Calgary Oval X-Treme	7	3	1	4	0

RANCOUR, DOMINIQUE
Forward. #31 #77.

Born 1979-4-14. Grew up in Charlesbourg, QC, CAN.

Year - League - Team			GP	G	A	PTS	PM
2000-01	NWHL	Sainte-Julie	7	2	9	11	0
2001	Nationals	Équipe Québec					
2002	Nationals	Équipe Québec	6	2	2	4	0
2002-03	NWHL	Avalanche du Québec	7	0	1	1	2
2003	Nationals	Équipe Québec	5	3	5	8	4
2003-04	NWHL	Avalanche du Québec	0	0	0	0	0
2007-08	CWHL	Phénix du Québec	1	0	0	0	0

RANDALL, CATHY
Defence. *1996-97 COWHL London Devilettes #7 (24 games, 3 assists).*

RANDELL, STACEY
Forward. *2001 Nationals Nova Scotia; 2002 Nationals (5 gp, 1 goal, 2 assists).*

RATHGEBER, TRINA
Defence. Shoots left.

Abby Hoffman Cup winner with Calgary on 2003-03-16.
Born 1979-01-31. Thompson, MB, CAN.

Year - League - Team			GP	G	A	PTS	PM	Year - Playoff	GP	G	A	PTS	PM
1998	Nationals	Tazmanian Devils	5	0	0	0	4						
2002	Nationals	Calgary Oval X-Treme	6	4	2	6	2						
2002-03	NWHL	Calgary Oval X-Treme	21	0	14	14	16	2003 NWHL-P					
2003	Nationals	Calgary Oval X-Treme	5	1	2	3	0						

RATTRAY, JAMIE-LEE
Forward. Shoots left. #26.

Clarkson Cup winner with Markham on 2018-03-25
Born 1992-9-30. Grew up in Kanata, ON, CAN. 5'6". Debut at age 16 on 2009-1-25.

Year - League - Team			GP	G	A	PTS	PM	Year - Playoff	GP	G	A	PTS	PM
2008-09	CWHL	Ottawa Senators	1	1	0	1	0						
2014-15	CWHL	Brampton Thunder	22	4	9	13	37						
2015-16	CWHL	Brampton Thunder	22	13	16	29	18	2016 C-Cup	2	0	1	1	0
2016-17	CWHL	Brampton Thunder	22	11	10	21	28	2017 C-Cup	2	1	1	2	12
2017-18	CWHL	Markham Thunder	28	22	17	39	22	2018 C-Cup	3	2	0	2	2
2018-19	CWHL	Markham Thunder	26	12	13	25	14	2019 C-Cup	3	0	1	1	2
CWHL Regular Season			121	63	65	128	119	Clarkson Cup	10	3	3	6	16
Totals from all Competitions			**131**	**66**	**68**	**134**	**135**						

CWHLPA Jayna Hefford Trophy in 2017-18... CWHL First All-Star Team in 2017-18 and CWHL Second All-Star Team in 2015-16... CWHL All-Rookie Team in 2014-15... finished 4th in the Angela James Bowl scoring race in 2017-18... scored 100th CWHL point on 2018 03 10.

RAVEL, BARABARA
Forward. *1999-00 NWHL Laval #57 (1 game); 2000-01 (5 games).*

RAWSON, JENNIFER
Forward. #4 #19

Year - League - Team			GP	G	A	PTS	PM
1996-97	COWHL	Mississauga Chiefs	24	2	6	8	0
2001-02	NWHL	Mississauga IceBears	24	10	7	17	33
2002-03	NWHL	Mississauga IceBears					
2004-05	NWHL	Oakville Ice	32	2	4	6	20
Totals from all Competitions			**80**	**14**	**17**	**31**	**53**

RAYMOND, JOSÉE
Forward.

Year - League - Team			GP	G	A	PTS	PM
1998-99	NWHL	Bonaventure	33	4	13	17	14
1999-00	NWHL	Wingstar de Montréal	34	7	9	16	12
Totals from all Competitions			**67**	**11**	**22**	**33**	**26**

RAYNARD, LILL
Forward. *2003-04 NWHL Durham Lightning #27 (19 games, 5 goals, 3 assists).*

REDDY, JANET
Forward. *2000 Nationals Newfoundland Labrador (5 games).*

REEVE, MEAGHAN
Charleston, ON. D. *2006-07 NWHL Etobicoke #21 (2 games).*

REEVE, RAYANNE
Defence. Shoots right. #18.

Born 1987-06-01.

Year - League - Team			GP	G	A	PTS	PM	Year - Playoff	GP	G	A	PTS	PM
2005-06	WWHL	Calgary Oval X-Treme	21	1	8	9	24	2006 WWHL-P	3	1	0	1	6
2006	Nationals	Calgary Oval X-Treme	7	0	1	1	4						

REIART, LESLEY
1998-99 NWHL North York #14 (5 games).

REICKER, JENNIFER
Defence.

Born 1967-01-05.

Year - League - Team			GP	G	A	PTS	PM
1995	Nationals	Maritime Sports Blades					
1996	Nationals	Maritime Sports Blades	6	0	0	0	6
1998	Nationals	Maritime Sports Blades	6	0	0	0	4
1999	Nationals	Team New Brunswick	6	1	0	1	
2000	Nationals	Team New Brunswick	6	1	0	1	

REID, AMANDA
Forward. Shoots right. #15 #61

Born 1978-7-21, Hamilton, ON, CAN. Grew up in Hamilton, ON, CAN. 5'8".

Year - League - Team			GP	G	A	PTS	PM	Year - Playoff	GP	G	A	PTS	PM
2002-03	NWHL	Mississauga IceBears											
2003-04	NWHL	Oakville Ice	4	0	0	0	2						
2004-05	NWHL	Durham Lightning	9	2	2	4	27						
2005-06	NWHL	Durham Lightning	27	3	5	8	32	2006 NWHL-P	2	0	0	0	4
2006-07	NWHL	Etobicoke Dolphins	19	0	3	3	30	2007 NWHL-P	3	0	0	0	8
2007	Nationals	Etobicoke Dolphins	7	1	2	3	8						
2007-08	CWHL	Vaughan Flames	6	0	1	1	10						
2008-09	CWHL	Vaughan Flames	4		1	1	4						
Totals from all Competitions			**81**	**6**	**14**	**20**	**125**						

REID, CASSANDRA
Forward. 2004 Nationals British Columbia (6 gp, 2 goals, 1 assist).

REID, KATHERINE
Forward. 2003 Nationals Newfoundland Labrador (5 games).

REID, SAMANTHA
2003-04 NWHL Oakville #14 (4 games).

REID, SARAH
Forward. Shoots left. #11 #28.

Born 1977-9-15. Grew up in Charlottetown, PE, CAN. Forward. Shoots left. 5'6".

Year - League - Team			GP	G	A	PTS	PM	Year - Playoff	GP	G	A	PTS	PM
1999-00	NWHL	Durham Lightning	36	5	9	14	78						
2000-01	NWHL	Durham Lightning	35	13	10	23	86						
2001-02	NWHL	Durham Lightning	28	13	11	24	69						
2002-03	NWHL	Mississauga IceBears											
2003-04	NWHL	Durham Lightning	33	1	8	9	54						
2004-05	NWHL	Durham Lightning	36	3	6	9	52						
2005-06	NWHL	Durham Lightning	28	1	0	1	36	2006 NWHL-P	2	0	0	0	0
Totals from all Competitions			**198**	**36**	**44**	**80**	**375**						

REINHART, STEPHANIE
Defence. 2006-07 WWHL Saskatchewan Prairie Ice #7 (21 games, 1 goal, 1 assist).

RENISSON, MELISSA
Forward. 1996-97 COWHL London Devilettes #5 (29 games, 11 goals, 3 assists).

RENLI, INGRID
Forward. 2012-13 CWHL Alberta #21 (3 games).

REPACI, GINA
Defence. Shoots left. #23.

Born 1993-05-13. Grew up in Toronto, ON, CAN. 5'8". Debut at age 25 on 2018-10-13.

Year - League - Team			GP	G	A	PTS	PM	Year - Playoff	GP	G	A	PTS	PM
2018-19	CWHL	Markham Thunder	27	0	2	2	6	2019 C-Cup	3	0	0	0	0

REVELL, SAMANTHA
Forward. #6 #24.

Year - League - Team			GP	G	A	PTS	PM	Year - Playoff	GP	G	A	PTS	PM
2005-06	WWHL	British Columbia Breakers	21	4	2	6	40						
2006-07	WWHL	British Columbia Breakers	23	0	4	4	62	2007 WWHL-P	2	0	1	1	6
2007-08	WWHL	British Columbia Breakers	24	2	0	2	54						
Totals from all Competitions			**70**	**6**	**7**	**13**	**162**						

REYNOLDS, BRENDA
Forward. #76 #7 #22.

Year - League - Team			GP	G	A	PTS	PM
1999-00	NWHL	Scarborough Sting	4	1	0	1	0
2002-03	NWHL	Durham Lightning					
2003-04	NWHL	Durham Lightning	24	8	9	17	20
2004-05	NWHL	Durham Lightning	31	3	6	9	28
Totals from all Competitions			**59**	**12**	**15**	**27**	**48**

REYNS, TRUDY
Defence. 2004-05 NWHL Durham Lightning #79 (10 games, 1 goal, 2 assists).

REZANSOFF, KELSEY
2004-05 WWHL Sask. (7 gp, 2 a.); 2005-06 (18 gp, 3 goals, 2 a.; playoff 2 gp, 1 goal).

RICHARD, BRENDA
Defence.

Abby Hoffman Cup winner with Aeros on 1991-03-17.

RICHARD, YOLANDE
Forward. 1995 Nationals PEI Esso Tigers; 1996 Nationals (4 gp, 1 goal).

RICHARDS, AUDRA
Forward. Shoots right. #21.

Born 1994-07-19. Grew up in Maplewood, MN, USA. 5'8". Debut at age 24 on 2018-10-06.

Year - League - Team			GP	G	A	PTS	PM	Year - Playoff	GP	G	A	PTS	PM
2018-19	NWHL/	Metropolitan Riveters	16	8	0	8	4	2019 I-Cup	2	2	0	2	2

RICHARDS, KRISTEN
Forward. Shoots right. #9.

Clarkson Cup winner with Markham on 2018-03-25

Born 1992-7-4. Grew up in Toronto, ON, CAN. 5'9". Debut at age 15 on 2007-11-11.

Year - League - Team			GP	G	A	PTS	PM	Year - Playoff	GP	G	A	PTS	PM
2007-08	CWHL	Mississauga Chiefs	1	0	0	0	0						
2015-16	CWHL	Brampton Thunder	24	2	11	13	18	2016 C-Cup	2	0	1	1	4
2016-17	CWHL	Brampton Thunder	24	1	2	3	18	2017 C-Cup	2	0	0	0	0
2017-18	CWHL	Markham Thunder	28	13	10	23	32	2018 C-Cup	3	0	0	0	2
2018-19	CWHL	Markham Thunder	28	2	5	7	36						
CWHL Regular Season			105	18	28	46	104	Clarkson Cup	10	0	1	1	8

Finished 15th in the Angela James Bowl scoring race in 2017-18

RICHARDSON, GENEVIÈVE *2003-04 NWHL Oakville Ice #15 (28 games, 1 goal, 7 assists).*

RICHARDSON, HEATHER *Forward. #14 #87 #21 #77 #15 #36.*

Year - League - Team			GP	G	A	PTS	PM
1993-94	COWHL	Toronto Junior Aeros	24	2	6	8	10
1995-96	COWHL	Peterborough Skyway	26	15	17	32	14
1996-97	COWHL	North York Aeros	31	11	19	30	10
1997-98	COWHL	North York Aeros	2	0	0	0	0
1998-99	NWHL	Scarborough Sting	25	2	6	8	35
1999-00	NWHL	Scarborough Sting	9	2	1	3	2
2000-01	NWHL	Toronto Sting	33	9	10	19	54
Totals from all Competitions			**150**	**41**	**59**	**100**	**125**

RICHARDSON, KYLIE *Forward. #7 #14 #41.*

Year - League - Team			GP	G	A	PTS	PM
1995-96	COWHL	Mississauga Chiefs	27	2	6	8	12
1996-97	COWHL	North York Aeros	14	5	9	14	11
1998-99	NWHL	Brampton Thunder	3	1	2	3	0
1999-00	NWHL	Brampton Thunder	5	0	1	1	0
Totals from all Competitions			**49**	**8**	**18**	**26**	**23**

RICIOPPO, NADINE *Defence. 2005 Nationals Alberta (6 games).*

RICKARD, KAREN *Forward. Shoots right.*

Abby Hoffman Cup winner with Aeros on 2005-03-13.
Born 1981-12-01.

Year - League - Team			GP	G	A	PTS	PM
1999-00	NWHL	North York Aeros	2	0	1	1	2
2004-05	NWHL	Toronto Aeros	16	3	7	10	4
2005	Nationals	Toronto Aeros	7	2	3	5	2

RIEGER, ANGIE *2004-05 WWHL Minnesota #6 (12 games, 1 goal; playoff 2games).*

RIGGS, ASHLEY *Forward. Shoots left. #10 #91 #11 #16 #93.*

Born 1985-3-25, Scarborough, ON, CAN. Grew up in Pickering, ON, CAN. 5'4".

Year - League - Team			GP	G	A	PTS	PM	Year - Playoff		GP	G	A	PTS	PM
2000-01	NWHL	Toronto Sting	10	5	3	8	4							
2003-04	NWHL	Durham Lightning	31	12	9	21	10							
2005-06	NWHL	Durham Lightning	2	2	2	4	0	2006 NWHL-P		2	1	0	1	0
2010-11	CWHL	Burlington Barracudas	6	1	0	1	0							
2011-12	CWHL	Brampton Thunder	23	9	11	20	4	2012 C-Cup		4	1	0	1	0
CWHL Regular Season			29	10	11	21	4	Clarkson Cup		4	1	0	1	0
Totals from all Competitions			**78**	**31**	**25**	**56**	**18**							

Finished 19th in the Angela James Bowl scoring race in 2011-12

RINGROSE, DONNA *Forward. Shoots left. #20 #18.*

Clarkson Cup winner with Montréal on 2011-03-27
Born 1986-2-25. Grew up in Campbell's Bay, QC, CAN. Debut at age 24 on 2009-10-3.

Year - League - Team			GP	G	A	PTS	PM	Year - Playoff		GP	G	A	PTS	PM
2009-10	CWHL	Stars de Montréal	28	15	7	22	18	2010 C-Cup		1	0	0	0	0
2010-11	CWHL	Stars de Montréal	23	4	2	6	12	2011 CWHL-P		2				
								2011 C-Cup		4	0	0	0	2
CWHL Regular Season			51	19	9	28	30	Clarkson Cup		5	0	0	0	2
Totals from all Competitions			**58**	**19**	**9**	**28**	**32**							

CWHL All-Rookie Team in 2009-10

RINGUETTE, NORA *1995 Nationals Maritime Sports Blades; 1996 (6 gp, 4 g.); 1998 (6 gp, 5 a.).*

RIOPEL, EMILIE *2000-01 NWHL Mistral de Laval #91 (19 games, 2 goals, 4 assists).*

RIOUX, EMILIE *2003-04 NWHL Québec.*

RIOUX, MARIE-FRANCE *Forward. 1998-99 NWHL Montréal #47 (10 games, 1 goal, 2 assists).*

RISSLING, TRINA *Defence. #9.*

Born 1978-3-11, Regina, SK, CAN. 5'0".

Year - League - Team			GP	G	A	PTS	PM	Year - Playoff		GP	G	A	PTS	PM
1995	Nationals	Regina Sharks												
2004	Nationals	Saskatchewan	6	1	1	2	6							
2004-05	WWHL	Saskatchewan Prairie Ice	21	0	0	0	10							
2005-06	WWHL	Saskatchewan Prairie Ice	24	0	1	1	26	2006 WWHL-P		2	0	0	0	4
2006-07	WWHL	Saskatchewan Prairie Ice	1	0	0	0	0							
Totals from all Competitions			**54**	**1**	**2**	**3**	**46**							

RITCHIE, MARTHA *Defence. 1993-94 COWHL Scarborough #12 (29 games, 1 goal, 5 assists).*

RITTMASTER, DANA *Forward. 2000 Nationals Équipe Québec (6 games, 1 assist).*

RIVARD, NATHALIE *Defence. #21 #72.*

IIHF champion. Abby Hoffman Cup winner with Aeros on 1993-03-28.
Born 1972-1-21. Grew up in Cumberland, ON, CAN.

Year - League - Team			GP	G	A	PTS	PM
1992-93	COWHL	Toronto Aeros	24	4	10	14	10
1992-93	COWHL	Toronto Aeros	28	8	11	19	34
1995-96	COWHL	North York Aeros	24	11	15	26	16
1996	Nationals	North York Aeros	5	1	3	4	0
1996-97	COWHL	Mississauga Chiefs	26	5	14	19	26
1998-99	NWHL	Mississauga Chiefs	26	8	7	15	42
1999	Nationals	North York Aeros	5	0	0	0	
1999-00	NWHL	Mississauga Chiefs	26	5	11	16	10
2000-01	NWHL	Mississauga IceBears	35	8	11	19	24
2001-02	NWHL	Mississauga IceBears	20	1	7	8	18
2002-03	NWHL	Mississauga IceBears					
Totals from all Competitions			**219**	**51**	**89**	**140**	**180**

RIVERS, JENNIFER — *2008 CWHL Burlington #25 (1 playoff gp).*

ROACH, MELANIE — *Defence. #4.*

Year - League - Team			GP	G	A	PTS	PM
2003-04	NWHL	Durham Lightning	33	4	7	11	64
2004-05	NWHL	Durham Lightning	28	1	9	10	80
Totals from all Competitions			**61**	**5**	**16**	**21**	**144**

ROBERT, LYNN — *Defence. #3.*

Year - League - Team			GP	G	A	PTS	PM
1992-93	COWHL	Scarborough Firefighters	28	0	7	7	26
1993-94	COWHL	Scarborough Firefighters	20	4	12	16	41
Totals from all Competitions			**48**	**4**	**19**	**23**	**67**

ROBERTS, BRITTANY — *Markdale, ON. 2007-08 CWHL Burlington #67 (3 games, 1 goal).*

ROBERTS, STACEY — *Cambridge, ON. Defence. 2009-10 CWHL Mississauga #18 (1 game).*

ROBERTSON, HEATHER — *Defence. 2004 Nationals Saskatchewan (6 games).*

ROBERTSON, KAILEY — *Forward. 2004 Nationals Manitoba (5 games, 2 goals).*

ROBINSON, BUSSIE — *Forward. #16.*

Year - League - Team			GP	G	A	PTS	PM
1992-93	COWHL	Scarborough Sting	26	3	1	4	16
1993-94	COWHL	Scarborough Sting	28	8	6	14	12
1996-97	COWHL	Scarborough Sting	34	8	8	16	24
1997-98	COWHL	Scarborough Sting	19	3	2	5	10
1998-99	NWHL	Scarborough Sting	27	2	1	3	6
Totals from all Competitions			**134**	**24**	**18**	**42**	**68**

ROBINSON, JENNIFER — *Forward. 1995 Nationals Britannia Blues.*

ROBINSON, LINDSAY — *Forward. Shoots right. #21.*

Born 1986-10-2. Grew up in Edmonton, AB, CAN. Forward. Shoots right. 5'5. Debut at age 25 on 2011-11-19.

Year - League - Team			GP	G	A	PTS	PM
2009-10	WWHL	Edmonton Chimos	17	5	5	10	10
2010-11	WWHL	Edmonton Chimos	17	5	4	9	6
2011-12	CWHL	Alberta	11	0	1	1	2

ROBINSON, LYNDA — *Forward.*

Abby Hoffman Cup winner with Calgary on 1998-03-22.

Year - League - Team			GP	G	A	PTS	PM
1998	Nationals	Calgary Oval X-Treme	7	2	1	3	2

ROBINSON, NICKI — *Defence. 2009-10 WWHL Strathmore #9 (17 gp, 2 goals, 5 a.); 2010-11 (10 gp, 1 goal, 1 a.).*

ROBINSON, SARAH — *1999-00 NWHL Durham #8 (6 games, 1 assist); 2000-01 NWHL (5 games, 1 goal, 1 assist).*

ROBINSON, STEFANIE — *London, ON. 2008-09 CWHL Mississauga #16 (1 game).*

ROBITAILLE, CHANTAL — *Forward. 2001 Nationals U. Manitoba; 2002 Nationals U. Manitoba (5 games).*

ROBITAILLE, JOANIE — *2003-04 NWHL Québec.*

ROBINSON, NANCY — *Defence. #23.*

Born 1973-05-20.

Year - League - Team			GP	G	A	PTS	PM
1996	Nationals	Équipe Québec	6	1	3	4	2
1998-99	NWHL	Bonaventure	32	5	8	13	36
1999-00	NWHL	Wingstar de Montréal	23	2	7	9	10
2000-01	NWHL	Wingstar de Montréal	38	2	10	12	12
2001-02	NWHL	Cheyenne	29	4	7	11	54
2002-03	NWHL	Avalanche du Québec	36	2	7	9	36
2003-04	NWHL	Avalanche du Québec	7	0	0	0	14
2005	Nationals	Prince Edward Island	5	0	1	1	2
2006	Nationals	Prince Edward Island	5	3	3	6	4
2007	Nationals	Prince Edward Island	5	2	2	4	6
Totals from all Competitions			**171**	**16**	**42**	**58**	**164**

ROCHE, JODY *1996-97 COWHL Newtonbrook #88 (1 game, 1 goal, 1 assist).*

ROCHE, LARISSA *Thorhild, AB. Forward. 2011-12 CWHL Alberta #16 (2 games, 1 assist); 2012-13 (1 game).*

ROCHE, TESSA *F. 2005 Nationals P.E.I. (5 gp, 1a.); 2006 Nationals (5 gp, 6 pts); 2007 Nationals (5 gp, 4 pts).*

ROCHON, CRYSTAL *F. 2002 Nationals Manitoba (5 gp); 2003 Nationals (4 gp); 2008 Nationals (5 gp, 2 goals).*

ROCKETT, CORRIE *2000-01 NWHL Brampton Thunder (1 game).*

RODGERS, NINA *Forward. Shoots right. #23.*
Born 1996-04-08. Grew up in Minnetonka, MN, USA. 5'5". Debut at age 22 on 2018-10-07.

Year - League - Team	GP	G	A	PTS	PM	Year - Playoff	GP	G	A	PTS	PM
2018-19 NWHL/ Connecticut Whale	15	2	2	4	14	2019 I-Cup	1	0	0	0	0

RODGERS, STACY *Forward. 2002 Nationals Newfoundland Labrador (5 games).*

RODRIGUE, ANNE *Forward.*
Born 1973-10-25.

Year - League - Team	GP	G	A	PTS	PM
1995 Nationals Équipe Québec					
1996 Nationals Équipe Québec	6	1	3	4	4
1998 Nationals Équipe Québec	6	1	1	2	4

ROESLER, CYDNEY *Shoots right. #21.*
Born 1994-02-21. Grew up in Stittsville, ON, CAN. 5'9". Debut at age 22 on 2016-10-09.

Year - League - Team	GP	G	A	PTS	PM	Year - Playoff	GP	G	A	PTS	PM
2016-17 NWHL/ Connecticut Whale	17	1	6	7	12	2017 I-Cup	1	0	0	0	0
2017-18 NWHL/ Connecticut Whale	14	1	1	2	8	2018 I-Cup	1	0	0	0	2
2018-19 NWHL/ Connecticut Whale	2	0	0	0	6						
NWHL Regular Season	33	2	7	9	26	Isobel Cup	2	0	0	0	2

ROFFEY, MARY *Forward. #44 #11.*
Abby Hoffman Cup winner with Aeros on 1991-03-17 and 1993-03-28.

Year - League - Team	GP	G	A	PTS	PM
1992-93 COWHL Toronto Aeros	14	5	8	13	4
1992-93 COWHL Toronto Aeros	28	16	33	49	14
Totals from all Competitions	**42**	**21**	**41**	**62**	**18**

ROGERSON, LAURA *Forward. Shoots right. #18 #12 #47.*
Born 1986-10-28, Millbrook, ON, CAN. 5'5". Debut at age 21 on 2007-9-15.

Year - League - Team	GP	G	A	PTS	PM	Year - Playoff	GP	G	A	PTS	PM
2007-08 CWHL Ottawa Capital Canucks	27	6	6	12	12	2008 CWHL-P	1	0	0	0	0
2008-09 CWHL Ottawa Senators	30	5	12	17	6	2009 CWHL-P	2				
2009-10 CWHL Ottawa Senators	17	3	4	7	2						
CWHL Regular Season	74	14	22	36	20						
Totals from all Competitions	**77**	**14**	**22**	**36**	**20**						

ROHRER, HEIDI *Right wing. #7.*

Year - League - Team	GP	G	A	PTS	PM
1992-93 COWHL Scarborough Sting	26	5	6	11	34
1993-94 COWHL Scarborough Sting	29	9	7	16	27
Totals from all Competitions	**55**	**14**	**13**	**27**	**61**

ROMBOUTS, KATHY *Forward. 1996-97 COWHL London Devilettes #50 (4 games, 2 assists).*

ROMEO, KRISTINA *Ottawa, ON. Forward. 2008-09 CWHL Ottawa Senators #12 (6 games, 1 assist).*

ROSA, DONNA-LYNN *Defence. #16 #9 #19.*
Abby Hoffman Cup winner with Aeros on 1991-03-17.

Year - League - Team	GP	G	A	PTS	PM
1992-93 COWHL Guelph Eagles	11	1	4	5	14
1993-94 COWHL Mississauga Chiefs	28	7	9	16	98
1995 Nationals Mississauga Chiefs					
1998-99 NWHL Brampton Thunder	30	1	13	14	91
1999-00 NWHL Brampton Thunder	36	7	9	16	60
2000-01 NWHL Brampton Thunder	33	4	20	24	50
Totals from all Competitions	**138**	**20**	**55**	**75**	**313**

Served as interim coach with CWHL Brampton... served as general manager with CWHL Brampton

ROSE, AMY *Defence. 2000 Nationals Nova Scotia Selects (6 games, 1 assist).*

ROSE, TEGAN *Defence. 2010-11 WWHL Edmonton Chimos #6 (16 games, 1 goal, 5 assists).*

ROSEN, CORRINE *Forward. 2002-03 NWHL Edmonton Chimos #5 (24 games, 1 goal, 1 assist).*

ROSENBERG, MICHELLE *Defence. #10 #8 #14 #51.*

Year - League - Team	GP	G	A	PTS	PM
1992-93 COWHL Scarborough Sting	15	0	2	2	0
1993-94 COWHL Scarborough Firefighters	21	6	2	8	2
1995-96 COWHL Peterborough Skyway	27	5	15	20	8
1996-97 COWHL Peterborough Pirates	2	1	0	1	2
1999-00 NWHL Scarborough Sting	6	0	0	0	2
Totals from all Competitions	**71**	**12**	**19**	**31**	**14**

ROSS, ANDREA — *Defence. 2003 Nationals Host Saskatchewan (5 games).*

ROSS, BOBBI — *Forward. 2002 Nationals Saskatchewan (6 gp, 3 pts); 2004 Nationals (6 gp, 5 pts).*

ROSS, LAURIE — *Defence. Shoots left. #83 #93 #18 #77.*
Born 1983-2-27, Manotick, ON, CAN.

Year - League - Team			GP	G	A	PTS	PM
1999-00	NWHL	Ottawa Raiders	7	0	1	1	6
2000-01	NWHL	Ottawa Raiders	7	1	1	2	8
2001-02	NWHL	Ottawa Raiders	30	3	8	11	40
2006-07	NWHL	Ottawa Raiders	33	0	7	7	74
Totals from all Competitions			**77**	**4**	**17**	**21**	**128**

ROSS, MEGAN — *Forward. 2010-11 WWHL Manitoba Maple Leafs #2 (5 games, 1 goal, 1 assist).*

ROSSIGNOL, LYSE — *F. 2006 Nationals New Brunswick (7 gp); 2007 Nationals (6 gp); 2008 Nationals (5 gp, 4 pts).*

ROSSLER, KYLIE — *Regina, SK. Forward. 2006-07 WWHI Saskatchewan #25 (4 games).*

ROSWELL, DENA — *Forward. 1999 Nationals Tazmanian Devils (4 games, 1 assist).*

ROTHON, MELANIE — *Defence. Shoots left. #12 #7 #17.*
Born 1988-11-25, Newmarket, ON, CAN. Grew up in Newmarket, ON, CAN. 5'7".

Year - League - Team			GP	G	A	PTS	PM	Year - Playoff		GP	G	A	PTS	PM
2004-05	NWHL	Toronto Aeros	1	0	0	0	0							
2005-06	NWHL	Durham Lightning	33	3	8	11	20	2006	NWHL-P	2	0	0	0	0
2006-07	NWHL	Etobicoke Dolphins	29	3	2	5	45	2007	NWHL-P	3	0	0	0	2
2007	Nationals	Etobicoke Dolphins	7	0	2	2	4							
2007-08	CWHL	Vaughan Flames	29	4	9	13	34	2008	CWHL-P	2	1	0	1	10
2008-09	CWHL	Vaughan Flames	30	7	7	14	22	2009	CWHL-P	2	1	1	2	0
2010-11	CWHL	Brampton Thunder	15	0	0	0	4							
CWHL Regular Season			74	11	16	27	60							
Totals from all Competitions			**153**	**19**	**29**	**48**	**141**							

ROUGEAU, LAURIANE — *Defence. Shoots left. #5.*
Olympic champion. Clarkson Cup winner with Montréal on 2009-03-21 and 2017-03-05
Born 1990-4-12, Pointe-Claire, QC, CAN. 5'8". Debut at age 16 on 2006-9-16.

Year - League - Team			GP	G	A	PTS	PM	Year - Playoff		GP	G	A	PTS	PM
2006-07	NWHL	Axion de Montréal	25	0	0	0	0	2007	NWHL-P					
2007-08	CWHL	Stars de Montréal	6	2	2	4	10	2008	CWHL-P	1	0	0	0	0
2008-09	CWHL	Stars de Montréal	2	0	0	0	0	2009	CWHL-P	0	0	0	0	0
								2009	C-Cup	3	0	0	0	0
2014-15	CWHL	Stars de Montréal	20	2	7	9	14	2015	C-Cup	3	0	2	2	2
2015-16	CWHL	Canadiennes de Montréal	22	2	17	19	10	2016	C-Cup	3	1	2	3	0
2016-17	CWHL	Canadiennes de Montréal	22	3	4	7	4	2017	C-Cup	3	0	1	1	0
2017-18	CWHL	Canadiennes de Montréal	2	0	0	0	0	2018	C-Cup	2	0	0	0	2
2018-19	CWHL	Canadiennes de Montréal	28	2	14	16	16	2019	C-Cup	4	1	3	4	4
CWHL Regular Season			102	11	44	55	54	Clarkson Cup		18	2	8	10	8
Totals from all Competitions			**146**	**13**	**52**	**65**	**62**							

Finished 18th in the Angela James Bowl scoring race in 2015-16

ROURKE, ERIN — *Forward. #34 #4 #44.*
Abby Hoffman Cup winner with Aeros on 1993-03-28.

Year - League - Team			GP	G	A	PTS	PM
1992-93	COWHL	Toronto Aeros	2	2	0	2	0
1993-94	COWHL	Toronto Junior Aeros	29	12	11	23	4
1995-96	COWHL	North York Aeros	25	11	19	30	19
1996	Nationals	North York Aeros	5	3	2	5	0
1996-97	COWHL	North York Aeros	35	16	27	43	10
1997-98	COWHL	North York Aeros	20	8	13	21	10
1998	Nationals	North York Aeros	6	3	2	5	0
1998-99	NWHL	North York Aeros	40	10	20	30	10
1999	Nationals	North York Aeros	5	1	1	2	
1999-00	NWHL	Durham Lightning	25	2	6	8	26
2000-01	NWHL	Durham Lightning	27	11	12	23	6
2001-02	NWHL	Durham Lightning	24	10	10	20	8
2002-03	NWHL	Durham Lightning					
Totals from all Competitions			**243**	**89**	**123**	**212**	**93**

ROUZES, CENA — *Forward. 2009-10 WWHL Edmonton Chimos #77 (5 games, 1 goal).*

ROY, BREANNA — *Orléans, ON. Defence. 2007-08 CWHL Ottawa Capital Canucks #23 (3 games).*

ROY, MÉLISSA — *Forward. Shoots left. #25 #86 #16 #77.*
Born 1983-12-13, Montréal, QC, CAN. 5'5".

Year - League - Team			GP	G	A	PTS	PM	Year - Playoff		GP	G	A	PTS	PM
2003-04	NWHL	Axion de Montréal	9	1	3	4	2	2004	NWHL-P	1	0	0	0	0
2004	Nationals	Équipe Québec	5	1	0	1	2							
2004-05	NWHL	Axion de Montréal	4	1	0	1	4							
2006-07	NWHL	Axion de Montréal						2007	NWHL-P					

Year - League - Team	GP	G	A	PTS	PM	Year - Playoff	GP	G	A	PTS	PM
2007-08 CWHL Stars de Montréal	25	7	11	18	34	2008 CWHL-P	2	2	1	3	0
2008-09 CWHL Stars de Montréal	7	3	2	5	4						
CWHL Regular Season	32	10	13	23	38						
Totals from all Competitions	**53**	**15**	**17**	**32**	**46**						

ROY, SABRINA
Defence. #5 #14.

Born 1977-11-4. Debut at age 21 on 2005-10-09.

Year - League - Team	GP	G	A	PTS	PM	Year - Playoff	GP	G	A	PTS	PM
1998-99 NWHL Bonaventure	33	2	10	12	26						
1999-00 NWHL Wingstar de Montréal	33	3	7	10	30						
2000-01 NWHL Sainte-Julie	34	6	13	19	28						
2001-02 NWHL Cheyenne	28	1	4	5	34						
2002-03 NWHL Avalanche du Québec	29	0	3	3	18						
2003-04 NWHL Avalanche du Québec	1	0	0	0	4						
2007-08 CWHL Stars de Montréal	6	2	1	3	4	2008 CWHL-P	2	0	0	0	0
Totals from all Competitions	**166**	**14**	**38**	**52**	**144**						

ROY, SANDY
Defence. 2004 Nationals Équipe Québec (7 gp); 2005-06 NWHL Québec #19 (4 gp, 1 assist).

ROY, STEPHANIE
F. 2006 Nationals Team NB (7 gp, 7 pts); 2012-13 CWHL Alberta (12 gp, 1 goal, 2 assists).

ROY, STEPHANIE
2000-01 NWHL Sainte-Julie #72 (3 games, 1 goal, 3 assists).

ROYER, DANIELLE
2006 Nationals British Columbia (6 games, 1 assist).

RUGGIERO, ANGELA
Defence. Shoots right. #7 #4.

Hockey Hall of Fame honoured member, Class of 2015
Olympic champion, IIHF champion.
Born 1980-1-3, Harper Woods, MI, USA. Grew up in Panorama City, CA, USA. 5'9".

Year - League - Team	GP	G	A	PTS	PM	Year - Playoff	GP	G	A	PTS	PM
2004-05 NWHL Axion de Montréal	10	2	9	11	12						
2005 Nationals Axion de Montréal	6	5	2	7	12						
2005-06 NWHL Axion de Montréal	0	0	0	0	0						
2007-08 WWHL Minnesota Whitecaps	15	8	10	18	20						
2008 Nationals Minnesota Whitecaps	3	3	1	4	10						
2008-09 WWHL Minnesota Whitecaps	12	7	8	15	14	2009 WWHL-P	2	0	1	1	0
						2009 C-Cup	3	2	1	3	4
2009-10 WWHL Minnesota Whitecaps	0	0	0	0	0						
2010-11 CWHL Boston Blades	20	10	15	25	36	2011 CWHL-P	2	1	0	1	2
CWHL Regular Season	20	10	15	25	36	Clarkson Cup	3	2	1	3	4
Totals from all Competitions	**73**	**38**	**47**	**85**	**110**						

CWHL Top Defender in 2010-11... CWHL First All-Star Team in 2010-11... finished 10th in the Angela James Bowl scoring race in 2010-11

RUHNKE, LAURA
Biel, SUI. Forward. 2006-07 NWHL Québec #71 (19 games, 4 goals).

RUMBLE, KERI
Defence. 2005-06 NWHL Brampton Thunder #7 (6 games, 1 goal, 1 assist).

RUMSEY, JANA
Forward. 2002 Nationals Newfoundland Labrador (5 games).

RUNDQVIST, DANIJELA
Forward. Shoots left. #55.

Born 1984-09-26, Stockholm, SWE.

Year - League - Team	GP	G	A	PTS	PM
2010-11 CWHL Burlington Barracudas	22	10	4	14	36

RUNYAN, KELLY
Defence. 2007 Nationals Manitoba (5 gp, 1 a.); 2008 Nationals (5 gp, 1 a.).

RUSCH,
2002-03 NWHL Ottawa Raiders (1 game).

RUSH, SAMANTHA
Defence. 2010-11 CWHL Boston Blades (13 games).

RUSHTON, SANTINA
Forward. 2007 Nationals Nova Scotia (7 games, 1 assist).

RUSSELL, AMANDA
Forward. 1998 Nationals Nova Scotia Selects (5 games).

RUSSELL, NAVADA
Defence. #12.

WWHL winner. Born 1981-6-30. Grew up in Calgary, AB, CAN.

Year - League - Team	GP	G	A	PTS	PM	Year - Playoff	GP	G	A	PTS	PM
1999 Nationals Calgary Oval X-Treme	6	0	0	0							
2003-04 NWHL Calgary Oval X-Treme	7	0	3	3	10	2004 NWHL-P					
2004 Nationals Calgary Oval X-Treme	5	0	0	0							
2004-05 WWHL Calgary Oval X-Treme	19	0	10	10	20	2005 WWHL-P	3	1	1	2	2
2007-08 WWHL Strathmore Rockies	22	0	5	5	26						
2008-09 WWHL Strathmore Rockies	12	0	1	1	21	2009 WWHL-P	1	0	0	0	0
Totals from all Competitions	**64**	**1**	**20**	**21**	**79**						

RUSSELL, REBECCA
Forward. Shoots right. #11.

Abby Hoffman Cup winner with Calgary on 2007-03-10. WWHL winner. Born 1982-8-7, St. John's, NL, CAN. Grew up in Clarenville, NL, CAN. 5'6".

Year - League - Team	GP	G	A	PTS	PM
2000 Nationals Newfoundland Labrador	5	0	0	0	
2001 Nationals Newfoundland Labrador					

Year - League - Team		GP	G	A	PTS	PM	Year - Playoff		GP	G	A	PTS	PM
2005-06	WWHL Calgary Oval X-Treme	22	20	30	50	8	2006	WWHL-P	3	0	2	2	0
2006-07	WWHL Calgary Oval X-Treme	24	20	32	52	4	2007	WWHL-P	3	3	2	5	0
2007	Nationals Calgary Oval X-Treme	6	3	8	11	4							
2007-08	WWHL Calgary Oval X-Treme	21	17	24	41	14							
2008	Nationals Calgary Oval X-Treme	3	2	2	4	2							
2008-09	WWHL Calgary Oval X-Treme	22	14	18	32	12	2009	WWHL-P	2	0	3	3	0
							2009	C-Cup	2	0	1	1	0
Totals from all Competitions		**113**	**79**	**122**	**201**	**44**							

RUSSO, REBECCA
Forward. Shoots left. #18.

Isobel Cup winner with Metropolitan on 2018-03-25
Born 1994-04-22. Grew up in Shelton, CT, USA. 5'4". Debut at age 22 on 2016-10-08.

Year - League - Team		GP	G	A	PTS	PM	Year - Playoff		GP	G	A	PTS	PM
2016-17	NWHL/ New York Riveters	18	3	13	16	0	2017	I-Cup	1	0	0	0	0
2017-18	NWHL/ Metropolitan Riveters	16	9	8	17	0	2018	I-Cup	2	1	1	2	0
2018-19	NWHL/ Metropolitan Riveters	16	5	3	8	2	2019	I-Cup	2	0	1	1	2
NWHL Regular Season		50	17	24	41	2	Isobel Cup		5	1	2	3	2

NWHL Fans' Three Stars Award in 2016-17

RUTA, NICOLE
F. 2008-09 CWHL Brampton #19 (27 gp, 4 goals, 5 a.; playoff 2 gp, 1 goal, C-Cup, 2 gp, 2 goals).

RUTH, VIKKI
Forward. 1999-00 NWHL Mississauga Chiefs #33 (1 game).

RUTH, WANDA
Defence. 2005 Nationals Nova Scotia (5 gp); 2006 Nationals Nova Scotia (4 gp).

RYAN, JENNY
Defence. Shoots right. #5.

Isobel Cup winner with Metropolitan on 2018-03-25
Born 1995-01-24. Grew up in Victor, NY, USA. 5'4". Debut at age 22 on 2017-10-28.

Year - League - Team		GP	G	A	PTS	PM	Year - Playoff		GP	G	A	PTS	PM
2017-18	NWHL/ Metropolitan Riveters	16	3	13	16	10	2018	I-Cup	2	0	0	0	0
2018-19	NWHL/ Metropolitan Riveters	16	1	3	4	12	2019	I-Cup	2	0	2	2	4

RYAN, JODY
1999-00 NWHL Brampton Thunder #71 (1 game).

RYAN, KELLY-RAE
Defence. #7.

Year - League - Team		GP	G	A	PTS	PM		
1998-99	NWHL Montréal Jofa-Titan	33	2	9	11	48		
1999-00	NWHL Sainte-Julie	32	4	6	10	32	2000	NWHL-P
2000-01	NWHL Sainte-Julie	37	3	13	16	53		
2001-02	NWHL Cheyenne	28	0	3	3	38		
Totals from all Competitions		**130**	**9**	**31**	**40**	**171**		

RYAN, SHANNON
Defence. #8 #88.

Year - League - Team		GP	G	A	PTS	PM
1995-96	COWHL Hamilton Golden Hawks	28	2	0	2	16
1996-97	COWHL Hamilton	29	3	5	8	12
Totals from all Competitions		**57**	**5**	**5**	**10**	**28**

RYAN, SYLVIA
Forward. 1996 Nationals Pictou County (4 gp, 1 goal); 2001 Nationals Nova Scotia.

RYCKMAN, KATHY
Forward. #64 #96.

Year - League - Team		GP	G	A	PTS	PM
1999-00	NWHL Durham Lightning	11	2	2	4	2
2000-01	NWHL Durham Lightning	37	6	7	13	32
Totals from all Competitions		**48**	**8**	**9**	**17**	**34**

RYDER, SAMANTHA
2007-08 WWHL British Columbia #77 (24 games, 4 goals, 4 assists).

SABEAN, KARA
Forward. 1995 Nationals Metro Valley; 2005 Nationals Prince Edward Island (5 gp).

SABOURIN,
2002-03 NWHL Québec (1 game).

SADLER, JEN
Forward. Shoots right. #9 #18 #22.

Born 1985-3-22. Grew up in Pickering, ON, CAN. 5'4".

Year - League - Team		GP	G	A	PTS	PM	Year - Playoff		GP	G	A	PTS	PM
2000-01	NWHL Durham Lightning	1	0	0	0	0							
2008-09	CWHL Burlington Barracudas	22	3	6	9	20							
2009-10	CWHL Mississauga Chiefs	1	0	0	0	0							
2011-12	CWHL Brampton Thunder	19	0	1	1	8	2012	C-Cup	4	0	0	0	0
2012-13	CWHL Brampton Thunder	1	0	0	0	0							
CWHL Regular Season		43	3	7	10	28	Clarkson Cup		4	0	0	0	0

SAFKA, KATHERINE
Right wing. Shoots right. #8 #10 #14

Born 1982-4-19. Grew up in Stoney Creek, ON, CAN. 5'7".

Year - League - Team		GP	G	A	PTS	PM
1999-00	NWHL Brampton Thunder	4	0	1	1	0
2000-01	NWHL Toronto Sting	4	0	2	2	4
2005-06	NWHL Toronto Aeros	35	9	7	16	0
Totals from all Competitions		**43**	**9**	**10**	**19**	**4**

SAGE, KELLY
Defence. Shoots right. #12.

Abby Hoffman Cup winner with Aeros on 2004-03-14.
Born 1980-11-01.

Year - League - Team			GP	G	A	PTS	PM	Year - Playoff	GP	G	A	PTS	PM
1995-96	COWHL	Peterborough Skyway	24	1	4	5	10						
1996-97	COWHL	Peterborough Pirates	31	13	16	29	49						
1997-98	COWHL	North York Aeros	19	3	2	5	4						
1998	Nationals	North York Aeros	6	0	1	1	0						
2003-04	NWHL	Toronto Aeros	27	5	6	11	27	2004 NWHL-P					
2004	Nationals	Toronto Aeros	6	1	1	2	4						
Totals from all Competitions			**113**	**23**	**30**	**53**	**94**						

SALATINO, MELANIE
Right wing. Shoots left. #15.

Born 1983-5-21, Thunder Bay, ON, CAN. 5'7". Debut at age 22 on 2005-09-17.

Year - League - Team			GP	G	A	PTS	PM	Year - Playoff	GP	G	A	PTS	PM
2005-06	NWHL	Ottawa Raiders	36	13	15	28	16	2006 NWHL-P	2	0	0	0	0
Totals from all Competitions			**38**	**13**	**15**	**28**	**16**						

SALES, JILL
Defence. #44 #21 #88.

Born 1985-3-27. Grew up in Edmonton, AB, CAN.

Year - League - Team			GP	G	A	PTS	PM	Year - Playoff	GP	G	A	PTS	PM
2002-03	NWHL	Edmonton Chimos	24	0	6	6	24						
2008-09	WWHL	Edmonton Chimos	23	3	9	12	62	2009 WWHL-P	1	0	0	0	2
2009-10	WWHL	Edmonton Chimos	1	1	1	2	2						
Totals from all Competitions			**49**	**4**	**16**	**20**	**90**						

SALVATORI, DIANNE
#10.

Year - League - Team			GP	G	A	PTS	PM
1998-99	NWHL	Scarborough Sting	34	1	0	1	2
1999-00	NWHL	Durham Lightning	38	4	2	6	0
Totals from all Competitions			**72**	**5**	**2**	**7**	**2**

SAMEC, MONICA
Defence. 1998-99 NWHL Scarborough #36 (12 games); 1999-00 Durham #13 (31 games).

SANCHEZ, ALLIE
Defence. Shoots left. #21.

Clarkson Cup winner with Minnesota on 2010-03-28
Born 1984-03-30. Grew up in St. Paul, MN, USA.

Year - League - Team			GP	G	A	PTS	PM	Year - Playoff	GP	G	A	PTS	PM
2007-08	WWHL	Minnesota Whitecaps	20	2	2	4	30						
2008	Nationals	Minnesota Whitecaps	3	0	0	0	4						
2008-09	WWHL	Minnesota Whitecaps	15	3	10	13	16	2009 WWHL-P	2	0	0	0	0
								2009 C-Cup	3	0	0	0	4
2009-10	WWHL	Minnesota Whitecaps	12	1	3	4	18	2010 C-Cup	2	0	0	0	2
2010-11	WWHL	Minnesota Whitecaps	12	5	9	14	16	2011 C-Cup	3	0	0	0	2
Clarkson Cup	8	0	0	0	8								
Totals from all Competitions			**72**	**11**	**24**	**35**	**92**						

SANDERS, KERRI
Saugus, MA, USA. Forward. 2012-13 CWHL Alberta #8 (10 games, 2 goals, 1 assist).

SANFACON, VERONIQUE
Left wing. Shoots left. #37 #7.

NWHL winner. Born 1982-6-26. Grew up in Beauport, QC, CAN. 5'7".

Year - League - Team			GP	G	A	PTS	PM	Year - Playoff	GP	G	A	PTS	PM
2000-01	NWHL	Mistral de Laval	4	0	2	2	6						
2005-06	NWHL	Axion de Montréal	36	1	6	7	22						
Totals from all Competitions			**41**	**1**	**8**	**9**	**28**						

SANTOIRE, KIM
2000-01 NWHL Laval (6 gp, 1 a.); 2002-03 Québec (13 gp, 2 a.); 2003-04 (13 gp, 2 a.).

SARGEANT, AMANDA
Forward. 1998 Nationals New Westminster (5 gp, 2 g.); 1999 Nationals (5 gp, 2 g.).

SARGAENT, LILY
Forward. 2009-10 CWHL Montréal #24 (30 games, 5 assists).

SARRAILLON, AMBER
F. 2000 Nationals Manitoba (5 gp, 3 pts); 2001 Nationals; 2002 Nationals (5 gp, 2 pts).

SATO, MASAKO
Forward. #21.

Born 1987-11-27, Yazu, JPN.

Year - League - Team			GP	G	A	PTS	PM
1998-99	NWHL	Mistral de Laval	20	6	5	11	4
1999-00	NWHL	Mistral de Laval	35	13	12	25	10
2000-01	NWHL	Mistral de Laval	22	5	11	16	8
Totals from all Competitions			**77**	**24**	**28**	**52**	**22**

SATO, RIE
Defence. #91.

Born 1972-01-31.

Year - League - Team			GP	G	A	PTS	PM
1998-99	NWHL	Mistral de Laval	20	0	0	0	2
1999-00	NWHL	Mistral de Laval	34	1	2	3	2
Totals from all Competitions			**54**	**1**	**2**	**3**	**4**

SAULNIER, JILLIAN   *Forward. Shoots left. #27.*

Clarkson Cup winner with Calgary on 2016-03-14
Born 1992-03-07, Halifax, NS, CAN. 5'5". Debut at age 23 on 2015-10-24.

Year - League - Team		GP	G	A	PTS	PM	Year - Playoff	GP	G	A	PTS	PM
2007	Nationals Nova Scotia Selects	7	0	0	0	0						
2015-16	CWHL Calgary Inferno	22	12	10	22	16	2016 C-Cup	3	1	3	4	0
2016-17	CWHL Calgary Inferno	20	11	7	18	12	2017 C-Cup	4	1	1	2	6
2018-19	CWHL Canadiennes de Montréal	20	11	18	29	12	2019 C-Cup	4	1	4	5	6
CWHL Regular Season		62	34	35	69	40	Clarkson Cup	11	3	8	11	12
Totals from all Competitions		**80**	**37**	**43**	**80**	**52**						

CWHL First All-Star Team in 2015-16... CWHL All-Rookie Team in 2015-16... finished 7th in the Angela James Bowl scoring race in 2018-19.

SAUNDERS, CHELSEY   *Right wing. Shoots left. #4.*

Born 1991-09-19. Grew up in Ottawa, ON, CAN. 5'6". Debut at age 23 on 2014-10-24.

Year - League - Team		GP	G	A	PTS	PM	Year - Playoff	GP	G	A	PTS	PM
2014-15	CWHL Stars de Montréal	19	1	2	3	0	2015 C-Cup	3	0	0	0	0
2015-16	CWHL Canadiennes de Montréal	22	0	5	5	4	2016 C-Cup	3	0	0	0	0
CWHL Regular Season		41	1	7	8	4	Clarkson Cup	6	0	0	0	0
Totals from all Competitions		**47**	**1**	**7**	**8**	**4**						

SAUNDERS, MICHELLE   *Forward. Shoots left. #5.*

Born 1992-01-22. Grew up in Oakville, ON, CAN. Debut at age 23 on 2015-10-24.

Year - League - Team		GP	G	A	PTS	PM	Year - Playoff	GP	G	A	PTS	PM
2015-16	CWHL Toronto Furies	19	0	1	1	16	2016 C-Cup	2	0	0	0	0
2016-17	CWHL Toronto Furies	15	0	2	2	35	2017 C-Cup	3	0	0	0	0
2017-18	CWHL Toronto Furies	26	1	2	3	47						
CWHL Regular Season		60	1	5	6	98	Clarkson Cup	5	0	0	0	0
Totals from all Competitions		**65**	**1**	**5**	**6**	**98**						

SAUNDERS, MICHELLE   *#12 #9 #17.*

Year - League - Team		GP	G	A	PTS	PM
1992-93	COWHL Scarborough Sting	29	4	5	9	26
1993-94	COWHL Scarborough Sting	29	3	4	7	18
2000-01	NWHL Toronto Sting	4	0	0	0	2
Totals from all Competitions		**62**	**7**	**9**	**16**	**46**

SAUVE, MELANIE   *1996-97 COWHL London Devilettes #54 (2 games).*

SAVAGE, PAIGE   *Forward. Shoots left. #27.*

Born 1994-07-25. Grew up in John Creek, GA, USA. 5'8". Debut at age 23 on 2017-11-11.

Year - League - Team		GP	G	A	PTS	PM
2017-18	NWHL/ Connecticut Whale	5	0	0	0	0

SAVARD, JULIE   *Centre. 1998-99 NWHL Ottawa (30 gp, 3 goals, 4 assists); 2000-01 (15 gp, 1 goal, 2 assists).*

SAVILLE, JEANINE   *Forward. 1999 Nationals New Westminster Lightning (5 games).*

SAVOIE, JOSÉE   *F. 1998 Nationals Maritime (6 gp); 2000 Nationals New Brunswick (6 gp, 1 a.); 2001 Nationals.*

SAWCHUK, COURTNEY   *Defence/Forward. Shoots left. #17.*

Born 1988-10-30, Sherwood Park, AB, CAN. 5'5".

Year - League - Team		GP	G	A	PTS	PM	Year - Playoff	GP	G	A	PTS	PM
2004	Nationals Edmonton Chimos	7	0	1	1	4						
2004-05	WWHL Edmonton Chimos	21	6	3	9	16	2005 WWHL-P	3	1	0	1	2
2005-06	WWHL Edmonton Chimos	22	8	11	19	39	2006 WWHL-P	2	0	0	0	2
2010-11	WWHL Edmonton Chimos	16	2	12	14	22						
2011-12	CWHL Alberta	15	1	1	2	14						
Totals from all Competitions		**86**	**18**	**28**	**46**	**99**						

SCACE, LIZ   *1998-99 NWHL Brampton Thunder #88 (1 game).*

SCAMURRA, HAYLEY   *Forward. Shoots left. #14.*

IIHF champion. Isobel Cup winner with Buffalo on 2017-03-19
Born 1994-12-14. Grew up in Williamsville, NY, USA. 5'8". Debut at age 22 on 2017-03-12.

Year - League - Team		GP	G	A	PTS	PM	Year - Playoff	GP	G	A	PTS	PM
2016-17	NWHL/ Buffalo Beauts	1	1	0	1	0	2017 I-Cup	2	1	3	4	0
2017-18	NWHL/ Buffalo Beauts	14	7	7	14	16	2018 I-Cup	2	0	1	1	2
2018-19	NWHL/ Buffalo Beauts	16	10	10	20	12	2019 I-Cup	2	0	2	2	0
NWHL Regular Season		31	18	17	35	28	Isobel Cup	6	1	6	7	2

NWHL Scoring Champion in 2018-19... NWHL Rookie of the Year in 2017-18... NWHL Fans' Three Stars Award in 2017-18

SCANZANO, JESSE   *Forward. Shoots right. #23 #15 #11 #10.*

NWHL winner. Born 1988-10-15, Montréal, QC, CAN. Grew up in Montréal, QC, CAN. 6'0".

Year - League - Team		GP	G	A	PTS	PM	Year - Playoff	GP	G	A	PTS	PM
2004-05	NWHL Axion de Montréal	18	5	4	9	26	2005 NWHL-P					
2005-06	NWHL Axion de Montréal	36	13	22	35	106	2006 NWHL-P	3	0	0	0	0
2006	Nationals Axion de Montréal	6	2	5	7	8						
2006-07	NWHL Axion de Montréal	35	22	15	37	52	2007 NWHL-P					

Year - League - Team			GP	G	A	PTS	PM	Year - Playoff	GP	G	A	PTS	PM
2011-12	CWHL	Toronto Furies	26	5	12	17	34	2012 C-Cup	3	0	2	2	0
2012-13	CWHL	Stars de Montréal	2	0	0	0	2						
2014-15	CWHL	Brampton Thunder	20	4	5	9	40						
2015-16	CWHL	Brampton Thunder	4	0	0	0	2						
CWHL Regular Season			52	9	17	26	78	Clarkson Cup	3	0	2	2	0
Totals from all Competitions			**153**	**51**	**65**	**116**	**270**						

SCARLETT, DANIELLE   *Burlington, ON. 2008-09 CWHL Mississauga #24 (1 game).*

SCHABKER, VANESSA   *Etobicoke, ON. 2005-06 NWHL Brampton #17 (1 gp); 2007-08 CWHL Montréal (1 gp).*

SCHADE, KELSEY   *Forward. 2010-11 WWHL Manitoba Maple Leafs #8 (3 games).*

SCHARFE, MARGOT   *Toronto. F. 2009-10 CWHL Mississauga (3 gp, 1 assist); 2015-16 NWHL New York (5 gp).*

SCHATZ, CARLA   *Forward. 1995 Nationals Regina Sharks; 1996 Nationals Saskatchewan (5 games).*

SCHEIBEL, CAROL   *Defence.*
Abby Hoffman Cup winner with Edmonton on 1997-03-09. Abby Hoffman Cup winner with Calgary on 1998-03-22 and 2001-03-11.
Born 1977-04-04. 5'6".

Year - League - Team			GP	G	A	PTS	PM
1997	Nationals	Edmonton Chimos					
1998	Nationals	Calgary Oval X-Treme	5	2	3	5	2
2000	Nationals	Calgary Oval X-Treme	7	0	2	2	
2001	Nationals	Calgary Oval X-Treme					

SCHERER, SUE   *Defence.*
Abby Hoffman Cup winner with Aeros on 1991-03-17.

SCHERPENBERG, MARY   *F. 1996-97 COWHL Newtonbrook Panthers #39 (1 gp, 1 goal, 1 assist).*

SCHILLING, JESSICA   *2000-01 NWHL Brampton Thunder (2 games).*

SCHIPPER, KATE   *Forward. Shoots right. #6.*
Isobel Cup winner with Minnesota on 2019-03-17.
Born 1995-06-28. Grew up in Brooklyn Park, MN, USA. Debut at age 23 on 2018-10-06.

Year - League - Team			GP	G	A	PTS	PM	Year - Playoff	GP	G	A	PTS	PM
2018-19	NWHL/	Minnesota Whitecaps	16	5	6	11	6	2019 I-Cup	2	0	1	1	2

SCHLAGAL, AMY   *Defence. Shoots left. #18.*
Born 1996-04-13. Grew up in Blaine, MN, USA. 5'7". Debut at age 22 on 2018-10-06.

Year - League - Team			GP	G	A	PTS	PM
2018-19	NWHL/	Minnesota Whitecaps	12	2	1	3	14

SCHLEPER, ANNE   *Defence. Shoots left. #15.*
IIHF champion. Clarkson Cup winner with Boston on 2013-03-23
Born 1990-1-30, St. Cloud, MN, USA. 5'10". Debut at age 23 on 2012-10-20.

Year - League - Team			GP	G	A	PTS	PM	Year - Playoff	GP	G	A	PTS	PM
2012-13	CWHL	Boston Blades	24	2	13	15	40	2013 C-Cup	4	0	1	1	4
2016-17	NWHL/	Buffalo Beauts	6	0	1	1	2						

CWHL All-Rookie Team in 2012-13... finished 19th in the Angela James Bowl scoring race in 2012-13

SCHMID, HAYLEA   *Forward. Shoots right. #91.*
Born 1990-09-10. Grew up in Oak Grove, MN, USA. 5'7". Debut at age 28 on 2018-10-07.

Year - League - Team			GP	G	A	PTS	PM
2018-19	NWHL/	Minnesota Whitecaps	6	0	1	1	2

SCHMIDT, SHERRI   *Defence. 2000 Nationals Britannia (5 gp, 1 assist); 2001 Nationals Vancouver Griffins.*

SCHNELL, AMANDA   *Defence. Shoots left.*
Born 1983-09-09. Sanford, MB, CAN.

Year - League - Team			GP	G	A	PTS	PM
2000	Nationals	University of Manitoba	5	0	0	0	
2001	Nationals	University of Manitoba					
2002	Nationals	University of Manitoba	5	0	0	0	2
2003	Nationals	University of Winnipeg	4	0	0	0	2
2004	Nationals	Manitoba	5	0	2	2	0

SCHNICKEL, JENNY   *Defence. Shoots left. #12.*
Born 1983-6-15, Coon Rapids, MN, USA. 5'9".

Year - League - Team			GP	G	A	PTS	PM	Year - Playoff	GP	G	A	PTS	PM
2005-06	WWHL	Minnesota Whitecaps	22	5	9	14	40	2006 WWHL-P	3	0	2	2	6
2006-07	WWHL	Minnesota Whitecaps	21	2	5	7	32	2007 WWHL-P	3	0	0	0	2
2007-08	WWHL	Minnesota Whitecaps	21	2	1	3	26						
2008	Nationals	Minnesota Whitecaps	3	0	1	1	0						
2008-09	WWHL	Minnesota Whitecaps	10	0	4	4	12	2009 WWHL-P	0	0	0	0	0
2009-10	WWHL	Minnesota Whitecaps	8	0	2	2	6						
2010-11	WWHL	Minnesota Whitecaps	13	1	9	10	2	2011 C-Cup	3	0	0	0	0
Totals from all Competitions			**107**	**10**	**33**	**43**	**126**						

SCHOLS, ASHLEIGH
Forward. #88 #16.

Born 1986-12-12, Edmonton, AB, CAN.

Year - League - Team			GP	G	A	PTS	PM	Year - Playoff		GP	G	A	PTS	PM
2002-03	NWHL	Edmonton Chimos	24	2	2	4	28							
2003-04	NWHL	Edmonton Chimos	11	0	0	0	10	2004	NWHL-P					
2004	Nationals	Edmonton Chimos	7	0	1	1	6							
2005-06	WWHL	Edmonton Chimos	24	4	14	18	24	2006	WWHL-P	2	0	1	1	0
2006-07	WWHL	Edmonton Chimos	24	7	11	18	40	2007	WWHL-P	2	1	0	1	4
2008-09	WWHL	Edmonton Chimos	16	1	3	4	10							
Totals from all Competitions			**110**	**15**	**32**	**47**	**122**							

SCHOLS, CASSEA
Defence. Shoots right. #88.

Born 1989-9-27, Edmonton, AB, CAN. 5'9".

Year - League - Team			GP	G	A	PTS	PM	Year - Playoff		GP	G	A	PTS	PM
2004-05	WWHL	Edmonton Chimos	21	1	5	6	20	2005	WWHL-P	3	0	0	0	0
2005-06	WWHL	Edmonton Chimos	24	2	9	11	16	2006	WWHL-P	2	0	1	1	0
2006-07	WWHL	Edmonton Chimos	23	3	9	12	32	2007	WWHL-P	0	0	0	0	0
Totals from all Competitions			**73**	**6**	**24**	**30**	**68**							

SCHOULLIS, JEN
Forward. Shoots left. #30 #23.

Clarkson Cup winner with Boston on 2013-03-23
Born 1989-3-7, Erie, PA, USA. Grew up in Erie, PA, USA. 5'9". Debut at age 24 on 2012-10-28.

Year - League - Team			GP	G	A	PTS	PM	Year - Playoff		GP	G	A	PTS	PM
2012-13	CWHL	Boston Blades	14	5	3	8	2	2013	C-Cup	4	2	0	2	4

SCHRIVER, COURTNEY
Forward. Shoots left. 2002 Nationals Nova Scotia Selects (5 games, 2 goals, 1 assist).

SCHROEDER, TEGAN
Defence. Shoots right. #28.

Born 1988-04-25. Grew up in Lumsden, SK, CAN. 5'6". Debut at age 25 on 2013-11-09.

Year - League - Team			GP	G	A	PTS	PM	Year - Playoff		GP	G	A	PTS	PM
2013-14	CWHL	Calgary Inferno	24	1	9	10	8	2014	C-Cup	3	1	0	1	0
2014-15	CWHL	Calgary Inferno	21	2	2	4	10	2015	C-Cup	2	0	0	0	2
CWHL Regular Season			45	3	11	14	18	Clarkson Cup		5	1	0	1	2
Totals from all Competitions			**50**	**4**	**11**	**15**	**20**							

SCHROKA, KAYLA
Forward. Shoots right. #19.

Born 1994-11-06. Grew up in Belleville, MI, USA. 5'7". Debut at age 22 on 2017-10-28.

Year - League - Team			GP	G	A	PTS	PM	Year - Playoff	GP	G	A	PTS	PM
2017-18	NWHL/	Buffalo Beauts	14	4	6	10	0	2018 I-Cup	2	0	0	0	2

SCHULER, JEN
F. 1993-94 COWHL Hamilton #44 (8 gp, 2 a.); 1997-98 Scarborough #22 (15 gp, 2 goals, 2 a.).

SCHULER, LAURA
Forward. #14 #27.

IIHF champion. Born 1970-12-3. Grew up in Scarborough, ON, CAN.

Year - League - Team			GP	G	A	PTS	PM
1993-94	COWHL	Scarborough Firefighters	14	9	7	16	38
1995-96	COWHL	Toronto Red Wings	16	6	11	17	12
1996	Nationals	North York Aeros	5	3	6	9	4
1996-97	COWHL	Newtonbrook Panthers	19	16	16	32	26
1998-99	NWHL	Brampton Thunder	14	6	10	16	10
1999-00	NWHL	Brampton Thunder	25	9	9	18	41
2000-01	NWHL	Brampton Thunder	29	15	22	37	32
Totals from all Competitions			**122**	**64**	**81**	**145**	**163**

SCHURMAN, CHERYL
Forward. 1996 Nationals PEI Esso Tigers (4 games).

SCHWARTZ, BLAIRE
Defence. 2003 Nationals Host Saskatchewan (5 games).

SCHWARZ, HEATHER
Forward. Shoots right. #37.

Born 1994-11-09. Grew up in Naugatuck, CT, USA. 5'7". Debut at age 22 on 2017-10-28.

Year - League - Team			GP	G	A	PTS	PM	Year - Playoff	GP	G	A	PTS	PM
2017-18	NWHL/	Boston Pride	16	1	1	2	4	2018 I-Cup	1	0	2	2	0

SCHWENZFEIER, SARAH
Forward. Shoots right. #19.

Born 1995-01-31. Grew up in Hingham, MA, USA. 5'5". Debut at age 23 on 2018-10-07.

Year - League - Team			GP	G	A	PTS	PM
2018-19	NWHL/	Connecticut Whale	4	0	0	0	0

SCOTT, JENNIFER
Defence. #73.

Year - League - Team			GP	G	A	PTS	PM
2003-04	NWHL	Durham Lightning	31	6	2	8	117
2004-05	NWHL	Durham Lightning	28	1	0	1	40
Totals from all Competitions			**59**	**7**	**2**	**9**	**157**

SCOTT, SANDRA
Forward. 1995 Nationals Calgary Classics.

SCRIVANICH, HEIDI
Forward. #9.

Year - League - Team			GP	G	A	PTS	PM
1995-96	COWHL	Peterborough Skyway	30	22	9	31	20
1996-97	COWHL	Peterborough Pirates	35	16	10	26	30
Totals from all Competitions			**65**	**38**	**19**	**57**	**50**

SCULLY, NATALIE	Defence. 2006 Nationals Nova Scotia Selects (5 games, 2 assists).
SEAMAN, SHELLEY	1995-96 COWHL London Devilettes #7 (26 games, 2 goals, 3 assists).
SEAWARD, TRINA	Forward/Defence. 2001 Nationals Newfoundland Labrador.
SEAWARD, TRULA	Forward/Defence. 2001 Nationals Newfoundland Labrador.
SEARS, WHITNEY	Defence. 2012-13 CWHL Alberta #15 (1 game).
SEATON, BRET	2010-11 WWHL Strathmore Rockies #16 (9 games, 1 assist).
SEEBOLD, JILL	Defence. 2002 Nationals Nova Scotia Selects (5 games).

SEEDHOUSE, ELLIE — Forward. Shoots left. #44.

Clarkson Cup winner with Markham on 2018-03-25
Born 1989-03-10. Grew up in Whitby, ON, CAN. 5'9". Debut at age 25 on 2014-10-19.

Year - League - Team		GP	G	A	PTS	PM	Year - Playoff	GP	G	A	PTS	PM
2014-15	CWHL Brampton Thunder	24	4	4	6	12						
2015-16	CWHL Brampton Thunder	12	1	1	2	2	2016 C-Cup	1	0	0	0	0
2017-18	CWHL Markham Thunder	16	1	2	3	0	2018 C-Cup	0	0	0	0	0
2018-19	CWHL Markham Thunder	2	0	0	0	0						
CWHL Regular Season		54	5	6	11	14	Clarkson Cup	1	0	0	0	0

SÉGUIN, AUDREY — Defence. Shoots left. #22.

Born 1985-7-20, Pointe-Claire, QC, CAN. 5'2". Debut at age 20 on 2005-09-25.

Year - League - Team		GP	G	A	PTS	PM	Year - Playoff	GP	G	A	PTS	PM
2005-06	NWHL Avalanche du Québec	35	0	7	7	22						
2006-07	NWHL Avalanche du Québec	29	3	9	12	50	2007 NWHL-P					
2007-08	CWHL Phénix du Québec	27	1	2	3	38						
CWHL Regular Season		27	1	2	3	38						
Totals from all Competitions		**91**	**4**	**18**	**22**	**110**						

| SEILER, SARA | Miesbach, GER. Forward. 2006-07 NWHL Ottawa #17 (32 gp, 5 a.; 2 playoff gp, 1 a.). |

SEKELA, CARRIE — Defence. #3 #33.

Year - League - Team		GP	G	A	PTS	PM
1995-96	COWHL Toronto Red Wings	29	1	10	11	20
1996-97	COWHL Newtonbrook Panthers	30	3	15	18	26
Totals from all Competitions		**59**	**4**	**25**	**29**	**46**

SELINA, BRITNEY	F. 2011-12 CWHL Brampton (27 gp, 4 goals, 8 assists; C-Cup 4 gp); 2012-13 (1 gp).
SELINGER, KATARINA	Defence. 2009-10 CWHL Burlington #15 (1 game).
SÉNECAL, KARINE	Defence. 2000-01 NWHL Laval (11 gp); 2002-03 Montréal (26 gp, 2 goals, 3 a.).
SENUK, LACEY	Defence. 2005 Nationals Alberta (6 games).
SETCHELL, CHERYL	Defence. 2000 Nationals Nova Scotia Selects (6 gp, 3 pts); 2001 Nationals Nova Scotia.

SGOIFO, LISA — Forward. Shoots left. #37.

Born 1983-1-25, Sudbury, ON, CAN. 5'5". Debut at age 24 on 2006-9-16.

Year - League - Team		GP	G	A	PTS	PM	Year - Playoff	GP	G	A	PTS	PM
2006-07	NWHL Ottawa Raiders	31	0	1	1	30	2007 NWHL-P	2	0	0	0	2
2007-08	CWHL Ottawa Capital Canucks	14	0	0	0	14						

| SHARKO, SHERILEE | Forward. 2004-05 WWHL Edmonton Chimos #22 (21 gp, 5 goals, 2 assists; playoff 3 gp). |
| SHARP, SARA | F. 2005-06 WWHL Calgary (24 gp, 5 goals, 10 a.; playoff 3 gp, 1 goal). |

SHARP, SARA — Forward. Shoots left.

Born 1988-09-26.

Year - League - Team		GP	G	A	PTS	PM	Year - Playoff	GP	G	A	PTS	PM
2005-06	WWHL Calgary Oval X-Treme	24	5	10	15	24	2006 NWHL-P	3	1	0	1	2
2006	Nationals Calgary Oval X-Treme	7	0	0	0	2						

SHAW, AMANDA — Defence. Shoots left. #25 #4.

Born 1987-5-12, St. Thomas, ON, CAN. 5'9". Debut at age 23 on 2010-10-23.

Year - League - Team		GP	G	A	PTS	PM	Year - Playoff	GP	G	A	PTS	PM
2010-11	CWHL Burlington Barracudas	23	0	1	1	16						
2011-12	CWHL Burlington Barracudas	25	0	4	4	22						
2012-13	CWHL Toronto Furies	15	0	1	1	16	2013 C-Cup	2	0	0	0	0
CWHL Regular Season		63	0	6	6	54	Clarkson Cup	2	0	0	0	0

| SHAW, ANNE | Forward. 2005 Nationals Prince Edward Island (5 gp, 1 goal); 2006 Nationals (5 gp, 2 goals). |

SHAW, ROBYN — Forward. #98 #19 #64.

Born 1983-1-26. Grew up in Brampton, ON, CAN.

Year - League - Team		GP	G	A	PTS	PM
1999-00	NWHL Brampton Thunder	2	0	0	0	0
2003-04	NWHL Durham Lightning	29	1	4	5	20
2007-08	CWHL Vaughan Flames	2	0	3	3	0
Totals from all Competitions		**33**	**1**	**7**	**8**	**20**

| SHEA, MEGAN | Forward. 2015-16 CWHL Boston Blades #23 (24 gp, 3 goals, 1 assist). |
| SHEA, ROBYN | Forward. 2000 Nationals Newfoundland Labrador (5 gp, 1 a.); 2001 Nationals Newfoundland. |

SHEARER, LAURA D. 2004 Nationals Nova Scotia (5 gp, 1 g.); 2006 Nationals (5 gp, 5 pts); 2008 Nationals (5 gp).

SHEARS, CATHERINE F. 2002 Nationals Newfoundland (5 gp); 2004 Nationals (5 gp, 7 pts); 2005 Nationals (5 gp).

SHEERAN, MELISSA   Forward. Shoots left. #20.
Born 1994-11-21. Grew up in Schagticoke, NY, USA. 5'2". Debut at age 23 on 2018-10-07.

Year - League - Team	GP	G	A	PTS	PM
2018-19 NWHL/ Connecticut Whale	2	0	0	0	2

SHERMAN, CASSANDRA   Centre. Shoots right. #9.
Born 1994-04-12. Grew up in North Smithfield, RI, USA. 5'1". Debut at age 23 on 2017-10-14.

Year - League - Team	GP	G	A	PTS	PM
2017-18 CWHL Boston Blades	13	0	0	0	6

SHERRARD, ALYSSA   Forward. Shoots left. #11.
Clarkson Cup winner with Montréal on 2017-03-05
Born 1992-06-26. Grew up in Bathurst, NB, CAN. 5'3". Debut at age 23 on 2015-10-17.

Year - League - Team	GP	G	A	PTS	PM	Year - Playoff	GP	G	A	PTS	PM
2015-16 CWHL Canadiennes de Montréal	20	1	2	3	8	2016 C-Cup	3	0	0	0	0
2016-17 CWHL Canadiennes de Montréal	12	0	0	0	0	2017 C-Cup	2	0	0	0	0
CWHL Regular Season	32	1	2	3	8	Clarkson Cup	5	0	0	0	0

SHERVEN, KRISTA   Forward. 2007-08 WWHL Strathmore Rockies #9 (23 games, 3 goals, 6 assists).

SHEWCHUK, TAMMY LEE   1997 Nationals Équipe Québec.

SHIELDS, KARLEE   Forward. 2007 Nationals Team New Brunswick (6 gp, 1 assist).

SHILLINGTON, KIMBERLY   Defence. #6.

Year - League - Team	GP	G	A	PTS	PM
1995-96 COWHL London Devilettes	28	1	4	5	2
1996-97 COWHL London Devilettes	25	1	5	6	8
Totals from all Competitions	**53**	**2**	**9**	**11**	**10**

SHIRLEY, SAMANTHA   Forward. Shoots right. #7 #71 #27.
Born 1983-5-2, Toronto, ON, CAN. Grew up in Mississauga, ON, CAN. 5'9".

Year - League - Team	GP	G	A	PTS	PM	Year - Playoff	GP	G	A	PTS	PM
2001-02 NWHL Mississauga IceBears	1	0	0	0	0						
2007-08 CWHL Vaughan Flames	19	4	6	10	20	2008 CWHL-P	2	2	0	2	2
2008-09 CWHL Vaughan Flames	26	6	7	13	28	2009 CWHL-P	2	1		1	4
2009-10 CWHL Vaughan Flames	26	4	9	13	24						
2010-11 CWHL Burlington Barracudas	24	4	11	15	6						
2011-12 CWHL Burlington Barracudas	26	7	4	11	14						
CWHL Regular Season	121	25	37	62	92						
Totals from all Competitions	**126**	**28**	**37**	**65**	**98**						

SHIRLEY, SOPHIE   Forward. Shoots right. #16.
Born 1999-10-20. Grew up in Saskatoon, SK, CAN. Debut at age 18 on 2017-10-21.

Year - League - Team	GP	G	A	PTS	PM	Year - Playoff	GP	G	A	PTS	PM
2017-18 CWHL Calgary Inferno	26	8	11	19	24	2018 C-Cup	3	0	0	0	4

CWHL Second All-Star Team in 2017-18... CWHL Outstanding Rookie in 2017-18... CWHL All-Rookie Team in 2017-18... finished 20th in the Angela James Bowl scoring race in 2017-18

SHOLZ, NANCY   Defence.
Abby Hoffman Cup winner with Calgary on 1998-03-22.

Year - League - Team	GP	G	A	PTS	PM
1998 Nationals Calgary Oval X-Treme	7	0	0	0	0

SHORT, SIMONE   Defence. 2002 Nationals Newfoundland (5 gp); 2004 Nationals (5 gp, 1 assist).

SHRIVER, COURTNEY   Forward. 2006 Nationals Nova Scotia (5 games, 2 goals, 1 assist).

SHUPAK, LORI   Forward. #18 #25.
Born 1980-8-22. F. Debut at age 26 on 2007-01-05.

Year - League - Team	GP	G	A	PTS	PM	Year - Playoff	GP	G	A	PTS	PM
2006-07 WWHL Edmonton Chimos	2	0	0	0	0	2007 WWHL-P	0	0	0	0	0
2007-08 WWHL Edmonton Chimos	19	9	10	19	4						
2008-09 WWHL Edmonton Chimos	1	0	0	0	0						

SHUREB, SARAH   Defence. Shoots right. #5.
Born 1995-06-20. Grew up in Livonia, MI, USA. Debut at age 22 on 2017-10-28.

Year - League - Team	GP	G	A	PTS	PM
2017-18 NWHL/ Buffalo Beauts	8	1	0	1	0

SIBLEY, JESSICA   Forward. Shoots left. #6.
Born 1995-07-10. Grew up in Luseland, SK, CAN.

Year - League - Team	GP	G	A	PTS	PM
2017-18 NWHL/ Buffalo Beauts	2	0	0	0	0

SILLJER, BOBBIE   Defence. Shoots right.
Born 1983-01-27. Outlook, SK, CAN.

Year - League - Team			GP	G	A	PTS	PM
1999	Nationals	Saskatchewan Selects	4	0	1	1	
2000	Nationals	Saskatchewan Selects	7	0	1	1	
2002	Nationals	Calgary Oval X-Treme	6	2	0	2	2

SILVEIRA, JESSICA — *Brampton, ON. F. 2009-10 CWHL Brampton #17 (1 game, 1 goal).*

SIMARD, MÉLISSA — *2001-02 NWHL Cheyenne (29 gp, 1 goal, 2 assists); 2002-03 Québec (16 gp).*

SIMMONDS, DANIA — *Defence. Shoots left. #19.*
Clarkson Cup winner with Markham on 2018-03-25
Born 1990-1-18. Grew up in Aurora, ON, CAN. 5'8". Debut at age 22 on 2012-10-20.

Year - League - Team			GP	G	A	PTS	PM	Year - Playoff		GP	G	A	PTS	PM
2012-13	CWHL	Brampton Thunder	24	0	2	2	20	2013	C-Cup	3	0	0	0	2
2013-14	CWHL	Brampton Thunder	24	0	1	1	30							
2014-15	CWHL	Brampton Thunder	24	0	4	4	20							
2015-16	CWHL	Brampton Thunder	24	2	1	3	28	2016	C-Cup	2	0	0	0	0
2016-17	CWHL	Brampton Thunder	24	0	4	4	10	2017	C-Cup	2	0	1	1	12
2017-18	CWHL	Markham Thunder	28	2	8	10	12	2018	C-Cup	3	0	0	0	2
2018-19	CWHL	Markham Thunder	2	0	0	0	0							
CWHL Regular Season			150	4	20	24	120	Clarkson Cup		10	0	1	1	16

SIMOURD, AMANDA — *2007-08 CWHL Ottawa Senators #20 (1 game).*

SIMPSON, AMY — *Forward. 2002 Nationals Nova Scotia (5 gp).*

SIMPSON, BECKY — *2007-08 CWHL Burlington Barracudas #12 (1 game).*

SIMPSON, BRITTANY — *Defence. Shoots right. #26.*
Born 1987-1-4. Grew up in Barrie, ON, CAN. 5'6". Debut at age 24 on 2010-10-30.

Year - League - Team			GP	G	A	PTS	PM	Year - Playoff		GP	G	A	PTS	PM
2010-11	CWHL	Boston Blades	16	2	3	5	6	2011	CWHL-P	2				
2011-12	CWHL	Boston Blades	24	3	4	7	18	2012	C-Cup	1	0	0	0	0
CWHL Regular Season			40	5	7	12	24	Clarkson Cup		1	0	0	0	0

SIMPSON, CARLY — *1999-00 NWHL Brampton Thunder #91 (1 game).*

SINCERNY, JOSÉE — *1998-99 NWHL Montréal (32 gp, 2 goals, 8 a.); 1999-00 NWHL Sainte-Julie (3 gp, 1 goal, 1 a.).*

SINCLAIR, CARRIE — *Forward. 2005 Nationals Manitoba (5 games).*

SINCLAIR, VICTORIA — *Forward. 2005 Nationals Manitoba (5 games).*

SINGH, JESSICA — *1999-00 NWHL Ottawa (4 gp, 1 goal, 1 a.); 2000-01 (37 gp, 4 goal, 14 a.).*

SINOW, KIRA — *Defence. 2000 Nationals Britannia (5 gp, 1 assists); 2001 Nationals Vancouver Griffins.*

SISK, SHANNON — *Forward. Shoots right. #7.*
Born 1987-5-29, Mercer, NJ, USA. Grew up in Plumsteadville, PA, USA. 5'9". Debut at age 23 on 2010-10-30.

Year - League - Team		GP	G	A	PTS	PM	Year - Playoff		GP	G	A	PTS	PM
2010-11	CWHL Boston Blades	22	2	3	5	4	2011	CWHL-P	2				
2011-12	CWHL Boston Blades	24	4	0	4	6	2012	C-Cup	3	1	1	2	4
CWHL Regular Season		46	6	3	9	10	Clarkson Cup		3	1	1	2	4

SITTLER, MEAGHAN — *Forward. Shoots left. #10 #72.*
Born 1976-3-12. Grew up in East Amherst, NY, USA.

Year - League - Team			GP	G	A	PTS	PM	Year - Playoff		GP	G	A	PTS	PM
1999-00	NWHL	Brampton Thunder	16	13	12	25	4							
2000-01	NWHL	Brampton Thunder	29	11	12	23	8							
2001-02	NWHL	Brampton Thunder	6	1	3	4	0							
2002	Nationals	Brampton Thunder	7	0	0	0	0							
2002-03	NWHL	Brampton Thunder						2003	NWHL-P					
2003	Nationals	Brampton Thunder	5	2	4	6	0							
2003-04	NWHL	Brampton Thunder	33	12	27	39	4	2004	NWHL-P	5	3	4	7	2
Totals from all Competitions			**101**	**42**	**62**	**104**	**18**							

SJOGREN, JARIN — *Forward.*

Year - League - Team			GP	G	A	PTS	PM
1998	Nationals	Saskatchewan Selects	6	0	0	0	8
1999	Nationals	Calgary Oval X-Treme	6	1	0	1	
2000	Nationals	Calgary Oval X-Treme	7	1	0	1	

SKARUPA, HALEY — *Forward. Shoots right. #22.*
Olympic champion, IIHF champion.
Born 1994-01-03. Grew up in Rockville, MD, USA. 5'6". Debut at age 22 on 2016-10-09.

Year - League - Team			GP	G	A	PTS	PM	Year - Playoff		GP	G	A	PTS	PM
2016-17	NWHL/	Connecticut Whale	16	11	11	22	0	2017	I-Cup	1	0	2	2	2
2017-18	NWHL/	Boston Pride	5	2	3	5	2							
2018-19	NWHL/	Boston Pride	13	6	12	18	6	2019	I-Cup	1	0	0	0	0
NWHL Regular Season			34	19	26	45	8	Isobel Cup		2	0	2	2	2

SKEATS, DEVON — *Forward. Shoots left. #21.*
Isobel Cup winner with Buffalo on 2017-03-19 and Clarkson Cup winner with Markham on 2018-03-25
Born 1991-06-12. Grew up in Whitby, ON, CAN. 5'5". Debut at age 24 on 2015-11-15.

Year - League - Team	GP	G	A	PTS	PM	Year - Playoff	GP	G	A	PTS	PM
2015-16 NWHL/ Buffalo Beauts	15	9	5	14	26	2016 I-Cup	5	2	2	4	2
2016-17 NWHL/ Buffalo Beauts	16	4	2	6	26	2017 I-Cup	1	0	0	0	2
2017-18 CWHL Markham Thunder	28	4	2	6	38	2018 C-Cup	3	0	0	0	8
NWHL Regular Season	31	13	7	20	52	Isobel Cup	6	2	2	4	4
CWHL Regular Season	28	4	2	6	38	Clarkson Cup	3	0	0	0	8
Totals from all Competitions	**68**	**19**	**11**	**30**	**102**						

SKIRROW, DANIELLE
Defence. Shoots right. #20.

Born 1991-05-28. Grew up in Trenton, ON, CAN. 5'3". Debut at age 22 on 2013-11-02.

Year - League - Team	GP	G	A	PTS	PM
2013-14 CWHL Brampton Thunder	24	5	10	15	20
2014-15 CWHL Brampton Thunder	22	1	3	4	12
2018-19 CWHL Markham Thunder	1	0	0	0	0
CWHL Regular Season	47	6	13	19	32

CWHL Second All-Star Team in 2013-14... finished 18th in the Angela James Bowl scoring race in 2013-14

SLATTERY, LEXI
Defence. Shoots right. #15.

Born 1994-01-28. Grew up in Hugo, MN, USA. 5'6". Debut at age 24 on 2018-10-07.

Year - League - Team	GP	G	A	PTS	PM	Year - Playoff	GP	G	A	PTS	PM
2018-19 NWHL/ Metropolitan Riveters	6	0	0	0	2	2019 I-Cup	1	0	0	0	0

SLATTERY, LORI-ANN
2003-04 NWHL Ottawa Raiders #17 (1 game).

SLEWIDGE, JENNIFER
Defence. Shoots left. #18 #17 #22.

Born 1984-3-29. Grew up in Carp, ON, CAN. 5'6".

Year - League - Team	GP	G	A	PTS	PM	Year - Playoff	GP	G	A	PTS	PM
2002-03 NWHL Ottawa Raiders	33	1	2	3	18						
2003-04 NWHL Ottawa Raiders	20	3	0	3	16						
2004-05 NWHL Ottawa Raiders	36	0	3	3	34						
2005-06 NWHL Ottawa Raiders	26	1	5	6	16	2006 NWHL-P	0	0	0	0	0
2007-08 CWHL Ottawa Capital Canucks	2	2	0	2	0						
Totals from all Competitions	**117**	**7**	**10**	**17**	**84**						

SLIVINSKI, TRINA
Defence. 2005 Nationals Alberta (6 games).

SLOMINSKI, LAURA
2004-05 WWHL Minnesota #21 (6 gp, 1 goal, 1 assist; playoff 2 gp, 1 goal, 1 assist).

SLUSAR, BOBBI JO
Defence. Shoots left. #11 #14.

CWHL winner. Born 1985-6-6, Swift Current, SK, CAN. 5'4". Debut at age 22 on 2007-11-17.

Year - League - Team	GP	G	A	PTS	PM	Year - Playoff	GP	G	A	PTS	PM
2002 Nationals Saskatchewan	6	0	1	1	4						
2007-08 CWHL Brampton Can.-Thunder	11	2	5	7	0	2008 CWHL-P	3	0	1	1	4
2008 Nationals Brampton Can.-Thunder	3	0	2	2	4						
2008-09 CWHL Brampton Thunder	25	7	15	22	10	2009 CWHL-P	2				
						2009 C-Cup	2	0	2	2	8
2009-10 CWHL Brampton Thunder	13	6	7	13	10	2010 C-Cup	2	1		1	
2010-11 WWHL Strathmore Rockies	6	3	0	3	4						
2011-12 CWHL Alberta	5	0	1	1	8						
2012-13 CWHL Alberta	12	0	0	0	16						
CWHL Regular Season	66	15	28	43	44	Clarkson Cup	4	1	2	3	8
Totals from all Competitions	**90**	**19**	**34**	**53**	**68**						

CWHL Second All-Star Team in 2008-09 and 2009-10... CWHL All-Rookie Team in 2007-08... finished 18th in the Angela James Bowl scoring race in 2008-09

SMALL, JILLIAN
Forward. Shoots left.

Born 1980-07-03. Grew up in Halifax, NS, CAN.

Year - League - Team	GP	G	A	PTS	PM	Year - Playoff	GP	G	A	PTS	PM
1998 Nationals Nova Scotia Selects	5		0	0	0	2					
2000 Nationals Nova Scotia Selects	6		0	0	0						
2001 Nationals Nova Scotia Selects											
2003 Nationals Nova Scotia Selects	6		0	1	1	2					

SMELKER, JORDAN
Left wing. Shoots left. #11.

Clarkson Cup winner with Boston on 2015-03-07 and Isobel Cup winner with Boston on 2016-03-12.

Born 1992-06-19. Grew up in Anchorage, AK, USA. 5'8". Debut at age 22 on 2014-10-18.

Year - League - Team	GP	G	A	PTS	PM	Year - Playoff	GP	G	A	PTS	PM
2014-15 CWHL Boston Blades	22	8	7	15	6	2015 C-Cup	2	0	1	1	0
2015-16 NWHL/ Boston Pride	17	9	10	19	8	2016 I-Cup	4	0	2	2	2
2016-17 NWHL/ Boston Pride	15	3	5	8	8	2017 I-Cup	1	0	0	0	0
2017-18 NWHL/ Boston Pride	14	3	2	5	12	2018 I-Cup	1	0	0	0	0
2018-19 NWHL/ Boston Pride	16	0	5	5	14	2019 I-Cup	1	0	0	0	0
NWHL Regular Season	62	15	22	37	42	Isobel Cup	7	0	2	2	2
Totals from all Competitions	**93**	**23**	**32**	**55**	**50**						

Finished 18th in the Angela James Bowl scoring race in 2014-15

SMILEY, SARAH
Forward. Shoots right.

Born 1982-08-24. Grew up in Toronto, ON, CAN. 5'2".

Year - League - Team			GP	G	A	PTS	PM	Year - Playoff		GP	G	A	PTS	PM
2000-01	NWHL	ClearNet Lightning	1	0	0	0	0							
2005-06	NWHL	Axion de Montréal	35	4	4	8	14	2006	NWHL-P	3	0	0	0	0
2006	Nationals	Axion de Montréal	6	1	1	2	2							

SMITH, AMANDA
Defence. #88 #7.

Year - League - Team			GP	G	A	PTS	PM
1995-96	COWHL	North York Aeros	1	0	0	0	2
1997-98	COWHL	Mississauga Chiefs	19	4	5	9	12
1998-99	NWHL	Mississauga Chiefs	36	9	14	23	32
1999-00	NWHL	Mississauga Chiefs	37	9	17	26	20
Totals from all Competitions			**93**	**22**	**36**	**58**	**66**

SMITH, BRITNI
Defence. Shoots right. #19.

Clarkson Cup winner with Toronto on 2014-03-22
Born 1988-10-13, Port Perry, ON, CAN. 5'10". Debut at age 22 on 2010-10-23.

Year - League - Team			GP	G	A	PTS	PM	Year - Playoff		GP	G	A	PTS	PM
2010-11	CWHL	Toronto Furies	26	7	18	25	18	2011	CWHL-P	2		2	2	4
								2011	C-Cup	4	1	2	3	0
2011-12	CWHL	Toronto Furies	27	5	6	11	18	2012	C-Cup	3	1	1	2	0
2012-13	CWHL	Toronto Furies	23	2	3	5	12	2013	C-Cup	3	0	0	0	0
2013-14	CWHL	Toronto Furies	14	1	7	8	8	2014	C-Cup	4	1	0	1	4
CWHL Regular Season			90	15	34	49	56	Clarkson Cup		14	3	3	6	4
Totals from all Competitions			**106**	**18**	**39**	**57**	**64**							

CWHL Second All-Star Team in 2010-11... CWHL All-Rookie Team in 2010-11... finished 12th in the Angela James Bowl scoring race in 2010-11

SMITH, CHRISTINA
2002-03 NWHL Avalanche du Québec (13 games).

SMITH, DANIKA
2009-10 CWHL Ottawa Senators #3 (17 games, 2 assists).

SMITH, ERIN
Forward. 2005 Nationals Alberta (6 games, 1 assist).

SMITH, JODY
Defence. 1998-99 NWHL Ottawa Raiders #7 (33 games, 2 goals, 8 assists).

SMITH, HEATHER
Defence. 1999 Nationals Prince Edward Island (5 games).

SMITH, KATHLEEN
Defence. 2008-09 CWHL Burlington #6 (25 gp, 6 assists; playoffs 4 go).

SMITH, KELLY
Defence. #10.

Abby Hoffman Cup winner with Aeros on 2000-03-12. NWHL Cup winner.
Born 1983-01-28. Grew up in Winnipeg, MB, CAN.

Year - League - Team			GP	G	A	PTS	PM	Year - Playoff		GP	G	A	PTS	PM
1993-94	COWHL	Toronto Junior Aeros	29	3	7	10	25							
1995-96	COWHL	North York Aeros	26	3	6	9	18							
1996	Nationals	North York Aeros	5	1	1	2	4							
1996-97	COWHL	North York Aeros	33	3	22	25	29							
1997-98	COWHL	North York Aeros	20	6	10	16	28							
1998	Nationals	North York Aeros	6	1	1	2	8							
1998-99	NWHL	North York Aeros	40	4	15	19	28							
1999	Nationals	North York Aeros	5	1	4	5								
1999-00	NWHL	North York Aeros	37	3	18	21	20	2000	NWHL-P					
2000	Nationals	North York Aeros	6	1	1	2								
2000-01	NWHL	North York Aeros	34	3	20	23	28							
2001	Nationals	North York Aeros												
2001-02	NWHL	North York Aeros	27	2	11	13	18	2003	NWHL-P					
2002	Nationals	North York Aeros	7	1	2	3	2							
2003	Nationals	University of Winnipeg	4	0	0	0	4							
Totals from all Competitions			**279**	**32**	**118**	**150**	**212**							

SMITH, MINDY
Calgary, AB. D. 2002-03 NWHL Edmonton Chimos #10 (20 gp, 1 goal, 1 assist).

SMITH, NATALIE
1999-00 NWHL Laval (3 gp); 2000-01 (3 gp, 1 goal); 2001-02 Montréal (30 gp, 2 goals).

SMITH, ROCHELLE
F. 2006 Nationals British Columbia (6 gp, 1 a.); 2007 Nationals BC Outback (5 gp, 2 pts).

SMITH, SARA
2006-07 NWHL Etobicoke #24 (14 games); 2007 Natoinals Etobicoke.

SMITH, SAVANNAH
Forward. 2005 Nationals British Columbia (7 games, 2 goals).

SMITH, STEPHANIE
Defence. 2003 Nationals Newfoundland Labrador (5 gp); 2004 Nationals (5 gp).

SMOLENTSEVA, YEKATERINA
Forward. Shoots left.

Born 1981-09-15. Grew up in Dmitrov, RUS (URS). 5'9". Debut in 2015-16.

Year - League - Team			GP	G	A	PTS	PM	Year - Playoff		GP	G	A	PTS	PM
2015-16	NWHL/	Connecticut Whale	13	3	5	8	2	2016	I-Cup	3	0	0	0	0

SNELL, CARLY
Defence. 2007-08 Ottawa Capital Canucks #23 (17 gp, 2 assists; playoff 1 gp).

SNEYO, SONYA
1993-94 COWHL Hamilton Golden Hawks #15 (8 gp, 1 goal) .

SNIDER, LINDSAY
2001-02 NWHL Brampton Thunder #4 (26 games); 2002 Nationals (7 games).

SNOW, PAM
Defence. 2001 Nationals Newfoundland Labrador.

SNOW, TARA
Defence. 2002 Nationals Newfoundland (5 gp); 2004 Nationals (5 gp, 1 a.); 2005 Nationals (5 gp).

SOBEK, JEANINE
Forward/Defence. Shoots left. #17 #11.

Born 1972-02-22, Coon Rapids, MN, USA. 5'5".

Year - League - Team			GP	G	A	PTS	PM
1995-96	COWHL	Toronto Red Wings	29	12	24	36	12
1996-97	COWHL	Newtonbrook Panthers	11	3	10	13	6
1997-98	COWHL	Mississauga Chiefs	11	4	10	14	2
1998-99	NWHL	Brampton Thunder	40	21	36	57	20
1999-00	NWHL	Brampton Thunder	38	21	27	48	4
2000-01	NWHL	Brampton Thunder	40	11	28	39	14
Totals from all Competitions			**169**	**72**	**135**	**207**	**58**

SOESILO, DENISE
Forward. 2004-05 WWHL Calgary #17 (21 gp, 8 goals, 5 assists, playoff 1 gp).

SOLBERG, KEARSTIN
Riley, AB. Forward. 2006-07 WWHL Minnesota #3 (17 gp, 2 goals, 2 assists).

SOLLOWS, SARAH
Defence. 2003 Nationals New Brunswick (4 gp, 2 g.); 2004 (5 gp, 1 a.); 2005 (6 gp, 2 g.).

SOMERTON, GARLENE
Forward. 2006 Nationals Nova Scotia Selects (4 games, 1 goal, 1 assist).

SORBARA, CHRISTINA
Centre. Shoots right. #7 #17.

Born 1978-05-15.

Year - League - Team			GP	G	A	PTS	PM
1995-96	COWHL	North York Aeros	1	0	0	0	0
2003-04	NWHL	Brampton Thunder	26	5	13	18	10
2004-05	NWHL	Brampton Thunder	27	4	9	13	8
2005	Nationals	Brampton Thunder	6	0	4	4	8
Totals from all Competitions			**60**	**9**	**26**	**35**	**26**

SOSTORICS, COLLEEN
Defence. Shoots right. #5.

Olympic champion, IIHF champion. Abby Hoffman Cup winner with Calgary on 2008-03-22, 2001-03-11, 2003-03-16 and 2007-03-10. WWHL winner.

Born 1979-12-17, Kennedy, SK, CAN. 5'4".

Year - League - Team			GP	G	A	PTS	PM	Year - Playoff		GP	G	A	PTS	PM
1998	Nationals	Calgary Oval X-Treme	7	1	2	3	4							
1999	Nationals	Calgary Oval X-Treme	6		1	1								
2000	Nationals	Calgary Oval X-Treme	7	1	2	3								
2001	Nationals	Calgary Oval X-Treme												
2002-03	NWHL	Calgary Oval X-Treme	16	5	13	18	32	2003	NWHL-P					
2003	Nationals	Calgary Oval X-Treme	5	2	1	3	10							
2003-04	NWHL	Calgary Oval X-Treme	6	5	5	10	2	2004	NWHL-P	2	0	0	0	0
2004	Nationals	Calgary Oval X-Treme	6	0	2	2	6							
2004-05	WWHL	Calgary Oval X-Treme	16	7	16	23	28	2005	WWHL-P	3	2	1	3	0
2006-07	WWHL	Calgary Oval X-Treme	20	15	21	36	31	2007	WWHL-P	3	1	0	1	0
2007	Nationals	Calgary Oval X-Treme	6	0	7	7	6							
2007-08	WWHL	Calgary Oval X-Treme	19	9	17	26	8							
2008	Nationals	Calgary Oval X-Treme	3	1	0	1	4							
2008-09	WWHL	Calgary Oval X-Treme	22	7	18	25	6	2009	WWHL-P	2	2	1	3	0
								2009	C-Cup	2	0	2	2	8
Totals from all Competitions			**151**	**58**	**109**	**167**	**145**							

SOULIOTIS, MALLORY
Defence. Shoots right. #47.

Born 1996-04-01. Grew up in Acton, MA, USA. 5'5". Debut at age 21 on 2018-03-03.

Year - League - Team			GP	G	A	PTS	PM	Year - Playoff		GP	G	A	PTS	PM
2017-18	NWHL/	Boston Pride	2	0	0	0	0							
2018-19	NWHL/	Boston Pride	14	3	3	6	4	2019	I-Cup	1	0	0	0	0

NWHL Foundation Award in 2018-19

SOUSAE, DEBBIE
Defence. 1995 Nationals Britannia Blues.

SPATARO, VANESSA
Left wing. Shoots left. #16.

Born 1993-05-04. Grew up in Stouffville, ON, CAN. 5'8". Debut at age 23 on 2016-10-15.

Year - League - Team			GP	G	A	PTS	PM
2016-17	CWHL	Toronto Furies	17	0	0	0	6

SPEAKE, MARCY
1996-97 COWHL Scarborough Sting #21 (1 game).

SPEARS, AMY
Ottawa, ON. 2006-07 NWHL Ottawa Raiders #5 (8 games).

SPEER, ALI
2000-01 NWHL Ottawa #4 (1 game); 2002-03 NWHL (1 game).

SPENCE, KAREN
Forward. Shoots left. #14.

Born 1964-07-06. Grew up in Toronto, ON, CAN.

Year - League - Team			GP	G	A	PTS	PM
1992-93	COWHL	Scarborough Sting	28	8	13	21	14
1993-94	COWHL	Scarborough Sting	30	9	18	27	12
1995-96	COWHL	North York Aeros	29	7	27	34	8
1996	Nationals	North York Aeros	5	1	1	2	6
1996-97	COWHL	Scarborough Sting	19	5	8	13	18
1997-98	COWHL	Scarborough Sting	18	3	7	10	12
1998-99	NWHL	Scarborough Sting	39	4	7	11	34

Year - League - Team			GP	G	A	PTS	PM	Year - Playoff	GP	G	A	PTS	PM
1999-00	NWHL	Scarborough Sting	39	3	10	13	32						
2000-01	NWHL	Toronto Sting	29	1	9	10	40						
2001-02	NWHL	Brampton Thunder	27	6	10	16	8						
2002	Nationals	Brampton Thunder	7	0	0	0	0						
Totals from all Competitions			**270**	**47**	**110**	**157**	**184**						

SPENCER, CORRY   *Defence. 1992-93 COWHL Scarborough #12 (3 games).*

SPERRY, CASSIE   *Southlake, TX. Forward. 2010-11 CWHL Boston Blades #21 (24 gp, 3 assists, playoffs 2 gp).*

SPIRES, HILARY   *Defence. 2002-03 NWHL Vancouver #55 (24 gp, 1 goal, 5 a.); 2005-06 WWHL B.C. (3 gp, 1 a.).*

SPIRES, HILARY   *Defence. Shoots right.*

Born 1986-03-18. Grew up in Tsawwassen, BC, CAN. 5'7".

Year - League - Team			GP	G	A	PTS	PM	Year - Playoff	GP	G	A	PTS	PM
2002-03	NWHL	Vancouver Griffins	24	1	5	6	10						
2003	Nationals	Vancouver Griffins	7	1	0	1	6						
2005-06	WWHL	British Columbia Breakers	3	0	1	1	2						
2007	Nationals	British Columbia	5	0	2	2	12						

SPLETT, LORI   *Defence. 1995 Nationals Regina Sharks.*

SPOONER, NATALIE   *Left wing. Shoots right. #24.*

Olympic champion.
Abby Hoffman Cup winner with Mississauga on 2008-03-15. Clarkson Cup winner with Toronto on 2014-03-22.
Born 1990-10-17. Grew up in Scarborough, ON, CAN. 5'10". Debut at age 16 on 2007-1-28.

Year - League - Team			GP	G	A	PTS	PM	Year - Playoff	GP	G	A	PTS	PM
2006-07	NWHL	Etobicoke Dolphins	1	0	0	0	0						
2007-08	CWHL	Mississauga Chiefs	1	0	0	0	0	2008	CWHL-P	3	0	0	0	2
2008	Nationals	Mississauga Chiefs	3	0	0	0	0						
2012-13	CWHL	Toronto Furies	24	15	8	23	6	2013	C-Cup	3	2	1	3	2
2013-14	CWHL	Toronto Furies	2	2	1	3	2	2014	C-Cup	4	1	3	4	0
2014-15	CWHL	Toronto Furies	20	7	8	15	8	2015	C-Cup	2	0	1	1	0
2015-16	CWHL	Toronto Furies	22	17	13	30	20	2016	C-Cup	2	1	1	2	0
2016-17	CWHL	Toronto Furies	20	13	7	20	8	2017	C-Cup	3	1	2	3	2
2018-19	CWHL	Toronto Furies	26	15	11	26	14	2019	C-Cup	3	2	1	3	0
CWHL Regular Season			115	69	48	117	58	Clarkson Cup		17	7	9	16	4
Totals from all Competitions			**139**	**76**	**57**	**133**	**64**						

CWHL First All-Star Team in 2015-16, CWHL Second All-Star Team in 2016-17 and 2018-19... finished 5th in the Angela James Bowl scoring race in 2015-16

SPRUYT, JOYCE   *Strathroy, ON. F. 2009-10 CWHL Ottawa #11 (14 gp, 6 goals, 3 assists).*

SPURLING, KAITLIN   *Left wing. Shoots left. #16.*

Born 1991-04-16. Grew up in Byfield, MA, USA. 5'8". Debut at age 26 on 2017-10-14.

Year - League - Team			GP	G	A	PTS	PM
2017-18	CWHL	Boston Blades	22	1	3	4	2
2018-19	CWHL	Worcester Blades	20	3	3	6	8

SPURLING, MEAGHAN   *Defence. Shoots left. #20.*

Born 1994-04-20. Grew up in Byfield, MA, USA. 5'6". Debut at age 23 on 2017-10-14.

Year - League - Team			GP	G	A	PTS	PM
2017-18	CWHL	Boston Blades	24	0	0	0	0
2018-19	CWHL	Worcester Blades	27	0	1	1	18

SQUIRES, NICOLE   *Forward. 2003 Nationals Newfoundland Labrador (5 games).*

ST-CROIX, LAURA   *Forward. 2008 Nationals Calgary Oval X-Treme.*

ST-GERMAIN, ANNE-MARIE   *2002-03 NWHL Montréal (30 games, 1 goal, 2 assists).*

ST-GERMAIN, CLARA   *Defence. Shoots right. #9.*

Born 1990-03-22. Grew up in Lunenberg, MA, USA. Debut at age 25 on 2015-10-17.

Year - League - Team			GP	G	A	PTS	PM
2015-16	CWHL	Boston Blades	22	0	0	0	4
2016-17	CWHL	Boston Blades	20	0	0	0	0

ST-GERMAIN, SADIE   *Forward. Shoots left. #5.*

Born 1992-04-16. Grew up in Lunenberg, MA, USA. Debut at age 23 on 2015-10-17.

Year - League - Team			GP	G	A	PTS	PM
2015-16	CWHL	Boston Blades	21	1	0	1	6
2016-17	CWHL	Boston Blades	22	0	2	2	16

ST-JACQUES, VALERIE   *Forward. #9.*

Year - League - Team			GP	G	A	PTS	PM
1999-00	NWHL	Mistral de Laval	34	4	8	12	14
2000-01	NWHL	Mistral de Laval	40	9	8	17	10
2001-02	NWHL	Cheyenne	21	4	2	6	4
2003-04	NWHL	Avalanche du Québec	36	3	8	11	6
Totals from all Competitions			**131**	**20**	**26**	**46**	**34**

ST-LOUIS, FRANCE
Centre. #3.

IIHF champion. Born 1958-10-17, Laval, QC, CAN. Grew up in St-Hubert, QC, CAN.

Year - League - Team			GP	G	A	PTS	PM
1995	Nationals	Équipe Québec					
1996	Nationals	Équipe Québec	6	5	2	7	4
1997	Nationals	Équipe Québec					
1998	Nationals	Équipe Québec	6	5	6	11	2
1998-99	NWHL	Bonaventure	17	13	11	24	4
1999	Nationals	Équipe Québec	5	2	8	10	
1999-00	NWHL	Wingstar de Montréal	16	12	16	28	14
2000-01	NWHL	Wingstar de Montréal	25	16	19	35	10

Women's National Championships Most Valuable Player in 1997 and 1998.

ST-LOUIS, SUE
Forward. 1999-00 NWHL Scarborough #10 (36 games, 1 goal, 1 assist).

STE-MARIE, ISABELLE
Forward. #12 #90 #6.

Year - League - Team			GP	G	A	PTS	PM	
1998-99	NWHL	Montréal Jofa-Titan	24	4	4	8	8	
1999-00	NWHL	Sainte-Julie	28	3	3	6	18	2000 NWHL-P
2000-01	NWHL	Sainte-Julie	2	0	0	0	0	
2001-02	NWHL	Cheyenne	29	3	3	6	8	
2002-03	NWHL	Avalanche du Québec	34	0	2	2	26	
Totals from all Competitions			**117**	**10**	**12**	**22**	**60**	

STACEY, LAURA
Forward. Shoots right. #7.

Clarkson Cup winner with Markham on 2018-03-25
Born 1994-05-05. Grew up in Kleinburg, ON, CAN. 5'10". Debut at age 22 on 2016-10-08.

Year - League - Team			GP	G	A	PTS	PM	Year - Playoff		GP	G	A	PTS	PM
2016-17	CWHL	Brampton Thunder	20	11	13	24	6	2017	C-Cup	2	0	0	0	4
2017-18	CWHL	Markham Thunder	2	2	2	4	0	2018	C-Cup	3	1	0	1	0
2018-19	CWHL	Markham Thunder	24	8	17	25	22	2019	C-Cup	3	0	0	0	2
CWHL Regular Season			46	21	32	53	28	Clarkson Cup		8	1	0	1	6
Totals from all Competitions			**54**	**22**	**32**	**54**	**34**							

CWHL Outstanding Rookie in 2016-17... CWHL All-Rookie Team in 2016-17... finished 7th in the Angela James Bowl scoring race in 2016-17

STACK, KELLI
Forward. Shoots right. #16.

IIHF champion.
Born 1988-1-13. Grew up in Brooklyn Heights, OH, USA. 5'5". Debut at age 24 on 2011-10-22.

Year - League - Team			GP	G	A	PTS	PM	Year - Playoff		GP	G	A	PTS	PM
2011-12	CWHL	Boston Blades	27	24	17	41	30	2012	C-Cup	3	2	3	5	2
2012-13	CWHL	Boston Blades	8	4	3	7	12							
2013-14	CWHL	Boston Blades	2	1	1	2	4	2014	C-Cup	4	1	5	6	0
2014-15	CWHL	Boston Blades	2	1	1	2	0							
2015-16	NWHL/	Connecticut Whale	17	8	14	22	24	2016	I-Cup	3	2	0	2	2
2016-17	NWHL/	Connecticut Whale	16	12	7	19	10	2017	I-Cup	1	1	1	2	2
2017-18	CWHL	Kunlun Red Star	28	26	23	49	40	2018	C-Cup	4	1	2	3	16
CWHL Regular Season			67	56	45	101	86	Clarkson Cup		11	4	10	14	18
NWHL Regular Season			33	20	21	41	34	Isobel Cup		4	3	1	4	4
Totals from all Competitions			**115**	**83**	**77**	**160**	**142**							

CWHL Most Valuable Player in 2017-18... CWHL First All-Star Team in 2011-12 and 2017-18... CWHL All-Rookie Team in 2011-12... Angela James Bowl scoring champion in 2017-18... scored 100th CWHL point on 2018-03-11

STADNYK, CHARISSA
Calgary, AB. D. 2012-13 CWHL Brampton #22 (8 games, 5 assists).

STAFFORD, SUE
1998-99 NWHL Ottawa Raiders #24 (34 games, 2 assists).

STASZEWSKI, JULIA
Forward. 2005 Nationals British Columbia (7 games, 1 goal, 2 assists).

STATHOPOULOS, CASEY
Centre. Shoots right. #12.

Born 1993-04-20. Grew up in Waltham, NY, USA. 5'3". Debut at age 24 on 2017-10-14.

Year - League - Team			GP	G	A	PTS	PM
2017-18	CWHL	Boston Blades	27	0	3	3	0
2018-19	CWHL	Worcester Blades	25	2	0	2	4

STATHOPULOS, ELISABETH
Forward. 2010-11 CWHL Toronto Furies (7 games).

STAUBER, EMMA
Defence. Shoots left. #7.

Isobel Cup winner with Minnesota on 2019-03-17.
Born 1993-04-06. Grew up in Duluth, MN, USA. 5'7". Debut at age 25 on 2018-10-06.

Year - League - Team			GP	G	A	PTS	PM	Year - Playoff		GP	G	A	PTS	PM
2018-19	NWHL/	Minnesota Whitecaps	16	1	4	5	12	2019	I-Cup	2	0	0	0	0

STEAD, JENINE
Forward. 2002 Nationals Newfoundland Labrador (4 games).

STEADMAN, KELLEY
Defence/Forward. Shoots right. #3.

Clarkson Cup winner with Boston on 2013-03-23 and Isobel Cup winner with Buffalo on 2017-03-19
Born 1990-5-11. Grew up in Plattsburgh, NY, USA. Debut at age 22 on 2012-10-20.

Year - League - Team		GP	G	A	PTS	PM	Year - Playoff	GP	G	A	PTS	PM
2012-13	CWHL Boston Blades	24	8	6	14	32	2013 C-Cup	4	3	0	3	12
2015-16	NWHL/ Buffalo Beauts	10	13	7	20	16	2016 I-Cup	4	2	1	3	4
2016-17	NWHL/ Buffalo Beauts	8	5	5	10	16	2017 I-Cup	2	0	0	0	0
NWHL Regular Season		18	18	12	30	32	Isobel Cup	6	2	1	3	4
Totals from all Competitions		**52**	**31**	**19**	**50**	**80**						

Finished 20th in the Angela James Bowl scoring race in 2012-13

STEARNS, COREY
Forward. Shoots right. #9.

Born 1990-12-27. Grew up in Falmouth, MA, USA. Debut at age 26 on 2017-11-11.

Year - League - Team		GP	G	A	PTS	PM	Year - Playoff	GP	G	A	PTS	PM
2017-18	NWHL/ Boston Pride	13	0	4	4	6	2018 I-Cup	1	0	0	0	0

STEBELESKI, SARAH
Forward. 2004 Nationals Manitoba (5 games).

STECH, AMY
Forward. 2010-11 WWHL Minnesota #77 (18 gp, 7 goals, 11 assists; C-Cup 3 gp).

STECKLEIN, LEE
Defence. Shoots left. #2.

IIHF champion. Isobel Cup winner with Minnesota on 2019-03-17.
Born 1994-04-23. Grew up in Roseville, MN, USA. 6'0". Debut at age 24 on 2018-10-06.

Year - League - Team		GP	G	A	PTS	PM	Year - Playoff	GP	G	A	PTS	PM
2018-19	NWHL/ Minnesota Whitecaps	16	1	10	11	8	2019 I-Cup	2	1	1	2	0

STEELE, CYNTHIA
Forward. 1995 Natoinals Metro Valley Selects.

STEELE, MICHELLE
Forward. #10 #9.

Year - League - Team		GP	G	A	PTS	PM
1992-93	COWHL Guelph Eagles	20	1	3	4	6
1996-97	COWHL Scarborough Sting	33	1	13	14	14
1998-99	NWHL Scarborough Sting	38	2	5	7	41
1999-00	NWHL Scarborough Sting	33	1	3	4	34
Totals from all Competitions		**124**	**5**	**24**	**29**	**95**

STEEVES, JILL
Forward. 1995 Nationals Maritime Sports Blades.

STEPHEN, JILL
1996-97 COWHL Hamilton Golden Hawks #12 (14 games).

STEPHEN, KARRAH
Defence. #8 #25.

Born 1985-3-23. Grew up in Morinville, AB, CAN.

Year - League - Team		GP	G	A	PTS	PM	Year - Playoff	GP	G	A	PTS	PM
2002-03	NWHL Edmonton Chimos	22	0	0	0	8						
2003-04	NWHL Edmonton Chimos	10	0	0	0	18	2004 NWHL-P					
2004	Nationals Edmonton Chimos	7	1	0	1	8						
2007-08	WWHL Edmonton Chimos	4	0	0	0	6						

STEPHENS, KELLY
Forward. 1999 Nationals New Westminster (5 gp, 6 pts); 20001 Nationals Vancouver Griffins.

STEPHENSON, ASHLEY
Defence. Shoots left. #39 #33 #12.

Abby Hoffman Cup winner with Mississauga on 2008-03-15.
Born 1982-11-22, Mississauga, ON, CAN. 5'5".

Year - League - Team		GP	G	A	PTS	PM	Year - Playoff	GP	G	A	PTS	PM
1998-99	NWHL Mississauga Chiefs	1	0	0	0	4						
1999-00	NWHL Mississauga Chiefs	3	0	0	0	0						
2000-01	NWHL Mississauga IceBears	8	2	1	3	2						
2001-02	NWHL Mississauga IceBears	9	0	0	0	2						
2005-06	NWHL Brampton Thunder	16	2	4	6	2	2006 NWHL-P	5	0	1	1	4
2006-07	NWHL Mississauga Aeros	33	0	12	12	10	2007 NWHL-P	5	0	2	2	2
2007	Nationals Mississauga Aeros	6	0	2	2	4						
2007-08	CWHL Mississauga Chiefs	28	2	10	12	16	2008 CWHL-P	5	0	2	2	2
2008	Nationals Mississauga Chiefs	3	0	0	0	2						
2008-09	CWHL Mississauga Chiefs	27	0	10	10	12	2009 CWHL-P	4		2		
2009-10	CWHL Mississauga Chiefs	26	2	12	14	10	2010 C-Cup	1	0	0	0	0
2010-11	CWHL Burlington Barracudas	21	0	4	4	8						
2011-12	CWHL Burlington Barracudas	17	1	7	8	6						
CWHL Regular Season		119	5	43	48	52	Clarkson Cup	1	0	0	0	0
Totals from all Competitions		**218**	**9**	**67**	**76**	**86**						

STEPHENSON, DARLENE
Left wing. Shoots left. #11.

Born 1981-12-3. Grew up in Virden, MB, CAN. 5'4".

Year - League - Team		GP	G	A	PTS	PM	Year - Playoff	GP	G	A	PTS	PM
2004-05	NWHL Oakville Ice	36	10	9	19	4						
2005-06	NWHL Oakville Ice	31	4	11	15	6	2006 NWHL-P	2	0	1	1	0
Totals from all Competitions		**69**	**14**	**21**	**35**	**10**						

STERANKO, ANDREA
Forward.

Year - League - Team		GP	G	A	PTS	PM	Year - Playoff	GP	G	A	PTS	PM
1998	Nationals Saskatchewan Selects	6	2	1	3	4						
2000	Nationals Saskatchewan Selects	7	5	4	9							
2004-05	WWHL Saskatchewan Prairie Ice	5	0	1	1	4						
2005-06	WWHL Saskatchewan Prairie Ice	9	0	3	3	0	2006 WWHL-P	2	0	0	0	0

STEVENS, EMILY — *D. 1995-96 COWHL Hamilton (30 gp, 1 assist); 1996-97 (35 gp, 3 assists).*

STEVENS, MICHELE — *C. 1993-94 COWHL Mississauga Chiefs #2 (28 games, 1 goal, 4 assists).*

STEVENSON, CHANTELLE — *Defence. 2005 Nationals Manitoba (5 games).*

STEVENSON, SARAH — *Toronto. Forward. 2015-16 CWHL Toronto #7 (24 games, 3 goals, C-Cup 2 games).*

STEWART, ASHLEY — *Forward. #23 #10 #11 #18.*

Born 1983-4-18, Toronto, ON, CAN. Grew up in Toronto, ON, CAN.

Year - League - Team			GP	G	A	PTS	PM	Year - Playoff	GP	G	A	PTS	PM
2001-02	NWHL	North York Aeros	4	1	1	2	0						
2006-07	NWHL	Oakville Ice	33	5	5	10	28	2007 NWHL-P	3	0	0	0	2
2008-09	CWHL	Burlington Barracudas	30	8	4	12	28	2009 CWHL-P	4		1	1	2
2009-10	CWHL	Burlington Barracudas	29	9	12	21	32						
2010-11	CWHL	Burlington Barracudas	25	4	7	11	14						
		CWHL Regular Season	84	21	23	44	74						
		Totals from all Competitions	128	27	30	57	106						

STEWART, CHERIE — *Lake Forest, CA. Forward. 2015-16 NWHL New York (4 gp, Isobel Cup 1 game).*

STEWART, ELLA — *Defence. Shoots left. #22.*

Born 1992-11-06. Grew up in Mississauga, ON, CAN. 5'3". Debut at age 23 on 2016-10-22.

Year - League - Team			GP	G	A	PTS	PM
2016-17	CWHL	Toronto Furies	13	0	1	1	8
2017-18	CWHL	Toronto Furies	26	0	1	1	28
		CWHL Regular Season	39	0	2	2	36

STEWART, KATELYN — *2004 Nationals British Columbia (6 games, 2 assists).*

STEWART, KATIE — *2004-05 WWHL Edmonton #77 (11 games, 2 goals, 3 assists; playoff 1 gp).*

STEWART, KELLY — *Defence. #23 #14 #66.*

Born 1983-4-18, Toronto, ON, CAN. Grew up in Toronto, ON, CAN.

Year - League - Team			GP	G	A	PTS	PM	Year - Playoff	GP	G	A	PTS	PM
2000-01	NWHL	North York Aeros	3	0	1	1	4						
2006-07	NWHL	Oakville Ice	34	0	6	6	42	2007 NWHL-P	3	0	0	0	4
2007-08	CWHL	Burlington Barracudas	13	0	2	2	8						
2008-09	CWHL	Burlington Barracudas	30		3	3	6	2009 CWHL-P	4		1	1	2
2009-10	CWHL	Burlington Barracudas	28	0	12	12	58						
2010-11	CWHL	Burlington Barracudas	25	0	2	2	36						
		CWHL Regular Season	96	0	19	19	162						
		Totals from all Competitions	140	0	27	27	214						

STEWART, SHANNON — *Forward. Shoots right. #10.*

Born 1993-04-07. Grew up in Pickering, ON, CAN. 5'5". Debut at age 24 on 2017-10-28.

Year - League - Team			GP	G	A	PTS	PM	Year - Playoff	GP	G	A	PTS	PM
2017-18	CWHL	Toronto Furies	26	0	4	4	4						
2018-19	CWHL	Toronto Furies	27	4	4	8	0	2019 C-Cup	3	0	0	0	0

STIEFEL, ANJA — *Forward. 2008-09 WWHL Calgary #3 (21 games, 2 goals, 3 assists; C-Cup 2 games).*

STIMSON, CAESARE — *Forward. Shoots left. #29 #14.*

Born 1981-12-17. Grew up Chisago Lakes, MN, USA. 5'5". Debut at age 24 on 2006-10-20.

Year - League - Team			GP	G	A	PTS	PM	Year - Playoff	GP	G	A	PTS	PM
2006-07	WWHL	Minnesota Whitecaps	16	6	2	8	8	2007 WWHL-P	3	0	0	0	0
2007-08	WWHL	Minnesota Whitecaps	16	6	3	9	10						
2008	Nationals	Minnesota Whitecaps	3	0	0	0	0						
2008-09	WWHL	Minnesota Whitecaps	6	1	0	1	2	2009 WWHL-P	0	0	0	0	0
2009-10	WWHL	Minnesota Whitecaps	9	2	2	4	2						
		Totals from all Competitions	53	15	7	22	22						

SIVER, LAUREN — *F. 1998 Nationals Tazmanian Devils (5 gp, 2 pts); 1999 (4 gp, 1 a.); 2001 Nationals Manitoba.*

STOBART, NICOLE — *Forward. 2003 Nationals Host Saskatchewan (5 gp); 2004 Nationals Saskatchewan (6 gp).*

STOCK, KELLY — *Forward. 2010-11 WWHL Manitoba Maple Leafs #11 (4 games, 1 assist).*

STOCKMAN, CATHY — *1996-97 COWHL Newtonbrook #9 (1 game).*

STONE, DANIELLE — *Forward. Shoots left. #17.*

Born 1986-08-19. Grew up in Prince Albert, SK, CAN. 5'6". Debut at age 27 on 2013-11-09.

Year - League - Team			GP	G	A	PTS	PM	Year - Playoff	GP	G	A	PTS	PM
2013-14	CWHL	Calgary Inferno	24	15	10	25	14	2014 C-Cup	3	3	1	4	4
2014-15	CWHL	Calgary Inferno	22	3	6	9	2	2015 C-Cup	2	0	0	0	0
		CWHL Regular Season	46	18	16	34	16	Clarkson Cup	5	3	1	4	4
		Totals from all Competitions	51	21	17	38	20						

CWHL First All-Star Team in 2013-14... finished 6th in the Angela James Bowl scoring race in 2013-14

STONE, EMILY — *Forward. 2008 Nationals Nova Scotia Selects (5 games).*

STONE, JANET — *1995-96 COWHL Hamilton #14 (1 game).*

STOSKY, LAURA *Defence. Shoots left. #5.*
Born 1982-10-21, Edmonton, AB, CAN. 5'6".

Year - League - Team			GP	G	A	PTS	PM	Year - Playoff	GP	G	A	PTS	PM
2003-04	NWHL	Edmonton Chimos	10	0	2	2	6	2004 NWHL-P	2	0	0	0	0
2004	Nationals	Edmonton Chimos	7	0	2	2	4						
2004-05	WWHL	Edmonton Chimos	21	1	3	4	4	2005 WWHL-P	3	0	0	0	0
2005-06	WWHL	Edmonton Chimos	22	4	5	9	10	2006 WWHL-P	2	0	0	0	0
2006-07	WWHL	Edmonton Chimos	21	3	4	7	24	2007 WWHL-P	2	0	0	0	6
2007-08	WWHL	Edmonton Chimos	24	1	3	4	14						
Totals from all Competitions			**114**	**9**	**19**	**28**	**68**						

STROUD, LORISSA   *2000-01 NWHL Toronto (17 games, 1 goal, 2 assists).*

STUART, KELLY *Defence. #12.*
NWHL Cup winner.

Year - League - Team			GP	G	A	PTS	PM	Year - Playoff	GP	G	A	PTS	PM
1999-00	NWHL	Beatrice Aeroes	1	0	0	0	0	2000 NWHL-P					

STURINO, LYNDA   *1998-99 NWHL Mississauga (1 game); 2000-01 (2 games).*

STYLES, CANDICE *Defence/Forward. Shoots left. #4.*
Born 1991-2-19. Grew up in Orangeville, ON, CAN. 5'3". Debut at age 18 on 2009-2-22.

Year - League - Team			GP	G	A	PTS	PM	Year - Playoff	GP	G	A	PTS	PM
2008-09	CWHL	Mississauga Chiefs	3	2	1	3	0	2009 CWHL-P	4	1	3	4	4
2014-15	CWHL	Toronto Furies	1	0	0	0	2						
2014-15	CWHL	Brampton Thunder	20	1	1	2	18						
2015-16	CWHL	Brampton Thunder	22	7	8	15	28	2016 C-Cup	2	0	0	0	0
2016-17	CWHL	Brampton Thunder	4	0	0	0	0						
CWHL Regular Season			50	10	10	20	48	Clarkson Cup	2	0	0	0	0
Totals from all Competitions			**56**	**11**	**13**	**24**	**52**						

SUDIA, KELLY *Defence. Shoots left. #12 #11.*
Clarkson Cup winner with Montréal on 2009-03-21, 2011-03-27 and 2012-03-25. NWHL winner.
Born 1980-7-3. Grew up in Pointe-Claire, QC, CAN. 5'2".

Year - League - Team			GP	G	A	PTS	PM	Year - Playoff	GP	G	A	PTS	PM
2005-06	NWHL	Axion de Montréal	36	5	2	7	2	2006 NWHL-P	3	0	0	0	0
2006	Nationals	Axion de Montréal	6	0	0	0	0						
2006-07	NWHL	Axion de Montréal	29	1	2	3	18	2007 NWHL-P					
2007-08	CWHL	Stars de Montréal	27	1	12	13	22	2008 CWHL-P	2	0	1	1	0
2008-09	CWHL	Stars de Montréal	27		7	7	14	2009 CWHL-P	2	0	0	0	0
								2009 C-Cup	3	0	0	0	2
2009-10	CWHL	Stars de Montréal	30	3	3	6	18	2010 C-Cup	1	0	0	0	0
2010-11	CWHL	Stars de Montréal	24	1	2	3	6	2011 CWHL-P	2				
								2011 C-Cup	4	0	0	0	0
2011-12	CWHL	Stars de Montréal	26	2	5	7	14	2012 C-Cup	4	0	0	0	2
CWHL Regular Season			134	7	29	36	74	Clarkson Cup	12	0	0	0	4
Totals from all Competitions			**226**	**13**	**34**	**47**	**98**						

SUDO, AKI   *Forward. 2000-01 NWHL Mississauga #16 (33 games, 6 goals, 7 assists).*

SUGGITT, JEN   *RW. 1995-96 COWHL Peterborough #8 (24 games, 2 goals, 1 assist).*

SULLIVAN, AMBER   *Defence. 2006 Nationals Manitoba (5 games, 1 assist).*

SULLIVAN, ARDEN   *Forward. 2005-06 NWHL Brampton Thunder #14 (2 games, 1 assist).*

SULLIVAN, JENNIFER *Forward. Shoots left.*
Born 1984-07-22. Grew up in Kensington, PE, CAN. 5'6".

Year - League - Team			GP	G	A	PTS	PM
2005	Nationals	Prince Edward Island	5	0	2	2	4
2006	Nationals	Prince Edward Island	5	1	0	1	6
2007	Nationals	Prince Edward Island	5	1	2	3	4
2008	Nationals	Prince Edward Island	4	0	1	1	0

SULLIVAN, TRACY   *Forward. 2000 Nationals Newfoundland Labrador (5 gp, 4 pts); 2001 Nationals Newfoundland.*

SUN RUI   *Forward. 2007-08 WWHL Edmonton Chimos #11 (17 games, 7 goals, 8 assists).*

SUNDQUIST, BREANNA   *Defence. 2008-09 CWHL Ottawa Senators (2 games).*

SUNOHARA, VICKY *Forward. Shoots left. #6 #61.*
Olympic champion, IIHF champion, CWHL winner.
Born 1970-5-18, Scarborough, ON, CAN. 5'7".

Year - League - Team			GP	G	A	PTS	PM
1992-93	COWHL	Scarborough Firefighters	21	12	8	20	16
1993-94	COWHL	Scarborough Firefighters	0	0	0	0	0
1995-96	COWHL	Toronto Red Wings	25	28	16	44	30
1996	Nationals	North York Aeros	5	3	1	4	0
1996-97	COWHL	Newtonbrook Panthers	29	42	28	70	12
1998	Nationals	North York Aeros	2	3	3	6	0

Year - League - Team			GP	G	A	PTS	PM	Year - Playoff		GP	G	A	PTS	PM
1998-99	NWHL	Brampton Thunder	24	22	18	40	18							
1999	Nationals	North York Aeros	5	6	0	6								
1999-00	NWHL	Brampton Thunder	31	18	34	52	18							
2000-01	NWHL	Brampton Thunder	30	19	31	50	30							
2002	Nationals	Brampton Thunder	7	3	4	7	4							
2002-03	NWHL	Brampton Thunder	30	20	27	47	24	2003	NWHL-P	1	1	0	1	0
2003	Nationals	Brampton Thunder	4	3	4	7	0							
2003-04	NWHL	Brampton Thunder	34	19	28	47	18	2004	NWHL-P	5	3	3	6	2
2004-05	NWHL	Brampton Thunder	31	28	28	56	33	2005	NWHL-P	2	1	2	3	2
2005	Nationals	Brampton Thunder	6	6	9	15	4							
2005-06	NWHL	Brampton Thunder	2	0	3	3	0	2006	NWHL-P	5	5	2	7	2
2006-07	NWHL	Brampton Thunder	33	20	33	53	36	2007	NWHL-P	5	1	2	3	2
2007-08	CWHL	Brampton Can.-Thunder	28	13	25	38	22	2008	CWHL-P	3	1	2	3	2
2008	Nationals	Brampton Can.-Thunder	3	2	3	5	4							
2008-09	CWHL	Brampton Thunder	21	5	14	19	22							
CWHL Regular Season			49	18	39	57	44							
Totals from all Competitions			**392**	**284**	**328**	**612**	**301**							

Finished 5th in the Angela James Bowl scoring race in 2007-08

SURASK, KIRSTEN
Forward. 1996 Nationals Britannia Blues (5 games, 1 goal).

SURPRENANT, ANNIE
Forward. #25 #22.

Year - League - Team			GP	G	A	PTS	PM
2000	Nationals	Équipe Québec	6	1	0	1	
2000-01	NWHL	Sainte-Julie	4	1	2	3	4
2001-02	NWHL	Cheyenne	27	6	13	19	10
2002-03	NWHL	Avalanche du Québec	12	1	0	1	0
Totals from all Competitions			**43**	**8**	**15**	**23**	**14**

SURPRENANT, ISABELLE
Defence. #95.

Year - League - Team			GP	G	A	PTS	PM	Year - Playoff	
1995	Nationals	Équipe Québec							
1996	Nationals	Équipe Québec	6	2	6	8	0		
1997	Nationals	Équipe Québec							
1998-99	NWHL	Montréal Jofa-Titan	26	3	8	11	18		
1999-00	NWHL	Sainte-Julie	28	3	11	14	28	2000	NWHL-P
2000-01	NWHL	Sainte-Julie	34	7	17	24	30		
2001-02	NWHL	Cheyenne	26	1	2	3	40		
Totals from all Competitions			**114**	**14**	**38**	**52**	**116**		

SUTTER, OLIVIA
Forward. #11.

Born 1992-1-31. Grew up in Red Deer, AB, CAN. 5'3". Debut at age 20 on 2011-10-28.

Year - League - Team			GP	G	A	PTS	PM
2011-12	CWHL	Alberta	13	2	2	4	2
2012-13	CWHL	Alberta	23	3	1	4	20
CWHL Regular Season			36	5	3	8	22

SUTTER, SALLY
D. 2003 Nationals Saskatchewan (6 gp, 1 a.); 006-07 WWHL Saskatchewan (12 gp, 1 assist).

SUZUKI, SENA
Defence. Shoots left. #6.

Born 1991-08-04, Tomakomai, JPN. 5'6". Debut at age 24 on 2015-10-17.

Year - League - Team			GP	G	A	PTS	PM	Year - Playoff		GP	G	A	PTS	PM
2015-16	CWHL	Toronto Furies	22	1	5	6	8	2016	C-Cup	2	0	0	0	2
2016-17	CWHL	Toronto Furies	6	0	0	0	2							
2018-19	CWHL	Toronto Furies	28	0	1	1	6	2019	C-Cup	3	0	0	0	0
CWHL Regular Season			56	1	6	7	16		Clarkson Cup	5	0	0	0	6

SWAN, CARISSA
Forward. 010-11 WWHL Manitoba Maple Leafs #15 (2 games, 1 goal).

SWANSON, KELLY
Defence. 1996 Nationals Winnipeg Sweat Camp (6 gp, 1 assist).

SWANSON, TARA
Wetaskiwin, AB. 2010-11 WWHL Edmonton (17 gp, 1 goal, 2 a.); 2011-12 CWHL Alberta (15 gp).

SWEENEY, CHRISTINE
Ottawa, ON. D. 2007-08 CWHL Ottawa #14 (17 games, 5 assists; playoff 1 gp).

SWEENEY, KATIE
Ottawa, ON. D. 2000-01 NWHL Ottawa (1 gp); 2001-02 (28 gp, 1 goal, 2 assists).

SWICK, KRISTA
Defence. 1996 Nationals Britannia Blues (5 games, 1 goal, 1 assist).

SWIRSKY, CORINNE
Centre. Shoots left. #17 #4.

Abby Hoffman Cup winner with Calgary on 2001-03-11 and 2003-03-16.
WWHL winner. Born 1977-8-19. Grew up in Thompson, MB, CAN. 5'5".

Year - League - Team			GP	G	A	PTS	PM	Year - Playoff		GP	G	A	PTS	PM
1995	Nationals	Winnipeg Sweat Camp												
2000	Nationals	Équipe Québec	6	4	4	8								
2001	Nationals	Calgary Oval X-Treme												
2002	Nationals	Calgary Oval X-Treme	6	7	7	14	2							
2002-03	NWHL	Calgary Oval X-Treme	17	17	9	26	12	2003	NWHL-P					
2003	Nationals	Calgary Oval X-Treme	5	5	5	10	2							
2004-05	WWHL	Calgary Oval X-Treme	2	0	0	0	0	2005	WWHL-P	0	0	0	0	0

Year - League - Team			GP	G	A	PTS	PM	Year - Playoff	GP	G	A	PTS	PM
2007-08	WWHL	Strathmore Rockies	14	5	7	12	12						
2008-09	WWHL	Strathmore Rockies	19	6	5	11	10	2009 WWHL-P	1	0	0	0	2
Totals from all Competitions			**70**	**44**	**37**	**81**	**40**						

SYME, HEIDI　　　　　　　　　　　　　　　　*Defence. Shoots right. #28.*

Born 1986-4-2. Grew up in Salmon Arm, BC, CAN. 5'6".

Year - League - Team			GP	G	A	PTS	PM	Year - Playoff	GP	G	A	PTS	PM
2007	Nationals	British Columbia	0	0	0	0	0						
2007-08	WWHL	Strathmore Rockies	23	2	10	12	8						
2008-09	WWHL	Strathmore Rockies	20	5	3	8	28	2009 WWHL-P	1	0	0	0	0
Totals from all Competitions			**44**	**7**	**13**	**20**	**36**						

SYMINGTON, NICOLE　　　　*2009-10 WWHL Edmonton #77 (1 game); 2010-11 (2 games).*

SZEPESI, JUDY　　　　　　　　　　　　*Defence. 1995 Calgary Classics.*

SZYMANEK, KELSEY　　　*Defence. 2007-08 WWHL Strathmore #14 (18 games, 1 goal).*

TABB, JESSICA　　　　　　　　　　　　　　*Forward. Right. #17 #15.*

Abby Hoffman Cup winner with Aeros on 2004-03-14 and 2005-03-13.
Born 1979-6-5. Grew up in Springfield, MA, USA.

Year - League - Team			GP	G	A	PTS	PM	Year - Playoff	GP	G	A	PTS	PM
2001-02	NWHL	North York Aeros	28	8	18	26	26						
2002	Nationals	North York Aeros	7	3	2	5	6						
2002-03	NWHL	North York Aeros	20	8	10	18		2003 NWHL-P					
2003-04	NWHL	Toronto Aeros	36	22	27	49	12	2004 NWHL-P	2	0	1	1	
2004	Nationals	Toronto Aeros	6	2	0	2	4						
2004-05	NWHL	Toronto Aeros	27	10	20	30	22	2005 NWHL-P	2	0	0	0	
2005	Nationals	Toronto Aeros	7	0	0	0	0						
Totals from all Competitions			**135**	**53**	**78**	**131**	**70**						

TADY, ERIN　　　　　　　　　　　　　　　　　*Forward. #11*

Born 1982-05-28. Grew up in North Battleford, SK, CAN.

Year - League - Team			GP	G	A	PTS	PM
2000	Nationals	Saskatchewan Selects	7	1	1	2	
2001	Nationals	Saskatchewan Selects					
2006-07	WWHL	Saskatchewan Prairie Ice	18	2	8	10	20

TAILLON, KAREN　　　*LW. 1995-96 COWHL Peterborough #16 (24 games, 1 goal).*

TAIT, AMY-LYN　　*D. 1999-00 NWHL Ottawa Raiders #15 (33 gp, 1 assist); 2000-01 #2 (38 gp, 2 assists).*

TANGUAY, DEE DEE　　　　　　　　　　　　*Defence. #5 #77 #58.*

Abby Hoffman Cup winner with Aeros on 1991-03-17.

Year - League - Team			GP	G	A	PTS	PM
1993-94	COWHL	Mississauga Chiefs	15	0	2	2	16
1999-00	NWHL	Scarborough Sting	32	0	3	3	22
2000-01	NWHL	Toronto Sting	31	0	3	3	30
2001-02	NWHL	Durham Lightning	5	0	0	0	6
Totals from all Competitions			**83**	**0**	**8**	**8**	**74**

TARDIF, STACIE　　　　　　　　*Defence. Shoots left. #79 #2.*

Born 1989-7-13. Grew up in Ste-Anne-de-Bellevue, QC, CAN. 5'5". Debut at age 18 on 2007-10-13.

Year - League - Team			GP	G	A	PTS	PM	Year - Playoff	GP	G	A	PTS	PM
2007-08	CWHL	Phénix du Québec	6	0	1	1	0						
2013-14	CWHL	Stars de Montréal	17	2	1	3	10	2014 C-Cup	3	0	1	1	4
2014-15	CWHL	Stars de Montréal	15	1	4	5	8	2015 C-Cup	3	0	1	1	2
CWHL Regular Season			38	3	6	9	18	Clarkson Cup	6	0	2	2	6
Totals from all Competitions			**44**	**3**	**8**	**11**	**24**						

TATLOCK, TAMMY　　　　　　　　　　　　　*Defence. Shoots left..*

Born 1978-05-10. Grew up in Plaster Rock, NB, CAN. 5'4".

Year - League - Team			GP	G	A	PTS	PM	Year - Playoff	GP	G	A	PTS	PM
1999	Nationals	Team New Brunswick	6	0	0	0							
2000	Nationals	Team New Brunswick	6	1	0	1							
2001	Nationals	Team New Brunswick											
2003	Nationals	Team New Brunswick	4	1	0	1	0						
2004	Nationals	Team New Brunswick	5	0	1	1	2						
2007	Nationals	Team New Brunswick	6	0	0	0	6						

TAVERNA, MAGGIE　　　　　　　　　　　　*Defence. Shoots right. #4.*

Born 1987-07-22 in Howell, NJ, USA. 5'8". Debut at age 26 on 2013-11-02.

Year - League - Team			GP	G	A	PTS	PM	Year - Playoff	GP	G	A	PTS	PM
2013-14	CWHL	Boston Blades	10	0	0	0	4	2014 C-Cup	4	0	0	0	0
2016-17	NWHL/	Boston Pride	0	0	0	0	0						

TAYLOR, BETH　　　*D. 1996-97 COWHL London Devilettes #2 (29 games, 1 goal, 5 assists).*

TAYLOR-BOLTON, LAURIE

Defence. #4 #44.

Year - League - Team		GP	G	A	PTS	PM
1992-93	COWHL	Scarborough Sting	21	0	3	3	26
1993-94	COWHL	Scarborough Sting	27	3	9	12	27
1995-96	COWHL	Toronto Red Wings	24	4	17	21	32
1996-97	COWHL	Newtonbrook Panthers	26	3	17	20	34
Totals from all Competitions		**98**	**10**	**46**	**56**	**119**

TAYLOR, CHELSEA
Defence. 2002 Nationals Saskatchewan (6 games).

TAYLOR, JOANNE
1993-94 COWHL Hamilton Golden Hawks #94 (1 game).

TAYLOR, JODY
Defence.

Abby Hoffman Cup winner with Edmonton on 1997-03-09.
Born 1975-09-29. Grew up in Sherwood Park, AB, CAN.

Year - League - Team		GP	G	A	PTS	PM	Year - Playoff	GP	G	A	PTS	PM
1997	Nationals	Edmonton Chimos										
1998	Nationals	Edmonton Chimos	7	0	2	2	2					
2002-03	NWHL	Edmonton Chimos	16	0	0	0	2					

TAYLOR, LINDSAY
Forward. Shoots left.

Born 1983-11-05. Grew up in Dartmouth, NS, CAN. 5'6".

Year - League - Team		GP	G	A	PTS	PM	Year - Playoff	GP	G	A	PTS	PM
2001	Nationals	Nova Scotia Selects										
2003	Nationals	Nova Scotia Selects	6	1	1	2	2					
2007	Nationals	Nova Scotia Selects	7	2	3	5	10					
2008	Nationals	Nova Scotia Selects	1	0	0	0	0					

TAYLOR, LYNSEY
2004-05 NWHL Brampton (1 gp); 2005-06 (3 gp); 2007-08 CWHL Montréal (1 gp).

TAYLOR, MELISSA
#4. #12

NWHL Cup winner.

Year - League - Team		GP	G	A	PTS	PM	Year - Playoff	GP	G	A	PTS	PM
1999-00	NWHL	Beatrice Aeros	1	0	0	0	0	2000 NWHL-P					
2000-01	NWHL	ClearNet Lightning	1	0	0	0	0					
2001-12	NWHL	Telus Lightning	28	0	1	1	14					

TAYLOR, RENAY
D. 1996-97 COWHL Hamilton #25 (22 games, 1 goal, 2 assist).

TEICHMAN, JAMIE
Forward. 2010-11 WWHL Strathmore Rockies #17 (11 games, 1 goal, 4 assists).

TERRY, KELLY
Forward. Shoots right. #10.

Born 1992-06-06. Grew up in Whitby, ON, CAN. 5'5". Debut at age 22 on 2014-12-20.

Year - League - Team		GP	G	A	PTS	PM	Year - Playoff	GP	G	A	PTS	PM
2014-15	CWHL	Toronto Furies	16	3	10	13	6	2015 C-Cup	2	0	1	1	4
2015-16	CWHL	Toronto Furies	16	3	5	8	8	2016 C-Cup	2	0	0	0	0
2016-17	CWHL	Toronto Furies	24	6	6	12	20	2017 C-Cup	3	1	1	2	4
CWHL Regular Season		56	12	21	33	34	Clarkson Cup	7	1	2	3	8
Totals from all Competitions		**63**	**13**	**23**	**36**	**42**						

TESSIER, MARIE-NOËL
Defence/Forward. Shoots left. #26 #22 #76 #89.

Born 1978-7-22. Grew up in Pont Rouge, QC, CAN. 5'3".

Year - League - Team		GP	G	A	PTS	PM
1999-00	NWHL	Mistral de Laval	9	0	1	1	2
2000-01	NWHL	Mistral de Laval	34	2	5	7	60
2001-02	NWHL	Wingstar de Montréal	19	0	2	2	28
2002-03	NWHL	Axion de Montréal	1	0	0	0	0
2003-04	NWHL	Avalanche du Québec	9	0	0	0	4
2004-05	NWHL	Avalanche du Québec	35	0	4	4	26
2005-06	NWHL	Avalanche du Québec	2	0	0	0	2
Totals from all Competitions		**109**	**2**	**12**	**14**	**122**

TETREAULT, ALISON
Defence. 1999 Nationals Tazmanian Devils (4 games).

THATCHER, KAREN
Forward. Shoots left. #20 #6 #5.

IIHF champion.
Born 1984-2-29, Douglas, MA, USA. Grew up in Blaine, WA, USA. 5'8". Debut at age 22 on 2006-10-27.

Year - League - Team		GP	G	A	PTS	PM	Year - Playoff	GP	G	A	PTS	PM
2006-07	WWHL	British Columbia Breakers	21	15	17	32	18	2007 WWHL-P	2	1	0	1	0
2007	Nationals	British Columbia	5	3	6	9	2					
2007-08	CWHL	Vaughan Flames	22	4	12	16	22	2008 CWHL-P	2	0	0	0	2
2008-09	WWHL	Minnesota Whitecaps	3	2	2	4	4	2009 WWHL-P	2	1	1	2	0
2009-10	WWHL	Minnesota Whitecaps	0	0	0	0	0					
2010-11	CWHL	Boston Blades	10	2	4	6	4	2011 CWHL-P	2				
2011-12	CWHL	Boston Blades	3	1	0	1	0					
2012-13	CWHL	Boston Blades	16	6	3	9	8					
CWHL Regular Season		51	13	19	32	34						
Totals from all Competitions		**88**	**35**	**45**	**80**	**60**						

THEAKER, NIKKI   *Forward. 2003 Nationals Host Saskatchewan (5 gp, 3 pts); 2004 Nationals (6 gp, 1 a.).*

THIBAULT, ANDREANNE   *D. 2002-03 NWHL Ottawa (7 gp); 2003-04 (33 gp, 3 goals, 1 assist; playoff 1 goal).*

THIBAULT, DOMINIQUE   *Forward. Shoots left. #26 #66 #96 #86.*
Clarkson Cup winner with Montréal on 2011-03-27 and 2012-03-25. NWHL winner.
Born 1988-8-26, Ottawa, ON, CAN. Grew up in L'Orignal, ON, CAN. 5'11".

Year - League - Team		GP	G	A	PTS	PM	Year - Playoff		GP	G	A	PTS	PM
2004	NWHL-P	2	0	0	0	0							
2004-05	NWHL Ottawa Raiders	2	0	0	0	2							
2005-06	NWHL Axion de Montréal	21	11	4	15	16	2006	NWHL-P	3	0	0	0	0
2006	Nationals Axion de Montréal	6	2	2	4	0							
2010-11	CWHL Stars de Montréal	17	6	8	14	10	2011	CWHL-P	2	1		1	2
							2011	C-Cup	4	3	3	6	2
2011-12	CWHL Stars de Montréal	7	3	3	6	6	2012	C-Cup	4	1	3	4	0
2012-13	CWHL Stars de Montréal	21	5	4	9	8	2013	C-Cup	4	2	0	2	2
2013-14	CWHL Stars de Montréal	17	10	6	16	2	2014	C-Cup	3	1	1	2	0
CWHL Regular Season		62	24	21	45	26	Clarkson Cup		16	7	7	14	4
Totals from all Competitions		**113**	**45**	**34**	**79**	**50**							

Finished 14th in the Angela James Bowl scoring race in 2013-14

THIBAULT, VANESSA   *Lachine, QC. Forward. 2007-08 CWHL Montréal #5 (4 games, 1 goal, 2 assists).*

THIEM, CASSANDRA   *Defence. Shoots right.*
Born 1983-11-23. Grew up in Winnipeg, MB, CAN.

Year - League - Team		GP	G	A	PTS	PM
2001	Nationals University of Manitoba					
2002	Nationals University of Manitoba	5	0	0	0	0
2003	Nationals University of Winnipeg	3	0	0	0	17
2004	Nationals Manitoba	5	1	0	1	2
2005	Nationals Manitoba	5	0	2	2	6

THOMAS, BREANNE   *Defence. 2005-06 WWHL British Columbia #16 (24 games).*

THOMAS, ELYCE   *Defence. 2006 Nationals British Columbia (6 games).*

THOMAS, JENNIFER   *Forward. 1998 Nationals Nova Scotia Selects (5 games).*

THOMPSON, CHRISSY   *1999-00 NWHL Brampton #28 (2 games); 2000-01 #18 (3 games).*

THOMPSON, KELLY   *D. 2004-05 WWHL British Columbia (20 gp, 9 pts); 2005 Nationals British Columbia (7 gp).*

THOMPSON, KRISTY   *2009-10 CWHL Vaughan Flames #61 (1 game).*

THOMPSON, REBEKAH   *Defence. Shoots right.*
Born 1985-07-24. Grew up in Dipper Harbour, NB, CAN. 5'5".

Year - League - Team		GP	G	A	PTS	PM
2005	Nationals Team New Brunswick	6	0	1	1	4
2006	Nationals Team New Brunswick	7	0	0	0	6
2007	Nationals Team New Brunswick	6	0	0	0	6
2008	Nationals Team New Brunswick	5	0	2	2	10

THOMPSON, ROBIN   *Forward. Shoots right.*
Born 1976-01-15. Grew up in Moncton, NB, CAN.

Year - League - Team		GP	G	A	PTS	PM
1995	Nationals Maritime Sports Blades					
2000	Nationals Team New Brunswick	6	2	3	5	
2001	Nationals Team New Brunswick					
2002	Nationals PEI Humpty Dumpty	6	2	1	3	0
2004	Nationals Team New Brunswick	5	2	2	4	0
2005	Nationals Team New Brunswick	6	8	3	11	4
2006	Nationals Team New Brunswick	7	2	2	4	4

THOMPSON, SHANNON   *Forward. #19 #17.*

Year - League - Team	GP	G	A	PTS	PM
1995-96 COWHL Hamilton Golden Hawks	28	10	4	14	36
1996-97 COWHL Hamilton	30	3	5	8	52
Totals from all Competitions	**58**	**13**	**9**	**22**	**88**

THOMPSON, SARAH   *2000-01 NWHL Mistral de Laval (3 games, 1 assist).*

THOMSON, MEGHAN   *Defence. 2003 Nationals Host Saskatchewan (5 games).*

THORSON, JESSIE   *Forward. 1999 Nationals Saskatchewan Selects (4 games).*

THUNSTROM, ALLIE   *Forward. Shoots right. #15 #9.*
Isobel Cup winner with Minnesota on 2019-03-17.
Born 1988-4-20. Grew up in Maplewood, MN, USA. 5'5".

Year - League - Team		GP	G	A	PTS	PM	Year - Playoff		GP	G	A	PTS	PM
2010-11	WWHL Minnesota Whitecaps	17	28	18	46	6	2011	C-Cup	3	1	0	1	2
2018-19	NWHL/ Minnesota Whitecaps	16	5	4	9	4	2019	I-Cup	2	0	1	1	0

TIBBO, LORNA   *Defence. 2004 Nationals Newfoundland Labrador (5 games).*

TIBERI, KIM — *Forward. Shoots right. #24.*
Born 1996-05-07. Grew up in Raleigh, NC, USA. 5'9". Debut at age 22 on 2018-10-07.

Year - League - Team	GP	G	A	PTS	PM
2018-19 NWHL/ Connecticut Whale	11	0	1	1	4

TICMANIS, ALLISON — *D. 2002 Nationals Équipe Québec (6 gp); 2003-04 NWHL Avalanche (25 gp, 4 assists).*

TILLEY, JENNIFER — *Forward. 2000 Nationals Newfoundland Labrador (5 gp, 2 goals, 2 assists).*

TOANE, JACKIE — *2008-09 WWHL Strathmore Rockies (20 games, 1 assist; playoff 1 game).*

TODD, ANGI — *1996-97 COWHL Hamilton Golden Hawks #15 (6 games, 1 goal).*

TODD, DIANE — *Forward. 2002 Nationals Saskatchewan (6 games, 1 goal).*

TODD, JUSTINE — *Forward. Shoots right. #5.*
Born 1983-07-04. Grew up in Smith Falls, ON, CAN.

Year - League - Team	GP	G	A	PTS	PM
2002 Nationals Calgary Oval X-Treme	6	0	0	0	0
2007-08 CWHL Ottawa Capital Canucks	1	0	0	0	0

Served as a referee in the Canadian Women's Hockey League and at the Winter Olympic Games.

TOLLFESON, CRISTIN — *Defence. 1999 Nationals Saskatchewan (4 gp, 2 goals); 2000 Nationals (7 gp, 1 g., 1a.).*

TOMASELLI, KATHRYN — *Forward. Shoots right. #27.*
Born 1993-05-12. Grew up in Cape Coral, FL, USA. 5'7". Debut at age 23 on 2016-10-07.

Year - League - Team	GP	G	A	PTS	PM
2016-17 NWHL/ Boston Pride	8	0	0	0	0
2017-18 NWHL/ Boston Pride	13	0	3	3	0

TOMIMOTO, TARA — *Defence.*
Born 1991-08-16. Grew up in Calgary, AB, CAN. 5'5". Debut in 2015-16.

Year - League - Team	GP	G	A	PTS	PM	Year - Playoff	GP	G	A	PTS	PM
2015-16 NWHL/ Connecticut Whale	13	1	0	1	6	2016 I-Cup	1	0	0	0	0

TOMKINS, LEE — *1996-97 COWHL Scarborough Sting #18 (29 games, 1 goal, 2 assists).*

TOOPE, JENNIFER — *Forward. Shoots left.*
Born 1979-11-26. Grew up in Mount Pearl, NL, CAN.

Year - League - Team	GP	G	A	PTS	PM
2000 Nationals Newfoundland Labrador	5	0	0	0	
2001 Nationals Newfoundland Labrador					
2002 Nationals Newfoundland Labrador	5	0	1	1	2
2003 Nationals Newfoundland Labrador	5	0	0	0	8
2004 Nationals Newfoundland Labrador	5	0	2	2	10
2005 Nationals Newfoundland Labrador	5	0	0	0	12
2006 Nationals Newfoundland Labrador	5	0	0	0	6

TOPOLNISKY, ELAINE — *Forward. 2001 Nationals Vancouver Griffins.*

TORRANCE, ANN — *Forward. 1998-99 NWHL Brampton Thunder #59 (4 games).*

TOUGAS, KAITLYN — *Forward. Shoots right. #94.*
Born 1994-11-05. Grew up in Thunder Bay, ON, CAN. 5'4". Debut at age 21 on 2016-10-08.

Year - League - Team	GP	G	A	PTS	PM	Year - Playoff	GP	G	A	PTS	PM
2016-17 CWHL Brampton Thunder	23	1	0	1	4	2017 C-Cup	2	0	0	0	0

TOWNSEND, JANYEA — *Defence. 2008-09 WWHL Edmonton Chimos (1 game).*

TRAPP, RHONDA — *Forward. #27.*
Abby Hoffman Cup winner with Aeros on 1991-03-17 and 1993-03-28.

Year - League - Team	GP	G	A	PTS	PM
1992-93 COWHL Toronto Aeros	26	8	10	18	22
1993-94 COWHL Toronto Aeros	26	13	18	31	40
Totals from all Competitions	**52**	**21**	**28**	**49**	**62**

TRAVERSA, SILVIA — *Forward. Shoots left. #19 #20 #17.*
Born 1980-11-14, Vancouver, BC, CAN. 5'3".

Year - League - Team	GP	G	A	PTS	PM	Year - Playoff	GP	G	A	PTS	PM
2002 Nationals Calgary Oval X-Treme	6	1	2	3	2						
2002-03 NWHL Calgary Oval X-Treme	2	0	0	0	2						
2005 Nationals Alberta	6	0	0	0	0						
2005-06 WWHL British Columbia Breakers	24	1	1	2	4						
2006-07 WWHL British Columbia Breakers	24	2	12	14	4	2007 WWHL-P	2	0	0	0	0
2007 Nationals British Columbia	5	0	2	2	0						
2007-08 WWHL British Columbia Breakers	24	2	4	6	10						
2008-09 WWHL British Columbia Breakers	14	2	2	4	2						
Totals from all Competitions	**107**	**8**	**23**	**31**	**24**						

TRAYLOR, KATHERINE — *Defence. 2004-05 NWHL Toronto Aeros #36 (6 games).*

TRAYNOR, KELLEIGH — *1995-96 COWHL Peterborough #24 (11 games, 7 goals, 2 assists).*

TREMBLAY, ÉLIZABETH — *Saguenay, QC. Forward. 2015-16 CWHL Boston Blades #14 (18 games, 2 goals).*

TREMBLAY, LAURIE

Forward. Shoots left. #90 #8 #77.

Year - League - Team		GP	G	A	PTS	PM	Year - Playoff	GP	G	A	PTS	PM
2004-05	NWHL Avalanche du Québec	1	0	0	0	0						
2005-06	NWHL Avalanche du Québec	9	2	2	4	10						
2006-07	NWHL Avalanche du Québec	4	0	1	1	2	2007 NWHL-PQuébec					
2007-08	CWHL Phénix du Québec	1	0	0	0	2						

TREMILLS, CHRISTIANNE

Defence. #16 #96 #27.

Year - League - Team		GP	G	A	PTS	PM
1992-93	COWHL Scarborough Firefighters	27	3	8	11	30
1993-94	COWHL Scarborough Firefighters	28	8	8	16	42
1995-96	COWHL Toronto Red Wings	23	2	11	13	55
1996-97	COWHL Newtonbrook Panthers	35	8	24	32	44
1999-00	NWHL Scarborough Sting	37	7	2	9	42
2000-01	NWHL Toronto Sting	38	4	6	10	62
2001-02	NWHL Durham Lightning	26	3	11	14	30
2002-03	NWHL Durham Lightning					
2003-04	NWHL Durham Lightning	32	3	7	10	12
Totals from all Competitions		**246**	**38**	**77**	**115**	**317**

TREPANIER, MYRIAM
Defence. 2003-04 NWHL Montréal (1 gp); 2004-05 (3 gp, 1 goal); 2005 Nationals (6 gp).

TRIMBLE, LINDSAY
Forward. 2000-01 NWHL Durham Lightning (1 game).

TRIMM-COMBES, LEIGH
Scarborough, ON. D. 2007-08 CWHL Burlington Barracudas (playoff 2 games).

TRITTER, NICOLE

Forward. Shoots right. #24.

Born 1987-5-31. Grew up in Toronto, ON, CAN. Debut at age 22 on 2009-10-4.

Year - League - Team		GP	G	A	PTS	PM	Year - Playoff	GP	G	A	PTS	PM
2009-10	CWHL Brampton Thunder	27	6	12	18	36	2010 C-Cup	2	0		0	2

CWHL All-Rookie Team in 2009-10

TRIVIGNO, DANA

Forward. Shoots right. #8.

Born 1994-01-07. Grew up in Setauket, NY, USA. 5'4". Debut at age 22 on 2016-10-09.

Year - League - Team		GP	G	A	PTS	PM	Year - Playoff	GP	G	A	PTS	PM
2016-17	NWHL/ Connecticut Whale	16	3	6	9	16	2017 I-Cup	1	1	0	1	2
2017-18	NWHL/ Boston Pride	13	3	5	8	24	2018 I-Cup	1	0	0	0	2
2018-19	NWHL/ Boston Pride	12	2	4	6	14	2019 I-Cup	1	0	0	0	2
NWHL Regular Season		41	8	15	23	54	Isobel Cup	3	1	0	1	6

TROOP, SOFIA
Georgetown, ON. Defence. 2009-10 CWHL Mississauga #18 (1 game).

TRUSSLER, EDITH
1999-00 NWHL Scarborough Sting #45 (3 games).

TUREK, AMY

Left wing. Shoots left. #6 #36.

Abby Hoffman Cup winner with Aeros on 2000-03-12. NWHL Cup winner.
Born 1975-7-20. Grew up in Brooklin, ON, CAN. 5'5".

Year - League - Team		GP	G	A	PTS	PM	Year - Playoff	GP	G	A	PTS	PM
1992-93	COWHL Guelph Eagles	27	7	8	15	6						
1993-94	COWHL Toronto Junior Aeros	26	17	23	40	18						
1995-96	COWHL North York Aeros	25	25	18	43	22						
1996	Nationals North York Aeros	5	4	3	7	0						
1996-97	COWHL North York Aeros	21	26	26	52	20						
1997-98	COWHL North York Aeros	19	7	7	14	14						
1998	Nationals North York Aeros	6	3	3	6	4						
1998-99	NWHL North York Aeros	20	13	12	25	10						
1999	Nationals North York Aeros	5	5	3	8							
1999-00	NWHL North York Aeros	38	26	25	51	20	2000 NWHL-P					
2000	Nationals North York Aeros	6	4	6	10							
2000-01	NWHL North York Aeros	39	35	34	69	18						
2001	Nationals North York Aeros											
2001-02	NWHL North York Aeros	28	25	17	42	18	2003 NWHL-P					
2002	Nationals North York Aeros	7	3	4	7	0						
2003-04	NWHL Toronto Aeros	0	0	0	0	0	2004 NWHL-P					
2005-06	NWHL Toronto Aeros	0	0	0	0	0						
Totals from all Competitions		**272**	**200**	**189**	**389**	**150**						

TURI, JESSICA
Mississauga, ON. Forward. 2007-08 CWHL Vaughan Flames #18 (1 game).

TURNBULL, BLAYRE

Forward. Shoots right. #26.

Clarkson Cup winner with Calgary on 2016-03-14 and 2019-03-24.
Born 1993-07-15. Grew up in Stellarton, NS, CAN. 5'7". Debut at age 22 on 2015-10-24.

Year - League - Team		GP	G	A	PTS	PM	Year - Playoff	GP	G	A	PTS	PM
2015-16	CWHL Calgary Inferno	22	7	9	16	16	2016 C-Cup	3	3	2	5	0
2016-17	CWHL Calgary Inferno	22	9	9	18	12	2017 C-Cup	4	1	0	1	4
2017-18	CWHL Calgary Inferno	4	0	0	0	4	2018 C-Cup	3	1	0	1	0
2018-19	CWHL Calgary Inferno	25	12	9	21	24	2019 C-Cup	4	1	2	3	4
Totals from all Competitions		**87**	**34**	**31**	**65**	**64**						

Finished 14th in the Angela James Bowl scoring race in 2016-17

TURNER, AMANDA — Forward. Shoots right.

Born 1989-02-03. Grew up in Kaslo, BC, CAN. 5'3".

Year - League - Team			GP	G	A	PTS	PM
2002-03	NWHL	Avalanche du Québec	33	1	3	4	20
2003-04	NWHL	Avalanche du Québec	8	1	0	1	4
2007	Nationals	BC Outback	5	2	0	2	2

TURNER, CASSANDRA — Defence. Shoots right. #21 #7.

Abby Hoffman Cup winner with Aeros on 2004-03-14 and 2005-03-13.

Born 1981-5-20.

Year - League - Team			GP	G	A	PTS	PM	Year - Playoff		GP	G	A	PTS	PM
1996-97	COWHL	Peterborough Pirates	34	1	9	10	31							
1997-98	COWHL	Scarborough Sting	19	1	1	2	14							
1998-99	NWHL	Scarborough Sting	31	2	4	6	24							
2003-04	NWHL	Toronto Aeros	34	2	15	17	18	2004	NWHL-P					
2004	Nationals	Toronto Aeros	6	0	2	2	4							
2004-05	NWHL	Toronto Aeros	35	2	15	17	26							
2005	Nationals	Toronto Aeros	7	1	1	2	4							
Totals from all Competitions			**166**	**9**	**47**	**56**	**121**							

TURNER, COURTNEY — Centre. Shoots right. #3.

Born 1994-06-17. Grew up in Milton, MA, USA. 5'3". Debut at age 23 on 2017-10-14.

Year - League - Team			GP	G	A	PTS	PM
2017-18	CWHL	Boston Blades	28	3	3	6	14
2018-19	CWHL	Worcester Blades	27	1	3	4	26

TURNER, MEGHAN — Forward. Shoots right. #26.

Born 1994-08-07. Grew up in Bedford, NH, USA. 5'6". Debut at age 24 on 2018-10-13.

Year - League - Team			GP	G	A	PTS	PM
2018-19	CWHL	Worcester Blades	21	0	2	2	6

TURNER, MORGAN — Forward. Shoots right. #81.

Born 1996-05-18. Grew up in Chicago, IL, USA. 5'8'. Debut at age 22 on 2018-10-13.

Year - League - Team			GP	G	A	PTS	PM
2018-19	CWHL	Worcester Blades	24	4	3	7	22

TURNEY, ALI — Forward. Shoots left. #10.

Born 1982-12-30, Milwaukee, WI, USA. 5'8".

Year - League - Team			GP	G	A	PTS	PM	Year - Playoff		GP	G	A	PTS	PM
2005-06	WWHL	Minnesota Whitecaps	24	5	4	9	26	2006	WWHL-P	3	0	1	1	4
2006-07	WWHL	Minnesota Whitecaps	13	3	1	4	6	2007	WWHL-P	0	0	0	0	0
Totals from all Competitions			**40**	**8**	**6**	**14**	**36**							

TURPLE, GLADYS — Defence. 1995 Nationals Metro Valley Selects.

TUTINO, KAYLA — Forward. Shoots right. #88.

Born 1992-12-18, Montréal, QC, CAN. Grew up in Lorraine. Debut at age 15 on 2008-10-4.

Year - League - Team			GP	G	A	PTS	PM	Year - Playoff		GP	G	A	PTS	PM
2008-09	CWHL	Ottawa Senators	4	1	1	2	0							
2016-17	CWHL	Boston Blades	24	2	3	5	8							
2017-18	CWHL	Canadiennes de Montréal	28	7	9	16	8	2018	C-Cup	2	0	0	0	0
2018-19	CWHL	Canadiennes de Montréal	5	1	1	2	0							
CWHL Regular Season			61	11	14	25	16	Clarkson Cup		2	0	0	0	0

TUTTLE, JENNIE — Forward. 2007 Nationals British Columbia (5 games, 1 goal).

TYRA, JESSICA — Forward. 2010-11 WWHL Manitoba Maple Leafs #7 (9 games, 5 goals, 6 assists).

ULRICH, ROBIN — Forward. 2003 Nationals Host Saskatchewan (5 gp, 1 goal, 1 assist).

UNRUH, COURTNEY — Forward. Shoots left. #6 #33 #27 #67.

Born 1987-2-7. Grew up in Fort St. John, BC, CAN. 5'4".

Year - League - Team			GP	G	A	PTS	PM	Year - Playoff		GP	G	A	PTS	PM
2002-03	NWHL	Vancouver Griffins	24	6	3	9	10							
2003	Nationals	Vancouver Griffins	6	0	1	1	0							
2004	Nationals	British Columbia	6	1	1	2	4							
2004-05	WWHL	British Columbia Breakers	20	6	8	14	19							
2005	Nationals	British Columbia	7	1	1	2	0							
2006-07	NWHL	Oakville Ice	35	3	9	12	24	2007	NWHL-P	3	0	0	0	2
2007	Nationals	British Columbia	5	4	2	6	6							
2007-08	CWHL	Vaughan Flames	5	3	1	4	4	2008	CWHL-P	2	0	1	1	0
2008-09	CWHL	Vaughan Flames	8	1	2	3	4	2009	CWHL-P	2				
2009-10	CWHL	Vaughan Flames	9	3	2	5	2							
2011-12	CWHL	Brampton Thunder	26	1	6	7	8	2012	C-Cup	2	0	1	1	0
CWHL Regular Season			48	8	11	19	18	Clarkson Cup		2	0	1	1	0
Totals from all Competitions			**160**	**29**	**38**	**67**	**83**							

URBAN, JOANNE — 1993-94 COWHL Hamilton Golden Hawks (1 goal).

URBAN, KAROLINA
Forward. Shoots left. #96.

Clarkson Cup winner with Markham on 2018-03-25
Born 1989-12-17. Grew up in Kamloops, BC, CAN. Debut at age 23 on 2012-10-20.

Year - League - Team			GP	G	A	PTS	PM	Year - Playoff	GP	G	A	PTS	PM
2012-13	CWHL	Toronto Furies	24	2	2	4	8	2013 C-Cup	2	0	0	0	0
2013-14	CWHL	Calgary Inferno	24	0	1	1	24	2014 C-Cup	3	0	0	0	4
2017-18	CWHL	Markham Thunder	28	2	3	5	30	2018 C-Cup	3	0	0	0	0
CWHL Regular Season			75	4	6	10	62	Clarkson Cup	8	0	0	0	4

URICK, NATALIE
2003-04 NWHL Durham Lightning #77 (33 games).

VACHON, CHRYSTAL
2000-01 NWHL Ottawa Raiders #12 (37 games, 2 goals, 5 assists).

VAILLANCOURT, MARIE-CLAUDE
Defence. Shoots right. #12 #77.

Born 1984-9-17, LaSalle, QC, CAN. 5'6".

Year - League - Team		GP	G	A	PTS	PM
2002-03	NWHL Avalanche du Québec	2	0	0	0	2
2003-04	NWHL Avalanche du Québec	11	0	2	2	0
2004-05	NWHL Avalanche du Québec	36	0	2	2	30
2005-06	NWHL Avalanche du Québec	32	1	6	7	30
Totals from all Competitions		**81**	**1**	**10**	**11**	**62**

VAILLANCOURT, SARAH
Forward. Shoots right. #40.

Olympic champion, IIHF champion. Clarkson Cup winner with Montréal on 2011-03-27
Born 1985-5-8, Sherbrooke, QC, CAN. 5'6". Debut at age 26 on 2011-1-15.

Year - League - Team			GP	G	A	PTS	PM	Year - Playoff	GP	G	A	PTS	PM
2010-11	CWHL	Stars de Montréal	12	10	15	25	8	2011 CWHL-P	2	1	2	3	2
								2011 C-Cup	4	7	0	7	6
2011-12	CWHL	Stars de Montréal	14	10	18	28	30						
2012-13	CWHL	Stars de Montréal	5	2	1	3	6	2013 C-Cup	4	1	2	3	2
2013-14	CWHL	Stars de Montréal	17	12	23	35	12	2014 C-Cup	3	0	0	0	2
CWHL Regular Season			48	34	57	91	56	Clarkson Cup	11	8	2	10	10
Totals from all Competitions			**61**	**43**	**61**	**104**	**68**						

CWHL First All-Star Team in 2010-11... CWHL Outstanding Rookie in 2010-11... CWHL All-Rookie Team in 2010-11...
Clarkson Cup Championship MVP in 2011... finished 2nd in the Angela James Bowl scoring race in 2013-14

VALENTI, MAREN
Forward. #90.

Born 1976-1-15, Freiburg, GER.

Year - League - Team		GP	G	A	PTS	PM
2000-01	NWHL Sainte-Julie	27	12	20	32	40

VALLEAU, LISA
Forward. 1995 Nationals Britannia Blues; 1996 Nationals (5 games, 4 assists).

VAN AGGELEN, ASHLEY
Forward. 2005 Nationals Manitoba (5 gp, 6 pts); .

VAN AGGELEN, ASHLEY
Forward. Shoots left.

Born 1982-04-21. Grew up in Winnipeg, MB, CAN.

Year - League - Team		GP	G	A	PTS	PM
2005	Nationals Manitoba	5	3	3	6	2
2006	Nationals Manitoba	5	3	5	8	2
2007	Nationals Manitoba	5	1	2	3	2

VAN BLOKLAND, TANYA
Forward. 1999-00 NWHL Mistral de Laval #11 (35 gp, 1 goal, 3 assists).

VAN DAM, JILL
Forward. 2000-01 NWHL Toronto Sting #2 (11 games, 5 goals, 1 assist).

VAN DAMME, SUE ANNE
Forward. #12 #7 #21 #10.

Year - League - Team		GP	G	A	PTS	PM
1996-97	COWHL Newtonbrook Panthers	9	7	4	11	8
1998-99	NWHL Scarborough Sting	32	4	3	7	120
1999-00	NWHL Scarborough Sting	36	8	5	13	116
2000-01	NWHL Toronto Sting	12	3	3	6	28
2003-04	NWHL Brampton Thunder					
Totals from all Competitions		**89**	**22**	**15**	**37**	**272**

VAN EERD, ANGELA
Forward. Shoots right. 2005 Nationals British Columbia (7 gp, 1 goal, 3 assists).

VAN OORDT, CHRISTY
Defence. 1998-99 NWHL Scarborough (38 gp, 1 goal, 1 assists); 1999-00 (4 games).

VANASSE, KARINE
Defence. 1998-99 NWHL Montréal (15 gp, 4 assists); 1999-00 Sainte-Julie (11 gp).

VANBLORIAND, TANYA
1998-99 NWHL Mistral de Laval #47 (2 games, 1 assist).

VANDENBERGHE, KENDRA
Forward. 2007 Nationals BC Outback (5 games).

VANDERHORST, LAURA
Defence. 1996 Nationals Winnipeg Sweat Camp (6 games, 2 assists).

VANDERLUGT, DANIELLE
Defence. 2009-10 CWHL Vaughan Flames #7 (12 games, 2 assists).

VANDIEPEN, EMILY
Defence. 2008 Nationals Prince Edward Island (3 games, 1 goal).

VANGALEN, HEIDI
Defence. 1992-93 COWHL Scarborough #17 (17 gp, 1 goal, 3 assists).

VANOOSTRUM, ELIZABETH
Forward. 2003 Nationals Team New Brunswick (4 games, 1 assist).

VASICHEK, JULIANNE
Forward. 2006-07 WWHL Minnesota (11 games, 3 goals).

VAUGHAN, KATE
F. 1993-94 COWHL Hamilton (2 games); 1995-96 Hamilton (27 gp, 9 goals, 7 assists).

VAUTOUR, JOANNE — *Forward. 1995 Nationals Maritime Sport Blades; 1996 Nationals (6 gp, 1 g., 4 a.).*

VAVASOUR, KATIE — *F. 2000 Nationals Newfoundland (5 gp, 1 a.); 2001 Nationals; 2002 Nationals (5 gp, 1 a.).*

VELLA, JESSICA — *Forward. Shoots right. #12.*

Clarkson Cup winner with Toronto on 2014-03-22
Born 1991-07-05. Grew up Pickering, ON, CAN. 5'2". Debut at age 22 on 2013-11-09.

Year - League - Team		GP	G	A	PTS	PM	Year - Playoff		GP	G	A	PTS	PM
2013-14	CWHL Toronto Furies	20	7	1	8	6	2014	C-Cup	3	0	0	0	0
2014-15	CWHL Toronto Furies	19	3	0	3	2	2015	C-Cup	2	0	0	0	2
2015-16	CWHL Toronto Furies	22	4	4	8	6	2016	C-Cup	2	0	0	0	0
2016-17	CWHL Toronto Furies	24	0	1	1	6	2017	C-Cup	3	0	1	1	4
2017-18	CWHL Toronto Furies	26	3	7	10	8							
2018-19	CWHL Toronto Furies	25	2	4	6	10	2019	C-Cup	3	0	0	0	2
CWHL Regular Season		136	19	17	36	38	Clarkson Cup		13	0	1	1	8
Totals from all Competitions		**149**	**19**	**18**	**37**	**46**							

VERDON, KARINA — *Defence. 1998-99 NWHL Ottawa Raiders #15 (24 games, 1 assist).*

VERHOEST, CYNTHIA — *2001-02 Montréal (1 gp); 2002-03 Québec (35 gp, 1 assist); 2003-04 (2 gp, 1 assist).*

VERLAAN PAGE, MARGOT — *Forward. Shoots right. #18.*

IIHF champion. Abby Hoffman Cup winner with Aeros on 1991-03-17 and 1993-03-28.
Born 1964-06-27, Kitchener, ON, CAN. Grew up in Lorne Beach. 5'6".

Year - League - Team		GP	G	A	PTS	PM
1992-93	COWHL Toronto Aeros	25	9	8	17	14
1992-93	COWHL Toronto Aeros	28	15	34	49	10
1995	Nationals Mississauga Chiefs					
1995-96	COWHL Mississauga Chiefs	19	12	11	23	20
1996-97	COWHL Mississauga Chiefs	35	44	48	92	24
1997-98	COWHL Mississauga Chiefs	10	4	3	7	10
Totals from all Competitions		**117**	**84**	**104**	**188**	**78**

VERMEULEN, AMY — *Forward.*

Born 1983-11-23, Rosetown, SK, CAN. Grew up in Melfort, SK and Saskatoon, SK.

Year - League - Team		GP	G	A	PTS	PM	Year - Playoff	GP	G	A	PTS	PM
1999	Nationals Saskatchewan Selects	4	1	1	2							
2000	Nationals Saskatchewan Selects	7	1	1	2							

Represented Canada Soccer in FIFA World Cup Qualifiers in 2006.

VERNON, RACHELLE — *Forward*

Abby Hoffman Cup winner with Edmonton on 1997-03-09.
Born 1969-09-28.

Year - League - Team		GP	G	A	PTS	PM	Year - Playoff	GP	G	A	PTS	PM
1995	Nationals Calgary Classics											
1996	Nationals Edmonton Chimos	7	0	5	5	2						
1997	Nationals Edmonton Chimos											
1998	Nationals Edmonton Chimos	7	2	6	8	2						

VESCI, ASHLEY — *Forward. Shoots right. #6.*

Isobel Cup winner with Buffalo on 2017-03-19
Born 1993-07-12. Grew up Pittsburgh, PA, USA. 5'7". Debut at age 23 on 2016-10-15.

Year - League - Team		GP	G	A	PTS	PM	Year - Playoff		GP	G	A	PTS	PM
2016-17	NWHL/ Buffalo Beauts	10	0	1	1	2	2017	I-Cup	2	0	1	1	6

VIBERB, NATALIE — *2001-02 NWHL Durham Lightning #27 (1 game).*

VIGUE, ABBI — *Defence. 2003 Nationals Vancouver (7 gp, 1 a.); 2007 Nationals BC Outback.*

VINE, LINDSAY — *Forward. Shoots right. #4 #19 #2 #91.*

Born 1981-10-3, Kirkland Lake, ON, CAN. 5'5".

Year - League - Team		GP	G	A	PTS	PM	Year - Playoff		GP	G	A	PTS	PM
1999-00	NWHL Mississauga Chiefs	39	11	13	24	18							
2004-05	NWHL Oakville Ice	36	9	10	19	40							
2005-06	NWHL Oakville Ice	34	14	19	33	34	2006	NWHL-P	2	0	2	2	2
2006-07	NWHL Oakville Ice	35	7	11	18	44	2007	NWHL-P	3	1	1	2	4
2007-08	CWHL Burlington Barracudas	30	10	11	21	22	2008	CWHL-P	3	0	0	0	0
2008-09	CWHL Burlington Barracudas	28	11	16	27	10	2009	CWHL-P	4	1	2	3	4
2009-10	CWHL Burlington Barracudas	30	18	26	44	28							
2010-11	CWHL Burlington Barracudas	22	5	4	9	12							
2011-12	CWHL Burlington Barracudas	23	2	4	6	8							
2012-13	CWHL Brampton Thunder	9	1	2	3	8	2013	C-Cup	3	0	0	0	2
2013-14	CWHL Brampton Thunder	24	3	2	5	18							
2014-15	CWHL Brampton Thunder	22	4	2	6	6							
CWHL Regular Season		188	54	67	121	112	Clarkson Cup		3	0	0	0	2
Totals from all Competitions		**347**	**97**	**125**	**222**	**260**							

CWHL First All-Star Team in 2009-10... finished 2nd in the Angela James Bowl scoring race in 2009-10... scored 100th CWHL point on 2011-01-09

VINEY, KRYSTAL — Defence. *2004-05 NWHL Durham Lightning #5 (31 games, 3 assists).*

VINT, REBECCA — Forward. Shoots right. #12.
Born 1992-5-5. Grew up in Caledon, ON, CAN. 5'10". Debut at age 17 on 2009-10-24.

Year - League - Team			GP	G	A	PTS	PM	Year - Playoff		GP	G	A	PTS	PM
2009-10	CWHL	Brampton Thunder	1	0	0	0	0							
2015-16	CWHL	Brampton Thunder	24	19	7	26	42	2016	C-Cup	2	2	0	2	4
2016-17	CWHL	Brampton Thunder	19	8	7	15	30	2017	C-Cup	2	0	0	0	2
2017-18	NWHL/	Buffalo Beauts	13	3	3	6	16	2018	I-Cup	1	0	0	0	0
CWHL Regular Season			44	27	14	41	72	Clarkson Cup		4	2	0	2	6
Totals from all Competitions			**62**	**32**	**17**	**49**	**94**							

CWHL All-Rookie Team in 2015-16... finished 9th in the Angela James Bowl scoring race in 2015-16

VISSEUR, KEIRSTIN — Defence. *2008 Nationals Prince Edward Island (5 gp, 1 assist).*

VLAHOVICH, TANJA — Defence. *1996-97 COWHL Hamilton #2 (20 games, 2 goals, 1 assist).*

VOLKART, TARA — Forward. *1998 Nationals Tazmanian Devils (5 games).*

VRIEND, JEN — *1999-00 NWHL Ottawa Raiders #96 (1 game).*

WADDEN, JENNIE — Defence. *2004 Nationals Newfoundland (5 gp); 2005 Nationals Newfoundland (5 gp).*

WADDEN, NANCY — Defence. *2004 Nationals Newfoundland (5 games, 1 goal).*

WAGNER, NADINE — Forward. *2005 Nationals P.E.I. (5 gp); 2006 Nationals (5 gp, 3 assists); 2007 Nationals (5 gp).*

WAKEFIELD, JENNIFER — Forward. Shoots right. #17 #11 #2.
Olympic champion.
Born 1989-6-15, Scarborough, ON. Grew up in Pickering, ON, CAN. 5'9". Debut at age 16 on 2005-11-29.

Year - League - Team			GP	G	A	PTS	PM	Year - Playoff		GP	G	A	PTS	PM
2005-06	NWHL	Durham Lightning	12	6	4	10	30	2006	NWHL-P	2	0	1	1	0
2006-07	NWHL	Etobicoke Dolphins	27	24	12	36	42	2007	NWHL-P	3	0	0	0	4
2007	Nationals	Etobicoke Dolphins		0	0	0								
2012-13	CWHL	Toronto Furies	24	12	5	17	34	2013	C-Cup	3	0	1	1	12
Totals from all Competitions			**71**	**42**	**23**	**65**	**122**							

Finished 16th in the Angela James Bowl scoring race in 2012-13

WAKEHAM, PEGGY — Defence. *2004 Nationals Newfoundland Labrador (5 gp, 1 goal).*

WALLACE, JANEELE — Forward. *2010-11 WWHL Manitoba #8 (3 games, 1 assist).*

WALLACE, KERRI — Defence. Shoots left.
Abby Hoffman Cup winner with Calgary on 2003-03-16.
Born 1984-06-10. Grew up in Rocky Mountain House, AB, CAN.

Year - League - Team			GP	G	A	PTS	PM	Year - Playoff		GP	G	A	PTS	PM
2002-03	NWHL	Calgary Oval X-Treme	17	2	5	7	19	2003	NWHL-P					
2003	Nationals	Calgary Oval X-Treme	5	0	2	2	0							
2003-04	NWHL	Calgary Oval X-Treme	5	1	4	5	2							
2004	Nationals	Calgary Oval X-Treme	6	0	0	0	4							

WALROTH, PATTI — Forward. *2009-10 NWHL Edmonton Chimos #88 (11 games, 1 goal).*

WALSH, JESSICA — Forward. *2006 Nationals Newfoundland Labrador (5 games, 1 goal).*

WALSH, LISA — Defence. *1998 Nationals Nova Scotia Selects (5 games).*

WALSH, PENNY — Forward. *2001 Nationals PEI Humpty Dumpty.*

WALSH, TAMMY — Forward.
Abby Hoffman Cup winner with Calgary on 1998-03-22.

Year - League - Team			GP	G	A	PTS	PM	Year - Playoff		GP	G	A	PTS	PM
1998	Nationals	Calgary Oval X-Treme	7	0	1	1	2							
2000	Nationals	Team New Brunswick	6	0	0	0								

WALSHE, KRISTIN — Defence. *2006 Nationals Newfoundland Labrador (5 games).*

WALTHER, URSULA — *1992-93 COWHL Guelph #7 (23 gp, 3 goals, 5 a.); 1993-94 Hamilton #7 (17 gp, 2 goals, 2 a.).*

WALTON, MEAGAN — Forward. Shoots right. #9.
Abby Hoffman Cup winner with Calgary on 2001-03-11 and 2007-03-10. WWHL winner. Born 1983-8-23, Edmonton, AB, CAN. 5'7".

Year - League - Team			GP	G	A	PTS	PM	Year - Playoff		GP	G	A	PTS	PM
2000	Nationals	Calgary Oval X-Treme	7	1	2	3								
2001	Nationals	Calgary Oval X-Treme												
2005-06	WWHL	Calgary Oval X-Treme	24	18	24	42	2	2006	WWHL-P	3	3	1	4	0
2006-07	WWHL	Calgary Oval X-Treme	21	7	23	30	8	2007	WWHL-P	3	0	4	4	2
2007	Nationals	Calgary Oval X-Treme	6	4	6	10	0							
2007-08	WWHL	Calgary Oval X-Treme	23	22	22	44	12							
2008	Nationals	Calgary Oval X-Treme	3	2	5	7	0							
Totals from all Competitions			**90**	**57**	**87**	**144**	**24**							

WALZ, DANIELLE — Forward. Shoots right. #22 #10.
Born 1986-05-18. Grew up in Kerrobert, SK, CAN.

Year - League - Team			GP	G	A	PTS	PM	Year - Playoff		GP	G	A	PTS	PM
2002	Nationals	Saskatchewan	6	3	0	3	2							

Year - League - Team			GP	G	A	PTS	PM	Year - Playoff	GP	G	A	PTS	PM
2003-04	NWHL	Edmonton Chimos	6	1	0	1	2	2004 NWHL-P	1	0	0	0	0
2004	Nationals	Edmonton Chimos	7	5	2	7	14						
2004-05	WWHL	Edmonton Chimos	11	1	2	3	16	2005 WWHL-P	2	0	0	0	0

WANG BO *Defence. Shoots right. #29.*

Born 1998-06-18. Grew up in Harbin, CHN. 5'6". Debut at age 19 on 2017-10-21.

Year - League - Team			GP	G	A	PTS	PM	Year - Playoff	GP	G	A	PTS	PM
2017-18	CWHL	Kunlun Red Star	28	0	0	0	0	2018 C-Cup	4	0	0	0	0

WANG LINUO *Harbin, CHN. Forward. 2007-08 WWHL Calgary #10 (15 gp, 2 goals, 6 assists).*

WANG WENZHUO *Centre. Shoots right. #21.*

Born 1998-05-29. Grew up in Qiqihar, CHN. 5'6". Debut at age 19 on 2017-10-21.

Year - League - Team			GP	G	A	PTS	PM	Year - Playoff	GP	G	A	PTS	PM
2017-18	CWHL	Kunlun Red Star	28	0	0	0	4	2018 C-Cup	4	0	0	0	0

WARD, CARLA *Defence. 1998 Nationals Nova Scotia Selects (5 games).*

WARD, CATHERINE *Defence. Shoots left. #18.*

Olympic champion. Clarkson Cup winner with Montréal on 2012-03-25.

Born 1987-2-17, Montréal, QC, CAN. 5'6". Debut at age 19 on 2005-11-26.

Year - League - Team			GP	G	A	PTS	PM	Year - Playoff	GP	G	A	PTS	PM
2005-06	NWHL	Axion de Montréal	3	0	2	2	4						
2011-12	CWHL	Stars de Montréal	27	2	29	31	28	2012 C-Cup	4	1	3	4	4
2012-13	CWHL	Stars de Montréal	21	1	12	13	18	2013 C-Cup	4	0	4	4	6
2014-15	CWHL	Stars de Montréal	0	0	0	0	0						
CWHL Regular Season			48	3	41	44	46	Clarkson Cup	8	1	7	8	10
Totals from all Competitions			**59**	**4**	**50**	**54**	**60**						

CWHL Defenceman of the Year in 2011-12 and 2012-13... CWHL First All-Star Team in 2011-12 and 2012-13... CWHL All-Rookie Team in 2011-12... Clarkson Cup Championship MVP in 2013... finished 11th in the Angela James Bowl scoring race in 2011-12... selected First Decade CWHL Team in 2017

WARD, DANIELLE *Forward. 2015-16 NWHL Connecticut (18 gp, 5 goals, 5 assists; I-Cup 3 gp, 1 assist).*

WARD, JEN *Orangeville, ON. Forward. 2009-10 CWHL Brampton (1 game).*

WARFORD, TANYA *Forward. 2003 Nationals Newfoundland Labrador (5 games).*

WARNICK, ALANA *Defence. 2007 Nationals Manitoba (5 gp, 7 assists); 2008 Nationals (5 gp, 3 assists).*

WARREN, LOUISE *Forward. Shoots left. #28.*

Clarkson Cup winner with Calgary on 2016-03-14 and 2019-03-24.

Born 1992-03-22. Grew up in Pembroke, ON, CAN. 5'8". Debut at age 22 on 2014-10-18.

Year - League - Team			GP	G	A	PTS	PM	Year - Playoff	GP	G	A	PTS	PM
2014-15	CWHL	Calgary Inferno	24	2	5	7	8	2015 C-Cup	2	0	0	0	0
2015-16	CWHL	Calgary Inferno	19	5	5	10	2	2016 C-Cup	3	0	1	1	0
2016-17	CWHL	Calgary Inferno	19	2	4	6	27	2017 C-Cup	3	0	0	0	0
2017-18	CWHL	Calgary Inferno	25	7	12	19	14	2018 C-Cup	3	1	2	3	6
2018-19	CWHL	Calgary Inferno	19	0	4	4	6	2019 C-Cup	4	0	0	0	0
CWHL Regular Season			106	16	30	46	57	Clarkson Cup	15	1	3	4	6
Totals from all Competitions			**121**	**17**	**33**	**50**	**63**						

WASH, LAUREN *Forward. Shoots left. #21.*

Born 1994-06-27. Grew up in Belle Mead, NJ, USA. 5'4". Debut at age 22 on 2017-01-14.

Year - League - Team			GP	G	A	PTS	PM	Year - Playoff	GP	G	A	PTS	PM
2016-17	NWHL/	New York Riveters	8	1	2	3	0						
2017-18	NWHL/	Metropolitan Riveters	6	1	0	1	0						

WASYLK, TAYLOR *Forward. Shoots left. #19.*

Born 1992-02-21. Grew up in Port Huron, MI, USA. 5'9". Debut at age 25 on 2017-10-21.

Year - League - Team			GP	G	A	PTS	PM	Year - Playoff	GP	G	A	PTS	PM
2017-18	CWHL	Boston Blades	12	4	2	6	10						

WATCHORN, TARA *Defence. Shoots left. #27.*

Olympic champion. Clarkson Cup winner with Boston on 2015-03-07.

Born 1990-5-30. Grew up in Newcastle, ON, CAN. 5'9.5". Debut at age 17 on 2007-1-28.

Year - League - Team			GP	G	A	PTS	PM	Year - Playoff	GP	G	A	PTS	PM
2006-07	NWHL	Etobicoke Dolphins	1	0	0	0	2						
2012-13	CWHL	Alberta	22	3	4	7	24						
2014-15	CWHL	Boston Blades	21	6	14	20	26	2015 C-Cup	3	0	2	2	4
2015-16	CWHL	Boston Blades	23	2	4	6	26						
2016-17	CWHL	Boston Blades	19	2	4	6	30						
CWHL Regular Season			85	13	26	39	106	Clarkson Cup	3	0	2	2	4
Totals from all Competitions			**89**	**13**	**28**	**41**	**112**						

CWHL Top Defender in 2014-15... CWHL First All-Star Team in 2014-15 and 2015-16... CWHL All-Rookie Team in 2012-13... finished 8th in the Angela James Bowl scoring race in 2014-15

WATERHOUSE, REBECCA *Forward. 2008-09 CWHL Ottawa Senators #25 (2 games).*

WATSON, EMILY *Defence. 2004 Nationals Team New Brunswick (5 games, 1 assist).*

WATSON, JENNIFER — *Forward. 2003 Nationals U. Winnipeg (4 games, 1 assist).*

WATT, LAURA
Defence. Shoots left. #21.

Abby Hoffman Cup winner with Mississauga on 2008-03-15.
Born 1985-11-22, Ajax, ON, CAN. Grew up in Ajax, ON, CAN. 5'6".

Year - League - Team		GP	G	A	PTS	PM	Year - Playoff		GP	G	A	PTS	PM
2000-01	NWHL Durham Lightning	2	0	0	0	2							
2001-02	NWHL Durham Lightning	5	0	0	0	0							
2007-08	CWHL Mississauga Chiefs	28	5	5	10	8	2008	CWHL-P	5	0	1	1	4
2008	Nationals Mississauga Chiefs	3	0	0	0	0							
2008-09	CWHL Mississauga Chiefs	8	1	1	2	2							
2009-10	CWHL Mississauga Chiefs	7	1	2	3	0							
CWHL Regular Season		43	7	8	15	10							
Totals from all Competitions		**58**	**7**	**9**	**16**	**16**							

Served as interim coach with CWHL Mississauga

WATT, SAMANTHA
Defence. #2.

WWHL winner. Born 1990-1-24.

Year - League - Team		GP	G	A	PTS	PM	Year - Playoff		GP	G	A	PTS	PM
2005-06	WWHL Calgary Oval X-Treme	23	2	5	7	58	2006	WWHL-P	3	0	0	0	6
2006	Nationals Calgary Oval X-Treme	7	0	0	0	16							
2006-07	WWHL Calgary Oval X-Treme	19	1	11	12	32	2007	WWHL-P	0	0	0	0	0
2007-08	WWHL Calgary Oval X-Treme	21	7	14	21	54							
2008	Nationals Calgary Oval X-Treme	3	0	0	0	2							
Totals from all Competitions		**76**	**10**	**30**	**40**	**168**							

WAUTERS, SHERI — *Forward. 2007 Nationals BC Outback (5 games, 5 goals, 2 assists).*

WEAFEN, PAULA — *1996-97 COWHL Newtonbrook #3 (1 game).*

WEATHERSTON, KATIE
Forward. Shoots right. #6 #24 #8.

Olympic champion, IIHF champion.
Born 1983-4-6, Thunder Bay, ON, CAN. 5'4". Debut at age 24 on 2007-9-22.

Year - League - Team		GP	G	A	PTS	PM	Year - Playoff		GP	G	A	PTS	PM
2007-08	CWHL Ottawa Capital Canucks	15	13	7	20	40							
2007-08	CWHL Stars de Montréal	2	2	4	6	4	2008	CWHL-P	2	2	1	3	10
2008-09	CWHL Ottawa Senators	4	2	2	4	12							
CWHL Regular Season		21	17	30	47	56							
Totals from all Competitions		**23**	**19**	**31**	**50**	**66**							

CWHL Eastern All-Star Team in 2007-08.. CWHL All-Rookie Team in 2007-08... finished 13th in the Angela James Bowl scoring race in 2007-08

WEAVER, KELLY
Forward.

Abby Hoffman Cup winner with Aeros on 1993-03-28.

Year - League - Team		GP	G	A	PTS	PM	Year - Playoff		GP	G	A	PTS	PM
1992-93	COWHL Toronto Aeros	16	0	0	3	6							
1993-94	COWHL Toronto Aeros	15	5	7	12	2							
1995	Nationals Mississauga Chiefs												

WEBER, JANINE
Centre. Shoots left. #26.

Clarkson Cup winner with Boston on 2015-03-07
Born 1991-06-19. Grew up in Innsbruck, AUT. 5'8". Debut at age 23 on 2014-11-15.

Year - League - Team		GP	G	A	PTS	PM	Year - Playoff		GP	G	A	PTS	PM
2014-15	CWHL Boston Blades	17	3	4	7	4	2015	C-Cup	3	3	0	3	0
2015-16	NWHL/ New York Riveters	18	3	6	9	4	2016	I-Cup	2	0	0	0	0
2016-17	NWHL/ New York Riveters	17	10	12	22	4	2017	I-Cup	1	1	0	1	2
2017-18	NWHL/ Boston Pride	13	3	4	7	6	2018	I-Cup	1	0	0	0	0
NWHL Regular Season		48	16	22	38	14	Isobel Cup		4	1	0	1	2
Totals from all Competitions		**72**	**23**	**26**	**49**	**20**							

WEBSTER, BROOKE
Centre. Shoots right. #26.

Born 1995-04-25. Grew up in Aurora, ON, CAN. 5'5". Debut at age 22 on 2017-10-28.

Year - League - Team		GP	G	A	PTS	PM	Year - Playoff		GP	G	A	PTS	PM
2017-18	CWHL Vanke Rays	26	9	17	26	26							
2018-19	CWHL Markham Thunder	23	2	4	6	6	2019	C-Cup	3	0	1	1	0

Finished 10th in the Angela James Bowl scoring race in 2017-18

WEBSTER, KELSEY
Defence. Shoots right. #26 #6 #3.

Clarkson Cup winner with Calgary on 2016-03-14. CWHL winner.
Born 1986-6-24. Grew up in Duncan, BC, CAN. 6'0". Debut at age 21 on 2007-11-18.

Year - League - Team		GP	G	A	PTS	PM	Year - Playoff		GP	G	A	PTS	PM
2007-08	CWHL Brampton Can.-Thunder	2	0	0	0	0	2008	CWHL-P	1	0	0	0	0
2008	Nationals Brampton Can.-Thunder	3	0	0	0	0							
2009-10	CWHL Brampton Thunder	8	0	2	2	8	2010	C-Cup	1	0	1	1	0
2010-11	WWHL Strathmore Rockies	6	3	1	4	16							
2011-12	CWHL Alberta	15	0	1	1	22							

Year - League - Team		GP	G	A	PTS	PM	Year - Playoff		GP	G	A	PTS	PM
2012-13	CWHL Alberta	23	1	1	2	38							
2013-14	CWHL Calgary Inferno	24	1	3	4	48	2014 C-Cup		3	0	0	0	16
2014-15	CWHL Calgary Inferno	24	0	7	7	18	2015 C-Cup		2	0	0	0	0
2015-16	CWHL Calgary Inferno	13	0	1	1	20	2016 C-Cup		1	0	0	0	0
CWHL Regular Season		109	2	15	17	154	Clarkson Cup		6	0	0	0	16
Totals from all Competitions		**125**	**5**	**16**	**21**	**186**							

WEBSTER, MARY JANE
Defence. Shoots right.

Born 1973-11-25

Year - League - Team		GP	G	A	PTS	PM
1995	Nationals PEI Esso Tigers					
1998	Nationals Nova Scotia Selects	5	0	0	0	8
2005	Nationals Prince Edward Island	5	1	3	4	12
2006	Nationals Prince Edward Island	5	1	3	4	8
2007	Nationals Prince Edward Island	5	0	1	1	4

WEEKS, JO-ANNE
Defence. Shoots right.

Born 1972-11-17. Grew up in Alberton, PE, CAN.

Year - League - Team		GP	G	A	PTS	PM
1995	Nationals PEI Esso Tigers					
1996	Nationals PEI Esso Tigers	4	0	0	0	2
1998	Nationals Prince Edward Island	5	1	1	2	2
1999	Nationals Prince Edward Island	5	0	0	0	
2000	Nationals Prince Edward Island	5	0	0	0	
2001	Nationals PEI Humpty Dumpty					

WEIBE, ANDREA
Defence. 2009-10 Strathmore Rockies (6 games).

WEILAND, KERRY
Defence. Shoots left. #44 #8 #2 #23.

IIHF champion. Born 1980-10-18, Pakmer, AK, USA. 5'4".

Year - League - Team		GP	G	A	PTS	PM	Year - Playoff		GP	G	A	PTS	PM
2003-04	NWHL Edmonton Chimos	1	0	1	1	0	2004 NWHL-P		2	0	0	0	2
2004	Nationals Edmonton Chimos	7	2	4	6	4							
2004-05	NWHL Brampton Thunder	30	6	18	24	32							
2005	Nationals Brampton Thunder	6	1	5	6	6							
2006-07	NWHL Etobicoke Dolphins	22	3	7	10	32	2007 NWHL-P		2	0	0	0	0
2007	Nationals Etobicoke Dolphins	7	0	2	2	10							
2007-08	CWHL Vaughan Flames	15	8	3	11	20	2008 CWHL-P		2	0	1	1	0
Totals from all Competitions		**94**	**20**	**41**	**61**	**106**							

WELCH, AMBER
Keswick. 2007-08 CWHL Mississ. (1 gp); 2009-10 Brampton (30 gp, 7 goals, 7 a.; C-Cup 2 gp).

WELLS, LAUREN
Port Alice, BC. Forward. 2005-06 WWHL British Columbia #2 (24 games, 1 assist).

WELSH, KATIE
Defence. #15

Born 1987-5-1, Abbotsford, BC, CAN.

Year - League - Team		GP	G	A	PTS	PM	Year - Playoff		GP	G	A	PTS	PM
2005-06	WWHL British Columbia Breakers	23	0	1	1	18							
2006-07	WWHL British Columbia Breakers	23	1	2	3	16	2007 WWHL-P		2	0	0	0	0
2007-08	WWHL British Columbia Breakers	24	0	4	4	22							
2008-09	WWHL British Columbia Breakers	14	0	1	1	12							
Totals from all Competitions		**86**	**1**	**8**	**9**	**68**							

WELTON, MELISSA
Forward. Shoots left.

Born 1978-06-10. Grew up in Middleton, NS, CAN.

Year - League - Team		GP	G	A	PTS	PM	Year - Playoff		GP	G	A	PTS	PM
1998	Nationals Nova Scotia Selects	5	2	2	4	0							
2004	Nationals Nova Scotia	5	1	4	5	4							
2005	Nationals Nova Scotia Selects	5	1	3	4	4							
2006	Nationals Nova Scotia Selects	5	3	1	4	4							
2007	Nationals Nova Scotia Selects	7	0	3	3	10							
2009-10	WWHL Strathmore Rockies	3	0	1	1	2							
2010-11	WWHL Strathmore Rockies	4	1	4	5	0							

WEN LU
Defence. Shoots right. #94.

Born 1994-04-21. Grew up in Harbin, CHN. 5'2". Debut at age 23 on 2017-10-21.

Year - League - Team		GP	G	A	PTS	PM	Year - Playoff		GP	G	A	PTS	PM
2017-18	CWHL Kunlun Red Star	28	1	3	4	4	2018 C-Cup		4	0	0	0	0
2018-19	CWHL KRS Vanke Rays	18	1	0	1	0							

WENDELL, KRISSY
Forward. Shoots left. #33 #7 #11.

IIHF champion. Born 1981-9-12, Brooklyn Park, MN, USA. 5'6".

Year - League - Team		GP	G	A	PTS	PM	Year - Playoff		GP	G	A	PTS	PM
2005-06	NWHL Oakville Ice						2006 NWHL-P		0	0	0	0	0
2006-07	NWHL Etobicoke Dolphins	22	9	23	32	41	2007 NWHL-P		2	2	1	3	0
2007	Nationals Etobicoke Dolphins		0	0	0								
2010-11	WWHL Minnesota Whitecaps	1	0	2	2	0	2011 C-Cup		2	0	0	0	0

WEST-McMASTER, BRANDY

Forward. Shoots right. #6.

Born 1979-4-22, Langbank, SK, CAN. 5'6".

Year	League	Team	GP	G	A	PTS	PM	Year	Playoff	GP	G	A	PTS	PM
1998	Nationals	Saskatchewan Selects	6	3	0	3	2							
1999	Nationals	Saskatchewan Selects	4	1	1	2								
2000	Nationals	Saskatchewan Selects	7	4	2	6								
2001	Nationals	Saskatchewan Selects												
2003	Nationals	Saskatchewan	6	5	5	10	4							
2004-05	WWHL	Saskatchewan Prairie Ice	21	6	5	11	22							
2005-06	WWHL	Saskatchewan Prairie Ice	24	13	9	22	14	2006	WWHL-P	2	0	0	0	0
2006-07	WWHL	Saskatchewan Prairie Ice	24	8	10	18	20							
Totals from all Competitions			**94**	**40**	**32**	**72**	**62**							

WEST, DANA

Forward. 2001 Nationals Saskatchewan.

WEST, SOMMER

Forward. Shoots left. #44.

Abby Hoffman Cup winner with Aeros on 2000-03-12 and 2004-03-14. Abby Hoffman Cup winner with Mississauga on 2008-03-15.

NWHL Cup winner. Born 1978-4-24, Houston, TX, USA. Grew up in Winnipeg, MB & Bowmanville, ON, CAN. 5'8".

Year	League	Team	GP	G	A	PTS	PM	Year	Playoff	GP	G	A	PTS	PM
1993-94	COWHL	Toronto Junior Aeros	29	12	3	15	18							
1995-96	COWHL	North York Aeros	24	9	17	26	45							
1996	Nationals	North York Aeros	5	1	0	1	0							
1996-97	COWHL	North York Aeros	32	36	24	60	32							
1997-98	COWHL	North York Aeros	19	10	6	16	14							
1998	Nationals	North York Aeros	6	0	5	5	0							
1998-99	NWHL	North York Aeros	33	11	22	33	38							
1999	Nationals	North York Aeros	5	2	3	5								
1999-00	NWHL	North York Aeros	31	21	26	47	42	2000	NWHL-P					
2000	Nationals	North York Aeros	6	1	1	2								
2000-01	NWHL	North York Aeros	31	23	18	41	47							
2001	Nationals	North York Aeros												
2001-02	NWHL	North York Aeros	19	11	13	24	47							
2002	Nationals	North York Aeros	6	2	5	7	2							
2002-03	NWHL	North York Aeros						2003	NWHL-P					
2003-04	NWHL	Toronto Aeros	29	19	26	45	34	2004	NWHL-P					
2004	Nationals	Toronto Aeros	6	4	3	7	6							
2004-05	NWHL	Toronto Aeros	35	23	22	45	64	2005	NWHL-P					
2005-06	NWHL	Toronto Aeros	36	28	27	55	68							
2006-07	NWHL	Mississauga Aeros	33	12	24	36	70	2007	NWHL-P	5	1	5	6	4
2007	Nationals	Mississauga Aeros	6	5	4	9	0							
2007-08	CWHL	Mississauga Chiefs	30	23	25	48	46	2008	CWHL-P	5	4	10	14	14
2008	Nationals	Mississauga Chiefs	3	0	2	2	4							
2008-09	CWHL	Mississauga Chiefs	27	16	22	38	34	2009	CWHL-P	4	2	1	3	
2009-10	CWHL	Mississauga Chiefs	30	11	24	35	68	2010	C-Cup	1	0	0	0	0
2010-11	CWHL	Burlington Barracudas	12	2	5	7	8							
2010-11	CWHL	Toronto Furies	4	2	2	4	2							
2011-12	CWHL	Burlington Barracudas	23	6	11	17	34							
CWHL Regular Season			126	60	89	149	192	Clarkson Cup		1	0	0	0	0
Totals from all Competitions			**535**	**297**	**356**	**653**	**741**							

CWHL First All-Star Team in 2009-10... finished 3rd in the Angela James Bowl scoring race in 2007-08... NWHL Player of the Year in 2005-06... scored 100th CWHL point on 2009-11-07... has served as head coach with CWHL Toronto... CWHL Coach of the Year in 2013-14

WESTENDORP, DEB

Defence. 1998 Nationals New Westminster Lightning (5 games, 1 assist).

WESTERVELT, VICKY

Defence. 1998-99 NWHL Mississauga #91 (1 game); 1999-00 (1 game).

WHALEN, KRISTY

Forward. 2005 Nationals Alberta (6 games, 1 assist).

WHEELER, KATELYN

Oakville, ON. Defence. 2005-06 NWHL Oakville #5 (1 game).

WHITE, BROOKE

Forward. Shoots left. #10.

Clarkson Cup winner with Minnesota on 2010-03-28

Born 1979-8-31, Berkeley, CA, USA. 5'5".

Year	League	Team	GP	G	A	PTS	PM	Year	Playoff	GP	G	A	PTS	PM
2004-05	WWHL	Minnesota Whitecaps	12	3	2	5	8	2005	WWHL-P	2	1	0	1	0
2005-06	WWHL	Minnesota Whitecaps	17	5	4	9	12	2006	WWHL-P	3	1	0	1	2
2006-07	WWHL	Minnesota Whitecaps	23	12	6	18	28	2007	WWHL-P	3	3	2	5	2
2007-08	WWHL	Minnesota Whitecaps	17	9	6	15	14							
2008	Nationals	Minnesota Whitecaps	3	0	0	0	2							
2008-09	WWHL	Minnesota Whitecaps	15	1	8	9	18	2009	WWHL-P	2	1	0	1	0
								2009	C-Cup	3	1	1	2	4
2009-10	WWHL	Minnesota Whitecaps	12	5	4	9	12	2010	C-Cup	2	1	2	3	0
2010-11	WWHL	Minnesota Whitecaps	1	0	0	0	0	2011	C-Cup	2	0	0	0	0
2018-19	NWHL/	Minnesota Whitecaps	2	0	1	1	2							
Totals from all Competitions			**119**	**43**	**36**	**79**	**104**							

WHITE, CATHERINE   *Brampton. F. 2007-08 CWHL Mississauga #10 (1 game); 2012-13 Toronto (8 gp, 1 assist).*

WHITE, CHERYL   *Forward. 2001 Nationals Manitoba; 2007 Nationals (5 gp, 6 pts); 2008 Nationals (5 gp, 2 pts).*

WHITE, KIM   *1992-93 COWHL Guelph #88 (15 games).*

WHITE, SHANLEY   *Forward. #51 #15.*

Year - League - Team			GP	G	A	PTS	PM
1998-99	NWHL	Scarborough Sting	16	2	0	2	22
1999-00	NWHL	Durham Lightning	37	2	4	6	26
2000-01	NWHL	Durham Lightning	38	8	9	17	100
Totals from all Competitions			**91**	**12**	**13**	**25**	**148**

WHITE, SHERRIE   *Neepawa, MB. Forward. 2004-05 NWHL Ottawa Raiders #27 (17 games, 5 goals, 8 assists).*

WHITNEY, BROOKE   *Forward. Shoots left.*

Born 1979-10-12. Grew up in Snohomish, WA, USA.

Year - League - Team			GP	G	A	PTS	PM	Year - Playoff	GP	G	A	PTS	PM
2002-03	NWHL	Brampton Thunder						2003 NWHL-P					
2003	Nationals	Brampton Thunder	5	4	0	4	0						

WHITTAKER, AIMEE   *Forward. #14 #12.*

Born 1986-9-11.

Year - League - Team			GP	G	A	PTS	PM	Year - Playoff	GP	G	A	PTS	PM
2003-04	NWHL	Edmonton Chimos	7	0	0	0	40	2004 NWHL-P					
2004	Nationals	Edmonton Chimos	7	0	4	4	14						
2005-06	WWHL	Edmonton Chimos	23	9	12	21	66	2006 WWHL-P	2	1	0	1	2
2006-07	WWHL	Edmonton Chimos	17	6	5	11	66	2007 WWHL-P	2	0	1	1	2
Totals from all Competitions			**58**	**16**	**22**	**38**	**190**						

WHITTAKER, LEAH   *Defence. Shoots right. #67 #25.*

Born 1989-08-15. Grew up in Cambridge, ON, CAN. 5'6". Debut at age 25 on 2014-11-15.

Year - League - Team			GP	G	A	PTS	PM	Year - Playoff	GP	G	A	PTS	PM
2014-15	CWHL	Brampton Thunder	14	0	3	3	10						
2015-16	CWHL	Brampton Thunder	24	0	0	0	6	2016 C-Cup	2	0	0	0	2
Totals from all Competitions			**40**	**0**	**3**	**3**	**18**						

WICKENHEISER, HAYLEY   *Forward. Shoots right. #23 #22.*

Hockey Hall of Fame honoured member, Class of 2019
Olympic champion, IIHF champion. Abby Hoffman Cup winner with Edmonton on 1997-03-09. Abby Hoffman Cup winner with Calgary on 1998-03-22, 2001-03-11 and 2007-03-10. Clarkson Cup winner with Calgary on 2016-03-14. WWHL winner.
Born 1978-8-12, Shaunavon, SK, CAN. Grew up in Shaunavon, SK, CAN & Calgary, AB, CAN. 5'9".

Year - League - Team			GP	G	A	PTS	PM	Year - Playoff	GP	G	A	PTS	PM
1995	Nationals	Calgary Classics											
1996	Nationals	Edmonton Chimos	7	4	5	9	6						
1997	Nationals	Edmonton Chimos											
1998	Nationals	Calgary Oval X-Treme	6	2	1	3	10						
1999	Nationals	Calgary Oval X-Treme	6	5	3	8							
2000	Nationals	Calgary Oval X-Treme	7	6	8	14							
2001	Nationals	Calgary Oval X-Treme											
2002-03	NWHL	Edmonton Chimos	11	4	2	6	16						
2003-04	NWHL	Calgary Oval X-Treme	5	10	3	13	6	2004 NWHL-P					
2004	Nationals	Calgary Oval X-Treme	6	5	6	11	8						
2004-05	WWHL	Calgary Oval X-Treme	18	22	36	58	20	2005 WWHL-P	3	2	2	4	0
2006-07	WWHL	Calgary Oval X-Treme	14	27	21	48	16	2007 WWHL-P	3	4	8	12	2
2007	Nationals	Calgary Oval X-Treme	6	11	8	19	8						
2007-08	WWHL	Calgary Oval X-Treme	19	19	30	49	20						
2008	Nationals	Calgary Oval X-Treme	3	3	4	7	6						
2015-16	CWHL	Calgary Inferno	23	3	13	16	10	2016 C-Cup	3	1	2	3	0
CWHL Regular Season			23	3	13	16	10	Clarkson Cup	3	1	2	3	0
Totals from all Competitions			**140**	**128**	**152**	**280**	**128**						

Women's National Championships Most Valuable Player in 1996, 1999, 2000, 2004, 2007 and 2008.

WIEBE, ALYSSA   *Forwad. 2004-05 WWHL Saskatchewan Prairie Ice #12 (17 games, 2 goals, 2 assists).*

WIEBE, JACKIE   *Defence. 2010-11 WWHL Manitoba Maple Leafs #15 (4 games).*

WIENS, CHERYL   *Forward. Shoots left.*

Born 1979-03-19. Grew up in Winnipeg, MB, CAN.

Year - League - Team			GP	G	A	PTS	PM	Year - Playoff	GP	G	A	PTS	PM
2015-16	NWHL/	Buffalo Beauts	17	1	4	5	14	2016 I-Cup	3	0	0	0	0
1998	Nationals	Tazmanian Devils	5	0	0	0	8						
1999	Nationals	Tazmanian Devils	4	0	0	0							
2002	Nationals	University of Manitoba	5	1	0	1	4						
2003	Nationals	University of Winnipeg	4	0	0	0	6						
2006	Nationals	Manitoba	5	1	1	2	2						

WIGGINS, LAUREN   *Forward. 2002-03 NWHL Durham #5; 2003-04 #15 (34 games, 2 goals, 3 assists).*

WILCOX, BARBARA   *1996-97 COWHL Scarborough #51 (1 game).*

WILDE, BARB — *Defence. 1998 Nationals New Westminster (5 gp, 1 a.); 1999 Nationals (5 gp, 3 pts).*

WILDMAN, JENN — *1996-97 COWHL Londeon Devilettes #27 (26 games, 7 goals, 7 assists).*

WILKINSON, BRENDA — *Forward. 1995-96 COWHL Hamilton (30 gp, 2 goals); 1996-97 (29 gp, 3 goals, 4 assists).*

WILKINSON, SARAH — *Defence. 2003 Nationals Nova Scotia (4 games).*

WILLARD, TAYLOR — *Defence. Shoots right. #27.*
Born 1995-11-02. Grew up in Bolingbrook, IL, USA. 5'6". Debut at age 22 on 2018-10-13.

Year - League - Team			GP	G	A	PTS	PM	Year - Playoff	GP	G	A	PTS	PM
2018-19	CWHL	Canadiennes de Montréal	26	2	5	7	4	2019 C-Cup	4	0	1	1	0

WILLEY, DAGNEY — *Defence. 2004-05 WWHL Minnesota (12 gp, 2 assists); 2009-10 (2 gp, 2 assists).*

WILLIAMS, BERNIE — *2008 Nationals Team New Brunswick (5 games, 1 goal, 2 assists).*

WILLIAMS, HAYLEY — *Forward. Shoots right. #3.*
Born 1990-06-03, Crete, IL, USA. 5'3". Debut at age 25 on 2015-10-11.

Year - League - Team			GP	G	A	PTS	PM	Year - Playoff	GP	G	A	PTS	PM
2015-16	NWHL/	Buffalo Beauts	17	1	4	5	14	2016 I-Cup	3	0	0	0	0
2016-17	CWHL	Brampton Thunder	14	0	0	0	2	2017 C-Cup	1	0	0	0	0
2017-18	CWHL	Toronto Furies	28	4	10	14	22						
CWHL Regular Season			42	4	10	14	24	Clarkson Cup	4	0	0	0	0
Totals from all Competitions			**63**	**5**	**14**	**19**	**38**						

WILLIAMS, JANINE — *Defence. 2001 Nationals Saskatchewan; 2002 Nationals Saskatchewan (6 games).*

WILLIAMS, KRISTA — *Forward. 2000 Nationals Newfoundland (5 gp, 1 assist); 2001 Nationals Newfoundland.*

WILLIAMS, LAUREN — *Defence. Shoots left. #7.*
Born 1996-09-09. Grew up in Windsor, ON, CAN. 5'9". Debut

Year - League - Team			GP	G	A	PTS	PM
2018-19	CWHL	Worcester Blades	24	0	2	2	6

WILLIAMSON, DEANNA — *Forward. 2007 Nationals BC Outback (5 games, 1 assist).*

WILLIAMSON, SARAH — *Forward. 2003 nationals Team New Brunswick (4 games, 1 assist).*

WILLIAMSON, SHARON — *Forward. #8 #19 #12.*

Year - League - Team			GP	G	A	PTS	PM
1992-93	COWHL	Scarborough Sting	26	4	10	14	8
1993-94	COWHL	Scarborough Sting	29	5	12	17	38
1995-96	COWHL	Mississauga Chiefs	14	0	6	6	4
1996-97	COWHL	Mississauga Chiefs	34	14	9	23	24
1997-98	COWHL	Mississauga Chiefs	20	11	5	16	14
1998-99	NWHL	Mississauga Chiefs	26	9	6	15	8
1999-00	NWHL	Mississauga Chiefs	9	1	1	2	6
2000-01	NWHL	Toronto Sting	37	8	17	25	34
2001-02	NWHL	Durham Lightning	27	2	7	9	10
2004-05	NWHL	Toronto Aeros	1	0	0	0	0
Totals from all Competitions			**223**	**54**	**73**	**127**	**146**

WILLIAMSON, TAYLOR — *Defence. 2010-11 WWHL Edmonton Chimos #25 (16 games, 2 goals).*

WILLOUGHBY, KAITLIN — *Forward. Shoots right. #17.*
Clarkson Cup winner with Calgary on 2019-03-24.
Born 1995-03-26. Grew up in Prince Albert, SK, CAN. 5'6". Debut at age 23 on 2018-10-13.

Year - League - Team			GP	G	A	PTS	PM	Year - Playoff	GP	G	A	PTS	PM
2018-19	CWHL	Calgary Inferno	27	1	5	6	2	2019 C-Cup	1	0	0	0	0

WILLSEY, ANNA — *Forward. 1998-99 NWHL Ottawa #5 (34 gp, 2 assists); 1999-00 #27 (32 gp, 2 assists).*

WILSON, CHRIS — *1993-94 COWHL Hamilton #35 (1 game).*

WILSON, JEN — *Defence. 2000-01 NWHL Ottawa Raiders #14 (36 games, 3 assists).*

WILSON, KATIE — *Forward. Shoots left. #8.*
Clarkson Cup winner with Toronto on 2014-03-22
Born 1991-04-03. Grew up in Winnipeg, MB, CAN. 5'8". Debut at age 22 on 2013-11-09.

Year - League - Team			GP	G	A	PTS	PM	Year - Playoff	GP	G	A	PTS	PM
2013-14	CWHL	Toronto Furies	23	5	9	14	12	2014 C-Cup	4	0	0	0	0
2014-15	CWHL	Toronto Furies	17	0	2	2	4	2015 C-Cup	2	0	0	0	0
2015-16	CWHL	Toronto Furies	5	0	0	0	0						
CWHL Regular Season			45	5	11	16	16	Clarkson Cup	6	0	0	0	0
Totals from all Competitions			**51**	**5**	**11**	**16**	**16**						

WILSON, SHANNON — *Forward. 1999-00 NWHL Durham #42 (7 games).*

WILSON, STACY — *Forward. Shoots left.*
Born 1965-05-12. Grew up in Moncton, NB, CAN. 5'7".

Year - League - Team			GP	G	A	PTS	PM
1995	Nationals	Maritime Sports Blades					
1996	Nationals	Maritime Sports Blades	6		7	5	12	2
1998	Nationals	Maritime Sports Blades	6		6	3	9	2

WINTER, BETHANY   Bloomington, MN. 2006-07 WWHL Minnesota (22 games, 1 goal, 2 assists).

WINTLE, LINDSAY   1996-97 COWHL Hamilton Golden Hawks #5 (2 goals).

WOHLFEILER, ALYSSA
Forward. Shoots right. #88 #8.

Born 1989-5-6. Grew up in Saugus, CA, USA. 5'7". Debut at age 22 on 2011-10-22.

Year - League - Team			GP	G	A	PTS	PM	Year - Playoff	GP	G	A	PTS	PM
2011-12	CWHL	Boston Blades	26	5	11	16	24	2012 C-Cup	3	1	0	1	0
2012-13	CWHL	Boston Blades	2	0	0	0	0						
2013-14	CWHL	Boston Blades	24	4	3	7	22	2014 C-Cup	4	0	0	0	6
2015-16	NWHL/	Connecticut Whale	17	3	4	7	20	2016 I-Cup	1	0	0	0	2
	CWHL Regular Season		52	9	14	23	46	Clarkson Cup	7	1	0	1	6
	NWHL Regular Season		17	3	4	7	20	Isobel Cup	1	0	0	0	2
	Totals from all Competitions		**77**	**13**	**18**	**31**	**74**						

WOLF, RAFFI
Forward. #19.

Abby Hoffman Cup winner with Calgary on 1998-03-22.

Year - League - Team			GP	G	A	PTS	PM
1998	Nationals	Calgary Oval X-Treme	5	0	1	1	0

WOLOSCHUK, ALEXIS
Defence. Shoots left. #10.

Abby Hoffman Cup winner with Calgary on 1998-03-22.
Clarkson Cup winner with Markham on 2018-03-25
Born 1994-04-06. Grew up in Winnipeg, MB, CAN. 5'7". Debut at age 23 on 2017-10-14.

Year - League - Team			GP	G	A	PTS	PM	Year - Playoff	GP	G	A	PTS	PM
2017-18	CWHL	Markham Thunder	14	1	1	2	14	2018 C-Cup	3	0	0	0	0
2018-19	CWHL	Markham Thunder	16	0	1	1	4	2019 C-Cup	3	0	0	0	0

WONG, JESSICA
Defence. Shoots left. #49.

Born 1991-03-29 in Sydney, NS, CAN. Grew up in Baddeck, NS, CAN. 5'7". Debut at age 22 on 2014-01-12.

Year - League - Team			GP	G	A	PTS	PM	Year - Playoff	GP	G	A	PTS	PM
2006	Nationals	Nova Scotia Selects	5	1	2	3	2						
2013-14	CWHL	Calgary Inferno	12	2	7	9	14	2014 C-Cup	3	0	0	0	2
2014-15	CWHL	Calgary Inferno	24	2	11	13	14	2015 C-Cup	2	0	0	0	2
2016-17	CWHL	Calgary Inferno	2	0	2	2	2						
2017-18	CWHL	Kunlun Red Star	28	10	14	24	22	2018 C-Cup	4	0	3	3	2
2018-19	CWHL	KRS Vanke Rays	28	3	12	15	12						
	CWHL Regular Season		94	17	46	63	64	Clarkson Cup	9	0	3	3	6
	Totals from all Competitions		**108**	**18**	**51**	**69**	**72**						

CWHL First All-Star Team in 2017-18 and CWHL Second All-Star Team in 2013-14... CWHL All-Rookie Team in 2013-14... finished 13th in the Angela James Bowl scoring race in 2017-18

WONG, KIMBERLEY   Mississauga. D. 2007-08 CWHL Mississauga #92 (3 gp, 1 goal); 2008-09 #11 (1 gp).

WONG, SAMANTHA   Forward. 2001 Nationals Vancouver Griffins.

WOO, MADISON
Right wing. Shoots right. #15.

Born 1994-09-24. Grew up in Plymouth, MA, USA. 5'8". Debut at age 23 on 2017-10-21.

Year - League - Team			GP	G	A	PTS	PM	Year - Playoff	GP	G	A	PTS	PM
2017-18	CWHL	Kunlun Red Star	28	3	7	10	10	2018 C-Cup	4	0	0	0	4
2018-19	CWHL	KRS Vanke Rays	28	3	3	6	10						

WOOD, BUSSIE
Forward. #16.

Year - League - Team			GP	G	A	PTS	PM
1999-00	NWHL	Scarborough Sting	32	4	4	8	37
2000-01	NWHL	Toronto Sting	29	7	11	18	32
	Totals from all Competitions		**61**	**11**	**15**	**26**	**69**

WOODCOCK, BRIANNE   Forward. 2002 Nationals Saskatchewan (6 games, 2 assists).

WOODFINE, EUNECE   Forward. 2003 Nationals Newfoundland Labrador (5 games).

WOODFORD, ASHLEY   Defence. 2003 Nationals Newfoundland Labrador (5 games).

WOODFORD, KATIE   Defence. 2002 Nationals Newfoundland Labrador (4 gp); 2003 Nationals (5 gp).

WOODS, EMMA
Centre. Shoots right. #67.

Born 1995-12-18. Grew up in Burford, ON, CAN. 5'8". Debut at age 21 on 2017-10-28.

Year - League - Team			GP	G	A	PTS	PM
2018-19	CWHL	KRS Vanke Rays	28	8	8	16	20

Finished 19th in the Angela James Bowl scoring race in 2017-18

WOODS, STEPHANIE   Forward. 2001 Nationals Team New Brunswick; 2007 Nationals (6 games, 1 goal, 1 assist).

WOODS, TAYLOR
Forward. Shoots right. #25.

Clarkson Cup winner with Markham on 2018-03-25
Born 1994-09-26. Grew up in Morden, MB, CAN. 5'2". Debut at age 22 on 2016-10-09.

Year - League - Team			GP	G	A	PTS	PM	Year - Playoff	GP	G	A	PTS	PM
2016-17	CWHL	Brampton Thunder	20	0	4	4	6	2017 C-Cup	2	0	0	0	2
2017-18	CWHL	Markham Thunder	28	4	1	5	18	2018 C-Cup	3	0	0	0	0
2018-19	CWHL	Markham Thunder	26	2	3	5	12	2019 C-Cup	3	0	0	0	0
	CWHL Regular Season		74	6	8	14	36	Clarkson Cup	8	0	0	0	2

WOODWORTH, DAKOTA
Centre. Shoots right. #9.

Clarkson Cup winner with Calgary on 2019-03-24.
Born 1994-03-17. Grew up in Carlisle, MA, USA. 5'7". Debut at age 22 on 2016-10-15.

Year - League - Team			GP	G	A	PTS	PM			GP	G	A	PTS	PM
2016-17	CWHL	Boston Blades	23	2	4	6	8							
2017-18	CWHL	Calgary Inferno	27	5	13	18	10	2018	C-Cup	3	1	1	2	0
2018-19	CWHL	Calgary Inferno	27	2	2	4	2	2019	C-Cup	4	0	0	0	0
	CWHL Regular Season		77	9	19	28	20	Clarkson Cup		7	1	1	2	0

WOOSLEY, SUE
Defence. 2007 Nationals Nova Scotia Selects (7 games).

WOOSTER, CAMI
Forward. Shoots left. #18.

Born 1986-12-03. Grew up in Salvador, SK, CAN.

Year - League - Team			GP	G	A	PTS	PM			GP	G	A	PTS	PM
2002	Nationals	Saskatchewan	6	1	0	1	4							
2004	Nationals	Saskatchewan	6	2	4	6	2							
2006-07	WWHL	Edmonton Chimos	241	11	7	18	14	2007	WWHL-P	2	0	0	0	2

WOOSTER, CARA
Forward. 2004 Nationals Saskatchewan.

WORSFOLD, HEIDI
Forward. 1998 Nationals New Westminster Lightning (5 games, 1 assist)

WOURNELL, MARLEY
Forward. 2007 Nationals BC Outback (5 games, 1 goal, 3 assists).

WOUTERS, SHAROLYN
1995-96 COWHL Peterborough #10 (18 games, 1 goal, 3 assists).

WRIGHT, ALISON
Oakville, ON. 2005-06 NWHL Oakville Ice #86 (? games).

WRIGHT, ELLEN
Forward. 2004 Nationals Nova Scotia Selects (5 games, 2 goals); 2005 Nationals (5 gp, 5 pts).

WRIGHT, KATHY
1996-97 COWHL London Devilettes #20 (5 games).

WRIGHT, SANDRA
Defence. 2008-09 WWHL Brisith Columbia #7 (14 games).

WRONZBERG, MELISSA
Forward. Shoots right. #28.

Born 1993-02-18. Grew up in Thornhill, ON, CAN. 5'5". Debut at age 23 on 2016-10-29.

Year - League - Team			GP	G	A	PTS	PM	Year - Playoff		GP	G	A	PTS	PM
2016-17	CWHL	Brampton Thunder	9	1	0	1	0	2017	C-Cup	1	0	0	0	0
2017-18	CWHL	Markham Thunder	23	0	1	1	4							
	CWHL Regular Season		32	1	1	2	4	Clarkson Cup		1	0	0	0	0

WYTON, DARA-LYNN
Forward. 2000 Nationals Manitoba (5 games, 1 assist).

XIAO JINQIU
Defence. Shoots right. #58.

Born 1995-08-30. Grew up in Harbin, CHN. 5'5". Debut at age 22 on 2017-10-28.

Year - League - Team			GP	G	A	PTS	PM
2017-18	CWHL	Vanke Rays	27	0	0	0	0

XIAOLIN DING
Harbin, CHN. Forward. 2013-14 CWHL BostonBlades #8 (4 games).

XING LIXUE
Left wing. Shoots right. #8.

Born 1999-10-13. Grew up in Harbin, CHN. 5'4". Debut at age 18 on 2017-11-19.

Year - League - Team			GP	G	A	PTS	PM	Year - Playoff		GP	G	A	PTS	PM
2017-18	CWHL	Kunlun Red Star	15	0	0	0	0	2018	C-Cup	4	0	0	0	0

XU JIACHAO
Defence. Shoots right. #90.

Born 1999-03-20. Grew up in CHN. 5'2". Debut at age 18 on 2018-01-20.

Year - League - Team			GP	G	A	PTS	PM
2017-18	CWHL	Vanke Rays	10	0	0	0	0

YAN HONGXIN
Defence. Shoots right. #19.

Born 1999-03-10. Grew up in Qiqihar, CHN. 5'3". Debut at age 18 on 2017-10-28.

Year - League - Team			GP	G	A	PTS	PM	Year - Playoff		GP	G	A	PTS	PM
2017-18	CWHL	Kunlun Red Star	20	0	1	1	0	2018	C-Cup	4	0	0	0	0

YANG LIYING
Centre. Shoots right. #18.

Born 1998-04-10. Grew up in Harbin, CHN. 5'5". Debut at age 19 on 2017-10-21.

Year - League - Team			GP	G	A	PTS	PM	Year - Playoff		GP	G	A	PTS	PM
2017-18	CWHL	Kunlun Red Star	27	0	0	0	0	2018	C-Cup	4	0	0	0	0

YEATS, KATHY
Forward. Shoots left. #19.

Abby Hoffman Cup winner with Edmonton on 1997-03-09.
Born 1967-5-5. Grew up in Coronation, AB, CAN. 5'6".

Year - League - Team			GP	G	A	PTS	PM	Year - Playoff		GP	G	A	PTS	PM
1997	Nationals	Edmonton Chimos												
1998	Nationals	Edmonton Chimos	7	0	1	1	6							
2002-03	NWHL	Edmonton Chimos	24	2	1	3	18							
2003-04	NWHL	Edmonton Chimos	11	1	1	2	10	2004	NWHL-P	2	0	0	0	2
2004	Nationals	Edmonton Chimos	7	0	0	0	4							
2004-05	WWHL	Edmonton Chimos	21	2	3	5	44	2005	WWHL-P	3	0	0	0	0
2005-06	WWHL	Edmonton Chimos	22	4	8	12	13	2006	WWHL-P	2	0	0	0	2
2006-07	WWHL	Edmonton Chimos	21	2	2	4	16	2007	WWHL-P	2	0	0	0	4
2007-08	WWHL	Edmonton Chimos	24	2	7	9	18							
2008-09	WWHL	Edmonton Chimos	24	0	5	5	8	2009	WWHL-P	1	0	0	0	0

Year - League - Team			GP	G	A	PTS	PM	Year - Playoff	GP	G	A	PTS	PM
2009-10	WWHL	Edmonton Chimos	18	0	0	0	12						
2010-11	WWHL	Edmonton Chimos	17	0	1	1	6						
Totals from all Competitions			**206**	**13**	**29**	**42**	**163**						

YOUNG, KELSEY   *Forward. 2006 Nationals British Columbia (6 gp, 1 goal); 2007 Nationals B.C. (5 gp).*

YU BAIWEI   *Defence. Shoots right. #8 #2.*

Born 1988-07-17. Grew up in CHN. 5'4".

Year - League - Team			GP	G	A	PTS	PM	Year - Playoff	GP	G	A	PTS	PM
2007-08	WWHL	Edmonton Chimos	17	0	1	1	2						
2017-18	CWHL	Kunlun Red Star	28	1	2	3	14	2018 C-Cup	4	0	0	0	2
2018-19	CWHL	KRS Vanke Rays	28	1	3	4	12						
Totals from all Competitions			**77**	**2**	**6**	**8**	**30**						

YULE, CHRISSY   *Forward. 1999-00 NWHL Mississauga (1 gp, 2 goals); 2000-01 (4 gp, 1 goal, 3 assists).*

ZABAN, CARISSA   *2000-01 NWHL Mississauga #47 (9 games, 4 goals, 5 assists).*

ZABRICK, JOCELYN   *Forward. 2008-09 WWHL Calgary Oval X-Treme #14 (3 goals, 2 assists).*

ZACH, ERIN   *Forward. Shoots left. #40.*

Born 1991-12-10, Kitchener, ON, CAN. Grewup in Elmira, ON, CAN. 5'3". Debut at age 24 on 2016-10-15.

Year - League - Team			GP	G	A	PTS	PM	Year - Playoff	GP	G	A	PTS	PM
2015-16	NWHL/	Buffalo Beauts	14	1	4	5	4	2016 I-Cup	5	1	0	1	0
2016-17	CWHL	Toronto Furies	19	0	2	2	0	2017 C-Cup	3	0	0	0	0

ZALEWSKI, ANNIKA   *Forward. Shoots left. #13.*

Born 1996-01-03. Grew up in New Hartford, NY, USA. 5'10". Debut at age 22 on 2018-10-07.

Year - League - Team			GP	G	A	PTS	PM	Year - Playoff	GP	G	A	PTS	PM
2018-19	NWHL/	Buffalo Beauts	16	3	9	12	2	2019 I-Cup	2	0	1	1	0

ZAMORA, KELLY   *Centre. Shoots left. #5 #96 #21.*

Clarkson Cup winner with Toronto on 2014-03-22

Born 1982-12-21. Grew up in Oakville, ON, CAN. 6'0". Debut at age 22 on 2005-09-30.

Year - League - Team			GP	G	A	PTS	PM	Year - Playoff	GP	G	A	PTS	PM
2005-06	NWHL	Brampton Thunder	2	0	0	0	2						
2006-07	NWHL	Brampton Thunder	4	0	0	0	0	2007 NWHL-P	3	0	0	0	0
2007-08	CWHL	Burlington Barracudas	27	7	10	17	14	2008 CWHL-P	3	0	4	4	2
2008-09	CWHL	Burlington Barracudas	26	1	10	11	18	2009 CWHL-P	4	1	1	2	4
2009-10	CWHL	Burlington Barracudas	30	11	13	24	30						
2010-11	CWHL	Toronto Furies	26	3	3	6	6	2011 CWHL-P	2		4		
								2011 C-Cup	4	0	0	0	2
2011-12	CWHL	Toronto Furies	26	2	6	8	30	2012 C-Cup	3	0	0	0	4
2012-13	CWHL	Toronto Furies	22	1	1	2	6						
2013-14	CWHL	Toronto Furies	18	2	2	4	8	2014 C-Cup	4	0	0	0	0
CWHL Regular Season			175	27	45	72	112	Clarkson Cup	11	0	0	0	6
Totals from all Competitions			**204**	**28**	**50**	**78**	**130**						

Finished 18th in the Angela James Bowl scoring race in 2009-10

ZAMORA, KRISTY   *Forward. Shoots left. #27 #9.*

Abby Hoffman Cup winner with Brampton on 2006-03-12. Clarkson Cup winner with Toronto on 2014-03-22

Born 1978-8-14. Grew up in Oshawa, ON, CAN. 5'11".

Year - League - Team			GP	G	A	PTS	PM	Year - Playoff	GP	G	A	PTS	PM
1996-97	COWHL	Peterborough Pirates	34	22	15	37	55						
1997-98	COWHL	Scarborough Sting	19	6	4	10	16						
1998-99	NWHL	Scarborough Sting	3	0	0	0	4						
2002-03	NWHL	Brampton Thunder						2003 NWHL-P					
2003	Nationals	Brampton Thunder	5	4	2	6	10						
2003-04	NWHL	Brampton Thunder	34	22	19	41	72						
2004-05	NWHL	Brampton Thunder	30	28	13	41	20						
2005	Nationals	Brampton Thunder	6	6	2	8	2						
2005-06	NWHL	Brampton Thunder	36	25	24	49	10	2006 NWHL-P	5	1	1	2	2
2006	Nationals	Brampton Thunder	6	3	1	4	6						
2006-07	NWHL	Brampton Thunder		13		13		2007 NWHL-P	6	3	3	6	0
2007-08	CWHL	Burlington Barracudas	21	1	0	1	42	2008 CWHL-P	3	2	1	3	0
2008-09	CWHL	Mississauga Chiefs	29	6	4	10	14	2009 CWHL-P	4	2		2	4
2009-10	CWHL	Mississauga Chiefs	23	13	4	17	40	2010 C-Cup	1	0	0	0	0
2010-11	CWHL	Toronto Furies	26	5	4	9	38	2011 CWHL-P	2		4		
								2011 C-Cup	4	0	1	1	0
2011-12	CWHL	Toronto Furies	25	1	8	9	22	2012 C-Cup	3	1	0	1	0
2012-13	CWHL	Toronto Furies	24	1	3	4	8	2013 C-Cup	3	0	0	0	0
2013-14	CWHL	Toronto Furies	23	4	3	7	36	2014 C-Cup	4	0	0	0	0
2014-15	CWHL	Toronto Furies	22	1	2	3	14	2015 C-Cup	2	0	0	0	0
2015-16	CWHL	Toronto Furies	24	1	2	3	8	2016 C-Cup	2	0	0	0	2
CWHL Regular Season			217	33	30	63	222	Clarkson Cup	19	1	1	2	2
Totals from all Competitions			**429**	**171**	**116**	**287**	**429**						

ZAMPERIN, STEPHANIE *Defence. 2009-10 CWHL Mississauga Chiefs #16 (1 game).*

ZAUGG, JINELLE *Eagle River, WI, USA. Forward.*

			GP	G	A	PTS	PM			GP	G	A	PTS	PM
2008-09	WWHL	Minnesota Whitecaps	8	3	3	6	2	2009	WWHL-P	2	1	1	2	2
2009-10	WWHL	Minnesota Whitecaps	1	0	1	1	0							

ZERAFA, JESSICA *2007-08 CWHL Mississauga Chiefs #20 (2 games, 1 assist).*

ZHAO QINAN *Defence. Shoots right. #88.*

Born 1997-08-29. Grew up in Harbin, CHN. 5'6". Debut at age 20 on 2017-10-28.

Year - League - Team			GP	G	A	PTS	PM
2017-18	CWHL	Vanke Rays	28	1	3	4	24
2018-19	CWHL	KRS Vanke Rays	27	0	4	4	10

ZHOU NAIXIN *Defence. Shoots right. #56.*

Born 1998-09-10. Grew up in Harbin, CHN. 5'6". Debut at age 19 on 2017-10-21.

Year - League - Team			GP	G	A	PTS	PM
2017-18	CWHL	Vanke Rays	27	0	0	0	0

ZHU RUI *Centre. Shoots right. #98.*

Born 1998-04-23. Grew up in Harbin, CHN. 5'2". Debut at age 19 on 2017-10-21.

Year - League - Team			GP	G	A	PTS	PM	Year - Playoff		GP	G	A	PTS	PM
2017-18	CWHL	Kunlun Red Star	27	2	0	2	2	2018	C-Cup	4	0	0	0	0
2018-19	CWHL	KRS Vanke Rays	24	0	1	1	2							

ZIADIE, CHELSEA *Defence. Shoots right. #20.*

Born 1995-09-14. Grew up in Pointe-Claire, QC, CAN. 5'3". Debut at age 23 on 2018-10-06.

Year - League - Team			GP	G	A	PTS	PM	Year - Playoff		GP	G	A	PTS	PM
2018-19	NWHL/	Metropolitan Riveters	16	1	3	4	2	2019	I-Cup	2	0	0	0	2

ZIBAROVA, PETRA *Most, CZE. D. 2006-07 NWHL Ottawa #18 (34 games, 4 goals, 4 assists, playoff 2 gp).*

ZIMMER, LESLEY *Forward. Shoots right. #15 #81 #10.*

Abby Hoffman Cup winner with Brampton on 2006-03-12.
Born 1975-2-2, Bolton, ON, CAN. Grew up in Toronto, ON, CAN. 5'5".

Year - League - Team			GP	G	A	PTS	PM	Year - Playoff		GP	G	A	PTS	PM
1993-94	COWHL	Mississauga Chiefs	29	7	7	14	18							
1995-96	COWHL	Mississauga Chiefs	14	4	2	6	16							
1996-97	COWHL	North York Aeros	0	0	0	0	0							
2002-03	NWHL	Durham Lightning												
2003-04	NWHL	Oakville Ice	27	0	6	6	18							
2005-06	NWHL	Brampton Thunder	26	1	1	2	20	2006	NWHL-P	5	0	0	0	0
2006	Nationals	Brampton Thunder	6	0	0	0	2							
2006-07	NWHL	Brampton Thunder	22	0	2	2	12	2007	NWHL-P	3	0	0	0	0
Totals from all Competitions			**132**	**12**	**18**	**30**	**86**							

ZIMMER, MARGARET *Forward. Shoots right. #19.*

Born 1994-06-07. Grew up in St. Charles, IL, USA. 5'7". Debut at age 22 on 2016-10-15.

Year - League - Team			GP	G	A	PTS	PM
2016-17	CWHL	Boston Blades	12	0	0	0	0

ZIMMERMAN, RUSH *F. 2006-07 WWHL Minnesota Whitecaps (6 gp, 3 goals, 3 a.; playoff 3 gp, 2 goals, 1 assist).*

ZUBECK, BRITTANY *Left wing. Shoots left. #19.*

Born 1993-05-02. Grew up in Thunder Bay, ON, CAN. 5'7". Debut at age 24 on 2017-10-14.

Year - League - Team			GP	G	A	PTS	PM
2017-18	CWHL	Toronto Furies	24	5	8	13	13
2018-19	CWHL	Toronto Furies	11	0	0	0	0

ZUBER, BIANCA *Calgary. 2012-13 CWHL Alberta #24 (5 gp, 1 goal); 2013-14 Calgary (17 gp, 1 a.; C-Cup 3 gp).*

ALL GOALIES

ANDERSON, CECILIA — *2006-07 NWHL Montréal; 2007-08 CWHL (6 gp, 4 wins, 1 SO 2.66 GAA).*

ANDERSON, JENNIFER — *1996-97 COWHL Hamilton Golden Hawks #30 (22 games, 11 losses).*

ANDERSON, JESSICA — *2007-08 CWHL Phénix du Québec #53 (3 games, 5.98 GAA).*

ANDERSON, SHANNON — *2007 Nationals British Columbia (3 games, 2.45 GAA).*

ANDERSON, TAMARA — *1995 Nationals Calgary Classics.*

ARCARO, SARAH — *2007-08 CWHL Burlington Barracudas #1 (did not feature).*

ASH, HEATHER — *2003 Nationals Winnipeg (3 games, 1 loss, 5.88 GAA).*

AUDET, JESSIKA — Goalie. #20 #1.

Osgoode, ON, CAN. Grew up in Charlesbourg, QC, CAN.

Year	League	Team	GP	W-L-T	SO	GAA	Year - Playoff	GP	W-L	SO	GAA
1999	Nationals	Équipe Québec									
2000	Nationals	Équipe Québec			2						
2000-01	NWHL	Wingstar de Montréal	27	18-6-3	6	1.89					
2001-02	NWHL	Wingstar de Montréal	23	7-11-4	3	2.67					
2002-03	NWHL	Axion de Montréal	19	8-6-2	2	2.36	2003 NWHL-P				
2003-04	NWHL	Avalanche du Québec	18	1-13-2	1	4.51					
Totals from all Competitions			**87**	**34-36-11**	**14**						

AVESON, SYDNEY — Goalie. #67.

Born 1991-09-17. Grew up in West Covina, CA, USA. 5'6". Debut at age 24 on 2015-11-01.

Year	League	Team	GP	W-L	SO	GAA
2015-16	CWHL	Canadiennes de Montréal	5	4-1	2	1.20

CWHL All-Rookie Team in 2015-16

BAIRD, LYNDSAY — Goalie. #1.

Abby Hoffman Cup winner with Calgary on 2007-03-10.
WWHL winner. Born 1983-4-7. Slave Lake, AB, CAN. 5'5".

Year	League	Team	GP	W-L-T	SO	GAA	Year - Playoff	GP	W-L	SO	GAA
2005-06	WWHL	Calgary Oval X-Treme	22	2-0-0	1	3.12	2006 WWHL-P	3	0-0-0	0	
2006	Nationals	Calgary Oval X-Treme	1	1-0	0	3.00					
2006-07	WWHL	Calgary Oval X-Treme	6	3-0-0	0	2.00	2007 WWHL-P	1	0-0-0	0	
2007	Nationals	Calgary Oval X-Treme	2								
2007-08	WWHL	Calgary Oval X-Treme									
2008	Nationals	Calgary Oval X-Treme	3	0-0	0						

BEARD, SHERRY — *2005 Nationals Manitoba (2 games, 2 wins, 2.50 GAA).*

BEATTIE, DANIELLE — *2009-10 CWHL Vaughan #33 (2 games).*

BÉLANGER, ANNIE — Goalie. #41.

Clarkson Cup winner with Calgary on 2019-03-24.
Born 1994-02-04 in Sherbrooke, QC, CAN. 5'9". Debut at age 24 on 2018-10-27.

Year	League	Team	GP	W-L-T	SO	GAA	Year - Playoff	GP	W-L	SO	GAA
2018-19	CWHL	Calgary Inferno	9	8-1	4	1.45	2019 C-Cup	0	0-0	0	-.--

BENELL, DIANA — *2006 Nationals Prince Edward Island (4 gp), 2007 Nationals (2 gp); 2008 Nationals (3 gp).*

BETTLES, SHANNON — *2005-06 NWHL Brampton #31; 2006-07 WWHL B.C. Breakers.*

BEUKER, LORENDA — Goalie.

Abby Hoffman Cup winner with Edmonton on 1997-03-09. Abby Hoffman Cup winner with Calgary on 1998-03-22 and 2001-03-11. Born 1977-03-18. 5'5".

Year	League	Team	GP	W-L-T	SO	GAA
1996	Nationals	Saskatchewan Selects	4	1-3	0	4.67
1997	Nationals	Edmonton Chimos				
1998	Nationals	Calgary Oval X-Treme	3			
1999	Nationals	Calgary Oval X-Treme				
2000	Nationals	Calgary Oval X-Treme		1		
2001	Nationals	Calgary Oval X-Treme				

BOE, ALI — Goalie. #33.

Abby Hoffman Cup winner with Calgary on 2007-03-10.
Born 1983-06-15. Grew up in Edina, MN, USA. 5'5".

Year	League	Team	GP	W-L-T	SO	GAA	Year - Playoff	GP	W-L	SO	GAA
2006-07	WWHL	Calgary Oval X-Treme	23	10-1-0	4	2.56	2007 WWHL-P	2	0-0	0	-.--
2007	Nationals	Calgary Oval X-Treme	3	3-0-0	3	0.00					

BOOTH, JOANNE — *1995 Nationals Regina Sharks.*

BOTEJU, CHARMAINE — *1996-97 London Devilettes #30 (6 games, 2 wins, 4.91 GAA).*

BOULAY, CATHERINE — *2003-04 NWHL Avalanche du Québec.*

BOUTIN, KRYSTEL *2005-06 Québec (4 games).*
BRADLEY, MAUREEN *2010-11 CWHL Boston #35 (3 games, 6.97 GAA).*
BRENNAN, ASHLEY *2005 Nationals Prince Edward Island (2 games).*
BRENNAN, LAURA *2016-17 NWHL Connecticut #33; 2017-18 (1 game); 2018-19 NWHL (1 game).*

BRIAN, DELAYNE *Goalie. #30.*
Clarkson Cup winner with Calgary on 2016-03-14
Born 1986-07-23 in Winnipeg, MB, CAN. 5'8". Debut at age 27 on 2013-11-10.

Year - League - Team		GP	W-L-T	SO	GAA	Year - Playoff	GP	W-L	SO	GAA
2013-14	CWHL Calgary Inferno	14	8-6	1	2.52	2014 C-Cup	2	0-2	0	3.54
2014-15	CWHL Calgary Inferno	18	11-7	1	2.47	2015 C-Cup	2	0-2	0	2.99
2015-16	CWHL Calgary Inferno	20	11-6	2	2.92	2016 C-Cup	3	3-0	0	2.67
2016-17	CWHL Calgary Inferno	7	7-0	1	1.84					
2017-18	CWHL Calgary Inferno	11	7-4	0	2.60	2018 C-Cup	3	1-2	1	1.01
CWHL Regular Season		70	44-23	5	2.56	Clarkson Cup	10	4-6	1	2.26
Totals from all Competitions		**80**	**48-29**	**6**	**2.52**					

Clarkson Cup Championship MVP in 2016... CWHL Goalie of the Year in 2013-14... CWHL All-Rookie Team in 2013-14

BRIDGEWATER, ERICA *Georgetown, ON, CAN. 2007-08 CWHL Vaughan Flames.*

BROWN, KEELY *Goalie. #1.*
Born 1976-07-28. 5'8".

Year - League - Team		GP	W-L-T	SO	GAA	Year - Playoff	GP	W-L	SO	GAA
1999-00	NWHL Scarborough Sting	39	2-15-3	0	4.63					
2000-01	NWHL Toronto Sting	27	5-16-3	2	3.41					
2001-02	NWHL Mississauga IceBears	12	6-3-3	2	2.40					
2002-03	NWHL Mississauga IceBears									
2003-04	NWHL Edmonton Chimos	6	1-5-0	0	5.33	2004 NWHL-P				
2004	Nationals Edmonton Chimos	4								
2004-05	WWHL Edmonton Chimos	15	6-3-1	2	2.55	2005 WWHL-P	3	0-1-1	0	1.50
2005-06	WWHL Edmonton Chimos	14	4-1-1	0	3.39	2006 WWHL-P	1	0-0-0	0	
2006-07	WWHL Edmonton Chimos	19	5-4-0	1	2.67	2007 WWHL-P	1	0-0-0	0	7.50
2007-08	WWHL Edmonton Chimos									
2008-09	WWHL Edmonton Chimos	12	8-4-0	0	3.17	2009 WWHL-P	1	0-1-0	0	4.07
2009-10	WWHL Edmonton Chimos	11	4-7-0	1	1.96					
2010-11	WWHL Edmonton Chimos	7	4-3-0	0	2.23					
Totals from all Competitions		**172**	**45-63-12**	**8**						

BROWN, SYDNEY *2009-10 CWHL Brampton Thunder #29; Vaughan Flames #18.*
BRULÉ, MELANIE *2010-11 WWHL Edmonton Chimos #31.*
BRYANT, SARAH *2016-17 NWHL New York Riveters #3 (2 games); 2018-19 Metropolitan.*
BUCK, JENN *Etna, NH, USA. 2001-02 NWHL Mississauga Ice Bears #35.*
BUGDEN, JANA *2000 Nationals Newfoundland Labrador; 2001 Nationals; 2002 Nationals (3 games).*
BUISSON, KARINE *2001-02 NWHL Cheyenne #41.*
BURKE, AMY *2011-12 CWHL Boston Blades #33.*

BURT, KATIE *Goalie. #33.*
Born 1997-01-26, Lynn, MA, USA.

Year - League - Team		GP	W-L-T	SO	GAA	Year - Playoff	GP	W-L	SO	GAA
2018-19	NWHL/ Boston Pride	16	10-5	0	2.42	2019 I-Cup	1	0-1	0	4.00

BUTTERS, DANIELLE *London, ON, CAN. 2014-15 CWHL Toronto Furies #61 (1 game, 3.69 GAA).*

CABANA, EMMANUELLE *Goalie. #30.*
Born 1980-12-3, Sainte-Hilaire, QC, CAN. Grew up in Sainte-Hilaire, QC, CAN. 5'6".

Year - League - Team		GP	W-L-T	SO	GAA
2000-01	NWHL Wingstar de Montréal	12	10-0-1	3	1.18
2001-02	NWHL Cheyenne	14	3-7-2	0	3.13
2002-03	NWHL Avalanche du Québec	29	6-18-4	1	3.34
2003-04	NWHL Avalanche du Québec	12	2-9-0	0	
2004-05	NWHL Avalanche du Québec	12	1-7-3	0	
2005-06	NWHL Avalanche du Québec	8	1-7-0	0	4.88
Totals from all Competitions		**87**	**23-48-10**	**4**	

CAMPBELL, KELLY *2016-17 CWHL Brampton Thunder #30.*
CAMPBELL, REBECCA *2009-10 CWHL Vaughan Flames #34.*
CUMMING, KAYLA *2008-09 WWHL British Columbia Breakers #30 (3 games).*

CARIDDI, AMANDA *Goalie. #1 92.*
Born 1993-05-11, North Adams, MA, USA. 5'9". Debut at age 22 on 2016-02-06.

Year - League - Team		GP	W-L	SO	GAA
2015-16	CWHL Boston Blades	3	0-1	0	6.75
2017-18	CWHL Boston Blades	4	0-1	0	6.13

CARON, DENISE *1995 Nationals Équipe Québec, 1996 Équipe Québec, 1997 Équipe Québec.*

CARTY, MEAGHAN *2010-11 CWHL Burlington Barracudas #31.*

CHAMPION, JENNIFER *1998 Nationals Prince Edward Island; 1999 Nationals; 2000 Nationals.*

CHARBONNEAU, VALÉRIE *Goalie. #27.*

Clarkson Cup winner with Montréal on 2011-03-27
Born 1991-1-2, Sudbury, ON, CAN. Debut at age 20 on 2010-10-30.

Year - League - Team		GP	W-L	SO	GAA	Year - Playoff		GP	W-L	SO	GAA
2010-11	CWHL Stars de Montréal	2	1-1	0	4.00	2011	CWHL-P	0	0-0	0	
						2011	C-Cup	0	0-0	0	

CHARTIER, BRITTONY *Goalie. #33.*

Abby Hoffman Cup winner with Calgary on 2003-03-16.
WWHL winner. Born 1986-1-25. Grew up in Saskatoon, SK, CAN.

Year - League - Team		GP	W-L	SO	GAA	Year - Playoff	GP	W-L	SO	GAA
2000	Nationals Saskatchewan									
2002	Nationals Saskatchewan				2.37					
2002-03	NWHL Calgary Oval X-Treme	9	8-0-0	3	1.32	2003 NWHL-P				
2003	Nationals Calgary Oval X-Treme	3	3-0	0	1.78					
2003-04	NWHL Calgary Oval X-Treme	6	5-1-0	2	0.83	2004 NWHL-P				
2004	Nationals Calgary Oval X-Treme	2								
2004-05	WWHL Calgary Oval X-Treme	20	11-0-0	4	1.00	2005 WWHL-P	3	2-0-0	1	0.00

CLEMAGO, ROBYN *2017-18 CWHL Boston #1 (1 gp).*

CHISHOLM, KENDRA *2011-12 CWHL Alberta #1.*

CHOLETTE, JOSÉE *1998-99 NWHL Bonaventure (1 gp); 1999-00 Montréal #1 (34 gp, 16 W, 7 SO, 2.17 GAA).*

CHULI, ELAINE *Goalie. #29.*

Born 1994-05-16. Grew up in Waterford, ON, CAN. 5'7". Debut at age 23 on 2017-10-28.

Year - League - Team		GP	W-L	SO	GAA	Year - Playoff	GP	W-L	SO	GAA
2017-18	CWHL Vanke	27	14-12	4	2.93					
2018-19	CWHL Toronto	14	6-7	2	3.03	2019 C-Cup	1	0-1	0	3.07
Totals from all Competitions		**42**	**20-20**	**6**	**2.96**					

CWHL All-Rookie Team in 2017-18

CLARK, DESI *Goalie. #1.*

Born 1982-5-11, Salmo, BC, CAN. Grew up in Salmo, BC, CAN. 5'7".

Year - League - Team		GP	W-L	SO	GAA	Year - Playoff	GP	W-L	SO	GAA
2005-06	NWHL Durham Lightning	28	17-6-5	4	1.96	2006 NWHL-P	2	0-2-0	8	2.00
2006-07	NWHL Etobicoke Dolphins			1		2007 NWHL-P	3	1-2-0	0	3.00
2007	Nationals Etobicoke Dolphins	4		2	1.09					
2007-08	WWHL British Columbia Breakers		0-0-0							
2008-09	WWHL British Columbia Breakers	9	0-9-0	0	4.28					

NWHL Goalie of the Year in 2005-06

CLARK, REBECCA *Keswick, ON, CAN. 2009-10 CWHL Mississauga Chiefs #1.*

CLAUSE, BETH *2011-12 CWHL Burlington Barracudas #35 (1 game).*

CLAYTON, MICHELLE *Goalie. #29.*

Year - League - Team		GP	W-L-T	SO	GAA
1993-94	COWHL Mississauga Chiefs	15			
1995	Nationals Mississauga Chiefs				
1995-96	COWHL Mississauga Chiefs	13			
1999-00	NWHL Durham Lightning	30	2-11-1	0	5.88

CLEGG, JANE *1995 Nationals Regina Sharks; 1996 Nationals Saskatchewan; 1997 Nationals Saskatchewan.*

CLEMIS, CARLI *2009-10 WWHL Strathmore (5 gp, 3 wins, 2.95 GAA); 2010-11 (4 games).*

CLOUTIER, KRISTA *2001 Nationals Vancouver Griffins.*

COOK, SAMANTHA *2009-10 CWHL Brampton Thunder.*

CONNELLY, LIZ *2008-09 CWHL Ottawa Senators #30 (2 games).*

CONVERY, JESSICA *Goalie. #30.*

Born 1996-07-16. Grew up in Commerce, MI, USA. 5'6". Debut at age 22 on 2018-10-14.

Year - League - Team		GP	W-L	SO	GAA
2018-19	CWHL Worcester	6	0-5	0	5.99

CONWAY, SEANNA *2002-03 NWHL Québec #33 (9 games, 1W-3L-1T, 4.55 GAA).*

COOK, TRACY *Goalie. #88 #30 #29.*

Year - League - Team		GP	W-L-T	SO	GAA
1995-96	COWHL Hamilton Golden Hawks	2			
1996-97	COWHL North York Aeros	21	5-0-0	3	0.22
1999-00	NWHL Scarborough Sting	40	1-19-0	1	5.49
2000-01	NWHL Toronto Sting	17	3-13-0	0	5.63

CORLEY-BRYNE, MEGHAN *Stittsville, ON, CAN. 2013-14 CWHL Montréal #33 (7 gp, 5W-1L, 1SO, 1.53 GAA).*

CÔTÉ, ANNIK *2000 Nationals Team New Brunswick.*

COUCH, SARAH *Goalie. #30 #75 #1.*

Year - League - Team			GP	W-L-T	SO	GAA
1993-94	COWHL	Toronto Aeros	29	?		
1995-96	COWHL	Toronto Red Wings	29	?		
1996-97	COWHL	Newtonbrook Panthers	35	15-1-5	5	1.94
1998-99	NWHL	Brampton Thunder	39	17-4-2	4	2.39
2000-01	NWHL	Durham Lightning	23	3-16-1	1	5.05
2001-02	NWHL	Durham Lightning	19	2-9-4	0	4.30
2005-06	NWHL	Durham Lightning	0	0-0-0	0	
Totals from all Competitions			**174**	**37-30-12**	**10**	

COUGHLIN, LINDSAY *2007 Nationals Team New Brunswick (2 games).*

COURCHENE, NICOLE *1999 Nationals Tazmanian Devils.*

COURTEMANCHE, SOPHIE *2005-06 NWHL Montréal (1 game).*

COUSINS, THERESA *1995 Nationals PEI Esso Tigers; 1996 Nationals PEI Esso Tigers (3 games).*

COX, J. *2002-03 NWHL Edmonton Chimos (2 games, 0W-2L).*

CRONIN, MANDY *Goalie. #1.*
CWHL winner. Born 1980-2-17, Kettering, OH, USA.
Grew up in York, ME, USA. 5'10".

Year - League - Team			GP	W-L	SO	GAA	Year - Playoff		GP	W-L	SO	GAA
2002-03	NWHL	Durham Lightning										
2003-04	NWHL	Durham Lightning	24	3-17-0	2	5.42						
2004-05	NWHL	Durham Lightning	23	2-18-0	0							
2005-06	NWHL	Toronto Aeros	24	9-10-3	1	2.98						
2006-07	NWHL	Brampton Thunder			1		2007	NWHL-P	0	0-0-0	0	
2007-08	CWHL	Brampton Can.-Thunder	18	12-5	2	2.29	2008	CWHL-P	1	1-0	0	2.00
2008	Nationals	Brampton Can.-Thunder		0-0	0	?						
2008-09	CWHL	Brampton Thunder	11	8-3	2	2.13	2009	CWHL-P	0			
							2009	C-Cup	0	0-0	0	
2009-10	CWHL	Brampton Thunder	??	??-??	1		2010	C-Cup	0	0-0	0	
2010-11	CWHL	Boston Blades	18	8-9	1	3.82	2011	CWHL-P	2	0-2	0	3.50
2011-12	CWHL	Burlington Barracudas	14	0-12	0	5.71						
Totals from all Competitions			**135**	**43-76-3**	**10**							

CUBBERLEY, ALLISON *Goalie. #31.*
Born 1987-1-7. Grew up in Bracebridge, ON, CAN. Goalie. Debut at age 23 on 2009-10-4.

Year - League - Team			GP	W-L	SO	GAA
2009-10	CWHL	Burlington Barracudas	13	9-4	2	2.05
2010-11	CWHL	Toronto Furies	0	0-0	0	
2011-12	CWHL	Burlington Barracudas	6	0-4	0	4.48
2012-13	CWHL	Brampton Thunder	0	0-0	0	

CWHL All-Rookie Team in 2009-10

CURRAN, DYANA *1998-99 NWHL Mississauga Chiefs #35 (1 game).*

DAHM, LAUREN *Goalie. #35.*
Born 1989-09-26. Grew up in Baldwinsville, NY, USA. 5'6". Debut at age 27 on 2016-10-15.

Year - League - Team			GP	W-L	SO	GAA
2016-17	CWHL	Boston Blades	22	2-18	0	5.35
2017-18	CWHL	Boston Blades	27	1-25	0	3.91
2018-19	CWHL	Worcester Blades	12	0-7	0	5.06

DANSEREAU, MARIE-FRANCE *1999-00 NWHL Montréal #30 (3W-0L-1T, 2 SO, 1.50 GAA).*

DAY, LUNDY *2010-11 WWHL Strathmore (6 games, 5L); 2011-12 CWHL Alberta (10 games, 4W-6L).*

DENEAULT, BRENDA *Goalie. #29 #37.*

Year - League - Team			GP	W-L-T	SO	GAA
1993-94	COWHL	Scarborough Sting	29			
1995-96	COWHL	Toronto Red Wings	22			
1996-97	COWHL	Newtonbrook Panthers	25	9-2-3	4	1.87
1997-98	COWHL	Mississauga Chiefs	16	6-2-3	2	2.29
1998-99	NWHL	Mississauga Chiefs	36	12-8-1	3	2.44
2000-01	NWHL	Mississauga IceBears	22	10-10-2	5	2.51
2001-02	NWHL	Mississauga IceBears	19	6-7-5	2	2.78
Totals from all Competitions			**169**	**43-29-14**	**16**	

DESBIENS, ANN-RENÉE *Goalie. #27.*
Clarkson Cup winner with Montréal on 2012-03-25
Born 1994-04-10. Grew up in La Malbaie, QC, CAN. 5'9". Debut at age 17 on 2012-03-24.

Year - League - Team			GP	W-L	SO	GAA	Year - Playoff		GP	W-L	SO	GAA
2011-12	CWHL	Stars de Montréal					2012	C-Cup	1	1-0	0	3.95

DESCHÊNES, MARIE-SOLEIL *Goalie. #35.*
Born 1994-05-09. Grew up in Ile-Bizard, QC, CAN. 5'3". Debut at age 23 on 2018-02-04.

Year - League - Team			GP	W-L	SO	GAA	Year - Playoff	GP	W-L	SO	GAA
2017-18	CWHL	Canadiennes de Montréal	1	1-0	1	0.00	2018 C-Cup	0	0-0	0	0.00
2018-19	CWHL	Canadiennes de Montréal	4	4-0	2	1.00					

DESJARDINS, KATHRYN Goalie. #1.

Clarkson Cup winner with Calgary on 2016-03-14
Born 1987-4-1. Grew up in Loretteville, QC, CAN. 5'3". Debut at age 26 on 2012-10-27.

Year - League - Team			GP	W-L	SO	GAA	Year - Playoff	GP	W-L	SO	GAA
2012-13	CWHL	Alberta	14	2-11	0	3.18					
2013-14	CWHL	Calgary Inferno	11	4-6	0	3.06	2014 C-Cup	1	0-1	0	6.00
2015-16	CWHL	Calgary Inferno	7	5-2	1	1.78	2016 C-Cup	0	0-0	0	-.--
CWHL Regular Season			32	11-19	1	2.86	Clarkson Cup	1	0-1	0	6.00
Totals from all Competitions			**33**	**11-20**	**1**	**2.97**					

DETENBECK, LAURA *1999 Nationals Team New Brunswick).*

DEVAULT, BRENDA *1992-93 COWHL Scarborough Sting #30 (29 games).*

DEVITO, DANI *1995 Nationals Britannia Blues.*

DEWAR, JENNIFER Goalie. #1 #31 #35.

Born 1973-12-08. Grew up in London, ON, CAN.

Year - League - Team			GP	W-L-T	SO	GAA
1992-93	COWHL	Guelph Eagles	28			
1993-94	COWHL	Hamilton Golden Hawks	26			
1995-96	COWHL	North York Aeros	27			
1996	Nationals	North York Aeros	4	3-1	1	1.85
1996-97	COWHL	North York Aeros	31	19-1-5	6	1.40
1997-98	COWHL	North York Aeros	20	10-1-1	2	1.47
1998	Nationals	North York Aeros	3			?
1998-99	NWHL	Mississauga Chiefs	36	11-7-1	6	2.16
1999-00	NWHL	Mississauga Chiefs	39	12-6-3	3	2.11
2000-01	NWHL	North York Aeros	21	22-1-3	9	1.64
2001	Nationals	North York Aeros				
2001-02	NWHL	North York Aeros	11	7-1-3	3	1.30
2002	Nationals	North York Aeros				0.00
Totals from all Competitions			**246**	**84-18-16**	**30**	

DIPETTA, MELISSA *2003-04 NWHL Ottawa (3 games, 1W-1L); 2004-05 (2 games, 1W-0L, 1 SO).*

DITONDO, JULIA *2018-19 NWHL Buffalo Beauts.*

DOUCETT, NICOLE *2005 Nationals Nova Scotia Selects (2 games, 1 loss).*

DOUGLAS, JULIE *1996 Nationals Britannia Blues (3 gp); 2000 Nationals Britannia Blues.*

DOYON-LESSARD, AUDREY *2011-12 CWHL Montréal (1 game, 1 win).*

DUBÉ, DANIELLE *1999 Nationals New Westminster Lightning.*

DUFOUR, CHRISTINE Goalie. #34.

Born 1984-2-5. Grew up in Rivière-du-Loup, QC, CAN. Debut at age 24 on 2007-9-16.

Year - League - Team			GP	W-L	SO	GAA
2007-08	CWHL	Phénix du Québec	13	5-6	1	3.12

CWHL All-Rookie Team in 2007-08

DYER, KELLY *1996-97 COWHL North York Aeros #35 (9 games, 4W-0L-1T, 2 SO, 2.18 GAA).*

DYOTTE, MARIÈVE Goalie. #29.

Year - League - Team			GP	W-L-T	SO	GAA
1998-99	NWHL	Mistral de Laval	34	4-11-2	0	6.01
1999-00	NWHL	Mistral de Laval	30	5-10-1	0	7.73
2000-01	NWHL	Mistral de Laval	3	0-0-0	0	21.82
Totals from all Competitions			**67**	**9**	**0**	

DZIOBA, LAURYN *2006-07 WWHL Edmonton Chimos #26 (1 game).*

EADIE, CINDY Goalie. #35.

Abby Hoffman Cup winner with Brampton on 2006-03-12.
CWHL winner. Born 1982-9-21, Brantford, ON, CAN. Grew up in Brantford, ON, CAN. 6'0".

Year - League - Team			GP	W-L	SO	GAA	Year - Playoff	GP	W-L	SO	GAA
2000-01	NWHL	Mississauga IceBears	16	11-5-1	1	2.37					
2005-06	NWHL	Brampton Thunder	19	10-6-3	2	2.18	2006 NWHL-P	5	4-1-0	6	0.22
2006	Nationals	Brampton Thunder	4	3-1	0	2.25					
2006-07	NWHL	Brampton Thunder		3			2007 NWHL-P	6	5-1-0	4	0.82
2007-08	CWHL	Brampton Can.-Thunder	14	10-3-0	2	1.37	2008 CWHL-P	2	1-0-1	0	2.83
2008	Nationals	Brampton Can.-Thunder	3	1-2	0	2.71					
Totals from all Competitions			**69**	**45-19-5**	**18**						

CWHL Central All-Star Team in 2007-08

EISNER, SHANNON *1999 Nationals Saskatchewan.*

ELAND, JODY *1995-96 COWHL Hamilton (28 games); 1996-97 (13 games, 1W-10L-0T).*

FENNER, ALIX _The Pas, MB. 2010-11 WWHL Manitoba #1 (9 games, 1W-6L)._
FERGUSON, AMY _1996 Nationals Pictou (1 gp); 2003-04 Edmonton Chimos (6 gp, 6 losses); 2004 Nationals (3 gp)._
FERGUSON, DEB _1992-93 COWHL Scarborough Firefighters (26 games); 1993-94 Scarb. Sting (22 games)._
FINI, LAURA _1996-97 COWHL Mississauga Chiefs #29 (1 game)._

FISHER, KENDRA
Goalie. #30 #31 #1.

Abby Hoffman Cup winner with Aeros on 2000-03-12, 2004-03-14 and 2005-03-13.
NWHL Cup winner. Born 1979-10-20, Kincardine, ON, CAN. Grew up in Kincardine, ON, CAN. 5'11".

Year - League - Team			GP	W-L	SO	GAA	Year - Playoff	GP	W-L	SO	GAA
1996-97	COWHL	North York Aeros	1								
1997-98	COWHL	North York Aeros	19	6-0-2	1	1.69					
1998	Nationals	North York Aeros	3			?					
1998-99	NWHL	North York Aeros	39	21-1-1	8	1.53					
1999	Nationals	North York Aeros									
1999-00	NWHL	North York Aeros	36	17-1-0	11	0.87	2000 NWHL-P				
2000	Nationals	North York Aeros			2						
2000-01	NWHL	North York Aeros	12	12-1-0	3	0.71					
2001	Nationals	North York Aeros									
2001-02	NWHL	North York Aeros	20	16-0-2	6	1.32					
2002	Nationals	North York Aeros				0.79					
2002-03	NWHL	North York Aeros					2003 NWHL-P				
2003-04	NWHL	Toronto Aeros	18	14-1-1	1	1.50	2004 NWHL-P	2	0-2-0	0	4.00
2004	Nationals	Toronto Aeros	2								
2004-05	NWHL	Toronto Aeros	15	9-4-1	4	1.88	2005 NWHL-P				
2005	Nationals	Toronto Aeros	3	2-1	1	2.00					
2005-06	NWHL	Durham Lightning	7	5-2-0	0	2.57	2006 NWHL-P	0	0-0-0	0	
2008-09	CWHL	Vaughan Flames	15	6-9	0	3.52	2009 CWHL-P	2	0-0-2	0	2.39
2009-10	CWHL	Vaughan Flames			0						
2010-11	CWHL	Toronto Furies	11	3-7	0	3.63	2011 CWHL-P	0	0-0	0	
							2011 C-Cup	1	0-1	0	1.50
2011-12	CWHL	Brampton Thunder	3	2-1	0	2.28					
							2012 C-Cup	0	0-0	0	
Totals from all Competitions			**209**	**113-31-9**	**37**						

FITZGERALD, BERNADETTE
2004 Nationals Team New Brunswick (3 games).

FITZGERALD, KATIE
Goalie. #35.

Isobel Cup winner with Metropolitan on 2018-03-25
Born 1994-04-13. Grew up in Des Plaines, IL, USA. 5'10". Debut at age 22 on 2016-10-08.

Year - League - Team		GP	W-L	SO	GAA	Year - Playoff	GP	W-L	SO	GAA
2016-17	NWHL/ New York Riveters	15	7-7	2	3.01	2017 I-Cup	1	0-0	0	4.14
2017-18	NWHL/ Metropolitan Riveters	15	12-3	1	1.87	2018 I-Cup	2	2-0	2	0.00
2018-19	NWHL/ Metropolitan Riveters	11	2-9	0	3.32	2019 I-Cup	2	1-1	0	1.55
NWHL Regular Season		41	21-19	3	2.68	Isobel Cup	5	3-1	2	1.43
Totals from all Competitions		**46**	**24-20**	**5**	**2.54**					

NWHL Goaltender of the Year in 2016-17... MVP of the Isobel Cup Playoffs in 2018

FITZGIBBONS, ERIN
1998 Nationals Nova Scotia Selects (1 game).

FRALICK, KELSIE
Goalie. #1.

Isobel Cup winner with Boston on 2016-03-12
Grew up in West Chester, PA, USA. 5'9". Debut in 2015-16.

Year - League - Team		GP	W-L	SO	GAA	Year - Playoff	GP	W-L	SO	GAA
2015-16	NWHL/ Boston Pride	1	0-0	0	0.00	2016 I-Cup	0	0-0	0	-.--

FRANCK, NICOLETTE
Goalie. #1 #31 #35 #25.

Born 1981-8-21. Grew up in Burlington, ON, CAN. 5'6".

Year - League - Team		GP	W-L-T	SO	GAA
1996-97	COWHL Hamilton	36	0-14-0	0	14.96
1999-00	NWHL Brampton Thunder	2			
2004-05	NWHL Brampton Thunder	12	11-0-0	1	
2005	Nationals Brampton Thunder	2	1-0	0	0.60

Year - League - Team		GP	W-L-T	SO	GAA
2005-06	NWHL Toronto Aeros	14	4-8-1	0	4.51
2006-07	NWHL Etobicoke Dolphins	0	0-0-0	0	
Totals from all Competitions		**66**	**16-22-1**	**1**	

FRIEND, JULIE
Goalie. #1.

Isobel Cup winner with Minnesota on 2019-03-17. Born 1993-06-08, Minnetonka, MN, USA.

Year - League - Team		GP	W-L	SO	GAA	Year - Playoff	GP	W-L	SO	GAA
2018-19	NWHL/ Minnesota Whitecaps	2	1-0	1	2.41	2019 I-Cup	0	0-0	0	0.00

FROATS, DAWN
1998 Nationals Saskatchewan Selects (5 games).
FROMKIN, ALISSA
2013-14 CWHL Boston Blades #30 (8 games, 2W-4L, 3.41 GAA).

FUJIMAGARI, MARIAH *Goalie. #1.*
Born 1994-04-17. Grew up in Markham, ON, CAN. 5'1". Debut at age 24 on 2018-10-13.

Year - League - Team		GP	W-L	SO	GAA
2018-19	CWHL Worcester Blades	16	0-10	1	6.53

FUJIMOTO, NANA *2015-16 NWHL New York #33 (4W-8L, 3.28 GAA; I-Cup 1 game).*

FUNKE, TARA *1996 Nationals Winnipeg Sweat Camp Storm (3 games).*

GARCIA, ALEXANDRA *2007-08 CWHL Montréal #73.*

GARDNER, WENDY *1993-94 COWHL Mississauga Chiefs (17 games).*

GASKA, GRACE *2009-10 WWHL Strathmore Rockies #31 (3 games, 1W-2L).*

GAUDIEL, ROXANNE *2006-07 NWHL Avalanche du Québec #30.*

GERBRANDT, LINDSEY *2001 Nationals U. Manitoba.*

GERMAIN, KATIE *Goalie. #1.*
Born 1981-2-11. Grew up in Sarnia, ON, CAN. G. 5'6".

Year - League - Team		GP	W-L	SO	GAA	Year - Playoff	GP	W-L	SO	GAA
2004-05	NWHL Oakville Ice	9	4-3-2	1						
2005-06	NWHL Oakville Ice	8	4-3-0	0	3.27	2006 NWHL-P	1	0-1-0	2	1.47
Totals from all Competitions		18	8-7-2	3						

GEYER, NINA *Graz, AUT. 2010-11 CWHL Burlington Barracudas #1 (6 games, 0W-6L).*

GIULIANI, KATRINA *Chateauguay, QC, CAN. 2008-09 CWHL Ottawa Senators #35.*

GOEURY, VANIA *Goalie. #53 #31.*
Born 1973-4-5, St-Sauveur, QC, CAN. Grew up in St-Sauveur, QC, CAN. 5'5".

Year - League - Team		GP	W-L	SO	GAA	Year - Playoff	GP	W-L	SO	GAA
1998-99	NWHL Mistral de Laval	34	5-10-2	1	4.98					
1999-00	NWHL Mistral de Laval	30	2-14-3	1	4.90					
2000-01	NWHL Wingstar de Montréal	1	1-0-0	0	2.00					
2003-04	NWHL Axion de Montréal	14	5-4-2	1	2.95	2004 NWHL-P	0	0-0-0	0	
2005-06	NWHL Ottawa Raiders	9	4-4-0	1	2.47	2006 NWHL-P	0	0-0-0	0	
2006-07	NWHL Ottawa Raiders	14	2-12-0	0	4.95	2007 NWHL-P	0	0-0-0	0	
Totals from all Competitions		102	19-44-7	4						

GOIN, KEIRA *Goalie. #31.*
Born 1994-07-22. Grew up in Dobbs Ferry, NY, USA. 5'7". Debut at age 23 on 2018-01-07.

Year - League - Team		GP	W-L	SO	GAA	Year - Playoff	GP	W-L	SO	GAA
2017-18	NWHL Connecticut Whale	1	0-0	1	7.64	2018 I-Cup	1	0-0	1	9.47

GOLDSTEIN, LAUREN *Goalie. #35.*
Abby Hoffman Cup winner with Aeros on 2000-03-12. NWHL Cup winner. Born 1979-5-25. Goalie.

Year - League - Team		GP	W-L-T	SO	GAA	
1998-99	NWHL North York Aeros	30	16-1-0	9	0.70	
1999	Nationals North York Aeros					
1999-00	NWHL North York Aeros	35	16-2-2	7	1.38	2000 NWHL-P
2000	Nationals North York Aeros				1	
Totals from all Competitions		65	32-3-2	17		

GRABAS, MELANIE *1996 Nationals Edmonton Chimos (4 games).*

GRAVELINE, TEENA *Goalie. #33.*

Year - League - Team		GP	W-L-T	SO	GAA
1995-96	COWHL Peterborough Skyway	24			
1996-97	COWHL Peterborough Pirates	36	10-19-4	3	3.92

GUSHNOWSKI, MELODY *Goalie.*
Abby Hoffman Cup winner with Edmonton on 1997-03-09.
| 1997 | Nationals Edmonton Chimos |

HAMERS, CONNIE *2000-01 NWHL Toronto Sting (1 game).*

HAMILTON, HEATHER *2000-01 NWHL Ottawa Raiders (1 game).*

HAMSDEN, SHELLY *1995-96 COWHL London Devilettes (26 games).*

HANDRAHAN, AMY *Goalie.*
Born 1981-02-04. Grew up in Peakef, PE, CAN. 5'5".

Year - League - Team		GP	W-L	SO	GAA
2000	Nationals Nova Scotia Selects			1	
2001	Nationals Nova Scotia Selects				
2003	Nationals Nova Scotia Selects	5	2-3	0	5.12
2005	Nationals Prince Edward Island	3	0-2	0	3.16

HANLON, KIM *2010-11 WWHL Minnesota Whitecaps #30 (5W-0L, 2.52 GAA).*

HANSON, LENITA *2001 Nationals Saskatchewan; 2003 Nationals Saskatchewan (3 gp, 3 wins).*

HARE, CAROLINE *1998-99 NWHL Ottawa Raiders #30 (3W-7L-2T, 4.20 GAA).*

HARRIS, JILLIAN *2004 Nationals Manitoba (3 games).*

HAUS, KARA *2004-05 WWHL Saskatchewan (0W-2L).*

HE SIYE
Goalie.

Born 1998-11-06. Grew up in Harbin, CHN. 5'7". Debut at age 19 on 2017-11-12.

Year - League - Team		GP	W-L SO GAA
2017-18	CWHL Kunlun Red Star	2	1-1 0 2.66

HEBERT, HAWLEY
1996-97 COWHL North York Aeros (1 game).

HECKMAN-MCKENNA, HEATHER
Salem, NH, USA. 2010-11 CWHL Boston Blades.

HENSLEY, NICOLE
Goalie. #29.

Born 1994-06-23, Lakewood, CO, USA. 5'6".

Year - League - Team		GP	W-L-T SO GAA	Year - Playoff	GP	W-L SO GAA
2018-19	NWHL/ Buffalo Beauts	6	5-1 2 1.50	2019 I-Cup	1	0-1 0 1.97

HERRITT, LISA
Goalie. #31.

Born 1977-01-13. Grew up in Shearwater, NS, CAN.

Year - League - Team		GP	W-L-T SO GAA	Year - Playoff	GP	W-L SO GAA
1999	Nationals Prince Edward Island					
2000	Nationals Prince Edward Island					
2001	Nationals Nova Scotia Selects					
2001-02	NWHL Brampton Thunder	10	1-6-3 0 4.53			
2003-04	NWHL Brampton Thunder			2004 NWHL-P		

HERRON, CATHERINE
Goalie. #31.

Clarkson Cup winner with Montréal on 2009-03-21, 2012-03-25 and 2017-03-05
Born 1983-6-24, Chambly, QC, CAN. Grew up in Chambly, QC, CAN. 5'8".

Year - League - Team		GP	W-L SO GAA	Year - Playoff	GP	W-L SO GAA
2001-02	NWHL Wingstar de Montréal	1	0-0-0 0 0.00			
2002-03	NWHL Axion de Montréal	1	0-1-0 0 2.00			
2008-09	CWHL Stars de Montréal	6	5-1 0 3.33	2009 CWHL-P	0	0-0 0 -.--
				2009 C-Cup	0	0-0 0 -.--
2010-11	CWHL Stars de Montréal	3	3-0 1 2.33			
2011-12	CWHL Stars de Montréal	4	2-1 0 2.27	2012 C-Cup	0	0-0 0 -.--
2013-14	CWHL Stars de Montréal	18	14-3 3 2.11	2014 C-Cup	3	1-2 0 1.90
2014-15	CWHL Stars de Montréal	6	3-3 0 2.47	2015 C-Cup	0	0-0 0 -.--
2016-17	CWHL Canadiennes de Montréal	9	6-3 1 2.45	2017 C-Cup	0	0-0 0 -.--
2017-18	CWHL Canadiennes de Montréal	5	3-1 0 3.72			
CWHL Regular Season		**51**	**36-12 5 2.53**	Clarkson Cup	3	1-2 0 1.90
Totals from all Competitions		**56**	**37-15 5 2.49**			

HOBBS, EMILY
Goalie.

Born 1981-08-19. Grew up in Fredericton, NB, CAN.

Year - League - Team		GP	W-L-T SO GAA	Year - Playoff	GP	W-L SO GAA
2003	Nationals Team New Brunswick	4	1-1 1 4.03			
2004	Nationals Team New Brunswick	4				
2005	Nationals Team New Brunswick	4	3-1 0 2.75			
2006	Nationals Team New Brunswick	6	2-4 1 4.00			
2007	Nationals Team New Brunswick	4	0 5.17			
2008	Nationals Team New Brunswick	4	1-3 0 2.95			

HORAK, JODY
2008-09 WWHL Minnesota Whitecaps #30 (3 games, 2W-1L-0T).

HOSIER, LAURA
Goalie. #29.

Born 1986-9-24, Newmarket, ON, CAN. Grew up in Sharon, ON, CAN. 5'7". Debut at age 22 on 2008-10-4.

Year - League - Team		GP	W-L SO GAA	Year - Playoff	GP	W-L SO GAA
2008-09	CWHL Brampton Thunder	19	14-5 1 2.10	2009 CWHL-P	2	1-1 0 5.63
				2009 C-Cup	2	1-1 0 3.03
2009-10	CWHL Brampton Thunder	?18	?8-10 0 ?.??	2010 C-Cup	2	1-1 0 3.00
2010-11	CWHL Brampton Thunder	19	12-6 3 2.98	2011 CWHL-P	1	0-0 0 2.00
				2011 C-Cup	1	0-1 0 7.00
2011-12	CWHL Brampton Thunder	1	0-1 0 5.00			
Totals from all Competitions		**65**	**37-26 4**			

CWHL Top Goaltender in 2009-10... CWHL First All-Star Team in 2009-10; CWHL Second All-Star Team in 2010-11...
CWHL Outstanding Rookie in 2008-09... CWHL All-Rookie Team in 2008-09

HOUSTON, ALI
Goalie. #30.

Born 1979-5-16, Kanata, ON, CAN. Grew up in Kanata, ON, CAN. 5'5".

Year - League - Team		GP	W-L SO GAA	Year - Playoff	GP	W-L SO GAA
2003-04	NWHL Oakville Ice	15	11-2-1 0 2.26			
2004-05	WWHL Edmonton Chimos	14	5-3-1 1 2.54	2005 WWHL-P	3	1-0-0 0 2.00
2005-06	WWHL Edmonton Chimos	15	4-1-1 1 1.55	2006 WWHL-P	2	0-1-0 0 7.00
2008-09	WWHL Strathmore Rockies	11	1-8-0 0 4.85	2009 WWHL-P	1	0-1-0 0 8.94
Totals from all Competitions		**61**	**22-16-3 2**			

HOWE, ERICA
Goalie. #27.

Clarkson Cup winner with Markham on 2018-03-25
Born 1992-07-17. Grew up in Ottawa, ON, CAN. 5'9". Debut at age 22 on 2014-10-19.

Year - League - Team	GP	W-L	SO	GAA	Year - Playoff	GP	W-L	SO	GAA
2014-15 CWHL Brampton Thunder	13	4-8	0	3.72					
2015-16 CWHL Brampton Thunder	17	9-6	2	2.66	2016 C-Cup	2	0-2	0	4.00
2016-17 CWHL Brampton Thunder	14	7-6	2	2.22	2017 C-Cup	1	0-1	0	7.00
2017-18 CWHL Markham Thunder	16	8-7	3	2.18	2018 C-Cup	3	3-0	0	0.96
2018-19 CWHL Markham Thunder	20	9-9	2	2.56	2019 C-Cup	3	1-2	0	3.67
CWHL Regular Season	80	37-36	9	2.62	Clarkson Cup	9	4-5	0	3.18
Totals from all Competitions	**89**	**41-41**	**9**	**2.68**					

CWHL Second All-Star Team in 2015-16 and 2017-18... CWHL All-Rookie Team 2014-15... Clarkson Cup MVP 2018

HUBER, RACHEL — *2006-07 WWHL Saskatchewan #20 (0W-5L-0T).*

HULS, JANELLE — *2005 Nationals Alberta (3 games, 3 losses).*

HUNT, CLARE — *2002 Natoinals Newfoundland Labrador (2 games).*

HUPE, GENEVIÈVE — *1999-00 NWHL Ottawa Raiders #30 (5W-5L-0T, 2SO, 4.46 GAA).*

HURLEY, KIRA — *Goalie. #31 #37.*

Born 1985-5-16, Toronto, ON, CAN. Grew up in Pickering, ON, CAN. Debut at age 25 on 2010-03-14.

Year - League - Team	GP	W-L	SO	GAA	Year - Playoff	GP	W-L	SO	GAA
2009-10 CWHL Mississauga Chiefs	1	1-0	1	0.00	2010 C-Cup	0	0-0	0	
2010-11 CWHL Brampton Thunder	3	3-0	0	1.67	2011 CWHL-P	2	0-2	0	2.53
					2011 C-Cup	2	1-1	0	2.50

HUTCHINSON, MEGAN — *1996 Nationals Pictou County Sobey's (1 game, 1 loss).*

JAGOE, MALLORY — *2004 Nationals Newfoundland Labrador (3 gp); 2005 Nationals (2 gp); 2006 Nationals (5 gp).*

JEAN, KRYSTEL — *2005-06 NWHL Axion de Montréal #20.*

JEFFERIES, JEN — *2003-04 NWHL Oakville Ice #31 (2 games).*

JETTE, CLAUDIA — *2000-01 NWHL Sainte-Julie (1 game).*

JIANAPOULOS, LIISA — *1999-00 NWHL Scarborough Sting #91 (1 game).*

JONCAS, MARIE-ANDRÉE — *Goalie. #36 #34.*

Born 1983-8-9, Murdochville, QC, CAN. Grew up in Laval, QC, CAN. 5'4".

Year - League - Team	GP	W-L	SO	GAA	Year - Playoff	GP	W-L	SO	GAA
2003 Nationals Québec	1	1-0	1	0.00					
2003-04 NWHL Avalanche du Québec	10	1-8-0							
2004 Nationals Québec	2								
2004-05 NWHL Avalanche du Québec	9	1-7-0	0						
2005-06 NWHL Avalanche du Québec	23	2-19-2	0	3.44					
2006-07 NWHL Avalanche du Québec	??	??-??	1	?.??	2007 NWHL-P				
2007-08 CWHL Phénix du Québec	22	3-15	0	4.57					
2009-10 CWHL Stars de Montréal	??	?-?	1	?.??	2010 C-Cup	0	0-0	0	-.--
Totals from all Competitions	**67**	**8-49-2**	**3**						

Served as CWHL emergency referee on 2008-02-17

JONES, STEPHANIE — *2007-08 CWHL Vaughan Flames #33.*

JORDAN, LESLIE — *1996 Pictou County Sobey's (2 gp, 2 losses); 1998 Nationals Nova Scotia (2 gp).*

KEARNS, JODI — *2003 Nationals Host Saskatchewan (3 gp, 1 wins, 2 losses, 1 shutout).*

KEHLER, BRITNI — *2003 Nationals Manitoba (2 gp, 1 win, 1 loss); 2004 Nationals (5 games).*

KELLOUGH, STACY — *Goalie. #29 #35.*

Born 1980-8-12. Grew up in Pickering, ON, CAN. 5'7".

Year - League - Team	GP	W-L	SO	GAA	Year - Playoff	GP	W-L	SO	GAA
1998-99 NWHL Scarborough Sting	40	1-22-2	0	6.36					
1999-00 NWHL Brampton Thunder	37	14-2-3	4	1.95					
2000-01 NWHL Brampton Thunder	19	12-4-1	1	2.50					
2001-02 NWHL Brampton Thunder	19	6-7-5	0	2.71					
2005-06 NWHL Brampton Thunder	1	0-1-0	0	6.00	2006 NWHL-P	0	0-0-0	0	
Totals from all Competitions	**116**	**33-36-11**	**5**						

KENNY, COLLEEN — *2003 Nationals Team New Brunswick (4 games, 2 losses).*

KERVIN, STEPHANIE — *1998-99 NWHL Brampton Thunder #93 (2 games).*

KESSLER, CHRISTINE — *Goalie. #35.*

Year - League - Team	GP	W-L	SO	GAA	Year - Playoff	GP	W-L	SO	GAA

Clarkson Cup winner with Toronto on 2014-03-22

Born 1988-5-28. Grew up in Oakville, ON, CAN. 5'6". Debut at age 22 on 2010-10-23.

Year - League - Team	GP	W-L	SO	GAA	Year - Playoff	GP	W-L	SO	GAA
2005-06 NWHL Toronto Aeros	0	0-0-0	0						
2010-11 CWHL Burlington Barracudas	19	5-14	0	3.69					
2011-12 CWHL Burlington Barracudas	10	1-9	0	5.22					
2012-13 CWHL Toronto Furies	17	5-12	2	3.12	2013 C-Cup	2	0-2	0	2.56
2013-14 CWHL Toronto Furies	14	3-11	1	2.84	2014 C-Cup	4	3-1	1	1.20
2014-15 CWHL Toronto Furies	19	6-12	0	3.41	2015 C-Cup	2	0-2	0	4.85
2015-16 CWHL Toronto Furies	19	4-14	2	3.44	2016 C-Cup	2	0-2	0	8.12
2016-17 CWHL Toronto Furies	17	6-11	1	2.20	2017 C-Cup	3	1-2	0	2.73

			CWHL Regular Season	116	30-84	6	3.32	Clarkson Cup	13	4-9	1	3.01
			Totals from all Competitions	**129**	**34-93**	**7**	**3.29**					

Clarkson Cup Championship MVP in 2014... CWHL First All-Star Team in 2013-14... CWHL All-Rookie Team in 2010-11

KLEIMAN, ARIELLA
Cote-St-Luc, QC. 2005-06 Québec (3 games, 0W-3L); 2007-08 CWHL Montréal (1 game).

KLEIN, NIKKI
1999-00 NWHL Ottawa Raiders #73 (2 games).

KNIGHT, SUSAN
1998 Nationals New Westminster Lightning (2 games).

KNOX, LIZ
Goalie. #31 #37.

Clarkson Cup winner with Markham on 2018-03-25
Born 1988-6-9. Grew up in Stouffville, ON, CAN. 5'5". Debut at age 23 on 2011-3-26.

Year	League	Team	GP	W-L	SO	GAA	Year	Playoff	GP	W-L	SO	GAA
2010-11	CWHL	Brampton Thunder					2011	C-Cup	0	0-0	0	-.--
2011-12	CWHL	Brampton Thunder	20	13-7	1	2.94	2012	C-Cup	4	2-2	0	2.50
2012-13	CWHL	Brampton Thunder	11	4-7	0	4.19	2013	C-Cup	1	0-1	0	3.43
2014-15	CWHL	Brampton Thunder	11	2-7	1	3.89						
2015-16	CWHL	Brampton Thunder	10	7-2	2	2.74						
2016-17	CWHL	Brampton Thunder	13	5-6	4	2.64	2017	C-Cup	1	0-1	0	4.04
2017-18	CWHL	Markham Thunder	13	6-7	0	2.23	2018	C-Cup	0	0-0	0	-.--
2018-19	CWHL	Markham Thunder	9	3-6	0	3.45	2019	C-Cup	0	0-0	0	-.--
CWHL Regular Season			87	40-46	8	3.09	Clarkson Cup		6	2-4	0	2.93
Totals from all Competitions			**93**	**42-46**	**8**	**3.08**						

KUNZELMAN, MELISSE
2010-11 WWHL Manitoba Maple Leafs #30 (3 games, 0W-3L).

KWASNEY, BRITTNEY
2007 Nationals BC Outback (2 games).

LABONTÉ, CHARLINE
Goalie. #32.

Olympic champion, IIHF champion . Clarkson Cup winner with Montréal on 2017-03-05. NWHL winner.
Born 1982-10-15, Greensfield Park, QC, CAN. Grew up in Boisbriand, QC, CAN. 5'9".

Year	League	Team	GP	W-L	SO	GAA	Year	Playoff	GP	W-L	SO	GAA
2000-01	NWHL	Mistral de Laval	14	1-12-1	0	5.08						
2001	Nationals	Équipe Québec										
2001-02	NWHL	Wingstar de Montréal	8	4-3-1	1	2.13						
2002	Nationals	Équipe Québec	2			0.00						
2002-03	NWHL	Axion de Montréal	18	9-8-1	5	2.19	2003	NWHL-P	2	1-1-0	0	2.00
2003	Nationals	Québec	4	4-0	1	1.23						
2003-04	NWHL	Axion de Montréal	25	14-7-3	3	1.93	2004	NWHL-P	4	2-2-0	2	3.01
2004	Nationals	Québec	7									
2004-05	NWHL	Axion de Montréal	27	18-7-1	6	2.14	2005	NWHL-P	3	2-1-0	0	3.26
2005	Nationals	Axion de Montréal	5	3-2	0	2.80						
2005-06	NWHL	Axion de Montréal	0	0-0-0	0	-.--	2006	NWHL-P	3	3-0-2	2	0.22
2006	Nationals	Axion de Montréal	5	3-1	1	1.38						
2012-13	CWHL	Stars de Montréal	14	10-4	1	2.19	2013	C-Cup	3	2-1	2	1.34
2014-15	CWHL	Stars de Montréal	16	9-7	2	1.89	2015	C-Cup	3	2-1	2	0.99
2015-16	CWHL	Canadiennes de Montréal	20	17-2	5	1.52	2016	C-Cup	3	2-1	0	3.02
2016-17	CWHL	Canadiennes de Montréal	15	11-4	5	1.53	2017	C-Cup	3	3-0	0	1.00
CWHL Regular Season			65	47-17	13	1.76	Clarkson Cup		12	9-3	4	1.59
Totals from all Competitions			**204**	**120-64-9**	**38**	**2.19**						

CWHL Top Goaltender in 2014-15, 2015-16 and 2016-17... CWHL First All-Star Team in 2014-15, 2015-16, 2016-17; CWHL Second All-Star Team in 2012-13... Clarkson Cup Championship MVP in 2015 and 2017... selected First Decade CWHL Team in 2017

LACASSE, GENEVIÈVE
Goalie. #33 #31 #60.

Olympic champion. Clarkson Cup winner with Boston on 2013-03-23 and 2015-03-07.
Born 1989-5-5. Grew up in Kingston, ON, CAN. 5'8". Debut at age 23 on 2012-10-21.

Year	League	Team	GP	W-L	SO	GAA	Year	Playoff	GP	W-L	SO	GAA
2012-13	CWHL	Boston Blades	14	13-1	3	1.26	2013	C-Cup	2	2-0	1	1.00
2013-14	CWHL	Boston Blades	2	1-1	0	3.00	2014	C-Cup	1	1-0	0	1.00
2014-15	CWHL	Boston Blades	12	10-2	1	1.79	2015	C-Cup	2	2-0	1	0.98
2015-16	CWHL	Boston Blades	23	1-22	0	4.90						
2016-17	CWHL	Calgary Inferno	9	8-1	1	2.00	2017	C-Cup	2	2-0	0	1.00
2018-19	CWHL	Canadiennes de Montréal	4	2-2	1	2.53	2019	C-Cup	0	0-0	0	-.--
CWHL Regular Season			64	35-29	6	2.90	Clarkson Cup		7	7-0	2	0.99
Totals from all Competitions			**71**	**42-29**	**8**	**2.71**						

CWHL Goaltender of the Year in 2012-13... CWHL First All-Star Team in 2012-13; CWHL Second All-Star Team in 2014-15... CWHL All-Rookie Team in 2012-13... selected First Decade CWHL Team in 2017

LACQUETTE, TARA
2012-13 CWHL Alberta #30.

LADEN, CHELSEA
2015-16 NWHL Connecticut (1 game, 1 win); New York (2 games, 0W-2L).

LAFRENIÈRE, LISA
2006 Nationals British Columbia Selects (3 games, 3 losses).

LAING, BRIANNA
Goalie. #42.

Born 1994-12-27. Grew up in Marblehead, MA, USA. 5'6". Debut at age 22 on 2017-11-11.

Year	League	Team	GP	W-L	SO	GAA
2017-18	NWHL/	Boston Pride	4	0-3	0	3.47

LALONDE, JULIE *2000-01 NWHL Ottawa #31 (1 game, 0W-1L); 2002-03 (0W-1L).*

LAVERGNE, RENEE *1995 Nationals Winnipeg Sweat Camp Storm.*

LAVIGNE, JENNY *Goalie. #35.*

Clarkson Cup winner with Montréal on 2009-03-21, 2011-03-27 and 2012-03-25. NWHL winner.
Born 1985-2-2, Lac-au-Saumon, QC, CAN. 5'8". Debut at age 19 in 2004-05.

Year - League - Team			GP	W-L	SO	GAA	Year - Playoff		GP	W-L	SO	GAA
2004-05	NWHL	Axion de Montréal	12	6-3-1	2	2.13						
2005	Nationals	Axion de Montréal	1	1-0	0	3.00						
2005-06	NWHL	Axion de Montréal	35	13-19-3	1	3.12	2006	NWHL-P	0	0-0-0	0	
2006	Nationals	Axion de Montréal	2	1-1	0	5.25						
2006-07	NWHL	Axion de Montréal				1	2007	NWHL-P				
2007-08	CWHL	Stars de Montréal	11	7-4	3	2.12	2008	CWHL-P	0	0-0	0	
2008-09	CWHL	Stars de Montréal	5	4-0	0	2.13	2009	CWHL-P	0	0-0	0	
							2009	C-Cup	0	0-0	0	
2009-10	CWHL	Stars de Montréal	??	??-1	3	?.??	2010	C-Cup	1	0-1	0	3.04
2010-11	CWHL	Stars de Montréal	7	6-1	0	2.96	2011	CWHL-P	1	1-0	0	0.92
							2011	C-Cup	0	0-0	0	
2011-12	CWHL	Stars de Montréal	23	19-4	2	2.39	2012	C-Cup	3	3-0	2	0.67
2012-13	CWHL	Stars de Montréal	7	6-1	0	2.71	2013	C-Cup	1	1-0	1	0.00
2014-15	CWHL	Stars de Montréal	0	0-0	0	-.--	2015	C-Cup	0	0-0	0	-.--
CWHL Regular Season			73	57?-11	8	2.27	Clarkson Cup		5	4-1	3	0.99
Totals from all Competitions			**109**	**68-34-4**	**15**							

CWHL Second All-Star Team in 2011-12

LEBLANC, EDITH *1999-00 NWHL Mistral de Laval #79 (1 game).*

LECLAIRE, ISABELLE *Goalie. #30 #31 #55.*

Year - League - Team			GP	W-L-T	SO	GAA	
1998	Nationals	Équipe Québec	2			?	
1998-99	NWHL	Bonaventure	25	10-11-2	3	3.73	
1999-00	NWHL	Sainte-Julie	35	9-2-2	2	2.34	2000 NWHL-P
2000-01	NWHL	Sainte-Julie	20	15-4-0	4	2.11	
2001-02	NWHL	Cheyenne	18	7-8-2	1	2.74	
2002-03	NWHL	Avalanche du Québec	3	1-1-1	0	5.00	
Totals from all Competitions			**103**	**42-26-0**	**10**		

Served as interim coach with CWHL Montréal

LEBLANC, LISE *Goalie.*

Born 1979-08-08. Grew up in Petit Cap, NB, CAN.

Year - League - Team			GP	W-L	SO	GAA
1996	Nationals	Maritime Sport Blades	1			1.33
1998	Nationals	Maritime Sports Blades	3			?
2000	Nationals	Team New Brunswick				

LEDUC, CATHY *2000 Nationals Britannia Blues.*

LEFEBVRE, SARAH *Goalie. #1 #33.*

Born 1985-2-22, Kanata, ON, CAN. Grew up in Kanata, ON, CAN. 5'7".

Year - League - Team			GP	W-L	SO	GAA	Year - Playoff		GP	W-L	SO	GAA
2002-03	NWHL	Ottawa Raiders	7	4-1-0	0	3.91						
2003-04	NWHL	Ottawa Raiders	17	4-12-1	0	4.35						
2004-05	NWHL	Ottawa Raiders	7	3-2-1	1							
2005-06	NWHL	Ottawa Raiders	2	0-1-0	0	5.18	2006	NWHL-P	0	0-0-0	0	
Totals from all Competitions			**33**	**11-16-2**	**1**							

LEGAY, ELIZABETH *2007 Nationals Prince Edward Island (3 games); 2008 Nationals (3 games, 2 wins).*

LEONOFF, JAIMIE *2015-16 NWHL Connecticut (7W-3L, 2.81 GAA; I-Cup 1W-1L, 1 SO).*

LEVEILLE, AMANDA *Goalie. #28.*

Isobel Cup winner with Buffalo on 2017-03-19. Isobel Cup winner with Minnesota on 2019-03-17.
Born 1994-06-10. Grew up in Kingston, ON, CAN. 5'7". Debut at age 22 on 2016-10-07.

Year - League - Team			GP	W-L	SO	GAA	Year - Playoff		GP	W-L	SO	GAA
2016-17	NWHL/	Buffalo Beauts	9	4-2	0	4.34	2017	I-Cup	1	1-0	0	2.00
2017-18	NWHL/	Buffalo Beauts	16	12-4	1	2.53	2018	I-Cup	2	1-1	0	1.49
2018-19	NWHL/	Minnesota Whitecaps	16	11-4	2	2.09	2019	I-Cup	2	2-0	0	0.99
NWHL Regular Season			41	27-10	3	2.71	Isobel Cup		5	4-1	0	1.39
Totals from all Competitions			**46**	**31-11**	**3**	**2.55**						

NWHL Goaltender of the Year in 2017-18

LITCHFIELD, MADISON *Goalie. #30.*

Born 1995-01-23. Grew up in Williston, VT, USA. 5'4". Debut at age 23 on 2018-02-18.

Year - League - Team			GP	W-L	SO	GAA
2017-18	NWHL/	Boston Pride	1	0-0	0	3.62
2018-19	NWHL/	Boston Pride	0	0-0	0	?

LOCKERT, STEPHANIE   *Goalie. #31.*

Abby Hoffman Cup winner with Mississauga on 2008-03-15.
Born 1983-9-25, Hearst, ON, CAN. Grew up in Cambridge, ON, CAN. 5'8". Debut at age 23 on 2006-9-16.

Year - League - Team		GP	W-L	SO	GAA	Year - Playoff	GP	W-L	SO	GAA
2008	Nationals Mississauga Chiefs	0	0-0							
2008-09	CWHL Vaughan Flames	15	3-12	0	4.69	2009 CWHL-P	0	0-0	0	
2009-10	CWHL Vaughan Flames									

LOPUCK, TANNIS   *2000 Nationals U. Manitoba.*

LOVE, SARAH   *Goalie. #31.*

Abby Hoffman Cup winner with Mississauga on 2008-03-15.
Born 1983-9-25, Hearst, ON, CAN. Grew up in Cambridge, ON, CAN. 5'8". Debut at age 23 on 2006-9-16.

Year - League - Team		GP	W-L	SO	GAA	Year - Playoff	GP	W-L	SO	GAA
2006-07	NWHL Mississauga Aeros	17	13-4-0	2	2.05	2007 NWHL-P	4	1-3-0	0	
2007	Nationals Mississauga Aeros	3		2	1.00					
2008	Nationals Mississauga Chiefs	3	2-1	0	3.15					
2007-08	CWHL Mississauga Chiefs	16	12-4	1	1.87	2008 CWHL-P	3	2-0	0	2.75
2008-09	CWHL Mississauga Chiefs	4	4-0	2	1.00	2009 CWHL-P	0			
Totals from all Competitions		**50**	**34-12-0**	**7**						

LUNDBERG, SHENAE   *Goalie. #1.*

Born 1993-03-14, Peterborough, NH, USA. 5'6". Debut at age 22 on 2015-10-11.

Year - League - Team		GP	W-L	SO	GAA	Year - Playoff	GP	W-L	SO	GAA
2015-16	NWHL/ New York Riveters	1	0-0	0	8.29					
2015-16	NWHL/ Connecticut Whale	2	2-0	0	1.97					
2016-17	NWHL/ Connecticut Whale	9	2-6	0	4.30					
2018-19	NWHL/ Connecticut Whale	3	0-2	0	3.43	2019 I-Cup	0	0-0	0	-.--
Totals from all Competitions		**15**	**4-8**	**0**	**3.92**					

LURA, JENNY   *North Vancouver, BC. 2006-07 WWHL B.C. (1W-4L).*

LUSK, ALEISHA   *Mitchell, ON. 2001-02 NWHL North York #35 (0 gp); 2005-06 Brampton #31 (1 gp, 1 win).*

LUTZ, TAMMI   *2002 Nationals Nova Scotia; 2003 Nationals (3 gp); 2004 Nationals (4 gp).*

MACCULLOCH, MARIE-MICHELLE   *2009-10 CWHL Vaughan Flames #35 (0 games).*

MACDOUGALL, ALYSSA   *Regina, SK. 2005-06 WWHL Saskatchewan #31 (5 gp, 1W-1L).*

MACISAAC, JILLIAN   *Goalie. #40.*

Born 1988-7-9. Grew up in Timberlea, NS, CAN. 5'4". Debut at age 23 on 2011-10-29.

Year - League - Team		GP	W-L	SO	GAA
2006	Nationals Nova Scotia Selects	3	3-0	1	1.98
2007	Nationals Nova Scotia Selects	5		0	10.29
2008	Nationals Nova Scotia Selects	4	2-2	0	2.33
2011-12	CWHL Alberta	5	1-4	1	4.80
2012-13	CWHL Alberta	12	1-9	0	3.68
Totals from all Competitions		**29**	**7-15**	**2**	

MACINNIS, KRISTA   *2006 Nationals Nova Scotia Selects (3 games, 1 win).*

MACKENDRICK, LORNA   *1995-96 COWHL Hamilton Golden Hawks #30 (16 games).*

MACKENDRICK, LORNA   *Goalie.*

Born 1968-10-25. Grew up in Birch Hill, PE, CAN

Year - League - Team		GP	W-L	SO	GAA
1995	Nationals Maritime Sports Blades				
1998	Nationals Prince Edward Island	5		?	
1999	Nationals Prince Edward Island				
2000	Nationals Prince Edward Island				
2001	Nationals PEI Humpty Dumpty Crunch				

MACKENZIE, CHELSEA   *2000-01 NWHL Ottawa Raiders #1 (11 games, 2W-9L).*

MACKRELL, MANDY   *Goalie. #1.*

Clarkson Cup winner with Boston on 2013-03-23
Born 1989-3-8, Cleveland, OH, USA. Grew up in Cleveland, OH, USA. 5'3". Debut at age 23 on 2011-10-30.

Year - League - Team		GP	W-L	SO	GAA	Year - Playoff	GP	W-L	SO	GAA
2011-12	CWHL Boston Blades	4	4-0	1	1.47	2012 C-Cup	0	0-0	0	
2012-13	CWHL Boston Blades					2013 C-Cup	0	0-0	0	

MACLELLAN, BRANDY   *2001 Nationals P.E.I.; 2002 Nationals; 2006 Nationals (2 games, 2 wins).*

MACLEOD, HAYLEY   *2004 Nationals Nova Scotia (3 games).*

MAINIL, ANDREA   *1998 Nationals Saskatchewan (1 game).*

MAKELA, AMANDA   *Goalie. #34.*

Born 1993-12-20, Thunder Bay, ON, CAN. 5'9". Debut at age 21 on 2015-11-22.

Year - League - Team		GP	W-L	SO	GAA	Year - Playoff	GP	W-L	SO	GAA
2015-16	NWHL/ Buffalo Beauts	?	1-2	0	2.69	2016 I-Cup	0	0-0	0	-.--
2016-17	CWHL Canadiennes de Montréal	0	0-0	0	-.--					
2017-18	CWHL Toronto Furies	10	4-6	1	3.72					

CHOLETTE, JOSÉE   *1998-99 NWHL Bonaventure (1 gp); 1999-00 Montréal #1 (34 gp, 16 W, 7 SO, 2.17 GAA).*

Year - League - Team		GP	W-L	SO	GAA
2018-19	CWHL Toronto Furies	1	1-0	1	0.00

MALCOM, JANICE   *1995 Nationals PEI Esso Tigers; 1996 Nationals PEI Esso Tigers.*

MALLORY, ANGIE   *1999-00 NWHL Ottawa Raiders (4 games).*

MANDERSON, ALYSHA   *2008 Nationals Team New Brunswick (2 games).*

MANWEILER, KRYSTIN   *2000-01 NWHL Brampton #1; 2001-02 #31 (2 games, 1W-0L).*

MARAZ, MICHELLE   *2002 Nationals Richmond Steelers (3 games).*

MAREK, DEB   *1995 Nationals Calgary Classics.*

MARSHALL, AMBER   *2001-02 NWHL Brampton Thunder #29 (1 game).*

MASCHMEYER, EMERANCE   Goalie. #38.

Born 1994-05-10. Grew up in Bruderheim, AB, CAN. 5'6". Debut at age 22 on 2016-10-08.

Year - League - Team		GP	W-L	SO	GAA	Year - Playoff	GP	W-L	SO	GAA
2016-17	CWHL Calgary Inferno	8	5-3	2	1.49	2017 C-Cup	2	0-2	0	3.07
2017-18	CWHL Canadiennes de Montréal	23	18-5	6	1.78	2018 C-Cup	2	0-2	0	2.42
2018-19	CWHL Canadiennes de Montréal	20	15-5	4	1.45	2019 C-Cup	4	2-2	2	2.03
	CWHL Regular Season	51	38-13	12	1.61	Clarkson Cup	8	2-6	2	2.39
	Totals from all Competitions	**59**	**40-19**	**14**	**1.71**					

CWHL Second All-Star Team in 2016-17... CWHL All-Rookie Team in 2016-17

MAY, CHELSEA   *2007 Nationals BC Outback (2 games).*

MAY, PAM   *2005 Nationals Manitoba (3 games); 2007 Natoinals Manitoba (4 games).*

MAYR, ASHLEY   *2004-05 WWHL British Columbia Breakers #1; 2005 Nationals British Columbia (3 games).*

MCCURDY, DARCY   *1995 Nationals Winnipeg Sweat Camp Storm.*

MCDONALD, LIZANNE   *1996-97 COWHL Peterborough Pirates #35 (1 game).*

MCDONNELL, JOAN   Goalie. #31.

Year - League - Team		GP	W-L-T	SO	GAA
1995-96	COWHL North York Aeros	28			
1996	Nationals North York Aeros	1	1-0	1	0.00
1996-97	COWHL Mississauga Chiefs	34	13-2-3	7	1.26
1997-98	COWHL Mississauga Chiefs	1			

MCGEE, JOLENE   *1995-96 COWHL Peterborough (29 games); 1996-97 (11 games, 1W-2L).*

MCKENZIE, CHELSEY   *1999-00 NWHL Ottawa Raiders #51 (6 games, 0W-2L-1T).*

MCLAUGHLIN-BITTE, BRIANNE   Goalie. #31 #20 #29 #1 #24.

Isobel Cup winner with Buffalo on 2017-03-19
Born 1987-6-20. Grew up in Sheffield Village, OH, USA. Debut at age 28 on 2015-10-11.

Year - League - Team		GP	W-L	SO	GAA	Year - Playoff	GP	W-L	SO	GAA
2010-11	CWHL Burlington Barracudas	0	0-0	0						
2012-13	CWHL Brampton Thunder	0	0-0	0						
2015-16	NWHL/ Buffalo Beauts	?	4-6	0	3.34	2016 I-Cup	5	2-3	0	2.60
2016-17	NWHL/ Buffalo Beauts	12	2-9	0	3.47	2017 I-Cup	1	1-0	0	2.00
	Totals from all Competitions	**?**	**9-18**	**0**	**3.21**					

MCLEAN, MANDY   *1998-99 NWHL Brampton Thunder #39 (1 game).*

MCMURTEN, SYDNEY   *2007-08 CWHL Mississauga Chiefs #30.*

MCNEIL, BONNIE   *1995 Nationals Metro Valley Selects.*

MCNICHOL, CASSANDRA   *2009-10 CWHL Ottawa Senators #30 (12 games, 2W-10L, 3.81 GAA).*

MERRELL, SASHA   Goalie.

Born 1979-03-20. Grew up in Winnipeg, MB, CAN. 5'3".

Year - League - Team		GP	W-L	SO	GAA	Year - Playoff	GP	W-L	SO	GAA
2002	Nationals University of Manitoba				9.68					
2003	Nationals University of Winnipeg	3	0-1	0	13.00					
2004	Nationals Manitoba	4								
2008	Nationals Manitoba	5	3-2	0	2.81					

METHOT, ISABELLE   *1998-99 NWHL Jofa-Titan de Montréal (7W-7L-1T, 1 SO, 4.33 GAA).*

MILLER, JAMIE   Goalie. #36 #1 #37.

Born 1989-5-18. Grew up in Richmond Hill, ON, CAN. Goalie. 5'5".

Year - League - Team		GP	W-L	SO	GAA	Year - Playoff	GP	W-L	SO	GAA
2004-05	NWHL Toronto Aeros	1	1-0	0						
2006-07	NWHL Mississauga Aeros	0	0-0-0	0		2007 NWHL-P	0	0-0-0	0	
2013-14	CWHL Brampton Thunder	3	0-3	0	5.33					
2016-17	CWHL Brampton Thunder	0	0-0	0	-.--					
2017-18	CWHL Markham Thunder	0	0-0	0	-.--					

MILNE-PRICE, ELIJAH   Goalie. #95.

Born 1995-09-07. Grew up in Port Credit, ON, CAN. 5'7". Debut at age 23 on 2019-02-02.

Year - League - Team		GP	W-L	SO	GAA	Year - Playoff	GP	W-L	SO	GAA
2018-19	CWHL Markham Thunder	1	1-0	0	1.00	2019 C-Cup	0	0-0	0	-.--

MINTO, KIERRA *2004 Nationals Saskatchewan (3 games).*

MOFFAT, JESSICA *Goalie. #30.*
Born 1983-8-25, Ottawa, ON, CAN. Grew up in Moose Creek, ON, CAN. 5'10". Debut at age 24 on 2007-9-15.

Year - League - Team		GP	W-L	SO	GAA	Year - Playoff	GP	W-L	SO	GAA
2007-08	CWHL Ottawa Capital Canucks	13	4-8	0	4.10	2008 CWHL-P	0	0-0	0	
2008-09	CWHL Ottawa Senators	15	3-12	0	5.58	2009 CWHL-P		0-0	0	

MORELAND, LISA *Goalie. #33.*
Born 1977-1-13. Grew up in Cole Harbour, NS, CAN. 5'9".

Year - League - Team		GP	W-L	SO	GAA	Year - Playoff	GP	W-L	SO	GAA
2004-05	NWHL Brampton Thunder	25	19-4-2	5	1.98					
2005	Nationals Brampton Thunder	5	4-1	1	1.38					
2005-06	NWHL Brampton Thunder	15	8-5-2	0	2.96	2006 NWHL-P	0	0-0-0	0	
Totals from all Competitions		**40**	**27-9-4**	**5**						

MORGAN, NATHALIE *1999 Nationals Team New Brunswick.*

MORIN, CYNTHIA *2005-06 NWHL Axion de Montréal (2 games).*

MORIN, NANCY *2000-01 NWHL Mistral de Laval #55 (2W-10L-1T, 6.23 GAA).*

MORRIS, NICKY *Goalie. #35 #32.*

Year - League - Team		GP	W-L-T	SO	GAA
1998-99	NWHL Scarborough Sting	33	0-15-0	0	7.50
1999-00	NWHL Durham Lightning	38	2-21-2	0	8.26
2000-01	NWHL Durham Lightning	17	0-16-0	0	6.68
Totals from all Competitions		**88**	**2-52-2**	**0**	

MORRISSEAU-SINCLAIR, GAZHEEK *2001 Nationals Manitoba; 2002 Nationals Manitoba.*

MURDY, DARCY *1996 Nationals Winnipeg Sweat Camp.*

MUTH, AMANDA *1998 Nationals Tazmanian Devils (4 games).*

NEUMANN, KELSEY *Goalie. #31.*
Born 1991-05-07. Grew up in China Grove, NC, USA. 5'5". Debut at age 25 on 2015-03-10.

Year - League - Team		GP	W-L	SO	GAA
2016-17	NWHL/ Buffalo Beauts	0	0-0	0	0.00
2017-18	NWHL/ Buffalo Beauts	0	0-0	0	0.00
NWHL Foundation Award in 2016-17					

NEWELL, KENDALL *Goalie. #33.*

Year - League - Team		GP	W-L	SO	GAA	Year - Playoff	GP	W-L	SO	GAA
2008-09	WWHL Calgary Oval X-Treme	10	9-1-0	3	1.60	2009 C-Cup	0	0-0-0	0	
						2009 WWHL-P	1	1-0-0	1	0.00

NEWELL, KIMBERLY *Goalie. #33.*
Born 1995-10-04. Grew up in Burnaby, BC, CAN. 5'8". Debut at age 23 on 2018-10-17.

Year - League - Team		GP	W-L	SO	GAA
2018-19	CWHL Shenzhen KRS Vanke Rays	10	5-3	2	2.19

NICOL, MAUDE *Goalie. #31.*
Grew up in Sherbrooke, QC, CAN.

Year - League - Team		GP	W-L	SO	GAA
2018-19	CWHL Canadiennes de Montréal	0	0-0	0	-.--

NUTTALL, ROBIN *2003 Nationals (3 games, 1 win, 2 losses).*

OIS, ISABEL *1995-96 COWHL Mississauga Chiefs #53 (1 game).*

O'NEIL, ERIN *Goalie. #27.*
Born 1996-05-11, St. Paul, MN, USA.

Year - League - Team		GP	W-L	SO	GAA	Year - Playoff	GP	W-L	SO	GAA
2018-19	NWHL/ Connecticut Whale	2	0-2	0	5.40	2019 I-Cup	1	0-1	0	4.22

OTT, BRITTANY *Goalie. #29.*
Clarkson Cup winner with Boston on 2015-03-07 and Isobel Cup winner with Boston on 2016-03-12
Born 1990-06-12. Grew up in St. Clair Shores, MI, USA. 5'3". Debut at age 23 on 2013-11-03.

Year - League - Team		GP	W-L	SO	GAA	Year - Playoff	GP	W-L	SO	GAA
2013-14	CWHL Boston Blades	17	10-6	1	2.63	2014 C-Cup	3	2-1	1	1.00
2014-15	CWHL Boston Blades	10	6-3	3	2.00	2015 C-Cup	1	1-0	0	3.00
2015-16	NWHL/ Boston Pride	?	13-2	1	1.98	2016 I-Cup	4	4-0	1	1.98
2016-17	NWHL/ Boston Pride	12	10-1	3	1.93	2017 I-Cup	2	1-1	0	3.39
2017-18	NWHL/ Boston Pride	13	4-9	2	2.50	2018 I-Cup	1	0-1	0	2.93
2018-19	NWHL/ Boston Pride	3	1-0	0	0.65	2019 I-Cup	0	0-0	0	-.--
CWHL Regular Season		27	16-9	4	2.39	Clarkson Cup	4	3-1	1	1.50
NWHL Regular Season		?	28-12	6	2.08	Isobel Cup	7	5-2	1	2.45
Totals from all Competitions		**?**	**52-24**	**12**	**2.18**					

CWHL Second All-Star Team in 2013-14... NWHL Goaltender of the Year in 2015-16

PANICCIA, NICOLE
Goalie. #31.

Born 1992-12-09. Grew up in Oakville, ON, CAN. 5'6".

Year - League - Team		GP	W-L	SO	GAA
2018-19	CWHL Calgary Inferno	0	0-0	0	-.--

PARADIS, LAURA
2000 Nationals Saskatchewan; 2001 Nationals Saskatchewan.

PARKER, GILLIAN
1992-93 COWHL Scarborough Sting #31 (16 games).

PARSONS, DEIDRE
2006 Nationals Newfoundland Labrador (3 games, 2 losses).

PATENAUDE, SABRINA
2004-05 NWHL Montréal; 2005-06 (1 game).

PAYNE, SHELLEY
Goalie. #31 #30.

Clarkson Cup winner with Minnesota on 2010-03-28
Born 1987-3-17. Grew up in Pelham, NY, USA. Goalie.

Year - League - Team		GP	W-L	SO	GAA	Year - Playoff		GP	W-L	SO	GAA
2009-10	WWHL Minnesota Whitecaps	4	0-0-0	0	3.87						
2009-10	CWHL Mississauga Chiefs	5	4-1	0	2.76	2010	C-Cup	0	0-0	0	0.00
2016-17	CWHL Boston Blades	1	0-0	0	9.23						

PELLERIN, ANDRÉE
2004-05 NWHL Ottawa Raiders #1 (2 games, 1W-0L).

PERRY, CARRIE-LYNN
Goalie. #1.

Abby Hoffman Cup winner with Aeros on 1991-03-17 and 1993-03-28.

Year - League - Team		GP	W-L	SO	GAA
1992-93	COWHL Toronto Aeros	28			
1993-94	COWHL Toronto Aeros	24			

PETERS, PENNY
1999-00 NWHL Laval #94 (0W-0L-1T); 2000-01 #49 (2W-11L-0T).

PETKAU, ROBIN
Goalie. #1.

Born 1982-5-7, Pense, SK, CAN. 5'6".

Year - League - Team		GP	W-L	SO	GAA	Year - Playoff		GP	W-L	SO	GAA
2004-05	WWHL Saskatchewan Prairie Ice	20	1-18-0	0	4.69						
2005-06	WWHL Saskatchewan Prairie Ice	17	3-8-1	0	4.17	2006	WWHL-P	2	0-2-0	0	5.50
2006-07	WWHL Saskatchewan Prairie Ice	10	0-8-0	0	6.57						
Totals from all Competitions		**49**	**4-36-1**	**0**							

PICKFORD, SARA
1998-99 NWHL Brampton Thunder #38.

PIGDEN, RACHEL
2010-11 WWHL Manitoba Maple Leafs #1 (4 games, 0W-3L-0T).

PIITZ, JENNIFER
Goalie. #33.

Born 1980-12-21, Oshawa, ON, CAN. 5'6".

Year - League - Team		GP	W-L	SO	GAA	Year - Playoff		GP	W-L	SO	GAA
2001-02	NWHL Durham Lightning	16	1-9-4	0	4.09						
2002-03	NWHL Durham Lightning										
2003-04	NWHL Durham Lightning	20	5-11-0	0	7.16						
2004-05	NWHL Durham Lightning	17	2-10-4	0							
2005-06	NWHL Durham Lightning	0	0-0-0	0							
2006-07	NWHL Etobicoke Dolphins			0		2007	NWHL-P	0	0-0-0	0	
2007	Nationals Etobicoke Dolphins	3		2	2.57						
2007-08	CWHL Vaughan Flames	13	4-7-0	0	3.78	2008	CWHL-P	0	0-0-0	0	
Totals from all Competitions		**69**	**12-37-8**	**2**							

PINELLI, TANIA
Goalie. #38 #1.

Born 1979-5-11. Grew up in Hamilton, ON, CAN

Year - League - Team		GP	W-L	SO	GAA	Year - Playoff		GP	W-L	SO	GAA
1995-96	COWHL Mississauga Chiefs	15									
1996-97	COWHL Mississauga Chiefs	34	13-3-2	5	1.22						
1997-98	COWHL Mississauga Chiefs	19	5-4-0	1	3.73						
2002-03	NWHL Mississauga IceBears										
2003-04	NWHL Oakville Ice	21	6-14-1	1	2.85						
2004-05	NWHL Oakville Ice	27	9-14-4	1							
2005-06	NWHL Oakville Ice	30	16-12-1	4	2.63	2006	NWHL-P	1	0-1-0	0	5.00
2006-07	NWHL Oakville Ice	??	??-??-??	2		2007	NWHL-P	3	1-2-0	1	3.00
2007-08	CWHL Burlington Barracudas	21	9-12-0	0	2.78	2008	CWHL-P	3	1-1-1	0	3.00
2008-09	CWHL Burlington Barracudas	16	3-13-0	1	3.05	2009	CWHL-P	2	0-1-1	0	3.82
Totals from all Competitions		**192**	**63-77-10**	**17**							

NWHL Goalie of the Year in 2004-05

PONTE, ALI
2009-10 CWHL Mississauga Chiefs #31.

POST, LINDSEY
Goalie. #33.

Clarkson Cup winner with Calgary on 2019-03-24.
Born 1994-01-11. Grew up in Calgary, AB, CAN. Goalie. Debut at age 23 on 2017-10-28.

Year - League - Team		GP	W-L	SO	GAA	Year - Playoff		GP	W-L	SO	GAA
2017-18	CWHL Calgary Inferno	13	7-5	2	2.21	2018	C-Cup	0	0-0	0	-.--
2018-19	CWHL Calgary Inferno	1	0-1	0	3.14	2019	C-Cup	0	0-0	0	-.--

PREFONTAINE, COLETTE *Goalie.*
Abby Hoffman Cup winner with Edmonton on 1997-03-09. Born 1969-07-07.
1997   Nationals   Edmonton Chimos

PRICE, BECKY *1993-94 COWHL Toronto Jr. Aeros #30 (29 games).*

PRICE, JENNIFER *Goalie. #31.*
Born 1977-8-13. Grew up in Victoria, BC, CAN. 5'5".

Year - League - Team		GP	W-L	SO	GAA	Year - Playoff	GP	W-L	SO	GAA
1998	Nationals New Westminster Lightning	3			?					
1999	Nationals New Westminster Lightning									
2001	Nationals Vancouver Griffins									
2002-03	NWHL Vancouver Griffins	21	9-11-0	2	3.83					
2003	Nationals Vancouver Griffins	6	2-3	0	4.79					
2004	Nationals British Columbia	5								
2004-05	WWHL British Columbia Breakers	21	4-6-1	0	5.91					
2005	Nationals British Columbia	5	0-4	0	4.73					
2005-06	WWHL British Columbia Breakers	24	0-11-1	0	4.49					
2006	Nationals British Columbia Selects	3	0-3	0	5.36					
2006-07	WWHL British Columbia Breakers	24	6-11-0	2	4.47	2007 WWHL-P	2	0-2-0	0	8.67
2007	Nationals British Columbia	2		0	3.50					
2007-08	WWHL British Columbia Breakers		0-0-0							
Totals from all Competitions		**116**	**21-51-2**	**4**						

QUIGLEY, KAREN *2004 Nationals Newfoundland (5 games); 2005 Nationals Newfoundland (3 games).*

QUINN, MELANIE *Goalie. #29 #35.*
Born 1981-3-20, Toronto, ON, CAN. Grew up in Newmarket, ON, CAN. 5'8".

Year - League - Team		GP	W-L	SO	GAA	Year - Playoff	GP	W-L	SO	GAA
2000-01	NWHL Brampton Thunder	1	1-0-0	0	1.00					
2001-02	NWHL Brampton Thunder									
2002	Nationals Brampton Thunder									
2002-03	NWHL Brampton Thunder					2003 NWHL-P				
2003	Nationals Brampton Thunder	2	2-0	1	0.65					
2004-05	NWHL Toronto Aeros	1	1-0-0	0						
2007-08	CWHL Vaughan Flames	21	8-11-0	2	3.03	2008 CWHL-P	2	0-2-0	0	6.00

RACKLEFF, JETTA *Goalie. #30 #21.*
Born 1991-09-30. Grew up in Bend, OR, USA. 5'8". Debut at age 25 on 2016-11-12.

Year - League - Team		GP	W-L	SO	GAA
2016-17	CWHL Brampton Thunder	0	0-0	0	0.00
	CWHL Boston Blades	8	0-4	0	6.06
2017-18	CWHL Boston Blades	2	0-0	0	0.88
2018-19	CWHL Boston Blades	9	0-5	0	4.84
Totals from all Competitions		**19**	**0-9**	**0**	**4.90**

RÄISÄNEN, MEERI *Goalie. #18.*
Born 1989-12-02, Tampere, FIN.

Year - League - Team		GP	W-L	SO	GAA
2018-19	NWHL/ Connecticut Whale	11	2-10	1	3.03

RANKIN, JESS *2005-06 NWHL Durham Lightning (1 game).*

RÄTY, NOORA *Goalie. #41.*
Born 1989-05-29. Grew up in Espoo, FIN. 5'5". Debut at age 28 on 2017-10-21.

Year - League - Team		GP	W-L	SO	GAA	Year - Playoff	GP	W-L	SO	GAA
2017-18	CWHL Kunlun Red Star	20	16-3	6	1.60	2018 C-Cup	4	2-2	1	1.40
2018-19	CWHL Shenzhen KRS Vanke Rays	20	8-12	2	2.46					
Totals from all Competitions		**44**	**26-17**	**9**	**1.96**					

CWHL Top Goaltender in 2017-18... CWHL First All-Star Team in 2017-18, CWHL Second All-Star Team in 2018-19

REDDON, LESLEY *Goalie. #30.*
IIHF champion. Abby Hoffman Cup winner with Aeros on 1991-03-17 and 1993-03-28.
Born 1970-11-15. Grew up in Fredericton, NB, CAN.

Year - League - Team		GP	W-L-T	SO	GAA
1992-93	COWHL Toronto Aeros	25			
1995	Nationals Maritime Sports Blades				
1996	Nationals Maritime Sports Blades	5			3.00
1998	Nationals Maritime Sports Blades	3			?
1999	Nationals Calgary Oval X-Treme				
2000	Nationals Calgary Oval X-Treme			2	
2001	Nationals PEI Humpty Dumpty Crunch				
2002	Nationals PEI Humpty Dumpty Crunch				3.56
2002-03	NWHL Edmonton Chimos	10	1-8-0	0	5.14
2007-08	WWHL Strathmore Rockies				
2008-09	WWHL Strathmore Rockies	4	0-3-0	0	10.12
Totals from all Competitions		**47**	**1-11-0**	**2**	

REES, MELANNIE — *2007-08 WWHL Edmonton Chimos #1.*

REILLY, MICHELLE — *1999-00 NWHL Durham Lightning (11 games).*

RHÉAUME, MANON — Goalie. #35.

IIHF champion. Born 1972-02-24. Grew up in Charlesbourg, QC, CAN. 5'7".

Year - League - Team			GP	W-L	SO	GAA	Year - Playoff	GP	W-L	SO	GAA
2000-01	NWHL	Wingstar de Montréal	4								
2007-08	WWHL	Minnesota Whitecaps	1	1-0-							
2008-09	WWHL	Minnesota Whitecaps	2	2-0-0	0	3.00	2009 C-Cup	1	1-0-0	0	2.71
							2009 WWHL-P	0	0-0-0	0	

RICARD, KELSEY — *2005-06 NWHL Oakville Ice #39.*

RIGSBY, ALEX — Goalie. #1.

IIHF champion.
Clarkson Cup winner with Calgary on 2019-03-24.
Born 1992-01-03. Grew up in Delafield, WI, USA. 5'7". Debut at age 26 on 2018-10-13.

Year - League - Team			GP	W-L	SO	GAA	Year - Playoff	GP	W-L	SO	GAA
2018-19	CWHL	Calgary Inferno	17	14-2	1	2.04	2019 C-Cup	4	3-1	1	1.52

CWHL Top Goaltender in 2018-19... CWHL First All-Star Team in 2018-19.

RIOUX, MARGOT — *2005 Nationals Team New Brunswick (2 gp, 2W); 2006 Nationals (1 gp, 1 W).*

RISLEY-CLARKE, KARA — *1998 Nationals Nova Scotia Selects (2 gp).*

RITCHOT, AMANDA — *2000 Nationals U.Manitoba.*

RITTMASTER, ROBYN — Goalie. #35.

Abby Hoffman Cup winner with Calgary on 1998-03-22 and 2001-03-11. Abby Hoffman Cup winner with Brampton on 2006-03-12.
Born 1979-7-27, Portland, ME, USA. Grew up in Halifax, NS, CAN. 5'5".

Year - League - Team			GP	W-L	SO	GAA	Year - Playoff	GP	W-L	SO	GAA
2004-05	NWHL	Ottawa Raiders	25	8-15-1	1						
2005-06	NWHL	Ottawa Raiders	27	17-6-4	6	1.79	2006 NWHL-P	2	0-2-0		1.00
1998	Nationals	Calgary Oval X-Treme	3			?					
1999	Nationals	Calgary Oval X-Treme									
2001	Nationals	Calgary Oval X-Treme									
2002	Nationals	Calgary Oval X-Treme				5.00					
2005	Nationals	Nova Scotia Selects	3	2-1	0	3.33					
2006	Nationals	Brampton Thunder	2	2-0	1	1.00					
2006-07	NWHL	Ottawa Raiders	23	5-17-0	1	3.24	2007 NWHL-P	2	0-2-0	0	4.03
2007-08	CWHL	Ottawa Capital Canucks	16	4-11-0	1	2.98	2008 CWHL-P	1	0-1-0	0	2.03
2008-09	CWHL	Ottawa Senators	17	1-13-0	0	5.32	2009 CWHL-P		0-1-0	0	
2009-10	CWHL	Ottawa Senators	18	3-15-0	0	4.10					
Totals from all Competitions			**131**	**38-83-5**	**9**						

Served as CWHL emergency referee on 2008-02-17

ROBERTSON, LISA — Goalie. #39 #36 #1 #94.

Born 1982-3-3.

Year - League - Team			GP
1998-99	NWHL	North York Aeros	2
1999-00	NWHL	North York Aeros	3
2004-05	NWHL	Oakville Ice	0
2008-09	CWHL	Vaughan Flames	0

RODRIGUEZ, ERIKA — *1995-96 COWHL Peterborough Skyway #1 (6 games).*

ROELOFSEN, STACEY — *2008-09 CWHL Burlington Barracudas #31.*

ROSS, LEANNA — *1996 Nationals Britannia Blues (2 games).*

ROSS, OLIVIA — *2015-16 CWHL Toronto Furies #33 (2 games, 0W-2L).*

ROSS, TONI — Goalie. #1 #31.

Born 1993-02-22. Grew up in Verwood, SK, CAN. Debut at age 24 on 2017-10-22.

Year - League - Team			GP	W-L	SO	GAA
2016-17	CWHL	Calgary Inferno	0	0-0	0	0.00
2017-18	CWHL	Calgary Inferno	6	3-2	0	1.91

ROSSMAN, SYDNEY — Goalie. #34.

Born 1995-05-17. Grew up in Excelsior, MN, USA. 5'5". Debut at age 22 on 2017-10-28.

Year - League - Team			GP	W-L	SO	GAA	Year - Playoff	GP	W-L	SO	GAA
2017-18	NWHL/	Connecticut Whale	16	3-13	0	3.14	2018 I-Cup	1	0-1	0	4.47
2018-19	NWHL/	Minnesota Whitecaps	0	0-0	0	-.--					

ROY, AMÉLIE — *Varennes, QC. 2011-12 CWHL Montréal.*

ROY, MARIE-CLAUDE — Goalie. #31.

IIHF champion. Born 1970-04-03, Montréal, QC, CAN. 5'3".

Year - League - Team			GP	W-L-T	SO	GAA
1995	Nationals	Équipe Québec				
1996	Nationals	Équipe Québec	3			1.60
1998	Nationals	Équipe Québec	4			?

Year - League - Team		GP	W-L	SO	GAA	Year - Playoff	GP	W-L	SO	GAA
1998-99	NWHL Axion de Montréal	32	5-10-4	2	3.94					
1999-00	NWHL Sainte-Julie	35	11-6-4	5	2.44	2000 NWHL-P				
2000-01	NWHL Sainte-Julie	20	7-11-2	2	3.07					
Totals from all Competitions		**94**	**23-17-10**	**9**						

Served as head coach with CWHL Montréal

RUDDOCK, JESSICA
1998-99 NWHL North York Aeros #1 (8 games).

RUDY, NIKKI
Goalie.

Born 1986-10-09, Port Hardy, BC, CAN. 5'4".

Year - League - Team		GP	W-L	SO	GAA
2002-03	NWHL Vancouver Griffins	7	1-3	1	3.53
2003	Nationals Vancouver Griffins	2	1-1	0	4.55
2004	Nationals British Columbia	3			

RUNNEY, ANGELA
1995-96 COWHL Hamilton Golden Hawks #33 (8 games).

SAGER, BECKY
Fort McMurray, AB. 2002-03 NWHL Edmonton Chimos (7 games, 1W-3L).

SANDAHL, SANYA
Goalie. #30 #20.

Born 1980-10-9, Duluth, MN, USA. 5'9".

Year - League - Team		GP	W-L	SO	GAA	Year - Playoff	GP	W-L	SO	GAA
2005-06	WWHL Minnesota Whitecaps	17	1-1-3	0	3.59	2006 WWHL-P	3	0-0-0	0	
2006-07	WWHL Minnesota Whitecaps	15	5-4-0	2	2.65	2007 WWHL-P	1	1-0-0	0	1.00
2007-08	WWHL Minnesota Whitecaps									
2008	Nationals Minnesota Whitecaps	1	1-0	0	4.00					
2008-09	WWHL Minnesota Whitecaps	9	5-1-0	0	1.98	2009 WWHL-P	1	1-0-0	1	13.00
						2009 C-Cup	2	1-1-0	0	2.02
2009-10	WWHL Minnesota Whitecaps	0	0-0-0	0	-.--					
2010-11	WWHL Minnesota Whitecaps	8	7-0-0	0	2.61	2011 C-Cup	1	0-1-0	0	6.00
Totals from all Competitions		**58**	**22-8-3**	**3**						

SASS, KIMBERLY
Goalie. #1.

Isobel Cup winner with Metropolitan on 2018-03-25
Born 1990-11-05, Buffalo, NY, USA. 5'5". Debut in 2015-16.

Year - League - Team		GP	W-L	SO	GAA	Year - Playoff	GP	W-L	SO	GAA
2015-16	NWHL/ Buffalo Beauts	2	1-1	0	4.64	2016 I-Cup	0	0-0	0	-.--
2017-18	NWHL/ Metropolitan Riveters	1	1-0	0	1.86	2018 I-Cup	0	0-0	0	-.--
2018-19	NWHL/ Metropolitan Riveters	4	1-2	0	4.17	2019 I-Cup	0	0-0	0	-.--

NWHL Foundation Award in 2018-19

SCHAUS, MOLLY
Goalie. #30 #31.

IIHF champion. Clarkson Cup winner with Boston on 2013-03-23
Born 1988-7-29. Grew up in Natick, MA, USA. 5'9". Debut at age 23 on 2011-10-22.

Year - League - Team		GP	W-L	SO	GAA	Year - Playoff	GP	W-L	SO	GAA
2011-12	CWHL Boston Blades	23	16-7	0	2.38	2012 C-Cup	3	1-2	0	3.32
2012-13	CWHL Boston Blades	11	6-4	2	1.99	2013 C-Cup	2	1-1	0	1.46
Totals from all Competitions		**39**	**24-14**	**2**						

CWHL Goaltender of the Year in 2011-12... CWHL First All-Star Team in 2011-12... CWHL All-Rookie Team in 2011-12

SCHELLING, FLORENCE
Goalie. #29.

Born 1989-3-9. Goalie. Debut at age 24 on 2012-10-21.

Year - League - Team		GP	W-L	SO	GAA	Year - Playoff	GP	W-L	SO	GAA
2012-13	CWHL Brampton Thunder	14	6-7	3	2.53	2013 C-Cup	2	0-2	0	3.03

SCHETTLER, CARISSA
Goalie. #1.

Born 1987-04-06. Grew up in St. Adolphe, MB, CAN. 5'5".

Year - League - Team		GP	W-L	SO	GAA	Year - Playoff	GP	W-L	SO	GAA
2006	Nationals Manitoba Selects	3	2-0	0	2.22					
2007	Nationals Manitoba	2		1	2.25					
2008	Nationals Manitoba	1	0-0	0	5.34					
2010-11	WWHL Manitoba Maple Leafs									

SCHIFF, ROSINA
2006-07 NWHL Oakville Ice #31; 2007-08 CWHL Burlington #31 (2W-7L).

SCODELLARO, JANINE
1999 Nationals New Westminster Lightning.

SCOTT, ALISON
2007-08 CWHL Brampton Thunder #29.

SCOTT, STACEY
2002-03 NWHL Ottawa Senators (13 games, 1W-10L).

SCRIVENS, JENNIFER
2015-16 NWHL New York (0W-3L).

SÉGUIN, CASSIE
2007-08 CWHL Ottawa Capital Canucks #31.

SHERBANUK, TASHA
2005 Nationals Alberta (4 games, 0W-3L).

SHIN SOJUNG
2016-17 NWHL New York Riveters #31 (1W-3L, 1 SO, 3.20 GAA).

SHIPE, O'HARA
2008-09 CWHL Mississauga Chiefs #30 (2W-2L, 3.00 GAA).

SILVA, ERIKA
Goalie. #30.

Born 1978-10-4.

Year - League - Team			GP	W-L	SO	GAA	Year - Playoff	GP	W-L	SO	GAA
2002-03	NWHL	Brampton Thunder					2003 NWHL-P				
2003	Nationals	Brampton Thunder	4	1-1	1	2.27					
2003-04	NWHL	Brampton Thunder									

SIMONOT, JACKIE
2004 Nationals Saskatchewan (5 games).

SKELHOM, PAULA
1995 Nationals Metro Valley Selects.

SKOUFRANIS, DANIELLE
2007-08 CWHL Burlington Barracudas #44.

SLADE, STEPHANIE
Goalie. #31 #30 #35 #29.

Year - League - Team			GP	W-L-T	SO	GAA
1992-93	COWHL	Guelph Eagles	15			
1993-94	COWHL	Mississauga Chiefs	27			
1995	Nationals	Mississauga Chiefs				
1995-96	COWHL	Mississauga Chiefs	27			
1996-97	COWHL	Scarborough Sting	34	6-15-4	2	4.19
1997-98	COWHL	Scarborough Sting	21	0-13-0	0	4.88
1998-99	NWHL	Brampton Thunder	37	13-3-1	7	2.22
1999-00	NWHL	Mississauga Chiefs	37	9-7-3	4	2.52
Totals from all Competitions			**198**	**28-38-8**	**13**	

SLEBODNICK, LAUREN
Goalie. #30 #24.

Isobel Cup winner with Boston on 2016-03-12

Born 1992-01-23. Grew up in Manchester, NH, USA. 5'8". Debut in 2015-16.

Year - League - Team			GP	W-L	SO	GAA	Year - Playoff	GP	W-L	SO	GAA
2015-16	NWHL/	Boston Pride	?	1-2	0	3.30	2016 I-Cup	0	0-0	0	-.--
2016-17	NWHL/	Boston Pride	6	6-0	0	1.22	2017 I-Cup	1	0-0	0	0.00

SMALL, SAMI JO
Goalie. #1.

Olympic champion, IIHF champion.

Abby Hoffman Cup winner with Aeros on 2004-03-14 and 2005-03-13. Abby Hoffman Cup winner with Mississauga on 2008-03-15. Clarkson Cup winner with Toronto on 2014-03-22

Born 1976-3-25, Winnipeg, MB, CAN. Grew up in Mississauga, ON, CAN. 5'8". Debut at age 23 in 1999.

Year - League - Team			GP	W-L	SO	GAA	Year - Playoff	GP	W-L	SO	GAA
1999-00	NWHL	Brampton Thunder	34	15-2-3	4	1.76					
2000-01	NWHL	Brampton Thunder	22	17-3-2	5	1.67					
2002-03	NWHL	North York Aeros	17	14-1-0	4	0.93	2003 NWHL-P				
2003-04	NWHL	Toronto Aeros	24	19-1-0	7	0.95	2004 NWHL-P				
2004	Nationals	Toronto Aeros	5								
2004-05	NWHL	Toronto Aeros	20	12-4-3	5	1.84	2005 NWHL-P				
2005	Nationals	Toronto Aeros	4	3-1	1	1.75					
2006-07	NWHL	Mississauga Aeros	18	14-4-0	4	2.17	2007 NWHL-P	1	1-0-0	0	1.00
2007	Nationals	Mississauga Aeros	3		0	1.77					
2007-08	CWHL	Mississauga Chiefs	15	9-5	2	1.93	2008 CWHL-P	2	1-1	0	2.32
2008	Nationals	Mississauga Chiefs	0								
2008-09	CWHL	Mississauga Chiefs	22	13-9	4	2.25	2009 CWHL-P	4	3-1	0	1.97
2009-10	CWHL	Mississauga Chiefs	23	16-7	5	1.77	2010 C-Cup	1	0-1	0	3.00
2010-11	CWHL	Toronto Furies	16	5-11	2	3.13	2011 CWHL-P	2	2-0	0	1.50
							2011 C-Cup	4	2-1	1	2.40
2011-12	CWHL	Toronto Furies	16	5-11	1	4.11	2012 C-Cup	2	0-2	0	6.06
2012-13	CWHL	Toronto Furies	8	3-2	1	2.49	2013 C-Cup	1	1-0	0	2.57
2013-14	CWHL	Toronto Furies	9	7-2	0	2.08	2014 C-Cup	0	0-0	0	-.--
2014-15	CWHL	Toronto Furies	7	2-3	0	3.70	2015 C-Cup	1	0-0	0	3.00
2016-17	CWHL	Toronto Furies	1	1-0	0	3.00					
2017-18	CWHL	Toronto Furies	4	2-0	1	2.55					
CWHL Regular Season			121	63-49	16	2.57	Clarkson Cup	9	3-4	1	3.40
Totals from all Competitions			**286**	**167-72-8**	**47**						

CWHL Second All-Star Team in 2008-09 and 2009-10... has served as general manager with CWHL Toronto.

SMART, LARA
Goalie. #31.

Born 1983-5-11, Airdrie, AB, CAN. 5'10".

Year - League - Team			GP	W-L	SO	GAA	Year - Playoff	GP	W-L	SO	GAA
2004-05	WWHL	Edmonton Chimos	10	3-2-0	2	2.45	2005 WWHL-P	0	0-0-0	0	
2005-06	WWHL	Edmonton Chimos	15	5-1-1	2	1.48	2006 WWHL-P	1	0-1-0	0	3.00
2006-07	WWHL	Edmonton Chimos	20	5-4-1	2	2.80	2007 WWHL-P	2	0-2-0	0	6.75
2008-09	WWHL	Edmonton Chimos	12	7-5-0	0	3.35	2009 WWHL-P	0	0-0-0	0	
Totals from all Competitions			**60**	**20-15-2**	**6**						

SOROKINA, MARIA
Goalie. #69.

Born 1995-08-19, Tver, RUS.

Year - League - Team			GP	W-L	SO	GAA	Year - Playoff	GP	W-L	SO	GAA
2018-19	NWHL	Connecticut Whale	0	0-0	0	-.--					
2018-19	NWHL	Metropolitan Riveters	3	1-1	0	5.68					

SQUIRE, AMANDA — *2009-10 WWHL Edmonton #31 (1W-4L); 2010-11 Strathmore #31 (0W-2L).*

ST-PIERRE, GENEVIÈVE — *Rouyn-Noranda, QC. 2005-06 NWHL Québec #81; 2006-07 Québec #33.*

ST-PIERRE, KIM — *Goalie. #33.*

Olympic champion, IIHF champion. Clarkson Cup winner with Montréal on 2009-03-21 and 2011-03-27 Born 1978-12-14, Châteauguay, QC, CAN. 5'9".

Year - League - Team	GP	W-L	SO	GAA	Year - Playoff	GP	W-L	SO	GAA
1999 Nationals Équipe Québec									
2000 Nationals Équipe Québec			3						
2001 Nationals Équipe Québec									
2002 Nationals Équipe Québec	4								
2004-05 NWHL Avalanche du Québec	17	3-13-1	1						
2005-06 NWHL Avalanche du Québec	0	0-0-0	0						
2006-07 NWHL Axion de Montréal			2		2007 NWHL-P				
2007-08 CWHL Stars de Montréal	10	9-1	1	1.51	2008 CWHL-P	2	1-1	0	2.32
2008-09 CWHL Stars de Montréal	20	16-4	5	1.80	2009 CWHL-P	2	1-1	0	1.89
					2009 C-Cup	3	2-1	0	1.93
2010-11 CWHL Stars de Montréal	15	13-2	3	2.13	2011 CWHL-P	1	1-0	0	3.00
					2011 C-Cup	4	4-0	1	1.75
2012-13 CWHL Stars de Montréal	2	1-1	0	3.50					
CWHL Regular Season	47	39-8	9	1.94	Clarkson Cup	7	6-1	1	1.69

CWHL Top Goaltender in 2007-08, 2008-09, 2010-11... CWHL Eastern All-Star Team in 2007-08; CWHL First All-Star Team in 2008-09 and 2010-11... selected First Decade CWHL Team in 2017... Women's National Championships Most Valuable Player in 2002.

STAGG, BONNIE — *2000 Nationals Team New Brunswick; 2001 Nationals Team New Brunswick.*

STAM, JENNELLE — *2007-08 WWHL Strathmore Rockies #31.*

STEIN, EMILY — *2002 Nationals Nova Scotia.*

STEWART, AMANDA — *2007-08 CWHL Brampton Thnuder #35.*

STOCK, NICOLE — *Goalie. #1 #24.*

Grew up in Buffalo Grove, IL, USA. 5'8". Debut on 2015-02-22.

Year - League - Team	GP	W-L	SO	GAA	Year - Playoff	GP	W-L	SO	GAA
2014-15 CWHL Boston Blades	1	1-0	1	0.00					
2015-16 NWHL/ Connecticut Whale	?	4-2	0	2.51	2016 I-Cup	1	0-0	0	3.04
2016-17 NWHL Connecticut Whale	10	3-7	0	4.07	2017 I-Cup	1	0-1	0	8.00
Totals from all Competitions	**?**	**8-10**	**1**	**3.52**					

STURGE, ALISON — *2001 Nationals Newfoundland Labrador; 2003 Nationals Newfoundland Labrador (3 gp).*

STURGE, KRISTY — *2000 Nationals Newfoundland Labrador.*

SUGIYAMA, KRISTEN — *2010-11 WWHL Edmonton Chimos #31 (6W-3L, 1 SO, 2.07 GAA).*

SULLIVAN, LAUREN — *Toronto, ON. 2013-14 CWHL Toronto Furies #61.*

SVENSON, BARB — *1998 Nationals Tazmanian Devils (1 gp); 1999 Nationals Tazmanian Devils.*

SZABADOS, SHANNON — *Goalie. #40*

Born 1986-08-06, Edmonton, AB, CAN. 5'8". Debut at age 32 on 2018-10-13.

Year - League - Team	GP	W-L	SO	GAA	Year - Playoff	GP	W-L	SO	GAA
2018-19 NWHL/ Buffalo Beauts	9	6-4	2	1.49	2019 I-Cup	1	1-0	1	0.00

NWHL Goaltender of the Year in 2018-19

TAKEDA, MEGAN — *Toronto, ON. 2007-08 CWHL Mississauga Chiefs #30 (1 playoff game).*

TALBOT, HILARY — *2005-06 WWHL British Columbia Breakers #30 (0W-2L).*

TAPP, AMANDA — *Goalie. #1.*

Abby Hoffman Cup winner with Calgary on 2003-03-16 and 2007-03-10. WWHL winner. Born 1981-5-19. Grew up in Calgary, AB, CAN. 5'9".

Year - League - Team	GP	W-L	SO	GAA	Year - Playoff	GP	W-L	SO	GAA
2002 Nationals Calgary Oval X-Treme				2.34					
2002-03 NWHL Calgary Oval X-Treme	14	13-1-0	4	1.61	2003 NWHL-P				
2003 Nationals Calgary Oval X-Treme	2	2-0	0	2.00					
2003-04 NWHL Calgary Oval X-Treme	6	6-0-0	2	0.67	2004 NWHL-P				
2004 Nationals Calgary Oval X-Treme	4								
2004-05 WWHL Calgary Oval X-Treme	21	7-0-1	2	0.71	2005 WWHL-P	3	0-0-1	0	0.00
2005-06 WWHL Calgary Oval X-Treme	24	10-0-1	4	2.63	2006 WWHL-P	3	3-0-0	0	1.67
2006 Nationals Calgary Oval X-Treme	7	3-3	2	2.84					
2006-07 WWHL Calgary Oval X-Treme	17	10-0-0	7	0.43	2007 WWHL-P	3	3-0-0	1	1.00
2007 Nationals Calgary Oval X-Treme	3		1	0.65					
2007-08 WWHL Calgary Oval X-Treme									
2008 Nationals Calgary Oval X-Treme	3	2-1	0	2.01					
2008-09 WWHL Calgary Oval X-Treme	10	8-2-0	1	1.79	2009 WWHL-P	1	0-1-0	0	2.00
					2009 C-Cup	2	0-2-0	0	3.04
2009-10 WWHL Strathmore Rockies	10	3-7-0	0	3.28					
Totals from all Competitions	**133**	**70-17-3**	**24**						

TARLETON, HOLLY — *2002 Nationals Saskatchewan.*

TAYLOR, LAURA — *2003 Nationals Host Saskatchewan (2 gp, 2L).*

TESSIER, JAMIE — *2011-12 CWHL Toronto Furies #30 (2W-1L, 1 SO, 3.89 GAA; C-Cup 1 gp).*

THERIAULT, TINA-ANNE — *1998-99 NWHL Brampton (1 game); 1999-00 (3 games); 2000-01 (1 game).*

THOMPSON, TRACEY — *1995-96 COWHL North York Aeros #29 (1 game).*

TILEY, SHEA   *Goalie. #35.*

Born 1996-12-02. Grew up in Owen Sound, ON, CAN. 5'11". Debut at age 21 on 2018-10-14.

Year - League - Team	GP	W-L	SO	GAA	Year - Playoff	GP	W-L	SO	GAA
2018-19 CWHL Toronto Furies	26	7-7	0	2.55	2019 C-Cup	2	1-1	0	1.51

TORRINGTON, JOYCE — *2001-02 NWHL Ottawa Raiders (8 games, 2W-5L-1T, 2.76 GAA).*

TOWNSEND, KALIE — *2006-07 WWHL Edmonton Chimos #30 (3 games, 1 playoff game).*

TRAN, GLORIA — *2008-09 CWHL Brampton Thunder #29.*

TRAUTMAN, CAMILLE — *2014-15 CWHL Calgary #1 (4W-2L, 2.51 GAA; C-Cup 1 game).*

TREMBLAY, GENEVIÈVE — *1998-99 NWHL Bonaventure Wingstar #1 (2W-5L-3T, 1 SO, 3.18 GAA).*

TROST, KIRSTEN — *2004-05 NWHL Durham Lightning #33 (1 game).*

TUCKER, CHRISTINE — *1995-96 COWHL London (28 games); 1996-97 (3W-6L-2T).*

TURGEON, MIREILL — *1999-00 NWHL Mistral de Laval (21 games).*

TURNER, TERI — *1998 Nationals Edmonton Chimos (3 games).*

VAN BEUSEKOM-SWEERIN, MEGAN   *Goalie. #39.*

IIHF champion. Clarkson Cup winner with Minnesota on 2010-03-28

Born 1981-12-14, Loretto, MN, USA. 5'8".

Year - League - Team	GP	W-L	SO	GAA	Year - Playoff	GP	W-L	SO	GAA
2004-05 WWHL Minnesota Whitecaps	7	2-1-0	1	2.00	2005 WWHL-P	2	0-0-0	0	10.00
2005-06 WWHL Minnesota Whitecaps	15	3-3-0	2	1.91	2006 WWHL-P	3	2-1-0	0	2.00
2006-07 WWHL Minnesota Whitecaps	13	2-3-1	1	2.14	2007 WWHL-P	3	1-0-0	0	1.00
2007-08 WWHL Minnesota Whitecaps									
2008 Nationals Minnesota Whitecaps	1	0-1	0	5.00					
2008-09 WWHL Minnesota Whitecaps	6	3-2-0	0	2.61	2009 WWHL-P	1	1-0-0	1	0.00
2009-10 WWHL Minnesota Whitecaps	12	10-2-0	2	1.80	2010 C-Cup	2	2-0-0	1	0.50
2010-11 WWHL Minnesota Whitecaps	7	5-1-0	2	2.13	2011 C-Cup	2	0-2-0	0	6.00
Totals from all Competitions	**74**	**31-16-1**	**10**						

VAN BRENK, DEB — *1995-96 COWHL London (1 game); 1996-97 (2W-18L).*

VAN DER BLIEK, SONJA   *Goalie. #30 #1.*

Grew up in Toronto, ON, CAN. 5'7". Debut at age 22 on 2012-2-22.

Year - League - Team	GP	W-L	SO	GAA	Year - Playoff	GP	W-L	SO	GAA
2006-07 NWHL Oakville Ice	0	0-0	0	-.--					
2011-12 CWHL Brampton Thunder	3	3-0	0	2.67	2012 C-Cup	0	0-0	0	-.--
2013-14 CWHL Brampton Thunder	18	4-13	0	3.62					
2014-15 CWHL Brampton Thunder	4	0-3	0	3.38					
2015-16 CWHL Toronto Furies	5	2-2	1	2.91	2016 C-Cup	2	0-0	0	2.60
2016-17 CWHL Toronto Furies	7	2-4	0	2.20	2017 C-Cup	0	0-0	0	-.--
2017-18 CWHL Toronto Furies	16	3-13	0	3.48					
CWHL Regular Season	53	14-35	1	3.25	Clarkson Cup	2	0-0	0	2.60
Totals from all Competitions	**55**	**14-35**	**1**	**3.24**					

VAN ROOYEN, ANITA   *Goalie. #39 #29.*

Year - League - Team	GP	W-L-T	SO	GAA
1993-94 COWHL Hamilton Golden Hawks	26			
1996-97 COWHL Scarborough Sting	34	5-4-1	1	4.83
1997-98 COWHL Scarborough Sting	19	0-7-0	0	7.71
Totals from all Competitions	**79**	**5-11-1**	**1**	

VANDERVEER, ERIKA   *Goalie. #37 #31.*

Born 1984-2-12, Bradford, ON, CAN. Grew up in Bradford, ON, CAN. 5'9". Debut at age 24 on 2008-10-25.

Year - League - Team	GP	W-L	SO	GAA	Year - Playoff	GP	W-L	SO	GAA
2008-09 CWHL Burlington Barracudas	14	8-6	1	3.33	2009 CWHL-P	2	1-0-1	0	1.94
2009-10 CWHL Burlington Barracudas	17	10-7	0	2.91					
2010-11 CWHL Boston Blades	5	2-3	0	3.90					
2010-11 CWHL Brampton Thunder	4	3-1	0	2.47	2011 CWHL-P	0	0-0	0	-.--
2011-12 CWHL Toronto Furies	9	2-6	1	2.97	2012 C-Cup	1	0-1	0	4.00
2012-13 CWHL Toronto Furies	2	2-0	0	2.00	2013 C-Cup	0	0-0	0	-.--
2013-14 CWHL Brampton Thunder	5	1-3	0	5.07					
CWHL Regular Season	56	28-26	2	3.25	Clarkson Cup	1	0-1	0	4.00
Totals from all Competitions	**59**	**29-27-1**	**2**	**3.24**					

VINEBERG, FLORA — *2000-01 NWHL North York Aeros (2 games, 1 win).*

VINGE, DANA — *2010-11 WWHL Edmonton Chimos #30 (2 games, 1 win).*

VOGT, SHARI

Goalie. #20 #30.

Born 1981-10-23, Richmond, MN, USA. 5'10".

Year - League - Team		GP	W-L	SO	GAA	Year - Playoff	GP	W-L	SO	GAA
2004-05	WWHL Minnesota Whitecaps	8	1-1-1	1	1.30	2005 WWHL-P	2	0-1-0	0	3.00
2006-07	WWHL Minnesota Whitecaps	19	6-4-0	1	2.96	2007 WWHL-P	2	0-1-0	0	7.00
2007-08	WWHL Minnesota Whitecaps									
2008	Nationals Minnesota Whitecaps	1	0-1	0	5.00					

WAGNER, LAURIE

2006 Nationals Manitoba Selects.

WALTIER, SAM

Goalie. #70.

Born 1995-07-16, Gambrills, MD, USA.

Year - League - Team		GP	W-L	SO	GAA
2018-19	NWHL Connecticut Whale	2	0-0	0	10.48

WANG YUQING

Goalie. #30.

Born 1994-05-06. Grew up in Harbin, CHN. Goalie. Debut at age 23 on 2017-11-11.

Year - League - Team		GP	W-L	SO	GAA	Year - Playoff	GP	W-L	SO	GAA
2017-18	CWHL Kunlun Red Star	10	4-3	1	1.98	2018 C-Cup	0	0-0	0	0.00
2018-19	CWHL Shenzhen KRS Vanke Rays	1	0-0	0	0.00					

WATERSTREET, KENZIE

2007 Nationals BC Outback (2 games).

WESTON, JOAN

1992-93 COWHL Scarborough Sting (23 games); 1993-94 (26 games).

WHALEN, JACQUELYN

2003 Nationals Newfoundland Labrador (3 games).

WHELAN, TRUDY

2000 Nationals Newfoundland Labrador.

WICKS, SANDY

1998-99 NWHL Mississauga Chiefs #33 (3 games).

WIDSTEN, JANINE

2002-03 NWHL Edmonton Chimos (9 games, 1W-8L).

WILLIAMS, SHAUNTELLE

2008-09 WWHL Strathmore (9 games, 1W-7L).

WILMANN, JAYNE

2002 Nationals Richmond Steelers (2 gp).

WOLFE, KRISTIN

2007 Nationals Nova Scotia (3 gp); 2008 Nationals Nova Scotia (1 gp).

WURM, BLYTHE

Goalie. #30.

Abby Hoffman Cup winner with Calgary on 2003-03-16.
Born 1984-04-12. Grew up in Swan Hills, AB, CAN.

Year - League - Team		GP	W-L	SO	GAA	Year - Playoff	GP	W-L	SO	GAA
2002-03	NWHL Calgary Oval X-Treme	2	2-0	0	2.00	2003 NWHL-P				
2003	Nationals Calgary Oval X-Treme	0	0-0	0	-.--					

YATES (NÉE MORIN), MARIE-FRANCE

Goalie. #1 #31.

Born 1976-3-22, Gloucester, ON, CAN.

Year - League - Team		GP	W-L-T	SO	GAA
1998-99	NWHL Ottawa Raiders	34	6-12-4	3	4.10
1999-00	NWHL Ottawa Raiders	25	4-13-4	1	3.54
2000-01	NWHL Ottawa Raiders	26	9-13-3	3	2.62
2001-02	NWHL Ottawa Raiders	22	12-5-5	4	2.18
2002	Nationals Brampton Thunder				2.37
2002-03	NWHL Ottawa Raiders	19	8-9-1	3	2.28
2003-04	NWHL Ottawa Raiders	17	4-10-3	1	3.53
Totals from all Competitions		**143**	**43-62-20**	**15**	

YOUNG, KRISTEN

2009-10 WWHL Edmonton Chimos #30 (2 games, 1W-1L).

ZAKARY, HEATHER

1993-94 COWHL Scarborough Sting #1 (27 games).

ZHANG TIANYI

Goalie. #39.

Born 1998-03-13. Grew up in Harbin, CHN. 5'3". Debut at age 19 on 2018-01-20.

Year - League - Team		GP	W-L	SO	GAA
2017-18	CWHL Vanke	4	0-2	0	7.29

ZISIS, ZOE

2014-15 CWHL Boston Blades #1.

ZUM-HINGST, PATRICIA

1995 Nationals Britannia Blues.

COACHES

AKAI, GARY *Coach.*

Year - League - Team			GP	W-L-O-S	Rank
2008-09	CWHL	Vaughan	1	0-1-0-0	

ALCORN, KRISTI *Coach.*
Please reference Alcorn's player record in this guide.

Year - League - Team			GP	W-L-O-S	Rank
2014-15	CWHL	Brampton	9	2-7-0-0	5th

AMBROZ, KASY *Coach.*

Year - League - Team			GP	W-L-O-S	Rank
2017-18	CWHL	Boston	14	1-12-0-1	7th

BATES, MARK *Coach.*

Year - League - Team			GP	W-L-O-S	Rank
2017-18	CWHL	Boston	1	0-1-0-0	

BEATTY, ROD *Coach.*

Year - League - Team			GP	W-L-O-S	Rank
2008-09	CWHL	Brampton	2	0-2-0-0	
2009-10	CWHL	Brampton	3	1-2-0-0	

BIRCHARD-KESSEL, COURTNEY *Coach.*
Please reference her player record in this guide.

Year - League - Team			GP	W-L-O-S	Rank
2018-19	CWHL	Toronto	26	14-12-0-0	4th
2019	C-Cup	Toronto	3	1W-2L	SF

BLAIR, BART *Coach.*

Year - League - Team			GP	W-L-O-S	Rank
2009-10	CWHL	Vaughan	29	9-19-0-1	5th
2010	CWHL-P	Vaughan	1	0W-1L	

BOIS, VALERIE *Coach.*

Year - League - Team			GP	W-L-O-S	Rank
2018-19	CWHL	Montréal	2	2-0-0-0	2nd *

* Montréal's assistant coach for balance of season

BOTHWELL, TIM *Coach.*

Year - League - Team			GP	W-L-O-S	Rank
2012-13	CWHL	Alberta	23	3-20-0-0	5th
2013-14	CWHL	Calgary	24	12-11-0-1	3rd
2014	C-Cup	Calgary	3	0W-3L	4th
CWHL Regular Season			**47**	**15-31-0-1**	**31 pts**
Clarkson Cup series			**3**	**0W-3L**	

BOYD, STEPHANIE *Coach.*
Please reference her player record in this guide.

Year - League - Team			GP	W-L-O-S	Rank
2008-09	CWHL	Vaughan	28	9-17-0-2	5th
2009	CWHL-P	Vaughan	2	0W-0L-2T	

BRENNAN, CHRIS *Coach.*

Year - League - Team			GP	W-L-O-S	Rank
2011-12	CWHL	Toronto	27	9-13-2-3	4th
2012	C-Cup	Toronto	3	0W-3L	4th

BRODT, JACK *Coach.*
Won Clarkson Cup with Minnesota on 2010-03-28
Won Isobel Cup with Minnesota on 2019-03-17

Year - League - Team			GP	W-L-O-S	Rank
2009	C-Cup	Minnesota	3	2W-1L	2nd
2010	C-Cup	Minnesota	2	2W-0L	1st
2011	C-Cup	Minnesota	3	0W-3L	4th
2018-19	NWHL/	Minnesota	16	12-4-0-0	1st
2019	I-Cup	Minnesota	2	2W-0L	1st

BRUGMAN, CASEY *Coach.*

Year - League - Team			GP	W-L-O-S	Rank
2017-18	CWHL	Boston	13	0-11-0-2	7th

BRUNET, DANY *Coach.*
Won Clarkson Cup with Montréal on 2017-03-05

Year - League - Team			GP	W-L-O-S	Rank
2013-14	CWHL	Montréal	23	19-2-0-2	1st
2014	C-Cup	Montréal	3	1W-2L	3rd

Year - League - Team			GP	W-L-O-S	Rank
2014-15	CWHL	Montréal	22	12-9-0-1	3rd
2015	C-Cup	Montréal	3	2W-1L	2nd
2015-16	CWHL	Montréal	24	21-3-0-0	1st
2016	C-Cup	Montréal	3	2W-1L	2nd
2016-17	CWHL	Montréal	24	17-5-2-0	2nd
2017	C-Cup	Montréal	3	3W-0L	1st
2017-18	CWHL	Montréal	28	22-5-0-1	1st
2018	C-Cup	Montréal	2	0W-2L	SF
2018-19	CWHL	Montréal	8	7-1-0-0	-
CWHL Regular Season			**129**	**98-25-2-4**	**111 pts**
Clarkson Cup series			**14**	**8W-6L**	
Totals from all Competitions			**143**	**106-31-2-4**	

CHASSIE, ERIN *Coach.*
Please reference Chassie's player record in this guide.

Year - League - Team			GP	W-L-O-S	Rank
2007-08	CWHL	Ottawa	1	0-1-0-0	

CHURCH, AMANDA *Coach.*
Please reference Church's player record in this guide.

Year - League - Team			GP	W-L-O-S	Rank
2009-10	CWHL	Mississauga	1	1-0-0-0	

CLOUTIER, YAN *Coach.*

Year - League - Team			GP	W-L-O-S	Rank
2007-08	CWHL	Montréal	16	14-2-0-0	

COCHRANE, BRADI *Coach.*
Please reference her player record in this guide.

Year - League - Team			GP	W-L-O-S	Rank
2008-09	CWHL	Mississauga	3	3-0-0-0	
2009	CWHL-P	Mississauga	1	1W-0L	
2009-10	CWHL	Mississauga	28	21-6-0-1	2nd
2010	C-Cup	Mississauga	1	0W-1L	
2010-11	CWHL	Burlington	2	0-2-0-0	
CWHL Regular Season			**33**	**24-8-0-1**	**49 pts**
Clarkson Cup series			**1**	**0W-1L**	

COCKLIN, PAT *Coach.*

Year - League - Team			GP	W-L-O-S	Rank
2007-08	CWHL	Burlington	16	5-11-0-0	5th
2008	CWHL-P	Burlington	3	1W-1L-1T	
2008-09	CWHL	Burlington	22	8-11-1-2	4th
2009	CWHL-P	Burlington	4	1W-1L-2T	
2009-10	CWHL	Burlington	28	18-7-0-3	3rd
2010	CWHL-P	Burlington	2	1W-1L	
2010-11	CWHL	Burlington	23	5-16-1-1	5th
2012-13	CWHL	Brampton	11	5-5-0-1	3rd
2013	C-Cup	Brampton	3	0W-3L	4th
2013-14	CWHL	Brampton	24	5-16-3-0	5th
2014-15	CWHL	Brampton	15	4-9-0-2	
CWHL Regular Season			**139**	**50-75-5-9**	**114 pts**
Clarkson Cup series			**3**	**0W-3L**	
Totals from all Competitions			**151**	**53-81-5-9 & 3T**	

COOPER, CAROL *Coach.*
Please reference her player record in this guide.

Year - League - Team			GP	W-L-O-S	Rank
2007-08	CWHL	Brampton	1	0-1-0-0	

CROSBY, PETER *Coach.*

Year - League - Team			GP	W-L-O-S	Rank
2008-09	CWHL	Mississauga	27	16-9-1-1	3rd
2009	CWHL-P	Mississauga	3	2W-1L	
2010-11	CWHL	Brampton	13	12-0-1-1	2nd
2011	CWHL-P	Brampton	2	0W-2L	
2011	C-Cup	Brampton	3	1W-2L	3rd
CWHL Regular Season			**40**	**28-9-2-1**	**59 pts**
Clarkson Cup series			**3**	**1W-2L**	
Totals from all Competitions			**48**	**31-14-2-1**	

DERANEY, BOB *Coach.*

Year - League - Team			GP	W-L-O-S	Rank
2018-19	CWHL	Shenzhen	22	11-10-1-0	-

DÉRY, NATHALIE *Coach.*
Please reference her player record in this guide.

Year - League - Team		GP	W-L-O-S	Rank
2012-13	CWHL Montréal	4	3-1-0-0	

DIAMANTOPOULOS, MICHEAL *Coach.*

Year - League - Team		GP	W-L-O-S	Rank
2016-17	CWHL Boston	2	0-1-0-1	

DOMITROVIC, DANIEL *Coach.*

Year - League - Team		GP	W-L-O-S	Rank
2007-08	CWHL Ottawa	6	2-4-0-0	

EQUALE, RYAN *Coach.*

Year - League - Team		GP	W-L-O-S	Rank
2017-18	NWHL/ Connecticut	16	3-11-2	4th
2018	I-Cup Connecticut	1	0W-1L	SF
2018-19	NWHL/ Connecticut	16	2-12-2	5th

EUSTACE, JOANNE *Coach.*
Please reference her player record in this guide.

Year - League - Team		GP	W-L-O-S	Rank
2009-10	CWHL Vaughan	1	0-1-0-0	

FINES, TYLER *Coach.*

Year - League - Team		GP	W-L-O-S	Rank
2015-16	CWHL Brampton	24	16-7-0-1	3rd
2016	C-Cup Brampton	2	0W-2L	SF
2016-17	CWHL Brampton	24	12-10-1-1	3rd
2017	C-Cup Brampton	2	0W-2L	SF

CWHL Coach of the Year in 2015-16

FLANAGAN, JEFF *Coach.*

Year - League - Team		GP	W-L-O-S	Rank
2017-18	CWHL Toronto	28	9-17-1-1	6th

HALLER, KEVIN *Coach.*

Year - League - Team		GP	W-L-O-S	Rank
2014-15	CWHL Calgary	17	11-4-1-1	

HEALY, SEAN *Coach.*

Year - League - Team		GP	W-L-O-S	Rank
2008-09	CWHL Brampton	7	5-2-0-0	

HILDERMAN, RYAN *Coach.*

Year - League - Team		GP	W-L-O-S	Rank
2018-19	CWHL Calgary	11	8-3-0-0	1st
2019	C-Cup Calgary	4	3W-1L	1st

HOFFMEYER, LEXIE *Coach.*

Year - League - Team		GP	W-L-O-S	Rank
2016-17	CWHL Toronto	8	2-4-2-0*	
2017	C-Cup Toronto	3	1W-2L	SF

* Sommer West's assistant for balance of season

HOLDGATE, GORD *Coach.*

Year - League - Team		GP	W-L-O-S	Rank
2008-09	CWHL Vaughan	1	0-1-0-0	

HUGHES, KAREN *Coach.*
Please reference Hughes' player record in this guide.

Year - League - Team		GP	W-L-O-S	Rank
2011-12	CWHL Brampton	27	18-7-1-1	3rd
2012	C-Cup Brampton	4	2W-2L	2nd

JACKSON, JIM *Coach.*
Won Clarkson Cup with Markham on 2018-03-25

Year - League - Team		GP	W-L-O-S	Rank
2017-18	CWHL Markham	28	14-7-4-3	4th
2018	C-Cup Markham	3	3W-0L	1st
2018-19	CWHL Markham	28	13-11-3-1	3rd
2019	C-Cup Markham	3	1W-2L	SF
CWHL Regular Season		**56**	**27-18-7-4**	**67 pts**
Clarkson Cup series		**6**	**4W-2L**	
Totals from all Competitions		62	31-20-7-4	

CWHL Coach of the Year in 2018-19

JAMES, ANGELA *Coach.*
Please reference James' player record in this guide.

Year - League - Team		GP	W-L-O-S	Rank
2010-11	CWHL Brampton	12	6-6-0-0	

JAY, BOBBY *Coach.*
Won Isobel Cup with Boston on 2016-03-12

Year - League - Team		GP	W-L-O-S	Rank
2016-16	NWHL/ Boston	18	14-3-0-1	1st
2016	I-Cup Boston	4	4W-0L	1st
2016-17	NWHL/ Boston	17	16-1-0	1st
2017	I-Cup Boston	2	1W-1L	2nd

JOHNSON, BRUCE *Coach.*

Year - League - Team		GP	W-L-O-S	Rank
2008-09	CWHL Ottawa	30	4-26-0-0	6th
2009	CWHL-P Ottawa	2	0W-2L	

JONES, RAY *Coach.*

Year - League - Team		GP	W-L-O-S	Rank
2007-08	CWHL Burlington	1	0-0-0-1	

KENNEDY, PAUL *Coach.*

Year - League - Team		GP	W-L-O-S	Rank
2018-19	CWHL Worcester	27	0-27-0-0	6th

KINDING, BJORN *Coach.*

Year - League - Team		GP	W-L-O-S	Rank
2009	C-Cup Calgary	2	0W-2L	

LADOUCEUR, VERN *Coach.*

Year - League - Team		GP	W-L-O-S	Rank
2007-08	CWHL Mississauga	2	1W-1L	

LANDRY, LYNE *Coach.*
Please reference her player record in this guide.

Year - League - Team		GP	W-L-O-S	Rank
2009-10	CWHL Ottawa	2	1-1-0-0	

LANGSTAFF, MIKE *Coach.*

Year - League - Team		GP	W-L-O-S	Rank
2007-08	CWHL Burlington	2	2-0-0-0	

LAZAZZERA, MIKE *Coach.*

Year - League - Team		GP	W-L-O-S	Rank
2018-19	CWHL Shenzhen	6	2-3-1-0	5th

LECLAIRE, ISABELLE *Coach.*
Please reference her goalie record in this guide.
Won Clarkson Cup with Montréal on 2009-03-21

Year - League - Team		GP	W-L-O-S	Rank
2008-09	CWHL Montréal	3	1-2-0-0	1st*

* Marie-Claude Roy's associate for balance of season

LEFEBVRE, CHRISTIAN *Coach.*

Year - League - Team		GP	W-L-O-S	Rank
2007-08	CWHL Québec	29	8-20-0-1	7th

LICHTERMAN, DAN *Coach.*

Year - League - Team		GP	W-L-O-S	Rank
2010-11	CWHL Toronto	26	8-13-0-5	4th
2011	CWHL-P Toronto	2	2W-0L	
2011	C-Cup Toronto	4	2W-2L	2nd

LINSTAD, HEATHER *Coach.*

Year - League - Team		GP	W-L-O-S	Rank
2016-17	NWHL/ Connecticut	17	5-12-1	4th
2017	I-Cup Connecticut	1	0W-1L	SF

LOFTUS, LORI *Coach.*
Please reference Loftus' player record in this guide.

Year - League - Team		GP	W-L-O-S	Rank
2008-09	CWHL Brampton	21	17-3-0-1	2nd
2009	CWHL-P Brampton	2	1W-1L	
2009	C-Cup Brampton	2	1W-1L	3rd
2009-10	CWHL Brampton	27	11-13-2-1	4th
2010	CWHL-P Brampton	2	2W-0L	
2010	C-Cup Brampton	2	1W-1L	2nd
CWHL Regular Season		**48**	**28-16-2-2**	**60 pts**
Clarkson Cup series		**4**	**2W-2L**	
Totals from all Competitions		56	33-19-2-2	

LOONEY, SHELLEY *Coach.*
Please reference her player record in this guide.

Year - League - Team		GP	W-L-O-S	Rank
2015-16	NWHL/ Buffalo	18	5-9-0-4	3rd
2016	I-Cup Buffalo	5	2-2-0-1	

LUCIBELLO, FRED *Coach.*

Year - League - Team		GP	W-L-O-S	Rank
2007-08	CWHL Burlington	1	0-1-0-0	
2008-09	CWHL Burlington	8	3-5-0-0	

MARA, PAUL *Coach.*

Year - League - Team		GP	W-L-O-S	Rank
2018-19	NWHL/ Boston	16	11-5-0-0	3rd
2019	I-Cup Boston	1	0W-1L	SF

MARSH, BRAD *Coach.*

Year - League - Team		GP	W-L-O-S	Rank
2009-10	CWHL Ottawa	28	4-22-1-1	6th
2010	CWHL-P Ottawa	1	0W-1L	

MASTEL, JACK *Coach.*

Year - League - Team		GP	W-L-O-S	Rank
2016-16	NWHL/ Connecticut	18	13-5-0-0	2nd
2016	I-Cup Connecticut	3	1-2-0-0	

MCATEER, MICHELLE *Coach.*

Year - League - Team		GP	W-L-O-S	Rank
2007-08	CWHL Vaughan	3	1-2-0-0	

MCAULIFFE, LAUREN *Coach.*

Please reference her player record in this guide.

Year - League - Team		GP	W-L-O-S	Rank
2011-12	CWHL Boston	25	19-6-0-0	2nd
2012	C-Cup Boston	2	1W-1L	3rd

CWHL Coach of the Year in 2011-12

MCCLOSKEY, BRIAN *Coach.*

Year - League - Team		GP	W-L-O-S	Rank
2015-16	CWHL Boston	24	1-23-0-0	5th
2016-17	CWHL Boston	22	2-19-1-0	5th

MCCORMICK, CODY *Coach.*

Year - League - Team		GP	W-L-O-S	Rank
2018-19	NWHL/ Buffalo	10	8-1-0-1	2nd
2019	I-Cup Buffalo	2	1W-1L	2nd

MCGUIRE, JAMIE *Coach.*

Year - League - Team		GP	W-L-O-S	Rank
2007-08	CWHL Vaughan	27	11-14-2-0	4th
2008	CWHL-P Vaughan	2	0W-2L	

MILLER, SHANNON *Coach.*

Year - League - Team		GP	W-L-O-S	Rank
2018-19	CWHL Calgary	16	14-1-0-1	-

MOIR, MIKE *Coach.*

Year - League - Team		GP	W-L-O-S	Rank
2009-10	CWHL Burlington	2	1-1-0-0	

MORGAN, ROB *Coach.*

Year - League - Team		GP	W-L-O-S	Rank
2017-18	CWHL Vanke	28	14-3-0-1	5th

MURPHY, DIGIT *Coach.*

Won Clarkson Cup with Boston on 2013-03-23
Won Clarkson Cup with Boston on 2015-03-07

Year - League - Team		GP	W-L-O-S	Rank
2012-13	CWHL Boston	22	17-4-0-1	1st
2013	C-Cup Boston	4	3W-1L	1st
2013-14	CWHL Boston	24	13-11-0-0	2nd
2014	C-Cup Boston	4	3W-1L	2nd
2014-15	CWHL Boston	22	17-2-0-1	1st
2015	C-Cup Boston	3	3W-0L	1st
2017-18	CWHL Kunlun	28	21-6-0-1	2nd
2018	C-Cup Kunlun	4	2W-2L	2nd
CWHL Regular Season		**96**	**68-25-0-3**	**135 pts**
Clarkson Cup series		**15**	**11W-4L**	
Totals from all Competitions		111	79-29-0-3	

CWHL Coach of the Year in 2012-13

NYHUUS, JIM *Coach.*

Year - League - Team		GP	W-L-O-S	Rank
2018-19	CWHL Toronto	2	0-2-0-0	4th *

* Toronto's assistant coach for balance of season

OUELLETTE, CAROLINE *Coach.*

Year - League - Team		GP	W-L-O-S	Rank
2018-19	CWHL Montréal	10	6-4-0-0	2nd
2019	C-Cup Montréal	3	2W-1L	2nd

PACINA, TOMAS *Coach.*

Year - League - Team		GP	W-L-O-S	Rank
2017-18	CWHL Calgary	28	17-7-1-3	3rd
2018	C-Cup Calgary	3	1W-2L	SF

CWHL Coach of the Year in 2017-18

PASTOREK, PETER *Coach.*

Year - League - Team		GP	W-L-O-S	Rank
2007-08	CWHL Ottawa	1	0-1-0-0	

PÖCK, THOMAS *Coach.*

Year - League - Team		GP	W-L-O-S	Rank
2017-18	NWHL/ Boston	16	4-8-4	3rd
2018	I-Cup Boston	1	0W-1L	SF

QUINTO, BERARDINO *Coach.*

Year - League - Team		GP	W-L-O-S	Rank
2011-12	CWHL Burlington	27	1-26-0-0	6th

RANKINE, PATRICK *Coach.*

Won Clarkson Cup with Montréal on 2011-03-27
Won Clarkson Cup with Montréal on 2012-03-25

Year - League - Team		GP	W-L-O-S	Rank
2007-08	CWHL Montréal	11	6-4-1-0	1st
2008	CWHL-P Montréal	2	1W-1L	
2009-10	CWHL Montréal	30	23-5-0-2	1st
2010	C-Cup Montréal	1	0W-1L	SF
2010-11	CWHL Montréal	26	22-2-0-2	1st
2011	CWHL-P Montréal	2	2W-0L	
2011	C-Cup Montréal	4	4W-0L	1st
2011-12	CWHL Montréal	27	22-4-0-1	1st
2012	C-Cup Montréal	4	4W-0L	1st
2012-13	CWHL Montréal	6	2-3-0-1	
CWHL Regular Season		**100**	**75-18-1-6**	**157 pts**
Clarkson Cup series		**9**	**8W-1L**	
Totals from all Competitions		113	86-20-1-6	

CWHL Coach of the Year in 2010-11
* Patrick Rankine co-coach with Yan Cloutier

REID, SCOTT *Coach.*

Won Clarkson Cup with Calgary on 2016-03-14

Year - League - Team		GP	W-L-O-S	Rank
2014-15	CWHL Calgary	7	4-2-0-1	2nd
2015	C-Cup Calgary	2	0W-2L	4th
2015-16	CWHL Calgary	24	16-6-1-1	2nd
2016	C-Cup Calgary	3	3W-0L	1st
2016-17	CWHL Calgary	24	20-4-0-0	1st
2017	C-Cup Calgary	4	2W-2L	2nd
CWHL Regular Season		**55**	**40-12-1-2**	**83 pts**
Clarkson Cup series		**9**	**5W-4L**	
Totals from all Competitions		64	45-16-1-2	

CWHL Coach of the Year in 2016-17

ROSA, DONNA-LYNN *Coach.*

Please reference Rosa's player record in this guide.

Year - League - Team		GP	W-L-O-S	Rank
2007-08	CWHL Brampton	29	22-6-0-1	2nd
2008	CWHL-P Brampton	3	2W-0L-1T	

ROY, MARIE-CLAUDE *Coach.*

Please reference Roy's goalie record in this guide.
Won Clarkson Cup with Montréal on 2009-03-21

Year - League - Team		GP	W-L-O-S	Rank
2008-09	CWHL Montréal	27	24-2-0-1	1st
2009	CWHL-P Montréal	2	1W-1L	
2009	C-Cup Montréal	3	2W-1L	1st

SAUVAGEAU, DANIÈLE *Coach.*

Year - League - Team		GP	W-L-O-S	Rank
2018-19	CWHL Montréal	8	6-2-0-0	2nd *
2019	C-Cup Montréal	1	1W-0L	2nd *

* Caroline Ouellette's co-coach for balance of season

SCHMIDT, JASON — Coach.

Year - League - Team			GP	W-L-O-S	Rank
2011-12	CWHL	Alberta	15	5-10-0-0	5th

SEILING, RIC — Coach.

Won Isobel Cup with Buffalo on 2017-03-19

Year - League - Team			GP	W-L-O-S	Rank
2016-17	NWHL/	Buffalo	17	6-10-1	3rd
2017	I-Cup	Buffalo	2	2W-0L	1st
2017-18	NWHL/	Buffalo	16	12-4-0	2nd
2018	I-Cup	Buffalo	2	1W-1L	2nd
2018-19	NWHL/	Buffalo	6	3-3-0-0	-

* Ric Seiling co-coach with Craig Muni

STONE, RYAN — Coach.

Year - League - Team			GP	W-L-O-S	Rank
2012-13	CWHL	Boston	2	2-0-0-0	1st *

* Digit Murphy's assistant coach for balance of season

SULLIVAN, SHANE — Coach.

Year - League - Team			GP	W-L-O-S	Rank
2007-08	CWHL	Ottawa	20	6-11-0-3	6th
2008	CWHL-P	Ottawa	1	0W-1L	

TRAHAN, PHILIPPE — Coach.

Year - League - Team			GP	W-L-O-S	Rank
2012-13	CWHL	Montréal	13	12-1-0-0	2nd
2013	C-Cup	Montréal	4	3W-1L	2nd

TRAUGNOTT, RICK — Coach.

Year - League - Team			GP	W-L-O-S	Rank
2012-13	CWHL	Brampton	13	5-7-1-0	

VELISCHEK, RANDY — Coach.

Year - League - Team			GP	W-L-O-S	Rank
2018-19	NWHL/	Metropolitan	16	4-12-0-0	4th
2019	I-Cup	Metropolitan	1	0W-1L	SF

WATT, LAURA — Coach.

Please reference her player record in this guide.

Year - League - Team			GP	W-L-O-S	Rank
2009-10	CWHL	Mississauga	1	0-1-0-0	

WEST, SOMMER — Coach.

Please reference her player record in this guide.

Won Clarkson Cup with Toronto on 2014-03-22

Year - League - Team			GP	W-L-O-S	Rank
2012-13	CWHL	Toronto	24	10-13-1-0	4th
2013	C-Cup	Toronto	3	1W-2L	3rd
2013-14	CWHL	Toronto	23	10-10-1-2	4th
2014	C-Cup	Toronto	4	3W-1L	1st
2014-15	CWHL	Toronto	24	8-13-1-2	4th
2015	C-Cup	Toronto	2	0W-2L	3rd
2015-16	CWHL	Toronto	24	6-16-1-1	4th
2016	C-Cup	Toronto	2	0W-2L	SF
2016-17	CWHL	Toronto	16	7-7-1-1	4th
CWHL Regular Season			**111**	**41-59-5-6**	**93 pts**
Clarkson Cup series			**11**	**4W-7L**	
Totals from all Competitions			122	45-66-4-5	

CWHL Coach of the Year in 2013-14

WHITE, STEPHANIE — Coach.

Year - League - Team			GP	W-L-O-S	Rank
2007-08	CWHL	Mississauga	28	20-7-0-1	3rd
2008	CWHL-P	Mississauga	5	3W-2L	

WHITTEN-HAMLEN, ERIN — Coach.

Year - League - Team			GP	W-L-O-S	Rank
2010-11	CWHL	Boston	24	10-13-1-0	3rd
2011	CWHL-P	Boston	2	0W-2L	
2011-12	CWHL	Boston	2	1-1-0-0	
2012	C-Cup	Boston	1	0W-1L	

WISEMAN, CHAD — Coach.

Won Isobel Cup with Metropolitan on 2018-03-25

Year - League - Team			GP	W-L-O-S	Rank
2015-16	NWHL/	New York	18	4-12-0-2	4th
2016	I-Cup	New York	2	0W-2L	SF
2016-17	NWHL/	New York	18	8-7-3	2nd
2017	I-Cup	New York	1	0W-1L	SF
2017-18	NWHL/	Metrop.	16	13-3-0	1st
2017	I-Cup	Metrop.	2	2W-0L	1st
NWHL Regular Season			**52**	**25-22-3-2**	**55 pts**

WISEMAN, WES — Coach.

Year - League - Team			GP	W-L-O-S	Rank
2007-08	CWHL	Burlington	10	4-6-0-0	
2008-09	CWHL	Brampton	2	0-2-0-0	

Coach Caroline Ouellette

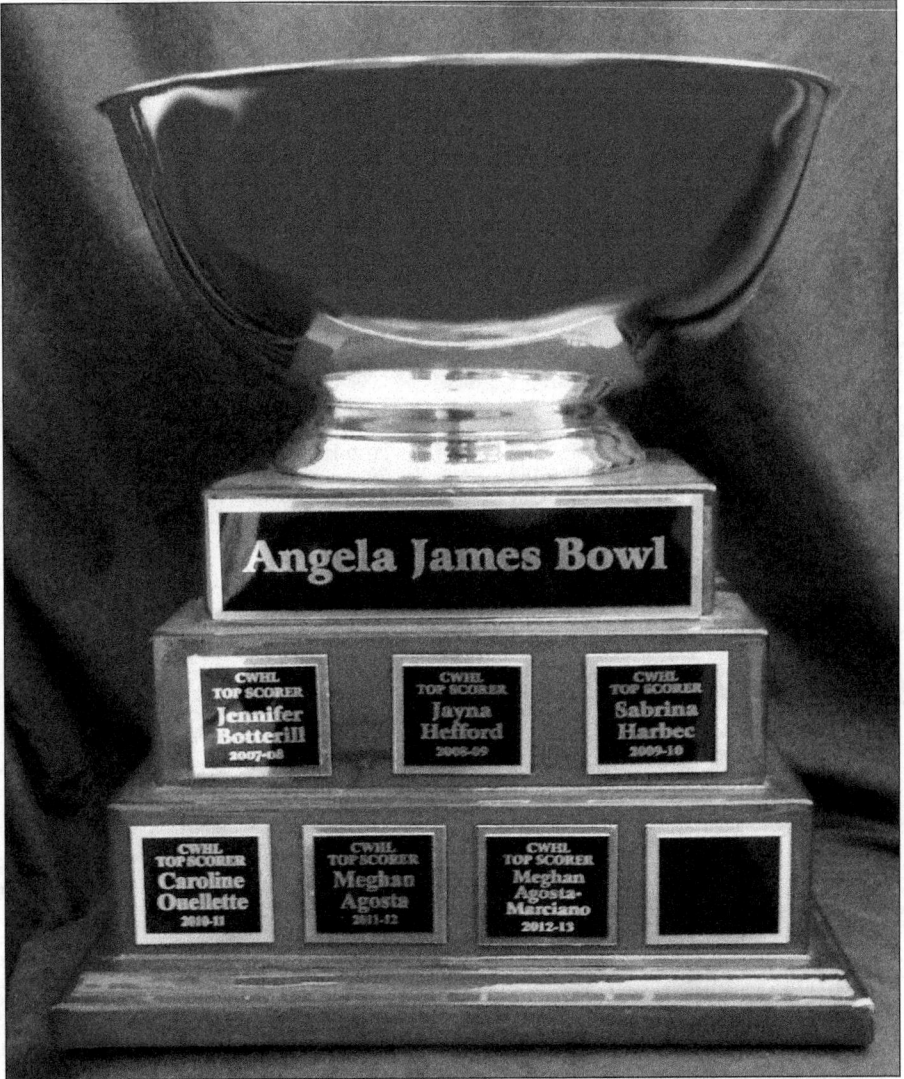

ANGELA JAMES BOWL

The Angela James Bowl was the oldest trophy associated with the Canadian Women's Hockey League, struck in the league's inaugural 2007-08 season. The trophy was awarded annually to the player who scored the most points during the CWHL's regular season.

The trophy is 28.8 centimetres tall. Each season's wi ner was recognized on a small black plaque that read "CWHL Top Scorer" (with the player's name and her winning season).

The trophy was presented for the first time on Saturday, March 22, 2008 at the Powerade Centre in Brampton, ON after the first CWHL playoff championship. Angela James, after whom the trophy was named, made the on-ice presentation to 2008 winner Jennifer Botterill.

HONOURS

Chairman's Trophy
CWHL LEAGUE WINNERS
2007-08 Stars de Montréal
2008-09 Stars de Montréal
2009-10 Stars de Montréal
2010-11 Stars de Montréal
2011-12 Stars de Montréal
2012-13 Boston Blades
2013-14 Stars de Montréal
2014-15 Boston Blades
2015-16 Canadiennes de Montréal
2016-17 Calgary Inferno
2017-18 Canadiennes de Montréal
2018-19 Calgary Inferno

CWHL Most Valuable Player
2007-08 Jayna Hefford, Brampton
2008-09 Caroline Ouellette, Montréal
2009-10 Sabrina Harbec, Montréal
2010-11 Caroline Ouellette, Montréal
2011-12 Meghan Agosta, Montréal
2012-13 Hilary Knight, Boston
2013-14 Ann-Sophie Bettez, Montréal
2014-15 Rebecca Johnston, Calgary
2015-16 Marie-Philip Poulin, Montréal
2016-17 Marie-Philip Poulin, Montréal
2017-18 Kelli Stack, Kunlun
2018-19 Marie-Philip Poulin, Montréal

Angela James Bowl
CWHL SCORING CHAMPIONS
2007-08 Jennifer Botterill, Mississauga
2008-09 Jayna Hefford, Brampton
2009-10 Sabrina Harbec, Montréal
2010-11 Caroline Ouellette, Montréal
2011-12 Meghan Agosta, Montréal
2012-13 Meghan Agosta-Marciano, Montréal
2013-14 Ann-Sophie Bettez, Montréal
2014-15 Rebecca Johnston, Calgary
2015-16 Marie-Philip Poulin, Montréal
2016-17 Jess Jones & Marie-Philip Poulin
2017-18 Kelli Stack, Kunlun
2018-19 Marie-Philip Poulin, Montréal

CWHL Goals Leader
2007-08 Jayna Hefford, Brampton
2008-09 Jayna Hefford, Brampton
2009-10 Noémie Marin, Montréal
2010-11 Jayna Hefford, Brampton
2011-12 Meghan Agosta, Montréal
2012-13 Ann-Sophie Bettez & Hilary Knight
2013-14 Ann-Sophie Bettez, Montréal
2014-15 Rebecca Johnston, Calgary
2015-16 Marie-Philip Poulin, Montréal
2016-17 Ann-Sophie Bettez, Montréal
2017-18 Kelli Stack, Kunlun
2018-19 Marie-Philip Poulin, Montréal

Top Defender
2007-08 Becky Kellar, Burlington
2008-09 Becky Kellar, Burlington

2009-10 Annie Guay, Montréal
2010-11 Angela Ruggiero, Boston
2011-12 Catherine Ward, Montréal
2012-13 Catherine Ward, Montréal
2013-14 Cathy Chartrand, Montréal
2014-15 Tara Watchorn, Boston
2015-16 Laura Fortino, Brampton
2016-17 Meghan Mikkelson, Calgary
2017-18 Cathy Chartrand, Montréal
2018-19 Erin Ambrose, Montréal

Top Goaltender
CWHL GOALIE OF THE YEAR
2007-08 Kim St-Pierre, Montréal
2008-09 Kim St-Pierre, Montréal
2009-10 Laura Hosier, Brampton
2010-11 Kim St-Pierre, Montréal
2011-12 Molly Schaus, Boston
2012-13 Geneviève Lacasse, Boston
2013-14 Delayne Brian, Calgary
2014-15 Charline Labonté, Montréal
2015-16 Charline Labonté, Montréal
2016-17 Charline Labonté, Montréal
2017-18 Noora Räty, Kunlun
2018-19 Alex Rigsby, Calgary

CWHL Outstanding Rookie
CWHL ROOKIE OF THE YEAR
2007-08 Marie-Philip Poulin, Montréal
2008-09 Laura Hosier, Brampton
2009-10 Danielle Blanchard, Vaughan
2010-11 Sarah Vaillancourt, Montréal
2011-12 Courtney Birchard, Brampton
2012-13 Ann-Sophie Bettez, Montréal
2013-14 Jillian Dempsey, Boston
2014-15 Brianna Decker, Boston
2015-16 Elana Lovell, Calgary
2016-17 Laura Stacey, Brampton
2017-18 Sophie Shirley, Calgary
2018-19 Victoria Bach, Markham

CWHL Coach of the Year
2010-11 Patrick Rankine, Montréal
2011-12 Lauren McAuliffe, Boston
2012-13 Digit Murphy, Boston
2013-14 Sommer West, Toronto
2014-15 Dany Brunet, Montréal
2015-16 Tyler Fines, Brampton
2016-17 Scott Reid, Calgary
2017-18 Tomas Pacina, Calgary
2018-19 Jim Jackson, Markham

CWHL Humanitarian of the Year
2012-13 Samantha Holmes-Domagala
2013-14 Cassie Campbell-Pascall
2014-15 Lois Mitchell
2015-16 Lisa-Marie Breton-Lebreux
2016-17 Jessica Campbell
2017-18 Brad Morris
2018-19 Michael Bartlett

Jayna Hefford Trophy
2015-16 Marie-Philip Poulin, Montréal
2016-17 Marie-Philip Poulin, Montréal
2017-18 Jamie-Lee Rattray, Markham
2018-19 Marie-Philip Poulin, Montréal

CWHL All-Star Team

CWHL CENTRAL ALL-STAR TEAM
2007-08 Goalie Cindy Eadie, Brampton
2007-08 Defender Becky Kellar, Burlington
2007-08 Defender Molly Engstrom, Brampton
2007-08 Forward Jayna Hefford, Brampton
2007-08 Forward Jennifer Botterill, Mississauga
2007-08 Forward Jana Harrigan (Head), Burlington

CWHL EASTERN ALL-STAR TEAM
2007-08 Goalie Kim St-Pierre, Montréal
2007-08 Defender Nathalie Déry, Montréal
2007-08 Defender Lyne Landry, Ottawa
2007-08 Forward Marie-Philip Poulin, Montréal
2007-08 Forward Leslie Oles, Montréal
2007-08 Forward Katie Weatherston, Montréal

CWHL FIRST ALL-STAR TEAM
2008-09 Goalie Kim St-Pierre, Montréal
2008-09 Defender Cheryl Pounder, Mississauga
2008-09 Defender Becky Kellar, Burlington
2008-09 Forward Jayna Hefford, Brampton
2008-09 Forward Caroline Ouellette, Montréal
2008-09 Forward Jennifer Botterill, Mississauga

CWHL SECOND ALL-STAR TEAM
2008-09 Goalie Sami Jo Small, Mississauga
2008-09 Defender Bobbi Jo Slusar, Brampton
2008-09 Defender Ashley Pendleton, Brampton
2008-09 Forward Jana Harrigan (Head), Burlington
2008-09 Forward Lara Perks, Mississauga
2008-09 Forward Sabrina Harbec, Montréal

CWHL FIRST ALL-STAR TEAM
2009-10 Goalie Laura Hosier, Brampton
2009-10 Defender Annie Guay, Montréal
2009-10 Defender Michelle Bonelle, Vaughan
2009-10 Forward Sabrina Harbec, Montréal
2009-10 Forward Lindsay Vine, Burlington
2009-10 Forward Sommer West, Mississauga

CWHL SECOND ALL-STAR TEAM
2009-10 Goalie Sami Jo Small, Mississauga
2009-10 Defender Shannon Moulson, Mississauga
2009-10 Defender Bobbi Jo Slusar, Brampton
2009-10 Forward Noémie Marin, Montréal
2009-10 Forward Lori Dupuis, Brampton
2009-10 Forward Jana Harrigan (Head), Burlington

CWHL FIRST ALL-STAR TEAM
2010-11 Goalie Kim St-Pierre, Montréal
2010-11 Defender Angela Ruggiero, Boston
2010-11 Defender Annie Guay, Montréal
2010-11 Forward Caroline Ouellette, Montréal
2010-11 Forward Jayna Hefford, Brampton
2010-11 Forward Sarah Vaillancourt, Montréal

CWHL SECOND ALL-STAR TEAM
2010-11 Goalie Laura Hosier, Brampton
2010-11 Defender Britni Smith, Toronto
2010-11 Defender Molly Engstrom, Brampton
2010-11 Forward Jennifer Botterill, Toronto
2010-11 Forward Sam Faber, Boston
2010-11 Forward Noémie Marin, Montréal

CWHL FIRST ALL-STAR TEAM
2011-12 Goalie Molly Schaus, Boston
2011-12 Defender Catherine Ward, Montréal
2011-12 Defender Molly Engstrom, Brampton
2011-12 Forward Meghan Agosta, Montréal
2011-12 Forward Caroline Ouellette, Montréal
2011-12 Forward Kelli Stack, Boston

CWHL SECOND ALL-STAR TEAM
2011-12 Goalie Jenny Lavigne, Montréal
2011-12 Defender Gigi Marvin, Boston
2011-12 Defender Tessa Bonhomme, Toronto
2011-12 Forward Gillian Apps, Brampton
2011-12 Forward Jayna Hefford, Brampton
2011-12 Forward Vanessa Davidson, Montréal

CWHL FIRST ALL-STAR TEAM
2012-13 Goalie Geneviève Lacasse, Boston
2012-13 Defender Gigi Marvin, Boston
2012-13 Defender Catherine Ward, Montréal
2012-13 Forward Hilary Knight, Boston
2012-13 Forward Meghan Agosta-Marciano, Montréal
2012-13 Forward Caroline Ouellette, Montréal

CWHL SECOND ALL-STAR TEAM
2012-13 Goalie Charline Labonté, Montréal
2012-13 Defender Kacey Bellamy, Boston
2012-13 Defender Tessa Bonhomme, Toronto
2012-13 Forward Jayna Hefford, Brampton
2012-13 Forward Rebecca Johnston, Toronto
2012-13 Forward Megan Duggan, Boston

CWHL FIRST ALL-STAR TEAM
2013-14 Goalie Christina Kessler, Toronto
2013-14 Defender Blake Bolden, Boston
2013-14 Defender Cathy Chartrand, Montréal
2013-14 Forward Ann-Sophie Bettez, Montréal
2013-14 Forward Danielle Stone, Calgary
2013-14 Forward Jillian Dempsey, Boston

CWHL SECOND ALL-STAR TEAM
2013-14 Goalie Brittany Ott, Boston
2013-14 Defender Jessica Wong, Calgary
2013-14 Defender Danielle Skirrow, Brampton
2013-14 Forward Jenna Cunningham, Calgary
2013-14 Forward Carolyne Prévost, Toronto
2013-14 Forward Alyssa Baldin, Toronto

CWHL FIRST ALL-STAR TEAM
2014-15 Goalie Charline Labonté, Montréal
2014-15 Defender Tara Watchorn, Boston
2014-15 Defender Blake Bolden, Boston
2014-15 Forward Brianna Decker, Boston
2014-15 Forward Rebecca Johnston, Calgary
2014-15 Forward Hilary Knight, Boston

CWHL SECOND ALL-STAR TEAM
2014-15 Goalie Geneviève Lacasse, Boston
2014-15 Defender Monique Lamoureux, Boston
2014-15 Defender Laura Fortino, Brampton
2014-15 Forward Ann-Sophie Bettez, Montréal
2014-15 Forward Jenelle Kohanchuk, Toronto
2014-15 Forward Caroline Ouellette, Montréal

CWHL FIRST ALL-STAR TEAM
2015-16 Goalie Charline Labonté, Montréal
2015-16 Defender Laura Fortino, Brampton
2015-16 Defender Tara Watchorn, Boston
2015-16 Forward Marie-Philip Poulin, Montréal
2015-16 Forward Natalie Spooner, Toronto
2015-16 Forward Jillian Saulnier, Calgary

CWHL SECOND ALL-STAR TEAM
2015-16 Goalie Erica Howe, Brampton
2015-16 Defender Julie Chu, Montréal
2015-16 Defender Courtney Birchard, Brampton
2015-16 Forward Ann-Sophie Bettez, Montréal
2015-16 Forward Brianne Jenner, Calgary
2015-16 Forward Jamie-Lee Rattray, Brampton

CWHL FIRST ALL-STAR TEAM
2016-17 Goalie Charline Labonté, Montréal
2016-17 Defender Meghan Mikkelson, Calgary
2016-17 Defender Laura Fortino, Brampton
2016-17 Forward Marie-Philip Poulin, Montréal
2016-17 Forward Jess Jones, Brampton
2016-17 Forward Caroline Ouellette, Montréal
CWHL SECOND ALL-STAR TEAM
2016-17 Goalie Emerance Maschmeyer, Calgary
2016-17 Defender Cathy Chartrand, Montréal
2016-17 Defender Renata Fast, Toronto
2016-17 Forward Brianne Jenner, Calgary
2016-17 Forward Natalie Spooner, Toronto
2016-17 Forward Ann-Sophie Bettez, Montréal

CWHL FIRST ALL-STAR TEAM
2017-18 Goalie Noora Räty, Kunlun
2017-18 Defender Jessica Wong, Kunlun
2017-18 Defender Cathy Chartrand, Montréal
2017-18 Forward Kelli Stack, Kunlun
2017-18 Forward Jame-Lee Rattray, Markham
2017-18 Forward Ann-Sophie Bettez, Montréal
CWHL SECOND ALL-STAR TEAM
2017-18 Goalie Erica Howe, Markham
2017-18 Defender Megan Bozek, Markham
2017-18 Defender Katelyn Gosling, Calgary
2017-18 Forward Cayley Mercer, Vanke
2017-18 Forward Zoe Hickel, Kunlun
2017-18 Forward Sophie Shirley, Calgary

CWHL FIRST ALL-STAR TEAM
2018-19 Goalie Alex Rigsby, Calgary
2018-19 Defender Kacey Bellamy, Calgary
2018-19 Defender Erin Ambrose, Montréal
2018-19 Forward Marie-Philip Poulin, Montréal
2018-19 Forward Brianna Decker, Calgary
2018-19 Forward Rebecca Johnston, Calgary
CWHL SECOND ALL-STAR TEAM
2018-19 Goalie Noora Räty, KRS Vanke
2018-19 Defender Renata Fast, Toronto
2018-19 Defender, Brigette Lacquette, Calgary
2018-19 Forward, Ann-Sophie Bettez, Montréal
2018-19 Forward Natalie Spooner, Toronto
2018-19 Forward Victoria Bach, Markham

CWHL All-Rookie Team
2007-08 Goalie Christine Dufour, Québec
2007-08 Defender Molly Engstrom, Brampton
2007-08 Defender Bobbi Jo Slusar, Brampton
2007-08 Forward Marie-Philip Poulin, Montréal
2007-08 Forward Leslie Oles, Montréal
2007-08 Forward Katie Weatherston, Montréal

2008-09 Goalie Laura Hosier, Brampton
2008-09 Defender Annie Guay, Montréal
2008-09 Defender Shannon Moulson, Mississauga
2008-09 Forward Noémie Marin, Montréal
2008-09 Forward Brooke Beazer, Brampton
2008-09 Forward Amanda Parkins, Burlington

2009-10 Goalie Allison Cubberley, Burlington
2009-10 Defender Ashley Johnston, Burlington
2009-10 Defender Sharon Kelly, Ottawa
2009-10 Forward Danielle Blanchard, Vaughan
2009-10 Forward Donna Ringrose, Montréal
2009-10 Forward Nicole Tritter, Brampton

2010-11 Goalie Christina Kessler, Burlington
2010-11 Defender Britni Smith, Toronto
2010-11 Defender Kacey Bellamy, Boston
2010-11 Forward Sarah Vaillancourt, Montréal
2010-11 Forward Sam Faber, Boston
2010-11 Forward Kori Cheverie, Toronto

2011-12 Goalie Molly Schaus, Boston
2011-12 Defender Catherine Ward, Montréal
2011-12 Defender Courtney Birchard, Brampton
2011-12 Forward Meghan Agosta, Montréal
2011-12 Forward Kelli Stack, Boston
2011-12 Forward Erika Lawler, Boston

2012-13 Goalie Geneviève Lacasse, Boston
2012-13 Defender Tara Watchorn, Boston
2012-13 Defender Anne Schleper, Boston
2012-13 Forward Hilary Knight, Boston
2012-13 Forward Ann-Sophie Bettez, Montréal
2012-13 Forward Rebecca Johnston, Toronto

2013-14 Goalie Delayne Brian, Calgary
2013-14 Defender Blake Bolden, Boston
2013-14 Defender Jessica Wong, Calgary
2013-14 Forward Jillian Dempsey, Boston
2013-14 Forward Alyssa Baldin, Toronto
2013-14 Forward Jill Cardella, Boston

2014-15 Goalie Erica Howe, Brampton
2014-15 Defender Monique Lamoureux, Boston
2014-15 Defender Laura Fortino, Brampton
2014-15 Forward Brianna Decker, Boston
2014-15 Forward Jamie Lee Rattray, Brampton
2014-15 Forward Jessica Campbell, Calgary
2015-16 Goalie Sydney Aveson, Montréal
2015-16 Defender Brigitte Lacquette, Calgary
2015-16 Defender Sarah Edney, Brampton
2015-16 Forward Elana Lovell, Calgary
2015-16 Forward Jillian Saulnier, Calgary
2015-16 Forward Rebecca Vint, Brampton

2016-17 Goalie Emerance Maschmeyer, Calgary
2016-17 Defender Renata Fast, Toronto
2016-17 Defender Katelyn Gosling, Calgary
2016-17 Forward Laura Stacey, Brampton
2016-17 Forward Kate Leary, Boston
2016-17 Forward Michela Cava, Toronto

2017-18 Goalie Elaine Chuli, Vanke
2017-18 Defender Ashleigh Brykaliuk, Vanke
2017-18 Defender Taryn Baumgardt, Calgary
2017-18 Forward Sophie Shirley, Calgary
2017-18 Forward Cayley Mercer, Vanke
2017-18 Forward Hanna Bunton, Vanke

2018-19 Goalie Alex Rigsby, Calgary
2018-19 Defender Mellissa Channell, Toronto
2018-19 Defender Halli Krzyzaniak, Calgary
2018-19 Forward Victoria Bach, Markham
2018-19 Forward Sarah Nurse, Toronto
2018-19 Forward Rebecca Leslie, Calgary

Top Forward
2007-08 Jennifer Botterill, Mississauga
2008-09 Jayna Hefford, Brampton
2009-10 Sabrina Harbec, Montréal
2010-11 Caroline Ouellette, Montréal
2011-12 Meghan Agosta, Montréal

2012-13 Hilary Knight, Boston
2013-14 Ann-Sophie Bettez, Montréal
2014-15 Rebecca Johnston, Calgary
2015-16 Marie-Philip Poulin, Montréal
2016-17 Marie-Philip Poulin, Montréal

First Decade CWHL Team
CWHL First Decade from 2007-08 to 2016-17
Goalie Charline Labonté, Montréal
Goalie Kim St-Pierre, Montréal
Goalie Geneviève Lacasse, Boston, Calgary
Defence Laura Fortino, Burlington/Brampton
Defence Catherine Ward, Montréal
Defence Becky Kellar, Burlington
Defence Cathy Chartrand, Montréal
Defence Molly Engstrom, Brampton/Boston
Defence Annie Guay, Montréal
Forward Caroline Ouellette, Montréal
Forward Jayna Hefford, Brampton
Forward Marie-Philip Poulin, Montréal
Forward Meghan Agosta, Montréal
Forward Ann-Sophie Bettez, Montréal
Forward Jennifer Botterill, Mississauga/Toronto
Forward Hilary Knight, Boston
Forward Rebecca Johnston, Toronto/Calgary
Forward Noémie Marin, Montréal

CWHL Playoff Winners
2008 Brampton Thunder

CWHL Championship MVP
2008 Lori Dupuis, Brampton

Clarkson Cup Winners
2009 Stars de Montréal
2010 Minnesota Whitecaps
2011 Stars de Montréal
2012 Stars de Montréal
2013 Boston Blades
2014 Toronto Furies
2015 Boston Blades
2016 Calgary Inferno
2017 Canadiennes de Montréal
2018 Markham Thunder
2019 Calgary Inferno

Clarkson Cup MVP
2009 Jenny Potter, Minnesota
2010 Julie Chu, Minnesota
2011 Sarah Vaillancourt, Montréal
2012 Caroline Ouellette, Montréal
2013 Catherine Ward, Montréal
2014 Natalie Spooner, Toronto
2015 Charline Labonté, Montréal
2016 Delayne Brian, Calgary
2017 Charline Labonté, Montréal
2018 Erica Howe, Markham
2019 Brianna Decker, Calgary

Clarkson Cup Top Forward
2009 Caroline Ouellette, Montréal
2010 Lori Dupuis, Brampton
2011 Sarah Vaillancourt, Montréal
2012 Erika Lawler, Boston
2013 Sarah Vaillancourt, Montréal

2014 Natalie Spooner, Toronto
2015 Brianna Decker, Boston

Clarkson Cup Top Defender
2009 Caitlin Cahow, Minnesota
2010 Molly Engstrom, Brampton
2012 Molly Engstrom, Brampton
2013 Catherine Ward, Montréal
2015 Monique Lamoureux, Boston

Clarkson Cup Top Goaltender
2009 Kim St-Pierre, Montréal
2010 Megan Van Beusekom, Minnesota
2012 Liz Knox, Brampton
2013 Geneviève Lacasse, Boston
2014 Christina Kessler, Toronto
2015 Charline Labonté, Montréal

Clarkson Cup Top Scorer
2009 Caroline Ouellette, Montréal
2010 Maggie Fisher, Minnesota
2011 Gillian Apps & Sarah Vaillancourt
2012 Caroline Ouellette, Montréal
2013 Hilary Knight, Boston
2014 Kate Buesser, Boston
2015 Brianna Decker, Boston
2016 Caroline Ouellette, Montréal
2017 Cathy Chartrand & Marie-Philip Poulin, Montréal
2018 Nicole Kosta, Markham
2019 Hilary Knight, Montréal

NWHL Regular Season
2015-16 Boston Pride
2016-17 Boston Pride
2017-18 Metropolitan Riveters
2018-19 Minnesota Whitecaps

NWHL Most Valuable Player
2015-16 Brianna Decker, Boston
2016-17 Brianna Decker, Boston
2017-18 Alexa Gruschow, Metropolitan
2018-19 Maddie Elia, Buffalo

NWHL Scoring Champion
2015-16 Hilary Knight, Boston
2016-17 Brianna Decker, Boston
2017-18 Alexa Gruschow, Metropolitan
2018-19 Hayley Scamurra, Buffalo

NWHL Best Defender
2015-16 Gigi Marvin, Boston
2016-17 Megan Bozek, Buffalo
2017-18 Courtney Burke, Metropolitan
2018-19 Blake Bolden, Buffalo

NWHL Goaltender of the Year
2015-16 Brittany Ott, Boston
2016-17 Katie Fitzgerald, New York
2017-18 Amanda Leveille, Buffalo
2018-19 Shannon Szabados, Buffalo

NWHL Rookie/Newcomer of the Year
2017-18 Hayley Scamurra, Buffalo
2018-19 Jonna Curtis, Minnesota

NWHL Denna Laing Perseverance
2015-16 Denna Laing, Boston
2016-17 Ashley Johnston, New York
2017-18 Jillian Dempsey, Boston
2018-19 Jillian Dempsey, Boston

Isobel Cup
2016 Boston Pride
2017 Buffalo Beauts
2018 Metropolitan Riveters
2019 Minnesota Whitecaps

NWHL Winners (Canada)
1998-99 Beatrice Aeros
1999-00 Beatrice Aeros
2000-01 Beatrice Aeros
2001-02 Beatrice Aeros
Missing 2002-03 and 2003-04
2004-05 Brampton Thunder
2005-06 Durham Lightning
2006-07 Mississauga Aeros

NWHL Playoff Champions (Canada)
2000 Beatrice Aeros
2001 Beatrice Aeros
2002 Beatrice Aeros
2003 Calgary Oval X-Treme
2004 Calgary Oval X-Treme
2005 Toronto Aeros
2006 Axion de Montréal
2007 Brampton Thunder

COWHL Playoff Champions
Missing earlier seasons
1992-93 Toronto Aeros
1993-94 Toronto Aeros
1995-96 North York Aeros
1996-97 North York Aeros
1997-98 North York Aeros

Women's National Championships
1982 Agincourt Canadians
1983 Burlington Ladies
1984 Edmonton Chimos
1985 Edmonton Chimos
1986 Hamilton Golden Hawks
1987 Hamilton Golden Hawks
1988 Sherbrooke
1989 Christin Automobiles
1990 Sherbrooke
1991 Toroto Aeros
1992 Edmonton Chimos
1993 Toronto Aeros
1994 Équipe Québec
1995 Équipe Québec
1996 Équipe Québec
1997 Edmonton Chimos
1998 Calgary Oval X-Treme
1999 Équipe Québec
2000 North York Aeros
2001 Calgary Oval X-Treme
2002 Équipe Québec
2003 Calgary Oval X-Treme
2004 Toronto Aeros
2005 Toronto Aeros
2006 Brampton Thunder
2007 Calgary Oval X-Treme
2008 Mississauga Chiefs

LEADERS

Most Points in the CWHL

ALL-TIME LEADERS		GP	G	A	PTS	PPG
1.	Ouellette, Caroline	176	131	184	315	1.79
2.	Bettez, Ann-Sophie	170	119	146	265	1.56
3.	Marin, Noémie	201	132	123	255	1.27
4.	Hefford, Jayna	128	130	104	234	1.83
5.	Poulin, Marie-Philip	93	87	96	184	1.98
6.	Botterill, Jennifer	76	62	92	154	2.03
7T	Dupuis, Lori	153	63	86	149	.97
7T	West, Sommer	126	60	89	149	1.18
9.	Harbec, Sabrina	85	49	90	139	1.64
10.	Blais, Emmanuelle	182	52	85	137	.75
11.	Apps, Gillian	126	68	66	134	1.06
12.	Head, Jana	140	63	70	133	.95
13.	Johnston, Rebecca	99	51	78	129	1.30
14.	Rattray, Jamie-Lee	121	63	65	128	1.06
15.	Agosta-Marciano, Meghan	50	57	69	126	2.52
16.	Chartrand, Cathy	144	30	93	123	.85
17T	Jenner, Brianne	114	56	65	121	1.06
17T	Vine, Lindsay	188	54	67	121	.64
19.	Spooner, Natalie	115	69	48	117	1.02
20T	Aarts, Meagan	193	61	49	110	.57
20T	Davidson, Vanessa	88	52	58	110	1.25
22.	Prévost, Carolyne	165	53	56	109	.66
23.	Breton, Lisa-Marie	180	46	58	104	.58
24.	Stack, Kelli	67	56	45	101	1.51
25.	Jones, Jess	120	52	49	101	.84
26.	Guay, Annie	80	31	64	95	1.19
27.	Piper, Cherie	77	43	51	94	1.22
28T	Vaillancourt, Sarah	48	34	57	91	1.90
28T	Hart, Kelly	144	30	61	91	.63
30.	Chu, Julie	92	18	72	90	.98
31T	Esposito, Brittany	93	36	47	83	.89
31T	Beazer, Brooke	143	30	53	83	.58
33T	Fortino, Laura	99	24	58	82	.83
33T	Bonello, Michelle	185	21	61	82	.44
35T	Knight, Hilary	65	38	41	79	1.22
35T	Déry, Nathalie	134	17	62	79	.59
37T	Cheverie, Kori	148	35	43	78	.53
37T	Deschênes, Kim	116	34	44	78	.67
39.	Clement-Heydra, Katia	102	28	49	77	.75
40.	Koizumi, Jessica	87	38	38	76	.87
41T	Oles, Leslie	87	35	40	75	.86
41T	Davies, Rebecca	126	32	43	75	.60
43.	Zamora, Kelly	175	26	45	71	.41
44T	Bram, Bailey	86	25	45	70	.81
44T	Engstrom, Molly	87	16	54	70	.80
46.	Saulnier, Jillian	62	34	35	69	1.11
47.	Bellamy, Kacey	117	16	52	68	.58
48.	Clarke, LaToya	100	20	47	67	.67
49T	Cunningham, Jenna	108	38	28	66	.61
49T	Moulson, Shannon	246	17	49	66	.27

Most Goals in the CWHL
ALL-TIME TOP-25 LEADERS
132 Noémie Marin, Montréal
131 Caroline Ouellette, Montréal
130 Jayna Hefford, Brampton
119 Ann-Sophie Bettez, Montréal
87 Marie-Philip Poulin, Montréal
69 Natalie Spooner, Mississauga/Toronto
68 Gillian Apps, Brampton
63 Lori Dupuis, Brampton
63 Jana Head, Burlington/Brampton

63 Jamie-Lee Rattray, Ottawa/Markham
62 Jennifer Botterill, Mississauga/Toronto
61 Meagan Aarts, Vaughan/Toronto
60 Sommer West, Mississauga/Toronto/Burlington
57 Meghan Agosta-Marciano, Montréal
56 Kelli Stack, Boston/Kunlun
56 Brianne Jenner, Mississauga/Burlington/Calgary
54 Lindsay Vine, Burlington/Brampton
53 Carolyn Prévost, Montréal/Toronto
52 Emmanuelle Blais, Montréal
52 Jess Jones, Brampton/Markham
52 Vanessa Davidson, Montréal
51 Rebecca Johnston, Toronto/Calgary
49 Sabrina Harbec, Montréal
46 Lisa-Marie Breton, Montréal
43 Cherie Piper, Mississauga/Brampton

Most Assists in the CWHL
ALL-TIME TOP-20 LEADERS
184 Caroline Ouellette, Montréal
146 Ann-Sophie Bettez, Montréal
123 Noémie Marin, Montréal
104 Jayna Hefford, Brampton
97 Marie-Philip Poulin, Montréal
93 Cathy Chartrand, Montréal
92 Jennifer Botterill, Mississauga/Toronto
90 Sabrina Harbec, Montréal
89 Sommer West, Mississauga/Toronto/Burlington
86 Lori Dupuis, Brampton
85 Emmanuelle Blais, Montréal
78 Rebecca Johnston, Toronto/Calgary
72 Julie Chu, Montréal
70 Jana Head, Burlington/Brampton
69 Meghan Agosta-Marciano, Montréal
67 Lindsay Vine, Burlington/Brampton
66 Gillian Apps, Brampton
65 Brianne Jenner, Mississauga/Burlington/Calgary
65 Jamie-Lee Rattray, Ottawa/Brampton/Markham
64 Annie Guay, Montréal

Most Games in the CWHL
ALL-TIME TOP-20 LEADERS
262 Shannon Moulson, Mississauga/Burlington/Toronto
217 Kristy Zamora, Burlington/Mississauga/Toronto
201 Noémie Marin, Montréal
193 Meagan Aarts, Vaughan/Toronto
188 Lindsay Vine, Burlington/Brampton
185 Michelle Bonello, Vaughan/Toronto
184 Emmanuelle Blais, Montréal
180 Lisa-Marie Breton, Montréal
176 Caroline Ouellette, Montréal
175 Kelly Zamora, Burlington/Toronto
172 Brooke Beazer, Brampton/Toronto
170 Ann-Sophie Bettez, Montréal
168 Mallory Johnston, Burlington/Brampton
165 Erica Kromm, Calgary
165 Carolyne Prévost, Montréal/Toronto
153 Lori Dupuis, Brampton
150 Dania Simmonds, Brampton
148 Kori Cheverie, Toronto
144 Cathy Chartrand, Montréal
144 Kelly Hart, Burlington/Brampton

Most Penalty Minutes in the CWHL
ALL-TIME TOP-10 LEADERS
359 Gillian Apps, Brampton
269 Michelle Bonello, Vaughan/Toronto

266 Shannon Moulson, Mississauga/Burlington/Toronto
222 Ashley Pendleton, three teams
222 Kristy Zamora, Burlington/Mississauga/Toronto
212 Nathalie Déry, Montréal
208 Lisa-Marie Breton, Montréal
196 Lori Dupuis, Brampton
192 Sommer West, Mississauga/Toronto/Burlington
182 Jocelyne Larocque, Brampton/Markham

Most Power-Play Goals in the CWHL
51 Noémie Marin, Montréal
35 Jayna Hefford, Brampton
27 Caroline Ouellette, Montréal
26 Ann-Sophie Bettez, Montréal
18 Sommer West, Mississauga/Toronto/Burlington
16 Gillian Apps, Brampton
16 Vanessa Davidson, Montréal
16 Brittany Esposito, Calgary
16 Jess Jones, Brampton/Markham

Shorthanded Goals in the CWHL
14 Ann-Sophie Bettez, Montréal
10 Caroline Ouellette, Montréal
9 Jayna Hefford, Brampton
9 Natalie Spooner, Toronto

Game-Winning Goals in the CWHL
22 Caroline Ouellette, Montréal
21 Marie-Philip Poulin, Montréal
20 Ann-Sophie Bettez, Montréal
20 Noémie Marin, Montréal
19 Gillian Apps, Brampton
19 Jayna Hefford, Brampton

First Goals in the CWHL
20 Ann-Sophie Bettez, Montréal
18 Caroline Ouellette, Montréal
15 Noémie Marin, Montréal
15 Marie-Philip Poulin, Montréal

Points-per-Game in the CWHL
ALL-TIME TOP-10 LEADERS
2.52 Meghan Agosta-Marciano, Montréal
2.03 Jennifer Botterill, Mississauga/Toronto
1.98 Marie-Philip Poulin, Montréal
1.90 Sarah Vaillancourt, Montréal
1.83 Jayna Hefford, Brampton
1.79 Caroline Ouellette, Montréal
1.66 Brianna Decker, Boston/Calgary
1.64 Sabrina Harbec, Montréal
1.56 Ann-Sophie Bettez, Montréal
1.51 Kelli Stack, Boston/Kunlun

Most Wins in the CWHL
Note: not all goalie stats are available from 2009-10
63 Sami Jo Small, Mississauga/Toronto
56 Jenny Lavigne, Montréal
47 Charline Labonté, Montréal
44 Delayne Brian, Calgary
40 Liz Knox, Markham
39 Kim St-Pierre, Montréal
38 Emerance Maschmeyer, Calgary/Montréal
37 Erica Howe, Markham
36 Catherine Herron, Montréal

35 Geneviève Lacasse, Boston/Calgary/Montréal
30 Christina Kessler, Burlington/Toronto
28 Mandy Cronin, Brampton/Boston/Burlington
28 Erika Vanderveer, four different teams
26 Laura Hosier, Brampton
24 Noora Räty, Kunlun
22 Molly Schaus, Boston
20 Elaine Chuli, Vanke/Toronto
16 Brittany Ott, Boston
16 Sarah Love, Mississauga

Most Shutouts in the CWHL
Note: not all goalie stats are available from 2009-10
16 Sami Jo Small, Mississauga/Toronto
13 Charline Labonté, Montréal
12 Emerance Maschmeyer, Calgary/Montréal
9 Erica Howe, Markham
9 Noora Räty, Kunlun
9 Kim St-Pierre, Montréal
8 Liz Knox, Markham
8 Jenny Lavigne, Montréal
7 Geneviève Lacasse, Boston/Calgary/Montréal

Most Wins by a Coach in the CWHL
98 Dany Brunet, Montréal
75 Patrick Rankine, Montréal
68 Digit Murphy, Boston/Kunlun
50 Pat Cocklin, Burlington/Brampton
41 Sommer West, Toronto
40 Scott Reid, Calgary
34 Peter Crosby, Mississauga/Brampton

Most Games by a Coach in the CWHL
139 Pat Cocklin, Burlington/Brampton
129 Dany Brunet, Montréal
111 Sommer West, Toronto
100 Patrick Rankine, Montréal
98 Digit Murphy, Boston/Kunlun
56 Jim Jackson, Markham
55 Scott Reid, Calgary
52 Peter Crosby, Mississauga/Brampton

Most Points in the Clarkson Cup

	ALL-TIME LEADERS	GP	G	A	PTS	PPG
1.	Ouellette, Caroline	30	16	28	44	1.47
2.	Knight, Hilary	17	14	12	26	1.53
3.	Blais, Emmanuelle	26	8	12	20	.77
4.	Bettez, Ann-Sophie	22	10	9	19	.86
5.	Poulin, Marie-Philip	11	10	9	19	1.73
6.	Chu, Julie	29	3	15	18	.62
7.	Johnston, Rebecca	16	8	9	17	1.06
8.	Marin, Noémie	29	7	10	17	.59
9.	Chartrand, Cathy	18	3	13	16	.89
10.	Harbec, Sabrina	12	5	11	16	1.33
11.	Spooner, Natalie	17	7	9	16	.94
12.	Jenner, Brianne	14	5	9	14	1.00
13.	Stack, Kelli	11	4	10	14	1.27
14.	Thibault, Dominique	15	7	7	14	.93
15.	Hefford, Jayna	14	3	10	13	.93
16.	Apps, Gillian	13	10	2	12	.92
17.	Bonhomme, Tessa	18	4	8	12	.67
18.	Buesser, Kate	9	6	5	11	1.22
19.	Decker, Brianna	7	8	3	11	1.57
20.	Saulnier, Jillian	11	3	8	11	1.00

Most Goals in the Clarkson Cup
16 Caroline Ouellette, Montréal
14 Hilary Knight, Boston/Montréal
10 Gillian Apps, Brampton
10 Ann-Sophie Bettez, Montréal
10 Marie-Philip Poulin, Montréal
8 Emmanuelle Blais, Montréal
8 Brianna Decker, Boston/Calgary
8 Rebecca Johnston, Toronto/Calgary
8 Sarah Vaillancourt, Montréal

Most Assists in the Clarkson Cup
28 Caroline Ouellette, Montréal
15 Julie Chu, Minnesota/Montréal
13 Cathy Chartrand, Montréal
12 Emmanuelle Blais, Montréal
12 Hilary Knight, Boston/Montréal
11 Sabrina Harbec, Montréal
10 Jayna Hefford, Brampton
10 Noémie Marin, Montréal
10 Kelli Stack, Boston/Kunlun

Most Games in the Clarkson Cup
30 Caroline Ouellette, Montréal
29 Julie Chu, Minnesota/Montréal
29 Noémie Marin, Montréal
26 Emmanuelle Blais, Montréal
22 Ann-Sophie Bettez, Montréal
20 Carly Hill, Montréal
19 Brooke Beazer, Brampton/Toronto
19 Lisa-Marie Breton-Lebreux, Montréal
19 Erica Kromm, Calgary
19 Kristy Zamora, Mississauga/Toronto
18 Kacey Bellamy, Boston/Calgary
18 Tessa Bonhomme, Calgary/Toronto
18 Cathy Chartrand, Montréal
18 Kori Cheverie, Toronto
18 Jessica Koizumi, Minnesota/Montréal/Boston
18 Lauriane Rougeau, Montréal

Most Minutes in the Clarkson Cup
720 Charline Labonté, Montréal
714 Christina Kessler, Toronto
636 Delayne Brian, Calgary
547 Erica Howe, Brampton/Markham
477 Emerance Maschmeyer, Calgary/Montréal

Most Wins in the Clarkson Cup
9 Charline Labonté, Montréal
7 Geneviève Lacasse, Boston/Calgary
6 Kim St-Pierre, Montréal
4 Delayne Brian, Calgary
4 Erica Howe, Brampton/Markham
4 Christina Kessler, Toronto
4 Jenny Lavigne, Montréal

Most Shutouts in the Clarkson Cup
4 Charline Labonté, Montréal
3 Jenny Lavigne, Montréal
2 Geneviève Lacasse, Boston/Calgary
2 Emerance Maschmeyer, Calgary/Montréal

Wins by a Coach in Clarkson Cup
11 Digit Murphy, Boston
8 Dany Brunet, Montréal

8 Pat Rankine, Montréal
5 Scott Reid, Calgary
4 Jack Brodt, Minnesota
4 Sommer West, Toronto
4 Jim Jackson, Markham

Games by a Coach in Clarkson Cup
15 Digit Murphy, Boston
14 Dany Brunet, Montréal
11 Sommer West, Toronto
9 Scott Reid, Calgary
8 Jack Brodt, Minnesota
6 Jim Jackson, Markham

Most Points in the NWHL

ALL-TIME LEADERS		GP	G	A	PTS	PPG
1T	Decker, Brianna	33	28	32	60	1.82
2T	Babstock, Kelly	65	27	33	60	.92
3.	Dempsey, Jillian	67	29	29	58	.87
4.	Packer, Madison	60	29	22	51	.85
5.	Knight, Hilary	27	23	25	48	1.78
6.	Skarupa, Haley	34	19	26	45	1.32
7.	Marvin, Gigi	47	19	25	44	.94
8.	Kunichika, Kourtney	50	15	27	42	.84
9T	Stack, Kelli	33	20	21	41	1.24
9T	Russo, Rebecca	50	17	24	41	.82
11.	Weber, Janine	48	16	22	38	.79
12T	Smelker, Jordan	62	15	22	37	.60
12T	Fratkin, Kaleigh	63	8	29	37	.59
12T	Burke, Courtney	40	5	32	37	.93
15T	Buie, Corinne	66	19	17	36	.55
15T	Duggan, Meghan	30	19	17	36	1.20
15T	Gruschow, Alexa	50	13	23	36	.72
18T	Scamurra, Hayley	31	18	17	35	1.13
18T	Kessel, Amanda	21	6	29	35	1.67
20.	D'Oench, Miye	36	13	21	34	.94
21.	Elia, Maddie	30	17	16	33	1.10
22.	Ketchum, Bray	51	17	15	32	.63
23T	Steadman, Kelley	18	18	12	30	1.67
23T	Field, Emily	64	14	16	30	.47
25T	Pelkey, Amanda	49	14	15	29	.59
25T	Carpenter, Alex	17	9	20	29	1.71
27.	Bolden, Blake	51	3	25	28	.55
28.	Browne, Harrison	51	10	17	27	.53
29T	Darkangelo, Shiann	29	17	8	25	.86
29T	Doyle, Shannon	61	5	20	25	.41
29T	Pfalzer, Emily	48	5	20	25	.52
29T	Gagliardi, Alyssa	65	3	22	25	.38

Most Goals in the NWHL
ALL-TIME TOP-10 LEADERS
29 Madison Packer, Metropolitan
29 Jillian Dempsey, Boston
28 Brianna Decker, Boston
27 Kelly Babstock, Connecticut/Buffalo
23 Hilary Knight, Boston
20 Kelli Stack, Connecticut
19 Haley Skarupa, Connecticut/Boston
19 Gigi Marvin, Boston
19 Meghan Duggan, Buffalo/Boston
19 Corinne Buie, Boston/Buffalo

Most Assists in the NWHL
ALL-TIME TOP-11 LEADERS
33 Kelly Babstock, Connecticut/Buffalo
32 Courtney Burke, Metropolitan
32 Brianna Decker, Boston
29 Jillian Dempsey, Boston
29 Kaleigh Fratkin, Connecticut/New York/Boston
29 Amanda Kessel, New York/Metropolitan
27 Kourtney Kunichika, Buffalo
26 Haley Skarupa, Connecticut/Boston
25 Blake Bolden, Boston/Buffalo
25 Hilary Knight, Boston
25 Gigi Marvin, Boston

Most Games in the NWHL
ALL-TIME TOP-20 LEADERS
67 Jillian Dempsey, Boston
67 Kiira Dosdall, New York/Metropolitan
66 Corinne Buie, Boston/Buffalo
65 Kelly Babstock, Connecticut/Buffalo
65 Alyssa Gagliardi, Boston
64 Emily Field, Boston
63 Kaleigh Fratkin, Connecticut/New York/Boston
62 Jordan Smelker, Boston
61 Shannon Doyle, Connecticut
61 Elena Orlando, New York/Connecticut
60 Madison Packer, New York/Metropolitan
59 Jordan Brickner, Connecticut
51 Blade Bolden, Boston/Buffalo
51 Harrison Browne, Buffalo/Metropolitan
51 Bray Ketchum, Boston/New York/Metropolitan
51 Tatiana Rafter, Buffalo/New York/Metropolitan
50 Alexa Gruschow, New York/Metropolitan
50 Kourtney Kunichika, Buffalo
50 Michelle Picard, New York/Metropolitan
50 Rebecca Russo, New York/Metropolitan

Most Wins in the NWHL
28 Brittany Ott, Boston
27 Amanda Leveille, Buffalo/Minnesota
21 Katie Fitzgerald, Metropolitan
10 Katie Burt, Boston

Most Shutouts in the NWHL
6 Brittany Ott, Boston
3 Katie Fitzgerald, Metropolitan
3 Amanda Leveille, Buffalo/Minnesota

Most Points in the Isobel Cup
14 Hilary Knight, Boston
14 Brianna Decker, Boston
10 Megan Bozek, Buffalo
9 Gigi Marvin, Boston
8 Kacey Bellamy, Boston
8 Emily Pfalzer, Buffalo

Most Goals in the Isobel Cup
10 Hilary Knight, Boston
6 Brianna Decker, Boston

Most Assists in the Isobel Cup
8 Kacey Bellamy, Boston
8 Brianna Decker, Boston
6 Gigi Marvin, Boston
6 Hayley Scamurra, Buffalo

Most Wins in the Isobel Cup
5 Brittany Ott, Boston
4 Amanda Leveille, Buffalo/Minnesota

TEAMS

Boston Pride

Year - League - Team		GP	W-L-OL	Finish
2015-16	NWHL Boston	18	14-3-1	1st
2016	I-Cup Boston	2	2W-0L	1st
2016-17	NWHL Boston	17	16-1-0	1st
2017	I-Cup Boston	2	1W-1L	2nd
2017-18	NWHL Boston	16	4-8-4	3rd
2018	I-Cup Boston	1	0W-1L	SF
2018-19	NWHL Boston	16	11-5-0	3rd
2019	I-Cup Boston	1	0W-1L	4th

British Columbia Breakers

Year - League - Team		GP	W-L-OL	Finish
2004-05	WWHL BC	21	5-15-1-0	4th
2005-06	WWHL BC	24	0-21-3-0	5th
2006-07	WWHL BC	24	8-15-0-1	4th
2007-08	WWHL BC	24	0-22-0-2	5th
2008-09	WWHL BC	24	0-22-0-2	5th

Buffalo Beauts

Year - League - Team		GP	W-L-OL	Finish
2015-16	NWHL Buffalo	18	5-9-4	3rd
2016	I-Cup Buffalo	2	1W-1L	2nd
2016-17	NWHL Buffalo	17	6-10-1	3rd
2017	I-Cup Buffalo	2	2W-0L	1st
2017-18	NWHL Buffalo	16	12-4-0	2nd
2018	I-Cup Buffalo	2	1W-1L	2nd
2018-19	NWHL Buffalo	16	11-4-1	2nd
2019	I-Cup Buffalo	2	1W-1L	2nd

Burlington Barracudas

Year - League - Team		GP	W-L-O-S	Finish
2007-08	CWHL Burlington	30	11-18-0-1	5th
2008	CWHL-P Burlington	3	1W-1L-1T	
2008-09	CWHL Burlington	30	11-16-1-2	4th
2009	CWHL-P Burlington	4	1W-1L-2T	
2009-10	CWHL Burlington	30	19-8-0-3	3rd
2010	CWHL-P Burlington	2	1W-1L	
2010-11	CWHL Burlington	26	6-18-1-1	5th
2011-12	CWHL Burlington	27	1-26-0-0	6th

Calgary Inferno

Year - League - Team		GP	W-L-O-S	Finish
2011-12	CWHL Alberta	15	5-10-0-0	5th
2012-13	CWHL Alberta	24	3-21-0-0	5th
2013-14	CWHL Calgary	24	12-11-0-1	3rd
2014	C-Cup Calgary	3	0W-3L	4th
2014-15	CWHL Calgary	24	15-6-1-2	2nd
2015	C-Cup Calgary	2	0W-2L	4th
2015-16	CWHL Calgary	24	16-6-1-1	2nd
2016	C-Cup Calgary	3	3W-0L	1st
2016-17	CWHL Calgary	24	20-4-0-0	1st
2017	C-Cup Calgary	4	2W-2L	2nd
2017-18	CWHL Calgary	28	17-7-1-3	3rd
2018	C-Cup Calgary	3	1W-2L	SF
2018-19	CWHL Calgary	28	23-4-0-1	1st
2019	C-Cup Calgary	4	3W-1L	1st

Calgary Oval X-Treme

Year - League - Team		GP	W-L-O-S	Finish
2004-05	WWHL Calgary	21	20-0-1-0	1st
2005-06	WWHL Calgary	24	22-0-1-1	1st
2006-07	WWHL Calgary	24	23-1-0-0	1st
2007-08	WWHL Calgary	24	24-0-0-0	1st
2008-09	WWHL Calgary	23	20-3-0-0	1st
2009	C-Cup Calgary	2	0W-2L	4th

* Played in Canada's NWHL in 2002-03 and 2003-04.

Connecticut Whale

Year - League - Team		GP	W-L-OL	Finish
2015-16	NWHL Connecticut	18	13-5-0	2nd
2016	I-Cup Connecticut	1	0W-1L	SF
2016-17	NWHL Connecticut	18	5-12-1	4th
2017	I-Cup Connecticut	1	0W-1L	SF
2017-18	NWHL Connecticut	16	3-11-2	4th
2018	I-Cup Connecticut	1	0W-1L	SF
2018-19	NWHL Connecticut	16	2-12-2	5h

Edmonton Chimos

Year - League - Team		GP	W-L-OL	Finish
2004-05	WWHL Edmonton	21	12-8-1-0	3rd
2005-06	WWHL Edmonton	24	16-5-3-0	2nd
2006-07	WWHL Edmonton	24	15-8-1-0	2nd
2007-08	WWHL Edmonton	24	9-11-0-4	4th
2008-09	WWHL Edmonton	24	14-10-0-0	3rd
2009-10	WWHL Edmonton	18	7-7-0-4	2nd
2010-11	WWHL Edmonton	17	11-5-0-1	2nd

* Played in Canada's NWHL in 2002-03 and 2003-04.

Markham Thunder

Year - League - Team		GP	W-L-O-S	Finish
2007-08	CWHL Brampton	30	22-7-0-1	2nd
2008	CWHL-P Brampton	3	2W-0L-1T	
2008-09	CWHL Brampton	30	22-7-0-1	2nd
2009	CWHL-P Brampton	2	1W-1L	
2009	C-Cup Brampton	2	1W-1L	3rd
2009-10	CWHL Brampton	30	12-15-2-1	4th
2010	CWHL-P Brampton	2	2W-0L	
2010	C-Cup Brampton	2	1W-1L	2nd
2010-11	CWHL Brampton	26	19-5-1-1	2nd
2011	CWHL-P Brampton	2	0W-2L	
2011	C-Cup Brampton	3	1W-2L	3rd
2011-12	CWHL Brampton	27	18-7-1-1	3rd
2012	C-Cup Brampton	4	2W-2L	2nd
2012-13	CWHL Brampton	24	10-12-1-1	3rd
2013	C-Cup Brampton	3	0W-3L	4th
2013-14	CWHL Brampton	24	5-16-3-0	5th
2014-15	CWHL Brampton	24	6-16-0-2	6th
2015-16	CWHL Brampton	24	16-7-0-1	3rd
2016	C-Cup Brampton	2	0W-2L	SF
2016-17	CWHL Brampton	24	12-10-1-1	3rd
2017	C-Cup Brampton	2	0W-2L	SF
2017-18	CWHL Markham	28	14-7-4-3	4th
2018	C-Cup Markham	3	3W-0L	1st
2018-19	CWHL Markham	28	13-11-3-1	3rd
2019	C-Cup Markham	3	1W-2L	SF

Metropolitan Riveters

Year - League - Team		GP	W-L-OL	Finish
2015-16	NWHL New York	18	4-12-2	4th
2016	I-Cup New York	1	0W-1L	SF
2016-17	NWHL New York	18	8-7-3	2nd
2017	I-Cup New York	1	0W-1L	SF
2017-18	NWHL Metropolitan	16	13-3-0	1st
2018	I-Cup Metropolitan	2	1W-1L	1st
2018-19	NWHL Metropolitan	16	4-12-0	4th
2019	I-Cup Metropolitan	2	1W-1L	3rd

Manitoba Maple Leafs

Year - League - Team		GP	W-L-O-S	Finish
2010-11	WWHL Manitoba	12	1-11-0-0	3rd

Minnesota Whitecaps

Year	League - Team	GP	W-L-O-S	Finish
2004-05	WWHL Minnesota	12	8-3-1-0	2nd
2005-06	WWHL Minnesota	24	11-8-4-1	3rd
2006-07	WWHL Minnesota	24	13-9-1-1	3rd
2007-08	WWHL Minnesota	24	15-6-1-2	
2008-09	WWHL Minnesota	22	18-4-0-0	2nd
2009	C-Cup Minnesota	3	2W-1L	2nd
2009-10	WWHL Minnesota	12	10-2-0	1st
2010	C-Cup Minnesota	2	2W-0L	1st
2010-11	WWHL Minnesota	18	17-0-0-1	1st
2011	C-Cup Minnesota	3	0W-3L	4th
2018-19	NWHL Minnesota	16	12-4-0	1st
2019	I-Cup Minnesota	2	2W-0L	1st

Mississauga Chiefs

Year	League - Team	GP	W-L-O-S	Finish
2007-08	CWHL Mississauga	30	21-8-0-1	3rd
2008	CWHL-P Mississauga	5	3W-2L	
2008-09	CWHL Mississauga	30	19-9-1-1	3rd
2009	CWHL-P Mississauga	4	3W-1L	
2009-10	CWHL Mississauga	30	22-7-0-1	2nd
2010	C-Cup Mississauga	1	0W-1L	

Canadiennes de Montréal

Year	League - Team	GP	W-L-O-S	Finish
2007-08	CWHL Montréal	30	23-6-1-0	1st
2008	CWHL-P Montréal	2	1W-1L	
2008-09	CWHL Montréal	30	25-4-0-1	1st
2009	CWHL-P Montréal	2	1W-1L	
2009	C-Cup Montréal	3	2W-1L	1st
2009-10	CWHL Montréal	30	23-5-0-2	1st
2010	C-Cup Montréal	1	0W-1L	SF
2010-11	CWHL Montréal	26	22-2-0-2	1st
2011	CWHL-P Montréal	2	2W-0L	
2011	C-Cup Montréal	4	4W-0L	1st
2011-12	CWHL Montréal	27	22-4-0-1	1st
2012	C-Cup Montréal	4	4W-0L	1st
2012-13	CWHL Montréal	24	18-5-0-1	2nd
2013	C-Cup Montréal	4	3W-1L	2nd
2013-14	CWHL Montréal	23	19-2-0-2	1st
2014	C-Cup Montréal	3	1W-2L	3rd
2014-15	CWHL Montréal	24	14-9-0-1	3rd
2015	C-Cup Montréal	3	2W-1L	2nd
2015-16	CWHL Montréal	24	21-3-0-0	1st
2016	C-Cup Montréal	3	2W-1L	2nd
2016-17	CWHL Montréal	24	17-5-2-0	2nd
2017	C-Cup Montréal	3	3W-0L	1st
2017-18	CWHL Montréal	28	22-5-0-1	1st
2018	C-Cup Montréal	2	0W-2L	SF
2018-19	CWHL Montréal	28	21-6-0-1	2nd
2019	C-Cup Montréal	4	2W-2L	2nd

* Known as Montréal Stars from 2007-08 to 2014-15.

Ottawa Senators

Year	League - Team	GP	W-L-O-S	Finish
2007-08	CWHL Ottawa	30	8-19-0-3	6th
2008	CWHL-P Ottawa	1	0W-1L	
2008-09	CWHL Ottawa	30	4-26-0-0	6th
2009	CWHL-P Ottawa	2	0W-2L	
2009-10	CWHL Ottawa	30	5-23-1-1	6th
2010	CWHL-P Ottawa	1	0W-1L	

* Known as Ottawa Capital Canucks in 2007-08.

Phénix du Québec

Year	League - Team	GP	W-L-O-S	Finish
2007-08	CWHL Québec	30	8-21-0-1	7th

* Note: the team name Québec identifies the province of Québec (not the city). The team was based in Montréal.

Saskatchewan Prairie Ice

Year	League - Team	GP	W-L-O-S	Finish
2004-05	WWHL Saskatchewan	21	1-19-0-1	5th
2005-06	WWHL Saskatchewan	24	4-16-3-1	4th
2006-07	WWHL Saskatchewan	22	0-22-0-0	5th

Shenzhen Kunlun Red Star Vanke

Year	League - Team	GP	W-L-O-S	Finish
2017-18	CWHL Kunlun	28	21-6-0-1	2nd
2018	C-Cup Kunlun	4	2W-2L	2nd
2018-19	CWHL Shenzhen	28	13-13-2-0	5th

Strathmore Rockies

Year	League - Team	GP	W-L-O-S	Finish
2007-08	WWHL Strathmore	14	11-2-1-0	
2008-09	WWHL Strathmore	23	6-16-0-1	4th
2009-10	WWHL Strathmore	18	7-10-0-1	3rd
2010-11	WWHL Strathmore	11	0-10-0-1	4th

Toronto Furies

Year	League - Team	GP	W-L-O-S	Finish
2010-11	CWHL Toronto	26	8-13-0-5	4th
2011	CWHL-P Toronto	2	2W-0L	
2011	C-Cup Toronto	4	2W-2L	2nd
2011-12	CWHL Toronto	27	9-13-2-3	4th
2012	C-Cup Toronto	3	0W-3L	4th
2012-13	CWHL Toronto	24	10-13-1-0	4th
2013	C-Cup Toronto	3	1W-2L	3rd
2013-14	CWHL Toronto	23	10-10-1-2	4th
2014	C-Cup Toronto	4	3W-1L	1st
2014-15	CWHL Toronto	24	8-13-1-2	4th
2015	C-Cup Toronto	2	0W-2L	3rd
2015-16	CWHL Toronto	24	6-16-1-1	4th
2016	C-Cup Toronto	2	0W-2L	SF
2016-17	CWHL Toronto	24	9-11-3-1	4th
2017	C-Cup Toronto	3	1W-2L	SF
2017-18	CWHL Toronto	28	9-17-1-1	6th
2018-19	CWHL Toronto	28	14-14-0-0	4th
2019	C-Cup Toronto	3	1W-2L	SF

Vanke Rays

Year	League - Team	GP	W-L-O-S	Finish
2017-18	CWHL Vanke	28	14-3-0-1	5th

* Merged with Kunlun Red Star for the 2018-19 season.

Vaughan Flames

Year	League - Team	GP	W-L-O-S	Finish
2007-08	CWHL Vaughan	30	12-16-2-0	4th
2008	CWHL-P Vaughan	2	0W-2L	
2008-09	CWHL Vaughan	30	9-19-0-2	5th
2009	CWHL-P Vaughan	2	0W-0L-2T	
2009-10	CWHL Vaughan	30	9-20-0-1	5th
2010	CWHL-P Vaughan	1	0W-1L	

Worcester Blades

Year	League - Team	GP	W-L-O-S	Finish
2010-11	CWHL Boston	26	10-15-1-0	3rd
2011	CWHL-P Boston	2	0W-2L	
2011-12	CWHL Boston	27	20-7-0-0	2nd
2012	C-Cup Boston	3	1W-2L	3rd
2012-13	CWHL Boston	24	19-4-0-1	1st
2013	C-Cup Boston	4	3W-1L	1st
2013-14	CWHL Boston	24	13-11-0-0	2nd
2014	C-Cup Boston	4	3W-1L	2nd
2014-15	CWHL Boston	24	17-6-0-1	1st
2015	C-Cup Boston	3	3W-0L	1st
2015-16	CWHL Boston	24	1-23-0-0	5th
2016-17	CWHL Boston	24	2-20-1-1	6th
2017-18	CWHL Boston	28	1-24-0-3	7th
2018-19	CWHL Worcester	28	0-28-0-0	6th

SEASONS

2007-08 CWHL

EAST STANDINGS	GP	W-L-OL-SL	PTS
E1 Stars de Montréal	30	23-6-1-0	47
E2 Ottawa Capital Canucks	30	8-19-0-3	19
E3 Phénix du Québec (Montréal)	30	8-21-0-1	17

WEST STANDINGS	GP	W-L-OL-SL	PTS
W1 Brampton Thunder	30	22-7-0-1	45
W2 Mississauga Chiefs	30	21-8-0-1	43
W3 Vaughan Flames	30	12-16-2-0	26
W4 Burlington Barracudas	30	11-8-0-1	23

CWHL Playoffs - First Round
Burlington wins 2-1 over Ottawa (one game)
Mississauga wins both games over Vaughan (6-2, 6-2)
CWHL Playoffs - Second Round
Mississauga eliminates Montréal (Mississauga wins 4-3, loses 4-1, then wins the series in a shootout)
Brampton eliminates Burlington (Brampton wins 5-2, then draws even 3-3 in the second game)
CWHL Final - 2008 Championship
Brampton wins 4-3 over Mississauga

2008-09 CWHL

CWHL STANDINGS	GP	W-L-OL-SL	PTS
1 Stars de Montréal	30	25-4-0-1	51
2 Brampton Thunder	30	22-7-0-1	45
3 Mississauga Chiefs	30	19-9-1-1	40
4 Burlington Barracudas	30	11-16-1-2	25
5 Vaughan Flames	30	9-19-0-2	20
6 Ottawa Senators	30	4-26-0-0	8

CWHL Playoffs - First Round
Mississauga eliminates Ottawa with back-to-back wins
Burlington eliminates Vaughan (both games end 2-2 before Burlington wins the series in overtime)
CWHL Playoffs - Second Round
Montréal eliminates Burlington (Montréal wins 6-1, loses 3-1, then wins the series with an overtime goal)
Brampton eliminates Mississauga (Brampton wins 3-2, loses 4-1, then wins the series with an overtime goal)
Montréal and Brampton join two WWHL teams (Calgary and Minnesota) in the inaugural Clarkson Cup playoffs
Clarkson Cup - Day One
Minnesota Whitecaps win 4-3 over Montréal
Brampton wins 4-3 over Calgary Oval X-Treme
Clarkson Cup - Semi-Final
Minnesota wins 2-1 over Calgary
Montréal wins 4-1 over Brampton
Clarkson Cup - 2009 Championship
Montréal wins 3-1 over Minnesota

2009-10 CWHL

CWHL STANDINGS	GP	W-L-OL-SL	PTS
1 Stars de Montréal	30	23-5-0-2	48
2 Mississauga Chiefs	30	22-7-0-1	45
3 Burlington Barracudas	30	19-8-0-3	41
4 Brampton Thunder	30	12-15-2-1	27
5 Vaughan Flames	30	9-20-0-1	19
6 Ottawa Senators	30	5-23-1-1	12

CWHL Playoffs - First Round
Burlington wins 4-3 over Ottawa
Brampton wins 4-1 over Vaughan
CWHL Playoffs - Second Round
Brampton wins 2-1 over Burlington

Brampton joins Montréal, Mississauga and the WWHL's Minnesota Whitecaps in the Clarkson Cup playoffs
Clarkson Cup - Semi-Finals
Brampton wins 3-2 over Montréal
Minnesota wins 3-1 over Mississauga
Clarkson Cup - 2010 Championship
Minnesota wins 4-0 over Brampton

2010-11 CWHL

CWHL STANDINGS	GP	W-L-OL-SL	PTS
1 Stars de Montréal	26	22-2-0-2	46
2 Brampton Thunder	26	19-5-1-1	40
3 Boston Blades	26	10-15-1-0	21
4 Toronto Furies	26	8-13-0-5	21
5 Burlington Barracudas	26	6-18-1-1	14

CWHL Playoffs - First Round
Montréal wins both games against Brampton
Toronto wins both games against Boston
Montréal, Toronto and Brampton join the WWHL's Minnesota Whitecaps in the Clarkson Cup playoff
Clarkson Cup - Round Robin
DAY 1: Toronto 3-2 Brampton; Montréal 5-1 Minnesota
DAY 2: Toronto 6-0 Minnesota; Montréal 7-4 Brampton
DAY 3: Brampton 7-2 Minnesota; Montréal 2-1 Toronto
Clarkson Cup - 2011 Championship
Montréal wins 5-0 over Toronto

2011-12 CWHL

CWHL STANDINGS	GP	W-L-OL-SL	PTS
1 Stars de Montréal	27	22-4-0-1	45
2 Boston Blades	27	20-7-0-0	40
3 Brampton Thunder	27	18-7-1-1	38
4 Toronto Furies	27	9-13-2-3	23
5 Team Alberta (Calgary)	15	5-10-0-0	10
6 Burlington Barracudas	27	1-26-0-0	2

Clarkson Cup - Round Robin
DAY 1: Montréal 7-0 Toronto; Brampton 3-2 Boston
DAY 2: Montréal 2-0 Brampton; Boston 5-2 Toronto
DAY 3: Brampton 4-2 Toronto; Montréal 5-4 Boston
Clarkson Cup - 2012 Championship
Montréal wins 4-2 over Brampton

2012-13 CWHL

CWHL STANDINGS	GP	W-L-OL-SL	PTS
1 Boston Blades	24	19-4-0-1	39
2 Stars de Montréal	24	18-5-0-1	37
3 Brampton Thunder	24	10-12-1-1	22
4 Toronto Furies	24	10-13-1-0	21
5 Team Alberta (Calgary)	24	3-21-0-0	6

Clarkson Cup - Round Robin
DAY 1: Boston 3-2 Toronto; Montréal 5-0 Brampton
DAY 2: Boston 2-0 Brampton; Montréal 2-0 Toronto
DAY 3: Montréal 1-0 Boston; Toronto 4-3 Brampton
Clarkson Cup - 2013 Championship
Boston wins 5-2 over Montréal

2013-14 CWHL

CWHL STANDINGS	GP	W-L-OL-SL	PTS
1 Stars de Montréal	23	19-2-0-2	42
2 Boston Blades	24	13-11-0-0	26
3 Calgary Inferno	24	12-11-0-1	25
4 Toronto Furies	23	10-10-1-2	23
5 Brampton Thunder	24	5-16-3-0	13

Clarkson Cup - Round Robin
DAY 1: Toronto 3-2 Calgary; Boston 1-0 Montréal
DAY 2: Boston 2-1 Toronto; Montréal 5-4 Calgary
DAY 3: Toronto 2-1 Montréal; Boston 6-2 Calgary
Clarkson Cup - 2014 Championship
Toronto wins 1-0 over Boston in overtime

2014-15 CWHL

CWHL STANDINGS	GP	W-L-OL-SL	PTS
1 Boston Blades	24	17-6-0-1	35
2 Calgary Inferno	24	15-6-1-2	33
3 Stars de Montréal	24	14-9-0-1	29
4 Toronto Furies	24	8-13-1-2	19
5 Brampton Thunder	24	6-16-0-2	14

Clarkson Cup - Semi-Finals
Boston eliminates Toronto (wins 3-0 and 7-3)
Montréal eliminates Calgary (wins 4-0 and 2-0)
Clarkson Cup - 2015 Championship
Boston wins 3-2 over Montréal in overtime

2015-16 CWHL

CWHL STANDINGS	GP	W-L-OL-SL	PTS
1 Canadiennes de Montréal	24	21-3-0-0	42
2 Calgary Inferno	24	16-6-1-1	34
3 Brampton Thunder	24	16-7-0-1	33
4 Toronto Furies	24	6-16-1-1	14
5 Boston Blades	24	1-23-0-0	2

Clarkson Cup - Semi-Finals
Montréal eliminates Toronto (wins 5-1 and 7-1)
Calgary eliminates Brampton (wins 4-2 and 4-3)
Clarkson Cup - 2016 Championship
Calgary wins 8-3 over Montréal

2015-16 NWHL

NWHL STANDINGS	GP	W-L-OL	PTS
1 Boston Pride	18	14-3-1	29
2 Connecticut Whale	18	13-5-0	26
3 Buffalo Beauts	18	5-9-4	14
4 New York Riveters	18	4-12-2	10

Isobel Cup - Semi-Finals
Boston 2-0 New York; Buffalo 2-1 Connecticut
Isobel Cup - 2016 Championship
Boston wins 2-0 over Buffalo

2016-17 CWHL

CWHL STANDINGS	GP	W-L-OL-SL	PTS
1 Calgary Inferno	24	20-4-0-0	40
2 Canadiennes de Montréal	24	17-5-2-0	36
3 Brampton Thunder	24	12-10-1-1	26
4 Toronto Furies	24	9-11-3-1	22
5 Boston Blades	24	2-20-1-1	6

Clarkson Cup - Semi-Finals
Montréal eliminates Brampton (wins 7-1 and 5-1)
Calgary eliminates Toronto (loss 2-5, wins 3-1 and 3-1)
Clarkson Cup - 2017 Championship
Montréal wins 3-1 over Calgary

2016-17 NWHL

NWHL STANDINGS	GP	W-L-OL	PTS
1 Boston Pride	17	16-1-0	32
2 New York Riveters	18	8-7-3	19
3 Buffalo Beauts	17	6-10-1	13
4 Connecticut Whale	18	5-12-1	11

Isobel Cup - Semi-Finals
Boston 8-2 Connecticut; Buffalo 4-2 New York
Isobel Cup - 2017 Championship
Buffalo wins 3-2 over Boston

2017-18 CWHL

CWHL STANDINGS	GP	W-L-OL-SL	PTS
1 Canadiennes de Montréal	28	22-5-0-1	45
2 Kunlun Red Star	28	21-6-0-1	43
3 Calgary Inferno	28	17-7-1-3	38
4 Markham Thunder	28	14-7-4-3	35
5 Vanke Rays	28	14-3-01	29
6 Toronto Furies	28	9-17-1-1	20
7 Boston Blades	28	1-24-0-3	5

Clarkson Cup - Semi-Finals
Markham eliminates Montréal (wins 2-1 and 4-1)
Kunlun eliminates Calgary (loss 0-3, win 3-2 and 1-0)
Clarkson Cup - 2018 Championship
Markham wins 2-1 over Kunlun in overtime

2017-18 NWHL

NWHL STANDINGS	GP	W-L-OL	PTS
1 Metropolitan Riveters	16	13-3-0	26
2 Buffalo Beauts	16	12-4-0	24
3 Boston Pride	16	4-8-4	12
4 Connecticut Whale	16	3-11-2	8

Isobel Cup - Semi-Finals
Metropolitan 5-0 Connecticut; Buffalo 3-2 Boston
Isobel Cup - 2018 Championship
Metropolitan wins 1-0 over Buffalo

2018-19 CWHL

CWHL STANDINGS	GP	W-L-OL-SL	PTS
1 Calgary Inferno	28	23-4-0-1	47
2 Canadiennes de Montréal	28	21-6-0-1	43
3 Markham Thunder	28	13-11-3-1	30
4 Toronto Furies	28	14-14-0-0	28
5 Shenzhen KRS Vanke Rays	28	13-13-2-0	28
6 Worcester Blades	28	0-28-0-0	0

Clarkson Cup - Semi-Finals
Montréal eliminates Markham (win 3-0, loss 4-3, win 5-0)
Calgary eliminates Toronto (loss 3-1, win 3-0 and 4-1)
Clarkson Cup - 2019 Championship
Calgary wins 502 over Montréal

2018-19 NWHL

NWHL STANDINGS	GP	W-L-OL	PTS
1 Minnesota Whitecaps	16	12-4-0	24
2 Buffalo Beauts	16	11-4-1	23
3 Boston Pride	16	11-5-0	22
4 Metropolitan Riveters	16	4-12-0	8
5 Connecticut Whale	16	2-12-2	6

Isobel Cup - First Round
Metropolitan 5-2 Connecticut
Isobel Cup - Semi-Finals
Minnesota 5-1 Connecticut; Buffalo 4-0 Boston
Isobel Cup - 2019 Championship
Minnesota wins 2-1 over Buffalo in overtime

CPSIA information can be obtained
at www.ICGtesting.com
Printed in the USA
LVHW102345270320
651480LV00014B/380

9 780464 437680